THE THIRD REPUBLIC OF FRANCE

THE
THIRD REPUBLIC
OF FRANCE

THE FIRST PHASE 1871–1894

BY

GUY CHAPMAN

Sometime Professor of Modern History in the University of Leeds

ST MARTIN'S PRESS
1962

MACMILLAN AND COMPANY LIMITED
St Martin's Street London WC2
also Bombay Calcutta Madras Melbourne

THE MACMILLAN COMPANY OF CANADA LIMITED
Toronto

ST MARTIN'S PRESS INC
New York

PRINTED IN GREAT BRITAIN

PREFACE

In the preface to his selection of extracts from the Greek and Latin historians, Dr. M. I. Finley reminded us that 'history in its root sense means inquiry'. All historical writing is, or ought to be, directed to the elucidation of a problem. It is in a way a high-class *roman policier*. It is comparatively simple if it is limited to a short period or an incident from which nothing came. But an inquest on the body of a society is more difficult than an inquest on a human being. Evidence of substance is hard to collect, harder to verify and harder still to interpret. The problem to which this history is directed is the discovery and dissection of the events in France that led to the defeat and downfall of the Third French Republic in 1940.

This is not a straightforward narrative history of France over seventy years, though that will come later. It is neither economic nor political nor social history, but all three are drawn on. It attempts an explanation by synthesis. In every country, in every society, there are new things and old things. Renan said that nothing that happened in his day was unrelated to the Revolution. But one must go back further. Anyone who has studied *Les caractères originaux de l'histoire rurale française* by Marc Bloch, published thirty years ago, will know how deep are the roots. My friend and partner, the late Hamish Miles, drew from M. André Maurois the story of how he contested the rights of his local villagers to fish certain waters on his land, which is in the Dordogne. The village deputation said that they had the right. 'From whom did you get it?' asked M. Maurois. 'The English gave it to us', they cried. By the year 1500 the English had gone for ever, but the rights they had granted remained. Writing soon after the war of 1914–18 the great geographer, Vidal de la Blache, wrote: '*Le régime politique actuel met en jeu, non seulement des passions et des intérêts, mais des réminiscences plus ou moins défigurées, des préjugés, des légendes.*'

It appears to me that in this dark epoch, the nineteenth century, in spite of more abundant evidence (it may not be reliable) than ever existed before (it may never exist again: the telephone is an enemy to the historian), we are faced by problems of historical writing that did not appear when the powers could dismiss a gang of Diggers with a few smacks over the buttocks with the flat of the sword, or reduce Levellers with a touch of decimation. Such minor incidents are unimportant

v

except to those seeking justification for later rebellion. But it is impossible to conceive pure political history after 1848.

The impact of demos on the structure and behaviour of national assemblies and politicians is fundamental to an understanding of the history of the later nineteenth and early twentieth century. The democratic drive towards levelling has had consequences which were foreseen and dreaded by even the most liberal of English statesmen. In France it was different. For whereas the English politicians kept control of the electorate as the suffrage was widened in stages, the French lost it by their impetuosity in 1848. With universal suffrage, democracy had arrived, and as Léon Blum told his followers it was universal suffrage and not parliamentary government which was the insignia of a democratic country.

The great changes which have taken and are taking place in countries regarded half a century ago as mature and stable have not come initially from outside pressures. They have been due to failures to solve internal problems, which in the end have led to failure to prepare against external enemies. '*Les pays sont comme les fruits. Les vers sont toujours à l'intérieur.*' But the worms started often long ago.

It is for this reason that I have found myself driven back to periods far earlier than 1870. War and peace alternate; régimes come and go, but, as the historian of Vergigny has shown, even after an error has been amended, it returns.

In his *Ancien Régime*, published in 1856, Alexis de Tocqueville wrote: 'When I reflect on this nation in itself, I find that it is more extraordinary than any of the events in its history . . . the most brilliant and the most dangerous of the nations of Europe, and most by nature apt to become turn by turn an object of admiration, of hatred, of pity, of terror, but never of indifference.' It was a saying in the eighteenth century that no war could happen in Europe without the French. In the twentieth, French governments were to be seen evading their responsibilities, deserting their allies and finally succumbing. Explanation of this behaviour has tempted a number of publicists and historians, and these are ready enough to inculpate individual politicians, journalists, industrialists, bankers and soldiers. If these responsible men were *fainéants*, how was it they arrived in their positions of responsibility? 'A nation with responsible parliamentary government is not the victim but the author of its government's blunders, and if it seeks to transfer the responsibility to politicians and the party system, or to some other scapegoat, it is guilty of the lie in the soul.' How came it that France, which has produced so many stout-hearted leaders to support a heroic soldiery, gave itself a series of governments which prepared its collapse in sixty days? The answer to the question is many-sided, and, in some aspects, of great age. A body may die of one stroke, but usually it expires through a number of small ills. It is these I propose to examine.

Guy Chapman

CONTENTS

ix

LIST OF MAPS

Introduction

France in the Eighteen-Seventies

(i)

In the year of the Paris Exhibition, 1867, monarchs, princes and lesser folk had thronged the City of Light, admired, as many Frenchmen did not, the new boulevards and palaces and churches which had risen at Haussmann's command, and had been fascinated by the high-stepping horses, the shining landaus and cabriolets and the elegance and luxury of the costumes, as the pageant of high society passed up and down the Champs Elysées. Europe had applauded and laughed at the musical comedies confected by Offenbach, Meilhac and Halévy, *La Belle Hélène, Barbe-Bleue, La Vie Parisienne* and *La Grande Duchesse de Gérolstein*. All Europe, says M. Daniel Halévy, had been tickled by the froth and glitter of France: but it was England that Europe copied.[1]

Of the serious and sober France that lay beyond the city's ramparts Europe had scarcely caught a glimpse. In 1870 German officers on reading captured correspondence expressed their amazement that French men and women showed love, affection, faith and loyalty to each other: French novelists, dramatists and journalists had shown only treachery, deceit and frivolity.[2] A few Englishmen who had visited the Exhibition had presented to their government a thoughtful report which stressed the alarming fact that the industrialists of Western Europe, including those of France, were rapidly overhauling England and in some directions had already outclassed English methods.

From the point of view of the foreigner, the French were an enigma. What was France? Was there one? Or two? Or several? Did the frequent changes of régime since 1789 — eleven constitutions were promulgated between 1791 and 1875 — betoken deep fissures in French society; or were these constitutions no more than modifications in the light of circumstances? Were the unmistakable cleavages between Legitimists, Imperialists, Constitutional Monarchists and Republicans deep or superficial? Or did the variations between these loyalties cover an undisclosed, undiagnosed malady? Were the passions roused by the revolutions significant of a permanent hostility between the privileged

xi

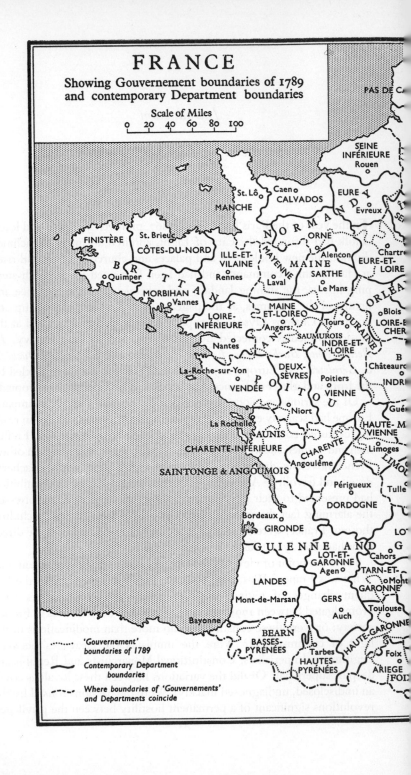

FRANCE

Showing Gouvernement boundaries of 1789
and contemporary Department boundaries

Scale of Miles

0   20   40   60   80   100

PAS DE C

SEINE
INFÉRIEURE
Rouen

St. Lô   Caen   EURE
CALVADOS   Evreux
MANCHE   SE

N O R M A N D Y

ORNE
FINISTÈRE   St. Brieuc   Chartr
CÔTES-DU-NORD   ILLE-ET-   Alencon   EURE-ET-
VILAINE   MAINE   LOIRE
B R I T   SARTHE
Quimper   Rennes   Laval   Le Mans   ORLÉA
T T A   MAINE
MORBIHAN   N Y
Vannes   MAINE-   Blois
LOIRE-   ET-LOIRE   LOIRE-E
INFÉRIEURE   Angers   Tours   CHER
A N J O U   TOURAINE
Nantes   SAUMUROIS
INDRE-ET-
LOIRE   B
La Roche-sur-Yon   DEUX-   Châteauc
SÈVRES   Poitiers
VENDÉE   P O I T   INDR
O U
Niort   Gué
La Rochelle   HAUTE-M
AUNIS   VIENNE
CHARENTE-INFÉRIEURE   CHARENTE   Limoges
Angoulême   LIMO
SAINTONGE & ANGOUMOIS
Périgueux   Tulle
DORDOGNE
Bordeaux
GIRONDE   LO
G U I E N N E   A N D   G
LOT-ET-   Cahors
GARONNE
Agen   TARN-ET-
LANDES   Mont
GARONNE
Mont-de-Marsan   GERS   Toulouse
Auch   GARONNE
Bayonne
BEARN   HAUTE-GARONNE
BASSES-
PYRÉNÉES   Tarbes   Foix
HAUTES-   ARIEGE
PYRÉNÉES   FOI

.... 'Gouvernement'
boundaries of 1789

——— Contemporary Department
boundaries

- - - - Where boundaries of 'Gouvernements'
and Departments coincide

FLANDERS
Lille
ARTOIS
Arras
NORD
HAINAULT
OMME
miens
PICARDY
Beauvais
ISE
Laon
AISNE
Mézières
ARDENNES
MEUSE
Metz
MOSELLE
Territory annexed
by Germany, 1871
DE FRANCE
INE
Paris
Versailles
OISE
SEINE-
ET-
MARNE
Melun
MARNE
Châlons-
sur-Marne
CHAMPAGNE
Bar-le-Duc
LORRAINE
Nancy
MEURTHE-ET-
MOSELLE
BAS-
RHIN
Strasbourg
IS
LOIRET
rleans
YONNE
Auxerre
Troyes
AUBE
HAUTE-
MARNE
Langres
VOSGES
Epinal
HAUTE-
RHIN
Mulhouse
ALSACE
HAUTE-
Vesoul
Belfort
CHER
Bourges
RY
NIVERNAIS
Nevers
NIÈVRE
CÔTE-D'OR
Dijon
BURGUNDY
SAONE
FRANCHE
Besançon
DOUBS
COMTÉ
JURA
Territory
of Belfort
Moulins
ALLIER
BOURBONNAIS
SAONE-ET-
LOIRE
Macon
Lons-le-
Saunier
HE
USE
PUY-DE-DÔME
Clermont-
Ferrand
RÈZE
N
AUVERGNE
CANTAL
Aurillac
RHÔNE
LYONNAIS
LOIRE
St.
Etienne
Bourg
AIN
Lyons
HAUTE-SAVOIE
Annecy
Chambéry
SAVOIE
HAUTE-LOIRE
Le Puy
Valence
ISÈRE
Grenoble
HAUTES-ALPES
CONY
AVEYRON
en
Albi
TARN
Rodez
LOZÈRE
Mende
ARDÈCHE
Privas
DRÔME
DAUPHINÉ
Gap
LANGUEDOC
HÉRAULT
GARD
Avignon
Nîmes
Montpellier
VAUCLUSE
BOURCHES
-DU-RHONE
Marseilles
Digne
BASSES-
ALPES
PROVENCE
VAR
Draguignan
ALPES-MARITIMES
Nice
arcassonne
AUDE
PYRÉNÉES
ORIENTALES
Perpignan
ROUSSILLON

BPL

or possessing groups and the poor and unprivileged? Or was it a con-flict between town and country? Again, were there, as a writer at the end of the century was to distinguish, two Frances, the Black and the Red, clerical and socialist, or perhaps spiritual and materialist?

An observant foreigner might have found some of the answers as he travelled the country, might have discovered, as elsewhere, the varia-tions from the common pattern in France, and even more the contrast with other countries of north-western Europe. If he was an English-man, he could not escape the fact that the area of forest-land in France was prodigious as compared with England. In England most of the forest-land had been neglected; many chases and woodlands were no more than names on the map. In France great blocks of oak and beech and fir survived in the Woevre and the Argonne, on the slopes of the Vosges, the forests of Fontainebleau, of Orléans, of Compiègne, of Othe, the *bocages* of lower Normandy and Vendée, the woods of Cher and Nièvre, the massed pines between the Pointe de Grave and the Adour. The country was still untamed. In 1876 twelve wild boars rushed through the main street of Bernay at midday, spreading dismay. There were still two or three thousand wolves in the Central Massif.

Another aspect as he roved from north to south would be the attitude to work. After he passed the Loire he would notice a change in the rhythm. In the north, production, whether agricultural or industrial, would be rational, calculated to an economic end. As he reached the south he would find the rhythm changing. It was not that men worked less hard; indeed they often worked longer, tilling poor soil near some village which had added '*le-chétif*' to its name. But except in the com-mercial vineyards, methods were traditional: time counted for less, and methods were still perhaps half a century behind those of Flanders, Artois and Picardy. One fragment of evidence, the workman's blouse, common in the north, had not yet become habitual south of the centre. In Brittany and south of the Sologne, probably — one cannot be sure — the old regional costumes were still being worn.[3]

For another thing, the distinction between the industrial and agri-cultural worker was not yet clear. Here and there the préfets in their departmental reports to the Minister of the Interior[4] (their date is 1872, but they were not published, and then only in précis, till 1875) say that the distinction is more apparent than in the past, that the agricultural force is declining, while the urban is increasing, and that men are now choosing industry where the rewards are higher: but the evidence is not universal. Even in Paris, owing to the lengthy dead seasons, many workers returned to the farms they came from. The salient feature of the reports is the absence of large-scale industry in most departments: the préfet of Seine-et-Marne could mention no more than the well-known faïence factory at Montéreau and a paper-mill; he of Finistère the Brest arsenal and one linen company; of Corrèze only the government arms factory at Tulle; of Var only the naval dockyards at Toulon. Of the active industrial population, a fifth was concentrated round Paris, while nearly a third of all heavy workers, coal and metals, were to be found in four of the eighty-seven departments, Seine, Nord, Pas-de-Calais and Loire.

So far only the preliminaries for expansion had been carried out, the lay-out of the main lines, the partial improvement of waterways and roads, the telegraph and cheap postal facilities. The railways had not opened up the country, but were constructed to serve industrial areas already in existence. The northern half of the country above the Nantes-Geneva line had far the greater share. The south as yet remained as it always had been, its back turned to the capital. Many towns, former centres of industry, bustling provincial capitals, had averted their eyes from the new world, had renounced the struggle and relapsed into crystallised hierarchies, indifferent to the growth of more active communities. There is Rennes, capital of Ille-et-Vilaine, with a tradition of hostility to the capital since the days of Le Chalotais and the Duc d'Aguilhon. 'In this antique city,' wrote André Siegfried, 'the *noblesse* of Upper Brittany . . . finds the aristocratic atmosphere that suits it. The sons of the family do their law training, army officers discover a brilliant garrison. The boulevard de Sévigné, the rue de Paris, form the nucleus of a miniature faubourg Saint-Germain, in which the *noblesse* lives in isolation, remote. The upper bourgeoisie of tradition, another aristocracy, today [i.e. 1910] almost extinct, scarcely mixes more. . . . And the religious atmosphere of the West, the piercing sound of bells morning and evening, the preoccupation with the affairs of the Church weigh like an obsession on even its adversaries . . . they invade the whole circumambient air.'[5] Rennes, remarked Taine, is a city of enormous piety and enormous squalor.[6]

Or there is Poitiers, the fief of Monsignor Pie, that redoubtable Legitimist prelate, dictator to a society of *bien-pensants* without brains or energy, who dress their domestic servants in the costumes of the eighteenth century. Grass grows in the streets; the lamps are extinguished soon after dark. 'Thirty-eight religious houses in a single town, and the Jesuits' boarding-school has 750 pupils', comments Taine in

1864. At Ste Radegonde's shrine miracles are known: a leprous woman was cured — and died three days later. The University is the public enemy: woe betide any priest that dares to become Rector; he is ostracised. Toulouse possesses sixty-four religious houses;[6] its area is exactly that fixed by Raymond VII in 1229. There is Montauban with its blood-red buildings, once a cloth town, now in decay, where, wrote Arsène Dumont, the main occupation is waiting for dead-men's shoes.[7] So far these and other cities and regions have scarcely been touched by the nineteenth century. Many communes had no horizon beyond the market town, itself remote from the provincial capital. Their sky-line was limited and they imagined nothing beyond it.

'The ignorance of the French peasantry is difficult to believe when you do not know them, and still more when you know them well, because their intelligence and tact seem incompatible with ignorance. . . . [The rustic's] ignorance is incredible. He does not really know what the word *France* means. During the war many patriotic Frenchmen were indignant at the conduct of the peasantry, at their indifference to the invasion of Alsace and Lorraine. . . . You tell them that the war has ended in the loss of Alsace and Lorraine. This conveys no distinct idea to their minds — why should they make sacrifices for the people of Alsace who were always foreigners to them?'[8]

Their interests were local, their policies the same, *querelles de clocher*. Many were illiterate. In 1875, 20% of newly-wed husbands and 31% of young wives were officially recorded as such. In 1872 the préfet of Gironde, the wealthiest department of the south-west, stated that 55% of those over twenty were unable to read or write, 86% of those over forty: in 1876, the figure of 57% of those over six is given for Indre-et-Loire. Most of those who lived in the frontier departments scarcely understood French. Basque, Catalan, Breton, Flemish, Walloon, Alsatian, Savoyard, Italian might be their language, but everywhere there were used dialects and dialect words, so deformed over years that neighbouring valleys had difficulty in communicating. The Marquis de Vogüé noted that at the end of the Second Empire the peasant of the Vivarais did not know who sat on the throne of France. Of 1894 Bodley records that there were peasants in the French Alps who thought Napoleon III still reigned.[9]

Yet in spite of illiteracy and ignorance, the people themselves were intelligent. 'You go to Saint-Cloud, and you find there a population which has never heard of *Tartuffe*! . . . Molière is not read by the peasants, for the good reason that they either cannot read or have not the time. Neither is he read by the workers: and the recent studies which we have been able to make of the Tuesday audiences at the Comédie-Française, have revealed to us that the ladies of the upper classes resemble in this respect the women of the people: they don't know Molière. The only difference between them is that when by chance they see him staged, the women of the people listen with all their heart, understand, laugh and are delighted, while the others purse up their mouths, affect to have no interest in these antiques and talk to their neighbour about clothes.'10

In the country, in spite of revolutions and social upheaval, in many parts the local landowner still ruled. The Vendéen squire could speak of '*mes gars!*' and the village labourer — the worst paid in France — would say '*Je suis de la sujétion de M. le vicomte*'.11 M. de Tusseau in the hard years of 1871 and 1872 distributed bread to the poor and gave them money. 'Later, even after his fortune began to decline, he would send over to the café after mass for the small change and throw it from the steps of the church to the destitute and the children.'12

Elsewhere control might reside in the local doctor or the innkeeper, even in the lay school-teacher, possibly a positivist, believing that most problems could be solved by the discovery of a formula: he might be a freemason, a member of Jean Macé's Ligue d'Enseignement. In the west, in the Vannetais, or in Léon dominated by the Chapter of the Cathedral of St Pol, clerical influence was strong enough to defeat even the noble landowners.

Only a few years before the defeat of 1870, Taine, who as an army examiner was touring France, wrote: 'I come back again and again to the same conclusion that France is a democracy of well controlled peasants, with a narrow parsimonious bourgeoisie, and ill-paid public servants who wait for promotion and grow no roots.'13 True as this might be for Guéret, or Le Puy, Bar-le-Duc or Mont-de-Marsan, it is too sweeping. There were regions and towns which Taine had not visited and social groups he had not entered. There were brains in unconsidered towns, Commentry, Tourcoing, Pont-à-Mousson, Longwy. What was ripening there would appear in the next half-century.

(ii)

In the nineteenth century, in which every social group is fluid and changing under economic pressures, the divisions in society are blurred. The hierarchy of French society had been much modified after 1789 by the changes in the régimes. In 1789 there had been thirty-seven *ducs et pairs*, fifteen *ducs*, *non pairs* and sixteen *ducs à brévets*. There had then arrived the creations of the First Empire, followed by those of the Restoration. Louis-Philippe had been a fairly modest creator: only two dukes. Napoleon III had restrained himself to no more than four. This, however, did not prevent usurpation of titles by the ambitious. The distinguished genealogist, the Baron de Woelmont,[14] declared in 1919 that of 989 marquises of that date, 645 could show no justification for the use of the title.

In any case the French *noblesse* was an astonishing imbroglio. Its origins, extractions and affiliations could be traced only by an expert, and between two great houses even a Charlus would flinch from giving one *duc et pair* precedence over another, so complex were the considerations. According to Chateaubriand, the aristocracy had three ages, that of ability, that of privilege and that of vanity. By 1871 the third age was well on its way, and though they would not believe it, the last patent of nobility had been granted.

Those who in 1871 looked forward to the re-establishment of the monarchy were those whose names and titles recur through French history, whose origins go back to long before 1400, and are of the darkest obscurity, names such as La Rochefoucauld, Crussol, Rochechouart, Harcourt. These remained nominally loyal to the Bourbons and to the Church. But the generation of the late nineteenth century differed markedly from their ancestors. Before the Revolution the *noblesse* was woven into the fabric of society: in the great mansions of the Faubourg all classes met: noble and artisan jostled shoulders as they passed in the courtyards. In that aristocracy there had been, even in its egotism and ineptitude, a vitality, a lack of self-consciousness, a freedom of mind, some taste in art, letters and life. These had died, as they had died in England. By the eighteen-fifties the privileged *noblesse* had surrendered to the Church and took its code of conduct from its spiritual directors. Monsignor Dupanloup and Father Didon led it the way it should go. That section of the VII arrondissement which lies between the south bank of the Seine, the rue des Saints-Pères, Saint-François Xavier and the Avenue de la Bourdonnais, is the Faubourg. Here, when it was in Paris, lived the *gratin*, the 'upper ten', possibly a thousand individuals. 'The dominant idea in the *gratin*', wrote Madame de Clermont-Tonnerre, herself a Gramont, 'is the certainty of a superiority which subsists in spite of an appearance to the contrary. The families of the *gratin* are all linked to each other and form a compact mass.'[15] Distinguished by its arrogance, its meanness and its lack of hospitality, the *gratin* existed largely to reproduce itself and to maintain the positions to which it believed itself entitled. In these interests its men did not disdain to ally themselves with wealthy *roturiers*. 'The Polignac family lives on champagne, sewing-machines and the *Petit Journal*', it was remarked, with a glance at its alliances with Pommery, Singer and Dupuy. In the cause, foreigners, even Jews, were, if not welcomed, admitted, Rothschild, Haber, Ephrussi, Bischoffsheim, Mirès, Heine.

This taunt could not be cast at Sosthène de la Rochefoucauld, Duc de Bisaccia, presently to succeed to the title of Doudeauville, *duc et pair*, Grandee of Spain, President of the Jockey Club, member of the National Assembly and of the Chamber of Deputies from 1871 to 1898, married to a Polignac, wealthy landowner with estates in Seine-et-Marne, Seine-et-Oise, Oise, Sarthe and Charente, not to mention Sicily. 'He married twice and being forbidden by his religion, had no adventures. His personality, as distinct as possible from that of an intellectual, filled to perfection the duties to which he had been born, that is to represent the party of monarchy with all possible ostentation, to have many children, all handsome, all well-dowered, well-married and highly procreative. . . . In the Chamber he did not speak: he represented. To represent with such strength, one must from the beginning have a high idea of one's person and rights.'[16] The duke's parliamentary interventions, it is true, were rather by way of interruption than oratory.

In contrast, there were members of the *noblesse* who, while valuing the monarchy as a strong component of the social structure, put the Church before the throne. Of these the most outstanding were the Comte Alfred de Falloux of the older generation, author of the Education Law of 1850, and, of the younger, Comte Albert de Mun and the Marquis de la Tour du Pin. Falloux, 'who was Legitimist by birth and education, [he had retired to the country after the July Revolution] and, if you like, by taste, at bottom served only the Church. He had no confidence in the victory of Legitimacy and through the thickets of our resolutions sought a way to bring the Catholic religion back to power.'[17] Adviser to the Right, counsellor to the younger enthusiasts, Falloux straddled the gulf between the Legitimists and Orleanists and nourished the minds of those who would one day espouse the policy of Leo XIII, of the Ralliement. Nevertheless he failed to close the gap between the Church and the Orleanists. For the latter were Liberals, who looked on the Church as an organ of the State, sceptics who rejected a blind Ultramontanism, followers of, or at least affected by,

Montalembert. Distrusted by Monsignor Dupanloup the Gallican, and by Monsignor Pie the Ultramontane, intellectually they could find no common ground with militant Christians such as de Mun.

These Orleanists were in a way a caste. Though by birth and lineage of the *noblesse*, they were not ostentatious; they were, perhaps, virtuous. Falloux[18] gives a charming sketch of a dinner of a few members of Broglie's cabinet at Versailles in 1873, which exhibits their decency and simplicity. But they were not inspiring. To Louis Veuillot, the coarse Ultramontane editor of *L'Univers*, they are the Coquelets.[19] 'Coquelet is not Prudhomme, but of a higher rank: he has been more carefully brought up. Coquelet is the favoured child of the universities. Prudhomme admires Coquelet: Coquelet despises Prudhomme. Prudhomme is a small tradesman; Coquelet is the cultivated writer, poet, artist, barrister, high executive, politician. In the National Guard Prudhomme never gets beyond a captaincy: Coquelet is a colonel.' Coquelet is part of the institution, perhaps a deputy, or a judge, or even a magistrate, often a fifth-rate academician: and finally the Coquelets were and are practically the exclusive contributors to the *Revue des Deux Mondes*, that most worthy product of the stuffed-shirt school. Earnest, solemn, intelligent, reasonable, with little humour and no common touch, they could never inspire. With the Legitimists, they could not live down 1830. For the Bonapartists on the other hand, who had ridden in on the fight of Louis-Philippe, they had obsessive hatred.

They were, however, in some measure linked with a section of the *haute bourgeoisie*. The Duc d'Audriffet-Pasquier, a leading Orleanist, and Casimir-Périer, biggest shareholder in the richest coal-mine in France, Anzin, had married sisters. The Duc Decazes, whose dukedom was of 1819, was a shareholder in the Decazeville mines and ironworks. For if the Revolution had broken aristocratic privilege, it had also freed the noble from the penalties attached to derogating from rank by trading. They were now to be found on the boards of many companies. Not only such magnificoes as the Marquis de Vogüé, ambassador, Academician, on the board of the P.L.M. railway, the Suez company, the Saint-Gobain glass and chemical corporation, but comparatively small industrialists, iron-masters and paper-manufacturers. There is banking with its own aristocracy, the fifteen regents of the Banque de France, some of them industrialists, some Trésoriers-Payeurs, who though State servants, in some way descend from the tax-farmers of the Ancien Régime, but above all the representatives of the members of the *Haute Banque*, the international financiers, Mallet,

Hottinguer, Rothschild, Pillet-Will, André. Many of these were comparatively late arrivals who had been buying up the great estates in the vicinity of Paris. There were the ten thousand acres of Ferrières which Rothschild had acquired; there was Vaux-le-Vicomte, Fouquet's famous palace near Melun, bought by Sommier, the sugar-millionaire; there was Courances, purchased by Haber, the Viennese banker, for his daughter; Armainvilliers and Vaux-de-Cernay, both Rothschild; Guermantes, owned by Hottinguer; and Champs by Cahen d'Anvers.

Nonetheless, for many the *noblesse* remained what they had been, the enemy of the people. 'All these emperors, kings, archdukes and princes are great, sublime, generous and proud, and their princesses are as you please, but I hate them mercilessly as one hated years ago in '93, when they called that ass Louis XVI the accursed tyrant. . . . Between us and those people there is war to the death.' So Georges Clemenceau.[20] And in another vein, a fanatically Republican lady, the wealthy Juliette Adam, said to Gambetta:[21] '*J'aime mieux ma roture, dont ma grande-mère de très vieille souche bourgeoise disait, "une branche de ma famille s'est laissée anoblir au XVIIIe siècle".*'

On the other hand, provincial wealth was not tempted to ostentation; Lyon, the world-capital of silk, was austere. Charles Benoist speaks of the great Lyonnais dyer, Gillet, one forerunner of the vast chemical combine, Progil-Kuhlmann, 'who led me through his workshops, which surprised me by their plainness and air of a family business; he was wearing an old wool jersey which was in sharp contrast with what one knew of his fortune.'[22]

Certainly there was a turning away from the gay frivolity of the sixties. After Sedan, Meilhac wrote to his partner Ludovic Halévy:[23] 'It is not courage we lack, but discipline . . . we have killed respect, and in doing it, of course, we were stupid and short-sighted. . . . When relics go by, one should bow one's head and not laugh at the donkey that carries them. We jeered at the donkey and the relics lost their potency.'

There were many sober bourgeois who thought the same, who had been profoundly shocked by the brashness and extravagance of the Empire, its lack of political foresight, its open immorality. Many looked forward to the revival of a Republic which would exhibit the republican virtues: justice, sobriety, decency. 'These believers wanted the Republic to be the signal for the regeneration of France, the redemption of the, to them shameless, immorality which marked the end of the Second Empire. I am reminded of an exchange between my father and mother — it must have been in 1876. My mother expressed her surprise that

La Belle Hélène, La Grande Duchesse and so on were no longer staged. "You ought to get it firmly into your head," said my father severely, "that with the Republic, that's over, all that silliness." "It's queer," my mother tranquilly replied; "it seems to me that there is just as much immorality as there used to be." My father had not long to wait before recognising that the establishment of the Republic in no way implied the reign of Republican virtues.'[24]

These were the so-called 'enlightened classes'. Of the rest it is difficult to speak. The *petite bourgeoisie* was scarcely a class; it is scarcely conscious of itself other than of not being what is called 'working class'. During the Empire it had obeyed the imperial authorities. On the outbreak of war it joined the National Guard. It accepted the Republic and 100,000 joined the Communards. In fact, the central committee consisted of many *petits bourgeois* inspired by nothing better than distrust of the Government and a feeling for humanity. It contains, on the one hand, men such as Delescluze, who would die on the barricades, or on the other such figures as Ludovic Halévy's 'Monsieur Cardinal'. The one certain thing is that it is bourgeois in the sense given by André Siegfried, to the question, 'what is a bourgeois?' — 'He is one who possesses reserves.'

Georges Duveau writes: 'Two facts of a general kind during the Second Empire created a social climate which day by day made the worker more aware of the separation of the classes.'[25] The first was the increasing primacy of money. In the old days a congeries of traditional links had held men of all ranks together, religious, feudal, corporative, and *compagnonage*. These were breaking, and the relationship between master and workman had chilled. Secondly, it was becoming increasingly impossible for the workmen to rise. The reign of Napoleon III saw the last generation of masters of popular origin. In other words, something which can be called 'a working class' was about to become self-conscious. (It is to be noticed that the *chambres syndicales* which embraced all members of a trade, masters and men, were suppressed by Thiers in 1872.) The distinction between worker and bourgeois, the classification by function, was about to be made.

1793, 1848 and now 1871 would pass into the mythology. In 1882 Ludovic Halévy heard a girl, a model for Sarah Bernhardt, singing:

> *Le bourgeois est un monstre, vomi par l'enfer,*
> *Pour boire le sueur du pauvre prolétaire.*

Chapter One

The Political Pattern I:
From Sedan to the Fall of Thiers

(i)

The news of the defeat at Sedan on September 2, 1870, and of the surrender of the Emperor and MacMahon's army reached Paris by six o'clock that evening; it was not public property for another twenty-four or thirty-six hours. On September 4, in a turmoil of insurrection and war-fever, the Corps législatif dissolved under the eyes of the followers of that old firebrand, Blanqui, who had invaded the Palais Bourbon. The Empress escaped to England. At the Hôtel de Ville a government was set up by members of the Opposition, and the Republic was proclaimed. The head of this self-styled 'Government of National Defence' was General Trochu, Military Governor of Paris. The catastrophe was beyond redress. MacMahon's army had been captured, Bazaine's had retreated into Metz where it was beseiged. Only a few strongholds stood; Strasbourg, which would surrender on September 27, Bitche, Langres, Mézières and Belfort. Only one army corps still existed, though another was being built up of unincorporated troops. Preparations were put in hand to defend the fortified area of which Paris was the kernel. From Metz, Bazaine staged a few demonstrations but made no serious attempt to break out. He believed that if he could maintain his army intact, he would become the inevitable arbiter of the future of France.

Adolphe Thiers, one of the few surviving politicians with a European reputation, who had carefully avoided taking any responsibility in the crisis, was despatched to the courts of Europe to seek intervention on behalf of France. In London, Vienna and Saint-Petersburg he was received with sympathy, but little more: no one was going to risk trouble with the most formidable military power on the continent and already fully mobilised. Thiers returned to Paris on October 30, and on the following day, the Russian government circulated to the interested Powers its unilateral denunciation of the Black Sea clauses of the

Treaty of Paris of 1856, thereby throwing the other co-signatories into something like panic.

The Government of National Defence would have liked to come to terms with the Germans, but as Trochu told the National Assembly some nine months later: 'Public opinion had reached such a pitch of excitement, that if the Government had at that moment thought it right to announce that they were going to make peace they would have been swept out in an hour.' There is certainly every indication that with the exception of the still naïf Gambetta, who took the war seriously, the members of the Government and the leading Bonapartists were much more afraid of the Paris mob and the armed National Guard than they were of the Prussians. Unhappily Favre, the Foreign Minister, had declared publicly to the world that France would surrender not a stone, not an inch of territory to the invader, and no compromise could be reached with Bismarck, who required Alsace. There followed a criss-cross of negotiation through the Empress Eugénie in England, Bazaine in Metz, and an irrelevant adventurer called Regnier, with Bismarck never failing to let Trochu and his associates know that, if necessary, he would come to terms even with Napoleon III. In the early days of November, Thiers, having returned empty-handed to Paris, saw Bismarck at Versailles to ask for an armistice. After three days the parleys broke down.

The German troops had reached Paris on September 18, and slowly invested the city. All attempts during the next four months to break the circle from both within and without failed. On October 27, with the agreement of Canrobert, Changarnier, Frossard, Ladmirault and Desvaux, Bazaine surrendered Metz and the last army of professional soldiers. The loss of the fortress put three marshals and fifty generals into the hands of the Germans. They could be spared, but not the 6000 officers, 152,827 combatant soldiers, the 1665 guns, the 278,289 rifles, the 23 million catridges and the three million shells, not to mention the 15,462 wounded and sick, of whom 11,000 would die in German prisons. On October 31 a group of revolutionaries in Paris seized the Hôtel de Ville and some members of the Government, who were with difficulty rescued.

Before the complete investment of Paris, the Government had despatched a delegation, Glaise-Bizoin, Adolphe Crémieux and Admiral Fourichon, the minister of Marine, to Tours to organise resistance in the provinces. On October 5 Gambetta, Minister of the Interior, left Paris by balloon to reinforce them.

The months from October to the end of January 1871 were filled by a medley of incidents comic, tragic, heroic, absurd or merely melodramatic. Gambetta had no administrative experience; nevertheless he went to work with unquenchable if confused energy and vociferous confidence. Since he was unable to decide whether he desired to defeat the Germans more than to create the Republic, one aim constantly undermined the other. Immediately after September 4 he had replaced the imperial préfets throughout the country by republican nominees, many of them incompetent, many rightly considered dangerous by those they administered. Through them he tried to purge the departments of Bonapartist officials, though these alone were capable of forwarding his military plans. He reached the ultimate point of contradiction when on December 25 he dissolved the *conseils-généraux*, the departmental councils, on the ground that they were disloyal to the Republic. On the military side there was equal chaos. Tours was filled with the flotsam that gathers in time of war and revolution, financiers, dealers in arms, place-seekers — among these last, the novelist Emile Zola, who was rebuffed. A few survivors from the fallen régime, Charles de Freycinet, an engineer of the Ponts-et-Chaussées, Rolland, Governor of the Banque de France, Chaudordy from the Foreign Office, and discreetly in the background, Magne, a former imperial finance minister, assumed responsibility and succeeded in curbing the extravagant expedients of the ardent and loquacious 'dictator'. The operations of the southern armies, amateur, badly armed and rottenly administered, were hampered by the disagreements of the commanders with each other and with Gambetta. Although the volunteers, the *mobiles*, fought with great courage, all attempts to relieve Paris and Belfort foundered. On January 1, 1871 Mézières, after a sharp bombardment which killed a number of civilians, surrendered. By the end of the month, the improvised forces had lost two-fifths of their effectives, and at the conclusion of hostilities, only 350,000 men remained to face 600,000 Germans.

In Paris, food and fuel had been gradually diminishing. In early December there were bread riots. Jules Ferry as *maire*, attempting to secure fair distribution, earned the title of 'Ferry-Famine'. By January the city was on the edge of starvation. On January 5 the Germans opened a slow bombardment. On the 6th there appeared on the streetwalls an '*affiche rouge*', a violent attack on the Government for its military failures. On January 18 the German Empire, with the King of Prussia as German Emperor, was proclaimed in the Hall of Mirrors in the Palace of Versailles. On the 19th a sortie of the garrison towards Buzenval was mismanaged, and some 3,000 dead and wounded were left on the field. On the night of January 21 those condemned for the October revolt were released, and on the very next day the revolutionaries once more tried to seize the Hôtel de Ville: they were dispersed by Breton troops. On the 27th, at midnight, Jules Favre on behalf of the Government accepted Bismarck's terms for an armistice, which included the capitulation of Paris, disarmament of the garrison, save for 12,000 men, an exchange of prisoners, head for head and rank for rank, an indemnity from the capital of 200 million francs,* the occupation by German troops of twenty-five departments and the forts of Paris,** and no fighting for twenty-one days, to enable the election of a National Assembly to meet at Bordeaux to decide whether the war should continue. On the other hand, the Paris National Guard was not to be disarmed, and owing to a bungle Bourbaki's army near Pontarlier was omitted from the convention and eventually driven to retreat into Switzerland where it was disarmed and interned.

(ii)

Bismarck had been lucky. Until the surrender he had been faced by the fact that there was no authority in France with whom he could come to terms. The Bourbon and Orleanist claimants were in exile, forbidden to return. Napoleon was a prisoner of war; his surrender had been followed by the proclamation of the Republic. The Government of National Defence had been improvised by no more than those deputies who happened to be in Paris; it had no legal or constitutional status, and it had no contact with the rest of France. As Picard, the Finance Minister, had told Gambetta: 'We are merely provisional and in consequence cannot legislate.' The Tours delegation, which in December had been forced to retreat to Bordeaux, was at best no more than a branch of the Paris Government, and in any case ineffective; for Gambetta, partly from his dictatorial methods and the uncontrolled

---

* The Germans took tribute from other places. Orléans had to find 600,000 francs, Tours 1.1 millions, the department of Seine-inférieure 26 millions, of which Rouen paid 6.5 millions.

** The area was roughly the whole of northern France except Nord, Pas-de-Calais and the Le Havre region, the southern boundary running from Pont-l'Evêque to the junction of Côte-d'Or, Nièvre and Yonne. In the area beyond this point the situation was obscure. Later, Doubs, Jura and Côte-d'Or were occupied. The fortresses of Givet and Langres which had not surrendered, remained unoccupied inside perimeters of ten kilometres.

requisitions on the countryside by his amateur appointees — 'Gambetta's préfets' were not to be soon forgotten, — partly through his reputation for 'red republicanism', had much of the south against him. Above all, Bismarck had needed a responsible body which could engage the French people and which he could trust to be both willing and able to carry out the terms of the treaty Germany would impose. Otherwise he would have on his hands a 'people's war', and for Germany, or more properly Prussia, he did not relish a situation in which jealous members of the now shattered Concert of Europe might intervene. He had not scrupled to threaten the bulliable Favre with a re-imposition of Napoleon.

The terms arranged, the Paris Government despatched to the Bordeaux delegation a telegram announcing the armistice and directing that elections be held with a view to convoking a National Assembly on February 12. The elections would take place on February 8. Among the members of the Government there was some uneasiness as to how Gambetta would take these orders. Jules Simon, Minister of Education and since 1857 an Opposition deputy, was hurried off, armed with full powers to take appropriate action should the Bordeaux delegation challenge the Paris decisions. Simon reached Bordeaux at noon on February 1. He found that Gambetta had already published a decree excluding from candidature for the Assembly practically all servants of the fallen régime, even those who had been unsuccessful government-sponsored election candidates. Moreover he had sent out a proclamation calling for a continuation of the war. These manifestos had been telegraphed to the préfets in all departments. During the next five days there raged a wordy battle, coupled with violent threats, between Gambetta and those who supported Simon. Other members of the Government hurried from Paris to Simon's aid, but by the time they met him on February 6, Gambetta, finding that some of his préfets disagreed with him, had given way. He resigned his portfolio, and Emmanuel Arago was appointed in his stead. He was not to forget Simon.

The system of election was a revival of that brought in by the Second Republic, the system known as *scrutin de liste*, that is to say, the constituency is the department and each voter elects the whole departmental representation. The basis was universal male adult suffrage. The election was carried out in chaotic conditions. The registers were incomplete. Many electors were prisoners of war; many had fled from their homes before the enemy: the wealthier Parisians who had undergone the siege had moved to the country. Gambetta's préfets had had too short a time to get to know their departments: some, too, had resigned, and their successors had not yet been appointed. The electorate was bewildered. Under the Empire it had been accustomed to receive clear indications from the government-appointed maires as to whom to vote for. This practice the as-yet-virginal Republic frowned on, though, like its predecessor of 1848, it was soon to lose its innocence. Thus the compilation of the lists of candidates fell to the prominent men in the departments, and to some extent to the clergy. In Seine-et-Marne[1] and Loire[2] the task was undertaken by the local gentry and the choice was difficult. Some candidates, indifferent to political creeds, allowed their names to appear on all lists: indeed, in some departments, the word 'Republican' appeared on all, even those with Royalist connections. Hence Dorian, Minister of Public Works, was elected on both lists in Loire, but in Tarn-et-Garonne Freycinet, Gambetta's right hand at Tours, fell between them. Frequently names appeared on lists without their owners' knowledge, while in regions where there was a dearth of suitable men, popular figures were entered, such as Thiers and Trochu in Loire. Save in Corsica, no Bonapartist stood openly as such, but, concealed as 'Conservatives', a number, not large, were elected: for, up to the war, the Empire had been popular in the rural areas; both Weiss and Ludovic Halévy found sympathisers with the fallen Emperor. There was in fact only one issue: peace or war, and Gambetta's proclamation had alarmed many. In Haute-Garonne Gambetta's préfet, Duportal, stood as a Republican and had the mortification of receiving only 18,000 votes against the 84,000 given to the conservative leader: the Republicans did not win a seat, and Duportal[3] telegraphed to his colleagues that the countryside had given a crushing majority to 'the Prussians of the interior'.

The elected representatives straggled into Bordeaux as best they could. Some were still prisoners of war, some did not even know they had been elected. They were of all classes and conditions. Two of the sons of Louis-Philippe had been chosen in Oise and Haute-Marne, the Prince de Joinville and the Duc d'Aumale, both, by the laws of the Second Republic, forbidden to return to France. Some were Gambetta's préfets, illegally elected. There was Garibaldi, a foreigner, who had fought for France and who would be ejected from the Assembly as soon as he appeared. There were ghosts of 1848, Louis Blanc of the Ateliers Nationaux, and Edgar Quinet. There was Victor Hugo. There were the professional politicians of the Left. In a famous passage J. J. Weiss has described the scene:[4]

'Those who saw Bordeaux in the early days of 1871 will recall the pervasive atmosphere of expectation, the groups of five or six deputies come up from their departments, who had to be bullied to prevent them from proclaiming the monarchy up and down the Allées de Tourny, even before the Assembly had secured a place in which to deliberate, those unexpected Legitimist faces, which looked as if they had been cut out of some pre-1830 tapestry, all come to plunge into the invigorating waters of universal suffrage and to find again their youth and confidence. There was Thiers, still uncertain of the number of constituencies that had elected him, affecting to gather round him first of all the "fusionists" (i.e. those who were working for a reconciliation of the Bourbon and Orleanist claimants). There was Gambetta preparing his retreat to San Sebastian, while his intimates could think of nothing better than to accuse Jules Favre of losing our armies and smothering the dynamism of the revolution. Everyone was hungrily searching for Joinville and Aumale in the teeth of the incomprehensible pains they took to hide; while for the last figure in the picture, old Blanqui who had stolen into Bordeaux to see if there was the faintest hope of throwing this assembly of backwoodsmen into the Garonne, saying in a discouraged voice to his lieutenants: "Nothing doing, my friends: not one single thing for us to do".'

The first business was the constitution of the Assembly. Jules Grévy, an old eighteen-forty-eighter, was elected President. In 1848 he had proposed that the Constituent Assembly should reserve to itself the election of the President of the Republic. They had preferred to leave it to the 'Nation', and the 'Nation' had elected Louis-Napoleon.

After the appointment of the Assembly's officers, there followed the verification of mandates. Some elections were contested; four of Gambetta's most forcible supporters, accused of using administrative pressure in Vaucluse, resigned before the Assembly decided on their case. The full number of the body, 768, was far from complete. Thiers had been elected in twenty-six departments and chose to represent Seine — it is significant that neither Haut-Rhin, Bas-Rhin, Meurthe nor Moselle, the four departments to be ceded to Germany, had voted for him. Gambetta had been chosen by ten; it is no less significant that the four which had denied Thiers had voted for him, and that, save Paris and Seine-et-Oise, the rest were in the Midi and Algeria. A number of members resigned at once. Thus the Assembly of February would prove to be some eighty to ninety members short.

In the immediate business of finding a man to lead a Government, the choice almost automatically fell on Thiers. To a former chief minister, a professional politician, a strong and clear-headed critic of the

Second Empire and the obvious negotiator with the formidable Bismarck, there could be no rival. The Commission formed to work out the organisation of the Government hesitated over the employment of the word 'Republic' before accepting it, but agreed to his appointment as Chief of the Executive (*chef du pouvoir executif*). 'The National Assembly, depositary of the sovereign authority; considering that, while awaiting decisions as to the institutions of France, it is essential to provide for the needs of government and the conduct of negotiations, DECREES: M. Thiers is nominated chief of the executive of the French Republic; he will carry out his duties under the authority of the National Assembly, with the collaboration of the ministers he shall select and preside over.'[5]

On this day, February 17, before business began, the delegations from the four departments to be ceded protested against their annexation to Germany. The protest was read by Keller, later to represent Belfort. Thiers, not yet appointed, warned the Assembly that on the acceptance or rejection of the protest depended the issue between war and peace. The speech testifies both to his wisdom and astuteness. The Assembly left the matter to the negotiators, and proceeded to confirm Thiers in office. On the next day he formed his ministry. The appointments indicated only to the sharpest and most experienced what would come. Most of the political offices went to men who called themselves Conservative Republicans, or, perhaps better, friends of Thiers. Dufaure, once a minister under Louis-Philippe, of upright and judicial mind, became Minister of Justice and Garde des Sceaux (Keeper of the Seals). Jules Favre was reinstated at the Foreign Office. Ernest Picard, recently Minister of Finance, took the Interior. Jules Simon was continued at the Ministry of Public Instruction, with simultaneously the Ministry of Public Worship. The Admiralty and War Office, regarded as technical ministries, were taken by an admiral, Pothuau, and a general, Le Flô, Minister of War in the provisional Government. The other two technical ministries, Commerce and Agriculture, and Public Works, were given to Lambrecht, a Legitimist, and de Larcy, also a Legitimist but an old friend of Thiers. There remained the all-important office of Finance. Thiers invited Buffet, who for a short time had held this portfolio in the ill-fated Ollivier Government of 1870. Buffet, who was by creed a Monarchist but had rallied to the Liberal Empire, first accepted, then declined. Thiers turned to Pouyer-Quertier, a Rouen cotton-spinner, a strong protectionist, who had quarrelled with the Imperial Government over the 1860 Cobden-Chevalier commercial treaty and had in consequence lost favour. 'A character', as has been said, 'from the pages of Balzac', Pouyer-Quertier had no hesitations. The ministry appeared before the Assembly on February 19.

On that same day, accompanied by Favre, Thiers left for German headquarters at Versailles to discuss the preliminaries of peace. The terms called for the cession of what would be known as Alsace-Lorraine, roughly the equivalent of three departments, the whole of Haut-Rhin and Bas-Rhin, two-thirds of Moselle and one-third of Meurthe — otherwise, the loss of 1,300,000 citizens, the cities of Strasbourg and Metz, of the great textile centre of Mulhouse, of the Saarbrucken coal-field and the iron measures and works round Thionville. Beyond this, France was to pay an indemnity of six milliard gold francs, later reduced to five milliard, scarcely 'indemnity', since German war costs were about two-fifths of this sum. Only 40,000 French troops were permitted to remain north of the Loire.

It is doubtful if Thiers, clever as he was, as yet perceived his unique advantage, that he was the single Frenchman on whom Bismarck could rely to negotiate with a sense of realities and to carry out the terms of a treaty. Had he appreciated this fact, as later he was to do, he might possibly have secured less harsh treatment. The negotiations, which lasted from February 21 to 25, were stormy. Attempts to defy Bismarck over the surrender of Metz failed. But in addition to the scaling down of the indemnity, Thiers, by conceding an increase of annexed territory west of Thionville and a German 'victory march' through Paris, secured the retrocession of the fortified city of Belfort, which, under Colonel Denfert-Rochereau, had fought to the last cartridge and from which after the armistice the garrison had marched out with the honours of war. In addition, Thiers gave up a more material object, the Moyeuvre-Ottange metallurgical region, with the exception of Villerupt, which Pouyer-Quertier persuaded Bismarck to spare.

In the general world opinion of the day, the terms were harsh. The indemnity was believed crippling, while the annexations, particularly that of the purely French province of Lorraine, shocked Europe. The discussion of the terms by the National Assembly took place on March 1. The committee on the terms, fortified by the evidence of the military that the war could not be continued, recommended acceptance. It was opposed by the forty representatives of the lost provinces and some members of the Extreme Left. A slighting reference to Napoleon III provoked a protest from the Corsican group, but they were howled down. A motion of forfeiture (*déchéance*)[6] put forward by a Norman member, Target, confirming the deposition of the Emperor and his family, was carried almost unanimously, only four of the Corsican delegation and one bold Imperialist, Haentjens of Orne, voting against it. Then, after a hot debate, the vote on the terms of peace was taken and the ratification of the preliminaries of peace carried by 546 to 107. Of the minority, more than a third were the Alsatians and Lorrainers. Of the others, twenty-seven were representatives of Paris and the whole of the Côte-d'Or representation. The minority was almost wholly of the Left. Only three of the twenty-six generals voted against the terms. The representatives of the ceded provinces then withdrew, among them Gambetta. Of the ten constituencies which had elected him, he had opted for the single one for which under no circumstances could he sit, Bas-Rhin. He disappeared from Bordeaux and was next heard of ruminating at San Sebastian.

On March 3 German troops began to enter a Paris of empty streets and shuttered windows.

With the preliminaries of peace ratified,[7] the Assembly after some discussion agreed to move to Versailles. From Bordeaux it was impossible for the Chief Executive to negotiate with the German Chancellor, impossible to consult the Banque de France on the liquidation of the indemnity. All the government offices had remained in the capital. On the other hand, the majority of the Assembly refused to sit in the city which had demonstrated its insurrectionary temper, not once but three times since Sedan. The choice therefore fell on Versailles, only fifteen miles from Paris and linked by rail.

Before the Assembly rose, Thiers outlined his policy. Already on February 19, in presenting his cabinet, he had said that pacification, reorganisation, the resurrection of credit and the renewal of work must be undertaken first. 'When we have carried out our reconstruction under the Government of the Republic, we shall be able to pronounce our destiny.' Now on March 10 he reiterated the declaration. 'What is my personal duty? It is loyalty to all the parties which divide France and divide the Assembly. What we promise to all is to deceive none, . . . to prepare no solution on constitutional questions behind your backs. From me that would be treachery itself.'[8] With these words, what was to be known as the Bordeaux Pact was sealed.

(iii)

In making this promise to the National Assembly, Thiers was possibly unaware that he was raising fears in the minds of all those who looked forward to the end of monarchs and emperors. Like other popular risings, that called the Commune was in part prompted by the ignorance and indifference of the governing groups, which gave to men of both good and ill will the excuse to excite the emotions of the common man to revolt. In Paris there had been various explosions since September 4. The latest had been on January 29 when two battalion-commanders of the National Guard tried to set up a military dictatorship and were at once arrested by the Préfet of Police.

Apart from these, and such extravagants as the professional revolutionary followers of 'le Vieux', Auguste Blanqui, now in hiding, there were enough discontents in all classes of Parisians to bring the populations quickly to boiling-point. A vast body of the able-bodied had no work to return to and nothing to live on but the thirty sous a day paid to a National Guardsman. The Government of National Defence on February 15 had decreed that pay should only continue if the Guardsman could produce a certificate of indigence. Payments indeed continued, but each man knew that if he was to feed himself and his family, the National Guard must survive.

There was no work because all industry and commerce were at a standstill and indeed could not be resumed until the banks had once more opened their doors, and few had. Nevertheless on March 10, the day of the Bordeaux Pact, Dufaure, Minister of Justice, secured from the Assembly the raising of the moratorium which had been placed by the imperial Government on debts existing at August 13 or contracted thereafter; these were to be paid at the end of seven months, which implied that the earliest must be liquidated in three days' time. For business men this was absurd. The Chambers of Commerce appealed to the Government; they were ignored. For the small man the law spelt ruin. It is said that some 50,000 bills were protested, and that if the law had been carried out in fact, there would have been tens of thousands of bankruptcies. At the same time nothing was done to protect those unemployed who owed for their rent.

Also, it was shocking to Paris to find that the National Assembly was not to sit in the capital. Louis Blanc declared that it would bring on

c

civil war, and it is certain that the move to Versailles played some part in what followed.

Whether, as some think, Thiers all along intended to 'finish with all that', cannot now be decided; in his *Souvenirs*, he puts the conclusion of peace side by side with the submission of Paris as his two earliest objectives. At least we know that he had marked the lessons of 1848 and drawn conclusions from Windischgraetz's occupation of Vienna, which he proposed to follow should the occasion arise.

In Paris were a number of guns. Before the German victory march, one of the National Guard battalions had removed them out of the German route to various points in the city. Thiers on his arrival in Paris on March 15 decided that the guns must be brought away by the regular army. Unfortunately the army, which consisted largely of men awaiting release and new recruits, was ready to fraternise with the Parisians. Thiers accompanied his orders to bring away the guns from Montmartre by a manifesto denouncing the evil men of an 'occult committee', which was the committee of the National Guard battalions. The operation failed. The troops fraternised with the populace. Two generals were taken and shot by determined insurgents and the Commune had begun. Thiers, apprised of the failure of his scheme, withdrew to Versailles where he was joined by other members of the Government and many of the administration of Paris.

The title 'Commune' harked back to the days of 1792–94 when, led by Hébert, the Paris mob had dictated to the Government and to France. There is too much legend in Paris for such things to be forgotten. The Commune has been called a protest against the Second Empire. If this was so, it was also against the Second Republic and the July Monarchy. It was in fact not an appeal to history but a spontaneous revolt against blundering authority and the 'assembly of bumpkins' the provinces had elected, a popular insurrection in which all classes were involved. It was not a revolutionary socialist movement, although members of the International Workingmen's Association were involved and indeed produced some sensible reforms. The Commune was as a whole aimless. For some it was a social cause, for others an attempt at administrative reform, for the criminals an opportunity for plunder, for the oppressed a protest against stupidity, for the patriot a gesture against the terms of peace. Nothing of this could be understood by Thiers, nor have his sympathy. He had no interest in understanding the causes of the revolt. To him it was merely a dangerous mob to be put down with a strong hand. Hence the ghastly ferocity of those last days after May 21 when the government troops entered the city, the pointless murder of hostages by the Communards, the travesty of justice in the courts-martial and the executions on the Satory plateau after the savage pacification. Many innocents died, many guilty got their deserts, while others of equal guilt escaped and fled the country. Many of those whose share in the revolt was negligible were condemned to transportation as pitilessly as those whose share in the revolt was great. Old scores were paid off. Henri de Rochefort, owner and editor of the *Lanterne*, 'vaudevillist escaped into journalism', was sent to New Caledonia. Arthur Ranc, Gambetta's police chief at Tours, one of the Seine representatives who had tried to mediate between the Commune and the Government, was tainted, later accused and eventually driven into exile. Rossel, the regular soldier, Captain of Engineers, who had joined the revolt as a protest against the stain of the surrender of Metz, was shot; seventy years later another rebel of the same kidney would become the leader of the French. Monstrous and absurd, the Commune forms a page in socialist mythology. Its place there cannot be justified, for many bourgeois with no thought of socialism received exactly the same retribution as the manual workers.*

Immediately after March 18 other restless cities, Lyon, Marseille, Toulouse, Limoges, Narbonne, Cette, Perpignan, Saint-Etienne, Le Creusot, followed the example of the capital. The only dangerous outbreak was that in Marseille, which took a week to put down. Few of the others lasted more than a couple of days.

* The employment of the terms 'communism', 'collectivism' and 'communardism' needs some elucidation. The first and third of these are often confused in documents of 1871 and thereafter, owing in part to the appearance of a few members of the International Workingmen's Association during the Commune. Communist was the term at this date given to the followers of Karl Marx, who in France were few. Collectivist on the other hand denoted Bakunin's disciples, the Anarchists, opponents of Marxism. But in France and Belgium about 1876–77, these groups exchanged labels, and from this date collectivism stands for Marxist theory, of which Jules Guesde becomes the champion, while communism becomes identified with anarchism.

The Communards, unfortunately often called communists, were not Socialists but decentralisers. They harked back to the Hébertist movement of 1793–94, preaching the autonomy of each commune, which should be a member of a national federation of communes. It was not a class movement, and Delescluze, its leader, was a Radical and not a Socialist.

In connection with Gambetta, deputy for Belleville, it should be noted that 'Bellevillois' in 1870 was synonymous with pillage, arson, etc., and frequently interchangeable with 'communist', i.e. Anarchist.

Zévaès, A., *De la semaine sanglante au congrès de Marseille, 1871–79*, p. 22, fn. 1.

Guillemin, 'Les origines de la Commune, Paris, août, 1870' (II), in *Les Temps Modernes*, Sept., 1955.

In the meantime, the negotiations for the definitive treaty had continued, first at Brussels, later at Frankfurt-am-Main. The Germans were stiff. They refused to accept anything other than currency, bar-gold or bar-silver. On the matter of the release of prisoners of war, urged by the French in order to hasten the winding-up of the Commune, they relented only in return for the right to occupy at French expense a number of departments until such time as they, the Germans, considered order restored and the French Government in a situation to carry out the terms. Bismarck wished to incorporate the railways of the annexed departments in the German system, but agreed to the deduction of 235 million francs from the indemnity in payment, leaving the French Government to make its own terms with the Est Railway. The commercial treaty between the French Empire and the Zollverein, having been annulled by the war, was replaced by a clause granting reciprocally 'most favoured nation' terms. As regards the people of Alsace-Lorraine, those who wished to emigrate were to be allowed to move their domicile to France provided they declared before October 1, 1872. In the end, though some 160,000 made the declaration, the German authorities rejected 110,000 on the ground that the declarations were fictitious.* As to the indemnity, it was arranged that 500 million francs should be paid one month after the capture of Paris from the insurgents, and a further milliard during 1871, followed by another 500 million, making two milliards in all by May 1, 1872, while the payment of the remaining three milliards was to be completed by March 2, 1874, this sum bearing 5% interest until liquidated. The transfer was to be made in either bar-metal or currency or in English, Dutch, Belgian or Prussian banknotes. The final discussion, at which France was represented by Favre and Pouyer-Quertier, took place between May 6 and 10, on which date the treaty was signed. Brought before the National Assembly, it was ratified on May 20.

(iv)

The Assembly had been summoned with no precisely defined object other than the discussion of the terms of peace. When they reached Bordeaux, the representatives were not members of political parties, but they did not take long to discover friends of their own colour. By the time of the move to Versailles, there had already appeared a dis-

* See Appendix I.

tinction between Monarchists and Republicans, but the exact line of the schism was far from clear. The Royalists were in three groups, meeting as a party at the Hôtel des Reservoirs. For the time being differences were sunk, yet they were patent. On one side were the Monarchists of the purest water who adhered to the legitimate Bourbon claimant, Henri, Comte de Chambord, grandson of Charles X, and in the eyes of his adherents Henri V. His life had been spent in exile, chiefly in Austria at Frohsdorf, where he was now living. He had, says Bodley, 'modelled his life on a rule more fitting for a cloister than a palace, a council-chamber, or a parade-ground; and in marrying a princess whose vocation was that of a Carmelite, he displayed in the circumstances of his life and death that there are heights of virtue and perfection to which it is expedient that the secular leaders of people should not attain.'⁹ That he was a believing and practising Catholic was known to all, which in many ways warmed his followers in the Assembly to him.

Among these few had political experience; most came from families which, after the Revolution of July 1830, had retired to their estates to await the restoration. Although among them were to be found men bearing historic names, a La Rochefoucauld, a La Rochejacquelin, the greater number were unknown country gentlemen, chiefly from the west, Brittany and the Vendée, and devout Catholics to a man. 'The Legitimist party', says de Meaux in his *Souvenirs*,¹⁰ 'did not belong to a single class, or, as their opponents said, to a caste. Whether of the Extreme or Moderate Right, its most active members bore obscure names. Of modest estate, often by the exercise of some hard-working profession, they had proudly maintained the traditions, which hitherto had kept them on one side, but in their own circles made them respected.' 'I belong', wrote one such to the Duc d'Audriffet-Pasquier in 1873, 'to that provincial aristocracy, honourable and full of respect for God and King, who live in modest ease, careful and happy to hand it on to their children with the blessed independence it gives.'¹¹ Their leader, Joseph de Carayon-Latour, was the pipe-line to Frohsdorf. Their number is difficult to estimate: at the highest perhaps ninety to a hundred, of whom something between fifty and sixty were out-and-out Extremists, regarding the Orleanist family as usurpers and the Orleanists as little better than traitors. Men such as the Breton La Rochette or the Marquis de Franclieu combined God and the King in their political faith with an obstinacy disastrous to their cause. One of the most active figures was that of Monsignor Dupanloup, Bishop of

Orleans, who had dared oppose the Pope in the matter of the Decree of Infallibility in 1870 and no less daringly opposed the Germans in his own diocese of Orleans; yet it was rather as the defender of the Church that he supported the claimant. Loyal, God-fearing and simple, the Legitimists were to prove a powerful instrument in the creation of the Republic they abhorred.

The second distinct Royalist group was that to be known as the Right Centre, a mixed body, partly of wealthy landowners, many from famous families, partly of business men, who preferred the twilight of the Bourgeois Monarchy to the glitter of pure Royalism or the glare of democracy. Usually liberal-minded, unimpassioned, they asked no more than a return to 1830–48. Their candidate was the grandson of Louis-Philippe, the Comte de Paris, their patrons the claimant's uncles, the Prince de Joinville and the Duc d'Aumale. Even more than to the revival of a constitutional monarchy, they looked forward to the foundation of strong conservative institutions as bulwarks against the rising flood of democracy. They came from no particular region, but it is noticeable that the great majority of the hard-headed Normans, representatives of Seine-inférieure, Calvados, Eure and Manche, were members of this group. At the opening of the Assembly they were by far the most numerous section, something above 200, perhaps 230. They were, however, as divided as the Legitimists. There were those who were uncompromising Orleanists, such as the impetuous Duc d'Audriffet-Pasquier and the Duc Decazes; there were others who called themselves 'fusionists', that is, they would support the claims of the childless Comte de Chambord, provided the breach between the two branches was healed and the Comte de Paris was recognised as heir-apparent. Of these the chief was Duc Albert de Broglie, at this hour, under Thiers' pressure, French Ambassador in London: for Thiers knew that Broglie, son of his old patron and political rival in the thirties, Duc Victor, was a trained, if unpractised politician, of considerable and possibly dangerous ability.

Between these two groups there hovered an indeterminate body of moderate Royalists, free of the mysticism of the Legitimists, yet not devoted to the Orleans family, who would vote as it seemed to them the occasion demanded and who would in the end find themselves on the wrong side of the blanket. Possibly 180 strong, they were led by Ernoul.

There remain the scattered and temporarily disheartened Bonapartists. Except for the four militant Corsicans, most of them remained as yet under cover, partially disguised under the word 'Right'. There were perhaps a dozen, such as Admiral La Roncière — the navy, re-created by the Emperor, was largely imperialist — and the Montauban merchant, Prax-Paris. Beside the Corsicans only two, Haentjens, a Nantais ship-owner, and Valon, a dismissed civil-servant from Cahors, had dared to vote against the *Loi de déchéance*. During the latter half of 1871 Haentjens was to found the Appel au Peuple group of faithful Bonapartists to revive the Napoleonic doctrines of democratic imperialism and free trade, and to win seats, particularly among the wealthy vinegrowers of the south-west.

The followers of the three dynastic branches were unable to shed the hatreds of the past. The Legitimists could never forgive the cadet line for the usurpation of 1830; nor would they ever forget it. The Orleanists hated the Bonapartists for the *coup-d'état* of 1851 and the resurrection of the Empire and, as a final item, the seizure of the private property of the Orleans family. The Bonapartists, issue of two revolutions, hated and despised the Monarchists with the fierceness of arrivistes for those they have supplanted. Each group nevertheless had its internal frictions. Among the Legitimists were those, for example, who in no circumstances, not even the death of Chambord, would recognise the Orleans line. And when in 1883 Chambord expired, they would throw their devotion at the feet of Don Carlos and earn the soubriquet of 'Blancs d'Espagne'. In the Orleans family the Comte de Paris did not by any means see eye to eye with his uncles, particularly with Aumale, who had his private ambitions. Inside the Bonapartists' ranks, latent but ready to come to the surface after the Emperor's death, there simmered a conflict of doctrine, policy and personalities. On the one side were the servants of the Emperor, such as Rouher, who had disliked the liberal régime of 1869 and had no use for democracy except as a tool. On the other, that queer fish, the eccentric but intelligent cousin of the Emperor, Prince Napoleon, beetle-browed, swarthy, a hark-back to the founder of the dynasty — 'a tragic head, the mask of a Roman emperor', wrote one diarist (Hérault); *'un César déclassé'*, scoffed Edmond About. Long before 1870 he had understood democratic sentiment, and had begun to think in terms, it might be, of the Consulate rather than the Empire. Between him and a Rouher there could be no alliance. Moreover, he was a friend of Rouher's supplanter, Emile Ollivier.

(v)

The Left was as heterogeneous as the Right, and in the first six months of the Assembly far weaker. As yet only two groups could be identified, the Left, otherwise the Republican Left (both terms are used by its members indifferently) and the Extreme Left. In the latter were future Communards who would soon go off to Paris, Delescluze, who sought and found death on the barricades, Pyat, who carefully avoided this fate, the comic Gambon and Razoua, and democratic sympathisers such as Clemenceau, Lockroy and Ranc. There were the survivors of the Mountain of 1848, Louis Blanc and Quinet, romantic, wordy and out-of-date. 'The *montagnard* believes that the man who has lived a good life is called by the Supreme Being to a privileged country where he will pass eternity in constructing barricades and invading the Tuileries and the Chamber of Deputies.' Beside these there was the as yet small group of Gambettists, the Republican Union, now, since the tribune's retreat to San Sebastian, leaderless. On the one hand, it comprised constructive intelligences such as Edmond Adam, the banker; on the other, inexperienced enthusiasts from the law and journalism, Brisson, Floquet and Proudhon's executor, Langlois, intemperate in speech, unpractical in policy.

The Republican Left, more moderate in tone, had three of its leaders in high positions: Jules Grévy, President of the Assembly, Jules Simon and Jules Favre, members of Thiers' cabinet. Their future leader, Jules Ferry, had made his mark under the Empire as the critic of the schemes of Haussmann, the préfet and rebuilder of Paris, and more recently, while préfet of Seine, by his energy in the repression of revolutionaries. In June 1872 he was to be sent as Minister to Athens, where he remained until after the resignation of Thiers. These Republicans were as yet a watching group, determined but not fanatical, though some of its members inscribed their names on the manifestos of the Republican Union. Probably the most influential of the group was Duclerc, 'the most eloquent of mutes', who had friends in every group and who remains an enigma. The strength of the group lay chiefly in the east, in the departments of small-scale working landowners and handicraftsmen, Meurthe-et-Moselle, Vosges, Doubs, Jura, Isère. They were firm and uncompromising Republicans and anti-clericals. Together the two groups numbered about a hundred, of which the Extreme Left appears to have been less than twenty-five. (A calculation of these groups on the eve of the election of July 1871 gives sixty-five Republican Left, and twenty-one Extreme Left, with sixteen on both lists.)

In the first half of 1871 what was eventually to become the Left Centre had not yet crystallised. In the early days of the Assembly a small group of business men had come together under the lead of Féray, a paper-manufacturer at Essonnes, chiefly to support Thiers and guard their own interests. A little later, a few conservatively-minded men were brought together by de Marcère, a Catholic lawyer from Avesnes (Nord), with the intention of opposing a monarchical reaction. By July they had chosen the title Conservative Republicans, and as it slowly became clear that Thiers was retreating from thoughts of a restoration, others of hitherto undecided opinions joined them, including men of such distinction as Léon Say and Edouard Lefebvre de Laboulaye. Much about the same time, the Féray group broke up on the political issue, some going off to the Right Centre and the rest coming over to the Conservative Republicans. By mid-July (after the election) the group numbered possibly eighty-five and soon thereafter it became the Left Centre, the group in which Thiers would take his place ('I am more conservative than all of you') after his resignation in 1873. Drawn from all parts of the country and elected for their personal qualities rather than for their political views, these it would be who would bring the republic about by their firm refusal to accept any other form of régime.

Thus a rough calculation of the strength of Right and Left at mid-summer 1871, before the bye-elections, gives the Right, including six open and perhaps twenty-four crypto-Bonapartists, a total of 412 seats against 102 Republicans and another hundred ready to become so.*

On July 2 elections were held to fill the empty seats in the Assembly. The full figure of seats was 123, of which 118 were for vacancies within the frontiers of France, with four of the remaining five for Algeria and one for French Guiana. Of the 118, 91 went to advertised Republicans, only eighteen to Monarchists; the remaining nine were multiple elections, the byes for which would take place in January 1872. To the Right it was a warning, which perhaps they did not take seriously. But it was not a triumph for the Left. Thiers had rightly predicted that they would be 'republican elections, wise, very wise, very moderate'. Though thirty-three of the new members were of the Extreme Left, it was more significant that in 'red' Paris, of twenty-one seats filled in February by Extremists and Revolutionaries, who had vanished, fifteen

* Cf. Appendix II.

now went to deeply conservative Republicans or moderate Royalists, and only six to the Extreme Left: Clemenceau, Floquet, Ranc and Victor Hugo were not elected. In Marseille the pattern was much the same. It was in fact a victory for Thiers. Although as Clemenceau remarked to Ranc that night: 'The word Republic has not scared the provinces', the republicanism was staid.

A few days later the Monarchists received a severe shock. The Comte de Chambord, who scarcely knew France and knew few Frenchmen outside his devoted followers, was a mystic. He claimed that the traditional emblem of the royal house was the White Standard. It was not; it had been invented after the Restoration of 1815, but none of his followers were able to persuade him of this. He had already declared against the tricolor, which he said was the symbol of the Revolution. Now under the tricolor had fought not only plebeians, but all France, nobles, bourgeois, priests, peasants and artisans, even the Orleans family. It had been on this question that the attempted reconciliation with the Orleans family had broken down in 1857. Immediately after the armistice, Chambord had reiterated his refusal to his closest friends, and he remained immovable in the face of their protests and entreaties. In April 1871 he had gone from Frohsdorf to Bruges. Then suddenly he decided to enter France. On July 1, the eve of the elections, he travelled incognito to Paris. His friends begged him to renounce the standard. He refused and went off to Chambord. The horrified Royalists had the temerity to send a delegation after him to warn him of the consequences, but it made no impression. Monsignor Dupanloup drove from Orleans to Chambord to beseech him to change his mind, and was rebuffed. On the next night the Comte de Chambord took train to Brussels. During his visit he had drawn up a manifesto, which he had sent to the Legitimist paper, the *Union*. It appeared in the issue of July 6. The gist of the message lay in the last line: 'Henri V cannot abandon the White Standard of Henri IV.' It was, as more than one Royalist foresaw, the claimant's farewell to the throne; it was abdication.

At first the Right was almost unanimous in its horror at the declaration. Then the Extremists began to suspect the Orleanists of trying to bring about the rejection of Chambord. Broglie was known to be cool towards fusion. They hinted that the question of the flag was 'reserved', and shortly afterwards they set up a new headquarters in the Impasse des Chevau-légers (whence their later nickname), leaving the Moderate Right to form the Réunion Colbert. From the point of view of the

Right Centre, the worst had happened; they could not, without split-ting their ranks, substitute for the stiffnecked head of the house his heir-apparent, the Comte de Paris. The profiteer could only be Thiers.

(vi)

Thiers already had other and better reasons for satisfaction. The first loan of 2000 million francs towards the payment of the indemnity had been issued and immediately taken up. The preliminaries of peace had required the payment of 500 million on the signature of the Treaty. The Commune had thrown the scheme into disarray. Bismarck, taking advantage of the embarrassment of the French Government, screwed up the total for 1871 to 1500 million of which 500 must be paid within thirty days of the pacification of Paris, otherwise June 27. On June 6 a bill for the issue of a loan was submitted to the Assembly, in support of which Thiers a fortnight later made a financial statement. He estimated that the total cost of the war amounted to a little under 8000 million, of which the major item was the indemnity and the cost of the German occupation. The balance included the 325 million due to the share-holders of the Alsace-Lorraine railways and various amounts due for interest on loans raised during the war. In the debate Henri Germain, one of the founders of the Crédit Lyonnais, spoke in favour of the adoption of income-tax. Thiers seized the chance to crush this heretic. Income-tax above all would shake the confidence of which they all stood in need. 'I look on this tax as so dangerous, I look on it as so fatal, that I will never consent to accept it. . . . I would rather cut myself off from the Government than consent.'

Apart from his beliefs, Thiers needed above all the confidence of the investing groups, and it was to these rather than the Assembly that his reply to Germain was directed. It was indeed so vital for the loan to succeed that the terms of issue were more than generous: interest at 5% and the issue at 82.5% gave a net return of 6.25%. The loan was taken up with enthusiasm. When at the end of the first day the offices were closed, 4897 million had been subscribed, of which Paris alone had taken two and a half milliards. It was a national, and, since foreigners had subscribed more than a milliard, an international, token of belief in the stability of France and its Government. The delivery of the first 500 million of the indemnity was completed on July 10.

Thiers might indeed triumph. The loan was a success. The elections had been 'Thierist'. On June 29, at a great review of 120,000 troops at Longchamps, he had taken the salute. And now the Comte de Chambord had signed the death-warrant of the monarchy. 'I am accused', he said to Falloux a few nights later 'of wanting to found the Republic. Observe how I am covered against the charge. Henceforward no one will contest that the founder of the Republic in France is M. le Comte de Chambord. Posterity will call him the French Washington.'[12]

In April he had turned seventy-four, but his energy was in no way diminished: the briskness which Carlyle had noted had not deserted him. Small, plump, in his chestnut frock-coat he looked almost a toy, 'like a ninepin.' Beneath closely cut hair was a round head. The eyes were grey, the nose small and aquiline. The face was a gift to caricaturists who depicted him sometimes as a wise and benevolent owl, sometimes as a bird of prey, sometimes as an imp of mischief, sometimes satanic. A méridional, he retained all the vivacity of the South, its quickness of mind and speech. His was in no wise a speculative mind: he was no reformer. '*Thiers!*' had written a journalist in 1855, '*c'est M. de La Palisse ayant le courage de ses opinions.*' There is no more penetrating comment, for he was a brilliant manipulator of familiar tools and ideas. Outside that equipment he was helpless. He had spent forty years in politics, but by now his experience had crystallised, and, perhaps unfortunately for France, had crystallised in the ideas of the thirties and forties. That he was a statesman and no mere politician, though he was a master of the techniques of politics, is not to be gainsaid. He believed in authoritative government, and his republicanism was in no way democratic. As he said to Marcère: 'What attracts me to the Republic is that primarily it is an admirable instrument of government.' Hence on one hand, his remorseless crushing of the Commune, on the other his clinging, in the teeth of the majority of the Assembly, to the centralised Napoleonic structure.

After his death in 1877 Gaston de Saint-Valry[13] speculated on whether, from the very hour he knew that he had been elected in twenty-six departments, he had not intended the Republic. 'Did he not wonder whether it would not be better to economise on a king, all the more as this king could be found nowhere? . . . Did not the old rascal come to say to himself: "Really, I am more intelligent, more perspicacious, more educated than all these people! Just me alone — that's enough!" ' The belief is debatable. Thiers was a practising, practised and practical politician. 'I hold to the principle that in politics one takes the facts as one's starting point. . . . Are we not living in a republic? . . .

Therefore I am Republican today as I was Monarchist in the past and from the same motive.'[14] True, this was after his fall from power, but from July 1871 restoration of monarchy had begun to fade. Therefore, if the State was to be reconstructed — and if it was not to lapse into anarchy it must be reconstructed rapidly — the Republic was the only instrument. His irritation with the Monarchists can be understood. In the circumstances of 1871 the form of the régime was secondary.

For there was so much to be done. Thiers flung himself into the problems with the zest of a younger man. There was the problem of the indemnity, the problems of war-damage, the problems of taxation, the problem of the delimitation of the new frontier and that of its fortification, the problem of the reconstruction of the army, the problem of the restless cities tainted with Communardism. He had his ministers, but they were merely his agents for the transaction of ordinary business. He corresponded with the préfets over the head of his Minister of the Interior — he had six in twenty-seven months, of whom the only independent was Casimir-Périer — and made and unmade préfets without reference to his colleagues. It had been his vanity to claim omniscience. As Chief Executive he showed something like omnicompetence; even though some of his measures were wrong and costly, he did not shirk responsibility. Not for Thiers the 'culte de l'incompétence' dear to later ministers.

Moreover, with this ferocious appetite for administration went a no smaller appetite for political debate. In spite of the chaotic circumstances of the elections of February 1871, the Assembly proved to be an excellent body of men, devoted, hard-working and, even after political differences had embittered the debates, sincere, as two Radicals, Gambetta and Goblet, were later to testify. It must be said that, for all its royalism, the Right was in many ways more liberal in outlook than the Republicans. They had experienced the paralysing hand of centralised government under the Empire and they desired to give back to the local councils a certain measure of autonomy and freedom of initiative. In April, in the middle of the Commune, whose raison d'être was a national system of federated autonomous councils, a bill on municipal elections was brought in. The debate turned on the appointment of the maires of the 35,000 communes. The Second Republic had left this to the electors; the Second Empire had appointed through the préfets. The Right, partly from principle, partly from interest as landed proprietors — many were maires in their own villages — desired a return to election. The bill, sponsored by Picard, Minister of the Interior, required nomination by the Government in all communes of 6,000 inhabitants and over. An amendment in favour of universal election was carried. To Thiers, historian of the Consulate and Empire, decentralisation was anathema. Thiers claimed he could not maintain order if nomination was excluded, and hinted resignation. The Assembly compromised and allowed government appointment in towns of above 20,000.

More friction arose between June and August over the *conseils-généraux*, the departmental councils. Here again the liberal elements in the Assembly wished to enlarge the powers of the local bodies. 'France must be restored to herself,' wrote the Catholic polemist, Veuillot of the *Univers*, 'and lest she should a second time be murdered and die through being stricken at one single point. The only method of securing this is to revive the greatest possible liberty in the provinces.'[15] The Assembly proposed to set up within the councils committees to keep an eye on local administration, and restrain the activities of the préfets. Thiers sharply retorted that these would be 'a syringe up my préfets' backsides: there will be no means of governing'.[16] After an acrimonious debate, a compromise was once more reached, but the power of the préfet was in no way diminished (L. August 29, 1871).*

Strong as the position of Thiers was, he still needed the support of the majority of the Assembly. He had been forced to compromise on the law for the conseils-généraux, even though he successfully maintained the préfets' power. In August a proposal signed by 164 members that the National Guard be disbanded was approved by the *rapporteur*, General Chanzy. Thiers treated the proposal as if it were merely another caprice of the Right, although in a number of cities, particularly Lyon and Saint-Etienne, where the préfet had been murdered, the situation was explosive. Again after a threat of resignation, a compromise was reached through the intervention of one or two army officers for whom the Chief Executive had a tenderness. It was left to the Government to dissolve the Guards on 'its own responsibility and as soon as possible'. They were in fact disbanded within three months by decree. Thiers' irritation was excusable. He was daily involved in external business, the payments to the Germans, the budget, the unceasing correspondence with the French ambassadors, especially with Saint-Vallier, attached to German occupying headquarters. It infuriated him to be dragged into conflicts, particularly those between unbridled Monarchists and undisciplined Republicans over minor affairs. He

* Cf. Appendix III.

needed a title more solid and more durable than that of Chief Executive 'under the authority of the National Assembly'.

How far he was the instigator of Rivet is not known. On August 12 this Conservative Republican deputy moved a resolution to confer on Thiers the title of President of the Republic with a prolongation of office for three years, provided there had been no dissolution. The proposal gave him executive powers, but placed ministerial responsibility on the cabinet. The Right had already met the newly-formed Left Centre and bargained. For the Right, the main object was to buy time and to prevent a dissolution which the more extreme members of the Left were already advocating. The debate turned on the constituent power of the Assembly, denied by the Left. A compromise bill between the Rivet proposal and the amendments of the rapporteur, the Right Centre deputy Vitet, was carried on August 31. The main point of the final version was that it linked the President to the life of the Assembly. Art. 1 ran: 'The Chief Executive will assume the title of President of the French Republic, and will continue to carry out, under the authority of the National Assembly, until the completion of its tasks (*tant qu'elle n'aura pas terminé ses travaux*), the duties which have been delegated to him by the Decree of February 17, 1871.' In addition, it was laid down that 'each of the acts of the President of the Republic must be countersigned by a minister. The President of the Republic is responsible to the Assembly' (L. August 31, 1871). The question that was neither asked nor answered was what would happen in a situation in which the President fell out with and was defeated by the Assembly.

The law had been voted by 491 to 94, the minority being composed of the extreme Monarchists and the Extreme Left, Brisson, Naquet and Gambetta. Since his election for Paris in July, Gambetta had scarcely spoken. In this debate he had raised his voice against the pretentions of the Assembly to be a constituent body, denying its competence to settle the future of France. It was the beginning of the campaign for dissolution.*

While the purely political questions had been in the foreground, other laws of importance were being placed on the Statute book. Between July 8 and September 16, six fiscal laws were approved. These did nothing to alter the structure of taxation, but they raised the percentages taken. Customs and excise, postage rates, licences, stamp duties, registration duties, some of which had not been raised since their original establishment, were all increased, some by as much as 100%.

* Cf. Appendix IV.

In the same period was discussed and voted (L. Sept. 6, 1871) payments to those whose property had been damaged by the war. Thiers refused to consider full compensation — the finances of the State were far too precarious — but 100 million francs were earmarked to assist the worst cases.

(vii)

In mid-September, the Assembly rose, not to resume its sittings until the beginning of December. In October, Thiers or Thierism received further confirmation in the results of the elections for the 1850 seats on the *conseils-généraux*. The Germans were slowly withdrawing towards the east. The transfer of the indemnity to Germany was being carried out with little disturbance of exchange-rates. The price of the Indemnity loan had risen very rapidly from 82.50 to 96. In October it suddenly slumped. The Banque de France, whose note-circulation was limited, had been driven to sell part of its holding of the Indemnity loan so as to recover currency. Thiers at once had the ceiling raised.

The Assembly reopened on December 4 to discuss the budget for 1872. All through the latter part of 1871 committees had been working over the organisation and finances of the ministries. *Rapporteur* after *rapporteur* denounced the administrative jungle, the useless departments, the armies of underpaid and underworked subordinates, the highly-paid but obsolete senior officials, the large staffs of ministers lodged on State premises, which cost a fortune in heating, lighting and upkeep. The economisers raised their voices and the *République Française*, the paper founded for Gambetta by his friends Scheurer-Kestner and Edmond Adam, claimed that this vast administrative parasitism was the creator of monarchies, which only the Republic could clean up. Gambetta's young men were still in the state of innocence. The permanent civil servants naturally fought the reformers tooth and nail, and they had ample support from the President, who declared that in fifty years' experience he had not known one day when it was possible to save fifty million francs.

So too with the budget. Pouyer-Quertier proposed to derive practically the whole new revenue required from indirect taxes which in the previous year had provided more than 80% of the revenue. The budget commission, through its spokesman, the economist Léonce de Lavergne, put forward an income-tax scheme on the English model. But it was vain for Wolowski, Féray, Germain, economist, industrialist and banker, to plead its equitability. Some asserted that income-tax would hinder initiative, others that it was a re-establishment of the abominable levies of pre-Revolution days. Pouyer-Quertier, ardent protectionist, said it was the worst of systems, with its mendacious declarations and vile inquisitions. Finally Thiers claimed the French system to be the most equitable work of the Revolution and the fairest in Europe. In a tempestuous appeal he insisted that the French worker was far more lightly taxed than the English. Income-tax was rejected by a large majority and the Assembly turned to Thiers' darling scheme, duties on imported raw materials, which he insisted were an absolute necessity. His audience was cool to him. The manufacturers said that any other form of tax was preferable; the diplomats pointed out that he could not unilaterally vary the commercial treaties then in force. On January 18 Thiers asked the Assembly to accept his scheme. Féray proposed an amendment to send the question to a committee, and carried his point. It was the President's first defeat; what was worse, it had been inflicted by the Left Centre. 'I have devoted myself to them for a year', he complained:[17] 'they have no political brains; they will never be a governing party.' Next day he sent a letter of resignation to Grévy. The Assembly was shocked; they must either lose Thiers, indispensable for so much, including the negotiations with Bismarck, or capitulate. After hours of parley they passed a motion appealing to his patriotism. The little man appeared touched and accepted the invitation. If earlier he had believed himself indispensable, now that he had tamed the Assembly he was doubly sure.

He had not tamed the Assembly. The permanent hostility of the Right to the Republic could not be weakened. The Left Centre were becoming dubious of their reactionary leader. 'The reorganiser of the ruin of France', the *Revue Bleue* had called him a year earlier. Through the next six months debate followed debate on items of revenue. Any proposal outside the established framework was resolutely combatted, and with the support of the Left, Thiers won. As André Siegfried said at a later date: 'The political economist of the Right is an economist, the political economist of the Left is a politician.' The great scheme to fill the gap in the budget by duties on imported raw materials was reached in July.

Once more the industrialists, regardless of party, fought the President; but the mass of the Assembly, timid, disspirited and tired, would not risk another crisis. The project was passed in principle (July 20 and

D

26). Thiers had his way — and nothing happened. Foreign Governments put up a lively opposition to what they rightly considered an infringement of treaty rights. Only a tiny revenue was derived from the duties, and a year later the scheme was quietly interred.

These disappointments had not yet appeared. Two other matters of future importance occupied the Assembly during the summer. The first was the bill on the Conseil d'Etat. The Conseil d'Etat was descended from the Conseil du Roi, its official existence going back to the sixteenth century. Much changed during the Revolution, it was reorganised by the Consulate (Constitution of 22 Frimaire An VIII, December 13, 1799, Secs. 52, 53), and became the lynchpin of the great Napoleonic administrative system, a body of experts to advise the executive on the relations between the State and the citizen. Among its members were Cambacérès, Merlin, Portalis, and it was largely responsible for the legal Codes, the law on mines, the regulation of the University. Like much of the Napoleonic system, it survived during the Restoration chiefly as an advisory body on legislation, but also as final judge in cases of conflict between the ministries or private individual and the State. Under the Second Empire, its powers had been much enlarged. The Organic Decree of 1852, while depriving the members of the Corps législatif of the initiative in legislation, gave the Conseil d'Etat the business of drafting bills and adopting or rejecting amendments as it chose. This practice lasted almost unmodified up to the Senatus Consultus of September 8, 1869, which set up the Liberal Empire, when the Conseil d'Etat was reduced to a mere advisory body in case of disagreement between the Government and legislature. Popularly believed an engine of tyranny, it had been replaced after Sedan by a body of commissioners appointed by the Government of National Defence (Decree September 15, 1870). The commissioners had been far from efficient, and by the beginning of 1872 their work had fallen badly in arrear: the branch handling conflicts of law had only disposed of 459 cases whereas the imperial institution had dealt with 1,400 a year. Moreover, the old quarrel between the tribunals and the administration had again broken out.

It is easy to see that a body such as the Conseil d'Etat would be anathema to an Assembly devoted to decentralisation. It was agreed that some such court must exist, but the Assembly flinched from placing so useful a tool in the hands of the arch-centraliser, Thiers. On the other hand, the doctrine of separation of the powers conflicted with the suggestion of placing judicial appointments in the gift of the President, or Chief Executive, and of having the Minister of Justice as chairman of the Conseil. It was contended on the other hand that if a Chamber of Deputies made the nominations, the choice of councillors would become a party matter. Hence, it was finally agreed that the appointment of the *conseillers en service ordinaire* should be by open voting in the Assembly, while that of *conseillers en service extraordinaire*, that is to say, specialists brought in from other ministries — usually the senior official — should be by presidential appointment. To sweeten the rebuff to Thiers, the number of ordinary councillors was reduced from 28 to 22. A third of the membership was to retire every third year, but be eligible for re-election. Thiers did not contest the conclusion.*

(*viii*)

The second series of debates, concerning the reorganisation of the army, is of more than passing interest, since the recreation of 1872 was to have bearing on both the war of 1914–18 and that of 1939–40. The Army Committee had been sitting since 1871; its report was ready in April, 1872. The Committee, all soldiers, was aware that the defeat of 1870 had been due to deep-seated evils in the structure of the forces, and that one of the chief of these had been the absence of reserves. Soult's law of 1832 had in effect called for seven years' service with no further obligation. This had been diluted by the July Monarchy, and even further by the Second Empire. Although the conscript system remained, exemption could be purchased at 2000–2500 francs a head, the money being employed to build up a fund to provide bonuses to encourage enlistment by time-expired soldiers. The army had become almost entirely professional. All attempts to solve the problem of reserves had failed. An attempted imitation of the Prussian Landwehr broke down in the face of public hostility. Marshal Niel's scheme of 1866–67 on these lines was emasculated beyond recognition, and the National Guard, under the Law of February 2, 1868, remained, as 1870 had shown, untrained for warfare.

The war of 1870–71 bred a number of legends. There was the myth of the Prussian schoolmaster, which would be one of the weapons in the approaching anti-clerical struggle. Another was 'the nation in arms', adopted by both Right and Left. The Left, imbued with the traditions of the Revolution, believed in the *levée en masse* and in democratic

* Cf. Appendix V.

equality in national defence. The Right, many of whom or many of whose sons had fought with the army or the improvised militias, believed that universal service might do much to heal class divisions. Further, the generals in the Assembly, who had commanded the untrained levies of the later months of the war, were now far less enthusiastic about the merits of long-term service than they had been.

All this was awkward for Thiers. As early as January 1872 he had been turning his mind towards the problem of paying off the last three milliards of the indemnity and getting rid of the German army of occupation. He hoped to secure an early withdrawal by the substitution of financial for territorial guarantees. This plan was already partly compromised by the German distrust of French military reorganisation. After the Longchamps review of June 1871 the Germans had shown suspicious curiosity as to the strength of French effectives, and the *chargé d'affaires* in Paris had hinted that too many troops were being kept round the capital in defiance of the Treaty of Frankfurt. In January 1872 Thiers wrote to the Comte de Saint-Vallier, intending him to pass it on to the German commander, von Manteuffel, who was sympathetic to the beaten enemy:[18] 'I do not want compulsory service, which would inflame the hotheads and put a rifle on the shoulder of every socialist. I want a professional army . . . very limited in numbers but of high quality.' When, in April, the Committee's report was published, Thiers insisted on the prior discussion of the bill on the Conseil d'Etat, probably to allow him time to prepare his ground on the army bill. Already it was being said in Berlin that the French were thinking in terms of renewed war, and von Arnim, the German Ambassador in France, warned Gontaut-Biron, the French Ambassador in Berlin, that the Emperor thought the French army too big and too expensive. Thiers replied at once:[19] 'I am only concerned with reconstituting the French military forces according to the views I have expressed for forty years and which I have always described as France on a peace footing.' One of his difficulties was that the Duc de Gontaut-Biron in Berlin, in spite of being a Legitimist, wholly faithful to Thiers, was too simple-minded and also extremely shy of Bismarck, whom he appears to have seen as seldom as he could. Hence Thiers was continuously driven to use the more roundabout way of communication through Saint-Vallier and Manteuffel.

The debates began on May 27. Thiers to his deep disquiet found he was unable to obtain rejection of compulsory military service. He himself still sincerely believed in the Soult system, and that short-term service led to an incompetent army and untrained n.c.o.'s. He therefore tried to make service as long as possible. Claiming eight years, he eventually compromised for five. The generals thought otherwise. Trochu asked for three, Chareton, the *rapporteur*, went to four. General Guillemaut defied anyone to prove to him that 210,000 soldiers with five years' service were worth more than 350,000 with four.

Thiers was in serious trouble. On the one hand, the negotiations for the liquidation of the indemnity and the evacuation of the occupied territory were already in the hands of de Gontaut and von Arnim, the one too simple, the other too unstable and intriguing: on the other, this infernal patriotic Assembly, with no understanding of the delicacy of the situation, was doing its best to create an army, or the semblance of an army, which would do anything but reassure the Germans as to France's peaceful intentions. While doing full justice to Thiers's policy, the Germans feared that his tenure of office was none too secure and that, if he fell, there might follow a presidency of the bogeyman Gambetta, whose recent speech at Le Havre had stimulated the German press to renewed attacks on France; and it would be Gambetta with a formidable army at his back. Thus in the teeth of the Assembly Thiers obstinately persisted in his demands. 'I tell you that if you do not vote the five years, I shall leave this place deeply wounded. Further I could not accept the responsibility of carrying out the law. You can take this declaration as you please. It is my duty and my right to make it!' Once more the Assembly, intimidated by the threat of resignation, gave way. The four-year amendment was defeated. All save three of the generals voted against their beliefs, and two hundred members, including most of the Left, salved their consciences by abstaining. On June 1 Thiers could write[20] to de Gontaut of 'this stupid army law which has kept me a week in the saddle. . . . At Berlin, it may be that they will tell you that I have myself turned to compulsory service. Emphasise that there is nothing in it and that I have yielded on words to win realities. A kind of coalition, not deliberate but real, of the Left and Right has forced on me a committee enamoured of the Prussian system. I have resisted for fifteen months; but if I have given way, it is because they have accorded me, in the place of the levy of a whole class, only a half, 75,000 in place of 150,000, a modest figure; plus five years' service in place of three. The whole basis of the law is there; and I see with regret that if I had resisted . . . I should have beaten this lunatic mob, which sacrifices good sense, real patriotism, to the patriotism of the parade-ground.'

Thiers had won, but universal service was hamstrung. The army budget could not support more than 464,000 men with the colours; thus five years' service could not employ a whole annual contingent of 150,000. By devious methods, exclusion of certain groups under certain conditions etc., the annual call-up under the law of July 27, 1872 could not rise above 110,000, and their service to more than fifty months. As a later critic was to write: 'At the origins of all theories which bid fair to destroy the effective organisation of the nation in arms, one is sure to find Thiers.'[21] It has been said that during the negotiations with Bismarck in 1871, Thiers gave a verbal promise that the armed forces should never be raised to a level which would alarm Germany.[22]

(ix)

While these debates were in progress, the negotiations with Germany for the liquidation of the remaining three milliards of indemnity and the evacuation of the occupied departments were proving none too easy. On March 6 Pouyer-Quertier had been driven to resign from the Finance Ministry. He had given evidence in favour of Janvier de la Motte, one of the tough imperial préfets accused of malversation of public funds, and had very naturally not been believed: to a great many people Pouyer-Quertier smelt a good deal too much of himself. His place had been taken by a very moderate member of the Right Centre, de Goulard, who had recently been appointed Minister of Commerce. Relations with the Germans were complicated by the unwelcome efforts of German bankers to participate in the financing of the indemnity. Further, von Arnim, ambitious and unstable, had conceived a complicated plan for ousting and succeeding Bismarck, in which the removal of Thiers and the restoration of the French monarchy were included. Bismarck, so far as he could trust anyone, trusted Thiers, who, he believed, could both damp down French irredentism and find the three milliards. He also favoured a French republic, believing that it would find no allies in a monarchical Europe. This good will brought the conversations to a conclusion. On June 29 a convention was signed. By this, it was agreed that 500 million francs should be paid within two months of ratification of this instrument, a further 500 on February 1, 1873, and the fourth and fifth milliards on March 1, 1874 and 1875 respectively. In return, the Germans agreed to withdraw from Marne and Haute-Marne after the first payment, from Ardennes and Vosges after the penultimate milliard, thus retaining Meurthe-et-Moselle,

Meuse and Belfort up to the end. The Assembly ratified the convention, but without enthusiasm; naïvely they had expected much better (L. July 17, 1872).

On July 8 the bill for the necessary loan was tabled. Thiers had evaded the attempt of the German financiers to force themselves on him. This second loan was also at 5%, but at a slightly, very slightly, higher price of 84.50. The subscription was opened on July 27, and the savings of the world seemed drawn to Paris by an irresistible magnet. The ground had been well prepared by the financial houses of Europe and the methods of subscription were singularly easy. For the three milliards asked, 43 milliards were subscribed, of which 26 came from abroad. Naturally the price leapt up. On July 31 it had reached 89.25.

Early in August the Assembly rose. Since January a slight but recognisable change had taken place in the party shading. Since the beginning of the year twenty-one bye-elections had been held. Fifteen had been won by Republicans, nine of them members of the Extreme Left. 'It is not only the monarchy which has been beaten, it is and above all the moderate republic. The Republic of M. Gambetta has triumphed over the Republic of M. Thiers.' So the *Journal des Débats* of June 12. Beyond this, another influence was beginning to be felt. Before the end of 1871 the hitherto crypto-Bonapartists had come into the open and formed the group of the Appel au Peuple in defiance of both Left and Right, not hesitating to claim to be truer democrats than the Republicans, not blushing to jeer at the impotent Monarchists, and not flinching from outfacing Thiers over his hatred of the imperial low tariff treaties. In February Rouher, once chief minister to the fallen emperor, joined them. From now onward they would show that Bonapartism, though overthrown, was still to be reckoned with.

At the same time, if almost imperceptibly, the Conservative Republicans, otherwise the Left Centre, were gaining in strength from the Independents and the lukewarm Monarchists.

In May 1872 a long absent figure re-appeared. Duc Albert de Broglie threw up the embassy to the Court of St James's, in which Thiers had astutely confined him in 1871, and returned to his seat in the Assembly. By descent on the one side from marshals of France, on the other from a temporary liaison of Germaine de Staël with Benjamin Constant, he united both tradition and genius. His father, Victor de Broglie, had trained him for politics. The Second Empire had barred his entrance to the profession. A sceptic by heredity and training, a Liberal Catholic of the school of Montalembert, perhaps alone of the Right he had penetrated what lay beneath the disputes of the claimants; at least as clearly as Gambetta he perceived the social conflict and thought he knew what was required: in 1871 he had drawn the attention of the Right to the fact that the interests of their class were not identical with those of this or that claimant to the throne. He had known Thiers from childhood, knew from his father of Thiers's work in the July Revolution, had seen his desertion of Louis-Philippe in 1848, and had learned not to trust one who was a pure politician, a pure opportunist. Since the Orleans family, in the person of the Comte de Paris, had submitted to the elder line, and since Chambord was obdurate, there was, he knew, now no hope of a monarchical restoration until Chambord's improbable repentance or his death: and he was no more than fifty-two. Hence it was necessary to provide for the interim. The main task of the Right was therefore to produce some solid if provisional structure of government which would permit at the appropriate hour the transition to the monarchy.

Albert de Broglie had the analytical brain of an historian, which he was; he had studied politics and learned much of his father's wisdom. He was a cultivated gentleman with a subtle appreciation of the theatre: he claimed to have seen Rachel fifty times in *Phèdre* and could discuss acutely the respective excellences of her and Bernhardt. Lucid in mind, he knew everything in theory; in practice he had no experience. In strategic planning he had vision; as a tactical leader he could never hold his forces together. Plump features, a pendant and petulant lower lip, a high weak voice and a slurred pronunciation, coupled with an inability to improvise, detracted from his presence at the tribune. His bearing was dignified, but his manner was stiff; he was in fact, as his memoirs unconsciously show, diffident. 'Worthy' wrote Saint-Genest, 'but as repellent as an article in the *Revue des Deux Mondes*.' He was brave and loyal, but his sense of honour was too clean for the manipulations required by politics.

During the summer he was feeling his way. The Right's distrust of Thiers was growing. Already in January some of them had planned to defeat him at the appropriate moment, and had suggested the Duc d'Aumale as a possible successor with the title of Lieutenant-General of the Realm. That suggestion had been vetoed by Chambord, while the proposal had roused the suspicions of the Extreme Right that this might be an Orleanist scheme to circumvent their candidate. Broglie, however, casting about, had already descried his man in Marshal MacMahon; but he held his tongue. At the leftward trend of the elec-

tions since January Thiers showed no signs of alarm. The Right considered it was time to approach and warn him. A committee tried to
secure the co-operation of the Left Centre, but the Left Centre would
join them only if the Right would formally declare their acceptance of
the republican form of government. In consequence, only the Right
committee saw Thiers on June 20, and Thiers, asserting that he was
more conservative than they were and that it was not his business to
oppose republican elections, laughed them out of countenance. 'What
do you expect? The Republic is one of the things we have inherited
from the Empire, with a lot more. . . .' When the Assembly was prorogued, it looked as if Thiers was invincible.

   In the last months of 1870, Thiers had referred to Gambetta as a
'raging madman'. Since that date, the latter had learned to respect the
President, though they had few contacts. Nevertheless, while proclaiming his conservatism, Thiers was in touch with the leader of the
Extreme Left through an intermediary, that Charles de Freycinet who
had been Gambetta's chief assistant at Tours. Freycinet carried re-
assurances to Gambetta. 'Your friends,' had said Thiers, 'need not
worry. As long as I am here, I shall not let the form of government be
touched. After me, they will contrive. If your friends are discreet, they
will be masters of France.'[23] To Edmond Adam and his wife Juliette,
Thiers had also said: 'Be careful, otherwise you [Gambettists] will appear as if you were following my policy, and I yours, and the monarchists will be even more exasperated.'[24]

   Gambetta accepted the warnings. Since his return to the Assembly
in July 1871 he had been careful. The Right, of course, hated and
despised him. The Conservative Republicans, and they extended far
beyond the limit of the Left Centre, distrusted him. In the Assembly,
his speeches were interrupted, and he was not helped by the loud
counter-cries of his friends. He had much to live down, the demagogy
of the days of the Second Empire, when in 1869 he had accepted as his
programme the Radical propositions put forward by the Republicans
of Belleville; the appalling mismanagement of his three months quasi-
dictatorship of 1870–71; the fact that his speeches could and did excite
popular audiences. 'What do you expect?' said his lawyer friend
Clément Laurier:[25] 'there is a degree of malevolence that an orator,
whoever he may be, can never overcome. Besides, when one has followed the trade of a god for six months, it is not easy to change.'

   Nevertheless, he could not merely support Thiers. For, though he
might enjoin discretion on his closest colleagues, there were outside that

circle ardent Republicans, the committees in the provinces, who could not understand the elaborate battle-field at Versailles. Further, for many, Gambetta incarnated the new battle with Germany. This image he had striven to dissipate: at Saint-Quentin on November 16, 1871 he had said: 'Never let us talk of the foreigner, but let him understand, we think of him always.' He had turned to purely domestic themes, to the dangers of clericalism, and more vehemently to the unrepresentative character of the Assembly, calling for its dissolution. At Toulouse, at Angers, at Le Havre in the spring of 1872 he had repeated these attacks.

The Left Centre began to feel something of the alarm of the Right. Staunch Republicans though they were, they did not want the Republic according to Gambetta. Their own numbers were only increasing by desertions from the Right, while in the bye-elections they were actually losing seats, to the profit of the Republican Union, which in June took three seats of four — the fourth being a Bonapartist in Corsica. Thiers, in spite of his flouting of the Right, knew that his conservative followers must be heartened, and in July he publicly rejected the campaign for the dissolution. Further, privately, he let Gambetta know that he was becoming a nuisance and forbade him to make public addresses during the recess. Gambetta, through his *République Française*, suspended the dissolution campaign. But he largely ignored the injunction on public meetings. In September he travelled through Dauphiné and down to Provence, acclaimed everywhere. The culmination of this oratorical pilgrimage came at Grenoble on September 26, with the famous and, for many, shattering speech in which he summoned the emergent forces to play their part — 'a new electoral personnel, a new personnel out of universal suffrage. Have we not seen the labourers in the cities and the country make their entry into politics? May not that presage imply that, having tried many forms of government, the country at last purposes to call on a new social stratum (*nouvelles couches sociales*) to risk the republican form. Yes! I foresee, I feel, I proclaim the arrival and the presence in politics of a new social stratum, which during these eighteen months has been in action, and which, be very sure, is far from inferior to its forerunners.'[26] No less certainly than Broglie had Gambetta discerned the future. The major question, obscured by the manoeuvrings of Monarchists and Republicans, was what class would secure control of the Republic.

The reverberation of the Grenoble and other speeches rolled round France. It shocked French Conservatives. It shocked Conservatives all over Europe. It embarrassed Thiers. Summoned from Trouville by the

Committee of Permanence, which the Assembly had appointed to guard its interests during the recesses, he condemned the speech, but alas! not for its Republicanism but for its foreshadowing of a class-war. 'He who distinguishes between the classes, to attach himself only to one, becomes factious and dangerous.' The Committee accepted his declaration, but they had their own views as to his meaning.

(x)

At the re-opening of the Assembly on November 13, the presidential message, the 'report to the nation', was the first item. It was the opening of the crisis. Thiers spoke at length, relating the negotiations with Germany, the success of the loan, the hopes of the liberation of the country. Then came the thrust. 'The Republic exists; it is the government of the country; to resolve anything else would be a new revolution, and the one to be feared most of all. Let us not waste time in proclaiming it, but let us use it to stamp it with the character we desire and require. A committee selected by you ... gave it the title of Conservative Republic. Let us seize this title and watch that it be deserved. ... The Republic will be conservative or it will not exist.'

It would seem that this theme had not been originally intended. Up to two days before, negotiations in a conservative sense had been going on between the two Centres, perhaps with the good will of the less radical members of the Republican Left (Grévy, President of the Assembly, is thought to have been encouraging);[27] but the parleys broke down on November 11, and Thiers, tired of relying on a fortuitous majority, decided to make this advance to the Left. On the Right there was consternation. The reference to the Republic was hailed by a sharp interruption: 'And the Bordeaux Pact?' A committee was appointed to draft the Assembly's reply to the message. Five days later Broglie, aiming to dislocate the Left, put up General Changarnier to interpellate the Government on its attitude to the Grenoble speech. Thiers remained silent. Lefranc, Minister of the Interior since February, replied, but his reply permitted Broglie to remind Thiers of his words to the Committee of Permanence. The President's rejoinder was choleric and violent; he threatened to ask for a dissolution. There might have been a break, but at the moment all hesitated. The Left Centre was alarmed by the Gambettists. The Right was not yet prepared to take responsibility. A motion of confidence, which included the Assembly's reprobation of the doctrines professed at Grenoble, was accepted for the Government by Dufaure. The two Centres united against the Extremists, but two-fifths of the members abstained.

The reply to the message, moved by the Orleanist Batbie, proposed a law on ministerial responsibility defining the rights of the President and the Assembly. Thiers seized the opportunity to carry the matter further, to enlarge the committee in order that it might consider constitutional and electoral laws and the creation of a Second Chamber. In principle the Right Centre were not opposed, but they did not wish the committee to work under Thiers's eye. The bill, however, was carried, Thiers getting the support of the united Left. But the Committee to study and draft the bill, the Committee of Thirty, save for nine members of the Left Centre, was drawn from the Right.

Thiers's troubles were far from diminished. On the one hand, with the aid of the Banque de France, since July he had been busily collecting the necessary foreign, particularly German, currency, gold and silver, with the intention of paying off the whole of the balance of the indemnity within the next twelve months, and freeing the country eighteen months before the expected date.[28] But, for the Germans, Gambetta was still and always 'the black spot'. The Chancellor, understanding perhaps little of Socialism, confounded Gambetta's democratic speeches, in which no socialistic tinge can be discerned, with those of the sponsors of the German Socialist programme. While he desired no restoration of the French monarchy, he wanted no revolutionary democracy on Germany's frontiers. And if Thiers was to carry through the final negotiation, he must reassure Bismarck.

On the other hand, the Right, although now ready to hunt Thiers down, knew that they would be incapable of dealing with Bismarck on the terms that Thiers could. Alphonse de Rothschild[29] claimed that by his persuasion of the Right, he kept Thiers in office for six months, that is from the end of November until May. From Berlin Gontaut-Biron warned Thiers against lending himself to the Left, and at the same time Broglie, through Cumont, against shaking Thiers's pedestal.[30]

January and February of 1873 passed in an atmosphere of expectation. Thiers, now alert to the dangers of his apparent carelessness of democratic manifestations, accepted a law which removed the turbulent city of Lyon from the charge of its maire and municipal council, and divided it into its six arrondissements, each (as in Paris) under its own maire, and placed the central control in the hands of the préfet of Rhône. But for the awkwardness of the Gambettists, Thiers was confident, though he knew that his majority could slip away from him. He, or rather his Minister of the Interior, Victor Lefranc, who had translated himself from the Right to the Left Centre, had been blamed on November 20 by the Assembly for allowing the publication of congratulatory addresses sent by some town councils to Thiers, in which the dissolution of the Assembly was recommended. Lefranc resigned, to be replaced by Goulard of the Right Centre from the Ministry of Finance, this office going to Léon Say, up to now, December 7, préfet of Seine. Yet if the Assembly remained cold and critical, Thiers was sure that he had the body of French opinion behind him. But that opinion, vague, ignorant and emotional, required of him a sign. Could he give it?

(xi)

The talks with Berlin were going smoothly. Thiers had told von Arnim that the fourth and penultimate milliard would be paid before March 1, 1873 and asked for a reduction in the occupying forces; fifty thousand German soldiers were far too many to be accommodated in Meuse, Meurthe-et-Moselle and Belfort. By January, he could tell Gontaut-Biron that the Banque de France had control of all except the last quarter of a million francs, which could easily be borrowed on French government credit from the international banking houses.

In January, too, another shadowy menace was removed. At Chiselhurst Napoleon III had determined once more to try his luck by a *coup-d'état*. The venture was perhaps not as mad as it may seem. The army and much of the civil service were still staffed by men of the former régime; the peasants had not forgotten the prosperity that had come to them during the Empire. Napoleon proposed to travel secretly to Geneva and then go to Lyon to seek the aid of the local army-corps commander, Bourbaki. In preparation, he agreed to undergo the operation he should have had many years before. His star was not to be tempted. On January 9, 1873 he died. The restoration of the Bonaparte dynasty might linger on as an idea for another twenty years; its reality was gone.

In March the Committee of Thirty were ready to present their recommendations. Broglie had been the brain of the committee; he knew what he was about, but, as he says in his memoirs, his trouble was with the Extreme Right, who wanted no accommodation with Thiers.

Yet the bill on ministerial responsibility which became law on March 13 was, as it proved, a weapon in the hands of the Right. Broglie accepted the Republic provided there was no bar to a monarchical restoration. In return, Thiers made concessions: first, to introduce a bill to modify universal suffrage — this would have no future — second, not to appeal, as hitherto he had done, to the Assembly on all occasions, but to speak only as President of the Republic, after giving notice; and, when he had finished, to leave the Assembly to its deliberations. The law had also importance in marking a stage in the process of driving the President of the Republic back from the direction of policy towards a final position of no responsibility: it did this by making the Garde des Sceaux the Vice-President and the mouthpiece of the President for ordinary business. That this would be its result now seems clear; at the time it was not perceived.

The bill was carried by 407, the united Centres, to 225, the Extremists on both sides. In the debates Thiers intervened on March 4, stressing the impossibility of any other course than the continuation of the existing régime, but calling for its improvement by the creation of the needed institutions. 'The Bordeaux Pact continues unmodified: for you (the Right) the future is open; for the other side of the Assembly the Republic loyally practised.'

During these debates, telegrams had been passing continually between Paris and Berlin concerning the final payments of the indemnity and the withdrawal of the German troops. Much bargaining had gone to the evacuation of Belfort, on which Thiers's heart was set. Finally it was agreed that Verdun should be substituted. The whole of the remaining departments, with this single exception, were to be evacuated on July 5, and Verdun within a fortnight of September 5, the date of the payment of the fifth and last milliard. Thiers received the news of agreement on the evening of March 15. He was triumphant, but he had no illusions — or had he? Some weeks earlier he had said to some friends: 'As soon as the convention is signed, the majority will pass a handsome decree that I have deserved well of the country, and then lay me out.' On the other hand, he still believed he was indispensable. To Jules Simon, who had remarked he could say his *Nunc dimittis*, he replied: 'But they have no one.' Simon, however, knew or, since he was very acute, had guessed Broglie's candidate. He replied: 'They have Marshal MacMahon', to which Thiers retorted: 'Oh, for that, I will answer for him; he'll never accept.'[31] For in April 1872, when Mac-Mahon's name had been mentioned, the Marshal had asked General de

Cissey, the Minister of War, to assure Thiers, who had placed him in command of the army, that he must not believe the ridiculous talk that was going about, and that he would not take the Presidency.[32]

The news of the final convention with Germany was communicated to the Assembly on March 17. It was greeted by a *'Vive la République'* from the Left, and a *'Vive la France'* from the Right. A proposal from the Left Centre to vote that Thiers had 'deserved well of the country' was amended to include not only the Assembly, but also the country itself. Thus far had hostility to the President gone.

A fortnight later, a minor incident removed one of the President's tactical strong-points. Grévy of the Left, President of the Assembly, finding himself at loggerheads with members over some trifle, resigned in a pet, and, in spite of being re-elected, stuck to his resignation. It seems that, among other grievances, he was tired of Thiers's party manoeuvres, and was probably cognisant of the fact that Thiers disliked the Republican Left (Grévy's own group) as he did the Gambettists. On April 4 the monarchical majority secured the election of their candidate, the Orleanist Buffet.

In April and May came thirteen more bye-elections, among them one in Seine. Thiers wished, indeed forced his extra-parliamentary Foreign Minister, Charles de Rémusat, who had replaced Jules Favre in August 1871, to stand. Shortly before polling day a Radical candidate, Désiré Barodet, the dismissed maire of Lyon, was 'spontaneously' put up. Barodet seems to have had no backing from any of the Left groups of the Assembly, but they could not oppose him. It is suggested that he was the candidate of the Freemasons, and Gambetta, although he had originally favoured Rémusat as Thiers's man, dared not oppose the Masons' candidate. On April 27 Barodet was elected by a clear majority over both Rémusat and a candidate of the Right. Thiers abounded in assertions that the electors had gone to the polls shouting *'Vive Thiers!'*, and that the result was favourable to him. Gabriel Charmes, then of the *Journal des Débats*, believed that the intention was to drive Thiers further to the Left, and quotes a Paris workman as saying: 'He must be wedged home'[33] (*'il faut le caler'*).

In the other elections the Right lost nine seats. It was this decline in their strength that brought the leaders of the Right to their decision. During the Easter recess, at a meeting of all their groups it was resolved to defeat the President. Some of the Right Centre, the Orleanist Duc d'Audriffet-Pasquier and the Duc Decazes, wished for the Duc d'Aumale to be chosen. Broglie, well though he knew that the duke would be rejected by the Extreme Right, nevertheless accompanied the delegation to Aumale. Aumale appears to have accepted, but as Broglie had foreseen, the Legitimists would have nothing to do with the usurper's family. On this Broglie proposed MacMahon and earned himself the reproaches of Audriffet-Pasquier.[34]

(*xii*)

The Assembly re-opened on May 19, after a recess of nearly six weeks. Dufaure, as Vice-President, introduced a government bill for the organisation of the public powers as envisaged by the Law of March 13. Dufaure's bill, laid on May 20, 1873, proposed that the Government of the French Republic should consist of a Senate, a Chamber of Deputies and as chief executive, a President (Art. 1). The Senate was to be composed of 265 members, aged not less than 35, the Chamber of 537, aged not less than 25, the President to be not less than 40 (Art. 2). The Senate was to be elected for ten years, renewable by one-fifth every second year, the Chamber for five years, at the end of which the body was wholly renewable. The President would be elected for five years and could be re-elected (Art. 3). Each of the eighty-six departments was to have three senators, and Belfort, Algiers, Constantine, Oran, Réunion, Martinique and Guadeloupe one each, elected by direct suffrage and by *scrutin de liste*. Each of the 362 arrondissements including Belfort was to have one deputy, but those with above 100,000 inhabitants should have two, while the three Algerian departments and Réunion, Martinique, Guadeloupe, Guyane, Sénégal and Indres Françaises were to have two (Art. 7). The President was to be elected by a college consisting of the Senators, Deputies and three members from each conseil-général (Art. 9). The President was to have the right of dissolving the Chamber on the authority of the Senate (Art. 15).[35]

The Assembly refused to listen to Dufaure and the Right presented an interpellation requiring an explanation of the changes in the cabinet during the recess. For Jules Simon and Goulard, respectively Ministers of Public Instruction and Interior, had quarrelled: both had resigned and their places had been taken by Waddington and Casimir-Périer, both of the Left Centre. The debate was called for May 23. The Right, temporarily united, attacked venomously. They accused the Extreme Left of subversive tendencies, pointed to the demands for amnesty for the Communards, the demands for dissolution of the Assembly, the demands for the raising of the state of siege. The recent changes in the Government, said Broglie, were even stronger evidence of concessions to the Radicals.

Under the terms of the recent law, Thiers was not permitted to reply until the following day. Dufaure, while strong on the cabinet's repugnance to left-wing tendencies, was otherwise weak. On the next day Thiers spoke, claiming that the Right, much as they attempted to disguise themselves as no more than Conservatives, were impenitently Monarchist, when they well knew that a monarchy was impossible. What was now needed was the legal organisation of government which would permit the ensuance of a conservative policy between the extremes. He concluded with a warning: 'It has been thrown in our teeth that we are the protégés of the Radicals. We reply to our adversary that he will be the protégé of a protector whom the former Duc de Broglie would have repelled with horror: he will be the protégé of the Empire!' Meaux says that it was the most persuasive speech Thiers had ever uttered, but it availed him nothing. At its conclusion he must withdraw from the audience. He asked Buffet what would happen if he came back. The President replied that he would at once close the session by leaving the chair. The debate continued during the afternoon. A resolution 'regretting that the recent ministerial modifications have not given the conservative interests the satisfaction they had the right to expect' was moved. For a short time it looked as if it might be defeated. Then Target of the Left Centre, the same who had in 1871 proposed the *Loi de déchéance*, rose to say that he and his small group of business men would vote for the resolution, so as to press the Government back to conservatism. The resolution was carried by 368 to 344, the Target fifteen having decided the day.

The next step lay with Thiers. He could not be forced to resign; his tenure was co-terminous with the life of the Assembly. He could, if he chose, embroil matters by forming a purely Republican Government and working for a dissolution. But all his life he had been a parliamentarian: he could not flout parliamentary conventions; he could not defy the majority. Besides, in his words to Simon, they had no one; he might, he would, as had happened before, be recalled by a repentant Assembly. So he wrote his letter of resignation and sent it to Buffet.

The Assembly met again at night. The letter was read, and the resignation accepted by 362 to 331. The proposal was put forward that Marshall MacMahon should succeed: it was carried by 390 to 1, Jules Grévy. The rest of the Left abstained.

E

The Marshal, innocent of all these intrigues, was at his home. Buffet, taking with him the officers of the Assembly, went to his house. MacMahon had only just been informed of events, and was protesting against his impossible situation. He had gone across to see Thiers, who had told him that his resignation was final, and warned him that the Presidency was 'a wasps' nest, in which the heart of a soldier like you will lose patience in eight and forty hours'.[36] Buffet took MacMahon in hand, told him that his election was not an offer but a command from the sovereign body of the nation. MacMahon, loyal soldier, was shaken, and after further objections capitulated, asking plaintively to be shown the 'regulations'. The future lay in the hands of the Duc de Broglie.

From the autumn of 1872 Thiers had been able to rely on no constant majority. Every vote was a vote of circumstance, and the groups themselves lost confidence. From then onwards it is impossible to divide the Left Centre from the Right Centre and the latter from the Moderates. Moreover, there existed small fragments such as the fifteen business men round Target; even smaller groups, as when Casimir-Périer with his son-in-law, de Ségur, broke from the Left Centre; even individuals, such as would later be known as '*sauvages*'. There were Thiersists in politics who were anti-Thiersists in economics, such as Lavergne, who later collected a group Right Centre by conviction, Constitutionalist by necessity. The Extremists at either end were wholly unreliable. Broglie would never be able to depend on the whims of the Chevau-légers: Thiers could never guess when the Extreme Left would from political tactics desert. And at all times the Bonapartists were wreckers. With Gambetta, Thiers was at sea. 'Sometimes he seems to want to make himself possible and adopts the language and precautions of a government man; then he is alarmed that he will lose his following and gives us a new edition of the Grenoble speech. But he has not and never will have the clear-cut ideas of a real statesman . . . he will always retreat into the role of tribune . . . which he plays most naturally.'[37] Thiers could have no other policy than that of balance; his survival to May 1873 had been a triumph of political dexterity.

Now it was finished. 'The great political career of M. Thiers ended on May 24. Thenceforward he lived rather for his resentment than for his glory.'[38]

Chapter Two

The Political Pattern II: the Government of Moral Order

(i)

It is usual to speak of MacMahon as an honest, honourable simpleton. There are many comic stories at his expense, some, to be sure, invented during the electoral campaign after the Sixteenth of May (1877). It is true that he was unversed in politics: he had not sought office; he was, to borrow an American term, drafted. Had he been less simple, he would probably have withstood Buffet's pressure; but those who chose him, knew that they would not appeal in vain to his sense of loyalty to France and his duty to the highest authority in the land, the Assembly. All things considered, he was a good President in an extremely difficult period. He had a certain natural shrewdness; he understood something of men, witness his recommendation to Broglie not to take the Ministry of the Interior himself. His complete honesty could call forth a like response. He trusted the duke, and Broglie gave him in return both affection and loyal support, even, it may be thought, to his own political ruin. Dufaure, also, he trusted, and Dufaure too gave him complete loyalty. On the other hand, for those who took advantage of his slowness of apprehension, such as Decazes, he had no forgiveness; yet he resisted the attempts of Thiers to replace Decazes by Jules Simon in 1877.[1] His chief faults were primarily his dislike of politics and political manipulation — probably his biggest error was his refusal to have anything to do with Gambetta. And, secondly, his lack of *panache*, his inability to play the public figure, the hero of the Malakoff Redoubt. How he disliked crowds! he even disliked being recognised in the street. His virtue lay in his sense of duty, which held him so long in office, in spite of the many merciless attacks on him, at a time when scarcely another man could have filled the position.

The first public action of the new Government was the issue of a presidential message to the Assembly indicating the MacMahon policy. 'With God's help and the devotion of our Army, which will always be an army of the law, with the support of all loyal men, we shall together continue the work of liberating the country and re-establishing the moral order in our land.' To those who expected a fanfare, it sounded like the retreat, and the phrase 'moral order' passed into familiar speech to qualify Broglie and all his works.

Broglie, responsible for the coalition which had brought down Thiers, was marked out for the Vice-Presidency and representative of the Marshal in the Assembly. His position was delicate. The forces he had welded for the battle of May 23 had been only temporarily united. To keep them together, he must offer a share of the direction to groups other than his own. From the Extreme Right, he took in the Comte de la Bouillerie as Minister of Commerce and Admiral Dompierre d'Hornoy, who though nominally a Legitimist was in fact a Moderate, as Minister of Marine. To Justice he invited Ernoul, the proposer of the motion against Thiers, an implacable Conservative and Clerical, who at once distinguished himself by accusing Arthur Ranc of membership of the Commune and driving him into exile. The Bonapartists were sweetened by the appointment of Pierre Magne, though once a minister of the Empire, the mildest of Imperialists, to the Ministry of Finance, while a non-political general, du Barail, was given the War Office. A man of the Centre, though whether of Left or Right cannot be determined, became Minister of Public Works, Alfred Desseiligny, a director of the Crédit Lyonnais and of Le Creusot, and son-in-law to Schneider. From the Orleanists he took the law professor, Batbie, the critic of Thiers, for Public Instruction and Public Worship. For the key ministry, the Interior, the choice was difficult. For an hour he thought of taking it himself, but the Marshal warned him, saying roughly that he would upset all the deputies with whom he had to deal. He therefore invited Beulé, a scholar and archaeologist, who had shown some spirit in debate: 'it is an experiment', Broglie told de Meaux.[2] Realising that it was a gamble, he reinforced Beulé by the reappointment of Goulard's assistant, an ex-préfet, Pascal, as under-secretary, and as secretary-general at the Place Beauvau another préfet, Baron Le Guay. Broglie himself took the Foreign Office. It was not a sparkling team.

The even more serious problem was the discovery of a policy. The country expected an immediate *volte-face* towards the restoration: but without the co-operation of Chambord, no restoration could be made. Except on the subject of the standard, all Chambord's declarations had been obscure. Broglie made it quite clear to Ernoul that neither he nor the other Orleanists would act unless they received guarantees that the claimant would accept constitutional institutions and the tricolor.[3] Chambord held his tongue. There was thus nothing to do except carry on the necessary government business and preserve order.

In informing the préfets of the resignation of Thiers and MacMahon's succession, Broglie had added to the message: 'Nothing will be changed in the existing institutions', intending thereby to emphasise that there would be no *coup-d'état*. It was perhaps unwise; later the phrase was quoted as evidence that he had accepted the Republic.[4] Meanwhile, the immediate task was to purge the executive of Thiers' agents. Between May 26 and June 1 there was a wholesale removal of préfets, sous-préfets, secretaries and maires, and their replacement by those believed to be favourable to an anti-republican régime: not, be it observed, a Royalist administration, since once again the dearth of experienced functionaries among the Royalists demonstrated the truth of Thiers's gibe that the Duc de Broglie would be the protégé of the Bonapartists. The substitutes in most places were imperial ex-préfets. Moreover, the inexperience of Beulé soon became embarrassing. His under-secretary circulated a notice to the préfectures asking for information on the status, colour and financial situation of the press in their departments. Brought to the notice of the Assembly by Gambetta, the document was weakly defended by the Minister of the Interior, and although the Government escaped defeat, Pascal had to be transferred to the préfecture of the Gironde. (After May 16, 1877 he turned Bonapartist.) Thus unable to offer any positive progress, Broglie could only fall back on the prevention of occasions for popular excitement. Forty-three departments had been put under martial law by Thiers; they remained so. The celebration of July 14 and of the fall of the Bastille was forbidden. Recruits joining the colours were forbidden to march in formed bodies; they might not sing the *Marseillaise*. The Universities were warned that professors, as State servants, should not contribute to Republican news-sheets. And finally, when the German troops at last marched out in September, there were to be no public rejoicings.

(*ii*)

It was not only on the Republican side that Broglie had trouble. As much, indeed more, came from the provincial Royalists, who believed the restoration imminent, and more still from the Clericals.

In August 1870 the Declaration of Papal Infallibility completed the campaign which since the early fifties Pius IX had undertaken against Liberal Catholicism. Almost at the same hour, the Pope lost his temporal sovereignty. The French Government, in desperate straits, on August 5, 1870 withdrew the garrison which had so long guarded the Sovereign Pontiff against the encroachments of the lay State of united Italy. On September 20 the Italian government troops entered Rome and Pius IX retreated into the Vatican. The Pontifical Zouaves, the French Catholic volunteers, were released and in France, under Charette, won for themselves great glory at Bellesme, Patay and Le Mans. Shortly before this, knowing what would follow the withdrawal of his troops, Napoleon III had sent the French battleship *Orénoque* to lie off Civita Vecchia at the disposal of the Pope should he choose to abandon the Eternal City. These incidents, although obscured by the war, served to keep the Roman Question alive in French Catholic circles.

In June 1871, Veuillot, the rudely combatant editor of the Catholic *Univers*, opened a campaign for, among other objectives, the restoration of the Pope's temporal power, the recovery of the Papal States by French force of arms. The campaign was supported by the French Archbishops and bishops who petitioned the Government to concert with other powers to 're-establish the Sovereign Pontiff in the conditions necessary for his liberty of action'. These untimely manifestations not only inflamed the Italian press and led King Victor Emmanuel to approach Prussia, where the *Kulturkampf* was on the point of breaking out, but gave the French Republican newspapers the chance of accusing the Catholics, and by extension the Monarchists, of fomenting war. On the eve of the election in July 1871 several Monarchist candidates disclaimed all such intentions, and were publicly upbraided by Veuillot. Thus they lost supporters on both Left and Right. In July Thiers put it to the Assembly that diplomatic action by France could only rouse distrust, and that the utmost possible was to secure the religious independence of the Pope. His speech did not satisfy the more extreme Catholic members, but the Right, which as a body thought the movement injudicious, joined with the Left in a vote on July 22 to leave the matter in the hands of the ministry.

During 1872 the dissension between the zealots and the Erastians became embittered. Relations between the Vatican and the Italian Government were non-existent, and the representatives of France at the Vatican and the Quirinal were not on speaking terms. Bismarck, involved since October 1871 in the *Kulturkampf*, at war with half the

German nation, required the support of the Powers against the pretentions of ultramontanism. On May 15, 1873 Falk's 'May Laws' against the German Catholics were signed by the Kaiser. Nine days later Broglie's ministry of 'moral order' took office.

To Bismarck, Chancellor of an empire which by force of arms had demonstrated to the world that it was the strongest power on the continent of Europe, but which by reason of its geographical position was vulnerable to a coalition of other powers on its frontiers, the appearance of a French Government ostensibly dedicated to the revival of the Bourbon monarchy was unwelcome. Through two years Bismarck had treated France, for Bismarck, gently. He had made little trouble over the liquidation of the indemnity; the trouble had come from Arnim and the soldiers in Berlin. In Bismarck's eyes, Thiers was the ideal ruler in France, first, a Republican, and thus unlikely to find an ally in either the Emperor of Austria or the Tsar — when Thiers made an approach to Russia, Bismarck had given him a friendly but categorical warning. Secondly, Thiers had none of 'the whimpering sentimentality that sees a martyr in every discontented rebel on the barricades', and was unlikely to encourage in France a socialism to link up with that now rising in Germany — all the same, he had warned him after his half-sketched gesture towards Gambetta in 1872. And finally he was *un homme de gouvernement*, little favourable to the outbursts of ultramontane French prelates. Broglie was another pair of shoes. Bismarck did not hesitate to make his sentiments clear to Gontaut-Biron: the election of MacMahon by a provisional assembly was irregular; though he, Bismarck, had no difficulty in recognising the Marshal as the Chief Executive in France, 'your Sovereign Assembly might later appoint a President who would inspire less confidence . . . if Gambetta, for example, by some means, succeeded in being elected President, you, a Conservative, would find our refusal to acknowledge him a great advantage.' Gontaut-Biron adds to his report that he was sure Bismarck was thinking as much of Chambord as of Gambetta.[5] The question was let fall, but the warning had been given and understood. Bismarck in power would tolerate neither radicalism nor ultramontanism.

Long before May 24 pilgrimages to shrines had been set on foot by the faithful, but with the arrival of the MacMahon-Broglie combination the movement, skilfully organised by a member of the Augustine Fathers of the Assumption, an Order of plebeian demagogic tendencies, which was later to create a powerful politico-religious press and to figure prominently in the Dreyfus case, was accentuated. In May 1873 thousands of pilgrims sought Lourdes, La Salette, Chartres: to the last went 40,000, including fourteen bishops, 140 members of the National Assembly and many préfets and sous-préfets. Paray-le-Monial, Mont-Saint-Michel and other sacred shrines were the scenes of like manifestations later in the year. Before Thiers fell, the Archbishop of Paris, Monsignor Guibert, had put forward the conception of an expiatory sanctuary at Montmartre. Thiers and Jules Simon, Minister of Public Worship, had agreed to support the idea. The Assembly had set up a committee to examine the project. In July 1873 its report approving the sanctuary of the Sacré Coeur as of 'public utility' was voted by the Assembly, although it refrained from voting any funds for the construction: the Right Centre, Gallicans and Liberals, refused to intermingle political action with an act of faith. The combined Centres, rejecting all amendments, whether from *dévots* or from free-thinkers, carried the bill.

These religious movements and, coupled with them, episcopal denunciation of the proceedings of the German and Italian governments against the Church — on May 26 the Italians had decreed the confiscation of 400 religious houses, including some the property of French Orders — were a sore embarrassment to Broglie. Pastorals from the Archbishop of Paris, the Bishops of Angers and Nîmes, at the moment when the German garrisons were on the point of quitting France, might lead to serious trouble. Bismarck told Gontaut-Biron that the French Church was fomenting revolt in the German Empire, threatened war, and required that the offending prelates should be brought either before the Conseil d'Etat for overstepping the limits of their duty, or before the courts for insults to a foreign sovereign. Broglie did not comply: the French Church might be governed by the Concordat of 1801, but the leader of the Right in the French Assembly could scarcely take steps against churchmen.

Above all, Broglie needed order. As he was to write in his memoirs, 'eighteen months of calm and strength' might have led to a different conclusion. Order he obtained. For the moment the Radical cry for dissolution was hushed. But until Chambord declared, he could do little more; he could only wait. In answer to the criticism of one of his younger supporters, Charles de Lacombe, he said: 'We are no more than sheep-dogs. We guard the flock, but we do not drive it.'[6] At the end of July the Assembly rose with no progress made.

(*iii*)

Early in August the Comte de Paris was received at Frohsdorf, and a vague understanding was reached. But nothing more illuminating emanated from Chambord. Broglie felt the ground slipping from under his feet, the future escaping. In October a committee of Nine representing the coalesced Right groups despatched Chesnelong of the Moderate Right, with three Extremists, to interview the claimant. Chesnelong, a prosperous pork-butcher from Orthez, who since 1848 had changed colour with every régime, was of sanguine temperament and vivid speech. He talked Chambord down, and at the end believed he had secured his assent to the proposal that the standard should remain an open question until after the restoration. The document he brought back was, however, indecisive, as Broglie and Audriffet-Pasquier recognised, but the Comte de Paris and Decazes thought otherwise. Some version of the contents became known and it was out and about that Chambord had abandoned the flag. The news reached Frohsdorf that he had accepted a parliamentary régime and the tricolor. Without a word to his closest adherents, without a word to MacMahon, he wrote a letter to Chesnelong and simultaneously sent a copy to his own paper, the *Union*, for publication (it appeared on October 30), in which he denied having withdrawn in any degree from his original principles.

The Monarchists were thrown into confusion. But Chambord had not abdicated. With some vague plan in his mind, he travelled incognito to Versailles and sent a follower to request an interview with the President. MacMahon refused to see him. It was the end. Chambord remained at Versailles for another ten days, then went back to Austria.

Now that the undetermined question had been dissipated, Broglie at last saw his way. On the re-opening of the Assembly on November 5 a message from the President was read saying that the time had come to give the Government stability and authority. There followed a bill to confer the executive power on the Marshal for ten years, to be exercised in the current conditions until such modifications as might be made by constitutional laws came into force. It called for the immediate nomination of a Commission of Thirty to prepare such laws. The Extreme Right smelt treason, but a threat of resignation from Broglie brought them momentarily to heel. After a noisy debate in which a Bonapartist submitted a counter-proposal for a plebiscite, Monarchy, Republic or Empire, Broglie's bill was voted in principle. The committee on the bill, which through the luck of that month's draw had a Left Centre majority, wanted the term reduced to five years. Broglie countered with an offer of seven, which was accepted. He had threatened them with MacMahon's resignation, and they, for all their republicanism, trembled at the prospect of a dissolution. The bill for the Septennate was passed on November 20 by 378 to 310. It was Broglie's moment of triumph, his highest point.

'The Duc de Broglie', writes Lajusan, 'was heart and mind completely Monarchist; his plan of restoration had an amplitude which was as much that of a historian as of a strategist. He dared . . . to plan for a decision seven years distant.'[7] The comment is just. Given seven years, it would be possible for one of his schemes to mature: either Chambord's conversion to realism or Chambord's death, with the succession of the constitutional Orleanist régime, or at worst, the foundation of a republic so hedged about with safeguards that the Conservatives could survive. But that plan depended on certain imponderable conditions, one, the survival of MacMahon, another, less certain, the survival of the monarchist coalition.

The committee of thirty members to examine the constitutional laws under Article 2 of the Septennate Law was to be chosen in public session of the whole Assembly. By this means the committee would not, unlike that for the Septennate Law, be dependent on the chance of the draw for the bureaux. In electing the Committee of Thirty by the whole Assembly (between November 26 and December 4) the Right was able to secure a majority of ten.

With the passage of the Law of the Septennate, Broglie was faced by a ministerial crisis. Already he had met a popular movement for the restoration in the West and South. If the Septennate was to run its term, it was clear that such movements must be scotched at once. Now he was faced by opposition from the most important Monarchist in the cabinet, La Bouillerie, who resigned, to be at once followed by the competent Ernoul, who feared the displeasure of Chambord. Moreover, both Beulé and Batbie had shown that they were not up to their work and must be shed. At the same time, Lucien Brun, one of Chambord's mouthpieces, let it be known that no Legitimist would take office in a MacMahon cabinet. With MacMahon's help, a new ministry was secured which included Thiers's one-time Minister of Public Works, Larcy. Of the others, the most important for the future was the Duc Decazes, to whom Broglie surrendered the Foreign Office, while he himself went to the Interior. There are in history certain characters who never come into the light but whose influence from the shadows is unmistakable. Of such is Decazes. Little but his public acts is apparent. A keen Orleanist — he had been the host of Joinville and Aumale at his château of Lagrave, when they came to Bordeaux in February 1871, and he had been one of the backers of the latter as Lieutenant-General of the realm — he was a far keener enemy of the Bonapartists. Yet it may be suspected that of all his emotions the strongest was self-love. Alone of the ministers of the Right, he successfully held office uninterrupted from November 1873 to December 1877, in both Left and Right cabinets, the indispensable man. Broglie, while testifying to his character, allows it to be seen that although he could never point to a definite action, he suspected him. 'The friendship which bound me to Decazes was of long standing, and I never saw him do me a bad turn. But that he wished to bring about the remodelling of the cabinet, through which, by withdrawing from the alliance with the Right, a wheel, or at least a quarter wheel could be made to the Left Centre, is scarcely to be doubted.'[8] It is a hint, no more, that in Broglie's opinion, Decazes was, if not its author, at least responsible for his defeat on May 16, 1874.

The other new minister was Bardy de Fourtou, a lawyer from the Dordogne, reputed energetic, who for a few months had been a member of Thiers's cabinet, although a member of the Moderate Right.

At the opening of the session in January 1874 Broglie brought in a bill to place the nomination of the maires of the capitals of cantons in the hands of the Minister of the Interior, of the communes in those of the préfets. The Extreme Right, having by now cogitated on the Septennate and concluded that it implied the postponement of a restoration until 1880, broke away. They refused to vote urgency for the bill, and the ministry was defeated. Broglie resigned, but MacMahon refused his resignation. Broglie, returning to the Assembly, secured a vote of confidence on January 12, and a week later the law on the appointment of maires was passed (L. January 20, 1874).

The trouble lay in the interpretation of the Law of November 20, 1873. The Extreme Right claimed that the appointment was personal to MacMahon: if he died or retired, the Septennate lapsed, while if the claimant returned to France, MacMahon must resign. On the contrary, said the Left: the Septennate consecrated the Republic for seven years, and, by the law on the appointment of maires, which was directed against Republicans, the Government was attacking the State. Between these two theses Broglie was careful not to declare. There was a yet further question: although the Government was the Marshal's, did a defeat of his ministry imply his defeat or merely that of his ministers?

In March two bills were simultaneously tabled; one, from the Committee on Decentralisation, on the municipal franchise, the other, by the Committee of Thirty, on the national franchise. The bills had many points in common, though the former favoured the more conservative elements in the country. Immediately after Easter Broglie circulated a draft plan for an Upper Chamber. This was to be composed of members by right of office, such as cardinals, appeal-court judges, etc., members by presidential appointment, and members elected on a restricted departmental franchise, in short, a wholly conservative body. 'If the Duc de Broglie's scheme is adopted', said Gambetta, 'goodbye to democracy in France for fifty years.' The bill was read on May 15 in almost complete silence; only the Right Centre approving. The Extreme Right looked on the bill as an attempt to erect institutions exclusive of the King; the Left as a bulwark against the Republic. Therefore, when on the following day the choice as to which of the two franchise bills should have priority came before the Assembly, and Broglie made that of the Committee of Thirty a question of confidence, the Chevau-légérs and the Bonapartists deserted him: he secured only 317 votes against 381, and at once resigned. In destroying Broglie, the Extreme Right, though they knew it not, had destroyed their own cause.

(iv)

On Broglie's advice MacMahon summoned Thiers's former Minister of the Interior, Goulard, of the Moderate Right. For a few days it appeared that a Centre ministry with its axis to the Right might be built up, but the negotiations broke down once more on the interpretation of the Septennate. Then, under heavy pressure from MacMahon, Decazes went to work and in twenty-four hours got together a team, largely from the Right Centre, with Fourtou at the Interior and the Bonapartist Magne still at the Ministry of Finance. General de Cissey, Broglie's Minister of War, was appointed Vice-President of the Council and representative of the Marshal in the Assembly. This was on May 22. Two days later a half-forgotten menace was suddenly revived.

The defeat of Thiers in the previous May had shocked many of the rural areas. After this the conservative peasant scarcely knew which way to turn. He feared the Monarchists, but he feared the Republicans as much. Since the fall of Thiers, the Monarchists, being in power, disturbed him the more, but he was not reassured by the Gambettists. Thus the atmosphere was peculiarly favourable to Bonapartism. On May 24 the electors of Nièvre, who in the previous October had elected an uncompromising candidate of the Extreme Left, Dr Turigny, now gave their votes to a former officer of the Imperial household, the Baron Philippe de Bourgoing, by an absolute majority over the combined votes of the Republican and Legitimist candidates. The disaster was all the more galling in that Bourgoing had stood undisguisedly as a member of the Appel au Peuple group, and on the announcement of the result, hurried to Chiselhurst to pay his homage to the Empress. Accusations laid by Cyprien Girerd, a Left member for the same department, of bribery on a vast scale, of pressure brought to bear on government servants in Nièvre, and finally of a vast Bonapartist conspiracy, were made public. An enquiry was at once voted by an alarmed Assembly and put into the hands of the préfet of Police, Léon Renault. Renault, an ambitious and dexterous lawyer, had been appointed by Thiers, but being an advertised Orleanist he had been maintained by Broglie. Furthermore, on the ground that the police, whose jurisdiction was limited to the boundaries of Seine, were unable to protect the Assembly at Versailles in Seine-et-Oise, Broglie had added to Renault's authority the direction of the Sûreté, which covered the whole of France.

The resurrection of Bonapartism sent a shudder of alarm through the Assembly. The Left were naturally vociferous, but the agitation was even stronger in the Right Centre, since the Orleanist hatred for the Empire was implacable, and their fear of its revival was not to be exorcised.

It is possible that the effects of the Nièvre election have been overestimated, at least if Broglie is to be believed. The Appel au Peuple group had grown little since its formation in 1871: it had won no more than five seats between January 1872 and January 1874, one in Charente-inférieure, a Bonapartist region, two in Pas-de-Calais and two in Corsica, both previously held by Bonapartists. It was in fact acting up to neither its opportunities nor its principles. It claimed to be a democratic, indeed to be the only democratic party: yet it was neglecting the popular touch. As J. J. Weiss pointed out in 1878,[9] its strategy was inept. The Bonapartists acquiesced in Broglie's policy, the maintenance of the state of siege, the decrees against the circulation of political pamphlets, in everything that militated against democratic sentiment, while later they, the party of mass appeal, were tamely to accept single-member constituencies (*scrutin d'arrondissement*) when they should have fought for departmental constituencies (*scrutin de liste*). Instead of going to the country, 'they stayed at Versailles, where the ministries were staffed by imperialists.' They 'lost the chief instrument of action which remained to them after the disasters of 1870, that is to say, the permanent imperialist spirit of the army, the civil service and the peasant'. The high officers in the services were aging and year by year retiring, the vacancies being filled by Anti-imperialists, while the peasant, as long as crops were good — and good they were in the early seventies, bumper wheat in 1874, record wine in 1875 — was content to do no more than argue with the authorities. The fact was that their leader, Rouher, was not a politician but a good man of business. To impose himself, he needed at his back the weight of the old imperial service, its préfets *à la poigne*, its well-supported maires, its authoritative press, and the public funds. The local committees tried to improvise a shadow service, but without the power or the activity from the Centre, they were only partly successful. 'Jupiter has aged', wrote the *Revue bleue* of Rouher in July; 'he has lost his thunder.'

Yet even in spite of their supineness, the lethargy, the almost self-exculpatory attitude of the Bonapartist leaders before the Assembly, Girerd's accusations were enough to alarm the Orleanists, enough to frighten and discipline the Left.[10] A decision on the future organisation of the country became imperative. On June 15, Casimir-Périer, with Left Centre backing, proposed that the Committee of Thirty should evolve from the existing laws and institutions a republican constitution on a two-chamber basis under the Septennate. The word 'republic' had been taken from the bill tabled by Dufaure on May 20, 1873, which had never been discussed. Its presentation in the first paragraph of Casimir-Périer's resolution was too much for the Right, and an amendment was submitted which, after referring to MacMahon's seven-year tenure, proposed the constitution of two chambers; at the end of seven years these would again consider the type of government for France. Other amendments followed, but in the end the Casimir-Périer resolution was passed by a majority of four, 345 to 341. Thirty-two of the Right Centre rallied to the majority, eleven others abstained, while the Left and the Republican Union turned about and, by voting for the resolution, recognised the constituent powers of the Assembly. On the same day a counter-proposition in favour of the monarchy was defeated without a division, but on June 16 additional articles to Casimir-Périer's resolution were tabled by Wallon, a specialist in constitutional questions. Although rejected on July 14, the proposals were to be heard of again.

On July 2 Chambord issued through the *Union* yet another manifesto. The Minister of the Interior, Fourtou, already shaken by the attacks of the Left over the Nièvre election and probably also criticised in the cabinet by Decazes, used his powers under the 'state of siege' to suspend the *Union*. Interpellated by the Extreme Right, he defended himself by re-affirming the Septennate which put the Marshal above the parties for seven years, claiming that these powers could not be questioned. Once more bitterness of feeling overcame good sense. A motion in support of Fourtou's contentions was negatived. The ministry was defeated.

Broglie counselled Decazes and Fourtou to secure from the Marshal a stiff message, which would re-assert his right of tenure of office. Although watered down by the cabinet, it yet recalled the members of the Assembly to their duty. 'The powers with which you have invested me have a fixed term. . . . Now the Assembly has no duty more imperious than to guarantee calm, security and tranquillity to the country through established institutions. I charge my ministers without delay to acquaint the Committee of Thirty . . . with the points on which I think it essential to insist.' The phrase 'my ministers' denoted the continuation in office of the defeated ministry. On July 14 the Committee of Thirty countered the Casimir-Périer proposal with their own. There followed debates on both proposals, whereon the Right, momentarily reunited, defeated both.

In the meantime the astute Léon Renault had made it known that the Bonapartist lines in Nièvre ran back to the Ministries of Finance and the Interior, to Magne and Fourtou. Magne, tainted by his prominence under the Empire, was the first victim. In attempting to balance the budget by increasing a tax, he was attacked by the chief agent of the interests of the Orleanist princes, Bocher. His proposal was defeated, and on the next day he resigned. Fourtou, realising the need to hold together the majority of which the Appel au Peuple group was an essential piece, desired that another Bonapartist should succeed Magne. Decazes, perfervid Orleanist, and the indispensable member of the cabinet, rejected the suggestion, whereon Fourtou, opposed in vital policy, perhaps feeling himself undermined by his brilliant subordinate, the préfet of police and director of the Sûreté, perhaps also uncertain of his ability to control the crypto-Bonapartist préfets, followed Magne. The two ministers were replaced, at Finance by Mathieu-Bodet, president of the Budget Committee, member of the Lavergne group (otherwise, the financial interest), and at the Interior by General Chabaud-Latour, with, as his under-secretary, Guizot's son-in-law, Cornelis de Witt. All were Orleanists, and thus Decazes had succeeded in his aim of securing a preponderantly Right Centre cabinet. But this success meant a further unbalancing of the ministry, the further isolation of the Right Centre and the enmity of the Bonapartists.

At the beginning of August, frayed with disappointment and acrimony, the Assembly was prorogued for four months, with the problem of the future no nearer solution. During the recess there were ten bye-elections. Of these seven went to Republicans, of whom only two were of the Centre, while two open and one reputed Bonapartists secured the other three. Even in those departments where they were beaten the Bonapartists received a by no means despicable number of votes, and the Republican press did not fail to rub in the peril. After the election of Le Prévost de Launay, one of the toughest imperial préfets, in Calvados, there was something like panic among the Orleanists. 'But the Orleans princes!' wrote the editor of the *Revue Bleue*, Yung:[11] 'what will happen to their persons, their property and their titles, if the Assembly continues to draw its recruits from the préfets of the Empire?'

In October the poll for the *conseils-généraux* showed a Republican majority over the combined vote of the Right, and in forty-three departments the Republicans secured control, while at the municipal elections in November, many of Broglie's appointees were not re-elected. The omens could be read only too easily; it was time for the Right Centre to come to terms.

On the reopening of the Assembly, the first signs of Right disintegration were seen when Pasquier, so linked with the Orleanist princes, almost lost the vice-presidency, the Legitimists turning their votes against him. On December 3 came the Marshal's message in which he called on all men of good will to sink their personal preferences before the needs of the hour and the interests of the country. The conclusion was significant. Recalling that the executive power had been conferred on him in the interests of peace for seven years, he added: 'The same interests make it my duty not to abandon the post where you have placed me, and to occupy it up to the last day with unshakeable firmness and scrupulous respect for the laws.' As Broglie commented, the passage was an error. Thiers had tamed the Assembly by his successive threats to resign. MacMahon, by stating his intention to stay, showed his opponents that they could act as they pleased against the ministry without provoking a crisis. The Extreme Right showed their comprehension by rebuffing every approach from the Right Centre on the question of the Senate.[12] The message was equally appreciated by the Left Centre. They could see that the Marshal no longer excluded the possibility of a Republic. All that they asked of him was not to obstruct its creation. The two important points, said Casimir-Périer to Decazes, were the transmission of powers (i.e. the passage to the Republic), and a permissive but not obligatory revision of the constitution in 1880. Decazes replied that MacMahon had at length understood that, should he die with the interpretation of the Septennate still obscure on the personal-impersonal issue, chaos would follow: his mind was therefore now open to the passage of the Republic. For the second point, Casimir-Périer made revision a condition of co-operation with the Right Centre.[13]

At the end of December MacMahon tried to solve the problem by a conference of the leaders of the Right, the Right Centre and the Left Centre. In principle they were not divided. The Right would accept a *de facto* Republic to the end of the Septennate, the Left Centre a conservatively organised Senate: but the Right insisted on the priority of the Senate, the Left on that of the proclamation of the Republic. Moreover, Audren de Kerdrel for the moderate Right held to the personal Septennate, Pasquier for the Right Centre to the impersonal, and quarrelled. Once again no agreement was reached. Broglie, however, noticed that both Buffet and Pasquier were insensibly moving towards the Republican solution.

In January 1875, therefore, on the reopening of the Assembly, the Marshal by message repeated that further delay was intolerable and requested the constitution of a Senate as the first and necessary complement to his Government, coupled with the postponement of a declaration as to its final form until 1880. After a confused debate, conducted by the dialecticians, the ministry asked for priority for the bill on the Senate, and on January 6 was defeated owing to yet another desertion by the Chevau-légers. It resigned. MacMahon invited Broglie to form a

F

ministry, and Broglie, feeling the Republic inevitable and his impotence to find support on either side, declined.[14] Left in a vacuum, the Marshal made no move to find a successor; he maintained the ministers in office for the transaction of current business, and by this put the responsibility for the future firmly on the Assembly's shoulders. By now the members were mentally and morally exhausted; they could only repeat the stale arguments and display their energy in the rancour of their speeches. The caretaker Government was not even capable of marshalling its aims. The direction passed to the Committee of Thirty.

It is at this point that Gambetta began to show those political qualities which were to make him the leader of the Left. During the previous summer he had expected the defeat of the Government and a dissolution. It had not come. During the autumn he had done his best to weld the Left by yielding the choice of Republican candidates to Thiers and the Left Centre. But within the Left Centre there were Conservatives such as Dufaure and Léon Say, who he knew might strike a bargain with the Right Centre to the disadvantage of the Left. The crisis now opening might uncover the President, might lead to another Broglie ministry, and then to a dissolution with all the power of the executive in the hands of the Monarchists; there might even follow a Bonapartist reaction.[15] It was time to drop the idea of dissolution and time to compromise.

On January 20 the debate was opened on the proposal laid by the Committee of Thirty for the organisation of the public powers, that is to say, on the form of government. After three days of tedious wrangling, the first reading was carried by a large majority. Many of the Orleanists voted in the majority: it is possible that they were influenced by the alarms of the men at their back, the Orleans princes. On January 25 the bill on the Senate was to be introduced.

Now, on January 20, 25, 26 and 27, Léon Renault gave his evidence before the committee set up to examine the Nièvre election and the alleged Bonapartist conspiracy. The Préfet of Police had done his work well. From remarkably vague facts he had deduced that the country was covered by a network of Bonapartist conspirators linked not only to a central committee, but — a pretty touch — even with the Commune. The weak point was that the conspirators had regrettably kept on the right side of the criminal law. 'His deposition', wrote Broglie,[16] 'was a trifle of oratory of the highest water, in which facts he had known for six years, of which he had talked to me a hundred times, and which, by mutual agreement, we had looked on as too insignificant to make a fuss about, were now artistically arrayed with the intention of making a synchronised demonstration of the risks society was running and the worth of the vigilant administrator who had brought them to light.'

Thus under the menace of what Saint-Valry called the 'clever romantic report of M. Léon Renault',[17] the Assembly passed the first reading of the bill on the Senate by 498 to 173, among the minority being found such oddly-assorted beings as Lucien Brun, Rouher, Gambetta, Louis Blanc and the Duc de la Rochefoucauld.

(vi)

On January 28 the Assembly returned to the 'public powers' bill. In the Committee's draft, the first clause ran that MacMahon should 'continue to exercise, with the title of President of the Republic, the executive power with which he had been invested by the Law of November 20, 1873'. This affirmation of the Republic choked the Right. After six amendments had been discussed that of Laboulaye was heard. Laboulaye reminded the Assembly of the incontestable fact that they were living in a republic and that government was being carried on. It was well to preserve what existed. He argued that the monarchy could not be restored, that the difference between the President and a constitutional monarch was merely one of heredity, a matter of form 'in a country in which during the last eighty years we have never seen the monarch succeeded by his heir'; the Empire was unreliable: only the Republic, which for four years had had a *de facto* existence, remained. The speech was received with bursts of applause: but other speakers intervened, and the enthusiasm died. The vote was postponed until next day when the Laboulaye proposal was defeated by 359 to 336, with twenty abstentions.

On January 30 was discussed a further counter-proposition submitted by Henri Wallon, representative of Nord, and a member of the small Lavergne group, which though of the Right was the hyphen with the Left Centre. A far from colourful speaker, Wallon addressed the Assembly in a quiet reasoned speech at first scarcely listened to. At length he reached the point he wished to make. 'We must abandon this provisional situation. If the monarchy is possible, show that it is acceptable; propose it. If on the contrary it is impossible, I do not say, "Propose the Republic", but I do say constitute the government at present established, which is the government of the Republic. I do not ask you to declare it definitive. What, after all, is definitive? But no longer call it provisional. I appeal to all those who put the common weal above questions of party. . . .'

Wallon's thesis was effectively the same as that of Laboulaye, but his draft possessed one small but all-important virtue: it did not in the first line proclaim the Republic: the odious word did not appear until the second article, and even then almost casually at the point where the President of the Republic was mentioned. After half a dozen members had opposed the proposal and Wallon had replied, the vote was taken. Wallon's amendment was carried by 353 to 352, a majority of one, with nineteen abstentions. In the minority were members of the Extreme Right, of the Bonapartists and of the Left. The press showed little enthusiasm; it had perhaps gauged the inevitability of the Republic more accurately than the Assembly.*

Two days later, on February 1, the Assembly turned to the articles of the law on the public powers. The lengthy debates were chiefly on interpretations. On the third day a new article proposed by Ravinel of the Extreme Right maintained the seat of the Executive and Parliament at Versailles. This exclusion of Paris, the capital both of the country and the Revolution, was an insult to the Left. Their protests were overwhelmed by a vote of the whole Right, and to gain their major end they accepted the decision.

On February 11, however, with the second reading of the bill on the Senate, there was a sudden explosion of uncalculating whim on the Left. The Committee's article on the system of senatorial election was based on Broglie's project of the previous May and recommended a Senate of 300, divided into senators by right of office, nominees of the President, and elected members. An amendment from Pascal Duprat of the Extreme Left, running: 'The Senate is elective; it is nominated by the same electors as the Chamber of Deputies', was carried by 322 to

---

* Some historians make much of the single vote, and imply that the conversion of a single member produced the Republic. This is nonsense. It is obvious from everything that preceded the vote that the Republic would be accepted provided a formula could be found. As for the swing of some dozen votes, it was not, as Deslandres says in his *Avènement de la Troisième République* (355), the action of the Target group, at least the group of May 24, 1873. Of the 36 members whose votes changed between that for the Laboulaye and that for the Wallon amendments, only four belonged to the old Target group. The greater number who instead of voting against, either abstained or voted for the Wallon proposal, belonged to the Lavergne group or the Right Centre, Adrien Léon, Beau, Gouin, de Ségur etc. led by Broglie's nephew, Haussonville. Alfred Desseiligny, Broglie's minister, whom Broglie thought a Republican, voted against Laboulaye and abstained on Wallon.

310. The Extreme Right had abstained, and twenty-eight Bonapartists, posing as champions of universal suffrage, voted with the Republicans. There followed total confusion. The aim of the two Centres had been to ensure a conservative Senate. If it was elected on exactly the same basis as the Chamber of Deputies, it would not only be of the same colour as the Chamber, but would become its creature. The Committee threw in its hand and formally withdrew from any further action, merely reserving its right to intervene according to circumstances, while, on behalf of the Marshal, de Cissey let it be known that since, contrary to his intention, the conservative nature of the Senate was compromised, his ministers would no longer take part in the debates. Realising its error, the Assembly rejected a motion to pass to the third reading by twenty-three, and another for dissolution by 143.

In the welter of reproaches, bargaining, new proposals and confused debate, the intervention of Gambetta was perhaps decisive. With greater prescience than his followers, with that *coup d'oeil prophétique* and sense of political tactics which mark his prime, he had seen that, provided the Senate was not overloaded with Life Senators, then, even with indirect voting in the electoral colleges for the remaining seats, if this was based on universal suffrage, the Republicans must sooner or later control the Upper House. Perhaps alone of the Left he had understood the change in the temper of the country: the summons of September 1872, at Grenoble, was being answered; the *nouvelles couches*, the provincial politicians, the country lawyers, the doctors, the tavern-keepers, even the better-educated peasants, were seeing the promised land with his eyes. The communes in many regions would no longer be the electoral fiefs of the squires. Power would pass to the new groups, and the small men would become the great electors. The constitution was of no serious significance: it was power that counted. His speech to the Assembly, although phrased as a denunciation of the Right Centre for its failure to respond to the sacrifices of the Left — 'we have agreed to the division of power, to the creation of two Chambers; we have consented to give you the strongest executive power that has ever been constituted in a land of democratic franchise: we have granted you the right of dissolution . . . we have allowed you the right of revision; we have given you everything, we have surrendered everything' — was in effect an appeal for reconsideration and conciliation. 'It was', says Broglie, 'one of the happiest improvisations I have heard not only from him but from any orator.'

To bring his reluctant, doctrine-ridden followers to take the last step and accept the nomination of Life Senators, Gambetta did not scruple to threaten the revival of Bonapartism, with a hint that certain generals were even at the moment ready to carry out a *coup*. At the same time Ferry put the screw on the Republican Left. Then, with the rebels tamed, Gambetta let the Left Centre know that provided universal suffrage remained as the basis of the Senate's electoral system, he and Ferry would support any transaction with the Right, on one condition, that the nomination of Life Senators should be taken from MacMahon, still believed to have a hankering for the Empire he had served.

On this Ricard for the Left Centre and Wallon for the Lavergne group drafted a short bill. It proposed a Senate of 300, seventy-five to be elected for life by the National Assembly (vacancies to be filled by election within the Senate), 225 by departmental electoral colleges composed of the deputies, the *conseillers-généraux*, the *conseillers-d'arrondissement*, and one delegate from each commune; with one-third of the elected senators retiring every third year. Legislative initiative was to be on an equal footing with that of the Chamber of Deputies, except in financial laws.

The only obstacle to agreement between the negotiators was the question of the Marshal's surrender of the prerogative of nominating the Life Senators. However, the fears which had influenced the Left to make concessions were no less lively among the Orleanists. Yet another Bonapartist had won a bye-election in January, while in February two others, though defeated, had secured a heavy vote, enough to show that the popularity of the Empire was not extinct. The Orleanist princes were still alarmed. They told their friends, Decazes and Pasquier, to come to an arrangement. Decazes sprang the question of nomination to MacMahon hurriedly at a cabinet meeting, and MacMahon, scarcely comprehending what was involved, acceded. He was later to regret it, and never forgave Decazes for what he regarded as a trick.[18]

After three days debate, the Wallon-Ricard bill, substantially unamended, was voted by 435 to 234, the majority consisting of Left, Left Centre and Right Centre (Constitutional Law of February 24, 1875). The decisive hour had passed. On the same and the following days, the third reading of the Public Powers bill was hurried through in spite of the protests of some wise and some fanatical critics. Raoul Duval contested every paragraph and was overwhelmed. It was time to consummate the sacrifice. 'You are not legislators; you are conspirators', shouted the honest Raudot. The way of the political idealist is stony.* On February 25, the bill passed its third reading by 425 to 254. Eighty-three members of the Right Centre, including Decazes, Pasquier and Broglie, reluctant but resigned, were in the majority. Thus the two fundamental constitutional laws which were to stand in principle unchanged for the next sixty-five years, were, after four years of sound and fury, brought to birth, with, be it said, no serious discussion. The Republic was founded. Its creator, some said, had been the Comte de Chambord. But there were others who had some share, the Orleans princes, the Préfet of Police, the Baron de Bourgoing and the venal electors of Nièvre.

(vii)

The 'constitutional laws' were in fact nothing of the kind, the word constitution being used to give the State a kind of sanctity. What emerged from these tedious and often frivolous debates was a treaty between two groups, neither of which at the time, January and February 1875, could coerce the other and both of which feared a longer delay. The National Assembly majority, afraid to tempt providence by a dissolution after the fulfilment of the Treaty of Frankfurt, arrogated to itself constitutional power. It had no juridical right to do this. It continued the arrogation of powers by creating (with no consultation with the nation) a National Assembly consisting of two Chambers, with power to modify the Constitution as it pleased, but again without consulting the universal suffrage from which it said it derived its powers. This claim is repeated *ad nauseam* throughout the history of the Republic, but it has no substance. The so-called constitution was related entirely to the Parliamentary game (as is the so-called English constitution) and rarely affects the citizen, who, however, in France is protected by the Conseil d'Etat.

The law of February 25 on the Public Powers laid down that the legislative power is exercised by two assemblies, the Chamber of Deputies, elected by universal suffrage and the Senate (Article 1). The President of the Republic is elected by an absolute majority of both parliamentary bodies united as a National Assembly, to hold office for seven years. He is re-eligible (Article 2). This last meant that he could not be independent. To be independent he must be elected for life or not be re-eligible. If he is re-eligible, he will have to make play with his

* Cf. Appendix V.

electors, i.e. the Chamber. The President's duties included the surveillance of the execution of the laws. Otherwise his rights and duties were purely formal, since each of his acts must be countersigned by a minister (Article 3). There was given back to him the appointment of the Conseillers d'Etat *en service ordinaire* (Article 4).* Article 5 gave him the right to dissolve the Chamber before the end of its term with the concurrence of the Senate. Article 6 declared that the ministers were jointly responsible for the general policy of the cabinet, and individually for their personal actions. Article 7 laid down the procedure in case of the President's death, and Article 9 named Versailles as the place of the executive and the legislature. Article 8 stated that the Chambers after separate deliberation, either spontaneously or at the President's request, might declare that there was occasion to revise the constitutional laws. They must then unite in a National Assembly. Any revision to take effect must be passed by an absolute majority. The implementation of this was postponed until the end of the Septennate, up to when revision could only be at MacMahon's request. This article was important in that it prevented the meeting of the National Assembly without an agreed agenda. It would thus be impossible for it to discuss the abolition of the Senate, as the Radicals desired.

The Law of February 24 on the Senate followed the Wallon-Ricard draft. Article 8 gave the Senate the same right as the Chamber in the initiation of laws, but financial bills must be presented to the Chamber first. The Senate could also sit as a court of justice to try the President or ministers or authors of acts against the security of the State.

(*viii*)

Immediately after the announcement of the passage of the two bills, Cissey and his caretaker Government resigned. That the ministry should be reconstructed was inevitable. The question was what kind of a ministry could survive. Broglie by now knew that he would not unite the Right, and that he was too well hated to command the support of the Left. He could do no more than advise MacMahon, for whom if asked he would sacrifice himself. That would not mend matters. Buffet, President of the Assembly, Orleanist, combative, honest and without

---

* The Conseil d'Etat, which had been the creation of the first Napoleon and the political engine of the third, under the Third Republic became increasingly independent and the tenacious guardian of the rights of the citizen against the centralised State. The Radicals regarded it as the citadel of reaction; but in fact it was the bulwark against jacobin tyranny.

guile, had believed that a cabinet of the Right could direct affairs, if it could get some Left Centre support. MacMahon entrusted him with the negotiations. The ministry was slow to form; but after some give and take a hybrid ministry containing two members of the Left Centre, Dufaure (Justice) and Léon Say (Finance), with Wallon of the Lavergne group, 'the Father of the Constitution', (Public Instruction) and de Meaux from the Moderate Right (Commerce) was got together. The others were members of the Right Centre who had voted the Constitution, while Decazes remained at the Foreign Office. Buffet took the Interior. The cabinet took office on March 11.

The trace of the in-and-out running of January and February is a labyrinth mapped with difficulty, but there is one clue which leads from the gate to the heart of the maze. The Left would not agree to any bill for a Senate without a guarantee of the law on the organisation of Public Powers. They suspected that if the Senate bill was passed before the latter, the Right, which meant Broglie, could defeat the Public Powers bill. It would then take office, reorganise the administration to its own liking, and perhaps dissolve, fighting the election with the state of siege, press control and its own obedient préfets as weapons. The Right Centre, on the other hand, would not accept the law on Public Powers without the organisation of a Senate as a barrier against a Radical Chamber. The united Right could, of course, dispose of both bills: but the Right Centre and many of the Moderates feared their Bonapartist allies as much as the Radicals. To create a Senate, a price must be paid; the Republic. Some, like the Lavergne group, believed the price of a Republic in name not too high to pay; others that the Republic could be governed with pure Right support; Buffet was one such. He, Pasquier, Decazes and Bocher, chairman of the Right Centre, were much influenced by Joinville and Aumale, who had much less fear of the Left Centre, where they had many contacts, than they had of the Bonapartists.

Thus everything had depended on the priority of the laws, coupled with compromises on detail, of which the outstanding, though perhaps not the most important one, was the veiled affirmation of the Republic. The achievement had been the work of the Left Centre and the 'hyphen' Lavergne group, Casimir-Périer, Léon Say, Ricard, Wallon, Laboulaye and Luro, with the support of Broglie's nephew, Haussonville, leader of the Right Centre compromisers, and of Ferry and Gambetta. The last two had permanent trouble with their followers, and, in point of fact, the Louis Blanc group was never coerced. There was considerable conflict over Article 9 of the Public Powers bill: 'The seat of the Executive and the two Chambers is at Versailles.' This had nearly brought down the whole structure. It was with great difficulty that Gambetta and his followers were persuaded to swallow the insult to Paris and allow the article to pass at the third reading without even challenging it to a vote.[19]

The passage of the two constitutional laws, while removing some of the tension of the previous six months, had by no means solved the problems of the Assembly. For the Republicans, true, it was the Republic; but it was not theirs, only a construction made by the two Centres. 'We entered the Republic backwards', Gambetta's paper had said. The elder purists of 1848, the 'Anabaptists' as Ferry was to call them, looked on the transactions of February as dishonest. And now they saw two members of the Left Centre in a cabinet led by the implacable Monarchist, Buffet.

On the Right, in spite of the conservative cabinet, there was irritation and simmering anger. The resigned Monarchists who supported Buffet had formed a group with the title of 'Constitutionalists'. Others broke away into minor groups. The hatred of the Legitimists for the Orleanists was not to be appeased.

Outside these were men whose thought was not in terms of parties, but of institutions, a Raoul Duval, a Raudot. Yet perhaps the majority of the Right — it is always to be remembered that the Assembly, however unenlightened some of its members, had as a body an intense sense of duty — were still confused. 'If we are not mistaken,' wrote Charles de Lacombe in his diary, 'several of those who voted the organisation of the Republic have whispered their envy of those that did not, while others who did not vote have from the bottom of their hearts thanked those who did.'

On April 23 Gambetta delivered to an audience from Belleville and Charonne one of his master orations, in justification of the Left's actions. Welcoming the Constitution, he approved the election of the President of the Republic by the National Assembly: 'he will not have those facilities which were so lightly and rashly conceded to his predecessor's predecessor [Napoleon III].' He was at pains to show how the Senate had been weakened as a citadel of reaction, and was now based on all that was most democratic: the spirit of the commune, that is the 36,000 communes of France. 'What will emerge from the ballot-box? A Senate? No, citizens, the Great Council of the Communes of France.' He skated lightly over the fact that the Senate held the executive and the legislature in its hand. In any case, the Constitution could be revised: 'I would not have voted it had it been otherwise.'

As Saint-Valry said, Gambetta was not talking to Belleville, except for an occasional explosion of violence 'obligatory in the circumstances of place and audience', but to the Assembly. 'Although superficially demagogic, the speech is at bottom a policy of compromise . . . a reply to the Louis Blancs, the Marcous, the whole group of the *Rappel*. . . .' Indeed, Gambetta's evolution since Grenoble had been constant. 'He has a political plan which is not one of ordinary ambitions; he believes it is a matter of building up cadres and drawing from them a new governing personnel, destined to replace the present governing class.'[20]

At the beginning of May, Dufaure introduced a third constitutional bill, 'on the relationship of the Public Powers,' and a bill on the method of electing the Senate. The Assembly refused to send either bill to the Committee of Thirty, which now dissolved. A new Committee of Thirty was elected. The schismatics of the Right in their bitterness preferred to elect enemies rather than those they considered false allies, with the result that the Thirty were made up of twenty-five members of the Left to five of the Right.

The third constitutional bill was in fact no more than a bundle of unrelated regulations concerning points previously overlooked. The most important article (Article 8), was the one which stated that the President ratified treaties and gave the terms to Parliament when the interest and security of the State allowed. The alliances were the business solely of the President and the cabinet, a matter of considerable importance from 1890 onwards. On the other hand, treaties of peace, and commercial or financial treaties, were the business of Parliament. Article 6 repeated the law of May 1873 on presidential messages. It also allowed a minister to be heard in either house. Article 10 gave each body the decision on elections to itself. The whole (Constitutional Law, July 16, 1875) was passed by 520 to 84, the minority coming from both extremes.

The above three laws, being 'constitutional', could only be amended by a National Assembly. Two later so-called 'Organic Laws' — the one on the method of electing to the Senate, and a second, on the election of the Chamber of Deputies — could be amended in the same way as other laws. Both bills contain a vast amount of matter on the incompatibilities of State servants with legislators. The two important exceptions were the Préfets of Seine and Police, though after 1882 for the first post, and 1888 for the second, only civil servants were appointed.

The Senate law was carried without difficulty on August 2, and the Assembly was prorogued until November 4.

(ix)

The bill on the election of the Chamber of Deputies in its first guise had been produced in May 1874 and after discussion laid on the shelf. The original bill of 1874 was much modified by the new committee, and submitted on November 8 for the second reading. It consecrated universal manhood suffrage at twenty-one, but the great debate turned on the nature and size of the constituency. The *rapporteurs* and with them the Gambettists and some of the Left favoured the retention of *scrutin de liste*, of the departmental constituency. It was opposed by the champions of the single member constituency, or *scrutin d'arrondisse-ment*. Many theories were proffered and discussed, that *scrutin de liste* would produce a better type of deputy, that he would not be at the mercy of local influences, that minorities would secure some kind of representation. The *'arrondissementiers'* retorted that the list put the voter at the mercy of the electoral committees, that he would have to elect men whom he did not know. Theories mattered little compared with electoral calculations. The Right, seeing that with *scrutin de liste* the Left and the Bonapartists had been winning seat after seat during the past two years, were convinced that this 'demagogic' system was one of the causes of their own undoing. In this opinion they were re-inforced by those other conservatives, the Left Centre. It must be remembered that most of the members of these groups were themselves landowners, who believed that their importance in their communes — many of them were both maires and *conseillers-généraux* — would allow them to influence the electorate. They were further encouraged in this opinion in that Gambetta was a patron of the departmental candidature.

Now Gambetta, who could have won at least half of the five-hundred-odd single-member constituencies in France had he stood, held for the *scrutin de liste* purely in the belief that in small constituen-cies local greeds would play too great a part. At this date he did not at-tach as much importance to the system of election as he would in five years' time. So, since agreement appeared of greater weight at the moment, the question was not seriously contested, and *scrutin d'ar-rondissement* was voted.

Article 13 laid down '*Tout mandat impératif est nul et de nul effet*', meaning that, once elected, the deputy is no longer the representative of his constituency but of the nation; he is free to vote as his conscience bids, and he cannot be called on by his outraged supporters to explain himself or resign.

No less important for the future was the question of the size of the constituency. Should it be based on population or on voters? The latter figure was far smaller since it excluded women, minors and foreigners. Should the basis of population be chosen, then should there be a constituency per 75,000 or per 100,000? The Conservatives did not want a large Chamber, which by numbers would overwhelm the Senate: they were able to carry the larger figure. They also secured the basis of population. Hence it was later found that the frontier departments, all of which contained many foreigners, were over-represented by a disproportionate number of deputies to voters — in 1914 the five deputies of Basses-Alpes represented no more than 34,000 electors.

The Law was voted at the end of November (O.L. Nov. 30, 1875). The National Assembly had now but a month to live, but that last month was stormy.

(x)

Since midsummer, the question of control of the Senate had been exercising the minds of the leaders. Control would turn on whether the seventy-five Life Senators belonged to the Right or the Left. At the end of November, the approximate situation in the Assembly was that the combined Right (apart from thirty-three Bonapartists) amounted to 350–355 members, while the combined Left had 330. But the Right figure included fifty Chevau-légers, Legitimists who held that the cause of the monarchy had been betrayed by the Orleanists of the Right Centre. The future of the Senate therefore depended on what the Chevau-légers and the Bonapartists did. If either went over to the Left, the seventy-five seats would be lost to the Right Centre; if both abstained from the election, the situation might be no less bleak. The Right Centre would have liked to eliminate the Bonapartists, but, without their votes, they could not win.

The Republicans, however, were also divided. As much as the Right, the Left Centre needed a conservative Senate, but if they split from the Left, they must submit to the dictation of the Right.

Gambetta believed that a bargain was possible. In spite of the protest of Thiers, he approached Bocher, President of the Right Centre, and offered the Left vote in support of fifty Right Centre candidates, provided that they were men who had voted for the Republican constitution and had joined the group of Constitutionalists. In return for this support, the Right Centre must vote for twenty-five Republicans. Bocher refused on the ground that he could not favour one group at the expense of another. The Right Centre rashly believed that they held the cards; rashly they offered the Left Centre no more than thirteen seats, the remaining sixty-two to go to the Right. The voting was to begin on December 9. To be elected, a candidate must secure the votes of more than half the members of the Assembly. During these last days, Raoul Duval had taken up the battle against the Orleanists. He approached La Rochette, the leader or the Chevau-légers. Their plans were not completed by the morning of the opening of the election, and on that day the President of the Assembly, the Orleanist Audriffet-Pasquier, and Martel, an apostate from the Right Centre, were elected. That night, probably through the offices of Eugène Duclerc, nominally of the Left but the friend of every man, Duval and La Rochette were put in touch with Gambetta and through him with the Republican Committee. A pact was concluded by which in return for the support of the Left for fifteen Chevau-léger candidates, the fifty members of the Extreme Right would support the men put up by the united Left. From next morning, the proceedings followed this plan. There were violent and noisy scenes, exchanges of insults. The Right cried treachery; some of the Chevau-légers indignantly refused the candidature and turned on La Rochette, but the election of Republicans and Extreme Right went on. On December 16, when only five seats remained to be filled, the alliance broke down; the Left under the influence of Thiers proposed to admit some moderate Right candidates. There was a quarrel between Ricard and Gambetta and the groups resumed their liberty of action, Four of the last five seats went to very moderate men of the Centre. Cissey, Wallon, Admiral de Montaignac and the Marquis de Maleville, while the other seat was filled by the Bishop of Orléans, Monsignor Dupanloup, of the Extreme Right. But Broglie, Buffet and Decazes had not been elected, and the Royalist preponderance in the Senate was utterly compromised. Of the seventy-five seats believed safe for conservatism, twenty-seven had gone to the Left Centre, fifteen to the Republican Left, eight to the Gambettist Republican Union and seven to Lavergne's group of Constitutionals. The Right secured only eighteen seats, of which fifteen were taken by the irreconcilables. From hatred of the Orleanists, the Legitimists had not only killed their power, but had completed the ruin of their cause. The results had exhibited to the world the impotence of the monarchist party in France, while on the other hand the Republicans were relieved of a number of elderly and very antiquated relics of the past. It had been a triumph for Gambetta. 'My fine gambler', said Thiers, 'when the cards are running your way, you should sweat every penny out of them.'*

There still remained some business to be concluded before the Assembly could rise. On December 20 Naquet, the strange hump-backed chemist, a Jewish romantic who had already abandoned the Republican Union for an even extremer position, a visionary act he would repeat more than once, moved for an amnesty to the deported Communards languishing in New Caledonia. His plea was rejected. A more immediate question was the raising of the state of siege still existing in twenty-seven departments, which gave the ministry control of public meetings and the press. Dufaure and Buffet were only prepared to modify the situation in return for a press law which allowed the repression of subversive propaganda. The Right once again united; so, in spite of the hostility of the Left, a press law was passed and the state of siege was lifted everywhere except in Paris, Versailles, Lyon and Marseille.

On December 29, 30 and 31 a large batch of laws was hurried through. On New Year's Eve the President, the Duc d'Audriffet-Pasquier, addressed a farewell to the members. 'Do not fear that the country will reproach you with the concessions you have made . . . for there are two things you have given it back intact, its flag and its liberties.' Thus ended the National Assembly, which had arrived at Bordeaux in February 1871 to restore the Bourbons and instead had created the Republic. In spite of its quarrels and its seeming fickleness, it had been an honourable body, working according to its lights only for what it deemed to be the welfare of France.

In five years it had largely liquidated the costs of the war. The indemnity had been paid off, compensation of a kind given for war damage, and the army had been re-formed and re-organised. In 1873 Magne put the total extraordinary expenses at 9.287 millions; his successor, Mathieu-Bodet, at 12,898, Léon Say at half a milliard less: the exact figure must remain conjectural. The speed with which France had recovered amazed the world. The country had shown an immense

* See Appendix VI.

vitality. The budgets had been balanced; that of 1875 had shown a surplus of seventy-eight millions, that for 1876, passed by the National Assembly on its deathbed, would show nearly a hundred millions, an example of strict economy which would not be followed by the Assembly's successors. Aside from the constitutional battle, the Assembly's work had been thoughtful, sober, intelligent and constructive. It had deserved well of the country. 'There will have been few Assemblies so great', said the *Temps* in 1901, while two of its members, who during its existence had been violently hostile to the majority, Gambetta and Goblet, later looked back on it as the halcyon age of their political experience. After a dinner given by Ludovic Halévy in February 1881, the host noted in his diary that Gambetta had shown a real enthusiasm for this 'reactionary' body: 'it is better to have to do with intelligent enemies than with stupid friends'. Goblet in his memoirs wrote: 'The truth is that the National Assembly . . . was far superior to the Chambers that succeeded it, not only in the worth of its men, but by the spirit that animated it. If the fights between the parties were sometimes violent, they were sincere. They were for ideas and principles, not for personal ambitions.'[21]

Chapter Three

Population

(i)

What happened in and to France during the nineteenth century — and for France the nineteenth century ends with the derogation of the French Chambers in July 1940 — was influenced by two phenomena, for both of which the French people themselves were responsible. One was the slow growth of the native population, the other the land settlement arising out of the Revolution. In every difficult situation in which the French people and the French government were involved, whether it arose out of foreign relations and military strength, out of national and local financial weakness, out of political misunderstanding, or out of educational and religious conflict, one, often both of these factors will be found to lie somewhere near the root of the trouble.

There were also natural disadvantages which prejudiced French industrial development in the period, for one, the deficiency of coal in the coal age. Yet this, though a natural handicap, was here actively abridged by imports and by intelligent fuel economy: it was also passively diminished by the laggard development of industry, occasioned partly by the absence of demand due to the two fundamental conditions, the stagnation of the internal market and the self-sufficiency of a large agricultural population of small landowners. The minds of French physicists, chemists, biologists and engineers were no less able and no less imaginative than those of the other members of the Scientific International that emerged in the eighteen-forties, but there was no pressure to put their ideas to practical uses. Had there been that pressure, the absence of coal would have been redressed by the harnessing of the abundant water-power and the expansion of hydraulic energy, scarcely undertaken by 1914.

In this and the following chapters, these contingencies will be described. In 1849, Renan wrote that the French Revolution was 'the inrush of deliberate conscious purpose into human affairs: it marks the end of the irrational and the instinctive and its supersession by the rational and the conscious'. But the consciousness was dim; the

G

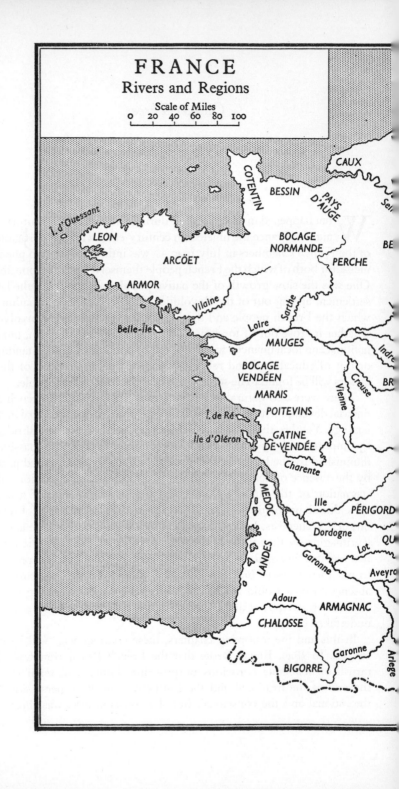

FRANCE
Rivers and Regions

Scale of Miles
0 20 40 60 80 100

CAUX

COTENTIN

BESSIN

PAYS D'AUGE

Sei

BE

I. d'Ouessant

LEON

BOCAGE NORMANDE

PERCHE

ARCÖET

ARMOR

Vilaine

Sarthe

Loire

MAUGES

Indre

Belle-Île

BOCAGE VENDÉEN

Creuse

BR

Vienne

MARAIS

I. de Ré

POITEVINS

Île d'Oléron

GATINE DE VENDÉE

Charente

MEDOC

Ille

PÉRIGORD

Dordogne

QU

LANDES

Lot

Garonne

Aveyro

Adour

ARMAGNAC

CHALOSSE

Garonne

Ariège

BIGORRE

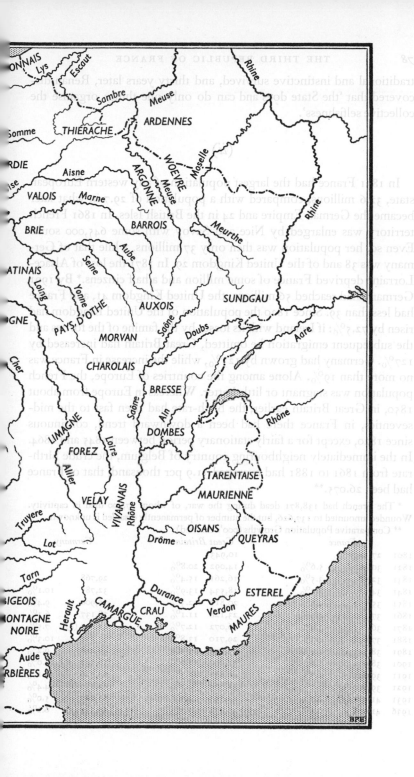

traditional and instinctive survived, and thirty years later, Renan discovered that 'the State does and can do only one thing: organise the collective selfishness'.

(ii)

In 1831 France had the largest population of any western European state, 32.6 millions, compared with a population of 29.7 in what later became the German Empire and 24 in the British Isles. In 1861 French territory was enlarged by Nice and Savoy with some 645,000 souls. Even so, her population was then only 37 millions, while that of Germany was 38 and of the United Kingdom 29. In 1871 the loss of Alsace-Lorraine deprived France of some million and a half citizens.* By 1901 Germany had reached 56 millions, the United Kingdom 41, and France had less than 39. Since 1820 the population of the United Kingdom had risen by 72.5%: if Ireland with its losses by the famine of the forties and the subsequent emigration be omitted, Great Britain had increased by 127%. Germany had grown by 123%, while the increase in France was no more than 19%. Alone among the countries of Europe, the French population was stagnant or little better. Whereas in Europe from about 1850, in Great Britain earlier, the birth-rate had risen fast to the mid-seventies, in France there had been a downward trend, continuous since 1820, except for a fairly stationary period between 1845 and 1864. In the immediately neighbouring country of Belgium, the crude birth-rate from 1861 to 1881 had averaged 31.9 per thousand, that of France had been 26.075.**

* The French had 138,871 dead during the war, of whom 17,000 died in captivity. Wounded amounted to 137,626, but the number of permanently disabled is unknown.

** Comparative Population Growths (000's omitted)

	France		Great Britain		Germany	
1801	27,349		10,943			
1821	30,462	5.6%	14,092	20.8%		
1831	32,569	3.5%	16,261	15.4%	29,768	
1841	34,230	5.1%	18,534	13.9%	32,785	10.1%
1851	35,783	4.5%	20,817	12.3%	35,900	9.4%
1861	37,386 (a)	4.5%	23,128	11.1%	38,137	6.2%
1871	36,103 (b)	−3.4%	26,072	12.7%	41,010 (b)	7.5%
1881	37,672	4.3%	29,710	13.8%	45,234	10.3%
1891	38,343	1.8%	33,028	11.1%	49,428	9.2%
1901	38,962	1.6%	37,000	12.0%	56,367	14.0%
1911	39,605	1.7%	40,831	10.3%	64,926	15.1%
1921	39,210 (c)	−1.0%	42,769	4.7%	62,130 (c)	−4.4%
1931	41,835 (d)	6.7%	44,795	4.7%	65,267	5.0%
1936	41,906	0.3%	(1939) 46,478	3.7%	(1939) 69,317 (e)	6.2%

It is calculated that there had occurred between 1846 and 1860, and would recur persistently after 1886, a phenomenon not yet observed in any other country, a fall in the net reproduction rate below unity, signifying that the French were not producing a sufficiency of girl children to maintain the population, unless the birth-rate rose.[1]

The age-structure of 1881 showed that the French were on the average older than their neighbours. The figures of that year showed that if the trend persisted, the French population would be smaller than that of Great Britain at a not distant date.

Ages	England & Wales		France	
	Population mns.	%	*Population mns.*	%
0–14	9.4	36.5	10.0	26.7
15–44	11.6	44.7	16.7	44.8
45–64	3.7	14.2	7.7	20.5
65 and over	1.2	4.6	3.0	8.0
	25.9	100.0	37.4	100.0

The relative smallness of the youngest French age-group and the size of the two oldest demonstrated that, unless some great social change were to take place, the reservoir in the future would not be able to furnish a working and fighting force large enough for security. The threat was increased by the knowledge that the German Empire, already larger than the French, showed an age-pattern similar to the English. Further, included in the French 37 millions, were over a million foreigners who might or might not become naturalised. Many of them, particularly the Belgians, who formed the largest group, 46% of the total, were taking advantage of the comparatively low French rents to settle for such time as they needed to save enough capital to return to their own country to buy land. France was a country of immigration, whereas everyone of her neighbours was a land of emigration. During the seventies, an average of 145,000 left the United Kingdom annually; during the eighties, this would rise to a quarter of a million. Between

(a) Annexation of Savoy and Nice. (b) Alsace-Lorraine, 559,000, loss to France, gain to Germany. (c) Re-annexation of Alsace-Lorraine: to France gain 1,710,000, but the net war loss was 2,105,000. This lost to Germany plus losses in Silesia etc. (d) 1,341,000 foreign immigrants since 1921. (e) Old Reich only. For Austria, Sudetenland and Memel, add 10.2 millions.
N.B. The German Imperial censuses are one year earlier.

1851 and 1910 French emigration did not amount to two million all told, of which less than 400,000 went to the French colonies.*

The reasons for the decline and perpetual weakness of the birth-rate are not wholly clear.** It is said that the fall is adumbrated in the structure of the population before 1789. Le Play and his school of sociologists believed it was due to the inheritance clause of the Code Napoleon, derived from the Revolutionary law of March 7, 1793, which decreed the partition of estates between the widow and children. In *Le Secret du Peuple de Paris*² of 1863 Corbon wrote that the *arrière-ban* of the working bourgeoisie, the lower middle-class, have 'perfected the science of sterile love-making. They say to themselves "We won't have any children", and they don't; or "We'll have only one child", and one they have.' '*L'ancien régime*', according to one critic, '*faisait des fils ainés; le régime actuel fait des fils uniques*.'³ In the debate on Méline's tariff bill, which began in May 1891, Eugène Raynal, combatting Méline's thesis that imports of foodstuffs were causing a flight from the land, said that everyone knew that there were departments in which the peasant believed it his interest not to have too many children: 'he has it set down in his marriage-contract that after the first child there shall be no more.'⁴ Fraix de Figon, writing in 1911 of the four hundred owners of *métairies* in Allier, said that they usually had only one child, the heir.⁵ On the other hand, it is said that those who wished to escape the inheritance terms of the Code could and did do so: there were many methods of circumventing the law, and in the regions where written law had not existed before the Revolution, the Code was openly flouted.

The decline was also ascribed to propaganda for small families in the late thirties and early forties, which Balzac, while also pointing to the inheritance laws, refers to in *La Fausse Maîtresse* of 1842. Yet it is impossible to believe that the peasant, largely illiterate, was affected by such doctrines, and it may well be asked why, alone of European peasantry, the French should have taken to birth control, why, in

---

* According to Ferenczi and Wilcox, *International Migrations*, II, 206, the average annual emigration in each decade 1871–1900 was respectively 17,050, 26,100 and 16,000. These are to Argentina, U.S.A., Canada, Uruguay, Paraguay, Brazil, Chile, Algeria, and after 1881, Tunisia.

** Mr Colin Clark has stated that the early decline was due to the institution of divorce. It is true that divorces were legalised by Law of September 20, 1792, but this was repealed in 1816, from which date until the Naquet law of 1884 there is nothing wider than legal separation. The figures for separations in my view are not sufficiently high to account for the lowness of the birth-rate. Nor was this pseudo-divorce used much by the peasantry. Professor Glass's opinion is that the age-structure before 1789 indicated a probable fall.

André Siegfried's phrase, they had become 'the first Malthusians without ever having read Malthus'?[6]

It is of course not beyond conjecture that the official figures are wrong. No English census earlier than 1851 is approximately accurate, and it is doubtful if the French have ever been absolutely true, since it is known that communes have deliberately falsified their figures to evade unwelcome additions to their duties which would burden their exiguous revenues.* On the other hand, it is possible that the birth-rate was higher than is reported. But infant mortality was also high, and it is improbable that the errors and omissions of the census-takers were sufficient to distort the general picture.

(iii)

Concentration of population, and urban growth, are inevitable features of industrialisation. In France, the contrast with Britain and Germany is again striking. In 1801, Great Britain had seventeen towns with a population of over 20,000, France had twenty-seven. In 1881 Great Britain had thirty of a population better than 75,000, France no more than twelve — she had, of course, lost Strasburg. True, the reports of many of the préfets on the industrial situation of 1872 speak of a movement to the towns, but the evidence is thin. Certainly towns were growing, but at no rapid pace, and largely by immigration. Paris, which was now stretching out towards Saint-Denis, grew little between 1872 and 1876, a mere 137,000, of which a third was natural growth. Between 1876 and 1881 the increase was 251,000, of whom 224,000 were immigrants — a great number seem to have been from Alsace and Lorraine. The increases of the provincial towns in the same periods were almost wholly from immigrants, 88.4% in the first period, 98.2% in the second.[7] No growths were in any way spectacular, nothing to indicate any revolutionary change. There seem to be no great aggregations of population. There is Paris, Lille and its two satellites, Roubaix

---

* In the *Temps*, May 27, 1932, there was printed the following: 'Nothing is less exact than the census. . . . A commune has no interest in publishing the exact figures of its population when this is growing and approaching either 5,000 or 10,000, because it may entail the obligation to provide a commissaire and policemen, whose budget and housing in the eyes of the central government are communal affairs. The figures will alter the rate of taxation. I know some mining communities in which whole areas are omitted.' The reference is to Houdain (P.-de-C.). Quoted in *Annales historiques de la Révolution*, XIX (1932), p. 353.

and Tourcoing, the agglomeration of the Saint-Etienne coal-field, Marseille and Lyon, but the only striking rises are those of Reims, the city of the wool-combers, Nice, and the 200,000 of Saint-Denis and Sceaux.

It is possible that in a number of cases the census figures do not give a realistic picture. This is due to the fact that a number of towns were fortified and still lay within walls, Paris itself, Lille, Maubeuge, Douai, Valenciennes, Troyes, Grenoble, to name only a few. The military did not wish the defence to be impeded by built-up areas close to the fortifications. Therefore it was natural to add height to the buildings within the enceinte rather than to spread. Accommodation was therefore limited. Further, the greater part of municipal revenues were derived from octroi duties on foodstuffs and building materials to be used in the town. Hence suburbs, country villages beyond the gates, which did not suffer from these duties, resisted the extensions of the city boundaries which would bring them within the dutiable area, and add to the cost of living. The example of Paris, however, would be followed by other cities in the next quarter of a century. Lyon took in the growing urban area east of the Rhône. Le Havre and Marseille, hampered in development by the insufficiency of their ports, dug new basins and extended their limits, thus artificially increasing their population. Some fortress towns, on being de-classified, pulled down their walls and replaced them with boulevards, as did Grenoble in 1883 and Douai in 1890.

With the increase of population and area, the cities repeated the common form of urban development, first, the abandonment of the areas of commerce and city-administration as residential quarters, and with this there were often changes in the nature of industry. In Paris, Lyon and Marseille, the cleaning up and rebuilding under the imperial préfets Haussmann, Charles-Marius Vaïsse, Besson and Maupas, were followed by a drop in the population in the centre and growth at the periphery. Partly as a consequence, the social pattern began to be transformed from one in which rich and poor lived side by side, often in the same building, to one of quarters inhabited exclusively either by the wealthy, their servants and tradesmen, or by the industrial workers. In Paris, more than half the inhabitants of the outer arrondissements from Montmartre eastwards down to the Seine at Bercy were working-class: in Arr. XII, XVIII, XIX and XX, domestic servants amount to between 1% and 2% of the inhabitants, while in VIII and XVI, Champs-Elysées and Auteuil, they form respectively 12% and 23%.

Similar shifts occurred in other growing cities. In the six cantons of

Rouen, dispersion had been continuous for half a century; but it was not until after 1856 that the desertion of the city centre began, while the fifth canton to the east and north-east and the sixth across the river expanded enormously. Also there began the expansion of the satellite towns, Saint-Nazaire, Roubaix, Villefranche-sur-Saône.

The development was to increase social strains. Ducarre, the rapporteur in 1875 of the préfets' reports, quoted an older metal-worker.[9] 'There used to be twenty of us in Père T——'s foundry. We all knew each other; in the evening we had our supper by candle-light with our master. Today there are 400, chaps picked up anywhere. . . . You have banished us to the other end of Paris. In the old days there were bonds of courtesy and, at need, of help between those on the fourth floor and the tenants of the first, and the mother on the first floor set a good example to the mother on the fourth. Now we are driven out to some isolated place and there are no models to look up to.'

(iv)

In spite of the lamentations of advocates of agricultural protection, there does not seem to be as yet any clearly defined drift from the land. Where the figures show a rapid decline, it is due in many cases to a catastrophe. The decline of the population of Var by some 22% between 1856 and 1881 is largely accounted for by the incorporation of the canton of Grasse in the newly annexed county of Nice in 1860; but both in Var and Vaucluse there was a decline, possibly as high as 10% owing to the ruin of the cultivators of garance and the other dye plants by the competition of the new chemicals. In the same period, Haute-Saône lost 22,000 from 318,000, following the gradual extinguishing of many charcoal forges with the arrival of coke-smelting; but it is quite possible that these emigrants moved to the reorganised department of Meurthe-et-Moselle, of which the population rose by 54,000 between 1872 and 1881. Aude, having largely escaped the phylloxera, was being swollen by vignerons migrating from the afflicted areas.[10] The population of Aude rose from 300,000 in 1876 to 332,000 in 1886 and then fell rapidly, whereas after falling from 445,000 to 439,000 in 1876-86, Hérault, with the replanting of the devastated vineyards, increased to 461,000 in 1891. Three departments of the Garonne basin, Gers, Tarn-et-Garonne and Lot-et-Garonne, were all smitten by the phylloxera. But here, as also in Eure, Orne and Calvados, the census-taker shows a death-rate above the birth-rate. Eure is described by Baudrillart as wholly peasant and the most criminal of departments, much given to hard liquor and rape,[11] while Orne was both clericalised and alcoholised.

There was some evidence of a desertion of marginal land, in, for instance, the Hautes- and Basses-Alpes, and perhaps in Meuse and Jura, but it is hesitant. Marginal land would not be seriously affected until there was a more decisive improvement in communications. On the whole, it cannot be said that migration from country to town was very marked in the seventies. There is really nothing that could be described as a flight. A publicist in the middle nineties insisted that the departures from the countryside were those of the younger sons and the landless labourers who could see no future for themselves.[12] Lessees and *métayers* rarely moved, and if their numbers had declined it was because they had become freeholders.

Of the two most significant facts in the early eighties the first is that only three of the eighty-seven departments showed a natural increase, Finistère with over 10%, Morbihan with 9% and Deux-Sèvres with 8%. Secondly, the growth of some regions was due largely to immigration from other countries. In 1872 there had been fewer than three-quarters of a million foreigners. In 1881 there were over a million, 2.68% of the population, and another 77,000 registered as naturalised. The main areas were the border provinces, Belgians in Flanders and Artois (nearly 10% of the active workers in Nord), Catalans in Roussillon, Basques in Béarn, Italians in Provence.

Chapter Four

Agriculture

(i) Ownership

'France being above all an agricultural country, it is agriculture which governs her economic life.'[1] According to the census of 1881, of a population of thirty-seven millions, a fraction under half was directly or indirectly dependent on agriculture for its living.

The pattern of agriculture in the eighteen-seventies had been there before the French Revolution. Though it brought changes in ownership, that upheaval caused no fundamental transformation in the structure of farming. The elimination of the Church as landlord had little effect on the systems of agriculture. The sequestration of the property of *émigrés* or those who perished as enemies of the nation either in massacre or by the guillotine was far from wholesale: a great number of estates were administered by relatives or faithful stewards on behalf of the heirs and remained intact.* The renunciation of feudal dues by the National Assembly on August 4–10, 1789 was in fact less damaging to the property of noble owners than was the division of estates among heirs, instituted by the Revolution and enshrined in the Civil Code. The consequence of this spectacular surrender was to transform a great section of the peasantry, *censitaires perpétuels*, copyholders, into freeholders, and in so doing to fasten on much of the country an agricultural system which, in the words of one commentator, was closer to that of Henry VIII than of George III. The attempts of ministers and intendants in the seventeen-fifties, -sixties, and -seventies, of Bertin, Trudaine and d'Ormesson, to get rid of 'the scandal of fallow' by suppressing common grazing and intercommoning, and encourage enclosure and agricultural individualism, broke on the conservatism of the peasantry and the hostility of the lawyers. The flow of edicts

---

* 'Contrary to an opinion more romantic than documented, it appears that the only persons to suffer confiscation were the *émigrés* not struck off the lists (of émigrés), who were later indemnified to the extent of about a quarter of the losses undergone. The majority of those decapitated, shot, massacred or killed had heirs who eventually succeeded in securing their property.' (Comte Guy de Courtine de Neufbourg in *Annales* (1936), VIII 250.)

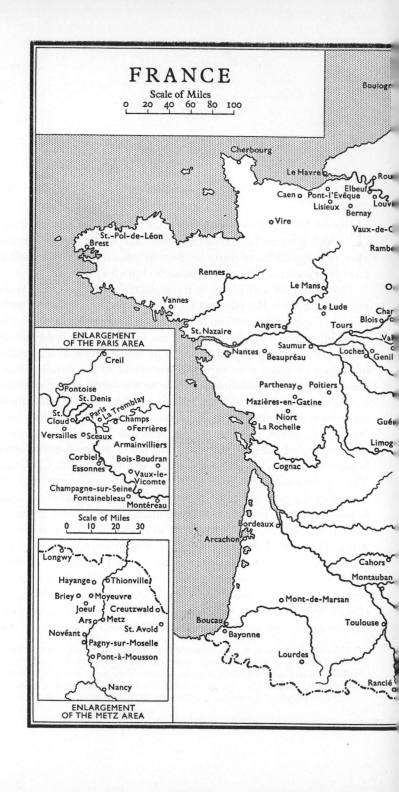

FRANCE

Scale of Miles

0   20   40   60   80   100

Boulogr

Cherbourg

Le Havre

Rou

Caen   Pont-l'Evêque

Elbeuf

Louvi

Lisieux   Bernay

Vaux-de-C

Vire

Rambe

St.-Pol-de-Léon

Brest

Rennes

Le Mans

Vannes

Le Lude

Char

St. Nazaire

Angers

Tours

Blois

Val

Nantes Beaupréau

Saumur

Loches

Genil

Parthenay Poitiers

Mazières-en-Gatine

Gué

Niort

La Rochelle

Limog

Cognac

Bordeaux

Arcachon

Cahors

Montauban

Mont-de-Marsan

Boucau

Toulouse

Bayonne

Lourdes

Rancié

ENLARGEMENT OF THE PARIS AREA

Creil

Pontoise

St. Denis

St.

Cloud Paris La Tremblay

Champs

Versailles Sceaux Ferrières

Armainvilliers

Corbiel Bois-Boudran

Essonnes Vaux-le-

Vicomte

Champagne-sur-Seine

Fontainebleau

Montéreau

Scale of Miles

0   10   20   30

Longwy

Hayange Thionville

Briey Moyeuvre

Joeuf Creutzwald

Ars Metz

Novéant St. Avold

Pagny-sur-Moselle

Pont-à-Mousson

Nancy

ENLARGEMENT OF THE METZ AREA

authorising the division of common lands and the suppression of *vaine pâture* dried up abruptly in 1777. 'The empire of custom which was opposed to both novel techniques and the reforms of agrarian law, prevailed in every class of society . . . nowhere was it more widespread and strong than among the mass of peasants, where it mingled with an obscure feeling of the dangers with which the agricultural revolution threatened the little people.'[2]

Thus reform was abortive. There was no reconstruction of parishes such as occurred in England, little rationalisation of agriculture, and such changes as were made during the nineteenth century were local and haphazard. For example, three plans of the village of Vergigny (Yonne), printed by its historian, dated XVIIIth century, 1810 and 1941 show only minor variations in the course of a hundred and fifty years.[3]

Such survival must not be exaggerated. In some areas the great estate was carved up, and disappeared as such. On the other hand, in some departments such as the Cher, where there were few *émigrés*, large estates (by which is meant an estate of over 250 acres) continued to occupy more than half the department.[4]

In France there was no aggregation of estates such as those shown on the English 'Return of Landowners' of 1873 etc., no group of magnates comparable to the forty-two persons who between them possessed some eight-and-a-half million acres in Great Britain and Ireland, with rent-rolls amounting to £2,750,000. True, much of these estates were of bog, moor and deer-forest, of little value. It is more important to know about estates less spectacular in size but of greater wealth. Were there, for instance, French estates comparable to the 44,000 acres of Holkham in Norfolk with its ten farms each of above 1,000 acres, thirty of 500–1,000, thirteen of 200–500, five of 100–200 and nine between 20 and 100 acres, and a revenue from rent of just under £60,000 a year?[5] It is possible. There is the Talleyrand estate at Valençay (Indre) which was spread over twenty-seven communes and covered 50,000 acres, half of which was leased to tenant farmers. But Valençay lies on the edge of the *triste* Sologne. Rents averaged ten francs the hectare,* say three shillings and threepence the acre, in contrast to the average twenty-five shillings of Holkham. There were large properties in the Camargue on which the little blue-black cattle were bred, estates owned by members of the *noblesse*, some running up to above ten thousand acres. In the Sarthe, the Marquis de Talhouët-Roy owned

---

* The hectare is 2.4711 acres. For these purposes, it is calculated at 2½ acres, 10 ares as 1 rood and 1 are as 121 sq. yards.

and farmed ten thousand acres at Le Lude. At Voré in the Perche, the
Comte d'Andlau owned the former estate of Helvétius, which now included 42 leaseholds and ten mills. Madame de Clermont-Tonnerre
says that the Duc de la Rochefoucauld owned properties in six
departments.[6]

Of course, a number of large estates had only a superficial connection
with agriculture. Of such are the châteaux in the Paris region, Rothschild's Ferrières, Greffuhle's Bois-Boudran, Vaux-le-Vicomte, bought
by the sugar-millionaire Sommier from the Choiseul-Praslin, and a
dozen more, summer residences and partridge shoots. Round Ram-
bouillet, the Pays d'Yveline was still the fattening ground for Berry
sheep and Breton cattle on their way to the Paris slaughter-houses, but
this pasture would be enclosed before the turn of the century and transformed into large estates for dukes and duchesses.[7]

There were big ranges of wasteland* in the Alps, the Pyrénées and
the Massif, which are indicated on the tax-schedules. In 1884 there were
recorded in the Hautes-Alpes 179 *cotes* (taxable area of a single tax-
payer in one commune) averaging close on 4,000 acres apiece, but it is
possible that the whole of this was the property of the communes,
whose aggregate amounted to more than half the department. There
are similar figures for Alpes-Maritimes, the Hautes- and Basses-
Pyrénées, Corsica, and for special reasons, the Landes. Richardson says
of the early eighties that there were at least a hundred owners of above
3,000 acres in the Berry and the Sologne.[8] Such figures as we have offer
little substance to the statement, but he can quote two estates as being
almost as large as Valençay. Nothing is less verifiable. What is a large
estate on Monday may by the death of the owner on Tuesday be reduced by the succession laws, which divide the property between the
widow and the children, to a group of smallholdings.**

The large landowner on the English scale was rare. In his account of
the western departments between the Poitevin marshes and the Caux,
which was really landlords' country, in the early years of the twentieth
century, André Siegfried displays comparatively modest estates.
Though they run up to 1,500 acres, they are more usually about five

---

* You never can tell. I remarked to a friend of mine who farms in the Var on the
wretchedness of a village in the hills of the Alpes-Maritimes. He snorted. 'Those people,'
he said, 'they own all the grazing as far as Vence and half Vence itself.'

** Entails (*majorats*) were prohibited in principle by Article 896 of the Code Civil,
though there were certain limited exceptions. Successions in perpetuity were forbidden in
1835, except for gifts by Napoleon I. These returned to the State on the extinction of the
direct line.

hundred. South of the Loire river round Beaupréau (Maine-et-Loire) ten estates covering more than half the commune averaged five hundred acres. At Saint-Sornin in the same department, three estates of five hundred covered two-thirds of the parish. In this department the tenant-farmers and share-croppers were double the number of owner-occupiers.[9] 'We are a country of moderation', says Augé-Laribé: 'when a property or a farm allows the cultivation of five hundred acres, we say, not unreasonably, that it is very large.' At the same time, he points out that behind the interplay of marriage and inheritance can sometimes be discerned the features of one he designates as the 'multi-proprietor', the owner of numerous smallholdings. The facts we shall never know. 'Yet it must be remembered that about 1880, the share of the land and the influence of the great landowner were bigger than we cared to admit.'[10]

This may be so, but probably the influence was restricted to one well-defined area with certain outlying provinces.* The twelve coastal departments from the Belgian frontier to the Poitevin marshes with the adjacent Eure, Orne, Sarthe, Mayenne and Maine-et-Loire held almost exactly half the tenant-farmers in the country, and in addition seven of these departments employed a fifth of the *métayers*.

Much more consideration should however be given to a figure who at this time was not much in evidence in England, the owner and occupier of a medium or small farm, ubiquitous in France. The most enduring of ambitions to the majority of Frenchmen of the nineteenth century was the possession of some piece of the soil. In the seventies, the industrial transformation, far gone in Great Britain, rapidly developing in Germany and Belgium, had scarcely touched France. Much manufacture was still rural, domestic and compatible with agriculture. Many factory-hands and mine-workers lived near enough to their place of employment to be able to cultivate some land. Land offered both investment and security, and to possess a rood, ten *ares*, he would pinch and scrape. In his report to the Minister of Agriculture for the Enquête of 1866, Granier de Cassagnac wrote of the 'retired farmhand, labourer or *métayer*, who has got together a modest capital of a thousand or fifteen hundred francs. . . . Its owner knows no peace until he has realised his dream by buying some corner of a field where he can build his humble dwelling.'[11] Cassagnac goes on to emphasise the

---

* 'To the west of Saumur, Le Lude and Le Mans, there is scarcely a commune and not a single canton that does not contain nobles. In Maine-et-Loire and the south of Mayenne, the *noblesse* pullulates.' (Siegfried, *Ouest*, 53.)

growth of the number of these little crofts, which 'are the result of the character stamped on the conservative elements of the family by the Revolution'.

This process had been continuous since the first *cadastres*, round about 1829–31, and was regarded by a number of publicists with growing misgiving. Léon Faucher, looking at the land-hungry peasants of the barren Creuse in 1836, wrote in a phrase that became famous: 'Ownership of land is falling into dust.'[12] Since then debate as to whether this fragmentation had gone too far had been perpetual. In every department, up to the time of the eighties, the area of the average *cote**** had decreased since the completion of the *cadastre*. In Seine in 1881, the *cote* had diminished by over 60%. In Nord, the smallest *cote*, under one *are* (roughly 11 × 11 yards), had more than doubled in numbers between 1829 and 1884. The prophets of woe asserted that soon it would be impossible to turn a horse out to grass or graze a cow, in spite of the objection that the number of animals was rising annually.

The fact was that most of these tiny fragments were not farmland at all. They were cottage gardens on the edge of the growing towns of Lille, Roubaix, Tourcoing and others. And in any case, the total of all the *cotes* smaller than a hectare, 2½ acres, amounted to only 2.2% of the whole agricultural land. The error was the confusion between possession and use, and a misconception of the meaning of the terms employed by officials. There were (in the year 1884) 14 odd million *cotes* in the country varying in size from a few yards upwards. Though each *cote* was chargeable to an individual (who might be an institution, such as a commune or a religious house), the individual (sc. the owner) might be responsible for any number of *cotes*. The figure of fourteen millions therefore did not mean, as some implied, fourteen million landowners. For example, there was no official information that the Duc de La Rochefoucauld possessed land in the Multien, the estate and château at Bonnétable in Sarthe, at least one hotel in Paris, and the château de La Rochefoucauld in Charente, and elsewhere. On the other

---

* The *cote* is the total of taxable land held by one individual in a commune. It contains all the parcels of land owned by that individual. These parcels need not be contiguous. Thus a *cote* does not imply a consolidated estate. (Cf. the Valençay estate quoted in the text.) A *parcelle* is a piece of land of no definite size situated in one commune, having one form of cultivation and belonging to one single owner. Hence an area held by ten men makes ten parcels, and so too does an estate with ten distinct fields. A single area of a single type of crop belongs to one man, but divided by a hedge, makes two parcels. (Foville, *Morcellement*, 136–37.)

hand, figures regarding *'exploitations'** merely informed the enquirer that the land in question was of such or such a size and was managed or worked by a tenant who might be the owner, or a leasehold-tenant for years, or a *métayer*, or indeed all three. It is however clear that, on the one hand, there were a number of fairly large landowners and on the other a great number of very small ones, whose contribution to agriculture was at best minimal, but in reality harmless.

(ii) *Tenures*

Ownership has not necessarily any connection with the uses the soil is put to, nor with the responsibility of the user to it. In France there were three main types of *patron*, the owner-cultivator, the lessee for years (*fermier*) and the share-cropper (*métayer*). A farm might include all three forms of tenure,** though it is rare to find leaseholds and *métairies* in conjunction. All three produce for the market, but the owner cultivator may in some cases be only a subsistence farmer, selling to the market only when he had a surplus beyond the needs of his family and his reserves for the future.

Tenants for years and *métayers* existed in far smaller numbers than working owners. There were less than a million lessees, less than three hundred and fifty thousand *métayers*, and half the lessees and a hundred and fifty thousand of the *métayers* also owned some fragments of land. The main areas let on lease were the North and West regions, 45% of the cultivated land of each area,*** and some departments of the Centre. The share-croppers, whose holdings amount to about half that of the lessees, were chiefly in the Centre and in the South-west: share-croppers could be trusted with vines, as lessees were not, since vines do not bear for vintage until the fifth year. The holdings of both types were as a rule larger than those of the owner-occupiers, but not everywhere. More than a quarter of the leaseholders were to be found in the largely royalist departments of the West, the Vendée and the whole of Brittany.

The share-cropper's situation showed a great deal of variety. For-

---

* That is, any piece of land worked by the occupier, including in this woodland, rough grazing, market gardens, etc.

** There were a number of variations of these tenures and of peculiar local forms, the *domaine congéable* of Brittany (Siegfried, *Ouest*, 150, fn. 2: Jenkins's report, p. 76), the wateringues and moerés round Dunkirk, etc.

*** It is stated in the Enquête of 1882 that the figures from which this is drawn do not include either woods and forests or uncultivated waste.

mally it implied that the landlord of the farm provided the house, the barns, the stock etc. and the *métayer* provided the tools and worked the soil either with his family or with hired labour, the produce being divided between owner and tenant either in kind or in cash. Apart from the *prestation colonique*, a sum payable and deducted from the *métayer*'s share, there were numerous modifications in practice as to the use of tools, of animals, amount of share etc. Agreements were usually verbal, often from year to year, and there was no compensation for tenant's improvements. Although popularly spoken of as the first step on the farming ladder for a man without capital, it was in fact a form of capitalist farming of long tradition. The great group of *métairies* lay in the Allier and adjacent departments, Cher, Saône-et-Loire and Indre. Here, during the troubles of 1789–91, the local leaders of the Revolution got a grip on the main properties and proceeded to work them through *métayers*.[13] Known locally as *fermiers-généraux*, they maintained themselves up to the twentieth century. Some in the eighties were paying as much as 100,000 francs in rent and running thirty or forty holdings.[14]

A different type were the resin-tappers, the *gemmiers*, who worked in the great pine forest area of the Landes and Gironde. A region of waste with dunes creeping in under the drive of the Atlantic rollers, there was a long history of failure to hold back the sand. It was not until the Second Empire that one of the Ponts-et-Chaussées engineers, Chambrelant, by draining the soil before planting, succeeded in rescuing this waste land. Napoleon III had put his weight behind the experiment and forced the communes to undertake the reconstitution of the region. The rewards to capital had been small. In the sixties land could be bought for about twenty shillings an acre. Resin-tapping offered little profit, except during the American Civil War. Hence the resort to *métayers*, who were brought in on what appeared to be unusually favourable profit-sharing contracts. In 1882 the area of pine forest in the two departments was well over two million acres and planting was still going on.[15]

Ordinary *métayage* was not small-scale. Throughout the country the average holding was almost forty acres. The average of those in the Bourbonnais was above a hundred acres. Six *métairies* in Allier owned by the same man averaged 140 acres. On the biggest of these were three men, a youth, a shepherd and two women permanently employed. The net profit to be shared between landlord and *métayer* amounted to 1200 francs[16].

(*iii*) *The Regions*

North
1. Aisne
2. Eure
3. Eure-et-Loir
4. Loiret
5. Nord
6. Oise
7. Pas-de-Calais
8. Seine
9. Seine-inférieure
10. Seine-et-Marne
11. Seine-et-Oise
12. Somme

West
1. Calvados
2. Charente
3. Charente-inférieure
4. Côtes-du-Nord
5. Finistère
6. Ille-et-Vilaine
7. Loire-inférieure
8. Maine-et-Loire
9. Manche
10. Mayenne
11. Morbihan
12. Orne
13. Deux-Sèvres
14. Vendée

East
1. Ardennes
2. Aube
3. Terr. de Belfort
4. Côte-d'Or

5. Doubs
6. Jura
7. Marne
8. Haute-Marne
9. Meurthe-et-Moselle
10. Meuse
11. Haute-Saône
12. Vosges

South-West
1. Ariège
2. Dordogne
3. Haute-Garonne
4. Gers
5. Gironde
6. Landes
7. Lot-et-Garonne
8. Basses-Pyrenées
9. Hautes-Pyrenées
10. Tarn-et-Garonne

Centre
1. Ain
2. Allier
3. Cher
4. Indre
5. Indre-et-Loire
6. Loir-et-Cher
7. Nièvre
8. Rhône
9. Saône-et-Loire
10. Sarthe
11. Vienne
12. Yonne

Massif Central
1. Ardèche
2. Aveyron
3. Cantal
4. Corrèze
5. Creuse
6. Loire
7. Haute-Loire
8. Lot
9. Lozère
10. Puy-de-Dôme
11. Tarn
12. Haute-Vienne

Midi and South-East
1. Basses-Alpes
2. Hautes-Alpes
3. Alpes-maritimes
4. Aude
5. Bouches-du-Rhône
6. *Corse
7. Drôme
8. Gard
9. Hérault
10. Isère
11. Pyrenées-orientales
12. Savoie
13. Haute-Savoie
14. Var
15. Vaucluse

Alsace-Lorraine
1. Moselle
2. Bas-Rhin
3. Haut-Rhin

According to the Enquête of 1882, something like three-eighths of the cultivated soil was worked by lessees and *métayers* (share-croppers), the balance, some forty-seven and a half million acres, being in the hands of owner-occupiers. Not even approximately accurate figures can be calculated, but from a comparison of the Enquête agricole of 1882 with the Census of Population of 1881, it seems probable that there

---

* Corse should be omitted from all statistics. Apart from these figures being rather less appropriate than most, the island has no reference to the economy of France. It merely sends the mainland a supply of tough policemen.

were between two and two-and-a-half million owner-occupiers, engaged in some form of agriculture.* If to these be added those tenant-farmers, *métayers* and day-labourers who owned some part of the land they worked, at least another million — the figures add up to 1,375,000 — might be added. How they were distributed through the country, what type of tenure preponderated, what form of husbandry, depended on soil and climate, tradition, communications and the type of the market.

(*a*)

In output and income, the northern region, and especially the Nord department, was closer to contemporary England than to the rest of France. Both countries had in the past learned from the Low Countries

* In a critical study of the French censuses between 1851 and 1951 published by the Institut national de la Statistique et des Etudes économiques in *Etudes et Conjonctures* (Mai–Juin, 1953), the author, Madame Cahen, stresses the impossibility of relying on the figures between 1856 and 1891 (when the basis of the census was altered), and particularly on those of women engaged in agriculture. For the men, 'the figures oscillate between 5.1 and 5.8 millions without the possibility of certainty that the oscillations correspond to an economic reality.' All that can be seen is a gentle decline in the male agricultural population up to the end of the century, after which the pace sharpens.

Nevertheless, from a more general point of view, some figures may invite examination. The census of 1881 stated that some 18¼ million souls lived directly or indirectly on agriculture. Leroy-Beaulieu, editor of the *Economiste Français* (Dec. 6, 1884) having deducted half a million depending on forestry, removed a further two million *vignerons* and market gardeners, and reduced the figure to about 15¾ millions. This was pure speculation, since up to 1924, no attempt was made to assess the number of *vignerons*. The Chamber report of that year gave a million and a half for a much reduced vine area which to some extent supports Leroy-Beaulieu.

As to landholding, there is a certain correspondence between the numbers given on the Census of 1881 and the Enquête agricole of 1882.

	Census 1881	Enquête 1882	Diff.
Owner-occupiers	2,425,500	2,150,696	− 274,804
Métayers and fermiers	1,010,999	662,632	− 348,367
Fermiers, métayers and day labourers owning land	772,339	1,374,646	+ 602,307
	4,208,838	4,187,974	20,864

While there can be no pretence that the figures are even approximate, we should probably be not far wrong in believing that the number of *chefs d'exploitation* was about 4¼ millions.

On the other hand, the figures for permanent, or at least year-to-year employees, foremen, carters, ploughmen, shepherds etc. are enormously at variance, as are those of landless day-labourers. It is pretty clear that the Enquête figures are wrong. It is probable that the two categories of permanent employees and day-labourers have been confused.

and had a long tradition of rational tillage. The north had long experience of working for a market, with Paris at the hub of the region and the industrial towns, Lille, Rouen, Amiens, and Reims at the periphery, served by good roads and excellent water and rail communications. Before the Revolution there had been farming on a large scale in the neighbourhood of Douai and Cambrai, units of five or six hundred acres.[17] Demangeon notes that the estate of the Abbaye of St. Waast was in 1905 exactly what it had been in 1789. With the development of the northern coal basin and its extension from Valenciennes through Pas-de-Calais to Lens and Bruay, more mouths to be fed arrived each year. Since 1851, the seven departments north of the Seine had increased by two million. It had fewer owners who farmed than any other region. Something approaching half the cultivated area* was leasehold — there were more than a quarter of a million Belgians living and working in Nord and Pas-de-Calais. Demangeon cites as typical of the villages round Arras, Achicourt, where of 122 cultivators only three were owners, the other 119 being in part lessees. At Wailly, 405 of 640 owners were absentee, the land being tilled by the other 235. Three-fifths of Mondicourt were owned by four absentees and were leased to the remaining cultivators. Three-quarters of the soil was arable. The yield of wheat was comparable with that of Norfolk, 25–26 bushels the acre, rising to 29 near Paris. So too with oats and barley. Here too was concentrated practically the whole of the sugar-beet production; well over four-fifths of the refineries were in the Aisne, Nord, Oise, Pas-de-Calais and Somme. The English commissioner described two prize farms worked by a single owner-lessee, twenty miles apart, on the Scheldt canal below Denain. Of one, 430 acres were owned, 350 leased; on the other, 550 were owned, 590 leased. There was a distillery and sugar factory at the northern farm. The beets were sent by boat to the factory and the pulp was returned to the other farm as cattle feed. There were 54 horses and 54 ploughing oxen, with 1300 sheep for fattening and 240–280 cattle for the meat market. The whole was placed on a proper commercial foundation.[18] In the northern region, only two per cent of the area was uncultivated, and of the arable, the bare fallow was no more than 1%, as in England. The ministry of Finance, when revising the land tax assessments in 1880, valued every one of the twelve departments of the northern region higher than the best elsewhere.[19]

* i.e. exclusive of woods and forests.

(b)

The West lay in three distinct sub-areas, lower Normandy, Brittany — Vendée and in part Poitou, and the area centred on Cognac. Calvados, which, with Seine-inférieure, formed the great dairying district, had been a country where reconstitution of the great estate had begun before the Revolution. In the eighteen-eighties the richest pastures were to be seen in the farms of over a hundred acres, which occupied three-quarters of the Seine-inférieure grazing and two-thirds of Calvados, chiefly in the Plain of Caen. Here in the famous Pays d'Auge, 'the farmer has an easy life. A maid and a man usually suffice him to plough his acres, milk the six or seven cows which graze round the homestead, while he fattens his stock on the valley meadows. In June he hires a few *botteliers* to bring in his hay. In August he joins his neighbour to cut the corn in one vast *corvée*, and in November, a few women and children help him pack his apples.'[20]

In contrast to the Norman departments, Brittany was a country of small farms, mostly leaseholds. In the Armorican peninsula and the adjoining departments, the population was denser than in any other agricultural area of comparable size. It was still so to speak 'colonial' country in process of being broken in, a harsh land of granite and furze. Of Finistère and Morbihan more than a third was uncultivated. An abundance of water-points had brought many tenants and also dispersed their holdings. In Ille-et-Vilaine, Côtes-du-Nord, Finistère, Morbihan and Mayenne, the average farm was no bigger than eighteen acres against a figure just about double for all France. At the western end, there was a certain amount of horse and cattle breeding, but the large numbers were due to the smallness of the cows; three Breton animals could be grazed on the area needed for one Norman. Much of the arable was given to cereals, wheat, barley, oats and rye, but the yields were poor, that of wheat being the lowest north of the Loire. The Bretons are, of course, a peculiar people, especially those of 'Bretagne bretonnante', scarcely French, and encouraged to remain Breton and speak Breton by their landlords, and even more by their priests, very often second sons of Breton farmers whose loyalty to God and Brittany was firmer than their loyalty to Republican governments.

The department of Loire-inférieure, historically part of Brittany, differed in many ways from the others, chiefly because the Loire valley is wine-producing. Vendée, largely a country of bocage and marsh, had scarcely changed from the country described by Balzac in *Béatrice*. Owned by royalist squires, worked by tenants and *métayers*, it was the chief breeding ground for draught oxen. All these departments possessed a quantity of day-labourers, wretchedly paid: the summer wages in the five Breton departments, without food, amounted to a fraction over two francs a day, in winter to a franc and a half. Probably their condition, shown in Perrochon's *Creux de maison*, was no worse than that of the cultivators who employed them. Southern Vendée, Deux Sèvres and the two Charente departments differed much from the area northward. The Poitevin marshes in which the Sèvre Niortaise loses itself before reaching the sea above La Rochelle, was one of the most fertile areas in France, real polder country, with no fallow and no need of fertilisers, 'rich', wrote André Siegfried, 'with a prosperity which the Empire had already made legendary.'[21] Here was a proliferation of small holdings: 'the day labourers, the small lessees are purchasers at any price, every time an opportunity occurs. . . . On the Maillezais and Niort sides, the subdivision goes to the limit . . . the price rises sometimes to £100 an acre.' This and the vine growing region round Cognac in Charente, smitten by phylloxera, was a country of cultivators, materially and mentally independent, indifferent in religion, Protestant by tradition, Bonapartist by interest.

(c)

The Centre, comprising chiefly the departments which run round the north of the Massif Central, in the valley of the Loire and across to the tributaries of the upper Rhône, was an area of mixed farming in which agricultural units of more than a hundred acres occupied half the region, though these were forest and waste rather than tillage, pasture or vine. Here and particularly in the old provinces of the Bourbonnais, the Berry and Poitou, cultivation was for the markets of Paris and the industrial centres of Montluçon, Saint-Etienne, Le Creusot, Bourges. More than half the arable and vines were worked by lessees and *métayers* — a good third of the Allier, the department of the *fermiers-généraux*, was under the share-cropping system. From here came the white Charolais cattle and the Berry sheep, bred specially for the capital's meat market. There was also much commercial lumbering by underpaid labour, sawyers who would form the first country labourers' union and be the first to bring strike action to success.

(d)

There could scarcely be a stronger contrast with the Centre than the Eastern region. From Givet to Sainte-Claude down the frontier the country is hilly and either wooded or uncultivated. The land west of this wall is uncongenial and uncovetable, acid and infertile. It was agriculturally far from wealthy. The Burgundian vineyard was comparatively small, and even with all the others, Champagne, the Jura, Alsace, the whole vine area amounted to under three per cent of the agricultural land. Only a few miles north of Dijon lies the once prosperous Châtillonnais, of which the persistent poverty is underlined by such village names as Toutifaut and Mauvilly. The population of the twelve departments was far sparser than in much of the country, the density well below the average. There were few large towns, only five with more than 40,000 inhabitants: headed by Reims with 98,000, then a rapid decline to Nancy, Dijon, Besançon, to Troyes with 47,000. The iron industry of the Haute Marne was struggling for survival, and the Lorraine iron-ore field would not begin serious development for another twenty years. The canton of Briey counted less than nine thousand souls — in 1926, it would have 147,000, 60,000 of them foreigners. There was a good deal of manufacture of small articles in Belfort and the neighbourhood, much domestic industry from the great firm of Japy, and this spread through to such towns as Montbéliard, the great provider of coffee mills, to Morez in the Jura with its spectacle-makers, to Besançon and its clock-makers, to Sainte-Claude with its tobacco-pipes, thriving small-scale trades.

In the region there were comparatively few large agricultural units, though more than in Brittany.* Three-quarters of the forest-land was in units of above a hundred acres. Much of this was public property. Of the 520,000 acres of forest in the Vosges, 140,000 belonged to the State and 292,000 to the communes. Of the 450,000 in Meuse, the State owned 80,000 and the communes 240,000. In Doubs, 250,000 were possessed by the communes: the State property amounted to only 30,000, but the Forêt de Caux near Dole was a model. In the Côte-d'Or, of which over half was in estates of above 100 acres, there were nearly 640,000 acres of timber: 350,000 of them were public property. The not very high amount of uncultivated land — a third of it was hill in Jura and Doubs — was also in large-scale units.

* There were large arable farms in the Marne.

Like all poor land, it was worked in the main by its owners, and its owners were farmers on a small scale, who if they needed help employed their own family. There were fewer landless day-labourers in this region than anywhere else in France. Scarcely more than a quarter of the cultivated land was worked by lessees and share-croppers.

The two most important vine-growing districts, the Côte-d'Or and Champagne, offered two distinct types of wine-making. Champagne was and is industrialised. It is not the growth of one vineyard, but a concoction made from grapes of which the origins at this time were many. Before the delimitation of 1911, the 30,000 acres of vines grown in the districts of Reims and Epernay could not produce enough for the demand, and grapes for blending had to be imported from the Vallage of Bar-sur-Aube, from the Saumurois and even from Lorraine. The Reims-Epernay grapes were grown by owners of extremely small holdings worked with the help of wife and children. In 1900, the canton of Avize in the Epernay arrondissement comprised 1381 vineyards of which 927 were smaller than one hectare (two-and-a-half acres) and 345 of between two-and-a-half and twelve-and-a-half acres. Of these 1272, 1071 employed no labour at all. This small-scale monoculture was highly aleatory. The English commissioner said that the grower would have to make about £26 an acre to survive. One thunderstorm could bring ruin.

On the other hand the producers on the long limestone ridge that runs south-west between Dijon and Chagny were both growers and vintners, highly skilled, working almost individually on a small, even tiny scale. On the Côte de Beaune Le Grand Montrachet is of ten acres. At Vosne, La Romanée covers two-and-a-half acres, La Romanée-Conti five. Le Clos Vougeot, created by the Cistercians in the twelfth century, although of 125 acres, was divided among a dozen growers, while Chambertin, including the famous Clos de Bèze, which goes back to A.D. 630, consisted of seventy acres held by twenty-five owners. Here, the grower made his own wine and sold it at the November auctions at Beaune. In the early eighties, the phylloxera had already moved up to Burgundy, and a bitter battle was engaged between those who wished to preserve the dying French vines and those who wished to plant American stocks and graft. The modernists won in 1886. But in one way the phylloxera had been a benefactor. The Côte-d'Or was already being undercut by the vinegrowers of the 'quatre gros' of the Midi. With replanting they were able to replace the coarser growth (the *'infame Gamay'*) by superior grafts and regain their previous reputation. In the meantime, they suffered, for here wine-producing is almost a monoculture since there are no fields. The villages with the presses and cellars lie on the old roads at the head of the *combes*: further out lie the modern buildings, and finally far away the railway.

Apart from the vine areas, there were serious structural problems. Probably less than any other region had the eastern departments been affected by the Revolution. In many parts there survived the pre-revolutionary, almost mediaeval communal practices. Unlike much of the country to the west, the amount of wasteland that could be used for grazing was negligible. In the four departments of Ardennes, Aube, Côte-d'Or and Marne, the uncultivated land amounted to between 2% and 4% of the whole, while the enclosed pasture was scarcely double (7.5%). Thus there survived the ancient custom of turning the animals on to the fields as soon as the crops had been lifted, on to the *vaine pâture*, while in some parts intercommoning was also still practised.

This was complicated by the survival in this region of the small unit, whose collection of fragments of land were not contiguous but scattered. The evils of this dispersal had been recognised in the mid-eighteenth century, but no remedy had been devised, and after 1789, what with the demand for land coupled with the division of property among heirs, the situation became inextricable. Attempts to reorganise the holdings in a commune failed against the ignorance and jealousies of the peasant owner, who at once suspected that he would be the loser in an exchange.*

---

* The trouble is illustrated by the account of a commune in the neighbourhood of Sens (Yonne). Here half the five thousand acres of the parish were in five consolidated farms. The other half was split into thirty-five units of anything between two and two hundred acres, all dispersed in 1603 separate pieces. The farm of 200 acres consisted of 120 scattered parcels. Others ran from five acres in sixteen parcels to forty-two acres in forty-two. On one twenty-five acre farm in twenty fragments it was reckoned that to grow corn in succession to clover, sixty-three days work was consumed. Harnessing, unharnessing, going and coming between plots, some of which were a mile from the stable, raised five hours effective work to nine. That access should not be denied to the main road, no piece was wider than seventy-five yards, and in consequence these could be worked only on the length, since ploughing across would need too many turns. Such squandering of time led to neglect of much necessary work. Probably, says the witness, this farmer walks some five or six hundred superfluous miles in the year. 'The first quality a farmer needs is to be a good walker, for to cultivate twenty-five acres he cannot do less than the distance between Paris and Marseille.' The problem was not confined to the eastern region. In Normandy in the Vexin, 'one of the most important farms at Saussay-la-Vache consisted of not less than thirty-four parcels to the seventy acres it occupied in the commune. One ten-acre field ran alongside the orchard, but the rest were dispersed in every direction. Many were no bigger than a quarter to three-eighths of an acre, while some were narrow rectangles of a hundred by twenty-five yards.' A further example, from the south, is of the

There was further complication. Round the basin of the Seine lay the departments where were raised the merino sheep which provided the fine wool for the French worsted cloth, Seine-inférieure, Somme, Oise, Aisne, Ardennes, Marne, Seine-et-Marne, Eure, Eure-et-Loire and Côte-d'Or. Now the merino-breeders were already feeling the competition of Australian and Plate wools which had been coming in in increasing quantities every year, not as was alleged so much because of the Franco-British commercial treaty of 1860, though this played some part, as by the fact first, that the French merino was regressing (the French were not skilled breeders: no flock books were kept until the twentieth century) and, secondly, because the small flock-master was unable to sort and clean the wool as the spinners required.*

The merino was thus doomed to decline. But here arose the problem of *vaine pâture* and *parcours*, for if these servitudes were needed to feed the sheep, the sheep were needed to dung the fields. 'Common pasture and common fields are in their original intention, and ever have been in their use inseparable as animal life and food.'[22] In 1880 it was said that if common grazing was abolished in Marne, half the sheep, and there were more than a quarter of a million, would have to go.[23] Hence in nearly all the departments where fragmentation and dispersion were far gone, Vosges, Haute Saône, Meuse, Saône-et-Loire, Yonne and Aube, there was resistance to suppression. Up to 1889, no serious encroachment on the practice had been made, but in that year Parliament by the Law of July 9 decreed the abolition of *vaine pâture* and *parcours*. There were immediate protests from the *conseils-généraux* and the deputies of Jura, Yonne, Saône-et-Loire and Aube. The Minister of Agriculture capitulated, and the question was left to the local authorities to arrange as best they could. Some did, some did not. In one Yonne commune, *vaine pâture* was not officially suppressed until 1926. Nevertheless, the practice continued.[24]

canton of Cadenat (Vaucluse) where there were seven hundred owners of five thousand non-contiguous parcels. Here is quoted a property valued at 6,000 francs which was in eight parcels each of 3 × 150 metres, an example admittedly extreme.

(Javal, A., 'La grande misère de la petite culture', in *RP*, 1933, March 15; Sion, J., *Les paysans de la Normandie orientale*, 417; Baudrillart, M. H., *Les populations agricoles de la France*, III, 230.)

* Since 1860, imports into France had tripled while French production had remained constant. The decline of the sheep flocks was at this date common to all industrialising countries in Europe, and was to continue. The numbers fell from 29 million in 1862 to 24 million in 1882 to 17 million in 1913. 'Owing to imports', wrote Tisserand, the director of the Ministry of Agriculture, 'wool is today largely an accessory.' Unfortunately the French merino proved to be very poor eating.

(e)

The Massif Central, which comprises the former *gouvernements* of Auvergne, Limousin and Marche together with the Velay and Vivarais, most of it hill country running up to 5000 feet in the Monts Dore and round the Plomb du Cantal, is of exquisite beauty in the spring with its fields of jonquil and orchis, but poor land, much of it uncultivated, with areas like the Mezenc wholly barren or, like the Cevennes *causses*, unimprovable. Roughly a third of Aveyron, Lozère and Corrèze and a quarter of Ardèche were uncultivated and on these hills during the summer grazed the largest sheep flocks, driven up from the valleys, even from the plains of the Garonne basin. The fleeces were not heavy and the sheep were bred chiefly to provide ewe milk for the manufacture of the noble cheese of Roquefort. The staple crop was rye: two-fifths of the whole French output came from this region. Most of the land, particularly in the valleys, was owner cultivated, and much, since communications were still thin, was subsistence agriculture. Except on the borders, for instance in the foothills of the Limousin where, on estates run as *métairies*, cattle were bred chiefly for veal to be sold for fattening, the small owner was everywhere. In Puy-de-Dôme, the whole Limagne and the country round Gannat and La Palisse was in the hands of small cultivators, largely owners, working the rich alluvial soil, in holdings from a few roods to ten or twelve acres, supplying Clermont-Ferrand, Riom and Vichy. But all the fertile part of this country was over-populated, and from Puy-de-Dôme and Creuse there was an annual exodus of surplus hands to Paris as masons and carpenters.*

(f)

In the ten departments of the south-west, a bigger area was devoted to the vine than in any other region. The vines in the Gironde alone covered almost as much ground as in either Hérault or Aude, and produced some of the finest wines in the world. The fifty odd classified growths of the Médoc were not big producers, nor were they on a very large scale, but their revenue was high. The big estates of the region

---

* There was a bigger area covered by the cultivators of less than 25 acres in Puy-de-Dôme than any other department. Excluding uncultivated, they held 45% of the soil.

were the fir plantations lying between the Gironde estuary and the Adour, mostly in large blocks and to a great extent communal property. The two Pyrenean departments were for the most part pasture or waste. Vines, maize and timber constituted the main cultures of the region. The greater number of the cultivators were owners, and after them *métayers*, chiefly in the Landes.

(g)

The south and south-east comprised Languedoc, the Dauphiné and Provence, together with the now incorporated Savoy departments and the canton of Nice. Much of the country is still remote from France, indeed scarcely French, with its Basques and Catalans and the wholly unintelligible dialects of the Pyrenean foothills, such as Gerson. The south-eastern corner was much Italianised, while the departments of Aude and Pyrenées-orientales were largely Catalan. More than half the region was covered by large estates, but these were for the most part either in the upper Alps or the Pyrenées, or again in Bouches-du-Rhône, on the unrewarding Camargue and Crau, where the pure-bred blue-black cattle were raised. Here too, the competition of foreign wool had led to the abandonment of breeding for the fleeces and to the crossing of the Arles sheep with English rams for milk and meat. (At this time, cow's milk was practically unknown in Provence.) In the summer, the sheep were driven into the high pastures of Dauphiné. Otherwise, the large properties were chiefly forest and waste, together with the large-scale vineyards.

Every department in the region grew vines, few notable. Most growers were small men, but in Languedoc, alongside the individual grower, there were large-scale plantations, worked by bailiffs with day-labourers. This was a comparatively recent development. In the thirties and forties it had been a region of mixed farming. The Narbonnais had been a wheat-producing area of more than half a million bushels a year, together with some rye and barley, exporting its surplus to Marseille and Nîmes. But costs were high, water was deficient and prices could not be reduced to compete with Russian wheat entering Marseille. By the middle fifties, the wheat area was shrinking. Then with the completion of the Bordeaux-Cette railway and its extension to Marseille, a revolution began. It was now possible to carry wine the length of France. There began the persistent reduction of the grain area and the corresponding planting of vines. In 1830, the Narbonnais had had 50,000 acres under corn. In 1879, cornland was less than 3000, while the eighty thousand acres of vine had quadrupled.[25] The four departments, Pyrenées-orientales, Aude, Hérault and Gard, 'les quatre gros', had been transformed into monoculturists, mass-producers of coarse strong wines for the cheap market. More than a million and a quarter acres in vineyards of all sizes, from a few rows to estates of well over five hundred acres, occupied some ninety-thousand owning-cultivators and 130,000 labourers, more than half the total number for the fifteen departments of the region. To a similar but lesser extent this system was repeated in Bouches-du-Rhône and Var, but in these two departments, together with that of Alpes-maritimes, there was greater variety of cultivation. Here two-thirds of French olive oil was produced as well as a large number of fruits, peaches, pears, apricots, plums, figs, medlars, loquots, pomegranates.

(iv)

A general survey of the whole extent of the French countryside demonstrates how vitally agricultural development depended on markets, and primarily on the French market. (Except for wine and spirits, a specialised trade, little agricultural produce was exported, butter, cheese and potatoes; export of cereals was sporadic and fell off from the late seventies.) By far the biggest market was Paris and its suburban satellites, nearly two and three-quarter million consumers, with the Lille-Roubaix-Tourcoing triangle, Rouen-Le Havre, Amiens, Versailles. Its importance is shown by the fact that the suburban market-gardens round Montmartre, Mont-Valérien, and Clichy were said to have a turn-over of about 4250 francs per acre (£175) against a mere 800 francs in the next department.[26] 'The whole of Seine-et-Oise', wrote an observer about 1880, 'depends on and works for Paris.' Some 9–10,000 workers migrated from the Orne each spring to work round Paris during the summer. The influence of the capital was spreading southwards and the graziers of the middle Loire departments were profiting. Similarly, agriculture in the Rhône valley was stimulated by the growth of Lyon and its ascendancy as far as Grenoble and Saint-Etienne. On the other hand, Marseille, progressing only since the opening of the Suez canal in 1869, was not enriching itself as fast as the rising city of Nice or its countryside. The other older cities, which did not grow, particularly the ports, were unable to influence agriculture to any great degree. Neither Bordeaux nor Nantes had at their back a hinterland which could attract trade. Gascony and Guienne remained the region of wine-export, wine and pit-props. Nantes, since the great days of colonial sugar and slavery had passed, declined from the pride of a great port to the canning of fish and vegetables.

Without easy communications, the agriculture of the rest of the country could only develop sluggishly. The Massif Central, a region nearly as large as Scotland and as rough as the Highlands, cut the south off from the developing north. So too did the Alps of Dauphiné and Provence. The railways penetrated only as far as a town of importance, which often already had water communications. Some departments had no more than one single line connecting the préfecture with that of the next department: some had not even this. Great areas remained isolated, and stagnated while the world outside changed. Readers of Jean Giono's *Les Ames Fortes* will remember the account of the busy relay post of the diligences at Châtillon-en-Diois (Drôme) in the Dauphiné mountains: '*A cinq heures du matin, tu avais d'abord le courrier de Luc, le courrier de Baurière, le petit courrier de Valence, la voiture de Die. . . .*' (Today Châtillon is on a by-road and has a population of less than six hundred.) But the railway was by no means the miracle-worker that politicians believed. The historian of Mazières-en-Gâtine (Deux Sèvres) which lies between Niort and Parthenay, says that, far from opening up the rural areas, the construction of one line from Saumur to Nantes and another from Poitiers to La Rochelle destroyed 'the natural order of communications', since the railway killed the trade of the carriers and long-distance hauliers, but provided no substitute. Parthenay, which was the hub of the road network north-south and east-west, was deserted, and the surrounding villages were more isolated than before the railways were opened.[27]

In 1880, there were 275 urban post-offices and 5718 country, i.e. approximately one for every six communes. 'Five-sixths of the rural communes were linked to the rest of the world only by the passing of the postman, the foot-slogger who circulated daily over some fifteen to twenty miles and whose leather box was a walking post-office, considered quite enough for people who did not write and rarely received letters.'[28] Parcels — parcel-post was inaugurated in 1881 — were delivered only in the villages that had railway stations. As for the disposal of produce, even in the best circumstances the small farmer sold only in the limited local market. He was dependent on a commission-agent who took advantage of his ignorance. It was only the vine-growers who, since they were so vulnerable, had learned to understand the meaning of prices, if not how to control them. But in the Alps or the Cantal or the Bas-Vivarais there were communes which had no contact with the outer world; others only that of the men who went down to the plains for haymaking and the harvest.

Apart from any question of the interpretation of the inaccurate statistics in the Enquête of 1882, there is no doubt that French agriculture at the beginning of the eighties was in difficulties. The agricultural mortgage debt amounted to £480,000 or one-sixth of the value of the whole land at interest rates running up to 7%.

It was inescapable that the French farmers, except the large-scale farmers in the north, producing cereals, sugar or meat, were not improving. Their tools were primitive. There was little machinery outside the north. There was a shortage of animals, and breeding, except on the farms of a few wealthy amateurs, was unscientific. As has been said, the French flock-masters had failed to compete with the South American and Australian merinos, and the French spinners were not buying local wool. Just as the French wool-men had failed over sorting and cleaning, so too the cheese and butter exporters were discovering that rivals in Denmark and the Netherlands were more hygienic, and were entering the English market. The small tenant-farmer got no compensation for improvements, while the vast majority of the ubiquitous cultivating-owners were without capital.

There were additional trials, some natural, some man-made. In the lower Rhône valley, there had long been the profitable cultivation of dye-plants, madder (*garance*), reseda (*gaude*), woad (*pastel*) and saffron, particularly in Vaucluse, where in the sixties some thirty thousand acres yielded some seven million francs worth of *garance*, while Gard, Drôme, the Camargue, the Crau and the banks of the Durance also sent quantities to the Avignon market. Then, in 1869 appeared the chemical dyes of the Swiss and Germans. The French army clothiers promptly abandoned *garance* and adopted the new stuff for the French infantry trousers. Within ten years, *garance* cultivation was dead and, wrote the editor of the Enquête of 1882, 'reseda, woad and saffron are on the way to extinction.' The Vaucluse growers were ruined; the value of their land fell by 40%. Hundreds of dye factories closed down and fifteen thousand were thrown out of work.

More widespread and costly was the assault of the phylloxera on the French vines. Introduced into France in American ornamental vines,

I

the disease first appeared in the Gard about 1865. The difficulty of dealing with it lay in the fact that the aphis attacks the root of the vine and
the first evidence of its action is the death of the plant. Up to the
mid-seventies the epidemic had been sporadic. Then it assumed the
character of a plague. In 1882, it was reported that something approaching two million acres of vines had been destroyed. The Languedoc
vineyards suffered worst. Nearly a million acres in Gard and Hérault
were killed, pretty nearly the complete vignoble; much the same happened in Vaucluse and Bouches-du-Rhône. The disease spread west-
ward as far as Charente-inférieure and also moved up the Rhône. No
remedy or prophylactic could be discovered. Sulphuring and flooding
were ineffective. It was not until the early eighties that C. V. Riley
solved the problem by importing American stocks which were immune,
and grafting on to them French vines.[29] In 1879, a cold wet year,
French vineyards had produced 567 million gallons. That figure, the
lowest in the seventies, would not be reached again until 1893. In the
meantime, the phylloxera had moved inexorably northward, had
plundered Burgundy and reached the Jura, and Marne and Aube.
Of the six million acres of vines of 1875, three and a half million had
been destroyed, but some two million had been replanted.

The French *vignoble* never again covered the area of the early seventies. By 1885 new diseases, mildew and black rot, added to the growers'
troubles. By 1914 the vine area was less than two-thirds of that of the
seventies, but the yields were no less. Partly this was due to the imports
which had begun to rise with the failure of 1879.[30] In the five years
1886–90, the average annual import was 250 million gallons. It was not
until 1900 that there was a serious reduction, to which the tariff law of
1892 contributed. For the Midi producers the worst feature was that the
Algerian colony had started to develop their vineyards. Although the
phylloxera appeared here too, in the mid-eighties, the bold strong
African wines had become a vigorous competitor, against which, since
Algeria was legally part of metropolitan France, no tariff protection
could be sought.[31]

The transformation of Languedoc from a balanced agricultural
economy to a region of monoculture meant that, with the destruction
of the vineyards, many of the population were ruined. The small men
without reserves were finished: if lucky, they sold their holding, it
might be to a man who would plant olives and could afford to wait: if
not, they abandoned their land and moved to as yet unaffected areas.
Aude and Pyrenées-orientales suffering less than Hérault and Gard be-

came departments of immigration. The Aude population rose from 300,000 in 1876 to 332,000 in 1886, the Pyrenées-orientales to a less extent. When these were in turn attacked, the growers moved on, some to Algeria, some even to the Argentine.[32]

Another bye-industry was also declining. In the four departments on the Rhône south of Lyon, one of the most profitable sidelines for the small farmer was the production of the silkworm cocoon. Much was done on a profit-sharing basis, the owner of the silkworms providing the hatch and the mulberry leaves, and the breeder, usually one of the women of the family, sharing the costs. In Ardèche a hatch of two ounces gave some ninety kilogrammes of cocoons valued at four francs the kilo, a handsome addition to the family income. In the forties, seven departments had produced more than 25 million kilos of cocoons worth 100 million francs. Then the region was smitten by the *pébrine*, the silkworm disease. By the time Pasteur had diagnosed the cause and shown the remedy, the Italians had cut in. They improved their breeding methods and with cheap labour undercut the French. By 1881 they were exporting 13 million kilogrammes, three times the weight they had sent in the sixties. The French continued, but the return from the cocoons — 69 million francs in 1872 —slid down. In 1881 it was only 41 million, in 1892 28.[33]

Even today one reads occasionally that the French peasant lives magnificently, and though no doubt some vignerons or market gardeners may be met whose prowess at table is gargantuan, they are rare. A close look at the evidence of the standard of existence of the French peasant in the last quarter of the nineteenth century shows burdened men struggling to provide the means of life for themselves and their families, often in debt and nearly always without reserves except a few acres of land. The late seventies were the last years of a long period of rising land values, and although, for special districts, like the already quoted Poitevin marshes, there was still stiff competition, by 1882 the fall in land values and rents had begun, to the dismay of landlords.

Did this seriously affect the peasantry? If a peasant can be distinguished from a farmer, it is that the farmer works for a market, develops those lines in which he can most easily produce and which he can dispose of most readily. A peasant is a freeholder, who lives on the produce of his land and sells the surplus. (There are of course cultivators who do both.) He is affected less by poor prices than by bad crops. So far as money is concerned he handles it with difficulty and some distrust. It was not until the nineties that the villagers of Mazières-en-Gâtine had 'partly adopted the habit of buying and selling, and of handling money; their outlook had widened; many had been to school. And the initiative which would lead to the foundation of a butter-making co-operative, instead of coming from above, from distant and unknown personalities, emerged from the region itself, *not, of course, from the peasants,** but from a local figure who enjoyed considerable authority . . .'.[34]

There were in the early eighties at least more than two and a half million landowners working properties of between two and twenty-five acres, and probably a number, not to be calculated, of those with less than two and a half. How many of these with their families habitually used money? No one can say. It is probable that many of the tiny hold-ings, for example in the island of Ouessant where the parcels averaged two-fifths of a rood, and a single furrow six-feet wide was tilled to grow early vegetables, or the smallholdings on the banks of the Rhône and the Erieux in Ardèche, were working for a market. But of the others, those who cultivated between five and twenty-five acres in the Basses-Alpes and the Cevennes, how many of these practised a small-scale autarchy, how many lived on what they drew from the soil and used money only for such transactions as taxes? All the evidence tends to support the view that south of the Loire, and perhaps to the north-east, a great number were cultivating to eat rather than to sell.

In the same period, seventeen to eighteen million acres were sown with wheat, producing in the best years about 20 bushels per acre; in bad years, like 1879, less than thirteen. It is pretty certain that little if any of the wheat grown in some of the Central Massif and Alpine de-partments, where normally no better than 13–15 bushels an acre was produced, came to market. It was given to the local baker in return for bread, particularly in communes where communications were poor. There is a report by Raoul-Duval, of about 1880, of Genillé, a com-mune near Loches. The population was 2,275 in 634 families. Of these families eighty harvested more wheat than they consumed. Of these, eight had a large surplus and seventy-two a small one, while another 240 families consumed all they harvested. The remaining 314 families, or just about half, had to import.[35]

* My italics.

A woman talking of her childhood in the nineties some twenty miles east of Albi (Tarn) said that 'we ate what we had and bought nothing. Before I was twenty and went into service, I had never tasted wine or eaten butcher's meat. Only the men drank and that only on fair days. When a young man married, he bought a suit: when he died, he was buried in it. The women spun the cloth for the family's clothing. There were twelve of us children and we ate white bread only on fête days.' The house had only one room, which is normal for the period. The stock consisted of five sheep and an ass. 'We ate nothing but soup made of potatoes and fat. We never had a sugar cake: we had no sugar, but we had a hive. In summer we went barefoot. Father made sabots for the children for the winter, and our clothes went on from child to child.'[36]

A different but parallel example is that of a rich peasant in the fertile Limagne, near Clermont-Ferrand, who inherited his estate in 1865. In 1869, his total expenditure on the farm, which includes labour, taxes, upkeep, renewal of stock and household expenses, amounted to 1,984.55 francs. He spent 25 francs on coal; he paid the priest 15 francs pew-rent for three seats, and the barber 10 francs to shave him twice a week all the year round. There were a few francs for the doctor and the vet., and a few for repairs. He bought a pair of slippers and a pair of trousers. But in the year his expenditure on food-stuffs came to 75.75 francs for 60 litres of wine, 4 francs worth of meat, 2.55 for oil, 15 for bread and 6 to the baker to bake the bread made in the house; and there was one bottle of quinquina. No groceries, no coffee, no sugar; like the Alban family, he had a hive. He leased some land; he had money out on loan. In this year, 1869, his total receipts were 8,947.30 francs, of which 3,090 came from interest and repayment of loan. At the end of the year, he had in hand some 6,000 francs of which 4,100 went out on loan and 1,200 were invested in 3% rentes. It was not until 1874 that he began to buy groceries for his household. As the investigator of these accounts remarks: 'What does he contribute to the economy of the country? Very little. Once assured of the subsistence of his family, what does he sell? A few sacks of corn — 13 in 1888, only seven in 1889; a few litres of wine, some roots. . . . Taxes? He pays as little as he can; all his financial operations are clandestine. His real business is to soak up the money of the peasants, who borrow to live, and to transform this money into Three Per Cents before sinking it in the abyss of the Russian loans.'[37]

(*vi*)

In the seventies and eighties, French agriculture with the exception of the north was still very much what it had been thirty years earlier. It was traditional and not rational. Apart from such physical obstacles to improvement as poor soil, broken country, absence or superfluity of water, poor roads and inadequate communications, agriculture was backward. Much of this was due to the pervasiveness of the small occupying-landowner, struggling to wring from the soil subsistence for himself and his family, certainly underfed, ignorant, superstitious and timid. He was undercapitalised, he was probably in debt. The English commissioner, Jenkins, reported that the land was mortgaged to a sixth of its value at rates running up to 7%, and from later figures this is certainly an underestimate. Lecouteux, editor of the *Journal d'agriculture pratique*, declared that three million landowners were indigent and paid no taxes. Richardson was of the opinion that not 15,000 landowners made as much as £325 out of their property. It was clear that in some areas the fragmentation of agricultural land (as distinct from suburban gardens) had reached the limit. In the eighties in the Ardennes, Meuse and Haute-Marne, it was considered that the parcels had become incapable of further division:[38] this situation was complicated by the dispersal of fragments.

A large section of French agriculture stood in need of a change of outlook. Materially it needed capital, tools, technical instruction, communications and markets. The railways were unhelpful. Their directors had seen the bankruptcy of those companies which had ventured their capital in peasant regions. Their prudence in holding back was seen when, thanks to the earlier enthusiasm of the Chamber of Deputies, the railways provided by the tax-payer had once again to be rescued by the tax-payer. Agricultural colleges were provided — and neglected.

From an economic point of view the fragments of agricultural land needed reconstituting into economic holdings. To bring this about a revolution was imperative, or, what was tantamount to a revolution, the education of the peasant. That was not to be. 'We', wrote André Siegfried, 'who know by experience what France owes to the peasant are instinctively reluctant to do anything against him politically,'[39] which is as much as to say that electoral candidates were the last people to advocate change to their constituents.

In any case, the peasant, ignorant, illiterate and suspicious, was not

to be persuaded to change his ways. To cause a voluntary transformation of the countryside, there must be external pressures such as an
increase, a rapid increase in the demand for country produce from
developing urban markets. But except in the north, such were not appearing. In other European countries, the towns were enlarged partly
through the ejection of peasantry by the process of enclosure coupled
with the supersession of bye-industries, by the development of mining
and by the breeding of an urban proletariat. Little of this occurred in
France. Further, whereas in a country of tenant-farmers such as
England, falls in prices could bring disaster, in a country of owner-
occupiers the peasant could and did survive. Although through the
eighties there was unceasing discussion of the agricultural crisis and of
a flight from the land, it was carried on largely by the landlords. There
is no evidence of what could be described as an exodus.[40] It is true that
more than two-thirds of the departments had passed their population
peak, but this was due rather to deaths outnumbering births. There is
evidence of some desertion of sub-marginal land, but not much. Siegfried writing of the Bas-Vivarais speaks of the peasant holdings on the
Cevennes hills, 'of an extreme frugality necessitating intense labour,
of a state of poverty in which the peasant by his own means can scarcely
improve his humble equipment. . . . When a peasant of the Ardèche is
compared with an American estate manager, one cannot but feel in the
presence of two different human races, of two periods of civilisation,
though the deep meaning of the needs of the earth is by no means
always, as might be thought, on the side of the new transoceanic
societies of the west.'[41]

Chapter Five

The Pattern of Industry

(i)

One of the weightiest factors in the history of the Third Republic is the lag in industrial development. It was, of course, inherited from an earlier epoch. The twenty odd years of war between 1789 and 1815 not only retarded progress in technique and organisation, but left behind a kind of economic timidity, a reluctance to take risks, which lingered on into the twentieth century. In 1815 France emerged from the wars battered and shaken, with a government it despised and a hated aristocracy which had learnt nothing. There was a heavy indemnity to be liquidated. Much of the overseas empire had gone for ever, and the merchant marine scarcely existed. French industrialists seemed to have changed their methods very little, let alone improved them. Why should they? With the continent of Europe prostrate at the Emperor's feet, they had enjoyed the monopoly of a vast market. Most of the army contractors, having made their fortunes, had moved into high finance. The *Haute Banque* was little interested in industrial promotion. The finance houses were dominated by foreigners, Swiss Protestant and German Jews, Hottinguer, Mallet, Rothschild, Thelusson, who gave their attention to government loans and arbitrage. During these years, the British had developed and adopted new inventions. Now it appeared that they might prevent French recovery. Hence French merchants and manufacturers had clamoured not merely for protection but in many cases for prohibition of imports. On the other hand, after the Peace of Paris, the English forbade the export of their prized machinery and the emigration of skilled artisans. Needless to say, smuggling flourished.

The most pressing need, if French industry was to expand, was accumulation, then mobility, of men, of raw materials, of finished goods, of information, of money. The waterways of France had been much neglected under the Empire, in spite of paper schemes, which were unfulfilled. From 1821 the Corps des Ponts-et-Chaussées began the completion of unfinished canals and the repair and widening of the rivers. After the abdication of Charles X in 1830, the work was carried on under the July Monarchy and concluded by 1843, but further projected canals were unfinished when Louis Philippe fled.

Canal systematisation had already been overtaken by the railroad. The success of the Manchester-Liverpool and the Stockton and Darlington in England, and of the Saint-Etienne-Lyon line, the first in France to employ locomotives (1832), though only on flat stretches, could not be missed, but in France the problem was more daunting than in England. There was a deficiency of materials, chiefly coal, the prime mover of nineteenth-century growth. In 1840 the French fields produced no more than three million tons to the 35 million of the United Kingdom. The workers were untrained in the new techniques. There was the relative absence or, rather, unavailability of capital. 'The slow convalescence of the country after domestic and foreign wars contributed to restrain the accumulation of capital during the Restoration. This is due to the predominance of agriculture to which the majority of Frenchmen were given; by the exaggerated customs duties which prevented the influx of foreign capital, and by the preference of the greater number of capitalists whose property was not land, for government securities, or, though more rarely, for public utilities.'[1]

Although the railway excited the interest of financiers and journalists, its realisation was slow. For one thing, the Corps des Ponts-et-Chaussées, which from its formation in the early eighteenth century had directed public works in France, considered that the railway should be the business of the State. Not only was this a matter of tradition, but there were also strategic considerations. Then there were budgetary obstacles. Many were still alive who could remember the great *assignat* inflation. On the other hand, while many members of the *Haute Banque*, of whom the most prominent in the railway world was Baron James de Rothschild, head of the Paris branch of the family, saw promise in railways, they could not from their own resources raise the capital for all the proposed lines. To extract money locked up in land, or hidden in stockings, the guarantee of the State was needed. The bankers considered that if they found the money and bore a large part of the risk, they were entitled to direct both the construction and the administration. The Government, on the other hand, feared the appearance of what must inevitably grow into powerful corporations capable of challenging the State's liberty of action. But without the co-operation of the bankers, the capital could not be found. Therefore, while ready to guarantee interest on invested money, the Government would only authorise short lines, under onerous conditions, and give concessions for short periods. In the end, the map was drawn by the engineers of the Ponts-et-Chaussées. In the main, six systems were envisaged, five radiating from Paris, north, east, south-east, south and south-west, with one across the south from Bordeaux to Marseille. Partly owing to financial stringency, partly to the inability of the Government to see its way clearly, the plan was not completed until 1842, but in June of that year the scheme was accepted by Parliament.

Meanwhile, apart from short lines to Versailles, there had been conceded the Paris-Orleans and Paris-Rouen railways. The latter, subsequently extended to Le Havre, was financed by an English group, many of whom were directors of the London and South-Western Railway. It was built by British engineers and British skilled labour, while the locomotives were constructed in Rouen by an English company. The possibilities excited optimism and, exactly as in Great Britain, the years 1844–46 saw a spectacular Stock Exchange boom in France. The main lines were conceded but always for limited distances, often with a parallel rival line. In 1845 was conceded to a Rothschild group Paris-Lille and Valenciennes with branches to Calais and Dunkirk, while Amiens-Boulogne was granted to a consortium partly English. What eventually became the Paris-Lyon-Marseille was financed by three different companies, Paris-Lyon, Lyon-Avignon, Avignon-Marseille. Lyon-Avignon went bankrupt in 1847, Paris-Lyon in the following year, and the concessions reverted to the State, their construction being continued by the Ponts-et-Chaussées. Avignon-Marseille, of which the chairman was the dynamic Paulin Talabot, hovered on the brink of insolvency, but survived.

The English railway crisis of October 1845 gave the French a warning and had a sobering effect. There was a pause in speculation. In 1846 disastrous floods and ruined harvest brought financial stringency and serious unemployment, particularly in those industrial areas where mechanisation had begun. At the end of 1847 though the fall of the Government was expected, none foresaw the outbreak of February 1848 and the expulsion of the 'timid, stingy, lethargic' régime of the Orleans family. [2] [3]

The revolution was accompanied by financial collapse, involving a number of investment bankers. When, after a fortnight's closure, the Bourse re-opened, government stocks had fallen by 25%, the shares of the Banque de France had slumped by a third, a number of financial houses had closed their doors and a great deal of money had taken refuge in London. The railway companies were in serious straits. Little construction had been completed. Except the northern lines in the Paris-Le Havre-Lille triangle, every track showed large gaps. The Est line had only reached Châlons-sur-Marne. The bankrupt and sequestrated Paris-Lyon, now under the Ponts-et-Chaussées, was approaching Tonnerre and had some permanent way completed between Dijon and Châlon-sur-Saône. The Orleans was working as far as Vierzon and Tours, but Lyon was reached only by diligence from Orleans, and Bordeaux was still isolated. The provisional Government had the choice of stopping work on construction, or of sustaining the surviving companies. In view of the violent strikes and incendiarism, the first was unthinkable. For a few days there was talk of State purchase of the railways, which Lamartine had more than once proposed. But the fear of inflation and the jealousies of financiers and industrialists caused the Assembly to reject the scheme.

During its existence, the Second Republic found no solution to the railway problem, while the engineering-industrial-investment-speculative groups wrangled over the carcase. There was much argument but little accomplishment. Nevertheless, experience had begun to produce a body of expert and determined engineers. They complained that while the Republican Government and the railway boards were fumbling, longer-sighted capitalists in England, Belgium and the Rhineland were alert to the future and France would soon see the traffic to the Mediterranean basin, which ought to pass through Marseille, annexed by rail systems running from Antwerp and Hamburg to Trieste.

The answer to the railwaymen's prayers came, on December 2, 1851, the *coup d'état* of Louis Napoleon, which 'offered a future to capital into which it would rush like air into a vacuum'.[4] It restored to adventurers the confidence and sense of security they had lost under the Second Republic, in particular to that group of enthusiasts, the disciples of Saint-Simon, who apart from the eccentricities of the Saint-Simonian church, had put their faith in expansion through public works, in industrial production and the bold employment of credit, 'socialism under capitalist direction'. Since the Prince-President had been attracted by the doctrine and had himself produced a pamphlet on the 'extinction of poverty', it is not surprising that within six weeks of the *coup d'état* the Government began to act. On January 3, 1852 the bankrupt Lyon-Avignon line was taken over by Paulin Talabot of the Avignon-Marseille and a group of leading iron-masters. On January 5 the slowly growing Paris-Lyon, the most necessary link in the whole communication system, was conceded to a group of three companies, on the boards of which were English engineers, contractors and company promoters, the directors of the Orleans and Nord railway companies, and pretty well the whole of the *Haute Banque*, headed by the Rothschilds of both Paris and London.[5] Within five years the skeleton of a national system was in operation. The short lines had been amalgamated into six groups, Nord, Est, P.L.M., Midi, Orleans (P.O.) and Ouest. By the end of the fifties, the frontiers had been reached.

A financial crisis in 1857, of which more later, was overcome without serious trouble, but the confused situation of competing lines and the problem of capital for what was known as the 'second network', expected to be less profitable than the trunk lines, led to a series of agreements between the State and the companies, the so-called Franqueville Conventions of 1859, by which the State guaranteed the interest on the capital for the new network up to an agreed level of 4%. When the profits on the old network reached 8% and on the new 6%, then the State was to participate. At the same time, the period of the concessions was extended to the reasonable length of 99 years, at the end of which the railways would revert to the State. The conventions were modified more than once between 1863 and 1868 but the principle remained unchanged.[6] On the eve of the Franco-Prussian war, neither the Nord, P.L.M., Est or P.O. had called on the Government, but the railways of the west and south were in trouble. At this date, there were 16,000 kilometres in operation, of which 13,000 had been built since 1851.

The railway expansion was of course not isolated, although it was the hastener of other development. The telegraph (another British undertaking), the extension and equipment of ports, the accelerated development of roads and waterways, followed. There was a drainage scheme for the morose Sologne, tree-planting in the Landais. Paris annexed eight suburbs on January 1, 1860 and the map of the city was redrawn. The Louvre was completed; a new opera house was put in hand. Some 25,000 houses were pulled down by the energetic préfet, Haussmann, and replaced by 70,000 new ones. Implacable straight boulevards were driven through warrens of narrow alleys, to the distress of many old Parisians. 'The transformation of Paris has forcibly expelled the labouring population from the centre towards the rim and made of the capital two towns, one rich, one poor, the latter round the former. The poor are like a rope round the neck of the rich.'[7] In Lyon, there was much rebuilding under the direction of the préfet, Vaïsse, and the suburbs across the Rhône were incorporated in the city. In Marseille, the Joliette basin was completed and a great number of public buildings erected. The Messageries fleet was increased from sixteen to fifty-eight between 1852 and 1858. Le Havre built an outer port and new docks.

(*ii*)

That this intense and complex activity would require a large and immediate expansion of credit was obvious. It was clear too that with the discoveries of gold in California and Australia, the time for this was ripe. The long winter of deflation, which had lain sullenly over Europe since 1820, was past. Even if the influence of the new gold has been exaggerated, it undoubtedly lent courage to timid finance. In February 1852 there was the authorisation of the Crédit Foncier de Paris, later in the year 'de France', a mortgage bank intended for the benefit of agriculture. Despite its mission, it was rather the urban landlord who profited from its creation. More spectacular was the Crédit Mobilier founded in November 1852 with government authority and a capital of sixty millions. Of its board, the most active members were Emile and Isaac Pereire, Bordeaux Jews, disciples of Saint-Simon, ambitious to modernise and transform French economic life. As Emile Pereire stated, the policy of the bank would be to supplement the insufficiency of capital available to industry by nursing selected businesses up to the day when they would be able to stand unsupported, and then to offer the shares to the public.[8]

It is undeniable that in these frenzied years at the beginning of the Second Empire, the French had undertaken construction on a scale beyond their equipment, their man-power and their financial resources. The Paris-Rouen-Le Havre railway was created largely by English money and English skilled labour. In addition to material organisation, there was much flimsy speculation. In the first years, champions of 'sound money' principles walked hand in hand with those of 'socialism under capitalist leadership' and gamblers both high and low, Rothschild with Pereire, Morny with Mirés, the Banque de France with the Crédit Mobilier, the piratical and rapidly bankrupt Grand Central Railway and the Caisse générale des Chemins de Fer. By 1855 the Banque de France was losing specie, partly externally (the Crimean War), partly internally to provincial centres, at a pace faster than the

Regents of the bank liked. As a bank of issue, the Banque de France began to draw in its horns. The crisis came in 1857 with the dividend of the Crédit Mobilier cut from 23% to 5% and the discount rate of the Banque de France up to 6.4%.[9] The problem was certainly no worse than one of growth but there was also a clash of principles. The Saint-Simonian creed was heresy to the Banque de France and the financial houses. Further, the Pereire had fostered competition with the established railway companies and the finance houses both at home and abroad. They had earned the personal dislike of Baron James de Rothschild. They had equally got across Paulin Talabot, master of the P.L.M. and involved in many interests in Marseille. Undoubtedly they were rash; they locked up too big a proportion of their reserves in affairs which could not show profits for a long time and were not easily disposed of. After the annexation of Savoy in 1860, they tried to acquire the Banque de Savoie with its rights of note-issue. In this they were challenged by the Banque de France and defeated. By 1867 the Crédit Mobilier was rocking. The resignation of the Pereire was insisted on as a condition of support. They capitulated. The Crédit Mobilier staggered on, but in 1871 it closed its doors. It was the end of Saint-Simonian finance for a long time. It is, however, to be noted that in the middle-eighties, an ex-employee of Isaac Pereire, one Edouard Drumont, took up the cause of the now dead financiers, declaring war on the Rothschilds and their kin with 'Down with the Jews' as his war-cry.

During the storms and stresses of the Crédit Mobilier's rise and fall, two banking institutions of a different character had come into existence. These were the Crédit Lyonnais in 1863 and the Société Générale in 1864, the equivalent of the English joint-stock banks. The Crédit Lyonnais was founded by Henri Germain of the Chatillon-Commentry iron-works, a personality in the region north-east of Lyon, deputy for Ain, and son-in-law of the President of the Conseil d'Etat, Vuitry. With him were others interested in heavy industry, Mangini, deputy for Rhône, Alfred Deseilligny of Le Creusot. On the board of the Société Générale were a number of railway directors. Both banks were inspired by the same idea. To quote the historian of the Crédit Lyonnais: 'The first objective to be pursued by credit establishments in the construction of a network is undoubtedly the accumulation of capital.'[10] At the beginning of the sixties, most banking outside Paris was narrowly local. Although practically every cantonal capital had one, two or even five small bankers, they were in fact usually no more than merchants or agents doing little beyond discounting paper in whatever trade they might be interested, silk, wool, wheat, wine, etc. None were powerful and most might at any moment be swept away by some unforeseen crisis: many had gone down in 1848 and went again in 1870–71. Often their calamities were due less to lack of means than to absence of liquidity. Besides these, there were the notaries who dealt in land and mortgages, money and securities, and as a rule were in touch with substantial men in their provincial capital, Bordeaux, Toulouse, Lyon. The Caisses d'Epargne were for the prudential saver and did nothing to fertilise trade.

The new banks set out deliberately to secure the money of the great public, most of which had neither knowledge nor experience of finance. 'The Bresse peasant is very distrustful of money', wrote an agent of the Crédit Lyonnais. The intention of the new banks was to drain the small towns of their savings and to generalise the use of these through the country. To encourage clients, they paid interest on current accounts. Yet strangely enough these forward looking bankers were in some ways as conservative as the leaders of the *Haute Banque* in Paris. They fought shy of industry. When, after two years' hesitation, the Crédit Lyonnais thought of opening a branch in the biggest glove-making centre in France, Grenoble, they made searching enquiries of merchants in the small hill-town of Annonay, which supplied the capital of Dauphiné with kid skins, before risking opening.[11] In spite of persistent representations from Schneider, it was not thought worth opening a branch at Le Creusot until 1900, because it was a town of manual workers and there could therefore be no savings. No one seems to have perceived that the vast Schneider pay-roll would return to the bank through the local shops in a few days.[12]

Indeed, from a banker's point of view, industry was scarcely respectable before the twentieth century: everyone knew that it was risky compared with commerce. 'The industrialist ties up capital; the merchant turns it over.' The customers of industry were nation-wide, even world-wide, and could not be identified, whereas in commerce and agriculture, the goods were there. There was nothing like cereals, 'a noble trade, universal and almost without risk since most of it is by cash transactions.' In 1877, at Chalon-sur-Saône, the volume of banking business (in millions of francs) was 15 for crops, 13 for cotton prints, $6\frac{1}{2}$ for wines and spirits, $4\frac{1}{2}$ for groceries, $3\frac{1}{2}$ for timber and no more than 3 for all the workshops, ironmongery, starch, glass, chemicals, masonry.[13]

The Crédit Lyonnais had, however, invested in the indemnity loans of 1871 and 1872 and after a couple of anxious years, the board's patriotism was rewarded when the 5% rentes rose from the issue price of 67/68 to 99.6. The profits of the Crédit Lyonnais for 1873 were 4.8 millions, for 1874, 13.5.[14] Truly, in the ironic phrase of the bank's historian, this was the 'heroic age' of French joint-stock banks.*

(iii)

The Emperor had observed the results of the British move over to free trade initiated by Peel in the early forties, and perhaps considered copying the policy if the occasion presented itself. Between 1853 and 1855 under the pressure of demand, decrees lowering the duties on a number of raw materials and semi-finished goods were confirmed, with some misgiving, by the Legislature. In 1856 a proposal to abolish all the remaining prohibitions and replace them by *ad valorem* duties ranging from 30% to 60% waked the jealous fears of the northern textile towns and the proposal was withdrawn. In 1853, owing to a short harvest, the sliding scale on cereals had been suspended, and although the situation improved during the next years, the sliding scale was not re-established until 1859, and then only under pressure.

However, on his return from the Italian campaign, in 1859, the Emperor, to allay anxieties of a public which imagined he was contemplating war with England, consulted the Pereire brothers and Michel Chevalier as to a reassuring public gesture. These Saint-Simonians counselled tariff reform as likely to bring back the fortunate days of 1852–53, and to stress a policy of international peace. In consequence, Napoleon published on January 5, 1860 a letter to his minister of State, Rouher, containing the outlines of national economic reform and improvement, including communications, rail and waterways, and a lowering of duties, and in some cases their abolition. The first spectacular step was the so-called Cobden-Chevalier commercial treaty with England. In this, the English agreed to recommend to Parliament some removal of duties and decreases, the French agreed to remove all prohibitions and generally to substitute specific duties not more than 30% *ad valorem* up to 1864 when the general limit would be reduced to 24%. The treaty came into force in January 1861. It was followed by similar treaties with other countries, Belgium in 1861, the German Zoll-

* See Appendix X.

verein in 1862, then between 1863 and 1867, with Italy, Switzerland, Sweden, Hamburg-Bremen-Lubeck group, Spain, Holland, Austria and Portugal.[15]

Further, beginning with the Belgian treaty, France granted Belgium the so-called 'conventional' tariff given to Britain, while there was a mutual guarantee of 'most-favoured-nation' terms. The 'general' tariff, that placed on the goods of states with whom France had no treaty, had the duties on many items reduced. Finally, the sliding scale on cereals was replaced by a small duty on imports.

In 1866 there followed reform of the French Navigation laws. Preferences to French ships in port dues and customs in the French colonies, and the *surtaxe de pavillon* on goods imported into France in foreign vessels, were abolished.

There were of course lamentations and bitter criticism, but on the whole they were overdone. This was not free trade, and in all except a few cases French goods were amply protected. Most of the difficulties of the sixties arose out of the American War of Secession, which hurt part of the cotton trade and brought about a financial crisis in 1864 due to the silver payments to India and Egypt for cotton. Otherwise producers had little to complain of. Under the fear of competition, the iron and steel industry speeded up its modernisation. Both imports and exports increased. The only sufferer of importance seems to have been the shipping and ship-building industry.

To soften the blow, the State offered loans to industries to allow them to renew machinery or to put in new. Altogether some 38 million francs were allotted, of which nearly 40% was given to textiles, the greater part to cotton. Nearly 25% more went to metallurgy, 9% went to mines and 8% to sugar. The loans were not all wise; an attempt was made to keep charcoal iron-smelting alive: in spite of its loan, the Decazeville works in Aveyron went bankrupt.[16]

It is argued that from the French point of view, the new tariff policy was mistaken, and that in the end, the lowering of duties put the French manufacturer at the mercy of more efficient foreigners. It is certain however that injury was not general. The English for example found the French worsted industry as good as their own. The error lies in the belief that infant industries cannot help but grow if sufficiently protected. This is true only when there is a market for them to grow to or with. In France there was not. It is possible that the commercial treaties had in fact little influence on French external trade or internal development.

K

(iv)

At the date of Sedan, the iron and steel industries in France appeared comparatively primitive. There was still a great deal of charcoal smelting. Coal in France was, for the needs of industry, at least 50% deficient, probably more. Further, except in a few areas, such as Lorraine and the Bourbonnais, the coal was distant from the iron measures. On the other hand, compared with Great Britain, France was abundantly forested. Even so, the need for fuel economy was always in the minds of ministers, from an early date. The council in the seventeenth century kept a sharp eye on the timber reserves, prescribing close limits to the amount of felling permitted to concessionaires in iron and chemical manufactures. At the end of the century, it became alarmed at the believed plundering of the woodlands and attempted to force the development of coal by easing the regulations on prospecting and exploitation. Although many mines were opened, the policy failed, largely owing to the lack of communications and the high cost of transport. In Paris, the price of coal from the Saint-Etienne field was fifteen times the pit-head price, while Bordeaux could supply itself more easily and cheaply by sea from England than from Carmaux (Tarn).[17] Similarly Normandy preferred the same source to Hainault. In 1744 the Crown, at Trudaine's suggestion, resumed the royal rights of ownership, administration and control of exploitation. Henceforward none, whatever his rank, might sink a pit without royal licence. This régime survived until the Revolution. In 1791 the Constituant, torn between conflicting political and economic theories, produced a compromise law which, while asserting the rights of the nation over the minerals of the subsoil, admitted the rights of landowners and concessionaires, and thus left the situation in confusion. In practice, however, the earlier régime continued until 1810, when by the law of April 27, the principles which were to govern mines of all kinds during the nineteenth century were laid down.

Under the law of 1810,[18] prospecting and mining could only be undertaken with government authority: but a landowner whose estate was believed to cover minerals, could not refuse to allow a survey. Thereafter an intending exploiter could obtain from the Conseil d'Etat a concession to work minerals, subject to payments both to the owner of the land and the State, the amounts being fixed by the State itself. These regulations did not hamper development, but they increased the authority of the State to intervene in many matters of administration, for instance in preventing monopolies through amalgamations.

The financial success of the first railways stimulated coal production which was also helped by the improvement in water transport in the thirties. The Loire basin for example doubled its annual output between 1835 and 1854 from one to two million tons. Except for the Nord mines, no other area approached the Loire region. The mines of Burgundy, the Nivernais and the Berry were scattered and small, while in the south, the coal of the mines of Alais (Gard), Aubin and Decazeville (Aveyron) and Carmaux (Tarn) was used locally. Then, in 1848, coal measures were discovered in Pas-de-Calais from Douerges and Courrières to Béthune: exploitation began in the fifties and it was soon seen that this area would become the most productive in France. In 1820 the total annual output had been a little over one million tons, in 1860 it was 8.3 millions, in 1870 13.3 millions.

As with other industries, the isolation from the leading industrial country, Great Britain, by war had kept the French iron-masters in ignorance of change: for example, it appears that until after 1815, puddling, practised in England for above forty years, was unknown, while until the end of the wars all steel had been imported from Prussia, Austria or England. Until, however, coal was more readily and more cheaply available, iron-masters found it more profitable to use wood. There had been some coke smelting before 1789. A younger brother of John Wilkinson of Brosley, William, in alliance with Ignace Wendel, the owner of foundries at Hayange (Moselle), built an iron-foundry and glass-works at Le Creusot in the Bourbonnais, where were both iron ore and coal, while transport was eased by the opening of the Canal du Centre joining the Saône to the Loire in 1793. Coke smelting seems to have begun here about 1785. But the political economists of the Revolution had views on liberty, monopoly and competition. They dissolved the Le Creusot organisation, divorced the coal from the iron and thus, though the foundry continued to produce cannon for the army, caused the owners serious loss. In 1813 Le Creusot was taken over by the principal creditor, Chagot, the owner of the neighbouring coal mine at Blanzy.[19]

The majority of iron-masters stuck to the familiar traditional methods in the scattered but easily worked iron-ore beds in Champagne, Lorraine, Franche-Comté, Berry and the Bourbonnais. Most forges were worked by water-power, hence foundries were near streams rather than at the pits. Owners had to obtain licences which set out the precise limits of the forest area they might fell. The works were thus a unit, and the estate often had the alternative function of agriculture: when the streams dried up or the demand for iron slackened, the workers moved to the fields. Unfortunately the Revolution decreed and the Napoleonic Civil Code confirmed the division of property between the immediate heirs on the owner's death. Under this successorial system, foundries gradually became separated from timber, and the iron-masters were compelled to purchase their fuel.[20] In charcoal smelting, fuel amounts to between two-thirds and four-fifths of the cost. So long as the demand for iron remained steady, this was not important, but with the coming of peace, it was found that English coke-smelted iron undercut the price. Although protected by a 60% tariff, the iron-masters sought further protection, which they secured when, by the law of July 27, 1822, the duty on imported coke-smelted iron was raised to the prohibitive rate of 120%, while in 1826 another law raised the duty on steel to 100%. In consequence, the price of iron rose and, to combat this, the Government began to grant licences for iron-foundries with alacrity. The Forest Commissioners, possibly influenced by the forest-owners, appear to have offered no opposition. But the iron-masters soon found that they had merely exchanged a foreign competitor for a less coercible rival at home.[21]

For, by the thirties, with the improvement in waterways and canals, coke smelting had begun in earnest. Terrenoire near Saint-Etienne appears to have taken to coke in 1818 and Anzin (Nord) a couple of years later. In 1826 the British expatriates Manby and Wilson, who had a large metal works at Charenton, acquired Le Creusot from Chagot, who, however, remained the chief shareholder. Probably hampered by the slump which began in 1827 and was prolonged, owing to the July Revolution, until 1832, Manby and Wilson failed and went into liquidation. Le Creusot passed into the hands of the financial group of Fould and Aguado. In 1836 this group sold the Le Creusot works and mines to the brothers Eugene and Adolphe Schneider, iron-masters from Bazeilles in Lorraine, who with the help of the banking house of Seillère formed the Société Schneider. The glass-works were sold to the Baccarat *cristallerie* which suppressed them. At this date, Le Creusot was producing about 40,000 tons of coal and 6,000 of iron: the population of the town was only 2,700. But the opportunities were immense. The company possessed Le Creusot and Montcenis and more coal at Montchanin. Yet further coal was available at Blanzy and Montceau-les-Mines, and northward at Epinac. Within fifteen miles, at Mazenay and Change, there was a large surface bed of brown haematite, which in the sixties was giving 300,000 tons of ore annually, though only 28% iron. Other haematite could be got from Chizeuil, near Bourbon-Lancy, and supplemented by the Berrichon pisolithics. Communications were assured through the Canal du Centre from Digoin to Chalon-sur-Saône. The Schneiders had arrived at the favourable hour, just when railroad and locomotive were about to call forth an enormous demand for iron. Nothing could stop the growth of Le Creusot. By 1870 the labour force had risen to 10,000 and the population of the town which Eugene Schneider had built (Adolphe died in 1845) was 29,000. In 1873 the capital of Le Creusot was put at 25 million francs with a turn-over of 35 millions. The works disposed of 15 blast-furnaces, 160 coke ovens, 130 puddling-furnaces, 30 steam-hammers and 41 rolling-mills. It was producing some 130,000 tons of foundry iron and 110,000 of puddled. Eugene Schneider was the foremost figure in the iron industry, alert, intelligent, forward-looking. No new invention that he did not examine, and, if found adaptable, take up. By 1870, when the local ores were already showing signs of exhaustion, he was drawing on the mines of Elba and Algeria. He was President of the Corps Législatif and when he died in 1870, leaving the firm in the no less capable hands of his son, Henri, he was chairman of the Comité des Forges.[22]

In 1836 there had been only six coke blast-furnaces and eight mixed coke and charcoal in France. By 1870 charcoal iron was almost gone, though the buoyant demand for iron helped obsolescent firms to survive.[23] Their inability to fill the demand had led to the reduction of the tariff in 1836, and the price of pig was being steadily lowered. In the twenties it had been round 250 francs a ton: by 1844 it had fallen to 128. Yet the decline in charcoal was slow. The railway expansion was followed by new uses for iron, armour-plating for battleships and a substitute for timber in building the swelling cities, Paris, Lyon, Marseille, Lille. In 1854 the railway companies, retarded in their construction, forced the Government to allow the import of English rails for the Nord, Lyon-Avignon and Midi railways.[24] In 1867 rails for French construction in Mexico were being manufactured at Middlesbrough.

Then came Bessemer, followed by Martin of Sireuil, and the substitution of steel for iron rails. In the sixties the price of foundry iron was down to 110 and in the last three years before the war to 90 francs a ton. Parallel with the price fall may be watched the progressive extinguishing of charcoal furnaces: from 445 in blast in 1839, the numbers fell to 385 in 1856, to 195 in 1865, to 82 in 1870.[25] In the department of Meurthe in 1860 were produced 14,000 tons of raw iron, of which half were from charcoal; in 1869 64,000 all from coke.[26] The extinguishing of the charcoal forges, which fell first on those works far from railheads, was the other side of the movement towards concentration of blast-furnaces either at the source of iron or coal, or later, on tide-water, coupled with a rapid increase in the height and capacity of the furnace. In 1875 France exported 1,042 tons of charcoal iron; in 1880 only 192; in 1888 none.

Almost step by step with Le Creusot, other iron-works from Nevers to the Brenne, based on scattered local ores and wood fuel, were modernising. Here concentration began with the opening in 1840 of the Berry canal connecting Montluçon with the Loire and encouraging the employment of the Commentry and Doyet coal-mines. From 1842, when the first blast-furnaces were lit, Montluçon began to grow, and its growth was hastened by the arrival of the railway from Orleans in 1861. From 5,000 in 1851, the population had quadrupled by 1872, and was over 25,000 in 1881. The Commentry coal-field had become the chief provider of the middle Loire valley, of Bourges and its arsenal, of Vierzon and its rail-centre, of Fourchambault and its iron-works, of Roanne. Amalgamations of firms had begun, Chatillon-Commentry and Commentry-Fourchambault, two of the steel giants of the future. Other industries, bottle- and plate-glass based on the Berrichon sands, as well as chemicals, settled in Montluçon and the neighbourhood.[27]

(ν)

The third great workshop of the Centre was the coal-basin that stretches from Firminy through Saint-Etienne by Terrenoire and Rive-de-Gier to the Rhône at Givors, up to 1870 the most productive coal region in France and the pioneer region of the iron industry. The first William Jackson is said to have introduced crucible steel at Chambon-Feugerolles as early as 1810. In 1830 his son moved the firm to Assailly and adopted the name of Jackson-Assailly. In 1837 one Pétin, who had been trained at the Arts-et-Métiers, and an iron-worker named Gaudet, set up a small forge with the modest capital of 500 francs at Saint Chamond which grew very rapidly, specialising in lock-gates. They put in their first steam-hammer in 1839. In the forties, they turned to boilers, marine-engines and crank-shafts, and, with the introduction of shell into naval gunnery, became the leading manufacturers of armour-plate. In 1854 Jackson and Pétin-Gaudet brought about a combination of the steel-works at Assailly and Lorette, a group of forges at Vierzon, their coke furnaces at Givors on the Rhône, and the works at Saint Chamond, in an amalgamation to be known as the Aciéries de la Marine et des Chemins de Fer with a capital of 27 millions, destined as 'La Marine' to become one of the great steel corporations of France. One other progressive Stéphanois firm to be noted was Terrenoire, whose directors bought up in 1867 a British patent for ferromanganese and by improving it became one of the leading manufacturers of mild steel for boiler-plates.[28]

In the north, before the fifties, metallurgy depended largely on the Anzin coal-mine corporation, acquired at the beginning of the century by the Périer family. Only round Denain was there iron in commercial quantities and this was acquired by Anzin. Forges were built here in 1836 by the more cautious of the Talabot brothers, Léon, who had already purchased the works at Saint-Juéry near Albi. In 1849, having acquired iron-deposits near Boulogne, he founded the Société des Forges de Denain et d'Anzin, which for the next twenty years remained the leading iron firm in the north. By 1868 the local ores at Denain were finished, and those of the Boulonnais were nearing exhaustion by 1878. This was no longer important. The northern region was served by excellent communications, with a fine river and canal network (for the canals, the Anzin board had been largely responsible), the best railway system in France and proximity to the sea. Further, with the extension of the coal-basin into Pas-de-Calais in the fifties, other iron-foundries had set up, the Forges et Aciéries du Nord et de l'Est, a blast-furnace group at Maubeuge, Hauts-Fourneaux de Maubeuge, later to be absorbed by Raty of Senelle near Longwy: at Maubeuge also, the Belgian La Providence and Vezin-Aulnoye, while at Isbergues near Béthune, Aciéries de France opened in 1882–83 to produce steel rails for the Orleans railway. Further south, near the great railway centre at Creil, appeared the Forges et Fonderies de Montataire.[29]

The Bessemer process was rapidly adopted by the French iron-masters, possibly because with later development of the industry than in England, there was less capital locked up in puddling. True, haematite was less easy to mine and more expensive to reduce than the lias ores, but it saved fuel, for the French iron-master a primary considera-tion.* There were haematite deposits all over France, at La Taillat near

* Lowthian Bell said that Pas-de-Calais coal, which was the best, cost almost double the price of English coal in 1871–78. He also claimed that the difference between the cost of producing pig from haematite and other ores ran from ten to fifteen shillings a ton in England, and in Westphalia and Lorraine sometimes almost double. (*Principles of the Manufacture of Iron and Steel*, 407 and 266).

Allevard (Isère) on which Le Creusot drew, at La Voulte near Privas on the Rhône, at Saint-Alban (Tarn) which supplied Léon Talabot's Saut-de-Sabo works, in Aveyron, taken by Decazeville. The richest area was between the Tech and Tet valleys in Roussillon, where the ore was said to be the purest in France, some ores giving as much as 92%, and there was also manganese. Some of this was smelted locally, but a quarter was exported through Port-Vendres, and the rest went north to the Alais field and Loire basin.

With the beginning of exhaustion of the known red haematite ores in the seventies, search was begun outside the frontiers. Denain-Anzin, which only adopted Bessemer in 1874, reckoned to get its ores more cheaply overseas. In 1876 it formed a syndicate with Montataire and the Belgian firm of Cockerill to bring haematite from Bilbao, the Société Franco-Belge de Somorastro. By 1880 43,000 tons of Bessemer and Martin steel were produced in Nord and Pas-de-Calais. A little later, in 1884, La Marine of Assailly set up blast-furnaces at Boucau at the mouth of the Adour for Asturian ores.[30] Before the seventies were out, the companies were looking further afield. Very early in their career, the Saint-Simonians had preached the development of the African territories. In 1857 Paulin Talabot had formed a company to exploit Mokta-el-Hadid, 'the slice of iron', west of Oran, which in 1879 opened Beni-saf, and far away to the east there was also Ouenza. All these gave ores yielding some 58%; though much was exported to England, much also went to the Gard and Loire coal-fields.[31]

The Siemens-Martin open-hearth process was adopted even more readily than Bessemer.[32] By 1869 nearly 18,000 tons of steel were being produced. Paulin Talabot had the whole length of the P.L.M. relaid with Martin rails. The process was more costly than Bessemer, but the price was continually falling. In the sixties steel rails averaged 556.50 a ton, in the seventies, 260, and in the eighties 156. Thus by the eighties steel-making in bulk was established.[33] In 1869 from twenty-four Bessemer converters and forty-four Martin furnaces had come 70,000 tons; in 1872, output had risen to 112,000, in 1878 to 283,000, of which Loire produced a third and Le Creusot a fifth.

(vi)

The north-eastern region, the Barrois and Lorraine, had like most regions a long history of iron-founding. Here the ores stretched from

Châtillon-sur-Seine to beyond the Moselle. The ores of Haute-Marne and Haute Saône were of poor quality but owing to the fortunate conjunction of iron, wood and water, the industry had survived and been kept alive by the Revolutionary and Napoleonic wars which produced an artificial revival, with the forging of swords and bayonets. Fortified by the Milan Decrees, propped by the prohibitive tariffs of the Restoration, the industry continued to thrive on the production of pig- and merchant-iron; blast-furnaces and forges multiplied. The main outlet of the region was through Saint-Dizier on the Marne, but the cutting of the Marne-Saône canal enabled producers to tap markets down the Rhône. Nevertheless, decline again began as coke-based producers enlarged their output. Also the forests were giving evidence of exhaustion, and Haute-Marne has no coal. From 1840, the low-cost producers of the Centre were making a better and cheaper article, and the Treaty of 1860, which the Haute-Marne iron-masters fought more bitterly than those from any other region, made the situation highly precarious.[34]

The Lorraine growth had been different. Here, too, for centuries iron had been worked, but only the surface ores. The main beds are composed of the so-called *minette*, with a high phosphoric content, which, until removed, makes the iron brittle. In 1701 one Jean-Martin de Wendel of Trèves, said to be of Croat origin, purchased a blast-furnace at Hayange, some five miles north-west of Thionville on the Fentsch. In 1811 his grandson François, son of the Ignace de Wendel who was part-founder of Le Creusot, purchased other furnaces at Moyeuvre on the Orne. In 1819 coke-smelting was begun, and in 1826 the Wendel became concessionaires of the Petite-Roselle coal-field at Forbach at the tail-end of the Saar coal-basin, though it was not until the opening of the Metz-Sarrebruck railway in the early fifties that the concession began to be worked. About 1854 the discovery of neighbouring deposits led to new acquisitions between Creutzwald, Saint-Avold and Forbach, which by 1869 had a coal output of 200,000 tons to add to the 160,000 of Petite-Roselle. Simultaneously, Wendel built blast-furnaces at Styring. By 1860 the Moselle department was producing some 91,000 tons of iron, of which between a third and a half was still charcoal smelted. Nine years later the output of the region had risen to 356,000 tons, of which an insignificant quantity only was from wood-fuel. Of this amount, something above 100,000 tons came from the Wendel works, while another 65,000 came from three other groups at Novéant and Ars-sur-Moselle.[35] In the previous year, transportation had been improved by the opening of the canal from Sarreunion to Sarrebourg where it linked up with the Marne-Rhine canal. Then came the war. By mid-1871 a third of Meurthe and two-thirds of Moselle were foreign territory; Hayange, Moyeuvre, Styring, Novéant and Ars were German towns, and the new frontier, west of the Moselle as far south as Novéant, included all the known iron-deposits, though the mines, foundries and forges remained the property of the owners.

Lorraine's misfortune benefited the iron-masters of the failing Haute-Marne, and they used the respite to re-adjust. Although the smaller units on the upper Marne and its tributaries went out of business, the survivors concentrated nearer the point of outlet, Saint-Dizier. Realising that to live they must specialise, they turned to forging axles, tires, wheels and so forth for the railways. Steam took the place of water-power, which in turn freed the rivers for transport and allowed the carriage of coal by barge. Though it never recovered its former importance, the Haute-Marne industry took on a new lease of life. The smaller manufactures did not die out, and round Nogent, Neufchâteau and Langres, a number of small factories developed out of an ancient domestic specialisation in bell-founding and knife-blades.[36]

On the annexation of Lorraine, the conquerors forcibly purchased the railways: the purchase price was knocked off the indemnity, which made the French Government liable to the shareholders. The railways of the Reichsland — such was the title given to the annexed provinces — were incorporated in the Prussian State system. The Wendel firm, Les Petit-Fils de François de Wendel et Cie., found the new owners stiffer on freight rates than the old Est company. Seeing that Styring would no longer be profitable, they closed it down, though still working the coal at Petite-Rosselle and Forbach. The French and Belgian firms at Ars and Novéant either sold out to the Germans or went into liquidation.

At the same time the Wendel 'could not resign themselves to the loss of the French market'.[37] Now in 1816 François de Wendel had obtained a licence to prospect for iron-ore between the rivers Orne and Fentsch, tributaries from the western bank of the Moselle with outfalls below and above Thionville. Flint (*rognon*) and phosphoric (*minette*) ores were discovered, and in 1834 Wendel obtained royal authority to work the area. The flint ore which was surface was soon worked out; the *minette* was considered too phosphoric — the proportion varied between 0.7 and 2% — and the undertaking was apparently abandoned:[38] at least the concession appears to have been either revived or renewed in 1875, when prospecting was begun just over the frontier from

Moyeuvre, at Joeuf in the Orne valley. Three years later, in 1878, there appeared Gilchrist Thomas's basic process, which by use of limestone in the converter, solved the problem of eliminating the phosphorus in the direct making of steel. 'To France and Central Europe, and above all, to the debatable land of Lorraine, he [Thomas] had given everything.' Clapham's sentence, while true in essence, over-dramatises the impact of the new process. Although some Thomas, otherwise basic, plants were installed, it was another quarter of a century before Lorraine became the most powerful iron and steel region in western Europe. Before 1893, when the patents ran out, there appear to have been no more than three French licencees: Schneider, who set up a Thomas plant at Le Creusot, the only one in the centre and south of France; Aciéries de Longwy, a recent amalgamation of iron firms at Le Prieuré, La Moulaine and Mont-Saint-Martin near the Luxembourg frontier, where the new plant was erected, and François de Wendel. In 1880, in co-operation with Schneider, a French subsidiary, *la Société de Wendel et Cie.*, was created, and in the following year was begun the construction of new works at Joeuf, where a rich *minette* deposit was discovered. Joeuf, of which the first furnace was lighted in July 1882, was planned for basic.[39] The Lorraine contribution to the 283,000 tons of Bessemer or Martin steel produced in 1878 had been negligible. In 1884 Meurthe-et-Moselle, the department created out of the rump of the annexed Meurthe and Moselle departments, produced 82,000 tons by basic. At this date, it was not yet clear that Lorraine was to become the new centre of metallurgy. Many difficulties lay in the way of expansion, absence of coal, poor communications, deficiency of labour, the proximity of the German frontier, the provision of capital for pit-sinking, machinery, factories and licences. One serious crisis would have to be passed, and the price decline which affected all Europe for the next twelve to fifteen years endured.

STEEL PRODUCTION
(Metric tons 'ooo's)

1860	30	1880	389	1897	1,325
1865	41	1882	458	1902	1,568
1869	110	1887	493	1907	2,750
1875	256	1892	825	1912	4,428

(Foville, *La France économique*, p. 217; *Sidérurgie*, I, p. 135.)

COMPARATIVE COAL PRODUCTION BY REGIONS

(Metric tons '000's)

The figures in brackets represent percentage of the total

Date	Nord	P.-de-C.	Loire	Gard	Nivernais & Burgundy	Rest	Total
1860	1,595 (19.2)	590 (7.1)	2,360 (28.4)	870 (10.5)	795 (9.6)	2,094 (25.2)	8,304
1870	2,418 (18.1)	1,895 (14.2)	3,351 (25.1)	1,300 (9.8)	1,029 (7.7)	3,338 (25.0)	13,330
1880	3,702 (19.2)	4,844 (25.0)	3,588 (18.5)	1,936 (10.0)	1,548 (8.0)	3,744 (19.4)	19,362
1890	5,135 (19.6)	9,077 (34.8)	3,587 (13.4)	2,005 (7.6)	1,915 (7.3)	4,364 (17.2)	26,083
1900	5,669 (17.0)	14,595 (43.7)	4,022 (12.7)	2,045 (6.2)	2,010 (6.0)	5,063 (15.2)	33,404
1910	6,600 (17.3)	18,893 (49.3)	3,750 (9.8)	2,062 (5.4)	2,134 (5.5)	4,911 (12.7)	38,350
1913	6,854 (16.7)	20,647 (50.5)	3,791 (9.3)	2,135 (5.2)	2,415 (5.9)	5,080 (12.4)	40,832

Of Nord, above 90% from Valenciennes basin:
of Loire, 98% from St-Etienne-Rive-de-Gier: of Gard, 98% from Alais group:
of Nivernais-Burgundy, 80% from Le Creusot-Blanzy, 9% from Decize (Nièvre).

The rest is composed of Tarn-Aveyron, Bourbonnais, Auvergne, Alps, Vosges, Hérault, Creuse-Corrèze, the West from the Vendée to the Cotentin peninsula, and Corsica. The only mines of importance were Aubin, east of Albi, supplying Decazeville, 20%, Carmaux, 15% and Commentry-Doyet, 15%.

(*Sidérurgie*, II, pp. 8-12.)

(vii)

In the early part of the century, much of the chemical industry was located in the south, chiefly in and about Marseille, the centre of the soap industry. Employing the Leblanc process, using coke from the Gard mines, Camargue salt, olive oil and local limestone, and after 1815 with ready access to Sicilian sulphur, Marseille prospered. But the fluctuations in the price of sulphur, coupled with the grant of the monopoly by Ferdinand IV to Marseille importers, induced their rivals to look elsewhere. Experiments with pyrites had hitherto failed, but under the stress of emergency, trials were renewed in 1839–40 and were successful. At this time there were some twenty-two manufacturers of Leblanc soda in Marseille, but most were small and unable to find the capital to establish pyrites roasting. Further, apart from soap, the chief market for chemicals was in the north, with its textiles and its sugar-beet growing and sugar-refining. It was cheaper for users in the north either to buy from local manufacturers or to import from Great Britain. By 1880 the Marseille firms had sunk to seven.[40]

In 1870 there were in the south two important chemical firms. In 1855 Henri Merle set up a chemical plant at Salindres on the Gard coal-field, and a salt-works on the Etang de Giraud west of the Rhône mouth. By 1870 this Cie. des Produits Chimiques d'Alais et de la Camargue was producing 10,000 tons of acid, 11,000 of sodium sulphate, and 6000 of soda. Its future was not to be on these lines. Merle died in 1877 and the company was acquired by A. R. Pechiney, of whom more later.

The other large southern factory was that of Perret, founded in 1837 at Saint-Fons, a suburb of Lyon, where large quantities of acid and copper sulphate were produced. Although the largest manufacturer of sulphuric acid in France, by 1870 Perret was already feeling the competition of the north and in 1872 sold out to Saint-Gobain. Produits chimiques de Saint-Gobain, Chauny et Cirey had been founded in the Forêt de Coucy in 1693 for the manufacture of glass. Early in the nine-teenth century it added chemicals to its activities, with the building of a Leblanc plant, employing among its managers the celebrated chemists Nicolas Clément and Gay-Lussac. The purchase of the Saint-Fons works foreshadowed the growth of what would become one of the biggest financial corporations in France.[41] At its head would be that remarkable figure Charles-Jean-Melchior, Marquis de Vogüé, Ambassador to the Sublime Porte in 1871, to Vienna in 1875, President of the Suez Canal company in 1895, Vice-president of the P.L.M. and P.O., and member of the Academy.

One other house was already rising, that of Charles-Frédéric Kuhlmann,* founded in 1824–25 at Loos between Lille and Roubaix. 'His aim was to sell alkali to the textile trade and acid to the manure works supplying the sugar-beet growers.' When these secured the imposition of high duties on colonial cane-sugar, beet-growing thrived and Kuhlmann profited. In 1847 he opened a second plant at La Madeleine and in 1852 a third at Saint-André to make sulphuric acid, nitric and hydrochloric acids. By the end of the seventies he was producing some 90,000 tons of heavy chemicals.[42]

Nevertheless, compared with that of the British, the French output was scarcely significant. In 1874 the total production of French alkali was only 74,000 tons; British export alone was 250,000. But the transformation of the industry was already beginning, and its growth. In 1865 Ernest Solvay, with the aid of his brother-in-law, Serret, who modified the Carvès oven for him, produced a method of making soda more efficiently and cheaply than by the Leblanc process. At his plant in Belgium, a year later, he was able to produce 1600 kilogrammes daily. In 1874 he built a factory at Dombasle near Nancy with a capacity of 15–20,000 tons a year. From this date the Leblanc process was doomed.[43]

In spite of the acknowledged superiority of French dyeing, French manufacture was in trouble. In the forties and fifties, vegetable dyes had predominated, and many acres in Provence and Languedoc were devoted to the cultivation of dye-plants. In the forties began the investi-

---

* C. F. Kuhlmann began in 1825 at Lille very modestly. Immediately after the 1914–18 war it ranked with Saint Gobain as the major producers of heavy chemicals, and Kuhlmann controlled the dye-stuff industry. Apart from coal, iron and steel, already noted, the whole Nord (Lille-Roubaix-Valenciennes) region expanded faster in more directions than any other: textiles, of course, but also sugar, brewing, engineering. Moreover, whereas the historian of the Bouches-du-Rhône says that the Marseillais industrialists do not found dynasties, in the Nord the most prominent names are found. There is the Motte family, of whom Alfred is to be seen in 1888–89 attempting the integration of eight textile firms, in the middle of the twentieth century it is spread through 'a labyrinth of cousinships'. These families have the habit of 'creating an enterprise for each son'. Being strongly Roman Catholic they are strongly progenitive. 'Eight Motte are to be found in cotton spinning, three Tiberghien, three Pollet and two Toulemonde in weaving.' There are the Masurel, the Lepoutre, the Prouvost: the last in wool-combing and spinning, in flax and linen, in knitwear, in sugar, in paint, brewing and publishing. 'Here there is no imcompatibility between the Catholic religion and the development of capitalism.' (R. Gendarme, *La région du Nord*, 177 ff., and for Motte, P. des Rousiers, *Les Grandes industries modernes*, III, 141.)

gation into the aniline process. In 1859 Renard Frères of Lyon patented a substance named Fuchsine, and then proceeded to sue for infringement of patent another company which had invented a somewhat similar but better and cheaper process. After some years of litigation, Renard in 1863 carried the day, securing what was tantamount to the grant of a monopoly of the aniline dye industry. The judgment put an immediate stop to further researches into aniline colours. In 1864, backed by the newly-established Crédit Lyonnais, Renard floated the Société la Fuchsine with a capital of four million francs. But instead of trying to improve and cheapen their products, their main activity was to prosecute infringers of their patent. The quality of their wares deteriorated and in 1868 the company foundered. The patents and licences were bought up by Poirrier of Saint-Denis, Fabrique des matières colorantes A. Poirrier. The Renard policy had been disastrous for France. Some firms gave up aniline dyes, others emigrated to Switzerland, while a number of chemists sought and found employment in Germany, England and Switzerland.[44]

These troubles came at a critical moment. The scientific, as opposed to empirical development of chemistry was beginning to give results. In June 1869 the first patents for synthetic alizarin, derived from coaltar distillation, were filed by the Badische Anilin- und Soda-Fabrik. This was followed by patenting in France which effectively forestalled French chemists. In 1878 Badische came to Neuville-sur-Saône. In 1881 the Meister Lucius und Brüning firm of Höchst, finding the French tariffs a nuisance, bought out a French firm at Tremblay and founded the Cie. Parisienne des Couleurs Anilines. In 1882 the Basle firm of Durand et Hugenin set up at Saint-Fons, and during the next fifteen years other German and Swiss chemical producers started branches in the neighbourhood of Lille and Lyon. In 1900 the French dye-stuff industry was either in the hands of foreigners or working up intermediaries. The only dye-stuff factory of any importance was the Poirrier business at Saint-Denis which had tried to compete in the manufacture of alizarin but had been defeated and gone back to aniline dyes.[45]

(viii)

In spite of the tripling of exports in the twenty years up to 1871–75, the French manufacturer remained interested primarily, and indeed in many instances solely, in the home market: only the surplus was exported. To keep the home market protected he had striven continuously from 1815 to 1860. While from the second date, some trades, iron and steel, worsted, silk, had quickly accommodated themselves to the regime of low tariffs, others campaigned to return to the previous system. In this they would not succeed until the nineties.

At the back of this apparent apprehension, of this absence of the 'capitalist ethos', lies a creed which was summed up by Balzac in *Mémoires de deux Jeunes Mariées*: 'A country is strong when it consists of rich families of which every member is concerned in the defence of the common wealth.' Behind so many of the actions of Frenchmen there is to be discerned that profound sense of the family, that personalisation of *'le trésor commun'*. As evidence is the persistence of the unlimited partnership, *société en nom collectif*, in French commercial life during the Third Republic. Huge businesses of great wealth refused the insurance which the *société anonyme*, the limited liability company, afforded them. Some, to be sure, became *sociétés en commandite par actions*, which limited the liability of the shareholder to the value of the share, but gave him no control of voting power, the responsibility being assumed by the directors. In 1880 among such were the great iron firms of Le Creusot, Chatillon-Commentry, Commentry-Fourchambault, Aniche-Anzin, the ship-builders Chantiers de la Méditerranée, and many of the Pas-de-Calais coal-mines. But the Bruay mine was a simple partnership, while in 1871, the Wendel family, trading as 'Les Petits-Fils de François de Wendel', having lost the French market by the annexation of Lorraine in which lay their forges, mills and mines, founded in France a *société en commandite*, 'De Wendel et Cie.', in the articles of which it was laid down that the shares be confined to direct descendants of François de Wendel; should a branch die out, the shares were to be divided among the others. Other firms remained as simple partnerships, among such in 1939 were the famous distilling house of Pernod and the automobile firm of Peugeot.

There were in fact two opposed views in French economic life, which might be called those of advance and of resistance. On the one hand were entrepreneurs such as the Schneiders, ready to control and direct policy with full personal responsibility. Actively engaged from the beginning in railway construction, they had grown rich and extended their range. The growth of Le Creusot from the two blast-furnaces of 1836 to the huge congeries of engineering and armament works of 1914 testified to the imagination and energy of the Schneider family. At the other end, there was a timidity which hampered development. By far the greater number of manufacturing businesses were small, and a great number of masters, especially those employing rural domestic workers, had themselves only just risen from the ranks. About them was the prudence of the peasant, the prudence of one who has learned from experience what a half-hour's hail-storm can do. There is the persistence of the mediaeval practice of keeping one's private and professional money in the same account — if indeed there were even serious accounts. André Maurois has given in his memoirs a delicious description of his family firm, the Fraenkels, optants from Mulhouse who came to Elbeuf in 1871. There is also secrecy, the same secrecy which keeps the landowners almost wholly obscured. One of the strongest traits is the reluctance to borrow. Until the price has been saved a new machine will not be installed although to do so will be an economy. All developments must be financed from profits.[46] If one borrows publicly, then one's assets must be disclosed. What indiscretion!

To active business men, this pusillanimity was disheartening. 'If all our manufacturers were good salesmen,' growled Raoul-Duval to the parliamentary commission on the economic situation in 1870,[47] 'what immense strength we should have, the strength that England possesses.' In 1884 Ferry, replying to an interpellation on the unemployment in Paris, said that France suffered from a lack of industrial courage, of which the lamentable story of Renard Frères and Fuchsine (q.v. above) is an example, though not necessarily outstanding. In 1921 the economic journalist Delaisi wrote:[48] 'As soon as he has won an important place in his industry, the French business man has only one worry; to come to an arrangement with his rival in order to get rid of all internal competition — this is the only kind of trade-union he can imagine; then to secure from the Government a protective tariff which will shelter him from external competition. Then having got rid of the risk, he abandons the effort. Every slightly risky opportunity to extend his business seems superfluous. Every experiment towards technical perfection looks like a threat to his security. . . . For him it is sufficient to exploit the domestic consumer who has been handed over to him by his accomplice, Parliament.'

There was of course more to it than mere timidity or lethargy. The great number of firms were neither large nor wealthy; many no more than workshops. Manufacturers hesitated to buy new machinery unless it was fool-proof, and were reluctant to adopt new inventions until they

L

were perfect enough to allow immediate large-scale economies. This, for example, accounts for the slowness in the introduction of the self-actor in spinning.[49] No doubt such delays allowed the hand-loom weaver to survive in some regions through the last quarter of the century. Though the linen-producer was largely eliminated, two of the three main textile industries could face competition, especially English, with reasonable equanimity.

In silk and wool mechanisation was slow. In silk, there were still unsolved problems. Although throwing had long been mechanised, it was difficult to accommodate the fragile thread to the power-loom. Further, from about 1852, there had been the *pébrine*, the silkworm disease, which had reduced the output of cocoons in the Rhône valley by three-quarters. By the time the rescuing genius of Pasteur had produced the remedy, the Italians had improved their methods and with cheap labour had successfully cut the price. Although the production of cocoons in the Rhône valley survived, production did not seriously improve. In 1882 the trade that had earned some 100 million francs a year in 1851 sunk to a mere 41 millions. Further, the modernisation of Japan and the opening of Suez soon brought even cheaper raw silk from the east. These events influenced some of the leading merchants and *fabricants* to turn away from the hand-loom. They did not however set up in Lyon, but built factories in Isère and on the Monts Lyonnais. No doubt, as had the English in the thirties, they discovered that the domestic worker could not be disciplined to the power-machine.

Thus, at the end of the seventies, of the 13,000 French power-looms, 4,505 were in Isère and 2,890 in Loire. In Rhône were no more than 650, but of the 60,000 silk hand-loom weavers, more than 40,000 worked in Lyon, mostly in the turbulent Croix-Rousse quarter.* [50]

Lyon silk-manufacturers in alliance with the Paris dress houses could easily withstand all rivals. In the woollen and worsted trade competition was more vigorous, and the transition from domestic to factorised industry more marked. The great centre for the wool-trade was in the north from the Belgian frontier to the Somme and Marne rivers. Here alone could it be said with truth that the industrial revolution was in progress. Here were coal and excellent communications by both water

---

* All the figures are suspect. Those above quoted are from the *Annuaire Statistique* of 1878, which vary from the figures of 1876. Baudrillart (III, 549–50) gives for 1875 105,000 handloom weavers in Lyon, a figure repeated by Pierre George in *Les Pays de la Saône et du Rhône*, p. 152. Since the population of Lyon between the rivers in 1875 was 218,000 and for the new quarters 133,000, the figure of 105,000 appears exaggerated.

and rail. Here was a thriving agriculture with growing urban markets. Here was the edge of the great area of the merino sheep, though the clip was now declining before imports of Australian and Plate wool. And above all here was a rapidly growing population: the nine northern departments increased by 20% between 1851 and 1876 against 6% for the whole country. This was the workshop of France. And here was to be found a happy combination of mechanic and artisan in the worsted-manufacture. In 1876 Bradford, which had been suffering for some years from French competition in England, sent a delegation of two members of the Chamber of Commerce to spy out the land of Picardy. Illingworth's notes are illuminating.[51] The main centre of wool-preparation was Reims with its combing and carding firms, where those two Yorkshire adventurers, Lister and Holden, having bought up all the mechanical comb patents, had established their business. Here were 13 mills using carded and 8 combed wool. There were about 8,000 power-looms and in the neighbouring country 7,000 hand-looms. It had one important firm of machine-makers. It had a splendid technical school and the municipality ran a more than adequate hospital service. Roubaix was the main spinning centre and here and in Fourmies were more than a third of the French spindles, as well as a high proportion of cotton spindles. Roubaix possessed as many power-looms as Reims, while according to the English delegates there were more than 23,000 hand-looms in the region: even this may be an underestimate. At this date, in England, the hand-loom weaver was practically extinct. He had been unable to stand up to a machine which could produce about forty times as much as a hand-loom at only two-and-a-half to three times the cost. Unlike his English counterpart, the French hand-loom weaver survived. The quadrilateral Le Cateau-Cambrai-Péronne-Saint-Quentin was the centre of the sugar-beet area with the refineries along the canals, the sugar-beet that needed constant work during the growing season. The same workers were by heredity and training highly skilled weavers, as well as being smallholders or tenants on peculiarly advantageous local traditional terms. Take Bohain. Soon after Napoleon's Egyptian campaign, the Paris dressmakers suggested shawls of wool and silk and pure cashmeres. They sent the necessary wool and silk and the patterns to Bohain and the product was enormously successful. These weavers were not merely craftsmen, they were often artists, who could devise their own patterns. They were invincible in their ability to change rapidly in accordance with the dictates of the Paris fashion houses, procedure which could not be followed by manufacturers of cheaper goods, based on long runs.* In 1884 there were said to be 10,000 such weavers round Bohain and another 10,000 round Saint-Quentin. In 1909, the rapporteur of the mixed-wool section of the standing committee on export trade bewailed the disappearance of the Picard weavers, who like the *canuts* of the Croix-Rousse could marry up all kinds of materials on the loom. Now, he lamented, 'fancies' have gone out of fashion and women have gone over to the *tailleur*. 'This has brought ruin to Picardy. From 1870 to 1900 this hive of 30,000 workers was the nursery for the weaving shops of the world.' Half had gone away, and the rest made broderies and tulles, or even had entered the factories.⁵²

Thus in Picardy the hand-loom weaver temporarily survived, though in the end he must yield to the 'multiple, tyrannical and ephemeral decrees of fashion'. Other branches of the textile industry suffered more severely at the hands of the Paris couturier. In the early seventies lace was no longer admitted for apparel, hence by 1876 it was almost 'out'. For Calais and Saint-Pierre the change was disastrous — until, after a few years, the ban was lifted. In 1880 the earnings were 43 million francs; 1881 82 millions.**

In contrast to the prosperity of Picardy were the departments of Seine-inférieure and Eure, with the cotton centre of Rouen and the woollen towns of Elbeuf and Louviers. Before 1871 cotton-manufacture had been mainly round three centres, Rouen, Roubaix and Mulhouse. The industry of Mulhouse had been very successful. Recognising that since all raw cotton was landed at Le Havre, the transport to Alsace would add heavily to the cost, the Mulhousiens had deliberately cultivated the luxury market, developing fine spinning, and weaving the most delicate organdies and muslins. They encouraged invention: from Mulhouse came the Heilmann comb. They did not import machinery but made their own. By 1830 they had abandoned hand-spinning. By

---

* This was one of the great advantages over the Yorkshire worsted-manufacturers, who in the sixties, after the Cobden-Chevalier treaty, seem to have imported much into France. But the question is very complex. There is the technical problem of short-wool merino which Bradford machines could not spin, while to adapt the machines was too costly. There was also the change in fashion about 1868 when the crinoline, for which the stiff English worsteds were most suitable, was dropped. The English never recovered the position they had held in the French market. But after 1871 there was a good deal of reciprocal trade, the English in fact through the seventies and eighties never taking less than half the French merino export, sometimes even three-quarters.

** Lace seems to have been finally killed by the same executioners after 1925, when Jenny and Lelong, who specialised in lace dresses, turned against them. There was no recovery before 1939.

1861 more than half their spinning machinery was self-actors. Further, as they were far from the sea, they had warehoused large quantities of cotton; hence though a number of small houses had failed, Mulhouse, as a whole, did not suffer during the cotton famine. By 1870 most of the 50,000 power-looms were run on water-power from the Vosges streams. Then, in 1871, these and more than two million spindles were in German territory, and though a few firms emigrated to France, not many, and not the biggest were able to.[53]

In Rouen up to 1870 the industry had been very different. 'Normandy does not do fine spinning or weaving', Waddington told the Commission of 1870: 'we make coarse cottons.'[54] The Rouen industry was confined to coarse yarns, and, compared with the English, not particularly good. At this date, much of the weaving was by Cauchois hand-loom weavers. The Caux at any time is cold and unsympathetic, a poor country of chalk. Its agriculture was not highly productive. Much of the land was given to the colza bean: the introduction of paraffin in the late sixties was finishing off the colza. The loss of Mulhouse led to the construction of factories in Rouen. In 1873 there were 13,000 power looms to 60,000 hand-looms in Seine-inférieure. Wages in 1878 fell to 9–14 francs a week. The hand-loom weaver, unlike the Cambrelot, was not an artist but a humble tool. He either sought the town or left the region.[55]

Yet, in the case of a product such as knitwear made by the *bonnetières* of Troyes and the neighbourhood, it was still possible for the hand-loom to flourish and down to the middle of the eighties to support some ten thousand.[56] Concentration was of course on the way. In cantonal capitals, small textile factories appeared which gradually attracted hands from the surrounding communes, only themselves in time to be defeated.

Some trades survived down to 1914 owing to a long tradition and good organisation. There were the locksmiths of the Vimeu, the region between the Bresle and the mouth of the Somme, where the division of labour had been carried to fantastic lengths. Each of some thirty villages had its speciality, here padlocks, there bolts, at others strong-boxes, spring-locks, keys of all kinds, wine-racks and so forth. These artisans drew their materials from distant places, iron from France or Luxembourg, special steels from England and Germany, copper from Chile, coke from Belgium. Of their products they exported to Germany, Spain and South America goods to the value of six or eight millions a year.[57] Or there is Thiers, whose cutlery trade goes back to the fifteenth century, and, like Sheffield, was a centre of artisan production based on the precipitated waters of the Durolle. Here after the Treaty of 1860, German and English competition in the trade of cheap knives was met by the introduction of cutting-presses, stamping and other machinery. Here again the raw materials came from a distance, special steel from Sweden, iron from Argentine and Brazil, ebony from Gaboon.[58] In the south, there were still the iron-miners of Rancié in Ariège, a mine owned by the commune where the winter work was nail-making.[59] Or again in the Jura hills, the spectacle-makers of Morez, the cutters of semi-precious stones between Arbois and Nantua, the makers of horn articles at Oyonnax, the watch-makers of Montbeliard and the neighbourhood, and the domestic glove-makers in Grenoble, Millau and Niort.[60] And everywhere to the main industry of a region, there were the subsidiaries, wine-casks and bottles, wicker bottle-carriers, fish-baskets. Throughout the countryside, particularly in the forest areas, were to be found the sabot-carvers, the makers of rakes and forks, the makers of hives. It was still a world of craftsmen, some, possibly, artists, whose names will never be known, the world into which Charles Péguy had just been born and of which he was to write: 'These workmen did not serve. They worked. They had their honour and it was absolute. That the rail of a chair should be well made was a necessity: that was understood. It was not on account of the master that it must be well made or for connoisseurs or the master's clients. It was that the rail itself must be well made, in itself, for itself, in its very being.'[61]

(ix)

The up-swing in French external trade between 1850 and 1875 reflects rather the general European trend than any particular French activity. It is difficult to attribute the increase to the Anglo-French commercial treaty of 1860, which came into force in 1861, or to the subsequent treaties with other countries. It is possible that they had some influence, but the changes in exports and imports in 1861–66 are much obscured by the cotton-famine resulting from the War of Secession. Compared with the trade of the United Kingdom, French figures are not impressive. They are higher than those of all the German states or, after 1871, of the new-fledged German Empire, and of the United States. But within two decades, they would be far outdistanced by the

German and American.* The active balances up to 1869 had provided
the resources in foreign currencies which eased the liquidation of the
indemnity in 1873. Nevertheless, the relaxations of the régime of the
commercial treaties had a considerable body of opponents, though the
hostility was far from universal. The silk-merchants of Lyon, who
disposed of the great part of their output abroad, and the wine-ex-
porters of Bordeaux and Burgundy, were natural free-traders. The
worsted-manufacturers professed themselves satisfied, while the iron-
masters asked only for duties on specific products. The clamorous
group were the less efficient trades, the woollen-weavers of lower Normandy and the cotton-spinners of Rouen whose leader was the sten-
torian Pouyer-Quertier. The attempt of Thiers to return to the former
régime and to re-impose the *surtaxes d'entrepôt et de pavillon* had been
thwarted even before his fall and had later been interred. The treaty with
the United Kingdom of 23 July, 1873 confirmed the extension of the
1860 and 1866 conventions. In 1875 de Meaux, then Minister of Commerce and Agriculture, circularised the Chambers of Commerce as to
their choice between *ad valorem* and specific duties. The majority of
these bodies professed indifference, provided they could be assured of
no further amendments; the only thing they asked for was the abolition
of the 'most favoured nation' clause, which, owing to the Treaty of
Frankfort, was now appearing in every commercial treaty.[62]

The evidence points to the fact that in the seventies, the French
manufacturer and the French agriculturist stood in little danger except
from the competition of his countrymen. The *fabricants* of Elbeuf,
Louviers and Lisieux were being driven out not by foreign competition
but by the power-looms of Reims and Roubaix, as were the cotton
hand-loom weavers round Rouen. No protection, no prohibition, could
save them.[63]

The three main articles of export were silk and woollen piece-goods
and wines.[64] During the sixties, silk had been an exceptional earner,
bringing in, up to 1874, between 400 and 500 million francs, but with
the fall in the price of raw silk in the seventies, the revenue dropped to
something between 250 and 300 millions. The leading place was taken
by wool cloth of which the British took as a rule something about a
quarter. In spite of the phylloxera depredations and the consequent reduction in the volume of wine exports by about a quarter, the revenue
fell by only 5%, from 258 to 246 million francs. For the rest, raw silk,
raw wool, leather goods and hides, toys, fancy goods, *articles de Paris*,

* Statistics of foreign trade are printed at p. 357.

clothing and *lingerie*, gloves, ribbons, millinery and artificial flowers all contributed, and during the next twenty years there was little change. The weakest of the exports was that of cotton piece-goods. In 1875, the manufacturers sold no more than 82 million francs worth and this was the best figure in the decade. Roughly a third of this went to Algeria. Of all exports, more than half were manufactured goods, about a fifth were food-stuffs and the balance was raw materials.

Of imports at least half consisted of raw materials, silk, wool, cotton, timber, coal and coke, skins, oil-seeds, cattle and sheep, with some machinery. The most variable was cereals. As in England, the series of bad harvests in the late seventies led to a heavy increase in imports. After an import costing a mere 207 millions in 1877, there came five successive years in which the average cost of grain import amounted to 623 millions. Almost simultaneously with the onset of phylloxera, imports of wine rose to staggering proportions. In 1875, this had been a mere 291,830 hectolitres (6 million gallons); in 1878, it was 35 million gallons; in 1880, 159 millions. From an importation which had never cost more than 30 million francs, the value shot up to over 300 million in 1880 and to about 500 million in 1886. Although it then began to fall, it was not until 1900 that the value of exports rose above that of imports.

A glance at the components of external trade shows that the exports from France were neither bulky nor heavy, while of the imports, the bulky and heavy items came chiefly from Great Britain (coal, coke and machinery) which were carried in British ships. Napoleon III had hoped with the commercial treaties to stimulate the building up of the merchant marine. Thiers' proposal to reimpose the *taxes d'entrepôt et de pavillon* also had this in mind. For a country with colonies scattered about the world, the merchant marine was insignificant. In 1874–75 the merchant fleet consisted of 3,780 sailing ships with a tonnage of 736,000 and 315 steamers of 319,000. At that date the British owned 20,338 sailing ships and 3,082 steamers, these latter with a tonnage of 3,016,000. Of French commerce, only about 30% was being carried by French boats in the seventies. The committee set up in 1874 to examine the problem declared the only method of improving the situation was to subsidise the building of ships, and in 1881 a system of bounties was inaugurated. This did not offer a serious solution for ships were increasing in size and the French dockyards did not possess slips capable of taking such. Further, the desire for self-sufficiency in foodstuffs meant that French ships would not obtain cargoes in foreign ports. To most Frenchmen, these questions had little significance; their meaning would only become clear after the outbreak of war in 1914.

France's best customer was Great Britain. In the five years 1871–75 the British share was 22%. With no other country was this figure approached. The main items taken from the British were raw and combed wool, some cotton and wool piece goods, and coal. After the British the Belgian trade was most important, 13%, with as the chief item coal and coke, Jeumont on the frontier east of Maubeuge taking more than any sea port. After Belgium came Germany with 9.5%, Italy with 8%, U.S.A. normally about 7%, but this would fluctuate enormously according to the harvest. With Spain and Switzerland, the amount was between 5% and 6%. As for Russia, this was almost wholly one-way traffic, the Russians taking very little other than wine. As for the overseas Empire, in 1873 it amounted to no more than 505 million francs, of which over half was with Algeria.

Chapter Six

The Church and Education

(i)

While the religious and educational question occupies so large a part of the political stage, until the Separation of Church and State in 1905, it is arguable that the prominence given to it in the history books is exaggerated and that the conflict itself is in fact peripheral.

In the seventies, the relationship of the State to the Roman Catholic Church was governed by the Concordat of July 15, 1801, between Pope Pius VII and Napoleon. This was in effect the charter for a Church which had been destroyed and despoiled by the Revolution. The agreement, enforced, since the Pope was in no state to resist the First Consul, did not put the Church back in the unique situation it had occupied in 1789. Its property was not handed back; in compensation for *el grande latrocinio*, its members received from the State modest salaries. Further, while the Catholic Church was accepted as the official Church of the State, both Protestant and Israelite faiths were not only recognised (their adherents amounted respectively to some 2.8% and 0.22% of the population), but their pastors and rabbis were as much on the State's pay-roll as were the bishops and curés.

In the Concordatory instrument, it was set down that the State controlled the Catholic episcopate, and that the power of the Pope over the archbishops and bishops could be exercised only with the approval of the State, whose representative was the Minister of Public Worship (*Cultes*), a transient, not even necessarily a Catholic. In this way, the real power in the matter of appointment, translations, and discipline, gradually accrued to the permanent civil service director. The lower clergy were controlled by the bishops. Owing to the thinness of the original budget, curés were appointed only to the chief town in each canton, some 3,000. They were irremoveable. For the communes later provision was made of priests (*desservants* and *vicaires*) who could be removed and transferred by the bishops. No priest could leave his diocese without the leave of the bishop, and no bishop without the permission of the Minister. Hence there could be no national Church. On the other hand, it is to be observed that bishops were far more permanent than were other State servants — twenty to thirty years in a diocese is quite common — and therefore could acquire considerable influence.

The French Catholic clergy were formally independent of Rome in that they were obliged to subscribe to and to impose on the seminaries obedience to the Gallican Declaration of 1682, which laid down that, in temporal matters, the Pope had no *locus standi*, that in the spiritual sphere, although he had the chief voice in questions of faith, 'yet his decision is not unalterable unless the consent of the Church (i.e. the General Council) is given'; in other words, the Pope is not infallible. Finally that his authority in France was limited by the rules, customs and constitutions accepted in the realm and Church of France. Napoleon did not erect a system of religion but an organ of government. 'The people', he said, 'need religion, and that religion should be in the hands of the government.' It is significant that as a rule the Director of Public Worship was a stout resister to the claims of the Ultramontane.

This was the secular Church.* Of the religious Orders, Dominicans, Capucins, Jesuits and so forth, the Concordat made no mention. These, the Regulars, being, as their name implies, supranational organisations of the Roman Catholic Church, each with its own superior or general, responsible only to the Sovereign Pontiff, were not and could not be controlled by either the French State or the French Church. In the eighteenth century, they had been distrusted; the Jesuits had been expelled from France in 1764 and in 1773 the Order dissolved by the Pope. During the Revolution, the Regulars had disappeared. When they returned to France, they did not recover their former position for a long time. Nevertheless, Bonaparte, believing they might be useful in the field of empire-building, had authorised the existence of four bodies, les Prêtres des Missions étrangères, the Lazarists, les Prêtres du Saint-Esprit and the Company of St Sulpice, which in fact were communities of Seculars rather than true congregations. These four were French, with their superiors domiciled in France. After the Restoration, it was

---

* In the seventies, the Church consisted of 17 archbishops, 68 bishops, 3–4,000 curés, 30,000 *desservants* and 9,000 *vicaires*. The Archbishop of Paris received frs. 80,000, others 20,000, Bishops 15,000. The curés had, according to class, 1,200 or 1,500 francs, the *desservants* 900, and the *vicaires* 450. The staff of the Protestant Churches were some 600 for the Reformed (Calvinist) Church, and 61 for the Lutheran Augsburg Confession: more than 200 had gone with Alsace, where the Lutherans abounded. According to the size of the parish, these received between 1,500 and 3,000 francs. The rabbis were paid on much the same scale.

enacted (Law of January 2, 1817) that the authorisation of a men's Order must be recognised by a law, and in fact no law was passed after this date. On the other hand, congregations of men could by decree be recognised as of public utility for specific purposes, such in particular as teaching. Thus a number of congregations obtained recognition as members of the Institut des Frères des Ecoles chrétiennes. Though few women's Orders were authorised (again a law was required) many houses were set up and their existence winked at, until January 31, 1852, when a decree was issued giving the right of conditional authorisation to the Conseil d'Etat.

(*ii*)

Up to the Revolution, teaching had been in the hands of the Orders. With the Napoleonic reorganisation of the country, it soon became evident that trained laymen were needed to administer the imperial decrees and laws. Napoleon would have none of the Regulars: such do not possess 'the national spirit, the independence of mind which makes the teachers of a great society'. Hence the foundation in 1806 of the University of France, with the monopoly of higher, i.e. secondary and university, education. But it was impossible for the State to provide schools or teachers in sufficient numbers; the rules had to be relaxed, though the Government had no intention of allowing freedom. No private school could be opened without a State licence, and whether lay or congregationist, every teacher must hold a diploma from the University. Only seminaries for the training of the priesthood were excepted and these were limited in numbers. Primary school teaching was left in private hands, also subject to licence and inspection by University inspectors.

In 1815 the Bourbons returned to find that the centralised state for which their ancestors had struggled through centuries had been carried out by the Revolution and Bonaparte. They were shrewd enough to maintain it. The Church might denounce the Concordat: the Imperial system stayed. The Church, however, perceived that if the authority over education could be recovered, in due time it might be possible to obtain control of the State. In the meantime, the Jesuits and other Orders slipped back, and their schools and seminaries were filled with the children of the upper classes. But two difficulties stood in the way. The cadres of the teaching Orders had scarcely been re-formed, and no government was going to hand over to the Church the higher education of the voters of tomorrow. The most that could be obtained was Guizot's Law (June 28, 1833) on primary education. This, while ordering the foundation of a school in every commune and in every department either an école normale or a higher primary school, laid it down that the teaching should be moral and religious, that it should be given under the surveillance of the parish priest and that ecclesiastics might be teachers. By 1835 there were at work 1660 members of the Frères des Ecoles chrétiennes, otherwise known as the Institut des Frères de la Doctrine chrétienne, and also, from an old gibe, les Frères Ignorantins.

(iii)

It is at this point that politics, lay and ecclesiastical, began to bedevil education. The 1830 Revolution had placed a little devout but wholly Gallican king on the throne. The Church, having secured nothing, and by its origins Legitimist, followed Montalembert, the Liberal Catholic layman, peer of France, in his attack on the University, on Victor Cousin, Villemain, Michelet and all the 'sons of Voltaire'. An attempt at a compromise over secondary education was rejected by Montalembert and equally, in the name of the Revolution, by Cousin and Thiers, who followed up with an attack on the Jesuits. These, on the advice of their general, closed their houses and broke up into little groups (July 1845). Nevertheless, the University once more offered reform, though the new proposals did not satisfy the Catholics. Before the discussion could take place, 1848 and all that that date implies had occurred. Eighteen months earlier, Cardinal Ferretti, said to be Liberal, had been elected to the Triple Tiara as Pope Pius IX.

Two revolutions, albeit merely dynastic, had led to serious plebeian risings in Lyon, Paris, and the Loire coal-fields, and finally to the civil half-war of June 1848. The dread word 'socialism' had been forged and had alarmed the wealthier classes. They had long forgotten the glories of the Revolution, the last Jacobin was dead and Voltaire was no longer their philosopher. They turned back towards the Church. In 1850, the Comte de Falloux, Minister of Public Instruction in the first government of Louis-Napoleon, brought in a new bill for the reorganisation of public education. Falloux, a dyed-in-the-wool Clerical, knew that it was impossible to return to the system of 1789, but he would break the University monopoly by subordinating the obnoxious educationalists to the control of what were described as the 'great organs of society'. His law (March 15, 1850) instituted the Higher Council of Public Instruction. On it sat four Catholic archbishops or bishops, two Protestant pastors, one member of the Jewish Consistory, with three members of the Institute, three from the Conseil d'Etat and three Appeal Court Judges. To these, all of whom were elected by their respective bodies, were added eight members of the University and three from the private schools. But whereas the majority were elected by their peers, those from the University were appointed by government decree, as a permanent section. For the future, the non-educationalists controlled the discipline and promotions of the teaching body. Further, in 1852, after the resurrection of the Empire, the members of the University were appointed for one year only. Below the Higher Council were created local councils on which too the clergy would be represented. Henceforward, secondary schools could be freely opened by ecclesiastics, provided the director held a university degree. Of greater import was the article authorising the appointment of members of congregations as teachers on no more than a letter of commendation from a bishop. Higher education, however, remained in the control of the University.

Catholic militant journalists grumbled that the Church had not been re-established as before the Revolution, and had not taken over all the duties of the University. It had in fact secured much. The Public Worship budget was substantially increased, while, under a régime in which civil liberties were closely curtailed, the Church with its subservient press and the freedom of the pulpit was enjoying a status it had not had since 1789. There was a notable increase in the congregations. In 1851 they comprised 3100 men and 34,200 women. In 1861 the numbers were 17,676 and 89,243. Of the 17,676, approximately 12,000 were of the Frères Ignorantins. In a long report to the Emperor in 1860, Rouland, who as minister combined Public Instruction and Public Worship, had warned the Emperor that congregational education was favourable neither to the régime nor to the ideas of the century. In these establishments 'are to be found history books written for the purpose of glorifying monarchy and divine right, exalting the supremacy of religion and indirectly denigrating the civil and political principles laid down since 1789'.[1] He drew attention to the so-called charitable lay society of St Vincent de Paul, with its 500 committees through the country, which was in fact a widespread Ultramontane and Legitimist conspiracy for undermining the régime. As for the Pope, 'at the present moment, abusing the liberty accorded him, he affects to rule France as he rules a province of the Catholic Empire . . . he administers directly, as he would in Ancona or Perugia, the business of the episcopate and the Church, according to the well-known Ultramontane formula: "the Clergy of France is Catholic before it is French." '2

The Church — it could scarcely do otherwise — thought in terms of what was good for itself. In a country which had had some ten revolutions in less than three-quarters of a century, the Church could not but be opportunist. The bishops had welcomed the Second Republic; Princes of the Church, they did not flinch from coming to terms with the Devil; four years later they had rejoiced over the *coup d'état*; they had never felt quite certain of Napoleon III, but they only turned against him when they believed he would betray the Pope by encouraging the ambitions of Piedmont. When, in the belief that he needed Catholic support for government candidates at the election of 1863, the Emperor told the Italian government that he would, so to speak, be forced to fight for Rome, the French episcopate executed yet another volte-face. They would at least be spared these pirouettes under the Third Republic.

On the other hand, the bishops wished to live at peace with the Government, but they were torn between conflicting groups. There were the needs of the Secular Church, which was always suffering from the encroachments of the Regulars, ambitious on behalf of the Vatican, dyed-in-the-wool Ultramontanes. These, because as a rule they were better educated and often of higher social level than the parish priests, would be influential among the aristocracy and a power on the committees of the Société de St Vincent de Paul. The subordinate priesthood, as much as the important Catholic laymen, could make a bishop's life intolerable. More than one bishop was driven to resign by the treachery of an Ultramontane Vicar-general or by organised rebellion among his parish priests. A reader of the sordid stories of the launching of pilgrimage centres, La Salette, Lourdes and so forth in the teeth of the scepticism of the higher clergy, will appreciate their impotence. Moreover, Rome had no hesitation in striking, if it need, at Gallican churchmen: the day of Gallicanism had passed with the expulsion of 'the most Christian King' in 1830, a title no one could possibly apply to Louis-Napoleon Bonaparte. France, as Duruy was to observe, might be the 'eldest daughter of the Church'; she was also 'the grandchild of Voltaire'.

Pius IX also had an immense burden of responsibilities, which he was not of the stuff to manage. Heaviest were the advance in power of demos, and the rapid development of knowledge of physics, chemistry and biology, which was inciting men to question the traditional tenets of the Christian Church. Of democracy Pius had had one experience, in 1849, with the Roman Republic. If, which is doubtful, he had had earlier liberal leanings, after that he quickly smothered them. From this time, he became uncompromisingly reactionary. In the face of the development of scientific discovery and invention, Vatican policy became fiercely authoritarian. In 1854 the Dogma of the Immaculate Conception of the Virgin Mary was promulgated without reference to the General Council of the Church; there was no protest. From that success grew the attack on Liberal Catholicism, of which the culminating point was reached in 1864 with the issue of the Encyclical *Quanta Cura* and its appendix, the Syllabus of Common Errors, with its denunciation of freedom of thought and its curious mixture of materialism and transcendentalism, its condemnation of Socialism, of the Separation of Church and State, of toleration, and of the idea that the 'Roman Pontiff can, and ought to, reconcile himself to, and agree with, progress, liberalism and modern civilisation'. Finally, the announcement of the summoning of a General Council for the purpose of accepting the Declaration of Papal Infallibility widened the already wide gulf between Ultramontanes and Gallicans.[3]

In 1863 after the elections, Napoleon personally appointed Victor Duruy Minister of Public Instruction. Duruy, the son of a working man, had been Professor of History at the Lycée Henri IV, and was a champion of the University and lay teaching. Constantly hampered, bitterly opposed by the Church, particularly by the Orders, whose illegally-opened institutions he closed, often deserted by his colleagues, forced to endure his master's compromises for the sake of his throne, Duruy did all he could in the cause of compulsory, free and lay education and in the promotion of secondary education for girls. By the time he was dismissed (after the largely Catholic election of 1869) he had set an ideal before the Republicans. 'You ought to come along with us,' said the leader of the Gauche ouverte, Picard, to him: 'You're the only member of the Government we're afraid of.'[4]

The Church was not seriously interested in education to fit the younger generations to come to terms with life. Its policy was directed on the one side to morality, on the other to politics. This was true even of the Catholic laity. It is certainly no less true of the Republicans. Except for Duruy and some members of the University, there were few educationists. Republican historians make much of Jean Macé who in 1866 founded the Ligue d'Enseignement, a kind of workingman's educational association, but in fact it seems to have been little more than a Republican political agency, which was taken over by the freemasons. Apart from attracting a few distinguished supporters, Havin of the *Siècle*, Sainte-Beuve, Menier, of chocolate fame, its operations seem to have consisted largely of Republican propaganda.

For the Church the problem was highly complicated and was made the more difficult to unravel by the refusal of the Pope to come to terms with the contemporary world. True, the 'common errors' laid out in the Syllabus were not new: most, if not all, had been condemned in some earlier encyclical. But their presentation in a single document was tantamount to a declaration of war. As the French ministers said, a number of these eighty damnable propositions was to be found in the French constitution. They therefore refused to allow the episcopate to make the document known officially, and the two bishops who read it from the pulpit were prosecuted before the Conseil d'Etat.[5]

The situation was made the worse by the internal conflicts within the Secular Church, between the Secular Church and Rome, between the Regulars and the Seculars, between Rome, the Orders and the Imperial Government. There were bishops who were uncompromising Ultramontanes, such as Monsignor Pie of Poitiers. There were bishops who were critical of both the Government and the Vatican, Liberal Catholics, Monsignor Dupanloup and his friends. There were others critical of Rome, but friendly to the Government such as Archbishop Darboy of Paris, much distrusted by His Holiness. There were even bishops who were both Ultramontane and Bonapartist. There were even Gallican religious Orders, such as the Sulpicians.

On the other hand, the Pope could not but protest when a professor of the Collège de France (Renan) could openly describe Jesus as 'an incomparable man . . . so great that although here [in the College] everything should be judged from a scientific point of view, I would not contend with those who . . . call Him God'. How could a French cardinal not object when a university lecturer, the absurd Naquet, encouraged the medical students in their violence against the Government and the Church?

M

(iv)

In the seventies, primary education was still carried out under the Loi Falloux, the teachers in the schools being both lay and ecclesiastic. They taught some two and a half million children of whom roughly a fifth were in charge of Congregationists. Most of these were Frères de la Doctrine chrétienne, now about twelve thousand strong (to some 40,000 lay teachers). Since the rules of the Order forbade them to work except in groups of three, they were to be found rather in the towns than the villages, where a lonely lay teacher battled unassisted against the priest who could make his life a misery. The Ignorantins were much in favour in a number of the larger towns: in Roubaix, Elbeuf, Lyon and Rouen they are thought to have had from 66 to 88% of the boys under their control. The employers encouraged them, but they are said to have been popular as well with the workers, though this may be due to the fact that they did not demand the fees laid down by the Government to be paid by the parents unless certified by the town council as indigent. (The Government intervened and insisted on their collecting the fees.) The préfets considered them satisfactory since they did not play politics; but on the other hand, they did not help the municipal councils or the administration as the lay teacher, usually as secretary to the mairie, was able to.

If the priests taught no more than a fifth of the boys, the girls were largely in the hands of the women's Orders. In many cities and towns, Roubaix, Saint-Etienne, Le Creusot, all the girls' schools were run by the sisters.

Yet in spite of the seventy thousand schools, illiteracy was still high, 20% of all men marrying, 31% of all girls, in 1875; it would be much higher for their parents. Education was not compulsory and governmental insistence on the payment of fees by the parents led to children being kept at home, and, in spite of the law, set to work very early; it depended on the region. According to the reports, the non-attendance of children between seven and twelve was between 45 and 50% in the four Breton departments, in Loire-inférieure, Poitou, the Berry and the Marche, while for girls it was even higher: between 60 and 70%. On the other hand, in the eastern departments, Meuse, Vosges, Jura, Doubs, Côte d'Or, absenteeism was no more than 3%. Much depended on the municipal council which could take the burden of the fees off the parents if it so desired. At Vergigny (Yonne), the fee for a child under seven was one franc a month, over that age 1.75 francs, not a trifling sum to labourers earning no more than 600 francs a year.[6] In the poorer departments, the fees might run up to 15 to 20 francs. In Normandy, in a bad department like Eure, children were put to work as early as possible.[7] On the other hand, in some thriving centres such as Reims, the schooling was organised and run by the municipality gratis.[8]

In December 1871 Jules Simon, Minister of Public Instruction in the Thiers Government, introduced a bill for compulsory primary education. It did not propose that this teaching should be free, but the Committee on the bill was presided over by Monsignor Dupanloup, whose views on education were out of date and obstinately held. The majority on the committee were Catholic, and they guessed that parents could not be compelled to send their children to school unless the State paid the fees. If this happened, they believed the Catholic private schools would be unable to compete. They therefore submitted another bill proposing that the heads of families in each commune should choose whether teaching should be carried out by priests or laymen and that indigent parents should be compensated for the fees they paid by a draft on the communal funds. Simon, seeing that his bill had no future, dropped it but did not adopt the committee's bill.[9] No further educational improvements were proposed during the Thiers Government* and none under that of Broglie; they were well enough content with the Falloux law. But in December 1874, Cumont, Minister of Public Instruction, introduced a bill which would grant complete freedom of higher education: in other words, anyone might found a university. Since the only organisation which could finance this was the Church, the Republicans naturally opposed. The main battle turned on the grant of degrees. The opposition claimed that the State could not surrender its right of supervision; the examinations must be carried out by the professors of the appropriate faculties. The Catholics proposed to put their universities on a level with those of the State, in spite of the fact that their secondary teaching, as Duruy had shown, was on a far lower level than that in the State schools. A compromise was reached in July 1875, when it was laid down that examining boards should be mixed. With the bill become law, July 12, 1875, the Church made haste to found universities before the new Constitution came into force, in Paris, Lille, Angers, Lyon and Toulouse.

'*Le cléricalisme, voilà l'ennemi.*' Was it really so? Or was it merely a

---

* Except for the law of March 19, 1873 which increased the teaching members of Higher Council of Public Instruction to twelve, of whom five would be elected.

bogy useful to smother the need for enquiry into such other matters as the employment of children? About 1905 a cynical Radical deputy implored his party not to allow a settlement of the religious question and thus 'take the bread out of our mouths'. On the whole, the higher clergy was Legitimist, though by no means always Ultramontane, and the members of the Orders devoted to higher education were Ultramontane. Their influence, however, was not strong except among the wealthier classes and those (apart from Paris) chiefly in the west. For it is by no means certain that clerical influence was as universal as it was presumed to be, or as Republican politicians said it was. Nine-tenths of the lower clergy were recruited from the sons of artisans and farmers. They were deficient in numbers, often badly educated, passionately Ultramontane and disliked by many of their parishioners. Indeed it is to be questioned whether much of the population was in any but a formal sense Christian; the countryman was vastly ignorant, and vastly superstitious. As Drumont pointed out, worship with ordinary men and women was first a *corvée* and then merely a habit, 'adoration more or less mechanical of a painted image.' It is said that much of France had been 'dechristianised'; but it might be truer to say that it had remained pagan.[11]

In the seventies, the regions in which Catholicism seems to have been alive lay in several blocks. The west was the most solid: all the four departments of the Breton peninsula, with the border departments of Vendée, Deux-Sèvres, Loire-inférieure, Maine-et-Loire, Mayenne, western Orne and southern Manche, with further north the area of Rouen, Le Havre and the pays de Caux. Further north still, the Flemish speaking parts of Pas-de-Calais and Nord, that is near the coast, were said to be devout. The second region, much diminished by the loss of Alsace-Lorraine, covered Meurthe-et-Moselle with parts of Meuse, most of Vosges, Haute-Saône, Belfort and Doubs. There were patches through the Jura, Savoy and upper Dauphiné, and there was another large area in Rhône, Loire, Haute-Loire, Ardèche, part of Gard, Lozère, Aveyron, Tarn, Tarn-et-Garonne, pretty well the whole of the south-east quarter of the Massif Central. Finally, there was the Basque country as far north as the Adour, and eastward to Tarbes.[12]

Of these regions, four, Brittany, Flanders, the Alsatian border and Béarn, were all territories inhabited by people for whom French was a subsidiary language. Duruy attempted on several occasions to prevent the use of these tongues, but he was always frustrated. The clergy, all of course locally recruited, were not only permitted by their bishops but encouraged to use the local speech for sermons and religious teaching.

A second point to be noticed is that the area of the Central Massif was (and has remained) the stronghold of heresy. This had been the land of the Cathars, the Albigensians and of the Protestants, and remained so: in many of the constituencies in this part the political conflicts were rather between Catholics and Protestants than between Monarchist and Republican. In Nîmes, in Ardèche, the cleavages of centuries still appeared. Last of all, it should be observed that Catholicism flourished in the hill country, Protestantism in the plain.

In the huge area bordering these enclaves, the influence of the Church had apparently evaporated. In the Landes, at least in the plantation area north of the Adour, were to be found irreligious landowners, ignorant peasants and a predatory clergy: 'Apart from rare exceptions, the curés are not content with having the best house in the village, rooms for their friends, stables, a coach-house, farmyards, a hay meadow and a wheat field . . . and even a share-cropper to work it.' Here a village that protested was deprived of its priest for a year or so.[13] On the other hand, in the Charentes, no priest had influence unless a Bonapartist. In 1867, there had been riots in the belief that a counter-revolution was preparing. The Paris basin, Seine, Seine-et-Marne, Seine-et-Oise, Yonne, were indifferent: 'the population is little religious.' There was a shortage of priests. In the diocese of Meaux, many were said to drink too much.

Chapter Seven

The Sixteenth of May

(i)

The Organic Law of August 2, 1875 distributed the 225 electoral seats in the Senate on the basis of population; but since the highest number of senators for a department was five (Nord) and (save for the single seat for the Territory of Belfort) the lowest two, those departments with the lightest populations were heavily over-represented. Moreover Seine, which was one and a half times more thickly populated than Nord, was allotted exactly the same number of senators, five. Thus the Senate was weighted in favour of the rural electorate.

Election was indirect. The electoral colleges consisted of the deputies of the department, the conseillers-généraux and conseillers d'arrondissement, and one delegate from each municipal council. Since there were some 36,000 municipal councils in the country, the franchise was heavily weighted in favour of the smallest villages; the delegation from the commune of Saint-Nectaire had exactly the same weight as the delegate of the commune of Clermont-Ferrand. In many regions, but chiefly in the west, the villages were dominated by the landowners, many of whom were maires and many chosen as delegates. Thus the natural conservatism of the peasant was reinforced. The departmental and other councils were themselves usually conservative, even if republican. As Thibaudet[1] wrote, the councils deal with serious matters, such as the distribution of taxes, requests for State subventions and so on, which affect everybody. Whereas to the Chamber of Deputies one can elect a voluble hot-head, for the local council one prefers an experienced and hard-headed gentleman-farmer, who knows what's what in the countryside. Thus, even though the Republic was accepted, conservatism tended to remain in the Senate. The method of election was *scrutin de liste*. The candidate to secure election at the first or second polls must have an absolute majority. If, after that, the full number had not been elected, a relative majority sufficed for the third and last.

The election was held on January 30, 1876 preceded by little propaganda. MacMahon issued an address on January 13, colourless except for its stress on conservatism, order and peace, against those 'who may in the present disturb the security of lawful interests or threaten to in the future by the propagation of anti-social doctrines and revolutionary programmes'. In spite of its vagueness, the press criticised his intervention as contrary to Parliamentary conventions. On January 18 Gambetta spoke at Aix-en-Provence, once more emphasising the conservative part to be played by the Senate. Except the uncompromising Monarchists, most candidates favoured loyalty to the constitution. Omens of future Republican strains were to be observed in the choice of candidates for the five Paris seats. Four meetings of the Republican members of the electoral college were needed and at these it became clear that, between the delegates of the Left Centre and those of the Extreme Left, no list could be agreed. In the end thirteen Republican candidates stood. At the first poll only three obtained absolute majorities, Freycinet, Tolain and Hérold, all detested by the Radicals. At the second poll Victor Hugo was elected alone, at the last Gambetta's friend, the journalist Peyrat. Louis Blanc and Floquet were both rejected. 'The relative check to Victor Hugo and the absolute one to Louis Blanc have given the *Rappel* people the chance they have so long yearned for, to attack the *République Française*. . . . They were determined to beat us. The catastrophe of January 30, the incurable hurt to their *amour-propre*, the evil comments, the bitterness, the enmity, deadened but still persistent, all together have precipitated the break we wanted to avoid.'[2] So Gambetta to Ranc. Elsewhere the results were as expected. The Left won 93 seats, of which 51 went to the Left Centre and only 7 to the Extremists; the Right 132, of whom only 2 were pure Legitimists, and 91 Moderates, Orleanists and the self-styled Constitutionals. The unwelcome feature was the election of 39 Bonapartists, for the most part from the south-west. Thus, with the inclusion of the Life Senators, the balance between Left and Right was almost evenly divided, 151 to 149. But the more important permanent majority was that of the two Centres over the wings, 84 Left Centre and 81 Right Centre and Moderates with 17 Constitutionals. The forces of order were in command of the Senate, but their removal from the Chamber weakened conservatism in the lower House.

For the Chamber of Deputies, the election was by direct suffrage in single-member constituencies, with two polls. To be elected at the first, the candidate must have secured the absolute majority of the votes and the votes of at least a quarter of the electors on the register: a poll must be held even if there were only one candidate. In the event of there being no absolute majority for any candidate, a second poll must be held on the Sunday fortnight, when a relative majority sufficed.

By the law the vote was secret: in practice, it was not.* Nominally the register was correct: in fact, it rarely was. In theory, the constituencies were approximately equal, with an upper limit of 100,000 votes: in reality, they differed enormously. According to the politicians and the journalists, the French citizen was on fire to demonstrate his love for the Republic or the Monarchy: when it came to polling on Sunday, February 20, his lack of enthusiasm in many places was striking. In Var and Alpes-maritimes, less than 60% went to the poll; in nine other departments, including those centres of revolt, Marseille and Saint-Etienne, fewer than 70%. The average of abstention for the whole country was 24.0%. Contrary to what might be expected, the voting was heaviest in three of the departments of the Garonne basin, Lot, Lot-et-Garonne and Gers, where of thirteen seats, eight were captured by Bonapartists.

There had been little national campaigning. Gambetta, candidate in five constituencies, Paris XX, Lille 2, Avignon, Marseille 1, and Bordeaux 1, spoke in each. At Avignon and in the neighbourhood, roughs hired by his Legitimist opponent (who was later invalidated) broke up one of his meetings. In Paris, Louis Blanc insisted on pressing his candidature in three constituencies. The first poll gave a crushing victory for the Republic, with absolute majorities in 300 constituencies against 135 for the Right. At the second poll on March 5, they took 56 against 49. In twenty-four departments, the Left had won every seat. Gambetta was elected in Paris, Lille, Bordeaux and Marseille, but was beaten in Avignon, where every crude device and pressure, including the influence of the préfet, was employed. Blanc won all his three contests in Seine, while Buffet was defeated in four, and at once resigned the vice-presidency of the Council, Dufaure presiding *ad interim*.**

Both Chambers met on March 8, and there was a formal handing over by the President of the National Assembly to the oldest members of Chamber and Senate, before each body constituted itself. On the following day the new cabinet appeared. Except for Decazes at the Foreign Office and de Cissey at the rue Saint-Dominique, the ministry

* Cf. Appendix XI.

** In consequence of multiple elections, there were ten byes for six seats held by Republicans and four by Bonapartists. Seven went to the Left and three to Bonapartists, of which one (Ajaccio) to Prince Bonaparte. After the meeting of the Chamber, one Extreme Right, two Right Centre and seven Bonapartists were invalidated. The bye-elections to replace them were not completed until November. In that month, a count of the Chamber, was Left Centre. Dufaure, Prime Minister* and Minister of Justice, with Waddington (Public Instruction), Léon Say (Finance), Christophle (Public Works), Teisserenc de Bort (Commerce) and Admiral Fourichon (Marine). Casimir-Périer had refused the Interior, and the portfolio was given to Ricard, who had been defeated at Niort. Six days later, under pressure from MacMahon,[3] he was elected by the Senate to the life-seat vacated by the death of the Legitimist, La Rochette, whose intrigues in December had killed the Right majority.

(ii)

The appointment of the cabinet exposed the bogus parliamentary structure of the constitutional laws. It demonstrated that while the Marshal was, by the law of November 20, 1873, the head of the Government and thus entitled to select his colleagues as individuals regardless of their political affiliations, the ministry did not correspond to the majority of the Chamber, which was overwhelmingly further to the Left. Yet the cabinet contained two members who, while at present 'constitutional', were in fact of the Right. No single member was beyond Left Centre, or in other words was a loyal democrat. The Republicans took it ill. 'It is not a majority ministry, simply a coterie cabinet', wrote Challemel-Lacour in the *République Française*. Thiers asserted to all who would listen that to keep Decazes at the Quai d'Orsay was scandalous. Ricard at the Interior was held not to be doing his duty by a show of vigour. The profiteers of victory had got quickly to work. 'The Ministry of the Interior looked like a position taken by assault. The ante-chambers were filled with senators and deputies, escorted by candidates they had brought to introduce to the minister. . . . "You have seen," said M. Ricard bitterly [to Ernest Daudet, chief editor of the *Journal Officiel*] ". . . I should like to be able to keep you. Please try to stay. I will shield you, and you will be doing me a service.

which includes six byes due to death or election to the Senate (Dufaure), gives the following approximate groupings:

Extrème Right	28	Left Centre (Marcère)	75
Right Centre and Moderates	39	Republican Left (Ferry)	185
Constitutionalists	18	Republican Union (Gambetta)	86
Bonapartists	80	Extreme Left (Blanc)	21
Independent (Decazes)	1		
	166		367

* The Vice-president became President of the Council, by the Law of March 10, 1876.

There are seven men after your job, all equally well backed. If I take one, I shall annoy six, not to speak of their patrons." '⁴ At a full meeting on March 7, the Republicans had passed a resolution that the cabinet should be wholly Republican. They met again on March 12, both deputies and senators.

It is well to look at the composition of this meeting. Of the five hundred odd senators and deputies, no more than 120 were followers of Gambetta or the Extremists. The Left Centre, with Thiers, and the Republican Left, with Simon and Ferry, were in enormous preponderance. On the other hand, compared with Gambetta, they had few striking figures. Of the deputies, nearly two-thirds were new men, unversed in parliamentary tactics, most of them deeply provincial. Gambetta spoke. He may well not have wanted to, but he must hold his group together, and among the speakers were theory-ridden zealots, such as Brisson and Lepère. He attempted to walk the narrow path between such and the Conservatives. While disclaiming any lack of confidence in the cabinet, he insisted that the Republican majority could not be its passive instrument, that both the cabinet and the country should be made aware of its attitude. He dropped an acid comment on Ricard: 'it is curious that not one official, whatever his rank, has been touched or removed, ("Very good, very good", from the audience) and that there has not been a single minister, not one head of a department, to make an example. . . . These officials flung themselves headlong into the electoral battle: wiser than those who guided them, they knew they were fighting for themselves. For them, the real social peril was the loss of their jobs. . . . Those préfets we know so well, whom everyone points to, those préfets whom no one dares defend in public, there they are, threatening, mocking, saying they will soon bring the new majority to heel. . . . There are ministers . . . their past is not a sufficient guarantee of the future. So I end by saying: No want of confidence, but no confidence.'⁵ A resolution was carried 'hoping that the cabinet would take note of the demands of the situation' and expecting the replacement of administrators in office by loyal Republicans.

Gambetta had overdone it. Paul Cambon, writing to his brother in Algeria, remarked: 'Gambetta, carried away by his feelings, has set on foot a campaign which has consolidated the ministerial majority; he has tumbled head over heels into the net held out to him by Thiers and Jules Simon. The too violent attacks on the ministry have grouped behind the cabinet the Left Centre, the Left and the Right Centre. His attempted plenary conferences have alarmed many members of the Republican Left who were moving towards alliance with the Republican Union and who now are drawing back.'[6]

The Republican party remained disunited. The Republican Left seceded and reconstituted its group, electing Jules Ferry as chairman, and on March 24 the Left Centre re-formed under Paul Bethmont. Gambetta, demonstrating his fidelity to the conception of the single party, refused to reconstruct the Republican Union. But the criticism of his followers gradually wore his resolution down. In June the Republican Union was reconstructed.

Nor was this the only complication. As all far-seeing Republicans knew, at this stage it was vital not to alarm either the electorate or the 'interests' by demagogy and the advertisement of impossible policies. It was even more vital to keep the Dufaure Government both in power and active, particularly in power. If the position of the ministry was made impossible, if a Republican cabinet were to be defeated, the crisis believed to be desired by MacMahon's entourage would be created, a situation, that is to say, either favourable for the dissolution of the Chamber or as an alternative, 'the Republic without Republicans.' As much as Ferry or Bethmont, Gambetta was aware of this, but he appears to have been unable to rein in his followers, let alone the Radicals. Hence during the next nine months, he is to be found every now and then making a demonstration to please his followers. 'Yes,' said Thiers to Edmond Adam,[7] 'he is level-headed, he is prudent, he is discreet: but his tail! Think, he is deputy for Belleville, and there is the Belleville programme to be carried out. If you have not read that programme for some time, Adam, have a look at it. If Gambetta triumphs, that programme is no longer a weapon of opposition, it is a governmental programme.' More immediate, for Gambetta, there was always the infernal question of a full amnesty for the Communards.

Two subjects were capable of welding the Republicans into a united body, anti-clericalism and the préfets of the Moral Order. Ricard had not been slow to act, but neither fast nor thoroughly enough for indignant Republicans. Still, a little over a week after Gambetta's speech, he began. Five préfets were dismissed, including Auray de Saint-Pois of Deux-Sèvres, believed responsible for Ricard's defeat at Niort: three more were put on half-pay. Their offices were given to unimpeachable Republicans. In mid-April, there were further dismissals and a great number of transfers. But Ricard, perhaps the strongest member of Dufaure's team, died suddenly on May 11. His place was taken by his under-secretary, de Marcère, the original founder of the Left Centre, a writer rather than an orator, a Catholic who would in due time become disabused of the virtuousness of Republicans. On the day after his appointment, the ministry was interpellated on the question of the amnesty for Communards, by the new member for Montmartre, Georges Clemenceau, a Radical supported by the Extremists. Dufaure replied irritably; nevertheless the Chamber gave him an overwhelming majority — but Gambetta neither spoke nor voted. This was the prologue to a tempestuous six months. Anti-clericalism was bound to come up. Already the majority had voted an enquiry into the election of the ultraclerical Comte Albert de Mun at Pontivy (Morbihan), where he had been publicly supported by Monsignor Freppel, the tempestuous Bishop of Angers: '*cet homme est porteur d'un mandat impératif; Dieu le lui a donné.*' Waddington, Minister of Public Instruction, now brought in a bill to restore the grant of degrees into the sole hands of the State University, thus reversing the law of July 12, 1875. In this quarrel, the difference between Left and Right was too great to be capable of composition: while each side claimed liberty of education, each was in fact seeking to monopolise it. The bill passed the Chamber: the Senate rejected it at its first reading.

Almost simultaneously, Broglie's law of 1874 on the appointment of maires came under fire. Dufaure and Marcère knew well that too drastic a revision would meet with disaster in the Senate. Ricard had opposed any return to the liberal law of April 4, 1871. Marcère compromised by retaining the appointment of maires of cantonal capitals. Some of Gambetta's followers demanded a full municipal law. Gambetta himself intervened in favour of the government bill. Everyone knew that any further freedom than that offered by the ministry would meet the hostility of MacMahon and the Senate. For the moment there was a fear that the ministry would be beaten and since MacMahon had told the cabinet that he was strongly opposed to the law of 1871, a defeat might cause not only a ministerial but also a presidential crisis. The Extremists were therefore defeated, and Marcère's bill passed. The Senate, observing the Chamber's willingness to compromise, followed its example.

If the summer session ended with the cabinet still unbeaten, its life was precarious, and its situation in fact untenable. It could satisfy neither the President nor the Senate, nor could it withstand the Chamber Republicans if they took the bit between their teeth. In the Chamber, the Left Centre and the wiser members of the Left were keenly alert to the situation: Ferry's newsletters to a Bordeaux newspaper are illuminating.[8] Gambetta was no less aware. But the two hundred or so new Republican members were as yet without understanding of government or politics. They saw no reason why the majority should hesitate and manoeuvre, why they should not challenge the President and the Senate, and in this they were encouraged by Ernest Lefèvre's *Rappel* and the old-time Radicals. The cabinet itself was weakened; the breach between the Republican and Orleanist members could not be wholly closed. Dufaure was a lawyer who detested politics. He was content that the Republic was founded, but desired no further democratisation of government: good administration was everything; for that, experienced agents were needed and political colour was of no significance; only open hostility to the régime set up in 1875 called for action. Criticism in the Chamber, especially from the Extreme Left, he met with contemptuous anger. Dufaure wished to be let alone to run his Ministry of Justice. Since the death of Ricard, his colleagues were conservative, competent and colourless. Decazes withdrew deeper into the Foreign Office. Cissey, after a brush with the Chamber, resigned, while the rest devoted themselves to the routine of their offices. The ministry existed, but no longer led.

Just before the end of the recess, Gambetta, having failed to unite the Republicans, having failed to force the complete purge of the administration, realising that the routed opponents of the Republic had had time to prepare new positions, came round to the opinion of Grévy and Ferry that the constitutional Republic must be nursed. At Belleville on October 27, he turned on the Extremists, denounced the 'criminal insurrection of the Commune', and declared for a policy of results as against the street-corner clamouring of noisy wind-bags. He was, as usual, applauded.

The autumn extraordinary session opened on October 30 with sniping by the Extreme Left. To the eternal question of the amnesty was added a proposal to suppress the Foreign Office vote for the Vatican embassy, followed by a quarrel over whether military honours should be paid to civil members of the Order of the Legion of Honour, followed in turn by the rejection of several items on the Public Worship budget. The Senate responded by electing Chesnelong, the clerical Monarchist, to a vacant seat for life. The crisis was near. Early in November, a private member's bill to stop further prosecutions of Communards was passed in spite of a government offer of a compromise. The bill in its original form went up to the Senate, which disliked two clauses. The anomaly of the situation lay in the fact that Dufaure now had to defend in the Upper House the bill he had opposed in the Lower, and although he carried out the task with skill and dignity, the Senate voted him down. Next day, December 2, he resigned. 'You won't leave us for a little thing like that?' had enquired a member of the Right Centre. 'It is the little thing, my friend, that trips me up,' replied Dufaure quietly.

(iii)

The resignation raised a delicate problem. Did this imply the resignation of the whole cabinet? Dufaure thought not: all that was needed was a new leader of the Government acceptable to both Senate and Chamber. The Republicans declared for a cabinet in conformity with the majority in the Chamber, which would get rid of the préfets and maires of the 1873–75 period. For the Marshal there was the problem of whether resistance could be made to the chamber. After studying various combinations with the two Presidents, Audriffet-Pasquier and Grévy, he came back to Dufaure, but Dufaure failed to secure support from either side. MacMahon now consulted Audren de Kerdrel, leader of the Moderate Right, and Broglie. They recommended Jules Simon, senator of the Republican Left, and detested by Gambetta. Both believed that the situation would become impossible and that the Left would eventually plunge the country into chaos from which the Right would profit. The Marshal did not like Simon. He thought, as many others did, that he was too fluent and not to be trusted. Nevertheless he agreed. On December 9 he gave his views to the cabinet. He made two conditions: first, that as responsible head of the armed forces, he would not submit to criticisms of senior officers by deputies; secondly, that the appointment of judges was for life, and no more than Dufaure would he sanction their removal. As a concession to the Left, he would offer the Interior to Simon, but further than that he would not go. Gambetta's doctrine of the omnipotence of the Chamber of deputies must be resisted. The trouble was that among the majority there were so few men who could construct a Conservative cabinet. Duclerc, whom he liked, but who had been suggested by Freycinet, prompted by Gambetta, he would not have. He was too closely linked with Gambetta, and the inclusion of two members of the Republican Union was the term of Gambetta's support.[8a] 'Does M. Gambetta believe himself in a position to dictate a cabinet to me?' Léon Say was a paler and less authoritative Dufaure. Only a Dufaure-Simon combination could win the support of both Senate and Chamber. If this failed, he would have to appeal to the country; in other words, dissolve the Chamber.

Simon had neither more nor less ambition than other *ministrables*. He had let it be known that, if he became the leader of the Government, he would not interfere with the Army. As he intended, the words were conveyed to MacMahon. On December 10, he was called on by Audren de Kerdrel and offered the Interior under Dufaure. The Dufaure-Simon conversations came to nothing; Simon said that his substitution for Marcère was not enough, while Dufaure would not accept the implied condemnation of the judiciary: he resigned for good. So, much against his will, MacMahon accepted Simon as the president of the Council, provided that both Decazes and General Berthaut (Cissey's successor) were retained. 'I entered a cabinet I had not formed', relates Simon, 'but of which I had taken the presidency.'[9] The only other change was the replacement of Dufaure by Martel of the Left Centre. In his declaration to Parliament, Simon said he was profoundly republican and profoundly conservative: spiteful hearers alleged that to the Chamber he emphasised the first epithet, the second to the Senate. For the moment, he satisfied the Left by various minor activities: in January, eight préfets and fifty-one sous-préfets were removed, though not the préfet of Morbihan, for whom de Kerdrel had spoken when he brought MacMahon's invitation. Simon was an honest man, who paid his debts.

While the consultations over Dufaure's successor had been going on, the Senate, examining the Public Worship budget, had replaced the credits which the Chamber had suppressed. When the finance bill returned to the Chamber, Gambetta attacked the Senate amendments on the ground that the Upper House had no competence in the matter, claiming that Article 8 of the Law of February 25, 1875 gave the Chamber priority and that to replace a credit was an act of priority. Simon resisted Gambetta's motion and after a hot debate the cabinet's view was accepted. It was the first struggle between the Senate and Chamber; it was the second between Gambetta and Simon, and again Simon had won. 'The trial of the big debate of December has left him [Gambetta] no illusions.... He was acclaimed; but he was not followed. The success of his speech, as brilliant as deserved, did not give him a hold on the majority.'[10]

Simon, indeed, showed considerable dexterity and tact. In his own style, as an orator, he was Gambetta's peer. Mealy-mouthed he might be called, but he was infinitely persuasive. Not for him the thunderous summons to action, but honied reasoning. He had taken the diplomatic step of meeting the Republican committees of the Chamber and assuring them that, as long as he was not absolute master of the Government, he could promise no miracles, but with the support of the Chamber he would show his strength.

His trials began in February. Two newspapers, one of the Extreme Left, one Bonapartist, *Le Pays*, owned and edited by Paul de Cassagnac, deputy for Gers, were prosecuted, and Simon was faced by a coalition of both wings on behalf of freedom of the press. Simultaneously, Thiers in conjunction with Gambetta began hatching a scheme to remove Decazes, into which Gambetta's friend Raoul-Duval was brought. Now Decazes had been forced on Simon by MacMahon as a condition of his presidency of the Council. Simon did not want to lose Decazes, but he was being undermined by his own supporters. Thus, since MacMahon had accepted Simon in the belief that he alone could reconcile Republicans and Conservatives, his position was shaken, though he still appeared the only possible minister. Furthermore, he was overworked: he had no under-secretary and his son was his *chef de cabinet*.[11] By mid-April, he was worn out and his nerves were on edge. He began to complain of the Chamber: it was ungovernable, and to the cabinet, in front of MacMahon, he exclaimed: 'I see quite well that there must be a dissolution.'[12] *

Beyond these difficulties, he was disturbed by the reopening of the Roman question. In January, Pius IX publicly asked the faithful to protect him against the new anti-clerical measures of the Italian government. The Pope's appeals were taken up and publicised by the Bishop of Nevers, an ardent Legitimist. Highly indignant, the Republicans asked that this trouble-making official should be reprimanded. Simon blamed the bishop in his reply, but the storm was not wholly allayed. On May 3 — the Chambers had been prorogued over Easter — the Republicans interpellated on ultramontane activities which disturbed the country. Simon replied that on the whole the French episcopate was discreet, that he would use all the powers at his disposal to maintain order, and anyhow it was false or at least exaggerated to pretend that the Pope was a prisoner in the Vatican. On the following day, Gambetta riposted with one of the major political speeches of his career, offensive to all Catholics in asserting that no Catholic (because of his

---

* Daudet, 156 fn. who adds that MacMahon, telling the story, added: 'Devil take me if I let him', which may well mean that at least Simon should not, in the common phrase, 'preside over the elections', and that the formation of a government of the Right and a subsequent dissolution had already been thought out.

double allegiance) could be a patriot, and ending on the phrase: 'Clericalism! that is the enemy!'* Amidst a hurricane of applause from the Left, through a forest of hands stretched out to catch his, he returned to his seat to await the consequences. Was this to be the end of Simon? The sitting was suspended while the Republican leaders consulted, perceiving that they themselves might fall into a net. The fall of Simon could only open the way for Gambetta or a dissolution. A resolution drafted by Gambetta requested the ministry to repress clerical manifestations, but it contained no sentence of confidence in the Government. Simon protested, but was overborne by his closest supporters. But on the resumption of the sitting, a Left-wing deputy, Bernard Lavergne brought up an article which had appeared the previous day in *La Défense Sociale et Religieuse* of the bishop of Orleans, Monsignor Dupanloup. It stated that the Marshal had insisted on action by the Prime Minister in defence of the Catholics against the anti-clerical press. It also contained a threat that if he failed to act, means would be found to coerce him. Simon replied that the article lied and tore the paper into shreds. But the resolution, unamended and with all its distrust of the Government, was passed by 304 to 113. 'The Government', wrote Cassagnac, 'did not accept the motion; it swallowed it.' 'Now,' said Simon to Martel, 'we have only to look for the right way out.'[13]

To the Chamber, the vote looked like Gambetta's triumph; his enemy had been challenged and contemptuously disarmed. Was the road to power open? When the excitement had died down, the Left Centre and the Left would look on their work with misgiving. Mac-Mahon was naturally indignant at the insults to the Army, unanswered by Simon, and distressed by the anti-clericalism. Broglie once more counselled delay; a fight on the religious question would only harm the Church. This advice he repeated to the senators of the Right. The battle of clericalism and anti-clericalism would be a bad choice of ground.

---

* '*Ce qu'a dit mon ami Peyrat: "Le cléricalisme! Voilà l'ennemi."* ' Gambetta's friend Peyrat had in fact written nothing of the kind. In anticipation of the election of 1863 some anti-imperialist papers had mooted the possibility of an alliance of the Republicans with the Legitimists and Ultramontants. Peyrat, then editor of the *Avenir National*, a neo-jacobin, contested such a policy in a letter to the *Temps*, at that date run by Nefftzer, printed on April 9, 1863. 'It is a long time since you first argued against the Legitimists and Clericals: do you find them any more liberal than ten years ago? . . . Believe me, they are always the same, loving what we hate, detesting what we like. In short, in one sentence: — there is the enemy!' This has nothing to do with clericalism. Peyrat is warning the Republicans against an opportunist manoeuvre for the elections. The noun '*cléricalisme*' had not yet been coined.

'There is only one instrument of social safety today; the Marshal and the Senate: do not blunt it in a lost cause.'[14]

During the next ten days, two bills were discussed in the Chamber. The first on the publication of business in the municipal councils was discussed for a week. Simon scarcely appeared. The second, brought forward on May 14, was an amendment to the press law of December 29, 1875, with the intention of abrogating an article which had withdrawn certain misdemeanours, such as insults to foreign sovereigns, from the jury. The Marshal had required Simon to oppose, and Simon, struggling for his existence, had proposed that instead of dealing with a minor amendment, the whole press law should be revised. The Republicans, having shown that they could carry their point against the ministry, suddenly hesitated; they knew it was life or death for Simon. Discreetly, Simon made patent his situation, and Gambetta, perhaps unsure of the consequences, recommended a reference back to the committee, to give a night to think it over. The Chamber, losing its head, carried the original motion. This was May 15.

On the next morning, Marshal MacMahon rose early, summoned his orderly officer and dictated to him a letter to the President of the Council, which when signed was at once despatched to the Ministry of the Interior in the Place Beauvau. In it, MacMahon said that on reading the official report of the debate, he had observed that neither Simon nor Martel, Minister of Justice, had developed any serious arguments against the abrogation of the article of the press law, which was less than two years old, and which Simon himself had used, and this in spite of the cabinet's decision to oppose the bill. Equally, he had not opposed certain clauses of the bill on the municipal councils, the danger of which both Simon and he had agreed on. Would he explain? While Simon was responsible to the Chamber, he MacMahon was responsible to the nation.

It seems that MacMahon had not fully appreciated what would be the impact of his letter on the recipient; but the Marshal's staff were quick to see the advantage that could be taken of it. They attempted to recover it with the intention of replacing it with a smoother communication. They were too late. Simon had read the letter and saw that this could enable him to escape with some dignity from a situation which had become increasingly disagreeable. He therefore wrote out a letter of resignation[15] and went with it to the Elysée Palace. He saw the President and handed him his letter which, be it noted, insisted that MacMahon's letter 'imposes on me the duty of giving you my resignation'. In a brief colloquy, MacMahon said: 'I am a man of the Right; we cannot march in step. Better I should be overthrown than that I should remain under the orders of M. Gambetta.'

MacMahon's letter had neither dismissed Simon, nor had required his resignation. Simon's explanation (that he was ill on the day of the debate on the municipal councils, while on the press law he had only partially agreed with the Marshal) was evasive. He had resigned without consulting his colleagues. He seems to have ignored the joint responsibility of the cabinet. In his letter he wrote that as a 'citizen', not as a minister, he hoped he would be succeeded by men belonging, like himself, to the Republican party. On leaving MacMahon, Simon consulted Thiers, who told him he thought his resignation silly.

The news of the interview was spread by Simon himself, at the public funeral of Ernest Picard. The cabinet met at noon and appears to have accepted Simon's action as involving them all.* Some Republicans wanted a public demonstration and defiance. Simon put the suggestion aside. 'I left the Marshal face to face with the Constitution he had sworn to respect. I left him face to face with Parliament, face to face with the country.'[16] The news spread slowly; only on the following day was it known in the country. Gambetta proposed a full meeting of the Left during the evening, but the Left Centre refused. Nevertheless, his and Ferry's group voted a resolution to the effect that the confidence of the majority would be given only to a cabinet enjoying full liberty of action, determined to govern according to Republican principles 'which alone can guarantee order and property within and peace without'.

In the meantime on May 16, the Marshal who at this juncture had intended nothing more than a reconstitution of a Left Centre government with a leaven of Right Centre, had consulted the President of the Senate, Audriffet-Pasquier, and Decazes. The two dukes seem to have advised moderation. MacMahon invited Dufaure, but Dufaure, pleading ill-health, said that in the circumstances he could be of no use. On the next day, MacMahon wrote a letter to Decazes, inviting him to remain at the Foreign Office (the letter was published in the *Official Journal* on May 18), but it began with the rash sentence: 'Circumstances have not allowed me to retain the last cabinet of which you were a member', a sentence which lent colour to the charge that Simon had been dismissed.

* There is a conflict of evidence as to the cabinet's actions. According to Michel's life of Léon Say (303), Say heard 'from someone at Picard's funeral that the Marshal had broken with Simon, whereupon Say went to the Elysée Palace and gave his resignation to MacMahon, who expressed his regret at his separation from this colleague'.

(iv)

Having failed with Dufaure, MacMahon had an urgent summons sent to Fourtou who was in the country,[17] and during the afternoon brought together a cabinet to be led by Broglie, with Decazes, Fourtou, Paris of the Right Centre, de Meaux alone of the Moderates, and the Bonapartists, Brunet and Caillaux, with Baron Reille as under-secretary to the Interior.

Almost simultaneously, in the Chamber, a resolution moved by the Republican Left in the same terms as those voted on the previous night was carried by the whole body of Republicans. In speaking to the motion, Gambetta, while making no accusation against MacMahon, insinuated that his advisers were planning war to recover the Patrimony of St Peter for the Pope. 'Dissolution may be the preface to war.' It was a good theme for electioneering.

Broglie had not been responsible for the Marshal's action. He would not, however, desert the President he had created, but — 'who would have thought it of the Marshal? Well, it's no use crying. We've been thrown into the water. We've got to swim.'[18] To de Meaux on this evening as they walked through the Champs Elysées, he said, scrutinising the elegant strollers: 'These people look as if they were made for a coup-d'état much more than for the effort we are going to ask them to make.'[19]

On May 18, in the Chamber, after ten minutes of cries and counter-cries, Fourtou read a message from the President explaining that neither Dufaure nor Simon had been able to secure a reliable majority in the Chamber in defence of Conservative principles and that he would not lend himself to the 'Radical modifications of all our great administrative, judicial, financial and military institutions'. Until 1880, he, MacMahon, alone could propose changes: 'I meditate nothing of this character.' He therefore proposed to prorogue the Chamber under Article 2 of the Law of July 16, 1875,* and on the resumption of the session to have the budget for 1878 brought forward. Gambetta tried to speak, but the President of the Chamber, Grévy, refused to let him. After a stormy scene, the Chamber adjourned. A similar though less violent scene took place in the Senate, where the message was read by Broglie.

Fourtou had at once set to work at the Interior. On May 19, sixty-

* 'The President can adjourn the Chambers. Nevertheless, the adjournment cannot exceed the period of a month. . . .'

two of eighty-six préfets had either resigned, been dismissed or put 'at disposal'. In the next fortnight, an almost clean sweep was made of the sous-préfets and secrétaires-généraux. Their places were taken by vintage préfets of the Empire, among them Doncières, who had been responsible for Gambetta's defeat at Avignon, and Delorme who came over to the Right with a sprinkling of Royalists. A few remained, including the préfets of the Seine and Police, Ferdinand-Duval and Voisin.

On June 16, Broglie read to the Senate a presidential message claiming that the Republican manifestos contested his constitutional powers, that no ministry could live in the Chamber without submitting to the Radicals, and that in the disturbed situation, he could only ask the Senate, after certain urgent laws had been voted, to ratify a dissolution. Simultaneously in the Chamber, Fourtou gave the deputies the gist of the Marshal's message. Various bills were tabled amid interruptions. An interpellation on the composition of the cabinet was put forward by Bethmont. Fourtou replied with a fighting speech: 'We are the France of 1789 arrayed against the France of 1793. We have not your confidence, nor have you ours.' He went on to claim that the ministry was descended from that Assembly of 1871, which might be said to be the bringer of peace to the people and of liberty to the country. This called forth a protest from Gailly, deputy for Mézières, who pointed to Thiers and shouted: 'There he sits, there is the liberator' amid frantic cheering.

Gambetta could scarcely be silent. Once more he repelled the accusation that the Republic had approved the Commune, and ended: 'I say that we, the three hundred and sixty-three who depart, will return four hundred.' Ferry, interrupted at almost every sentence, earned Grévy's rebuke for questioning the action of the President. For three days 'the sons of Belial had a glorious time' of mutual invective, until on June 19 the majority voted no confidence in the ministry by 363 to 158; only five private members, three of them Bonapartists, abstained. On the next day, the Senate had a similar bout over the motion for dissolution. Simon made a long and somewhat disingenuous speech which avoided the main issues. Alone worthy of note was Laboulaye, imprecating the salon politicians who had placed the Marshal between 'humiliation and abdication'. The motion for dissolution was carried by 149 to 130 on June 22. Three days later, the Chamber, having refused to vote the direct taxes, in order to prevent the cabinet from delaying the elections,* was dissolved.

* The refusal to vote the direct taxes had a technical significance for the elections. Local revenue was created by adding the required number of centimes to the taxpayer's assess-

(v)

The business of Broglie and Fourtou was to prepare the ground and to concentrate the strength of the Right. It was difficult. According to de Meaux, the leaders of the Right Centre — he can only mean Audriffet-Pasquier, Decazes and perhaps Bocher and Batbie — still bore Broglie a grudge for the elimination of Aumale as President. Also, they feared that the profiteers of strong action would be the Bonapartists. Thus they came in reluctantly, chiefly because the rank and file of the group followed the ministry. For the Bonapartists the case was different. The appropriate conditions for the revival of Bonapartism, chaos and disintegrating parties, were absent. Strategically, the Bonapartist senators ought to have voted against dissolution and by defeating the motion, have created a deadlock. Thiers had hoped they would do so, but the Empress Eugénie and the wiseacres at Chislehurst forbade it. The Moderate Right, despite the disappointment of having only one member in the cabinet, rallied to the duke, while the Legitimists, after attempting to bargain, also came in, but as Clericals rather than Monarchists. Nevertheless, the cracks remained. The Legitimists disdained even to vote for Bonapartists. 'You ask us to procure the election of M. Rouher's candidates? Never!'[20]

Neither Broglie nor Fourtou were the men to dominate the electoral stage. Of Broglie, Saint-Valry had written: 'he is too well-bred — in the sense that a whole vulgar and hard side of life has remained to all intents unknown to him'.[21] For twelve years during the Empire, the Broglie family had suffered under Janvier de la Motte, the busy, noisy and unscrupulous préfet of Eure, the Broglies' own department. The duke now saw uses for Janvier and believed that with a Janvier in every préfecture he would be master of the situation: but what he could not do was to allow these vulgarians a free hand. He must, a Broglie could not but, remain within the expandable but still definite boundaries of legality. The old imperial hands found themselves hampered. Janvier

ment for direct taxes, to cover whatever sum was needed. The conseillers-généraux, who allotted the amounts between the cantons, met by law on the first Monday after August 15. Without the tax schedules, they would be unable to make the assessments. The Opposition thought that by holding up the vote, they could force the Government to bring the date of the elections forward, in fact hold them almost at once, and thus prevent the changes in the administrative personnel, of which they had seen the beginnings during May. Curiously enough, after the elections, the ministers thought that they had made a tactical error in postponing the election dates, and that they would have done better to have appealed to the country in May.

himself, consulted, replied: 'M. le duc, I have invariably observed during my long career that when you want a girl, nine times out of ten if you go at it squarely, you won't be snubbed: but, if you lift up her skirt to see what's underneath, she'll call the police. That's what I think of your policy.'²² Poor Broglie, he was no Strafford. Since his hope was to induce the electorate to form up behind the Marshal and the Law, he could scarcely lend himself to a policy of 'Thorough'. So he remained within the letter of the law, using only such means as the law winked at. The date for the election was postponed to the last possible hour under the constitution. Journals were suppressed or suspended. Republican posters were torn down or not licensed by the authorities. Drink shops, those centres of intrigue, were closed: one préfet made himself a place in history by shutting four hundred in his department in one day. Hostile maires and justices were relieved of office, while factious officials, schoolteachers and such, were summoned to their ministries in Paris and left there to kick their heels during the last days of the campaign. Each minister warned his subordinates not to mix in politics, and forbade them to work for parties hostile to those to whom they were responsible. The Church was recommended to silence, advice it did not follow. The Bonapartists complained that the Government had no spine: if they, the Bonapartists, had been in charge of operations, they would have proclaimed a state of siege, adjourned the elections *sine die* and remodelled the country. Finally the unhappy, tongue-tied Marshal was sent on a tour: Bourges, Tours, Périgueux and other cities saw him. He was greeted by the Church, but the city fathers grudged him the funds for a joyous entry. Hating the whole thing, he gallantly went round, and Republican journalists followed him with jeers and turned his simple remarks against him. Such were, in the phrase of Monsignor Pie, the pugnacious Bishop of Poitiers, the 'inconsequences of liberalism'. 'We do not pride ourself on being a politician: but we know enough of politics to be able to say that a *coup d'état* is not made against anyone or anything, but for something incarnated in somebody.'

The Republicans had two great advantages: they were in their familiar role of opposition — it is far easier to oppose; opposition carries no responsibility — and they were, for almost the last time, united. Moreover, they had stacked the cards; through Simon they had produced the myth of dismissal and the terror of war: the transfer of an infantry regiment from Wissembourg to Metz, and the despatch of a cavalry brigade into Alsace were spiritedly worked up. They had a figure-head, the Liberator, Thiers. He had in fact been useful, for his hatred of MacMahon made him keep the Left Centre, in June wavering towards the Right Centre, firmly Republican. They had an orator, bold and unscrupulous, Gambetta. They had, best of all, funds. Vincent Dubochet, who had carried out the amalgamation of the Paris gas-companies in 1847 and remained chairman, who was on the boards of the Est Railway and the Comptoir d'Escompte, connected through Arnaud de l'Ariège with the Republicans, became their treasurer, putting his mansion in the rue de Surène at their disposal. Here, sur-rounded by flunkies, Gambetta received deputations from the workers of Belleville and Menilmontant. The Republicans had an organisation of committees in each canton, the committees originally created in the autumn of 1873, drawn from Jean Macé's Ligue de l'Enseignement and the masonic lodges. In the shadow stood another powerful ally, Bismarck.

On May 9 the Emperor William had inspected the garrison of Metz. MacMahon and Decazes had sent Gontaut-Biron, who was in Paris, to make a courtesy visit. William was fond of the French ambassador; the German Foreign Office was not. The Emperor was warned that the French would want to exploit his sympathy at this moment, which was just after Disraeli had refused to sign the Berlin Memorandum on the Russo-Turkish conflict over Bulgaria, to Russia a hostile move. The Emperor appears to have told Gontaut something to the effect that he desired to keep England neutral. He may also have said that he did not feel any sympathy for the Republic.* Gontaut-Biron's report seems to have encouraged MacMahon. On the other hand, Bismarck, getting wind of what had passed, sent a stiff message to the Kaiser that unless foreign policy was left in his hands, he would resign. Although his messenger, Bülow, was snubbed, Bismarck circularised the German embassies with a despatch denying rumours of the Emperor's remarks. The last thing Bismarck wanted was a clerical French government; the Kulturkampf was not going well. Thus Gambetta's 'Dissolution the preface to war' was not implausible: and seizing on the phrase, Bis-marck told his subordinates to see the German press rubbed in the moral to the French elector: 'if he casts his vote for the cabinet in office, he votes for war.'[23]

During the summer, the excitement, or at least that of the politicians,

---

* One French newspaper reported that the Emperor had said: 'It is impossible to main-tain diplomatic relations with a revolutionary government like Simon's.' (Halévy, *République des Ducs*, 307.) In August, he told MacMahon's orderly officer, Gen. le Marquis d'Abzac, that he approved of the action of May 16: 'We have only one enemy, Radicalism. We have a mutual interest in fighting it.' (*First DDF* II, No. 198.)

increased. At Lille on August 15 Gambetta stated the issue clearly: 'When France has made her sovereign voice heard, one must either submit or resign' (*soumettre ou démettre*). Broglie and Fourtou decided to prosecute not only the bold speaker, but also those papers which had printed the speech, for attacks on the President and the cabinet. Gambetta was sentenced to three months' imprisonment and a fine of 2000 francs. He at once appealed and remained at liberty. His appeal rejected, he appealed to a higher court.

The crowning stroke for the Republicans came on September 3 when Thiers suddenly died. The Government offered a State funeral, but Madame Thiers refused any courtesy from Broglie's hands. Thiers was not loved in Paris, with good reason; yet he symbolised the Republic and twenty thousand followed the coffin to Père Lachaise, with Gambetta bare-headed in the front rank of the procession.

If no longer active, Thiers had been the figure-head of the Republicans. It was he who should succeed MacMahon. There was now no leader, and although Broglie had not yet published the dates, the elections were approaching. Thiers had been respectable and respected; foreign offices had valued him. Gambetta? Gambetta was looked on as the stoker of revolution. Gambetta's tail? Would not conservative Republicans shrink? The group leaders invited Dufaure, who refused. After that, they could think of no one better than Jules Grévy, President of the Chamber, known to bear no good will to the Tribune. For the party's sake, Gambetta once more accepted the decision.

On September 19, an official proclamation drafted by Fourtou was posted up in every village in the country on behalf of MacMahon. In every line, it showed where he stood. 'The Chamber of Deputies, daily moving further and further from the paths of moderate men, and more and more dominated by the open leaders of Radicalism, had come to ignore the share of authority vested in me, and which I could not allow to be weakened without compromising the honour of my name before you and before history.' Even the moderate press was roused to harsh words. On September 22, a decree gave the election dates as October 14 and 28. On October 4, Gambetta, in response to a letter from the Republicans of Belleville, repeated his challenge to the President to submit or resign. Again prosecuted, he was given three months and fined another four thousand francs.*

At the headquarters of the Right, Fourtou confidently claimed that they would not only hold their 158 seats, but win another 112, which

* Cf. Appendix XII.

would give a narrow majority. 'You are a bold gambler', said Broglie uneasily: then, 'Though the surface is ruffled, France is not shaken to the depths. The electors . . . seem to be afraid. What of? What are they hiding from? The Radicals? Or us? The quietness of the country frightens me. I fear the inertia of decent people.' Brunet, the Bonapartist minister, said to his son: 'The Conservatives are asleep, indifferent or snatching at an immediate satisfaction of their unrealisable demands; they are preparing our defeat, and when we have failed, they will not forgive us.'[24] On the night of October 14, as the telegrams came in the cabinet knew they had lost: only forty seats had been won, and at best they could count on no more than another ten.

The quietness that disturbed Broglie had concealed much. Over 80% of the electorate went to the polls; in Aube, the fief of Casimir-Périer, over 90%. So heavy a poll would not occur again for more than half a century. Many seats were won by narrow majorities. The calculations of neither Fourtou nor Gambetta were fulfilled. The Republicans lost forty-three seats; they came back not 400, not even 363, but 320: yet they still had a large majority. In the overall first poll, their lead was 700,000 in a vote of over eight millions. It was not wholly reassuring. But, for the Right, the result was disastrous. The cabinet discussed with MacMahon whether they should bring the Senate into action. 'If the Senate refuses?' asked Decazes. 'I shall stay,' replied the President. Fourtou, exhausted by his five months' toil and his disappointment, suggested to Broglie a military *coup d'état*. 'Not I,' said Broglie. 'Then,' said Fourtou, 'let us go.' Broglie rejected this weakness. 'We shall be attacked in the Chamber; we must be there to answer.' The pride and loyalty of the Broglies refused to retreat. Pouyer-Quertier had not approved of the Sixteenth of May. In spite of pressure during the week before the opening of Parliament, he held to his view that no ministry could be formed until Broglie had defended his actions.[25]

Parliament re-opened on November 7. The Republicans, fearing a *coup d'état*, had formed a committee of eighteen drawn from all four groups to meet the danger. In the Chamber, the same Bureau was elected as existed on May 16, in order to demonstrate the continuity. On November 12, Grévy's brother Albert tabled a motion to appoint a committee of enquiry into the actions of the ministry since May 16. The debate led to the inevitable clash between the leaders, Fourtou, Ferry, Broglie and Gambetta. Their speeches were not arguments for the deputies, but addresses to the outside world. Broglie accepted full responsibility, covering MacMahon's blunders; his most telling point was that the election had been won by the Left's raising of the bogey of war, 'the greatest humiliation France has yet endured. . . . Was it not in the agora at Athens that was summoned up the ghost of Philip of Macedon? And in the Polish diet that one looked over one's shoulder before voting, to see what the Empress Catherine's ambassadors were thinking and wanting?' Gambetta ignored the charge and concentrated on the imperialist methods employed, methods Broglie himself had denounced before 1870. The result was foregone. The Right was overwhelmed (November 15). Earlier, on the 10th, Broglie had tried to secure a vote of confidence from the Senate. In the name of the Right Centre, Audriffet-Pasquier refused. On the 19th, again in the Senate, Audren de Kerdrel raised the matter of the Chamber enquiry. Broglie insisted that, since the enquiry was political and not judicial, no one need appear to answer. Dufaure pointed out that the rights of parliamentary committees were not covered by the Constitutional Laws, and that to debate was not only futile, but dangerous. A colourless resolution reaffirming the separation of the powers was adopted. The vote had only been obtained on condition that the cabinet should resign, and thus covered, it now retired.

(vi)

Did Broglie remain the Marshal's counsellor, or did he withdraw? The subsequent actions of MacMahon indicate more passionate advisers, Monsignor Dupanloup, Cardinal Bonnechose. Another appeal to Pouyer-Quertier was met by a refusal on the 18th. On the 23rd MacMahon appointed a cabinet headed by General de Rochebouët, supported by officials, including one of the most active préfets, Welche, at the Interior. For the moment it looked as if the President was about to try a *coup de force*. The Republican committee of vigilance met. Exactly what passed is not known, save that Gambetta raised the question of the forfeiture of the Presidency, and of meeting force by force. Some of the Left Centre seem to have flinched, and perhaps resigned. The question was carried to Grévy as leader of the Republicans, and Grévy coldly answered that MacMahon was within his rights and that he, Grévy, would in no case associate himself with a civil war. The proposals were dropped. Although they had no serious belief in a military coup, the Republicans issued warnings, rather to intimidate

MacMahon than to rouse their followers.[26] On November 24, when the new cabinet appeared, the Chamber refused to hold communication with it. Rochebouët and his aides vanished.

MacMahon was at a loss. Should he fight, submit or resign? All advice was conflicting. The leaders of the two Centres recommended submission and the formation of a Left Centre cabinet. On December 6 Dufaure was invited and consented to constitute a ministry, but faced on the following day by MacMahon's insistence on appointing the Foreign, War and Marine ministers himself, gave up. Gambetta, through Freycinet, had already warned Dufaure that the appointment of all ministers must be in his (Dufaure's) hands if he was to secure the support of the Republicans. For some days MacMahon listened to the forceful group, but they could produce no plan. When they gave up, he said he would go with them. On this the ministers told him that he would be abandoning to the furies of the Left not only themselves but the officials who had supported his policy. In his manifesto of September, now regarded as impolitic, he had written that he would stay to protect the faithful officials who in an hour of difficulty had not let themselves be intimidated by threats. Pouyer-Quertier was again suggested — by Dupanloup it is said — but the astute Norman would not take the risk; he advised capitulation, particularly as the year was running out, the budget not yet voted and after December 31 no direct taxes could be collected. The Marshal's advisers had now reached the end of their expedients, and he could see that resistance was useless. He submitted; he would do his duty. 'I love my country well enough to sacrifice, I do not say my life — that has been done — but my last shred of honour.' Once more he summoned Pasquier, who once more commended Dufaure. Was this the advice of the Orleans princes? At least half the Right in the Chamber were Bonapartists. Dufaure was summoned and on the 13th brought the list of his civil ministers. The rugged Dufaure, stiff in his principles, had in fact much sympathy for the sore-beset MacMahon. While he stood firmly on his right to choose his colleagues, he put forward names which the Marshal could accept, and after a brief struggle with his feelings, MacMahon agreed. With one exception, the cabinet was drawn from the Left Centre. The exception was de Freycinet, senator of the Republican Left, Gambetta's right-hand man at Tours in 1870, put to the Ministry of Public Works — he had been an official of the Ponts-et-Chaussées — selected as the link with the Extreme Left. Simon was omitted, perhaps to please Gambetta. It was an error. Simon had excellent talents. Deprived of the opportunity to employ them, he later went into opposition in the Senate, with troublesome consequences.

One further sacrifice was required of the President, a public surrender, and an assurance against another recourse to dissolution. It was drafted by Léon Say. Once more MacMahon made difficulties, but he was shown that, without a guarantee of the Chamber's survival, the cabinet could not get support. So, 'The exercise of the right of dissolution is no more than the method of final consultation with a judge from whom there is no appeal: it cannot be set up as a system of government. I conform to the country's answer. The Constitution of 1875 has founded a parliamentary Republic by establishing my non-responsibility, and the collective and individual responsibility of the ministers. Our duties and rights are thus respectively determined; the independence of the ministers is the condition of their new responsibility. These principles are those of my government.' Given under *force majeure*, the message recorded the last stage in the development of the Presidency from the active executive of 1871 to the quasi-cipher of 1887. As Daniel Halévy has written: 'The Constitution of 1875 is not as clear as all that. It grants the President certain powers the importance of which implies a certain responsibility. The December message expunges that responsibility. . . . By his signature, Marshal MacMahon consented to this for all his successors.'[27]

The exact sequence of events leading to the crisis of the Sixteenth of May will probably never be established, nor will it be known what inspired the President to write his letter that morning. Hanotaux printed a story that on the previous night Broglie was brought from his bed to advise MacMahon. Hanotaux, contrary to his usual practice, gives no authority (Seignobos blandly repeats it, but his account of the crisis is thoroughly disingenuous). Judging from Broglie's conversations with Ernest Daudet and de Meaux, one can only say that the tale is without substance. Many years later, Paul Cambon, who though young was a trusted friend of Ferry, Léon Say, Jules Simon and the young Casimir-Périer, in a letter to his son said that those who inspired the Marshal to act where La Maréchale de MacMahon, a Harcourt, who hated the Republicans, Dupanloup, the Vicomte Emmanuel d'Harcourt, the Marshal's private secretary and a scatter-brain, and Durangel, a senior official in the Ministry of the Interior. It was certainly current property that the Maréchale and her relations had made the President's life miserable with their criticisms when he renounced his right to appoint the Life Senators.

It may be that historians have accepted too readily the view that MacMahon disliked politics and was stupid to the point of illiteracy. It is true he was limited and that he could not foresee the distant consequences of his actions. But by May 1877, he had been in office four years; he had learned something from Broglie, and perhaps Dufaure; he had learned his duties, and if he was not very clear on the rights of the President, those rights were highly debatable. Moreover, he had personality: the man who dictated the address to the Cabinet of December 9, 1876, was no fool; nor was the writer of the letter of May 16 to Jules Simon.

The situation of an uncomposable conflict between President and Chamber had long been foreseen, though how far plans had been made is not known. It may be that Simon's exclamation in the cabinet that a dissolution of the Chamber was the only method of dealing with that body, and MacMahon's resolve not to grant a dissolution to Simon at the Ministry of the Interior, precipitated the action of May 16. It seems clear that the articles in Dupanloup's paper after Gambetta's anticlerical speech indicated to observers (e.g. Saint-Valry) that something was in the wind. In short, the foreseen situation had appeared, and rather than let the occasion slip, MacMahon, without consultation, took action which had long been meditated. There is no reason to believe that anyone was consulted. The error lay, not in the letter to Simon, but in the subsequent actions: the failure above all to make it clear that Simon was not dismissed. Ernest Daudet[28] had no doubt that the action was spontaneous; neither had Broglie. There is no reason to differ from them.

(vii)

The Sixteenth of May crisis was more important than the mere question of what the actors did. For, out of the episode, some at least of the political misfortunes of the Third Republic came. The Sixteenth of May was not catastrophic, but what followed was harmful. The trouble lay in the incompatibility of the Law of November 20, 1873 and the Constitutional Law of February 25, 1875. The former appointed MacMahon President of the Republic for seven years, to November 1880. Otherwise it altered nothing. The President therefore accepts office under the same terms as Thiers, that is, under the Rivet law of August 31, 1871, which is an enlargement of the Resolution of February 17. Nothing in these two documents or in the Law of March

13, 1873, changed the fact that the President is the maker and executor of policy.

The Constitution of 1875 came into force on the day the two Chambers assembled, but nothing was said of the position of the President. The silence implies that he continues as before as the director of policy and that the cabinet is his cabinet. Under Article 3 of the law of February 25, 1875, he, as much as any deputy or senator, can initiate legislation. This passes so long as there is no conflict between the Council (with the President) and one of the Houses. But if either rejects a bill, what is the consequence? If procedure is governed by the law of February 25, 1875, then the whole cabinet is responsible under Article 6, and the cabinet should resign. But if the cabinet resigns what is the position of MacMahon, whose appointment runs until 1880? (Dufaure evaded the problem by saying that he alone need be replaced, though it cannot be decently pretended that a bill dealing with so political a matter as the prosecution of Communards is not a matter for the whole cabinet.) Where does he find his new cabinet? He cannot find one in the minority, and if he gets one from the majority, in what does it differ from the one that has resigned?

The dissolution was not unconstitutional. Article 5 of the Law of February 25, 1875 runs: 'The President of the Republic can, with the agreement (*avis conforme*) of the Senate dissolve the Chamber of Deputies before the legal expiration of its mandate.' Nothing is said of the circumstances in which this power may be exercised. In the debates of January and February 1875 the rapporteur, Ventavon, for the Commission of Thirty, stated dissolution to be 'an appeal in case of conflict between the President and the Chamber', that is to say, in a case such as that of May 1877. The only contestant of this proposition was the Republican Lenoel, who, while combatting the whole project, asserted that in a Republic dissolution should not be allowed, since a mandated delegate could not shed his mandate. All the other arguments turned on whether MacMahon's successors should be allowed this power. Bertauld's amendment (withdrawn but readopted by Depeyre) permitted the Marshal one dissolution, but denied it to his successors, the argument for the most part turning on the matter of the Senate's agreement. It was defeated. The Wallon text, which is incorporated in the Law of February 25, was carried, and since the Wallon constitution is impersonal, the rights of the President passed to MacMahon's successors. The Republicans did not like the clause, but they accepted it in return for the agreement to the Republic.

The right to dissolve remained, but was never again exercised. This was not due to the fact that the message of December 1877 blunted the weapon, but because the appropriate conditions for its exercise were never again present. The absence of a two-party system had already led to the point that no cabinet ever had control of the Chamber. Instead of the Chamber, it was the cabinet that dissolved. The only situation where the power to dissolve might be exercised was that of a deadlock between Senate and Chamber. When in later years that happened, either one or other, usually the Chamber, gave way and accepted the situation, which meant the resignation of the government, e.g. Léon Bourgeois in 1896 and Léon Blum in 1938.

The situation of the Sixteenth of May could have taken place only during the Septennate. After MacMahon's resignation, the President's rôle became subject to the constitutional laws of 1875. The message of December 1877 merely anticipated the future by fourteen months.

The final conclusion must be that while it was politically impossible for MacMahon to resign, it was constitutionally difficult for him to remain in office. Sensible men reviewing the situation coolly could have reached a compromise. But in the circumstances of 1876–77, no group leaders, even if not personally blinded by their political hopes, could so have flouted 'democracy' as not to give it a chance to make its 'sovereign voice' heard. Gambetta with his *soumettre ou démettre* put the question squarely if crudely. As can now be seen, MacMahon's mistake was to defy a dilemma. If he had given way, he could have saved the President's power to dissolve.

No doubt Dufaure, in saying that he alone need go, believed he was saving the situation. In fact, the long-term results of his action were much worse. For by ignoring cabinet responsibility in a political question, he was in fact destroying it. Within three years, the President (MacMahon's successor, Grévy) is seen to be ignoring the meaning of Dufaure's phrase and building cabinets out of the débris of their predecessors. In January 1879 Waddington took over four ministers from Dufaure, in December Freycinet five from Waddington, and in September 1880 Ferry recruited eight from Freycinet's team. Of the forty cabinets, from Dufaure's second to the election of May 1914, in no more than eleven was there a clean sweep.

The question of cabinet responsibility was suddenly raised again in 1913 by Franklin-Bouillon and Thalamas (Socialist-Radicals) and Violette (Independent Socialist). On March 18, Briand, who had become Prime Minister on Poincaré's elevation to the Presidency of the

Republic, resigned, having been defeated in the Senate on a bill for electoral reform passed by the Chamber. He was succeeded by Barthou, of whose twelve colleagues, five had been in Briand's ministry. The criticism was that there was neither unity nor homogeneity in the cabinet because (*a*) it was formed of elements of its defeated predecessors; (*b*) the cabinet could not possibly be in agreement on a number of matters in Barthou's declaration since one member wanted fiscal reform and another did not, one proportional representation, and another the current system. But Bonnard, the editor of the standard book on parliamentary rules of procedure, insists that the French have never followed English practice, and indeed, with a Chamber containing many groups, cabinet homogeneity could not be achieved, because a homogeneous cabinet which could only be drawn from a minority of deputies could scarcely survive more than a few days.[29] In fact, some questions were always 'reserved', and a single minister could not commit the cabinet. In the Combes cabinet of 1902–05, Rouvier and Pelletan disagreed on railway policy, and Pelletan spoke publicly against his colleague. Combes claimed that each was entitled to his view and that the cabinet represented the opinions of four parties.

Chapter Eight

The Republic of the Republicans

(i)

The year 1878, at least its first eight months, were superficially calm after the storms of the previous year. The Left decided to rally to the support of Dufaure. The important date lay a year ahead, January 5, 1879, when the first renewal of one-third of the Senate would take place. The Republicans recognised that, if they were to win the majority in the Upper House, the country must not be agitated: there must be no amnesty for Communards, no increase in taxation, no violent anti-clericalism; 'it would be rash', said Gambetta at Marseille, 'not to postpone some reforms up to the approaching moment when the country shall have given the Republican party the majority in the Senate. Up to that moment, I repeat, no imprudence, no dissidence, no mistakes.'[1] In earnest of this the proscribed International Workingmen's Association was refused authorisation to hold a congress in Paris. A number of delegates, nonetheless, slipped into the country, held a preliminary meeting and were swept up by the police. Among the thirty-four prisoners was a Nîmes journalist, who had fled abroad after the Commune, Jules Guesde. To the court, he claimed to represent an order separated from the rest of society, the Order of the Proletariat which was destined to supplant the others. No member of the court could have any sympathy for this ridiculous view: he was sentenced to six months imprisonment.

From December, apart from the passage of the budget for 1878, the major task was the invalidation by the Chamber of all Right deputies against whom some case of illegal influence, official, clerical or financial, could be made out. Seventy-one were expelled, the most massive execution the Third Republic was to carry out. At the consequent byes, only twelve of these seats were held. The Republican majority was now some 240, better than in 1876.*

*	Elected 14/28 Oct., 1877	Invalidated	Byes	Totals
Extreme Right	41	16	2	27
Right, inc. Constitutionals	59	24	3	38
Bonapartists	105 — 205	31 — 71	7 — 12	81 — 146

On January 8, 1878 Victor Emmanuel I died and was succeeded by his son, Umberto, on which Pius IX, himself at the edge of the grave, once more lifted up his voice against the spoliation of the Patrimony of St Peter. A month later, on February 7, he died. For the King, the French Republican leaders attended a solemn mass at the Madeleine. For Pius IX, the Chambers merely did not sit on the day of the funeral. Jules Ferry succumbed to the temptation to make a declaration of his anti-clerical principles. On February 20 the Conclave elected Joachimo Pecci, Archbishop of Perugia, a man of balanced judgment who, as Leo XIII, would bring about the composition of the Kulturkampf in a manner acceptable to Bismarck.

The great tranquilliser of 1878 was the Paris Exhibition. That of 1867, the terrible year of the shooting of Maximilian in Mexico, had attracted all Europe, Emperors, Kings, ministers. It had been all light and glitter, and a mile of cafés and restaurants in the grounds. In 1878 all ranks of society were determined that the Exhibition should outshine the imperial festival. Party differences were sunk, and the Republican director, Krantz, had agreed to work under the Government of the Sixteenth of May. There was one drop of poison. Foreign countries were displaying their wares, but Germany was absent. Then in December 1877 Gontaut-Biron, the innocent ambassador whom Bismarck distrusted and detested, was recalled and Saint-Vallier was sent in his place, Saint-Vallier, who through Manteuffel had been Thiers' private contact with Berlin. Bismarck made him welcome with all the charm the great junker could assume when he wished (the conversations, or rather the monologues, delivered to Saint-Vallier, and which were relayed to the Quai d'Orsay, display him in all his racy virtuosity), and relented. At the last hour, he decreed that German pictures and statuary should be sent to Paris. It was too late for the industrial exhibits, and the Chancellor earned the irritated comments of frustrated German business men.

The Exhibition opened on May 1, not yet dedicated to revolution, and it poured with rain. Nevertheless, the day was a success. Paris was

	Elected 14/28 Oct., 1877	Invalidated	Byes	Totals	
Left Centre	84	–	16	100	
Republican Left	141	–	19	160	
Republican Union	87	–	21	108	
Extreme Left	18 — 330	– — 0	3 — 59	21 — 389	
				Total	535

Two new seats were created for Guyane and Senegal.

gay with bunting, tricolor and light. The whole people took part, walking up and down the boulevards with flags and lanterns. The *Marseillaise*, by the permission of Marcère, Minister of the Interior, was played for the first time since May 1873. The Trocadero with its minarets and cupolas had been specially constructed. True, there was no Grand Duchess, no new music. But Sarah Bernhardt was at the Comédie Française: with Mounet-Sully, she was playing the masterpieces of Racine, Hugo and de Musset. On the other hand, the Salon rejected all Manet's pictures, and there was no Impressionist exhibition. The Impressionists had been attacked after May 16 by the Right press which accused them of producing Communard art, and associated them with Zola. To be just, Paris was ostentatious rather than discreet. Cheerful ostentation, however, was suited to one visitor, Albert Edward, Prince of Wales, who insisted — to the horror of good society — on lunching with Gambetta.

Gambetta was the lion of the Exhibition, the one Frenchman in the public eye of all Europe. But he had passed his zenith. Republican politicians were not in politics for their health. Gambetta had said publicly that the Republic was open to all sincere men. In February Freycinet had innocently repeated this at Nantes. At a party at Juliette Adam's house, he had been assailed by furious Republicans who had no intention of sharing the spoils of victory with late-comers.[2] There were, too, the *revanchards*, who began to find the leader growing lukewarm in his desire for the return match with Germany.[3] There were the Radicals who accused him of abandoning the Belleville programme: Clemenceau was shaking the dust from the standard of 1869.[4] Some of his old intimates were finding themselves pressed aside by newcomers. In September, at Romans in Dauphiné, he took up once more the anticlerical theme, 'the conflict fomented solely by the agents of ultramontanism. . . . Everywhere where the Jesuit spirit can slip in, the Clericals are infiltrating and aiming at domination: they are not the people to abandon a task.'[5] Education must be purged of these rebels; they must be penned within the law; the favours shown them must be withdrawn. The speech was a warning, and by Dufaure and the conservative Republicans it was not well received. Gambetta had to promise not to repeat his error.[6]

Another Congress had held the eye of Europe more fully than the spectacle at Paris. In June, to wind up the Russo-Turkish War, the representatives of the Great Powers met in Berlin and ratified the bargains they had already struck. In 1856 Prussia had been a humble guest at the Paris Congress. In 1878 it was the French Government's turn to be humble and to be the guest of the conqueror. The French representatives were spectators. France was gaining nothing, was impotent to snatch any spoils. French patriots had hoped that the Government would refuse the invitation. Not so Gambetta; he had already during 1877 received advances from Bismarck's unofficial agent in France, Henkel von Donnersmarck, and had responded. Now disabused of the possibility of recovering Alsace-Lorraine by force of arms, he perhaps believed that the provinces could be recovered by diplomacy. At least he seems to have thought that colonial offers might tempt Bismarck. How little he understood the Chancellor may be read in his letters. He had a long conversation with Waddington, though it does not seem that, as he boasted, he 'gave the chief French delegate his instructions'.[7] Waddington went to Berlin to see what he could secure: one condition of his presence was that there should be no discussion on Egypt, Syria or the Holy Places. He talked with Salisbury on topics of mutual interest. From this, he believed that he had obtained from the British a free hand in the Turkish vassal state of Tunisia, and that this had been confirmed by talks with both Beaconsfield and the Prince of Wales. The form of the future Tunisian government might be a protectorate, it might be annexation: at least it meant French occupation. In addition, Bismarck gave the project his benediction. On his return to Paris, Waddington at once told Harcourt, the ambassador in London, to secure formal confirmation from the British government.[8] To Harcourt, Salisbury was less decisive than Waddington had said he was, remarking that he would prefer not to see his reported conversation reproduced;[9] in fact he hesitated. He had already told Lord Lyons,[10] the ambassador in Paris, that he was prepared for the French to occupy Tunis, but to promise it publicly would be a little difficult, 'because we must avoid giving away other people's property without their consent, and also because it is no business of ours to pronounce beforehand on the considerations which Italy would probably advance.' Nonetheless, the French believed that the English would create no obstacle, and Roustan, the French consul-general in Tunis, was told[11] to prepare the way with discretion for an occupation in due time, while the ambassador to the Quirinal in Rome was ordered to make it clear to the Italian government that Italy should give up dreams of conquest.[12]

(ii)

The election for the renewal of one-third of the elected members of the Senate was held on January 5, 1879. The group of departments involved was those of Series B, those in order of initials from Haute-Garonne to Oise, with Constantine (Algeria) and Martinique. As chance would have it, these departments had returned in 1876 a heavier proportion of anti-Republicans than either of the other groups, above 40% of the elected senators of the Right. For them, the election was catastrophic. They had had the majority in twenty-nine departments: on the night of January 5, they held only six, Gers, Ille-et-Vilaine, Indre, Landes, Maine-et-Loire and Morbihan. They had occupied fifty-seven seats; now they had twenty. The Republicans had control in both Chambers, or so it appeared. The appearance was deceptive, for the new Republican senators were on the whole even less 'advanced' than the senators of 1876, and scarcely less hostile to the Extreme Left of the Chamber of Deputies than their predecessors of the Right. The Senate was Centre both in sentiment and principle.

Gambetta saw that this situation would check the Radical Extremists, but he did not yet perceive the dilemma in which he would be placed. For the moment, he may have thought that his colleagues would show the spirit he had once professed on their behalf, that they would not ask for places of profit in the administration. If he did, he had not only misread history, he had mistaken his men. Well before the Chambers met, delegates from the Left were accosting ministers, even threatening them, Coquelin the actor was among them — 'Gambetta's Talma', said a caustic critic. Dufaure, who had always striven to keep the services out of politics, rounded on the place-hunters, telling them he would remove the men aimed at only if proper compensation was given. But he had no illusion as to his power: members of the Republican Union and the Extreme Left told him that their support was only to be had if they wrote his programme for him. He drove them out. As in his earlier phase, he was torn between his regard for MacMahon, his sense of justice, and the demands of the Republicans. For the moment he stood his ground.

On the re-opening of Parliament on January 15, the approach of trouble was visible in the election of the dim Republican, Martel, to the Presidency of the Senate in the place of the Duc d'Audriffet-Pasquier. In the Chamber there were restlessness and muttering, though not open hostility: Gambetta had recommended calm until the ministry had declared its intentions. The declaration of policy was not to the taste of the Extremists. While it enumerated a large number of pardons and remissions for Communards, there was no hint of a general amnesty. It promised to remove anti-republican officials, but with the reservation that justice and respect were shown to the services. 'While we shall be severe, we shall continue to be just, and we would first be convinced of the fault before inflicting the penalty. . . . The country has approved of us, such as we are; nothing therefore is changed.' In the Senate, Dufaure was applauded; in the Chamber, Marcère hardly got a hearing. What did place-hungry deputies care for educational schemes, for equitable treatment of the religious Orders or for the protection of children employed in industry?

As a precursor of what was to follow, General Borel, the Minister of War, resigned, and General de Miribel, recognised as the best brain in the Army, was transferred from the head of the Staff. Gambetta had claimed the War Office for his client, General Farre. The Marshal had refused: Farre was too junior and too political. The post was offered to General Gresley, who told MacMahon that he would accept only on condition that all question of the removal of senior officers was reserved. 'This means war,' wrote Gambetta to his mistress;[13] 'they shall have it!' He was being incited by the Extreme Left to attack the cabinet, bring it down, and himself take Dufaure's place. He did not like their advice; he would be their prisoner, and the Left Centre would give him short shrift.

Rumours were already abroad that MacMahon was considering immediate resignation, and the leaders of the other groups were discussing his successor. Gambetta they would not have, both on the score of probable German hostility — they knew nothing of a proposed visit to Bismarck in the previous April — and on the score of the presidency itself; in Gambetta they did not see a non-responsible and inactive head of the State, content to preside at public ceremonies. Their man was the sober Grévy, very republican, but very moderate. Gambetta, between whom and Grévy no love was lost, appreciated the manoeuvre. He saw two possibilities: either to maintain MacMahon in power until the end of the Septennate in November 1880 or, if he resigned, the promotion of Dufaure. His supporters appear to have rebelled; at least an article warning Dufaure against procrastination appeared on January 20. Gambetta himself would not attack. On that day, the Left put up an elderly Republican of 1848 to question Dufaure on the details of his policy towards officials hostile to the régime; was he sure of the loyalty of his procureurs-généraux? Sénard proposed departmental commissions of senators and deputies to advise ministers. It was said of Dufaure that he was a watchdog who bit only members of the family. Like any sensible, courageous and responsible minister, he hit back. He rejected the proffered commissions; on the advice of such bodies, he would break no man who had served the state for twenty years. And looking forward, he prayed to Heaven that the critical moment of November 1880 would pass quietly and calmly. The Chamber was taken aback. For the moment, the group leaders did not see their way. The Right, knowing that with the help of the Extremists, the individualists and the hot-heads, they could defeat the Government, hung back; only worse would follow. Hesitating, the majority waited for a lead from one of the chiefs. Gambetta held his tongue; so did Ferry. Only the windbags intervened, Madier de Montjau ('When', asked Gambetta once, 'will this old harp cease vibrating?') and Floquet. Gambetta was still silent. 'It was this that saved the cabinet from a certain fall. The silence of the leader of the majority showed yet again that he did not desire power, and that in replacing the administration whose fate lay in his hands, only one, the Dufaure ministry without Dufaure, was possible.'[14] Floquet had asked for 'the pure and simple order of the day' which was not only less than a weak vote of confidence, but an insult. The sitting was suspended, and in the corridors the deputies wrangled over the terms of the motion. Dufaure insisted on a motion of confidence. On behalf of the Republican Left, Ferry bargained. It was not only the procureurs-généraux and the Ministry of Justice, but all the other ministries, which must be involved in the purge. Gambetta, looking to wider issues, required, it appears, the retirement of a number of Corps Commanders. Dufaure, examining the specific demands, yielded. A motion was patched up, stating that the Chamber, confident that 'the Government, henceforward in possession of its full liberty of action, would not [amended from "no longer"] hesitate to give to the Republican majority its legitimate satisfactions', a disingenuous translation of the war-cry, '*toutes les places et tout de suite*'. On the division, Floquet's motion was defeated and Ferry's carried by 208 to 116; neither the Right nor Gambetta voted. The verge of crisis had been reached. 'We are beaten; the ministry is beaten; the majority is split, the programme is at sixes and sevens, and I am pleased, for I didn't put a finger in the mess. The moment was not propitious for the decisive stroke.' So Gambetta that evening to Léonie Léon.

'The silence in which I wrapped myself, saved old Dufaure from foundering, him and his skiff; but he drank a good deal of salt water. . . . I am both satisfied and reassured. I have not crossed the line I set myself; shake the cabinet but not replace it, drive the Chamber and the Executive into a defile where they will argue hotly for several weeks, and out of this I shall be able to extract the best solution.'[15] In spite of their boldness, behind the words there seems to hang uncertainty.

The situation was not to be saved. MacMahon told Dufaure that the vote was not a vote of confidence, but a command: it would have been better for both himself, the President, and the cabinet to have defied the Chamber and fallen together instead of merely postponing the crisis. Small matters in the next days increased his irritation. Paul Andral, Vice-president of the Conseil d'Etat, one of his safest advisers, was forced into resignation. Ferdinand-Duval, the capable Préfet of Seine, who had survived all changes of government since May 24, 1873, had been driven to resignation because Marcère had not dared to support him against the Paris municipal council, which without authority had decreed the expulsion of the teaching members of the religious Orders from the schools. At the same time, the Préfet of Police, Gigot, was in trouble over scandals which had been publicised in Rochefort's *Lanterne*, while to add to the cabinet's embarrassment, the report of the committee on the activities of the ministries after the Sixteenth of May was about to be brought before the Chamber. MacMahon had come to the end of his patience. When, on January 25, a group of ministers headed by Léon Say began to bring him their lists of the victims, he reacted sharply. 'M. Léon Say is a minister who gets carried away; there is no need for it, or for the infliction of these executions,' he told Dufaure, who mildly replied that Say was only the first, and that every member of the cabinet would be appearing with a similar list. If the President refused to accept, the cabinet would have to resign and their successors would present the same lists. MacMahon gloomily surrendered, but on the third day, he first kicked against the dismissal of the lay director of Public Worship before signing the decree; then at the appearance of General Gresley, he who had said he would resist changes in the Corps Commanders, MacMahon turned obstinate: he would not strike good officers, his companions in arms. 'The Constitution entrusts me with the command of the Army, and I cannot permit its disorganisation. . . . What has Bourbaki done? And du Barail, one of our best cavalry generals, what have you against him? No more than you do I wish to see politics in the Army. . . .'* The ministers them-selves were unhappy; in their hearts they felt that MacMahon was right. Dufaure was perplexed; he said that the Marshal's resistance should have been made a fortnight earlier and that by accepting the Govern-ment's declaration, he had by implication approved the dismissals. It was now too late to remedy the situation; they could only insist on the Marshal's signing the decrees. On January 29, Dufaure tried to find a compromise, but MacMahon refused to budge and called a meeting of the cabinet for the following day.

The news of disagreement was already abroad and Gambetta was heard to say that MacMahon must resign and Dufaure take his place. The Republican senators met and Challemel-Lacour put forward Dufaure's name. Since he had been one of Dufaure's more active critics, the senators were well aware, even if Jules Simon had not maliciously rubbed it in, whence the proposal emanated; they forced him to with-draw. Grévy was their man. All the evening the ministers begged Dufaure to remain. He stubbornly refused: he would not be the pro-fiteer of a decision which MacMahon had taken through his action. Through Havas, he had had it published that he was not a candidate for the Presidency.

On January 30, the cabinet once more came to MacMahon, who, after enquiring if they had changed their minds, read them a letter of resignation. The news spread. The committees of the Republican groups met and decided to put forward Grévy's name. Gambetta, his combination torn in shreds, rallied, too late, to the candidature. Dufaure was not present. In the afternoon, the letter of resignation was read to both Houses. The National Assembly was at once summoned. Grévy was elected by an overwhelming majority of 593 to 107; the Right had put up General Chanzy, the Republican Governor-General of Algeria, without his knowledge. MacMahon at once came to shake his suc-cessor's hand before retiring into private life and absolute silence. Two days later, Dufaure tendered his resignation to the new President. Grévy coldly invited him to stay — he had no graces — but Dufaure declined. The new situation, he said, needed new men. Grévy called the Foreign Minister, Waddington. Gambetta, who had put himself at the disposition of the President, was not even consulted. A number of

* The Corps Commanders were appointed for three years, and could be re-appointed. All those who were to be retired were nearing the end of the second term. The question turned on whether, as Dufaure said, they were appointed 'at pleasure', or whether, as MacMahon asserted, they were appointed for the full term.

ambassadors, Harcourt in London, Le Flô in St Petersburg, sent in their resignations.

Gambetta quickly adjusted himself to the situation he had striven to avert. His hour he believed had not yet come.* He would withdraw to a position from which he could work from behind the scenes, the Presidency of the Chamber. On the evening of Grévy's election, he told Juliette Adam of his intention. She protested against his taking a subordinate place: moreover, he would earn the enmity of Brisson, who wanted the post himself. He angrily rejected her advice. 'You will see before long that I am not abdicating from my sovereign role. To end this argument I will add: I have had enough of truth.'[16] On January 31 he was elected. Among many of the older Republicans there was surprised dismay. What was the man about? 'No doubt,' said Bethmont, 'Grévy is keeping Gambetta back for better times.' 'Oh, Bethmont,' Duclerc rejoined; 'how can you be so simple? Keeping him back, yes, but for a worse situation.' 'What', wrote a commentator, 'will he do during the seven years, to keep himself ripe for the Presidency of the Republic? It is impossible. Gambetta is on the way to lose his influence and his raison d'être. Most of all, he will be the one to suffer.'[17] But Gambetta believed that now he could wield influence that, as a mere group leader (which in spite of being the silently acknowledged champion of the Republicans, he still was), he could not exercise. 'I have chosen the better part. . . . I am henceforth rid of this terrible campaign of eight years . . . standing above and outside the parties, I shall be able to choose my hour, my way, my means.'[18]

(iii)

The early years of Grévy's presidency were dominated by the public image of Gambetta. Confident and ebullient, Gambetta made the Presidency of the Chamber the most remarked if not the most important office in the State. At the Palais Bourbon, he kept open house, spending the eighty thousand francs of his salary in entertainment. Every day, his table was filled with solicitants, and among his guests were invariably the officers of the Chamber's military guard. He was,

* Some secondary writers say that Clemenceau called on Gambetta, and in the presence of Léonie Léon, urged him to stand for the Presidency of the Republic. Gambetta shook his head. 'Maybe you are afraid?' 'I have proved that I have no fear.' 'Are you tired?' 'Perhaps.'

said Adrien Hébrard of *Le Temps*, 'a romantic president. . . . A president is a success only on condition that he has the parts of a tenor, a herald and an acrobat.' Like other southerners, Gambetta was an actor. Every great orator, one who can kindle his audience and inflame himself with their response, has something of the *cabotin* about him — one has only to read the Midlothian campaign speeches of Gladstone: the effect is both edifying and debasing; in short, intoxicating.

Against such a figure, Grévy, old — he was now at least seventy-two — careful, provincial, *rangé*, perhaps tired, however much he might be valued by his ministers, could not, even did he want to, compete. He had not the necessary equipment. Did he not tell the director of the Salon, who said there were no outstanding pictures, that democracy needed a good average? 'He knows nothing, he does nothing, he thinks of nothing except saving pennies,' sneered Gambetta.[19] It was not Grévy, but Gambetta whose advice and recommendations suppliants sought; and not only clients, but ministers. Hence there became attached to Gambetta the attribution of omnipotence, of the possession of an 'occult power' which in fact he did not possess.[20] His recent leadership of the Republican Union led to the belief that he could and did control the existence of the Government, whereas in fact many members of that many-headed group believed him insufficiently resolute. The legend however persisted and stood between him and Grévy; and no doubt had something to do with the reluctance of the President to consult Gambetta, though by no means all that Gambettists believed.

It was generally considered by contemporaries and has been repeated by historians that Grévy's failure to invite Gambetta to form a government after Dufaure's resignation did infinite harm to the Republic. Allain-Targé, for one, held that Gambetta's conception of politics was far superior to the 'mean and petty calculations of those to whom the President would confide business'. Allain-Targé thought that Grévy intended to govern himself, and hence required weak and precarious cabinets. Gambetta would be too strong. On the other hand, the weight in the Republican party was not on the Left but in the Centre and Right (i.e. Left Centre), and the Senate was deeply conservative. It is unthinkable that in 1879 a Gambetta government could have survived twelve months. Either he must initiate (or support) legislation demanded by the Republican Union, such for instance, and almost unavoidable, as a full amnesty for the Communards, which would have been defeated by the anti-Republican Right in combination with the

Left Centre and the Moderates, or he must abandon all the Belleville programme and lose control of the Republican Union.

Moreover, it is to be remembered that he was not an experienced minister. In spite of having presided over the Chamber Finance Commission and having listened respectfully to Léon Say, his views on national finance were to say the least sketchy; but then, Léon Say, in spite of being a director of Rothschild's, was far less acute than he was thought and thought himself to be.

On the other hand, as Ferry wrote after Gambetta's death: 'He had political genius, and that is the rarest quality in our country . . . to be sure, he was not himself very fitted for governing, but what security it was to feel him there in reserve!'

The Waddington cabinet, in spite of containing three men of talent, Léon Say, Freycinet and the newcomer Jules Ferry, and two undersecretaries who would distinguish themselves, Carnot and Goblet, was colourless save for one striking trait. Of the ten ministers, five were Protestants, while Ferry was a free-thinker and a freemason. The only practising Catholic was the Minister of the Interior, de Marcère. The period between 1879 and 1885 has been characterised as one of purging, anti-clericalism and education. This is superficially true, but what in the end emerges is the conquest and subordination of the executive by the legislature.

Although, under pressure from the Chamber, Dufaure had carried out an extensive elimination from the Conseil d'Etat, the préfectures and the army, of men believed to be anti-Republican, the Chamber was not satisfied. There remained the magistrature, the law officers, the *magistrature assise*, the judges and the *magistrature debout*, the public prosecutors, the examining magistrates and so forth, who could not be dismissed. Many of these were with some reason suspected of hostility to the régime. Goblet, under-secretary at the Ministry of Justice, was eager to remove a number, but was damped down by Gambetta, who said that the purge could only be carried out when the Republicans could provide adequate replacements, and by Grévy who assured him that the country was uninterested and that there were more urgent tasks.

The cabinet was soon in trouble. In early March, as a result of attacks on the Paris police by Yves Guyot in the Radical *Rappel*, Marcère after much hesitation and changes of mind removed Gigot, the Préfet of Police, and being himself in turn attacked, resigned. His place was taken by Lepère from the Ministry of Commerce, who was replaced by

Tirard of the Republican Left, a business man and a free-trader. Gigot's place for some undiscoverable reason was given to a politician, Louis Andrieux, one of the deputies for Lyon, who had played an active part in the suppression of the Commune in that city, an appointment which would be regretted.

In this same month, the committee which had been investigating the actions of the Broglie government in 1877, presented its report. The rapporteur, Henri Brisson, demanded the prosecution of Broglie and his fellow-ministers. Now, before his election, Grévy had insisted that MacMahon should not be attacked, while it was unlikely that the Senate, which had voted the dissolution of the Chamber, would condemn itself. Brisson's proposals were rejected, but the Chamber passed a motion blaming the Broglie ministry for its acts.

One other burning question was that of the amnesty for the Communards claimed by the deputies for Paris. Waddington refused to produce a bill, and a proposal from the Extreme Left was negatived only with the support of the Right. Nevertheless a partial amnesty which included many already pardoned was passed.

A further concession to the Left was the abrogation of Article 9 of the Constitutional Law, making Versailles the seat of government, and the passage of a new law placing this in Paris. In view of the later controversies of 1884 it is to be noted that this was only carried out after negotiations with the Senate limiting the agenda of the National Assembly to this single item.

Of the dynastic parties, the only dangerous one was the Bonapartist. In June that threat disappeared with the death of the Prince Imperial, attached to the British army in South Africa, at the hands of Zulu tribesmen. The heir was Prince Napoleon, one of the black sheep of the family, certainly its most intelligent member. Like his cousin Napoleon III, he regarded democracy as a weapon to be employed against the 'governing classes'. He had sat in the Chamber of 1876–77 as Republican deputy for Ajaccio, an embarrassing comrade for the 'pures'. But he was a free-thinker, which made him odious to the Empress Eugénie's clique, led by the former Imperial minister Rouher. Rouher had persuaded the Prince Imperial to make a will barring Prince Napoleon from the succession and nominating his son, Prince Victor, as the claimant. Many of the old Bonapartists stood by Prince Napoleon, but Rouher and his intimates, the belligerent journalists Paul de Cassagnac and Jules Amigues, claimed that 'by accepting the Republic, Prince Napoleon has violated the contract between the nation and the dynasty of Napoleon'. A simulacrum of unity continued until the decrees against the Jesuits in the following year, which Prince Napoleon accepted. On this the Catholic group split off and rallied to Prince Victor.

By the autumn it was obvious that the Waddington government, largely Left Centre, had no control over the Chamber Republicans, and that its defeat was only a question of time. In December the War Minister, Gresley, interpellated on a minor issue, only survived by a tiny majority, and Royer went through the same ordeal. Both resigned, and Waddington in turn placed the resignation of the Government in Grévy's hands.

(*iv*)

Grévy did not consult or even see Gambetta on the choice of a successor. He had his eye on Freycinet. Charles de Saulces de Freycinet came from a Protestant family near Montauban, with a long tradition of State service. He himself had been in the Ponts-et-Chaussées, and during the sixties, after a mission to England, had submitted a report on English labour conditions. Like other superficially modest men, he had strong ambitions. He, however, insured himself by consulting the President of the Chamber and getting his promise of support, before accepting. In the Government, he took over the Foreign Office from Waddington and replaced Say, who also resigned, with Magnin, a senator, giving him as under-secretary the deputy for Loches, Daniel Wilson, the son of the Scottish engineer who had made a fortune in supplying Paris with gas. To Lepère at the Interior he gave as under-secretary one of the deputies for Toulouse, Constans, who succeeded Lepère when he retired in March. The most prominent figure in the cabinet was the Minister of Public Instruction, Jules Ferry, who had held the office in the previous ministry.

Member for Saint-Dié (Vosges), now almost on the German frontier, Ferry had been a Republican all his political life; an Opposition member of the Corps Législatif under the Empire, he had made a name for himself by attacking Haussmann's financing of the reconstruction of Paris. During the siege of 1870, he had been appointed 'administrator of the Seine', and his rationing scheme had earned him the nickname of Ferry-Famine. In March 1871 he had narrowly escaped murder by the Communards. A member of the National Assembly, he had been minister at Athens in 1872–73. On his return he had become one of the leaders of the Republican Left, and by 1876 its acknowledged leader. Like many other Republicans, he was a free-thinker, though not wholly uncompromising. Nevertheless he had that reputation, and his wholly civil marriage to a granddaughter of Goethe's Charlotte, who was the daughter of the Republican life-senator Scheurer-Kestner, was underlined by his enemies. Although a free-thinker and although, as he told Jaurès, he wished to organise society without either King or God, his letters display no fanaticism.

After Gambetta, he was probably the strongest influence in the Chamber. His relations with the tribune unhappily remain obscure. It is said that he opposed Gambetta's delegation to Tours in October 1870 and that Gambetta held it against him. In fact there seems little difference between the two men except temperament, Gambetta warm, popular, cordial, bohemian and meridional, Ferry, the frontiersman, cold, reserved, prickly ('My roses grow inside') and perhaps clumsy.

It was this man, now forty-seven, tall, broad, ugly with the enormous side-whiskers of a maître-d'hôtel, who for the next five years would drive France along paths which the country did not particularly want to take.

Chapter Nine

The Problem of the Orders

(i)

In March 1879 Ferry had introduced two bills on higher education. In effect, the first handed back to the University the sole direction of State education. It abolished the higher committee and its subsidiaries. The second bill, which reorganised higher education, was largely an institutional measure, but its seventh article was irrelevant to the bill and political in aim and character. It ran: 'No person is permitted to direct a public or private establishment, of whatever kind it may be, or to teach, if he is a member of an unauthorised congregation.' (This is the amended final text, not the original draft.) As Léon Blum remarked many years later: 'It is difficult to see why this was inserted in a bill relating to higher education. By its own terms it in fact applied to all the teaching Orders whatever they might be, also in fact it aimed at and could only aim at secondary education. . . . Higher ecclesiastical education was ceasing to be dangerous, while the powerful congregations which practised primary education were authorised.'[1]

The debate on the bill was long and bitter, raging from June 16 to July 9; Article 7 alone occupied five sittings. At the later date, the bill, including the notorious clause, was voted by 362 to 164. But although the debates had turned on points of history or law, it was recognised that the issue was political. This was Ferry's gross error, an error which he was to expand when the bill was discussed in the Senate in February and March 1880. For here Article 7 was opposed by that discarded Republican orator, the persuasive Jules Simon. Simon insisted that the Article was a direct infringement of liberty. Whether his arguments were valid is of little moment, but they drew from Ferry a fierce and clumsy retort to the effect that this was a battle between the Revolution and the Syllabus of Common Errors, between lay government and theocracy. In spite of a moderate and conciliatory speech from Freycinet, who claimed that the Article was a compromise, the Left Centre abandoned the Government and the Article was rejected. The amputated bill was passed on March 16. On the next day, in the

P

Chamber, a vote of confidence that the Government would take the appropriate action against the congregations under the existing laws was passed by a large majority.

Freycinet, strengthened by the vote, and on the advice of Gambetta and Ferry, now laid before the cabinet two decrees under the existing laws, the first dissolving the 'aggregation nominally of Jesus' within three months though allowing teaching establishments to carry on until the holidays, the second requiring all non-authorised congregations to apply for authorisation within three months or take the consequences under the laws. At the cabinet meeting,[2] Grévy criticised the issue of new decrees, which he said added nothing to the Government's existing rights: 'they seem rather to weaken them by admitting the belief that in your own minds you think the law insufficient.' Freycinet believed it necessary to make a demonstration to satisfy the Extremists in Parliament, and Grévy reluctantly acceded: 'you will find yourselves imprisoned in the decrees.' They were published on March 29.

There followed a spate of protests from the politicians and editors of the Right, and attempts to organise resistance. The Jesuits, on the strength of the opinion of an eminent lawyer, backed by a number of his confrères, contested the validity of the decrees. The case eventually came before the tribunal of legal conflicts, which dismissed it. A meeting of the heads of religious houses on April 2 led to a unanimous decision to stand by the Jesuits and make no applications, a decision confirmed by the provincial houses a week later. On the other hand, the moderate archbishops and bishops tried to reach an accommodation with the Government, and Maret, head of the theological faculty of the Sorbonne, asked Cardinal Lavigerie, Archbishop of Carthage and Algiers, to invite Leo XIII to intervene.[3] It was thought that if authorisation were left to the Ministry of Public Worship and not to the Chamber, requests for authorisation would be granted, since Flourens, the director, was sympathetic. Lavigerie hurried to Rome and secured from the Pope his agreement to the submission of the Orders, their recognition of the incontestable rights of the State in lay matters and their guarantee that they would not meddle in politics. The Jesuits, it was recognised, could not be saved.

Freycinet had already begun to fear that he had been too precipitate and too provocative. Lavigerie got a promise from him that the congregations in North Africa should not be touched. He then saw Dufaure, who offered to produce a bill covering the Orders. Everything now depended on the willingness of the congregations to follow the

Pope's advice and to make submission before June 29. Lavigerie drafted a declaration of submission for them which Freycinet agreed to — he hinted at it a few days later in answering attacks in the Senate — but he urged the need for speed on Lavigerie and on the Papal Nuncio, Monsignor Czaki. 'If the congregations should respond to me, they must do it at once; otherwise, it will be too late.' Nothing however was done and on June 30, the first decree expelling the Jesuits was put into force by Constans. More than two hundred law officers resigned rather than carry out the repugnant task of expulsion.

Freycinet, always moderate, always hesitant and possibly as a Protestant embarrassed at acting against Catholics, delayed moving against the other Orders. The consequence was that the Catholic politicos believed him frightened, and began to bring pressure on the congregations. '[The politicos'] unpublished but obvious design', says a Catholic writer, 'was to dominate the congregations and to make war on the Republic in the name of the interests of religion.'[4] Thus when on July 4, while some of the heads of houses accepted the Cardinal's compromise, the Catholic laymen rejected it, Lavigerie wrote to the Pope that the Catholics were putting themselves in a false position by failing to abjure political action as set out in his letter to Freycinet. The Church was becoming dominated by the most ardent Legitimists, who were in fact hoping for the execution of the decrees and a fight. He pointed out that this would lead to the rupture of the Concordat and the suppression of the Public Worship budget, which in turn would bring about the termination of the French financial contributions to the Vatican. Leo XIII, however, had not yet made up his mind, and there were further delays. Cardinal Bonnechose of Rouen became seriously alarmed. Cardinal Guibert of Paris was much disturbed.

The scandal of the imminent expulsions was accentuated by a simultaneous scandal in another field. Hitherto, every government had resisted all motions put forward by the Extreme Left of the Chamber for a full amnesty for those either imprisoned or deported or in exile for their actions during the Commune. The reply had always been that while individuals might be and were being pardoned, the time for a full amnesty had not yet come. At the beginning of 1880, more than 800 Communards remained to be dealt with, and in February, Freycinet, in opposing yet another motion from Louis Blanc, told the Chamber that pacification was not yet complete and until that time — he hinted at a year — an amnesty was out of the question. Gambetta had agreed with this view, but a number of Gambetta's group voted with the Louis Blanc minority.

In June there was a bye-election for a seat on the municipal council in Gambetta's constituency in the XXth Arrondissement. Gambetta had commended to the electors one of his followers. The constituency responded by electing Trinquet, a Communard deportee in the penal colony on the island of Nouméa. Gambetta appears to have lost his head. Having in February agreed that a full amnesty was impolitic, he now swung the other way and pressed Freycinet to bring in a bill. Freycinet protested: it would be impossible to carry such a bill; even should the Chamber accept it, the Senate would not. He agreed to pardon by decree the remaining prisoners and to bring in a bill for the amnesty in January. Gambetta, however, became more urgent, appealing to their old friendship, and Freycinet capitulated.[5] On June 19 he brought in the bill with considerable embarrassment, but Gambetta left the presidential chair and in an eloquent appeal carried the day. The Senate was more hostile, but allowed itself to be persuaded to give a narrow majority to the bill, which amnestied all Communards save those guilty of murder or arson. It became law on July 10. By July 14, many exiles were back in Paris, among them that bogus revolutionary Rochefort, who at once founded a new daily paper, *l'Intransigeant*, and in its first issue made a violent attack on those he called 'the Opportunists',* the government Republicans. Nearly 200,000 copies were sold.

There were some scathing comments on the policy which restored the Communards while expelling the Jesuits. Gambetta, however, recovered his confidence and now urged the wretched Freycinet to finish off the congregations.

Lavigerie was aware that a committee of Catholic laymen had been formed to take in hand the affairs of the congregations: he dreaded that these would drive both seculars and regulars to open war with the Republic. Time was short. Once again he saw Freycinet about the declaration by the congregations, but under the laymen's influence, the Superiors drew back. Once more Lavigerie approached the Pope, and Leo, through the Nuncio, instructed the Orders to make the declaration of loyalty to the Republic. This was drafted by Flourens, and, it seems, shown or read to Constans (now Minister of the Interior) and to his under-secretary, Fallières, neither of whom raised objections.[6]

---

* The word 'opportunism' had been coined by Gambetta in defence of a government policy of choosing the right moment to bring forward measures. It might be considered as a French parallel of Gladstone's doctrine of timing. It became a word of reproach against the Republicans.

The Chamber had now risen for the vacation. Freycinet appears to have confided nothing of the negotiations with the Vatican to any of his colleagues (although Constans and Fallières must have been aware of them), only to Grévy. Before leaving Paris, he told the Nuncio that he would speak openly on the matter at his home city, Montauban. He had failed to say anything to Gambetta. On August 18 he told his audience in veiled terms that the congregations would be regulated according to their behaviour, and foreshadowed a new law to deal with all associations, whether lay or religious. On August 23, Gambetta's *République Française* warned him that he was departing from the instructions he had received from the Chamber. In the meantime, though with hesitation, the congregations had begun to submit. By the end of the month, 152 men's and 224 women's had signed the declaration.

Then on August 30 a Bordeaux religious paper printed a version of the declaration, which at once started trouble. The ministers in Paris asked Freycinet to deny the statement. On September 6 an official note was issued: 'The Government has entered into no engagement with either the Vatican, the Apostolic Nuncio, or anyone regarding the execution of the decrees. Its freedom to act is unimpaired and its policy depends on none but itself.' Ministers stated that they knew nothing of the terms, but Freycinet and Grévy were asked to come back to Paris. After refusing they yielded and the cabinet met on September 17. It appears to have disagreed, Cazot, Constans and Ferry holding for the execution of the decrees, in order to assure their followers and constituents that they had had no part in the negotiations, Freycinet and Grévy desiring to postpone action until the meeting of Parliament, and then to submit a bill for all associations. It may be that on this day, in view of the submissions of so many congregations, the anti-clerical ministers were not uncompromising, but in the next twenty-four hours Gambetta seems to have stiffened those who belonged to the Republican Union. On September 18 Cazot and Constans threatened to resign.* The cabinet was breaking up, and Freycinet, having blundered at the outset — he now recognised that Grévy had been right in deprecating the decrees — threw in his hand and resigned.[7] The 'occult power' had shown it was not to be trifled with.

Freycinet says that this was the moment when Grévy should have sent for Gambetta, since he was in fact the author of the crisis. Yet the situation differed little from that of January 1879. Although in the

---

* Much remains enigmatic. Cambon says that Constans was publicly abusing Freycinet for having insisted on the decrees and for then having gone back on them.

current circumstances Gambetta could find a large majority in the Chamber, he would not in the Senate, as the vote on the amnesty had shown. Grévy called Ferry, who was the author of the original complication. There were a few minor changes in the cabinet. The Foreign Office was given to Barthélemy Saint-Hilaire, a solemn Greek scholar, once Thiers' private secretary, with as the under-secretary, Horace de Choiseul, the first aristocrat to rally to the Republic, both Left Centre and both impatient of Gambetta.

The problem of the Orders had not been solved. 'Nothing in this country should be taken tragically', wrote Flourens to Lavigerie,[8] '—at least in the political field. . . . The new cabinet is in reality no less embarrassed than its predecessor.' Nevertheless, under spur of their earlier attitudes, Ferry and Constans had to act. A limited expulsion of the men's congregations, Order by Order, was put in hand, and directions issued to the préfets.

The wiser members of the Church hierarchy were in despair. As the Archbishop of Rennes, Monsignor Place, wrote: 'Hitherto, it has been professed, at least in theory, that only the Pope and the bishops have the right to negotiate and to decide the internal policy of the Church: but such has not been the opinion of the *Univers* . . . still less that of the rash friends of the Jesuits and the fanatical Legitimists, and they have carried the day against the sacred hierarchy. M. Constans himself at the beginning accepted the declaration and only abandoned it in the face of the discredit with which lawyers and journalists, calling themselves Catholics, assailed it.'[9]

The appeal of the Jesuits was rejected by the Tribunal of Legal Conflicts, and the pursuit of the congregations sporadically begun. The chief of those dealt with were the foreign Orders, Dominicans, Recollets, Marists, Premonstratensians. In all 262 men's houses were closed either quietly or by force. Tactful préfets secured a free hand as to which Orders they would expel and often negotiated a voluntary abandonment of their house by the brethren.[10] Some resisted. It is related that the Dominicans in Paris barred their doors. Two sympathisers, Broglie and Cassagnac, visiting the house on the night before the expulsion, had to climb a ladder to an upper window. Half way up, Cassagnac growled savagely: 'Monsieur le Duc, if you had only shown a little more vigour on the Sixteenth of May, we should not be in this ridiculous position tonight.' To oust thirty-seven brethren from a monastery near Tarascon, a regiment of infantry, five cavalry squadrons and an artillery group were employed. On the whole, the public remained indifferent. At Roubaix a man was killed. Here and there were riots. Much was made of the fact that the cynical Andrieux, the Préfet of Police, in supervising the Paris expulsions, donned pearl-grey gloves, which for some unexplained reason was taken as the height of bad taste. In all, some 5–6000 men were expelled, rather less than a third of the full number. No action was taken against the women's congregations.

On the re-opening of Parliament in November, Freycinet gave the Senate a more or less accurate account of what had passed, and Ferry's Government secured a tiny majority. In the Chamber he had to meet a formidable attack from Clemenceau, who upbraided him for sparing the women's Orders, claimed that the police had arrested government supporters and that magistrates were condemning them. Anyhow, why was Ferry Prime Minister? 'We gave our confidence to M. Dufaure; he has disappeared: to M. Waddington; he is gone: to M. de Freycinet; M. de Freycinet has evaporated. We gave it to M. Ferry; he nearly went yesterday, and look, today the door is half open. . . . Today it is found that the majority is not supple or docile enough. Well, to those who say there is no majority, I say: "Take off your hats to this obedient majority, for you have seen the last of it." '11 Ferry got his majority, but twenty-six members of the Extreme Left voted against him and a number of Gambetta's followers abstained. Ferry complained bitterly to Gambetta.12 'You, my dear President, have supported me very loyally and very cordially, but not one of your disciples voted with me. It is worse than a vote of distrust, it is one of contempt. Brisson told Charles [Ferry] yesterday that it would be so, just as long as Gambetta failed to put an end to a false parliamentary situation by taking office. They [Brisson, Floquet, Allain-Targé] want office, but covered by the name and the popularity of Gambetta. They well know that by themselves they are not worth a hundred votes. Why should you not attempt a ministry which would discipline this disintegrating group and which would have the support of us all?'*

(ii)

The educational programme had been inaugurated by a series of tactical errors which permitted both oppositions, fanatical Clericals and fanatical Anti-clericals, to make trouble. Article 7 was irrelevant to the

* The letter is warm and personal. Ferry writes 'tu' to his 'cher Léon'. The Gambetta correspondence contains no reply.

rest of the bill, and Freycinet's handling of the question was morally cowardly. What had been an administrative matter was transferred to the metaphysical plane, permitting clerical polemists to represent the measures as religious persecution and anti-clerical demagogues to denounce them as timorous and weak.

'The unpardonable stupidity of our Republicans,' wrote Paul Cambon in 1894,[13] 'has been to fight the clergy not in the name of the interests of the State, of public order, of the hierarchy of public powers, etc., but in the name of free thought and positivism. This was the capital error of Gambetta and Jules Ferry. . . . The clergy is thus in a position of legitimate defence when it strikes at the Republic, and when the Republic does not attack it and persecute it for political motives but for philosophical reasons.' Whereas many Catholics were ready to welcome State lay education, many Republicans were sickened as much by the vulgar anti-clericalism and vociferous atheism of Paul Bert, 'cet Homaïs supérieur' as by the no less vulgar clericalism of the writers in the Univers and Croix.

Ferry learned nothing from his errors until it was too late. To the educational legislation passed between 1880 and 1886 was added a number of anti-clerical measures, often unnecessary, which envenomed the conflict.

In the strictly educational field, in 1880, there was the complete reorganisation of secondary education for girls (December 21), together with the institution of Ecoles normales supérieures for women-teachers in both primary and secondary schools, each under the direction of a well-known agnostic. By the law of June 16, 1881, free primary education was made compulsory between the ages of six and eleven and no religious instruction was to be given in any State school. In 1881 (law of March 18) the mixed juries for degrees were abolished and the Catholic Universities were denied the use of the title. By a second law on June 16, 1881, all teachers with less than five years experience were required to hold the certificate of an Ecole normale; letters of authorisation from a bishop were unacceptable.

In addition were the lesser molestations and provocations. In the Public Worship budget for 1881, the official salaries of archbishops and bishops were reduced by 5,000 francs, an economy of 385,000, although a sum of only 200,000 was used to augment the stipends of the lowest paid clergy by one hundred francs apiece. In 1881 the supplement paid to Cardinals was suppresssd. In both cases the Senate protested, but yielded. By an earlier law (July 12, 1880) a law of 1814 forbidding work on Sundays and certain holy days was abrogated. On

July 8 a law suppressed army chaplains. Between 1881 and 1884 a number of decrees intrinsically of little importance were aimed at the Church, the removal of military guards from episcopal palaces, the transfer of the charge of the church bells to the maire of the commune, whose permission was needed for their sounding, the grant of power to this official to forbid religious processions, all pin pricks, but pricks nonetheless. In addition the Public Worship budget was steadily reduced between 1884 and 1904, at the end by about twenty per cent.

Many difficulties remained. The number of lay teachers needed was quite inadequate: churchmen and nuns must still be employed. In 1886, after four years of troubled gestation, a bill presented in 1882 by Paul Bert was passed ordering the ejection from the schools of teachers belonging to religious bodies — women as vacancies occurred, and men within five years. Similarly, when the Paris municipal council substituted lay nurses for the nuns in hospitals, they found they had exchange bad for worse. The complete laicisation of these services was not completed until 1907.

The misfortune for both State and Church was that Ferry went into action almost simultaneously with a revolution in the Vatican. In 1878 Pius IX died. Leo XIII, who succeeded to the Triple Tiara, understood the atmosphere of the times and was willing to transact. It needed more than ten years for Ferry to understand that legislation cannot substitute new principles for old on unprepared soil and to perceive that, in a number of parts of France, the faith could and would defend itself. To do this, he must circumvent a Church which, while it spoke of freedom, sought domination. With Leo, a compromise might have been found. It is, however, very much a 'might', since the Church in France faced a practical dilemma. Much of its revenues came from the châteaux, and thus it was impolitic to acknowledge the régime. 'If I accept the Republic,' said Monsignor Turinaz of Nancy who claimed never to have combatted Republican institutions, 'I shan't have a penny.' How were church schools, seminaries and charitable organisations to be provided for?

In several directions, anti-clericalism was ineffective. In those areas where religion was strong, such as Brittany, the Ferry legislation was only formally implemented. The free Catholic schools continued side by side with those of the State, the free schools having the pupils, the State schools only the children of State servants. The free schools were supported solely by the contributions of the faithful, and such was their success that as late as 1900, it could be said that one-third of the school population was in them.

Chapter Ten

From Ferry to Gambetta

(i)

At the Congress of Berlin in 1878 Lord Salisbury by word of mouth to Waddington had as good as given the French a free hand in Tunisia, and had later confirmed this through Lord Lyons, the ambassador in Paris. Waddington had wanted to take immediate advantage of the situation, but MacMahon seems to have thought such a step premature.

Still formally a vassal of the Ottoman Empire, Tunisia for all practical affairs was independent.[1] Like other potentates, the Bey, Mohammed Sadak, liked money, and through the sixties had thoroughly entangled himself in the nets of European financiers. By 1869 he owed some 160 million francs and, at this point, the three most interested countries, Britain, France and Italy, set up an international commission to consolidate and control the Tunisian debt. The economic penetration of the country had already begun under the patronage of the European consuls. In the early seventies, the English consul had seemed the most successful, but the beginnings of the depression led to English withdrawal and the succession of the French with the energetic help of their consul, Roustan, to most of the concessions the English had failed to finance. The French stake in the country was almost purely financial; there were only 700 French nationals. But for many poor Italians, Tunisia was a land of promise, and at the end of the seventies there were more than 11,000 of them, as well as 7000 Maltese. In October 1878 a new Italian consul, Maccio, arrived and from this date there began feverish competition between him and Roustan which reached its peak in 1880 over various claims and concessions. More than once in this year Freycinet warned the Italian government against interference in French interests. Maccio secured for an Italian company, secretly financed by the Italian government, an important railway concession, while at the same time there were quarrels between the English, French and Italian consuls about the Enfida domain, an estate owned by a Marseillais group. This was the situation when Ferry succeeded Freycinet.

At this date, Ferry had shown little of the interest in the French Empire which would be so conspicuous in the next five years. No doubt the true motive for what happened in April-May 1881 was the desire to forestall the Italians. Bizerta had the makings of a magnificent, almost impregnable naval base, and the French could scarcely relish a possibly hostile fleet on the flank of Algeria. It must however be admitted that the events of March-May bear a resemblance to such conspiracies as the Jameson Raid or the birth of the Panama Republic. In mid-February, a small raiding party of Kroumirs from south of Tunisia entered Algeria. This had occurred many times before, and admittedly the Tunisian government had paid little attention to the protests of either Roustan or the Algerian governor-general. This official, Albert Grévy, brother of the President, now appealed for support to the French Foreign Office. A month later came a further appeal from the French colony in Tunis. On April 4 Ferry told the Chamber that the Government proposed to intervene and three days later obtained an almost unanimous vote of credit for an expeditionary force. That the Government was innocent of conspiracy seems clear from the fact that the force was a clumsy improvisation. There was no colonial army, and a scratch corps of odd battalions and squadrons was hastily mobilised and despatched to support the few Zouave units from Algeria.* By the time this force landed early in May, the raiders had vanished. Nevertheless the French swept down on Bey's summer residence at Bardo and on May 16 persuaded him to sign a treaty which placed his foreign and defence policies under French direction.

By now the Opposition in the Chamber saw an opportunity for criticising the Government. On May 21, when the draft Treaty of Kassar-Said (or Bardo) was presented to the Chamber, Ferry was hotly attacked from both Right and Left. Clemenceau accused him of endangering the security of France by the despatch of 20,000 troops overseas, and on the ground that the German press had approved the French actions, implied that Ferry was making approaches to the unforgivable enemy: 'I don't like this sudden explosion of friendliness.'[2] Ferry had no difficulty in rebutting the charges; the treaty was ratified with one dissentient and a few days later unanimously by the Senate.

---

* At this date, there were 4 Regiments (16 battalions) of Zouaves in Algeria and 3 regiments of Tirailleurs algériens, plus 18 squadrons of Spahi, some of which were in Senegal.

(ii)

Long before the end of 1880 it was well known that Gambetta had
become bitterly critical of the Chamber, this assemblage of *'sous-
vétérinaires'*, and complaining of its intellectual nullity. He had failed to
organise the Republican party, perhaps worse, he had failed to unite
even the Republican Union. He could see no other means of ridding
politics of the influence of the Café de Commerce than by the manipulation of the electoral system, by increasing the size of the constituency,
by going back to the *scrutin de liste* he had advocated in 1875. In
January 1881 it was known that he was prescribing this as part of a
general revision of the constitution.

These opinions were naturally disliked by those who held their seats
by their ability to pull wires in their own fiefs. Against the Gambetta
thesis they raised the shadow of a threat of dictatorship. Was not
scrutin de liste a masked form of plebiscite? Would it not lead to a
revival of the methods of the Second Empire? Grévy was known to be
opposed and much was made of this.

During the spring of 1881, Gambetta's authority in the Chamber
became more uncertain. Careless of criticism, he let fall unwisely disclosures of his influence on certain members of the cabinet, leading to
louder gossip about the 'occult power'. It was known that Bonapartists,
riven by the quarrel between Rouher and Prince Napoleon, were attracted to the Tribune: 'they want a master; they can see no other
possible despot; so: Put your money on Gambetta. They are Gambettist, not Republican.' So Déroulède and Octave Feuillet.[3]

Rochefort, whose hatred of the Republicans was unappeasable — he
believed they had deliberately left him on Nouméa — in spite of Gambetta's generosity to him, attacked him without remission. The fact
that he had lunched with aristocrats — once Albert Edward, Prince of
Wales was also a guest, that he was friendly with the Marquis du Lau,
with de Breteuil, the adviser of the Comte de Paris, with General
Galliffet, reputed executioner of the Communards, and with Alphonse
de Rothschild, was given damaging publicity in *L'Intransigeant*.[4]

At the end of April Agenor Bardoux, a deeply conservative Republican deputy, who had been in the Buffet and first Dufaure Governments, tabled a bill to replace *scrutin d'arrondissement* by *scrutin de liste*.
Ferry himself was highly dubious of both the wisdom of the change and
the success of the bill. On the other hand, he refused Grévy's request

that he should intervene against it. With Tunisia on his hands and the general election due in the autumn, he was not going to risk his cabinet in a fight not of his own making. He engaged the three acknowledged Gambettists in the cabinet to remain silent and neutral. In spite of the aloofness of the cabinet, Gambetta believed the bill could be carried, but he was taken aback when he discovered that a number of deputies had signed a request for a secret ballot,* which if passed would permit nominal friends to betray him. The secret vote, however, went in Bardoux's favour and the bill was sent to a committee which by eight to three disapproved it. The report was debated on May 20. Bardoux's arguments were the well-worn ones, which dwelt heavily on the venality of small constituencies and the contrasted freedom of the mass vote. One of the critics who opposed him argued that homogeneous parties left no room for the individual and that within the Republican ranks there were many shades of opinion, a plea which shows how far the deputies were from a conception of government. Finally, Gambetta himself left the President's chair and spoke warmly in support of the bill, which was carried by 268 to 204, with 47 abstentions.** The voting list was of exceptional interest, since every group was divided. The Monarchists were on the whole opposed, the Bonapartists slightly in favour. The Left Centre slightly against, but the other three Republican groups approved, though by no means unanimously. The cabinet, following Ferry's advice, abstained (none of them had spoken), but four of the under-secretaries voted, Martin-Feuillée, Raynal and Girerd, all Gambettists, in favour, Wilson, shortly to marry Grévy's daughter, against.

A few days later, Gambetta left Paris to pay a promised visit to his

---

* At this date, a secret ballot could be had of right on the demand of thirty members of the Senate, or fifty deputies, and took precedence over a public vote. It was suppressed by the Chamber in 1885 (Feby. 2), by the Senate in 1887 (Jany. 17). (Pierre, *op. cit.*, Sec. 1029.)

** My own count taken from *J. O., Chambre* differs from that of *Année politique*.

	For	Against	Abstained	Absent
Extreme Right	11	11	2	2
Right	14	22	–	–
Bonapartists	40	32	7	1
Left Centre	37	40	10	1
Republican Left	75	61	16	5
Republican Union	66	24	6	4
Extreme Left	25	14	6	–
	268	204	47	13

This gives 532, with three seats vacant, making the total of the whole House.

native city of Cahors where he was given an immense ovation, as though he were the personification of France, an ovation reported in full by the journalists. He was still absent when the Bardoux bill was debated by the Senate.

Whether, as Melchior de Vogüé alleged, the Cahors demonstration prompted the senators to see in Gambetta a nascent dictator, whether they were actuated by the indecisiveness of the Chamber vote, is impossible to decide. But forty-three Republicans joined the Right in defeating the bill by a majority of thirty-four. On the next day the Gambettist papers broke out into violent abuse of Ferry and Grévy, comparing the Senate division to that of the Sixteenth of May.[4] J. J. Weiss in an article in the *Revue bleue*[5] criticised Ferry's neutrality, which he asserted caused Gambetta to fail: '*ce ministère laissait tranquillement échouer M. Gambetta.*' He dates the coolness between the two men from June 9. De Vogüé, who saw Gambetta on the following day at the Palais Bourbon, was impressed by his bearing, but considered that he had been rebuffed and that his star had paled: '*les imbéciles le croient très touché.*'[6] On the other hand, Ferry and the cabinet had also been shaken by the fact that Ferry had maintained his neutrality in the Senate after the Chamber vote. From now onward, the Government was at the mercy of the pro-*liste* bloc in the Chamber, some seventy members of the Republican Union, whose mere abstention in a vital division would bring it down. If he desired to control the elections even negatively, Ferry must bring the session to a close as soon as it could decently be done.

Before that step could be taken a number of bills, one of some importance for the future, had to be passed, a law on the freedom of public meeting (June 30, 1881), a law on training of women teachers (July 13), and that on the press. Although this last was little more than a consolidation and classification of the existing mass of laws and decrees, it laid down, for better or for worse, that prosecutions of newspapers for press misdemeanours should be jury cases, which permitted Rochefort and his like to blackmail unhappy jurymen usually drawn from the Paris tradesmen. One item was that which made the *gérant*, the manager of the paper, responsible for the contents. This was excellent from the editor's point of view, since it was not he but an employee who went to jail.

On July 27 Ferry at length announced that the elections would be held on August 21 and September 4. The earliness of the date, which, owing to the calling up of reservists in August, had been expected a month later, took the Chamber aback. Clemenceau in a bitter interpellation accused Ferry of deceiving the deputies and put forward a motion of censure on what he described as an electoral manoeuvre.[7] Ferry replied by asking no more than the passage to the order of the day, which he carried by only thirteen votes, his majority including all the ministers, and the minority several conspicuous Gambettists. It was a narrow escape. Two days later Parliament rose.

(iii)

The next three weeks were occupied with electioneering. So far as the greater part of the electorate was concerned, the matter was one of indifference, and on the first poll this was made obvious by the numbers who did not trouble to vote. In some departments scarcely half the electors went to the poll: in Bouches-du-Rhône less than half. The only fierceness was to be seen in one or two cities, in chief Paris. The next Chamber would be increased from 535 to 557. Of the twenty-two new seats, seven went to Algeria and the colonies, and in Paris seven arrondissements were split into two, among them, Clemenceau's Montmartre (XVIII) and Gambetta's Belleville-Menilmontant (XX). Clemenceau stood in both constituencies and was elected in both on a clear Radical programme, the old Belleville manifesto. He stood down in XVIII (1), and on the subsequent bye, one of his later opponents, Lafont, was elected, offering himself as a Socialist-Radical, the first to adopt this label, while another candidate was put up by the Parti Ouvrier. Gambetta's passage was rough.[8] Radical candidates opposed him in both constituencies. He was faced by hostile and riotous audiences whom he could not silence. At one meeting, he was heard shouting 'drunken helots!'. In the first constituency he was elected on August 21, but in the other he did not secure the absolute majority and withdrew before the second poll, when a wild Radical was elected. Soon after this, he accompanied Grévy on a short presidential tour in Normandy during which, through no fault of his own, it was he who received the recognition of the crowds. Then he disappeared, believed to have gone incognito to Germany.

As soon as the count was finished, it was seen that in spite of Menilmontant Gambetta's stock was higher than ever. The Republican Union had gained nearly eighty seats and was now by far the strongest group in the Chamber. The Extreme Left too had gained, while Ferry's followers remained much the same. The losers were the Left Centre and the Right, the latter being little over ninety strong.

The next two months were to increase Ferry's difficulties. In July the situation in Tunisia had suddenly worsened, with raids by tribesmen over the southern border, and in Algeria the Oran area was attacked by raiders from Morocco. Again a provisional expeditionary force of odd battalions had to be mobilised and sent overseas to deal in summer heat with an elusive enemy. Now was seen that Ferry's choice of date for the elections was a blunder, since the mandate of the out-going Chamber ran until October 27: before this date, the newly elected deputies could not be summoned, while on the other hand, the old Chamber had lost its authority. Ferry could foresee the end of his ministry as soon as Parliament met. He was at the mercy of the newspapers at the very moment when the forces in North Africa were needing large reinforcements, and he was unable to ask for additional credits.

No one has ever denied to Ferry either courage or principles, but he lacked adaptability. As soon as the results of the election were known he decided to resign. It was to both his and Gambetta's interest that they should meet, negotiate and ally. Neither seems to have made a move. A deputation of Radical deputies, Louis Blanc, Barodet, Ménard-Dorian, Raspail and Camille Pelletan, summoned him to recall Parliament. He gave the 'five Anabaptists' a sharp refusal.[9] In the last week of September, he stayed with Grévy at the President's house in the Jura. It was clear that, as the leader of the largest group, Gambetta should have the firmest control of the Chamber and that he must form a ministry. Grévy agreed, on condition that the hot-heads of the Republican Union, Floquet and Allain-Targé, were left out of any combination and that Ferry should take a portfolio. Ferry excused himself, but Grévy retorted that though this might be in Ferry's interest, it was not in the interest of the Republic.[10]

On October 5, therefore, Ferry announced his future resignation. On October 13 Gambetta, who had returned from his visit to Hamburg, was summoned by Grévy, but of what passed between the two nothing is known.

The autumn session opened on October 28. Gambetta was at once re-elected President by 317 of 364 votes, but the abstention of nearly two hundred members indicated a growing dissatisfaction. He resigned a few days later and Brisson was elected in his place. On November 4 Ferry, still Prime Minister, was interpellated on what had happened in Tunisia. For five days the debate raged. On November 9 the order of the day 'pure and simple' was negatived by 326 to 205. Confusion followed with individualism rampant. Twenty-five different motions

were submitted and each in turn was defeated. Finally Gambetta resolved the difficulty by telling the Chamber that the situation required
the ratification of the Treaty of Bardo; what had happened since that
date could be neglected. The motion ('The Chamber, resolved to
execute in its integrity the Treaty of May 12, subscribed to by the
French nation, passes to the order of the day') was accepted by Ferry
and carried by 355 to 68. On the same evening Ferry resigned, and on
the following day, Gambetta was entrusted by Grévy with the formation of a ministry. Though he knew it not, he had dominated the
Chamber for the last time.

(iv)

Ever since Dufaure's resignation, the public had been led to believe
that Gambetta alone had the magic touch which would cure all the ills
of the commonwealth. Now it looked for the 'Grande Ministère', Gambetta heading a cabinet of all the talents, flanked by the ex-prime
ministers and the best of the *ministrables*. The expectations were disappointed. In spite of his agreement with Grévy, Ferry did not take
office: it is said that Gambetta's followers would not have him; it is also
said that he was chilled by Gambetta's ignoring the cabinet in his
speech of November 9. In any case, after the debate on Tunisia, no
government could survive with Ferry as a member. Beyond this,
Challemel-Lacour, the oracle of the *République Française*, refused the
Foreign Office and Brisson clung to the presidential chair. Worst of all,
Léon Say, guardian of the railway interests, refused, unless guaranteed
that there would be no proposal to carry State purchase of railways
further than it had already gone. It is possible that the purchase of the
Orleans railway by the State had certain economic advantages, but
there had been wild speculation in the autumn and money was tight.
Further, Say had some justification in believing that the Orleans railway would be only the first mouthful and that under Radical pressure the other systems would in turn be attacked. Gambetta would
not, perhaps politically could not, give way — there had been a
vicious attack on the railway companies by the *République Française*
in November — and Say declined the invitation, although in other
directions favourable to Gambetta, especially in his determination to
prevent the initiation of new expenditure by private members. On
Say's retreat, Freycinet, who had earlier accepted, rapidly withdrew

Q

into a cloud of very cogent excuses. The Great Ministry had collapsed.[11]

Gambetta took the bull by the horns. Ignoring the other *ministrables*, he constructed a cabinet, almost exclusively from untried men. The only survivors from Ferry's administration were Cazot, the Minister of Justice and his under-secretary, Martin-Feuillée, Raynal, the Bordeaux Jew coal-merchant, who had been an under-secretary, and Cochery, almost a permanency at the Post Office. At the Interior he put Waldeck-Rousseau, a rising barrister, son of an old Republican, at Commerce, Rouvier, a clever financier, who had worked his way forward from a humble clerkship in the office of a Greek merchant in Marseille. To Public Instruction he put Paul Bert, the anti-clerical. He himself took the Foreign Office. Further, without reference to the Chamber, he split the Ministry of Agriculture and Commerce, thus creating a new ministry, while to each office he appointed an under-secretary, among them, at the Foreign Office, his devoted adherent Spuller. Finally, in place of the cautious Léon Say, Allain-Targé, whom Grévy told Ferry he would not sanction, was given the Ministry of Finance. In public, Gambetta called it a ministry of talents (*capacités*): privately he knew that neither he nor the cabinet could long survive: to Marcellin-Pellet, he remarked, 'X is good enough for a ministry that can't last three months.'[12]

The announcement of the names of the new cabinet was greeted with murmurs. 'Gambetta takes twelve portfolios', said one paper. His opening address received a chilly welcome. Ribot, deputy for Boulogne, once Dufaure's private secretary, who, in spite of more than forty years in Parliament and having been five times the leader of a government, would always be a follower, in a speech of subtle malignance challenged the creation of a new ministry and eight under-secretaryships without reference to the Chamber. No one was certain what was to come. If the Chamber of 1877–81 had lost its coherence, the new Chamber with 140 new deputies failed to regain it. The Republican Union had already split. Inspired by the sinister Brisson, a new deputy (for Bourges), Alfred Chéneau, in alliance with Daniel Wilson, organised a group in the Chamber, the Gauche radicale, for the purpose of coercing the Prime Minister, a detachment of some fifty members, chiefly from the Republican Union. The remainder of this group fell back on Ferry's, and with it formed the Gauche démocratique.

The arrival of Gambetta, such was his reputation, sent a shiver through Europe. Fearing the worst, French ambassadors took fright. Some resigned at once; Saint-Vallier, who had gained Bismarck's confidence, if that were possible, threw in his hand, as did General Chanzy in Saint-Petersburg. There was resentment that Gambetta had appointed to the political directorate at the Foreign Office the brilliant journalist J. J. Weiss, a conseiller d'état, but tainted with Bonapartism. To top it all, Gambetta posted General de Miribel to Chief of Staff, Miribel, who was well known to be an ardent Catholic, who in 1877 had been nominated Chief of Staff by General Rochebouet, and who was suspected of disaffection to the Republic.

Nor was the coolness of the deputies improved when the new Minister of the Interior, Waldeck-Rousseau, circulated to the préfets a letter warning them against concessions to deputies on behalf of their constituents.[13] How was a deputy to live, or indeed to get re-elected if all the local patronage was left in the hands of the préfecture? It would be abominably undemocratic. Further, not much faith could be placed in the Minister of Finance, Allain-Targé. Gambetta seemed to be treating the Chamber with a high hand, and the talk of dictatorship grew louder. He did not trouble to conceal his contempt for the deputies, particularly those known as *arrondissementiers*. Cambon, watching the approaching disaster, remarked that Ferry had already fulfilled the policies connected with Gambetta's name and that he had nothing left but issues so controversial, so impossible, that he recoiled at the thought of them.[14] A number of bills were drafted but they would have no future. In January Gambetta brought in a bill for constitutional reform which included *scrutin de liste* for the Chamber.

On January 8 came the second renewal of the Senate. As in 1879, it was a Republican triumph. Of their 38 seats, the Right lost 24 and the Republicans came back with 61 of the 75 vacated. The vote was the complete confirmation of the Republic.

The committee to consider Gambetta's bill was from all groups, but it was patent that his enemies were in a large majority, Marcère, Choiseul, Ribot from the Left Centre, Dréo and Langlois from his own group, Clemenceau, Barodet, Camille Pelletan from the Radicals. They questioned him as to his intentions, first on the powers of the revising congress, which would consist of both senators and deputies together. He said that the congress must have an agreed agenda. The committee returned that the congress was a paramount assembly and could not be limited: it alone had the powers to interpret the constitution. Asked what would happen if it went outside the prescribed limits, he answered that this would be illegal and revolutionary, and in that case the President of the Republic should give his opinion. Clemenceau remarked that the President must, constitutionally, have a minister to counter-sign, to which Gambetta retorted that the President would not fail to find one. At this, the committee pretended shocked surprise and, on leaving the room, did not scruple to let it be known that Gambetta had practically threatened a *coup d'état*. The report on the bill, which was entrusted to Andrieux (who, Ferry told his wife — quite truly — , was more mischievous than a wagonload of monkeys) was entirely hostile to the bill and agreed to by the whole committee save two.

When the bill came before the Chamber for discussion on January 26, a majority decided to take out Article 2, on *scrutin de liste*, and deal with that alone. Andrieux attacked both the article and its author. He insisted that if it were voted there would appear two equally evil alter-natives. Either there must be an immediate dissolution, which was scarcely decent within six months of an election: and anyhow Gam-betta had declared that he was not thinking of proposing it. Or, if there was no dissolution, then the Chamber must continue until October 1885. What authority would a body elected under *scrutin d'arrondisse-ment* have under a system which itself had condemned? It would be at the mercy of every hostile journalist. Andrieux as good as accused Gam-betta of aspiring to dictatorship, and the Chamber applauded. Gambetta replied, but he knew he was beaten. On the motion ('to include Article 2, *scrutin de liste*, in the revision'), the government, of whom all the members including the under-secretaries abstained, was defeated by 288 to 107, with 121 members abstaining.* That evening, Gambetta resigned.

* The division list, although the members are not identical with those who voted in May 1881 (cf. p. 215 fn.), and the strength of the groups has changed, has an interest in showing the hostility to Gambetta.

	For	Against	Abstained	Absent
Extreme Right	1	21	1	1
Right	–	15	–	1
Bonapartists	1	39	3	3
Left Centre	7	28	14	–
Republican Left	24	63	37	6
Republican Union	64	68	61	5
Extreme Left	9	47	4	1
Independents	1	1	1	
	107	288	121	17 — 533

Bye-elections pending 24

557

Of the 50 identifiable members of the Gauche radicale, there were 13 for, 23 against, 13 abstentions and 1 absent.

(ν)

While the Chamber was demonstrating its determination to suffer no
control by a resolute Prime Minister, a temporarily shattering episode
was convulsing French business circles, the failure of the Union
Générale.

In spite of the expansion under the Second Empire, the railway map
had by no means been filled up by 1870. Except for the main lines, the
region south of the Loire had not tempted railway promoters, while in
the south-west between Nantes and Bordeaux, in Poitou, the Limousin
and the Charentes, where some small lines had been built, the companies were on the edge of bankruptcy. Moreover many rural districts
were worse off for the coming of railways because the long-distance
hauliers were going out of business, and small towns between the railways were becoming isolated.

The 1876 legislature, wishing to show itself no less benevolent than
the fallen régime, took up the whole question of communications, railways, rivers, canals and ports. Christophle, Minister of Public Works,
set the Ponts-et-Chaussées to produce a full report. This was completed
and approved by his successor under the Sixteenth of May Government.
On resuming office in December 1877 Dufaure appointed Freycinet to
the Ministry.

As a State engineer, Freycinet was a convinced believer in State
direction, even State ownership of everything pertaining to transportation. Hence in 1878 he brought forward what was to be known as the
Freycinet Plan, in the belief that this would tap the potential wealth of
the provinces and speed up the mobility of goods and population.

The finances of the railways were based on the so-called Franqueville
conventions arrived at in 1859, when, owing to the crisis of 1857, the
companies had been in difficulties and the State had intervened with a
loan at 4% per annum, to enable them to complete what was known as
'the second network', together with a guarantee of interest. But arising
out of the technicalities of the interest and amortisation between the
first and second networks, the companies were in a position to refuse
improvements making for efficiency, such as marshalling yards,
which demanded capital expenditure, and reduction of fares and freight
charges. They did not want to build unprofitable lines and would only
undertake them with a State subvention. Again, they did not want to
burden their revenue with interest to the State. Hence the State had had

to encourage small companies to build by providing capital, but these had overbuilt and were now in trouble with uncompleted projects. Of the main companies, the Nord, the Est, the P.L.M. and the Orleans were all strong and formed a powerful economic-political interest.

In 1872 Gambetta and his friend Clément Laurier had tabled a bill for the purchase by the State of all the railways. This had been defeated, but the railway interest henceforward looked on Gambetta as dangerous. In 1876 the Chamber once more took up the question. On this occasion they forced the Orleans and Ouest companies to take over the small tottering companies, but both soon refused to add lines of which the revenue would amount to about a twentieth of the lines they had built themselves. The matter came up again in March 1877, when the Chamber decided to buy up all these lines at cost, less the amount of government subsidies to date: thereafter the State would operate the existing system and complete the building. The provisional conventions were ratified by Parliament a year later (L. May 18, 1878). Freycinet was at pains to explain that this was not a preliminary to the acquisition of the whole French system, which many of the Left desired.

The year 1877 had shown rising prosperity. The indemnity had been liquidated. The slump that had followed the Austrian crash of 1873 had not seriously affected France since the indemnity loans had mopped up all the spare speculative money. At the end of 1877 there were abundant deposits flowing into the banks, a rise in share values and in January 1878 specie payments were resumed. In this same month, Gambetta and Freycinet met Léon Say, the Finance Minister, who was also a director of the Nord railway and the representative of the Rothschild house, the railway's biggest shareholder. As Finance Minister he had hitherto been caution itself, opposed to State intervention or loans. But imports were rising, and since a great part of the public revenue was drawn from customs, revenue was buoyant; he allowed himself to give Freycinet's scheme his blessing. No doubt he was more amenable in that the scheme being financed by the State in no way jeopardised the position or revenues of the great companies. He afterwards claimed that he agreed to the State borrowing no more than 4 to $4\frac{1}{2}$ milliard francs over ten years and that he had warned Freycinet that 'usefulness was not enough; there must also be necessity'. In fact, he does not appear to have examined the details or considered the scheme from the point of view of the country's interests. At the moment, with the abundance of money, the first condition he should have laid down was the precedence of a conversion loan. The 5% indemnity loans issued at 83 and 84 were standing at 115, and could have been converted to 4½ or even 4%. Say did nothing. Nor does he appear to have criticised the fact that nothing was said as to how the new, 'the third network,' was to be operated and by whom. The companies or the State? If the latter, how were these branch lines to be connected with the privately owned lines? If the former, what inducement was to be offered to the companies to take them over?

On receiving Say's agreement, Freycinet, during 1878 and 1879, produced his plans; three milliards for the railways and 500 millions for the purchase of the bankrupt lines, one milliard for rivers, canals and ports. The scheme was to be financed by the issue of a 3% terminable loan in shares of 500 francs, payable over seventy-five years and free of tax.

Neither minister had reckoned with the Chamber. 'The fault was less to have conceived an initially swollen scheme than to have failed to foresee the formidable impulsion which private and local interests would give to a plan to promote their own advantage, an impulsion which a government relying on an elected Parliament is less capable of withstanding than any other.' 'The plan was launched like a sort of rocket to the glory of the Republic.'[15] At once the deputies rushed forward to share in what is sometimes called 'the pork barrel'. Private motion after private motion for branch lines in the least profitable areas was put forward by deputies eager to hold their electors' confidence. Neither Say nor Freycinet appears to have offered more than weak opposition. To the originally proposed 4500 kilometres were added another 4000. By 1882 the State had in all adopted some 16,000 kilometres, the majority in non-productive regions. The companies let it be known that they most certainly would not take over the new network. And further, the simultaneous beginning of construction of the track-beds all over the country caused a critical shortage of labour and materials, while imports of railway iron in 1881, 1882 and 1883 were abnormally high and exports negligible.

Throughout 1879, 1880 and 1881, in spite of agricultural difficulties, prosperity continued. By the summer of 1881, there were boom conditions. Already many finance and other companies had been formed, including in December 1880 a company to pierce the Isthmus of Panama and construct a waterway, under the chairmanship of Ferdinand de Lesseps, the builder of the Suez Canal. That trouble would come of all this had been foretold by the *Economiste Français*[16] as early as November 1879 and a deputy had asked for the prosecution of the editor. Among these companies was a Lyon finance house called the Union Générale, founded in 1878 by Emile Bontoux, who had made a fortune in financing railways in Austria. Bontoux had been elected as a Monarchist deputy in 1877, but the Chamber had unseated him. He had formerly been an employee of Rothschilds and now, as a believing and practising Catholic, put his corporation forwards as the instrument to break the power of Jewish finance. The faithful bought the shares in the belief that their money would bring about the downfall of the atheist republic and the restoration of the monarchy and the Church.

The par value of the Union's shares was 500 francs, but only 125 had been paid up. In 1879 it had showed a profit of 9 millions, in 1880, 11½. During 1881 speculation in the shares suddenly increased. In July they stood at 1400; by the end of August they had risen to 1670. In mid-November, on the report of a new issue of bonus shares, they touched 2700. The price was wholly fantastic; speculators had lost all touch with reality.

Already the markets had begun to feel the pinch. In July the Finance Ministry had issued one milliard of the 3% Public Works loan with an initial subscription of one-fifth, the remaining calls to be made at monthly intervals until January. In previous loans, initial payments had been high in order to keep out men of straw. But money was tight; speculators were said to be paying 15% and 20% for loans. In October carry-over money was at 10%. During November and December the new Minister of Finance, Allain-Targé, had had to intervene, since the Treasury must have its 200 millions in January. The Treasury was forced to find 53 millions to support the carry-over in December. Meanwhile, the Union Générale shares were still rising. On December 15 they touched 3050; they sagged slightly to 2880 during the rest of the month; there were rumours, but on January 5 they were up to 3040. Then came a sudden wave of selling. The rumour spread that Rothschilds were behind the attack. Whatever the reason, by January 19 the shares were down to 1400 and on the 26th, the day of Gambetta's defeat, to 950. There was panic. In Paris the Bourse was in difficulties, but in Lyon there was disaster, for with the decline of the Union, its subsidiary Banque de Lyon et de la Loire closed its doors. By mid-February the Union share stood at 325 with no buyers. At the creditors' meeting on April 14 the company was shown to have a deficit of 135 million francs.[17] With its disappearance went a number of other dubious finance houses, 'twenty-eight so-called banks, in reality bucket-shops,

Crédit de France, Crédit de Paris, Banque nationale. . . . All these operate in the provinces . . . working through advertisement and bond-salesmen, who sell at a discount to the ignorant peasants; many of their shares are only 25% paid up.'[18] Leroy-Beaulieu went on to say that in consequence a number of industrial companies were in severe diffi-culties, gas, electro-metallurgy, coal-mining, as well as nineteen insur-ance companies. The receivers were calling up the unpaid balances and money was being poured into the abyss, while saving had practically stopped.

Bontoux, who by Freycinet's order was arrested on February 2, and the managing director, Feder, were prosecuted. It was proved *inter alia* that they had used the Union's money to support and inflate the market through nominees and that they had printed share certificates and put them in their pockets without payment. Condemned to five years' im-prisonment, they appealed, and then skipped the country. The respect-able guinea-pigs on the board, such as Broglie's son, were spared. The 12,000 creditors got nothing.

Possibly the most scathing comment was written a few months after the crash, again by Leroy-Beaulieu:[19] 'Then [in 1879] we said we would have no difficulty in naming three hundred senators or deputies, the majority without either competence or special vocation, on the boards of limited companies. Today we could go to four hundred.'

The Banque de France had done little. Bank rate had risen from $3\frac{1}{2}$ to 4% on August 25, to 5% on October 20. Thereafter it did not rise. Rouvier, almost the only financial head in Parliament, said: 'This wouldn't have happened if I'd been in charge.'[20] As for the Minister of Finance, Gambetta with appalling frivolity said to Allain-Targé: 'You want to cause a rise on the Bourse? It's quite easy, you have only to resign.'[21]

Chapter Eleven

The Pattern of French Government

(i)

During the six years between 1879 and 1885, the pattern of politics was so deeply stamped by events that all subsequent efforts to change it failed. The pattern resisted social changes in the structure of representation and in 1939 the Chamber would be less coherent than in 1879.

The defeat of Gambetta has more importance than that of any other minister or ministry in the years between 1877 and 1895. Hitherto, although individual ministers had been defeated and resigned without involving the whole cabinet, no Republican cabinet had been overthrown. Dufaure, Simon, Waddington, Freycinet and Ferry had each resigned without challenging a division. Gambetta alone had challenged opposition and been defeated. The defeat was the more significant in that the Chamber had expelled from office the most popular political figure in the country, whose popularity, if judged by the recent election results, was higher than ever. For the moment those who had voted against his bill may have shivered at the thought of what their constituents would say. It was soon perceived that the country, the electorate, would do nothing. The consequences of this indifference were far-reaching. It showed the Chamber that no minister was indispensable, that the deputies need not shrink from defeating lesser men. In future every cabinet would be at their mercy. It would not be the Government that would direct policy, but the legislature, which in the end would mean that there would be no policy at all.[1] Ministers instead of looking at the needs of the country and attempting to frame the appropriate policy would be seen canvassing the opinions of deputies as to what was to them acceptable.[2] The pernicious consequences would not be less, except in periods of exceptional difficulty, up to the end of the Third Republic and would be exhibited in the repeated overthrow of governments at short intervals and by irresponsible financial legislation.

Of the forty-six ministries between 1876 and 1914, forty existed for no longer than an average of five months. The instability can be attributed in large part to the failure to organise parties. The original pattern, Legitimist, Orleanist, Bonapartist and Republican, had a raison d'être; each group represented something. The later groups, or most of them, derived from splits and represented mere variations. The Extreme Left, whether it spoke through the mouth of Clemenceau or Louis Blanc or Madier de Montjau, talked of democracy and liberty but could not say for what purpose, and offered no practical policy. Each of the Right groups wanted power to restore a dynasty but nothing more. There was no clash of economic interest in the Chamber. Of economic interests there was one paramount, agriculture, and this was the interest of every deputy for a rural constituency, about three-quarters of the Chamber and a good deal more in the Senate. The other interests were not competitive and supported one another, the railways, shipping and ship-building lobby asking for subsidies, the cotton-spinners pressing for higher tariffs and so forth. The Comité des Forges and the Comité des Houillières scarcely needed political support before 1914, and until the late nineties a colonial lobby had not appeared. As yet nothing was heard or at least very rarely of social improvement. Labour, of course, was not yet an influence. The Chamber was in no way interested in education, its methods, its purpose except politically. Having voted the creation of agricultural schools, the Republicans neglected them. 'Once in power in the countryside, the Radicals were no longer interested in young peasants. . . . A resolutely protectionist attitude was a better guarantee of votes.'[3]

In the constituencies local interests and local influences prevailed, and the local committees were rarely nationally minded, while on the other hand, local interests prevailed because there were no national parties. In spite of the superficial creation of national organisations, the Union Républicaine, the Alliance Démocratique etc., about 1900, after the schisms caused by the Dreyfus case, no real party with funds and party discipline came into being until the conjunction of the socialist groups in 1905–06, and except for the Communist Party in 1921, there were no imitators.

One technical detail helped to prevent the formation of parties. In the autumn of 1872, once in Somme and once in Calvados, a Republican had been elected on a minority vote between a Monarchist and a Bonapartist. Hence in early 1873, the National Assembly passed a short act reviving a law of 1855, itself a revival of the practice of the July Monarchy.[4] This required for election at the first poll that the candidate should have an absolute majority. If this was not obtained, then a second poll would be held a fortnight later, when a relative majority was enough.* This system returned to the gerrymandering practices of the Second Empire, but the law was maintained until the fall of the Republic in 1940. It had effects not foreseen by its authors. Since there could be a second poll, rival groups were encouraged to put up outsiders who could be withdrawn at the second poll. A random example from 1910 at Reims shows seven candidates of whom four were Independent Socialists. Here was one of the hindrances to party formation. Had there been a single poll, the interested local politicians would have been forced to compromise on the choice of a candidate before the election and thus be gradually forced to accept party leaders and party discipline. Duverger claims that the second poll smoothed out exaggerations. But if the second poll had not existed, the exaggerations would have been smoothed out beforehand.[5]

(ii)

The Chamber elected in 1877 remained essentially bourgeois, not 'grand bourgeois', but in majority 'petit'. The professions of the deputies, so far as can be judged from far from reliable evidence, indicate that most had some financial backing, though few possessed large means. The majority of landowners owned modest estates: an English commentator says of the eighties that not more than 75,000 had an income of 9,000 francs a year from land:[6] the majority of industrialists were small-scale. On the whole the members had neither the incomes nor the style of the imperial Corps Législatif.

Nearly a third of the 530 odd members of 1877 were lawyers, but lawyer is a term covering many activities. Beyond the lawyers were some ninety or so landowners, of whom a quarter claimed to be engaged in agriculture. Some were living on the rents of their farms, but a number were also company-directors, as one only discovers after pursuing them through many annuals. Industry provided some sixty members, from every kind of trade, ships, machines, cotton, tanning, scent, paper: the biggest group were eleven iron-masters. Another group was of men retired from government service, the great majority former civil servants of the Empire, indeed this group was almost

---

* Under the 1919 Electoral Law, the second poll was dispensed with, but replaced in the Electoral Law of 1924.

wholly imperialist. There was a surprising number of doctors. Had they any patients? Did they find the 9,000 francs a year of a deputy more rewarding than the practice of medicine? Had Dr Turigny, who sat for a Nièvre constituency for forty years and never spoke, a practice? There were of course the journalists, some thirty, but journalism is the training ground of politics. Some must be regarded as professional politicians, Gambetta, Ferry, Brisson, for example. For the rest, a dozen professors, chiefly of law, a few engineers who may in fact have been industrialists or contractors, and a couple of former manual labourers. Little can be learned from the list, because so many of the labels are unreal.

On the other hand, it is to be noticed that 95% of the deputies represent their own home constituency. Only Seine and perhaps Seine-et-Oise elected men who had not been born there or at least had worked there for many years.

In the first thirty-five years of the Republic, no parties were organised; candidates were endorsed by no central office; there was nothing to prevent a local nonentity standing for the Chamber. Frequently, especially in the seventies and eighties, several candidates with no more accurate definition than Republican or Radical would stand against each other at the first poll, those with the fewest votes withdrawing before the second, sometimes voluntarily, sometimes in return for favours or money. Briand is said to have been paid to withdraw at Saint-Nazaire in 1898. When Clemenceau was defeated at Draguignan (Var) in 1893, he was opposed by four other Radicals. In Corsica in 1910 as many as seventeen candidates contested Sartène. In Paris in 1885 there were 270 candidates for 38 seats.

The new deputy arriving in Paris had no central office, no whip to welcome him. He might be a Republican in the eyes of his electors, but this counted for little. Having taken his seat, he would choose which group or sub-group he would join. Even so, when inscribed on a group list, he did not invariably support its leader, for across the pattern of political doctrines there ran the more important patterns of economic interests, of the vine-growers, of the silk-cocoon breeders, of the silk-exporters, and so forth, and across these again a further pattern of communal appetites. The *bouilleurs de cru*, peasant brandy-distillers of surplus wine in the south, were at daggers drawn with the commercial distillers of the north.

Few groups were not open, i.e. willing to allow members of other groups to join. Clemenceau alone would make no concessions, but by the middle nineties Radical was said to be 'the most elastic of epithets'.

More important is the relationship of the deputy to his constituents. Although the constitution makers rejected the *mandat impératif*, the arrondissements exercised it, not so much on matters of national politics as on those of local interest. Municipalities looked to the deputy for financial or quasi-financial help, a railway station, loans for schools, bridges, water supply. He was expected to provide important voters with jobs, to see to it that their children passed their examinations. No wonder that when Jules Simon asked Audren de Kerdrel, who brought him the invitation to become Prime Minister, what he could do for him, Kerdrel answered: 'Leave me my préfet.' Both Delcassé and later Anatole de Monzie, both southerners, were reputed to have filled the telephone service with their clients — useful ears in an emergency.[7] One has only to run one's eye over the supplements to the Freycinet scheme to observe electoral pressure at its strongest. The deputy, as Barrès said, 'remains a perpetual candidate.' To him the constituency was more vital than any party.

Chapter Twelve

Freycinet and Egypt

(i)

No sooner had the Gambetta Government gone than the absence of direction became acutely felt. The Republican Union, whose desertion of their chief had brought about the disaster, looked with jealous eyes at Ferry. But who else was there? In the Chamber were no personalities which could command a majority. Grévy called Freycinet, who in future would be the ever-ready stop-gap. Faced by the financial dislocation, Freycinet appealed to Say, and Say made his own terms — no forced purchase of any railway system.[1] The other ministers were secondary figures, the majority senators, without weight, except for Ferry who returned to the Ministry of Public Instruction. From the moment it took office, the Government was shaky.

The Chamber displayed its capriciousness. Having thrown over *scrutin de liste*, it had voted revision of the constitution, which the Government rejected, and on this voted confidence in the Government.* Then, the committee on the judiciary having rejected the election of judges, the Chamber voted the suppression of their irremovability and their election by universal suffrage. The Chamber voted a variation in the excise rates between wine and spirits in spite of the opposition of Léon Say. He at once resigned, on which the Chamber hastily went back on its vote. The Law of March 28 gave each town council throughout France the right and duty of electing its maire and his aides. The single exception was Paris, which continued to be administered by the city council, but in fact was ruled by the Préfets of Seine and of the Police. Goblet, Minister of the Interior, challenged on this, was evasive and the Government was rewarded with a vote regretting its indecision. On this the cabinet resigned, and the Chamber once more retired behind a vote of confidence.

In spite of this vacillation over domestic affairs, it was on a foreign issue that the Chamber finally overthrew Freycinet. This was Egypt.

* The Government refused to submit the motion for revision to the Senate on the ground that a Senate vote on the question ought to be spontaneous.

The financial condition of the Egyptian government had long been deplorable. The extravagance of the Khedive Ismail had built up a vast debt to European financiers, who lent him more money at ever increasingly fantastic discounts. In 1875 the British government had bought from him his holding of founder's shares in the Suez canal, in which the French government of the day was scarcely interested. In 1879, at the instigation of the French and British governments, the Sultan of Turkey, the nominal overlord of Egypt, removed Ismail and replaced him by his son Tewfik. An international commission was instituted to administer the Egyptian national debt, *la Caisse de la dette publique*, while ways and means finance was subjected to two controllers, one French, one English. At the same time, the size of the army was reduced, a reform causing considerable discontent among the officers, of whom a Colonel Arabi became the spokesman and leader of revolt. In the autumn of 1881, these forced the Khedive to summon an assembly of Egyptian notables, with the principal purpose of getting rid of the French and British financial controllers. In December Gambetta persuaded Gladstone's government to join, albeit reluctantly, in a 'Dual Note' to the Khedive that they proposed to support him and the European financial control. Instead of scaring the Egyptian nationalists, as had been hoped, it merely stimulated them to greater pressure on the Khedive. Intimidated by Arabi and his colonels, he appointed a new government on February 5, with Arabi as Minister of War, which led to a situation of anarchy.

Between the delivery of the Dual Note and the appearance of the Arabi-dominated Government, Freycinet had succeeded to Gambetta. During the spring, the English cabinet became seriously alarmed for the safety of the Canal, the route to India. Though at sixes and sevens and unable to agree on a policy, on this the ministers were united. The French were not as yet interested in the Canal to the same extent, but they did not wish to see the Turks, encouraged by Bismarck, send troops to Egypt. Neither French nor English wanted military action on land. Hence in May, each sent a naval squadron to lie in the harbour of Alexandria. This merely fomented further trouble. On June 11, there was a massacre of Europeans in Alexandria, and the Egyptians began to construct batteries on shore to command the shipping in the harbour. The British admiral proposed to bombard if the work continued, but the French cabinet to whom the proposal was submitted declined and withdrew their squadron.[2] On July 11 the British destroyed the batteries by gunfire. This merely had the effect of rousing the Arabists to further demonstrations.

On July 13 the British cabinet invited the French to a joint occupation of the Canal area. Freycinet agreed and brought the matter to the Chamber on July 18. At the end of the second day's debate he obtained a credit of some eight million francs for the Minister of Marine and Colonies for the purpose of securing the Canal, but he was much embarrassed[3] between Gambetta who considered the amount wholly insufficient for effective action and Clemenceau who was opposed to intervention in Egypt, partly on moral grounds, partly that it would distract forces from Europe. Moreover, the cabinet was split, four ministers, including both service chiefs, being opposed to action. Ten days later, when Freycinet asked for another nine millions, this time for the army, the Chamber was even cooler. After a confused debate, the motion was rejected by a coalition of all his critics, and he resigned. No French action was taken. The British entered Egypt alone, and having routed Arabi at Tel-el-Kebir on September 13, assumed sole control of the country.

Grévy was now in even greater difficulties. He consulted on all sides and found no solution. He suggested that Ferry might sew up the torn cabinet. Ferry refused, and writing that night (August 1) to his wife, said that the problem was not to find ministers but a ministry.[4] Since he shared Gambetta's policy of intervention in Egypt, he could not lead it. But now that Freycinet was gone, who was there? He appears to have suggested that 'ghost of 1848', Eugène Duclerc, negotiator over the life-senators in 1875, now over seventy and ailing. Duclerc in the end accepted, taking over the non-interventionists from Freycinet's cabinet, Tirard, Billot, Jauréguibery and de Mahy. It was a stop-gap government and knew itself to be so.

Owing to the parliamentary recess, the cabinet had more than three months law, but it had no more definite policy than its predecessor for dealing with Egypt. The hesitations, negations and timidities of the past six months had now to be paid for. When their expeditionary force landed, the British cabinet had not thought out a policy for the future. It now had the government of Egypt on its hands, and much as it disliked doing so, it had to act quickly if it was to forestall intervention by jealous neighbours. Even before Arabi was defeated, Gladstone began the preparations for settlement of the conflict and evacuation. He proposed that the Khedive should be restored and equipped with a loyal army, and that the British should leave the country as soon as possible. To this the cabinet agreed, adding that it was imperative to keep the Canal inviolate and inviolable by securing that no other nations should

R

dominate Egypt. In fulfilment of this resolve, they intimated to the French Government that withdrawal would not take place until the stability of the Khedivial régime was in British opinion assured and that for the future there should be a single financial controller. This unilateral denunciation of the 1880 agreement naturally galled the French, particularly the French holders of Egyptian bonds. The British were adamant, and in December established under a single Englishman the new system. They began to concentrate the garrison early in 1883 with a view to withdrawal, but in spite of repeated promises this was never completed. The French had only themselves to thank. It was not that they desired to occupy the country themselves: they merely wanted the British out, or compensation elsewhere for their own blunders. Yet offered the presidency of the *Caisse*, Duclerc declined, saying that France would resume her liberty of action. The Egyptian question remained to poison Anglo-French relations for more than another twenty years, poison all the more bitter for being self-administered. As the British ambassador in Paris, Lord Lyons, wrote: 'The really remarkable fact is that each government succeeded in bringing about the result which it least desired. . . . The efforts of the French Government were chiefly directed towards the prevention of Turkey or any other Power establishing its predominant influence in Egypt, and that French policy should have unconsciously and involuntarily thrust England into this unsought position is one of the real ironies of recent history'.[5]

(ii)

From the opening of the extraordinary session in November, the Duclerc Government was on the defensive, the target of a campaign opened by Léon Say against government extravagance, such as the increase in teachers' salaries and of teaching staffs at an hour of a deficit budget and a Bourse slump. Already there were indications that the fat years were over; there was a violent strike at Montceau-les-Mines where Schneider had dismissed a number of workers, and another of the Paris building trades. Though he did not admit it, the crisis was accentuated by Say's own errors. In preparing the budget, the Finance Minister took as the rate for each tax the level of the previous year, that is to say, in the budget for 1883, which should be debated and passed by Chamber and Senate before December 31, 1882, the rates shown would be those of 1881. Since 1876, owing to the rise of both the volume of trade and prices, each year had shown a surplus. Say seems to have believed that this rise would continue and had therefore had the rates reduced, a practice copied by his successor, Magnin, in 1880 and 1881. At the same time, non-recurrent capital expenditure had been taken out of the budget proper and placed in a category called extraordinary budget. Hence at the end of 1882, the Treasury was much embarrassed by falling revenue and burdened with the cost of the Freycinet Plan. In December, Hérisson, Minister of Public Works, admitted that the plan now amounted to 9–9½ milliards, double the total quoted by Say.[6]

(*iii*)

At the end of December, it was known that Gambetta was dangerously ill. During the previous two years, he had changed much in appearance: he had grown extremely fat, had lost much of his hair and his complexion had become pallid. An operation for peritonitis was unsuccessful. Just before midnight on December 31 he died at the early age of forty-four.

The world was startled. From abroad, the response showed the belief that France had lost her great leader, and those who bore the country no good will expressed their satisfaction. '*Ein Brausekopf weniger*', said the Kaiser briefly. In France, the sentiment among politicians was coloured by political convictions: relief from such as Grévy and Broglie; grief from his friends; regret from his allies. 'His exuberant personality', wrote Ferry, 'of which opinion still exaggerated the activity, often embarrassed government, but what security it was to feel him there in reserve. Certainly he leaves us diminished and impoverished.' And Grévy said, 'Destiny has not been just. Perhaps he deserved to fall; he certainly deserved to have time to pick himself up.'[7] But beyond the politicians there was France. The funeral was possibly the biggest Paris had ever seen. The procession took two hours and a quarter to pass a given point, some hundred thousand marchers. 'The whole Ecole polytechnique. Two to three thousand students. Carts filled with wreaths. Deputations from all over France. That was the oddest thing, this march past of two or three hundred groups of small-town politicians come from every corner of France, each with its own wreath. *The new social stratum, the petite bourgeoisie*, the real masters of France. Gambetta was their god. He had said: "Yours is the policy. Yours is France!" He had shown them the promised land.'[8]

(iv)

A few days later, Prince Napoleon, the imperialist claimant, impetuous, bold, eccentric, chose this moment to placard Paris with a manifesto against the obviously rotten parliamentarianism of the Republic, calling for a revival of the plebiscite and a return to the Empire. He was immediately arrested, but this was the kind of chance the Radicals loved. Floquet tabled a motion for the expulsion of the families of all claimants to the French throne. Since both the Comte de Chambord and the Comte de Paris lived abroad, Floquet's target was the three Orleans princes, particularly the Duc d'Aumale, who were either serving or had held commands in the forces and who were valued in many quarters. For Duclerc this was the last straw; he insisted that he was ill and on January 29 resigned, as did his two service ministers, Billot and Jauréguibery, neither of whom relished dismissing the popular princes. Billot was replaced by General Thibaudin, a general tinged with Radicalism, who alone of the soldiers was known not to shrink from the task. The cabinet remained under the nominal leadership of Fallières, Minister of the Interior. Meanwhile, Government, Chamber and Senate quarrelled over the question of the royal families. Fallières could not deal with the problem and he and the rest of the cabinet resigned. Grévy called Ferry.

For Ferry, the death of Gambetta, however regrettable, was a relief. No longer need he suffer the obscure and undesirable suggestions to ministers and deputies that had troubled him in 1881. Now while Gambetta's wilder followers would shift to the Left, a stable majority might be achieved with the more sober Gambettists, the Left Centre and his own friends.

The Government, which was to last for more than two years, was drawn from all groups. It included three Gambettists in Waldeck-Rousseau (Interior), Raynal (Public Works) and Challemel-Lacour (Foreign Office)* as well as Félix Faure as Under-Secretary for the Colonies. Among Ferry's own followers were Martin-Feuillée (Justice), Tirard (Finance), Hérisson (Commerce), Méline (Agriculture) and Jean Casimir-Périer as Under-Secretary for War. He himself returned to the Ministry of Public Instruction. The cabinet contained two future

---

* Challemel-Lacour fell ill in the summer of 1883 and resigned in November, when Ferry, who had already been acting for him, took over the Foreign Office.

Presidents of the Republic, one of whom with three others would become Prime Minister.

Ferry at once took up the question of the princes. A compromise had been invented. Expulsion would be abandoned but, under a law of 1834, the victims could be removed by decree from the services. This at least partially saved the faces of the princes' friends in Chamber and Senate.

Chapter Thirteen

Ferry

Ferry came to power for the second time with one advantage, and one disadvantage, both deriving from Gambetta's death. Though he need no longer fear the 'occult power' which, like Penelope's fingers, undid the previous day's work, he could no longer call on Gambetta's infusing warmth to rally the waverers against the injurious Clemenceau. In his old age, talking to his secretary Martet, Clemenceau[1] said Ferry was stupid, and added that he was heartless, alleging that when he and Barodet had approached Ferry with a request to support free education, he had rebuffed them. Neither comment is true. Ferry was not heartless; he had done much for education and he knew what he could not do, and he had no brutality of the Clemenceau kind. Nor was he stupid. But he was rigid and limited.

The new Government took office in an hour of serious financial difficulty, when the decline in trade, due largely to a new turn of the technical revolution, was superimposed on the liquidation of the crash of the previous February. In addition, the two major products of French agriculture, wheat and wine, were in severe trouble. The phylloxera, hitherto sporadic, had suddenly become endemic in Languedoc and was spreading through all the south: an import of 707,000 hectolitres in 1877 had risen to 1,603,000 in 1878, to 2,938,000 in 1879 and to 7,219,000 in 1880. At the same time, to a poor cereal crop in 1878 had succeeded a grim winter and a disastrous harvest in 1879: in 1879 22 million quintals of wheat had been imported, in 1880 20 million. Nor was there any sign of relief. In the years 1870–77, imports of wheat and wine had cost annually 264 million francs; in 1878–85, the yearly bill averaged 785 millions.[2] Further complications were due to the belief of Republican governments, fostered by Léon Say, that the prosperity which followed the payment of the war indemnity would continue and that their plans could be easily financed. Now it appeared that the schools authorised under successive education acts would by 1885 cost some 540 millions, of which four-fifths would be added to the public debt.[3] Worse was the problem of completing the Freycinet scheme, the exorbitance of which had recently been revealed in all its crudity by

Hérisson. Revenue was falling and unemployment was increasing, at least in Paris, while at the end of 1882 the floating debt had swollen to 1,179 millions, to which 1883 would add another 622 millions.[4]

On the other hand, Ferry had certain assets. He might be stiff, he might be limited, but he had character and courage, and no one even at the height of his unpopularity ever suggested he was corrupt. Further he had an excellent cabinet of his own group and Gambetta's, and, because they had no other choice, most of the rank and file of the Republican Union had come over to what would now be known as the Democratic Left (to distinguish it from the Radical Left). The attacks from the Right were normal and since they could not be supported by the Radicals presented no danger. Attacks from the Left were more difficult to repel. Usually they were interpellations on political themes, with no future, but there were also appeals to democratic principles which would seduce timid deputies from the Republicans. Clemenceau's reputation rests on his work in 1918, which veils the fact that had the Father of Victory died in 1914, it would be very different. During much of his early parliamentary career his activities were pernicious and often devoid of political understanding. The 'overthrower of cabinets' could not replace those he destroyed and his temporary allies in the shambles promptly deserted him, since Grévy refused to invite him to form a ministry: 'he would turn the country upside down.' Even less than Gambetta was he a judge of men, and his later connections with Boulanger, Laguerre, Andrieux and Cornelius Herz did his reputation no good. Still, he intimidated the simpler provincial deputies. 'He is Chocquard himself, the legendary Garde de Corps,' quoth Drumont, 'the terror of the estaminets, the barmaids' idol.'[5] Ferry privately spoke of him as a malevolent starling, and in October, 1883 in a speech at Le Havre denounced the Extreme Left. 'The monarchist danger lies buried beneath two grave-stones,' he said, referring to the death of the Prince Imperial and the recent demise of the Comte de Chambord. 'That danger is no more, but another succeeds and we must face it. . . . Whenever we talk of government, of stability, of method, the intransigents will not have it. Intransigence is the negation of all that. For government, it cares nothing. Whoever talks of government is a monarchist. . . . Stability! there, to Intransigence, stands the enemy!'[6] It was a declaration of war and the Radicals accepted it. In this denunciation is to be seen the essential Ferry. The liberty Radicals demand is licence. There is no liberty without order. A follower once said of Gladstone at the peak of his career: 'how he drove us!' Ferry too was hard. 'The kind of general,' wrote Freycinet, 'that takes no prisoners.'[7] It is a type that has followers, but not friends. When the crisis came in 1885, he was deserted.

The twenty-six months of the Ferry ministry added several important laws to the Statute Book. The entanglements of the finances of railway construction were unravelled by Raynal, the Minister of Public Works, and a bill brought in in June 1883. By the Freycinet scheme the State had backed the construction of some 16,000 kilometres of line all over the country, parts of which were leased to the six main systems. The State credit was now in peril, whereas that of the railway companies, which had not yet begun to feel the slump, was far better; their revenue in 1883 was better by 40% than a decade earlier and the three indebted companies were paying off. The Extreme Left took up once more the old theme of State purchase, in spite of the obvious impossibility of finding the money. The Raynal bill proposed that the companies should take over 12,000 kilometres of railway and complete the whole system, except some strategic lines. The State would construct bed, track and superstructure, the companies would build the stations and provide the equipment, with government help.[8] The existing distinction between old and new networks was to be suppressed and the State gave a general guarantee over the whole, of minimum interest and dividends plus amortisation. In spite of the opposition of the Left, the bill passed the Chamber easily, and the Senate even more easily. The law was promulgated on November 20. It was not observed, until much later, that the terminal date of the concessions had not been set out in the bill.

Other legislation included a law of purely political significance. Constitutionally, the judges (and other members of the *parquet*) were irremovable. Most of the senior law officers had been appointed under the Empire, some even had sat on the mixed commissions after the *coup d'état* of 1851. A great number had no love for the Republic, and, as has been seen, many had resigned rather than carry out the expulsion of the Orders in 1880. The Left, and in chief the Extremists, insisted that there were still many disaffected to the Republic. The method of getting rid of them had been discussed more than once since February 1882, when Martin-Feuillée, lately of Gambetta's cabinet, produced his bill. The solution of the difficulty was to suspend the attribution of irremovability of all the law officers for three months, and during that time to suppress as superfluous the offices held by those to be eliminated, their holders being retired on pension. There was considerable criticism in the Chamber before the bill was passed. 'Yes,' said Ribot, 'Republican magistrates are necessary, but before all, magistrates.' In the Senate, the measure was strongly opposed by Jules Simon and only passed by a majority of three. The law was promulgated on August 30, 1883. It was a dubious proceeding, the first approach towards the tampering with judicial independence which twenty years later would be laid to the charge of the political leaders.[9]

In 1884 came the great municipal law (April 5) which co-ordinated and regulated the system of local government. One clause was of political importance in that it laid down the number of members of each council on a basis of population.

Apart from the law referred to elsewhere (April 6, 1884) legalising trade unions, on July 27, 1883, a bill presented by Naquet was passed, re-establishing divorce, which had been abolished in 1816.

Meanwhile, agitation on the reform of the constitution had been growing. There had been no government move since Gambetta's defeat. More than one motion for revision, invariably of a nature to be lost in a National Assembly, was presented by the Extreme Left and rejected by the Chamber. But there still remained the promises of reform made light-heartedly by candidates at the election of 1881.* For the cabinet the crux of the matter lay in the limitation of revision. The Radicals wanted to discuss everything, including the abolition of the Senate, but the Senate somewhat naturally would accept no invitation to an Assembly without a guarantee of its own emergence from the congress unscathed. Ferry's bill restricted the agenda chiefly to the question of Senate elections, which had been given constitutional status in February 1875 with the purpose of protecting the Upper Chamber against attempts to destroy it. There were, however, other questions which the Senators themselves were willing to discuss, that of the extinction of Life Senators, that of the membership of the electoral colleges at senatorial elections. The Senate was ready to allow the Life Senators to disappear since thus they became masters of their own electoral system. As regards the electoral colleges, the National Assembly had given one vote to each commune, with the intention of giving a small commune with less than 500 souls the same weight as

---

* In February 1882 Barodet proposed that the Chamber should publish the election pledges of the deputies elected in general election. The proposal was rejected by the committee, but the deputies overrode it. These showed that 364 had promised the reform of the judiciary, 342 the revision of the constitution, 283 for divorce, 235 the legalisation of syndicats, 227 for the separation of Church and State. The majority in the full Chamber would be 279.

Paris or Marseille, thus strengthening the conservative rural vote against the Radical urban vote. This the Republican majority in the Senate was willing to change, and to admit electoral delegates according to the size of the municipal council, as laid down in Waldeck-Rousseau's law of April 5, from those of ten members having one delegate up to 24 delegates for councils of 36, and 30 for Paris. The critical question before the Assembly would be over Article 8 of the constitutional law of February 24, 1875: 'The Senate, concurrently with the Chamber of Deputies, has the initiative in the making of laws. Nevertheless, the financial laws must in the first instance be presented to the Chamber of Deputies and voted by it.' In 1884 the Senate refused to meet the Chamber unless guaranteed that Article 8 should be maintained. Léon Say had rightly claimed that the initiative in requests for credits was the prerogative of the Government. This condition was intolerable to the majority of the Chamber, which in any case wanted to deprive the Senate of any form of financial control. After considerable trouble, Ferry persuaded the two main Republican groups not to ask for any amendment to Article 8 and to the fury of the Extremists secured their unwilling consent. On this the Senate agreed to play its part.[10]

The Assembly met at Versailles on August 4. Both Right and Extreme Left behaved outrageously; the hall was in uproar. Yet in the end all the unagreed amendments from the extremists on either side were rejected. The agreed changes were passed on August 13 by 519 to 172.*

In consequence, an ordinary law for the new organisation of the Senate was needed to pass both Chambers. This proved almost as difficult as in 1875. After weeks of incoherent argument, with impossible proposals sometimes passed, sometimes withdrawn, the electoral law for the Senate was passed on December 9. The main feature was the gradual extinction of the Life Senators by non-replacement at death, and the attribution of the seat to a department by lot. It was not until 1916 that the last life member died. At that point the whole 300 seats would be elective for nine years.

---

* The Constitutional Law of August 14, 1884, laid down (a) that elections must be held within two months of the dissolution of the Chamber. This was to prevent a repetition of Broglie's manoeuvres of 1877. Further, that the Chamber must meet within ten days of the closure of the poll, this to avoid a repetition of Ferry's muddle of 1881: (b) the removal of the constitutional character of Articles 1–7 of the law of February 24, 1875, thus making the Senate master in its own house: (c) as a sop to the anti-clericals, the paragraph ordaining the daily saying of prayers was abrogated (Law of July 16, 1875, Article 1, para. 3): (d) 'The Republican form of government must not be made the aim of any proposition of revision. Members of families which have ruled over France are ineligible for the Presidency.'

The passage of the law was just in time for the triennial renewal of a third of the Senate, with in addition eight bye-elections of which two were to replace defunct Life Senators, a total of 82, 42 Left to 40 Right. The poll took place on January 25 and resulted in yet one more crushing defeat of the Right: of their 40 seats, 23 were lost. Except for the Life Senators the Senate had now had a complete turnover. The state of the membership gave 50 Republican Life Senators to 23 Right, and of the rest 177 Republicans to 50 Right. But, of the 227 Republicans, at least 70, probably more, were Left Centre and deeply conservative.

More important was the renewed introduction of Gambetta's fatal *scrutin de liste* proposal. The rapporteur was Constans who had always supported the change. He merely repeated the former arguments and left it at that. The bill was carried in the Chamber by 404 to 91, thus demonstrating that the division of January 1882 was influenced entirely by fear or jealousy of Gambetta.* The Senate suggested that the number of constituencies in a department should be based on the number of voters rather than the population, since the latter favoured the frontier departments swollen with foreigners. The Chamber agreed to the subtraction of the foreigners from the population. In the new system, the basis for one member would be 75,000 instead of 100,000. Although this raised the membership of the Chamber from 557 to 584, it caused fourteen departments to lose members, while thirty-two gained, Paris being increased from 32 to 38. The bill became law on June 16, two months after Ferry's defeat.

* In the spring of 1885, there were 246 deputies who had voted in all three divisions on *scrutin de liste* (May 1881, January 1882, and February 1885). Of these no more than 29 had voted 'aye' in all three, and only 43 'no'. But 78 had voted 'no' only against Gambetta, showing that they were against the man rather than against the principle.

Chapter Fourteen

Ferry and the Colonies

(i)

At the end of the Seven Years' War, France had lost the greater part of her overseas empire. With the Louisiana sale of 1803, the Napoleonic era saw the turning away from the colonies in the pursuit of an empire in Europe which also foundered. 'There are two charges to be levelled against Napoleon; the first, that of losing our colonial empire by his own fault (the neglect of the French navy); the second of destroying our appetite for colonisation.'[1] After 1815 the colonies were forgotten. All that remained were those territories which the English did not require, the sugar islands of Martinique and Guadeloupe, Réunion and a few small islands in the Indian Ocean, the trading stations on the coast of India, Pondicherry, Chandernagar and the rest, footholds on the West African coast in Guinea and Senegal, and the islands of Saint-Pierre and Miquelon in the mouth of the Saint Lawrence Gulf.

Between 1815 and 1870 a few acquisitions were made. Algeria, the invasion of which was begun under Charles X, was partly subdued during the thirties by the troops of Louis-Philippe, a conquest accepted by the country largely with indifference, but which opened opportunities to professional soldiers. Tahiti, the Marquesas, the Society Islands and New Caledonia, were acquired in the Pacific, in the belief that the Panama Canal was soon to be cut. New Caledonia was transformed into a penal settlement in 1863–64. In 1839 Gaboon, or at least the mouth of the Ogowe river, was annexed, but the hinterland was scarcely entered, while in the fifties the West African fragments were extended and the beginnings of penetration made under the initiative of General Faidherbe, who more than any other is the progenitor of the French colonial success of the twentieth century. Last, in 1858–61 there came the invasion of the Annamite Empire, a vassal state of China, and in the next six years, six provinces of Cochin-China were annexed and a protectorate established over Cambodia.

In the years after Sedan, the colonies were little valued. Between all of them and France there was little interchange; the total of commerce in 1873 amounted to little over 500 million francs and half of this was with Algeria. The empire was costing the taxpayer a considerable amount in subsidies. Except for a handful of devoted 'explorers', in fact almost all officers of the navy and marine infantry — the colonies were the business of the Ministry of Marine — Frenchmen were largely apathetic, even hostile to the idea of empire. Colonial expansion was a distraction from the main question, the recovery of the lost provinces. 'I have lost two children and you offer me twenty servants', Déroulède, the President of the noisily *revanchard* Ligue des Patriotes founded in 1882, is said to have thrown at Ferry in a moment of bitterness. There was the insecurity of the new frontier until General Séré des Rivières had completed the fortifications. There were the Jacobins of the Extreme Left opposing colonisation in any form on the ground that none had the right to impose an alien civilisation by force on primitive peoples. With the single exception of Leroy-Beaulieu, editor of the *Economiste Français*, French economists agreed that colonies were an expensive luxury. In token of this, Broglie in 1874 stopped the advance in Indo-China; a peace was signed with the Emperor of Annam, and at the same time, the Emperor, momentarily in conflict with his liege-lord the Emperor of China, placed himself under French protection.

(*ii*)

Throughout the history of French colonisation, there had been one unshakeable doctrine, even when it appeared temporarily forgotten. This was that the colonies existed for the benefit of metropolitan France. To this end, they had been subjected to a system analogous to the English Navigation Acts, the *pacte coloniale*. Under this, no colony could trade independently and its commerce was subordinated to French trade. Abrogated in 1789, the pact was re-imposed in 1802 and survived until 1861, when freedom of import and export was granted and five years later, partial fiscal autonomy. By 1868 the *pacte* was generally abolished. These measures were less acts of enlightened generosity than the alignment of the colonies with the French commercial treaties of the sixties.

It was the corollary of another doctrine, namely that the French Revolution and all that derived from it was of such perfection that the colonies must model themselves on France, or, in the official jargon, be 'assimilated'. Every colony should be a replica of a French department and the Napoleonic codes must be substituted for the local legal tradi-tions. That each territory had a different type of population, a different religion, a different economy and a different social hierarchy, carried no weight in Paris. In token of this, Saigon was provided with a cathedral, splendid government offices, and an opera house unrivalled in Asia, but was still watered by the primitive and insanitary system of the days of the Chinese domination. Governors, some of whom were politicians of awkward disposition, some arrivistes with an eye to easy wealth, were despatched, accompanied by large staffs of French officials ig-norant of both the country and the language, and frequently recalled within a year. Indo-China was to have seven governors-general within six years; Tahiti thirty-one between 1880 and 1920. New Caledonia required 3,000 functionaries for less than that number of colonists.[2]

The history of Algeria has a melancholy interest in that the French governments and ministries seem to have made every blunder that theorists could possibly make: not Bouvard and Pécuchet at their most visionary could compete. Whereas, in other colonies, there were mis-takes, some with lamentable results, in no other were the errors so many or so continuous. It would seem that no régime, July Monarchy, Second Republic, Second Empire, Third Republic, ever made up its mind as to what kind of colony Algeria could be, a colony of settlement or a colony of exploitation or, as was sometimes assumed, a province of France, a more southern Languedoc: or should it be a fusion of all three?

Algeria was the only region suited to European immigration. In spite of General Bugeaud's efforts between 1841 and 1847 to build up settle-ments of soldier-farmers, mattock and rifle in hand, the experiment failed. After this, there was no policy, only a kaleidoscope of half-hearted measures, each imagined on the failure of the latest. In a roman-tic mood, Napoleon III toyed with the idea of an Arab kingdom. In 1863 what had been known as *refoulement*, the pushing back of the indigenous inhabitants to the interior, was abandoned and a serious attempt begun to deal with the native problem and smooth out the difficulties of managing a diverse population with different ancestries and different ways of life. In the Kabylie hills, the Aurès ranges and the Mzab, lived the Berbers, the original non-Arabic natives, individualist groups of landowners, hard-working, grasping, xenophobic, with a lively dislike of the Arab conqueror of the past and the French of the present. The Algerian Arabs were nondescript, a people of mixed Turkish, Moorish and Negro stock, united solely in being, like the

Berbers, Moslem. The new policy, known as *cantonnement*, envisaged the settlement of each tribe in a reserve of land considered sufficient for its existence, the rest being retained by the State with a view to white settlement. This satisfied neither natives nor immigrants. In 1864 there were revolts in Oran and the Kabylie, followed by sporadic raiding up to 1869, while locusts, drought, famine in 1867 and cholera in 1868 contributed to undoing the work of the past. Settlers abandoned their farms and drifted back to the cities. In 1869, of nearly a quarter of a million Europeans, only 90,000 were on the countryside, and at least half of these were not French. Round Oran, hardworking Spaniards from Valencia and Murcia, conservative and anti-French, created what was to all intents a Spanish enclave. At the eastern end, below Constantine, Italians from poverty-stricken Calabria and Sicily, labourers rather than peasants, built another area of discontent, next door to their fellow-nationals in Tunisia. And the French?[3]

Between 1820 and 1924 the United Kingdom sent to the U.S.A. alone 8½ millions, Germany 6 millions; France sent at most half a million. France had no population to spare for overseas expansion. The landless labourer who fled from England had few counterparts in France. There was little pressure to drive the French peasant overseas. As Norre, a farmer in the Quercy, was to say to Daniel Halévy in 1920: 'Must one go to Africa or Asia to be a colonist? These journalists and ministers who talk to us about the colonies seem to have forgotten to know about France. Let us colonise our own land first.'[4] There were no sources from which a stream of colonial settlers might flow.

Although Algeria was represented in Parliament in Paris from 1848, the only voters were French citizens. French citizenship depended on the acceptance of French law and French institutions, impossible for a Moslem bound by Koranic law.* On the other hand, Algeria contained a large body of Jews of ancient stock, settled in the country from before even the Arab invasions. These had been recognised as French by the Second Empire in 1865, though remaining subject. In 1870 their enfranchisement was completed by Gambetta's delegation at Tours, the Crémieux decree of October 24. It was, however, not because of this, but because of the French defeat that insurrection broke out at Souk-Arrhas near the Tunisian frontier in January 1871. By March the whole Kabylie was up and the coastal towns between Alger and Philippeville

---

* Although polygamy, forbidden under French law, was permissible under Koranic law to a limited degree, it was very rare in Algeria, few being able to afford more than one wife.

invested. It was five months before General Saussier had the country in hand.

From 1864 the country had been under military government. The Republic in 1871 proposed to inaugurate the civil administration of the colony, but until 1879, this remained merely nominal, the governor-general in fact being a soldier supported by the armed forces. The punishment for the revolt was both brutal and foolish. A great area, some million acres, was sequestrated, a quarter of which was given to Lorrainers, who had opted for France. The gesture failed; most of them simply drifted back to the towns. Nevertheless a fresh start was made in 1878 when a system of official colonisation with free grants of land on terms was initiated. This brought from the phylloxera-stricken departments of Languedoc and Provence a number of trained vigner-ons, true peasants who would take whatever good land was offered. By 1881 the rural population had risen by half and more than half were French. Ten years later, the Algerian vineyard had grown to 110,000 hectares.[5]

The confiscations of native property were not carried out easily, nor was the imposition of French law. Under the latter, the individualisa-tion of tribal land led to natives disposing of their share to European speculators, involving tribes in endless litigation and legal costs. Be-tween 1883 and 1889 the Arabs lost some 40% of their property. At every corner French law conflicted with Koranic, while acquisition by Europeans meant not settlement, but sub-letting to an incompetent native cultivator without capital, using primitive tools and methods. In spite of the nominal pacification, revolts continued. There were re-newed outbreaks, in 1876 at El-Amri, in 1879 in the Aurès, in 1881 in southern Oran which had been seething for fifteen years, in 1882 revolt spread into the Mzab. By the middle nineties the area of controlled country was smaller than in 1864 and travellers south of the line of outposts were fortunate if they returned.

In 1881, after two years of civil government, a new theory was devised. Since 1848 certain branches of administration had been directed from Paris: Public Worship, Public Instruction, Justice (for Europeans) and Customs. In 1881 in the desire to complete the 'assimilation' of Algeria, the Government, by decrees of March 11 and August 26, ex-tended the 1848 system to all ministries. Each ministerial branch in Algeria in future would be *rattaché* to the appropriate ministry in Paris; it was simply the extension of the inland departmental system to the colony. Henceforward, Algeria was at the mercy of the Paris civil servants, wholly ignorant of local conditions and wedded to regulations often quite impracticable for a largely non-French province. The governor-general became a cypher; he was reduced, said Ferry, to 'an ornament as costly as it was useless, at the best an inspector of colonisation in the palace of a *fainéant* king'. Algerian business became the sport of parliamentary influences and bureaucratic rivalry, incompetence and delay. Tirman, governor-general 1881–91, was powerless; his successor Jules Cambon, 1891–96, spent his term in fighting for amendment, and only saw *rattachement* repealed as he was promoted elsewhere (December 31, 1896).[6]

(iii)

That, given intelligent leaders and confidence in them, the French were capable of successful colonisation is shown by the history of what became French West Africa.[7] In 1850 there had been little on the west coast other than the small fragment at the mouth of the Senegal with the moribund port of Saint-Louis and its four cantons. Here in 1854 Colonel Faidherbe, an engineer officer, was appointed governor. By the time he was recalled to France in 1866, he had organised the first regiment of native tirailleurs and fought his way up the right bank of the river as far as Medina, where he established French influence over the local chiefs. In 1861 and again in 1863–66 one of his officers, Magé, explored still further inland, reaching the Niger at Segou, while some time later, Binger, Faidherbe's orderly officer, began the penetration of Guinea. Meanwhile other explorers and traders had worked along the coast and established stations between the various English possessions. By 1870 French naval officers pushing inland were already aware of a possible rich empire in the hinterland. During these years, they broke the power of the religious leader El-Hadj Omar; they conquered Ahmadau, north of the upper Senegal, and finally after a long struggle subdued the kingdom of Samory near the upper Volta. From 1879 through the early eighties, economic missions and military patrols were pushing out eastwards. Bamakao was reached in 1883, Timbuktu by 1893. Segou was occupied in 1891, the foothold on the Ivory coast was extended and the occupation of Dahomey undertaken. By the middle nineties, there were four French colonies, Senegal, Sudan, Guinea and the Ivory Coast, ready to be welded into a colonial federation with extensions in progress northward and eastward.

s

In contrast to the failure in Algeria, which became neither a colony of exploitation nor a colony of settlement, the French penetration of West Africa was successful. Making no attempt to found settlements, the invaders maintained the native authorities and encouraged the development and rationalisation of native institutions. There was no expropriation of land; the native was encouraged to become a peasant farmer. There were no abrupt changes, and though later the Government influenced specialisation of production it was carried through without friction and according to well-conceived plans.

The success in West Africa was due initially to Faidherbe, whose policy was the improvement of the native. On his resignation from the governorship, he wrote:[8] 'I believe I quit the colony in a fairly satisfactory condition and I am persuaded that France can make of it a fine and useful possession if the interest of the natives is taken to be the rule of government. For this governors are needed who have neither repugnance, dislike nor disdain for races little favoured by nature as to human perfectability but which nonetheless are not unworthy of sympathy and which on their own soil and without being driven by unjust and inhuman methods can produce something to repay amply the European peoples and the merchants who are glad to interest themselves in them, to protect them and handle them with kindness.' Faidherbe created a tradition from which sprang all that was best in French colonial expansion, not only the thrusting explorers, Binger, Mizer, Monteil but also those who practised and extended Faidherbe's theories, such as Galliéni, together with Faidherbe's brilliant successors, Brière de l'Isle, Roume, Camille Guy, Joost van Vollenhoven, Merlin. The success in West Africa, apart from the personality of Faidherbe, was due to the fact that his work 'never agitated opinion in France, never called for money, reinforcements or discussion; it did not attract the ambitious or the parasite. It raised no international complications: it seemed enclosed in a poverty-stricken Africa and contemporaries never saw its originality.'[9]

(iv)

During the debates on Egypt in the summer of 1882, Ferry had not spoken. He was too angry with the indecisiveness of his colleagues and the pusillanimity of the Chamber. As he wrote later:[10] 'the doctrine of effacement was consummated on the day the Chamber . . . left England alone tête-à-tête with the Khedive. . . . When the new vision of English greatness materialises, and the British flag, either as protector or conqueror, floats over the whole Nile valley from Alexandria to the Great Lakes and from the Great Lakes to the Zambezi, perhaps French levity will understand the irreparable damage that was done to our future and our race by short-sighted policy.'

When he took office the second time in the spring of 1883, the colonial question was already being transformed, but not in Paris. On the fringes of the colonies, Frenchmen, whose names were still little known to the public, Rivière, Magé, Binger, Galliéni, were exploring deserts, rivers and forests and offering their discoveries to their countrymen — more, returning with treaties signed by foreign, often savage, potentates, on the frontiers of China, on the Senegal, Niger and Volta, on the Congo, on the Somali coast, in the kingdom of the Hovas, pledging, as it were, the forces of France. In the autumn of 1882 Savorgnan de Brazza, returning after four years in the Congo river basin, presented the Chamber with a file of treaties with African chiefs, largely cannibal, and in January 1883 was given a large credit to permit him to continue his work, which, strangely enough, had been undertaken on the authority of the Ministry of Public Instruction, Ferry.

Ferry was not the man to refuse such legacies. The great extension of overseas France was in the main prepared and in part carried out between 1883 and 1885. Hitherto, Ferry had shown small interest in the empire, but now he became the obstinate and pugnacious advocate of policies which he knew to be detestable to the majority of Frenchmen. Yet his attitude is ambiguous. The explanation of his aims and policy which he gave in July 1885, after his defeat, is rather a series of defensive arguments than the cogent exposition of a faith: the suspicion is unavoidable that his ideas had come from outside and had been imperfectly digested. It may be that he had been influenced by his brother Charles. Jules Ferry was no economist; his replies to interpellations on the depression are unimaginative, not to say commonplace. Charles Ferry, on the other hand, was a business man, a financier, director of the Franco-Egyptian Bank, on the board of which were to be found directors of the Banque d'Indo-Chine, possibly the strongest of all the French colonial banks. Whatever its origin, Jules Ferry's demonstration does not carry great weight: he gives the impression of a man rummaging through an armoury to find weapons without knowing how to handle them.[10] His first point was that with the rapid industrialisation of Europe, each country was now protecting its manufactures with tariff walls.* French production was rising, hence new markets must be sought, and where could they be found except in Asia and Africa? In Indo-China, the French were on the doorstep of the biggest potential market in the world, four hundred million Chinese. Further, since France had no surplus population to send overseas, and anyhow all the temperate regions suited to white settlement were already occupied, it was French capital that must migrate. To this he added a second argument: that Europe was spreading all over the world and that the wars of the future would be world-wide. Therefore the French navy must have bases and coaling-stations. 'It is not in the Mediterranean or the Channel that the decisive engagement will be fought; Marseille and Toulon will be defended as much in the China Sea as in the Mediterranean.'[11] Last of all, he spoke indignantly of British acquisitions. They had taken Cyprus in 1878; it was only tolerable that as compensation, the French occupy Tunisia for their own security. And now the British were in Egypt, and the French must have compensation. 'The occupation of Tonkin is the revenge for Egypt.'

There, 'his theory stopped. It never got beyond protection and colonial markets to the issues of raw materials and the best forms of colonial development.'[12] It was an abstract conception carried to an abstract conclusion. Ten years later, at the Paris Colonial Exhibition, he bitterly remarked to Spuller that 'la belle Fatma' and the *danse du ventre* were all that the empire meant to the French and that colonies were but pawns in the domestic political game. 'When they are occupied, they are described as deserts and marshes: when you use them for barter, people call them the flesh of the mother country. It would be better to have the Germans in Tonkin than in Nancy.'[13] That this had been Ferry's secret hope is possible, that by horse-trading with an esurient Germany the lost provinces might be recovered. Who could desire it more than Ferry, whose home lay only fifteen miles from the new frontier? The hope was vain, though Bismarck was ready enough to encourage illusions by hints to the French Ambassador, Courcel.

During the negotiations, in 1884-85, between the Portuguese, the British and the Germans with the International Association of the Congo (the philanthropic mask for the private estate of that astute merchant-prince, Leopold II of Belgium), over the delimitation of the Congo basin and the freedom of its commerce, Ferry was pressed by Bismarck to join some sort of alliance against the British. 'He translated

* Germany had gone over to full protection in 1879.

the world of Grimm's fairy tales into political terms. Ogres and witches were waiting to chop Germany into bits.'[14] In 1884 the German Chancellor, like Capek's dung-beetle, apprehensive that Germany's winnings would be snatched from her, had proposed through Courcel joint action in West Africa and offered support to drive the English out of Egypt. Ferry was cautious. Apart from Egypt, France had no serious quarrel with the English. What did the Germans offer? It was found to be nothing worth considering in the colonial sphere, and to a suggestion that there might be some modification in the commercial relations of the two countries, there was no response. Bismarck airily proposed some reconstruction of the Continental system of Napoleon I, an 'equilibrium of the seas' at British expense. Several times he told Courcel that he wanted the French to forgive Sedan as they had forgiven Waterloo. Bismarck was no historian; the changes in the French frontier after 1815 had been to the profit of Prussia and had not been forgotten. Ferry would pick no quarrel with the British on unguaranteed promises of German support. 'Our policy is to wait and to take no steps without the support of Europe.'[15]

Hence at the Berlin West Africa Conference, while the French obtained a large part of their claims, the right bank of the Congo (except the mouth) and a vast region extending to Lake Chad, relations with Germany, while pacific enough, did not grow cordial. After all, Ferry could count on Bismarck's hostility to Britain to provide support to French obstruction on the Egyptian Finance Commission. Further he need not go. Further he must not, if he was not to expose himself to the charge of treachery to Alsace-Lorraine.

(v)

The treaty of Saigon between France and Annam had left the latter independent but proclaimed a vague protectorate over the Annamese empire; in other words, the Annamese promised to subject their foreign policy to French advice.[16] The Annamese, taking the French to be soft, proceeded to ignore most of the articles they had agreed to, including the unimpeded export of rice. Now, the Emperor of Annam and Tonkin was a vassal of the Emperor of China, and since he and his mandarins had been much irked by the French, in 1881 he appealed to China. The Chinese informed the French that they did not recognise the treaty of Saigon and sent troops down to Tonkin, a difficult country and the stronghold of bandits and pirates, who were practically indistinguish-able from the Chinese troops. The French were under the impression that the English would get ahead of them in southern China. The Governor of Cochin-China, Le Myre de Vilers, was ordered to extend French influence in Tonkin. This he entrusted to Commandant Rivière with two hundred men, who captured Hanoi, but went no further until, being without orders and finding the Chinese troops cooperating with the bandits, he began to clear the Red River delta in the spring of 1883. In May Rivière was killed. This roused the Chamber, which voted credits for naval and military action. The Annamese capital Hué was bombarded and the Emperor, having sued for peace, in August signed a treaty recognising the French protectorate. Negotiations with the Chinese were resumed, while the conquest of Tonkin continued against the Chinese troops who had now become the official enemy. After dilatory and complicated diplomacy, which was made even more en-tangled by the number of French negotiators, a treaty was signed by the Chinese in May 1884 in which they agreed to evacuate Tonkin. They did not however do so, and in June ambushed a French column. In answer to protests, the Chinese promised to withdraw their troops by August. On their failing to do this, the French fleet bombarded Foo-Chow and landed on Formosa. Once more there was a resumption of negotiations, while the guerilla war went on.

Between July 1883 and the end of 1884 there had been seven debates on the Far Eastern war, most of which were coupled with a request for money. The opposition had been feeble. Only once, on December 10, 1883, had the opposition vote risen to 200. The single Senate division on December 20 was overwhelmingly favourable. Ferry had had 38 millions in August and another 43 in November. Nonetheless, by the beginning of 1885 the Chamber was beginning to show some im-patience at the failure to finish off the Tonkin affair. Ferry certainly had great difficulties. War had not been declared, since this would lead to international complications regarding blockade, and, since the French fleet depended for supplies on the English, the French had long resisted the temptation to bombard Chinese ports. Not many troops had been sent, perhaps fifteen battalions and only three from France, but in February Campenon, Minister of War, resigned. The press was now turning against the Prime Minister, the *Journal des Débats* (Conserva-tive Republican), *Justice* (Clemenceau), *Autorité* (Bonapartist), *Intran-sigeant* (Rochefort) harped perpetually on Ferry rather than on Ton-kin. In China mediation was being carried out by the Inspector of

Chinese Customs, Sir Robert Hart, and in spite of the lethargy of the negotiation was being successful.

On March 28, 1885, the Government survived only by accepting the 'pure and simple' order of the day by 259–209. On that day, General Brière de l'Isle in Annam cabled the report of a disastrous defeat at Lang-Son on the Chinese frontier and the retreat of the French force. The news was soon out. On March 30 Ferry brought to the Chamber a request for a credit of 200 millions to finish off the affair. He was met by a storm of accusations, largely baseless, of having squandered a milliard francs, of having caused the death of 35,000 Frenchmen. Clemenceau accused him of treason and Ribot, whose career as a spoiler was no wiser than Clemenceau's, followed. In an interval, the presidents of the two Republican groups begged Ferry to resign. He refused, faced the storm, and was overwhelmed. On the vote only 149 deputies remained faithful. He then left the Palais Bourbon to give his resignation to Grévy. A motion to impeach Ferry by a Bonapartist and a dissident Radical was negatived.

Before he had resigned, a second cable from Brière de l'Isle put the Lang-Son affair in perspective. It had been no more than a skirmish in which a senior officer had been wounded and there had been a slight withdrawal. On March 31 Ferry, acting pending the formation of a new cabinet, received a cable announcing the conclusion of negotiations with the Chinese.

(*vi*)

In spite of his defeat, in spite of the derisive soubriquet of 'le Ton-kinois', the criticism of his policy was not serious. There was no with-drawal from Indo-China. Money was found for a campaign of pacification that needed another twenty years to wind up. The extension of the colonial frontiers continued, unadvertised. Young Captain Monteil arriving in Paris with plans for the Senegal railway at the height of the Ferry trouble, was told that he would not get a penny. Then de Lanessan, ex-naval surgeon and a Paris deputy, who later became governor-general of Indo-China, offered his aid. He slipped the Senegal railway bill in with a batch of local bills which were being hurriedly passed at the end of a session, and behold, Senegal got the money for its railway.[17] Everywhere in the history of expansion there is contradiction. The French had had a kind of shadowy protectorate over the Hova kingdom in Madagascar since 1868. In March 1884 Ferry was attacked by the Radicals and the Right for not insisting on French rights and not implementing a forward policy.

At the back of the criticism, apart from the personal hostility to Ferry, lies the dislike of the Chamber for adventure. The politicians had no objection to picking up a colony cheaply, but a conquest involving a long war, the expedition of troops (even though they be Foreign Legionaries) and the expenditure of money on a grand scale for dubious rewards, was unthinkable. Nevertheless, the French found themselves being driven forward on a path they did not want to take, driven to the acquisition of vast territories in Asia and Africa without quite knowing why.

The need for markets overseas claimed by Ferry was, in the early eighties, exaggerated. At this date it was of little importance, but it might be in the future. The difference between the French and English approach to what is today called 'colonialism' is the difference between the large and the small producer. The English in the nineteenth century were not conquistadors but merchants. They had long practised capital export; the necessary condition for loans was the orderly government of the borrower. Where this was reasonably stable and the State was organised, the British lent money and asked for nothing more than peaceful commercial relations. Their industrial and shipping strength would do the rest. True, they often lost money; South America at moments appeared a bottomless pit, but, compared with the cost of conquering, organising and administering a vast uncivilised territory, the losses were negligible. Given free access to a market they were content, because they were confident in their competitive power — at least up to the middle of the nineties.

While English politicians regarded the occupation of Egypt as a regrettable necessity, the French could not believe that they did not want to stay there. For the French, alive to their own inferior productive strength, their commercial and financial weakness, they believed the British approach to the matter must be as their own. For them the market must be a monopoly. Therefore they must be able to control it, and to do that they must control the government and by tariff policy prevent a strong rival from competing. The fear that the British might conquer that mythical market of 400 million Chinese by opening up the Burma road to Taly in Yunnan was in part responsible for the Tonkin annexation. Similarly, the British, having, as they believed, secured reasonable freedom in the Congo, did not contest the French claims, nor, having control of the river mouths in the Bight of Benin, did they raise strong objections to the French advance in West and Equatorial Africa until the descent on Fashoda. The French therefore are found to be taking on more and more responsibilities of government between 1880 and 1914 in order to secure economic control, which from the point of view of exports was in fact burdensome. On the other hand, it is possible that as sources of raw materials the colonies became important, but this had not been foreseen at the dates of annexation.

Chapter Fifteen

The 1885 Election

Ferry's successor was not easy to find, and the embarrassment caused by the absence of parties with practical programmes could not be overcome. The old Left Centre had no following in the Chamber, while all the Republicans, the Opportunists, had been used up. Grévy would not hear of the suggestion of Clemenceau, in spite of his having been the overthrower of Ferry. Constans tried to collect a cabinet, but failed. Finally, Brisson was summoned from the Presidency of the Chamber; with his leaning towards mild radicalism, it was hoped he might bridge the gulf between the Opportunists and the Extremists. He got together a ministry from all the groups, if not of all the talents. Freycinet came back to the Foreign Office, Allain-Targé, of Brisson's own colour, went to the Interior, with another Radical, Goblet, at Public Instruction. The new Finance Minister, Clamageran, fell ill within a week and was replaced by the grandson of the 'organiser of victory' of the First Republic, Sadi Carnot. The rest were nonentities, except for another bearer of a historic name, Godefroy Cavaignac, appointed undersecretary to General Campenon, who went back to the War Office. It was a stop-gap ministry to tide over affairs until the elections in October.

The attempt to press the charges against Ferry and his cabinet had been foiled. His panic-stricken followers had now recovered their nerve, and Brisson, who took office on April 6, succeeded in getting a vote of credit to wind up the Tonkin campaign, but of only fifty millions. In July a great debate took place on colonial policy, in which Ferry, unrepentant and contemptuous of his adversaries, made a fighting defence of his proceedings.

Brisson was possibly the most negative Prime Minister in the history of the Third Republic. His single passion was anti-clericalism. Otherwise he was a shadow without decision or energy. In spite of the pressure of Goblet and Campenon to provide the Government with a policy, he refused to draft an electoral manifesto, on the ground that the ministry was drawn from differing groups, and he forbade all electoral activity by civil servants on behalf of government candidates. 'We are a cabinet of rabbits', the disgusted Goblet scribbled in his diary.[1]

Goblet had good reason to complain of Brisson's neglect of the most elementary precautions. In 1881 the Right had been at sixes and sevens, the Monarchists disheartened, the Bonapartists quarrelling between themselves. In mid-1884 most had deserted Prince Napoleon for Prince Victor, and the party chairman, the Duc de Padoue, reached an electoral alliance with the Monarchists in a 'Conservative Union'. At the other extreme, the Radicals drew up the so-called 'programme of the rue Cadet', in which stood the headquarters of the Masonic Grand Orient. This included the abolition of the Senate, the denunciation of the Concordat and the abandonment of colonial expansion. A few candidates added the adjective Socialist to Radical but a number of prominent Radicals would have nothing to do with the programme and so lost votes, among them Clemenceau. The Opportunists were squabbling among themselves and in many departments presented rival Republican lists. Comte Albert de Mun and his friends proposed the formation of a purely Catholic party (*Les Treize*) devoted to the interests of the Church but met with such hostility from the Monarchists that the Pope advised them not to proceed.[2] In Paris, where over 200 candidates contested thirty-eight seats, most spoke only of local politics.

The first poll on October 4 was a shock to the Republicans. Apart from Paris, which voted Radical, the poll was largely anti-governmental, with the Right receiving some hundred-thousand more than the Left. In some departments the Conservatives swept the board. In the coastal districts from Flanders to the Bidassoa, every department except Seine-inférieure and Gironde gave a majority to the Right, which in many cases secured all the seats. Seine-inférieure, administered by the highly competent and popular Jewish préfet, Hendlé, alone stood up, electing twelve Republicans. Here the Radical list, which included Clemenceau, got a pitiful 5,000 votes. In Gironde, the first poll was indecisive; only one Republican came through. In Marseille, Rouvier, who had lost his popularity owing to a tactless distribution of decorations, withdrew and went off to Nice.[3] In Paris, Déroulède got a mere 49,000 votes against the 272,000 of Lockroy. At the end of the first day, the Right had 179 seats, the Left but 129.

The seventeen western departments, with almost a quarter of the membership of the Chamber, returned 122 Right candidates to 29 Left. These departments had nearly exactly half of all the lessees of agricultural land in France: in fact, they were nearly double the number of owner-occupiers. This demonstrates the power of the landlord. Moreover, it shows how the mass rural vote could overwhelm such 'government' towns as Brest and Cherbourg, with their arsenals.

During the next fortnight, there was much agitated heart-searching. The préfets of those departments where the results were still in issue were summoned to Paris: there was to be no more nonsense about leaving demos to choose its representatives. Republicans and Radicals got together and after bargaining, agreed to produce joint lists at the second poll. This time no risks were to be run. On October 18, the Conservatives added very few to their earlier winners. The Republic was saved, but over a hundred seats had been lost and the situation of the Republicans was far from easy. The Right had 205 seats: the Left consisted of 257 Republicans and 115 Radicals, 372 in all.* Should the Radicals from whim or hatred desire it, they could unite with the Right and make government by the Republicans impossible. Only sixty-four of Ferry's faithful 149 came back. The Centre no longer dominated the Chamber.

It was clear that *scrutin de liste* had led to extremism. In only eight departments had both Conservatives and Republicans been elected. The other seventy-nine had given the whole representation to one side or the other. It was seen that, except in the constituencies where there was a large city, Paris, Marseille, Lyon and Bordeaux, the rural vote swamped the urban. The new system had been an unhappy experiment, and so far as could be seen, contrary to Gambetta's prophecy, the intellectual level of the Chamber had not been raised. Naturally the préfets were blamed, but the Government itself had hamstrung them. There were the usual denunciations to the Ministry of the Interior of improper pressure on the electors, and Goblet, Minister of Public Worship, deprived two hundred priests of their salaries. In the Chamber the Left with great promptitude invalidated all the Conservative deputies in five departments. At the subsequent bye-elections in February, the Republicans recovered twenty-one of the twenty-four seats. Thus when the bye-elections for these and the double elections were over, the strength of the groups in the Chamber was:

Monarchists	119		Republicans	279
Bonapartists	64	183	Radicals	122	401

leaving the Republicans still dependent on the good will, or at least the tolerance of their extremist allies.

Yet in spite of a turbulent four years, to be followed by two more restless parliaments, the Republicans were to survive as the party of government for another fifteen years. 'The Opportunists', wrote Léon

---

* Seven Radicals had been elected in two constituencies, which left seven seats to be filled at bye-elections.

Blum, then a young *rédacteur* on the Conseil d'Etat,[4] 'survived for ten years simply because they comprised men capable of understanding a financial decree, of formulating a customs tariff, or of drafting a criminal law. The utter dearth of specialists has condemned and today [1898] still condemns the Radical party to deplorable impotence in spite of their successes at the polls.'

The Chamber assembled in November. Nearly half the deputies were new. Among them were men destined to make their name in politics, a Paul Deschanel, who had been on the secretariats of Marcère and Jules Simon, and who married the daughter of Brice, member for Redon, wealthy banker and railway director; a lecturer from Toulouse University, Jean Jaurès, one of the hopes of the Centre Republicans; a school-inspector, Charles Dupuy, to be thrice Prime Minister; a young Béarnais lawyer, very intelligent, very cultivated and very unreliable, Louis Barthou; Jean Piou, the effective founder in due time of a Catholic political party; and a Socialist-Radical lawyer, journalist and municipal councillor of Paris, Alexandre Millerand.

The invalidation of the two dozen Conservatives by the Chamber reduced the opposition vote for the time being. Brisson seized the opportunity to apply for one more credit of fifty millions to finish off the annexation of Tonkin. He carried it by a tiny majority and a vote of confidence was only accorded him by 274 to 270: without the invalidation of the twenty-four deputies, he would have been defeated. It was clear that his Government could not live. But, before he resigned, Brisson must preside over the election of a new President since Grévy's seven-year term was nearly up. Brisson was pressed by some of his friends to stand, on which Freycinet let it be known that if Brisson stood, he too would. But neither had any backing and there was no serious candidate. The National Assembly re-elected Grévy on December 28 by 457 votes to 109 divided between a number of unofficial candidates.

Brisson stayed in office a few more days, long enough to see the passage of an amnesty bill for various political prisoners, including that of the famous Russian anarchist, Prince Kropotkin, on whose release the Russian ambassador, Mohrenheim, returned to Russia in protest. Brisson resigned and Grévy confided the formation of a new government to his favourite Freycinet. On January 7 the new Prime Minister took office with a cabinet of much the same shot colour as Brisson's. There were four old members; Carnot at Finance, Goblet at Public Instruction, himself at the Foreign Office and a lobbying quasi-Radical,

Sarrien, at the Interior. It included several second-rank men from the Centre. From the Radicals, he selected Lockroy, Victor Hugo's son-in-law, a scatterbrain, and Granet, who had sold himself to Clemenceau for a seat and who would be Clemenceau's go-between in any obscure negotiation. The most interesting figures were the two Service ministers, Admiral Aube, who was to alarm the British Admiralty with his *guerre de course* theory, and General Boulanger, whose activities for more than three years were to make every government's existence a misery.

Chapter Sixteen

The Rise of Boulanger

(i)

Between the fall of Ferry and the Chamber election of October 1893, little of French history is visible through a whirling dust-screen of humiliating but scarcely intelligible public scandals. The Boulanger episode, which begins in 1885, falls on either side of the Daniel Wilson scandal of 1887, and moves to its ineffectual climax in 1889. Then, after a short period of the abortive 'Ralliement', comes the inglorious farce of Panama. Little of all this had any serious or permanent consequence for the country. True, at the end, some familiar faces have disappeared and been replaced by new ones, but this might well have happened without the alarms and demonstrations which disturbed the country from 1886 to 1894.

The Boulanger episode grew from 'a cloud no bigger than a man's hand' into a political crisis, owing to the lack of character among the notables. General Georges Boulanger had had a fortunate career. With no particular advantages except physical courage and good health, he had been rapidly promoted. With four campaigns and half a dozen wounds to his credit, he had had the excellent luck to have been wounded during the Commune before the reprisals began. He had been promoted to General of Division at the early age of forty-eight; but he had held no important command and shown no particular talents in the higher military sphere other than energy. As director of infantry at the War Office, he had developed a somewhat clumsy taste for intrigue with politicians towards his own advancement and made a number of friends in journalism, whom he supplied with publicity about himself. He was far from well educated; he was not well bred; and he could not resist the lure of a skirt. Also he had a fine vanity coupled with the common military contempt for *pékins*. In 1884 he had been given command of the garrison in Tunisia as support to the Resident, Paul Cambon. For a year he had behaved circumspectly. But Cambon was a protégé of Ferry and, with that minister's fall, Boulanger issued some foolish and provocative military orders, which he refused to withdraw at Cambon's request. In the upshot, the quarrel was carried to Paris in July 1885, where Cambon spent six months struggling to stiffen the support given him by his Minister, the timorous Freycinet, while Boulanger sought that of the War Minister, General Campenon. During these months he obtained the backing not only of Rochefort but also of Clemenceau and his *Justice*. It was not until January 1886 that Freycinet, having become Prime Minister, closed the dispute. He had Cambon specially decorated and sent him back to Tunisia confirmed in his authority. At the same time he invited Boulanger to become his War Minister. Freycinet claims that he took Boulanger on the advice of Campenon, exacting from him promises that he would put through the army reforms outlined by Freycinet and that he would confine himself to technical military business. On the other hand, he had had six months' experience of Boulanger's methods. It is unbelievable that Freycinet, an aristocrat, who fifteen years earlier had warned Gambetta about his behaviour to generals, would have invited Boulanger, whom he knew to be a climber and trouble-maker, except under severe political pressure. The pressure had come from Clemenceau, who with his hundred-odd Radicals could at any moment break a government. Why did Clemenceau push this man? It is said that the Radical leader was aiming for universal compulsory service and the thorough republicanisation of the army. It may be so, but other contemporaries think he was imitating Gambetta who had made friends in the service. Certainly, except for the discredited General Thibaudin, Boulanger alone claimed to be Radical.

From taking office, Boulanger was in the public eye. He could touch no topic, however trivial, without magnifying it. He ordered two cavalry brigades to exchange garrisons on the ground that one was displaying royalist propensities, omitting to perceive that he was sending erring cavaliers from republican Tours to royalist Nantes. To questions in the Chamber, he replied in a declamatory democratic vein which enchanted the Radicals. When a mine manager had been murdered by strikers at Decazeville with conspicuous brutality and troops had been despatched to maintain order, he told the Chamber that it might well be that each soldier was sharing his rations with a miner. For a venial breach of the regulations by General Saussier, Military Governor of Paris and Commander-in-Chief designate in case of war, he sent a written reprimand and publicised the fact, at the same time transferring Saussier's chief-of-staff. Saussier at once requested to be relieved of his duties. Boulanger's impudence had gone too far. The cabinet refused Saussier's application.

On the other hand, Boulanger deployed much activity in a number of reforms in army conditions. If he had not secured exemption, the soldier was still spending five years with the colours under the normal wretched conditions of nineteenth-century army life. The modest improvements in his lot were no doubt welcome, and the press inspired by the War Office made much of them. There were indeed more fundamental projects, the re-arming of the infantry with the Lebel magazine rifle and the reduction of service from five to three years, neither of which would bear fruit during Boulanger's time at the rue Saint-Dominique. Freycinet claims that in both these matters his was the initiative. This is very likely true, for Boulanger had little of the constructive sense or long sight of the reformer: he had the virtue of rapid decision,* but often the rapidity was better than the decision. His views on military operations were summary, and the members of the Conseil supérieur de la Guerre hoped they would not have to undertake a campaign while Boulanger was at the War Office. '*Si un pareil fumiste nous conduit pendant que nous aurons les Prussiens dans le ventre, nous sommes foutus,*' said Galliffet.

In March one of the recurring minor squabbles between Right and Left induced a deputy to raise the question of the presence in France of the claimants and their families and to ask for their expulsion. Grévy had refused to take the responsibility for such an action, and Freycinet asserted that his powers were insufficient. But a reception given by the Comte de Paris in May on the occasion of the engagement of his daughter to the Crown Prince of Portugal roused the Extreme Left once more to plague Freycinet. Freycinet produced a bill giving him the right to expel as he desired. At this a Radical proposed an amendment making the expulsion of the claimants and their immediate heirs peremptory, and permissive only for the other members of their families. Some of the Centre Republicans, Fallières and Waldeck-Rousseau, were revolted by this and invited the Right to join them in defeating Freycinet and forming a Conservative cabinet. But Ferry found that at best he could get no better than sixty supporters. Freycinet, getting wind of what was afoot, acted with unaccustomed decision. He accepted the Radical amendment, and the bill was passed, though a number of his supporters abstained. The bill became law on June 22. The Comte de Paris and his son, the Duc d'Orléans, and Prince Napoleon and Prince Victor left the country.

* Boulanger in fact hustled the committee, which had been arguing for months on whether a magazine rifle was desirable, to produce a model in four months.

T

Article 4 of the law forbade the entry into the armed forces of any member of a royal family. On this, Boulanger, who was perfectly aware of the precise reason for the employment of the word, struck from the Army List the Duc d'Aumale, the Duc de Chartres, the Duc d'Alençon and the Duc de Nemours, as well as Prince Murat and his son. He had flouted the cabinet and broken the law. Aumale addressed a haughty letter to President Grévy pointing out that he had no power to take an officer's rank from him. On this a decree expelling the duke from France was issued. This was on July 13. On the following day came the National Fête, a review brilliantly staged, nominally in honour of the Army and the Republic, actually, since he commanded the parade, of the Minister of War. The crowd had no eyes for any other, nor applause, and that evening the popular cabaret singer, Paulus, produced a new song, *En revenant de la revue*, with a refrain in praise of *Not' brav' général Boulanger*. 'We get the actors we deserve', acidly commented the editor of *La Vie Parisienne*, 'Louis XIV — Molière; Napoléon — Talma; Gambetta — Coquelin; Boulanger — Paulus.'

On the previous day in the Chamber, the Duc de la Rochefoucauld had shouted: 'The Duc d'Aumale made you a general', and Boulanger had denied it. Within a fortnight, a former préfet produced a letter of thanks from Boulanger to his patron. Boulanger denied he had written it, indeed could not have done so. Two further sycophantic epistles were produced. He tried to ride it off with abuse, but even his supporters were shocked. Alone the termagant Rochefort continued to adulate him. Grévy was willing that he should be removed, but again Freycinet shrank back. Boulanger appears to have at last acquired a little discretion. During the remainder of the year he stuck to his ministry and his files.

In December Freycinet, whose majority had been slowly sinking, was defeated. The budget was still under discussion. Carnot, the Finance Minister, had been attacked at intervals by the Right for the increase in expenditure, by the Left for his rejection of income-tax. Freycinet had promised economies, but Carnot said he could do no more than suppress the extraordinary budget, and to do this he must have a loan to clear off the items. On this, Right and Radicals came together, and struck out the credits for the sous-préfectures. Carnot resisted and the Government resigned.

Grévy patched up the cabinet by inviting Goblet, Minister of Public Instruction, to take over. He suggested that Goblet should go to the Foreign Office, but Goblet appointed Flourens, formerly director of

Public Worship, who was now a conseiller d'état and not a member of Parliament. The cabinet was the Freycinet without Freycinet or Carnot.

Le petit père Goblet was an idealist and a man of peppery temper, also a fanatical believer in the separation of Church and State. He was simple and earnest with an earnestness which the Chamber found unsympathetic: 'he chilled the dishonourable with his uprightness and the honourable with his touchiness.' But at least he was not Freycinet, and being, as were most members of the cabinet, a Radical, he was temporarily safe from the malevolence of Clemenceau.

The popularity of Boulanger had been observed by the German Chancellor. There is no reason to suppose that Bismarck paid more attention to the reports of the military attaché than to the despatches of the ambassador, or that he took the manifestations of the French War Minister very seriously. But he perceived that Boulanger could be made into an excellent bogeyman, which he could use. In 1887 a new seven-year law would be needed for the German army and, as a precautionary measure, he wanted its strength raised from 400,000 to 472,000. To secure the increase he must have a docile Reichstag. The army bill was introduced on November 25. There was only one argument in its favour, the danger threatened from France. In his speech on January 11, Bismarck said: 'When France has any reason to believe that she is stronger than we are, on that day, I believe, war is certain. If Napoleon III declared war on us, was it not for reasons of internal politics? Why should not General Boulanger be tempted to act in the same way, should he come to the head of the government?' The bill nonetheless was rejected, largely by the agency of the Catholic Centre, and on January 14, the Reichstag was dissolved. In the interval before polling day on February 21, everything possible was done to impress on the German electorate the peril. At the end of January, there was a Bourse panic.

The reply of Boulanger was to order the construction of hutted camps near the eastern frontier. When in early February the German government called up 72,000 reservists for training, Boulanger proposed to do likewise and brought to Grévy the text of a decree for his signature. Grévy was thunderstruck. 'Don't you know that this means war?' 'Yes, I am ready.' 'My friend,' retorted Grévy severely, 'just as ready as Leboeuf under Napoleon III. I won't have the question even discussed.' 'Then, I resign.' 'Very good; do so.' But Boulanger did nothing. Also he renounced the recall of reservists. On February 21, the German voters gave Bismarck what he wanted, a large increase in the National Liberal group and a decline in both the Centre and Socialist membership.

(ii)

From the first the annexed provinces had been governed as imperial, not Prussian, territory, the Reichsland, under the direction of the German Chancellor, who was represented in the region by an Imperial administrator and a Council in Strasbourg. The Reichsland was treated as a protective glacis to transrhenan Germany and garrisoned by troops from the interior of Germany. Alsace-Lorraine was a useful whipping-boy to Bismarck, to be punished if the French misbehaved, or mal-treated if, for reasons of German internal politics, it was necessary to incite the French to bellicose demonstrations.

From January 1, 1874, the Reichsland sent fifteen elected representatives to the Reichstag. On their first appearance, they repeated the protest against annexation which they had made at Bordeaux in 1871, and seven refused to recognise the validity of the Treaty of Frankfurt. This early difference in their ranks became permanent. Those who rejected the treaty became known as the Protesters, the French party, *revanchard*, looking forward to re-annexation to France. Opposed to them were the Autonomists, who had already understood that however uncivilised had been the seizure of the provinces, they had little hope of cession by Germany and that they must therefore screw out of the Imperial government such rights as they could. Although, to philosophers like Renouvier, the French by the vote of 1871 having refused to fight to the death had forfeited their claim to Alsace-Lorraine, and the Alsatians and Lorrainers therefore had the right to dispose of themselves, such liberalism found few echoes in France. To Frenchmen on both sides of the frontier, the Autonomist party was the most dangerous enemy. Manteuffel, who, from 1871, had been the Statthalter, had done his best to win over the population by lenient administration and had encouraged the Autonomists, but his policy was unsuccessful. The Autonomist candidates for the Reichstag were beaten again and again. In 1881 and 1884 they had but a single seat. Manteuffel died in June 1885 and the German ambassador in Paris since 1874, Prince Hohenlohe-Schillingfürst, much to his dismay was appointed Statthalter. Although a liberal-minded man and ready to conciliate the Alsatians, he met serious difficulties. The rise of Boulanger, his popularity after July

1886, and finally Bismarck's references to him in January 1887, bewitched the electorate in the Reichsland. At the German election, the whole fifteen seats were won by the Protesters with nearly 80% of the poll and there was a general belief that Boulanger would soon be on his way to liberate them. This was reflected in a return to government severity, with the suppression of a number of local associations and (later in the year) the resumption by the government of the appointment of the burgomasters. One deputy was expelled from the Reichstag and another forced to withdraw.

In April, Schnaebele, a French frontier officer at Pagny-sur-Moselle, who was believed by the Germans to be working with the Alsatian irredentists, was lured by the German police across the frontier, arrested and spirited away. At the meeting of the French cabinet on April 23, the excitable Goblet talked of an ultimatum. Grévy asked Boulanger for his opinion, at which the War Minister produced a draft mobilisation decree and assured the President that the frontier cover could be in position in eighteen hours and the whole army ready in six days. Grévy mildly remarked that one could scarcely send the Germans an ultimatum before receiving the reply to the French note.* On April 30 the German government, finding their people to blame, made a grudging apology and released Schnaebele. In the end, it was revealed that Boulanger, without confiding in his colleagues, had used the French frontier police as intermediaries with French spies in Alsace-Lorraine and the discovery of this by the Germans lay at the origin of the affair.

This trivial episode would be unimportant but for the legend that grew after Schnaebele's release that the Germans had been frightened off by the *brav' général*. To the mob, Général Revanche had at last appeared.

To the more conservative politicians, to the more serious, the whole of Boulanger's history from the beginning was seen to be thoroughly mischievous and this sentiment was increased by the alarm of Herbette,

---

* Francis Charmes who was political director at the Quai d'Orsay gave a somewhat different version of the Grévy-Boulanger conversation. Boulanger wanted to have the issue of peace or war put to the Chamber. Grévy said: 'I am reproached for allowing my ministers too much independence, too much masters of their own decisions. So long as these matters are the particular concern of the ministries, I do not intervene. But over a question where the interest of France is concerned, I say: "This is my business and I will change my ministers twenty times rather than submit the question to the vote of the Chamber." ' Boulanger seemed not to understand and talked of resigning. Grévy coldly replied: 'I don't require that of you.' This time the general seemed to have understood. He had come to the cabinet very high and mighty. Now he crept away. (Clarétie, *Journal* under Nov. 1, 1906.)

the ambassador in Berlin. If this kind of gasconading continued, there might be an unexpected crisis and the unprepared country — there were only 25,000 of the famous new Lebel rifles — plunged into war. Ferry and his fellow deputies for the frontier departments had been warned by their friends among the Alsatian Protesters of the dangers. In January Ferry, on behalf of the Republican deputies, had made an approach to Grévy to tell him that at need they would provoke a crisis to rid the Government of Boulanger. During the Schnaebele incident, Baron Mackau, organiser and president of the Union des Droites, had made it clear to Goblet that the Right had no liking for war and no interest in either war or Alsace-Lorraine. Patriotic questions were in fact no more than minor instruments for bating the government in power. Indeed, as would subsequently appear, though as yet few observers had suspected, the Right's attachment to the monarchy was by no means as enthusiastic as the secretariat of the Comte de Paris would like to think.

By now it was known in all parliamentary circles that, outside France, Boulanger at the War Office was looked on as a national, nay, international danger. Grévy, too, was repeatedly saying he must go. But against this were the Radicals, the *Intransigeant* and the other sections of the general's press, Déroulède and the Ligue des Patriotes, and behind these again, the Paris mob. To avoid making him a martyr, the whole Government must fall. The operation was carried out on May 17–18. The Budget Commission told the Finance Minister that there were insufficient economies. Their disapproval of the budget was taken up by the Chamber and the Government handsomely defeated. Among the Republicans in the majority were Ferry, Raynal, Spuller and Méline. So well obscured was the purpose of the transaction that Goblet, according to his memoirs, believed it was entirely due to the jealousy of the president of the Finance Commission, Rouvier.

To find a successor was difficult; Freycinet, Ferry, Raynal, Rouvier, and Freycinet again all failed. Clemenceau would only support a team in which there was Radical preponderance. Grévy should have called him, as Ferry suggested. 'Never!' said the old President. Floquet was considered, until it was remembered that twenty years earlier he had shouted '*Vive la Pologne!*' at Alexander II and was therefore impossible. Fortunately, since Floquet seems to have believed that a combination of himself and Boulanger would be irresistible to France. Then on May 23, at a bye-election in Paris, Rochefort recommended the electors to add Boulanger's name to the voting slips, and 39,000 took his advice.

It was a sign. Freycinet, once more invited by Grévy, was, as usual, in favour of yielding to 'public opinion' and including Boulanger in a new cabinet. On this, all three Republican groups in the Senate made it known to the President that no ministry that included the general could count on the Senate Republican majority.

At this desperate juncture, Grévy accepted help from a source he would have turned away in horror a few months earlier. He saw Baron Mackau. Between them and Rouvier an understanding was soon reached. In return for attenuations in the laicisation policy, such as leaving the schools run by the Orders to function, and dropping persecution of State servants suspected of disaffection to the Republic, the Right agreed to allow a government to survive by not voting with the Radicals. Thus, on May 30, a Republican cabinet, headed by Rouvier, appeared to the Chamber, a cabinet drawn from the Centre, the only exception the Minister of Agriculture, Barbe, whose radicalism rarely stood the test of voting. The Minister of War, General Ferron, was said to owe his promotion to Boulanger through Clemenceau. Rouvier was immediately attacked by the Extreme Left for seeking the support of the Right. He denied that he was seeking support, a disingenuous answer, but pointed out that if the Government did not secure a Republican majority, it would resign. The Radicals might rage, but Clemenceau had been responsible for the fall of Ferry, Brisson, Freycinet and Goblet, four cabinets in two years; he had only himself to blame.

Boulanger refused an appointment to an army corps, but the Government was not going to risk a second Fourteenth of July with the now overwhelmingly popular idol in Paris. He was given command of XIII Army Corps at Clermont-Ferrand, though he had never yet commanded a division, and ordered to take over before the national holiday. He left the Gare de Lyon on July 8 amid scenes of extraordinary disorder. A crowd of many thousands stormed the station, shouting, 'Don't go!' coupled with snatches of the *Marseillaise, Revenant de la revue* and '*Vive Boulanger!*'. Déroulède who had made himself the impresario of the scene, having done his act, tried in vain to get the mob to disperse. The general was at last evacuated two hours late on a light engine and Louis Lépine of the Préfecture de Police spent another two hours clearing the streets.

It was probably that evening which settled Boulanger's destiny. He had appeared as the creature of Radicalism. Clemenceau suddenly saw what he had hatched. 'General Boulanger's popularity', he told the

Chamber, 'has come too soon to one who likes noise too much.' The noise did not cease with the general at Clermont. Crowds made themselves a nuisance in Paris, and Boulanger wrote letters to the deputy, Francis Laur, which Laur published. To Ferry, who in a speech at Epinal, called him a 'night-club Saint-Arnaud' (War Minister at the *coup d'état* of December 1851), he sent his seconds with unacceptable demands and on their refusal, published an insolent open letter.

Chapter Seventeen

Boulangism

(i)

In the autumn of 1887 the public learned — by a devious route involving two ladies of easy virtue — that the son-in-law of the President of the Republic, Daniel Wilson, had been abusing his position by trafficking in decorations. This Wilson, a tall man with a flaming beard, was the son of Daniel Wilson the Scotch engineer, some time of Le Creusot, who had later made a fortune out of the Paris gas companies. When he died his money was divided between his daughter, the wife of a scientist and the owner of the splendid château de Chenonceau on the Cher, and his son. This Daniel[1] seems to have run through his share of the money during the early sixties, and then, to recoup his fortune, had gone in for politics. In 1869 he was elected for Indre-et-Loire as an Independent, by methods which went as close to bribery as is possible without direct payment. After 1870 he had carried on his career as Republican deputy for Loches, a member of the Chamber Finance commission, and the permanent and unscrupulous enemy of Gambetta. In October 1881 he married Grévy's daughter and took up his residence in the Elysée Palace. He was spoken of as a 'business man', but this seems to have been no more than the foundation of some unimportant provincial papers, which, as son-in-law of the President, he forced on unwilling subscribers and unwilling advertisers. In addition he ran a brisk trade in decorations through the agency of various low-lived characters, coupled with a senator, and also one of the assistant chiefs-of-staff at the War Office, Caffarel, who had been appointed by Boulanger. This, since Boulanger was not involved, would have been unimportant but for the fact that, in an interview, the general asserted the enquiry was directed against him, and then criticised the War Minister for the delay in completing the provision of the Lebel rifles. On this Ferron gave him thirty days close arrest. Not a Radical came to his aid. Boulanger spent much of the time in the company of his mistress, a Madame de Bonnemains, who had taken up residence at a hotel a few miles away.

In the meantime the Wilson scandal grew. On November 5 the Chamber voted an enquiry, and four days later, on a report that some-one had been manipulating the contents of Wilson's files, ordered the laying of an information against 'Master Son-in-Law'. Rouvier was embarrassed, but the affair was all the more irksome in that he was in the middle of an important conversion operation.[2] On November 10 the Three Per Cents dropped to 80.50 francs. On November 15 the Chamber refused his request for the adjournment of an interpellation by Clemenceau. Rouvier resigned.

Grévy, who had known nothing of his son-in-law's commerce, be-lieved that he could hold himself apart: in any case, he was legally and constitutionally untouchable. He had reckoned without Parliament. Wilson had been instrumental in the fall of Gambetta, and he had always been a thorn in the side of the Opportunists. In 1883 he had campaigned against them over the railway conventions. As for Grévy, it had been he who had delayed Gambetta's taking office. Let him go. Outside the Elysée the mob already had its song: 'Oh, what misery to have a son-in-law.'

Grévy believed he could find a ministry to replace Rouvier's. He was mistaken. The faithful Freycinet slid away. The simple Goblet failed. Clemenceau scoffed. Brisson moralised.[3] On November 27 Grévy pro-mised Rouvier, who was acting *ad interim*, that he would resign on December 1. But who was to replace him? There would of course be a Right candidate, but he hardly counted. Who would the Republicans declare for? It was suddenly realised that Ferry was the man, 'Ferry-famine! Ferry-le-Tonkinois!' Against him was Déroulède and his Ligue des Patriotes, Rochefort and the street, the Paris municipal council, largely communard, the Anarchists and the unemployed. The Radicals were horrified. Having attacked Grévy for months, they now wanted to retain him until Ferry could be finally discarded.

On the night of November 28, a Radical group met first at the office of the Grand Orient in the rue Cadet, then at Durand's restaurant op-posite the Madeleine, Clemenceau, Laisant, Laguerre, Granet, Roche-fort, Eugene Mayer of the *Lanterne*, Déroulède. Goblet was invited but declined. Boulanger was brought by Déroulède. The only plan that seemed viable was to retain Grévy and to find a Prime Minister who would work with Clemenceau and Boulanger — either Floquet, the President of the Chamber, or Freycinet, or both. One party went off to ask Floquet, another to Freycinet. When they returned, they reported that both had visions of higher things, the Presidency of the Republic itself. A Clemenceau-Boulanger combination was refused by Clemenceau himself: in such a cabinet he saw himself being elbowed into the background.

On the following night, the same group with some reinforcements met in Laguerre's apartment in the rue Saint-Honoré. Andrieux the mischievous was remembered and a messenger went for him. At this point Boulanger was fetched away by his orderly officer, Captain Driant.* He had a private rendezvous at the apartment of the Comte de Martimprey which had been proposed by one of the deputies for Ille-et-Vilaine, Le Hérissé. At Martimprey's rooms was waiting Baron Mackau. Here it was proposed that the Right should put all their votes behind the feeble Freycinet as President, with Goblet as Prime Minister and Boulanger at the War Office. After this, there would be an appeal to the nation out of which the monarchy would be restored. If necessary, the army would be used.** Boulanger accepted Mackau's terms almost without amendment. All he wanted was the exclusion of Ferry and, for himself, the War Office. Mackau on November 30 sent a messenger to the Comte de Paris in England, but the text of the communication was obscure. The claimant was misled, and by the time the misunderstanding was rectified it was too late.

The conspirators at Laguerre's went home, having accomplished nothing. During November 30, there was a continuous coming and going at the Elysée. At one hour Grévy was resigned to his disappearance, at another he was ready with a new stratagem. Goblet was asked at least three times to be Prime Minister, and there was still Andrieux indulging his imagination.

On December 1 the Chamber met at 2 p.m. to receive the resignation of the President, while demonstrators from the Ligue des Patriotes and the Blanquistes made scenes on the Quai d'Orsay before being driven off by the cavalry patrols. Finally Rouvier had to inform the Chamber that he had received no message from Grévy and that the cabinet had

---

* Driant married one of Boulanger's daughters, Marcelle, in 1888. He retired from the army and later became deputy for a Nancy constituency, taking an active part in the debates on army reform just before the war of 1914. He was killed in command of a group of chasseur battalions on the first day of the battle of Verdun, 1916. Le Hérissé, a cuirassier officer, inherited a fortune and retired from the army. A Royalist at this time, he refused to recognise the Orleans family after the death of Chambord and became a *blanc d'Espagne*. In 1886, under the aegis of the great elector for Rennes, Le Bastard, he became deputy for one of its two seats, and continued to sit as whatever seemed to him popular until 1913.[4]

** It is to be noted that at this meeting Boulanger claimed that the army would obey him. To others, at other times, he said that the army would not follow him, which is far more likely. He was probably telling Mackau what he hoped would take place.

once more renewed its resignation. On the following day, the ministers once again found themselves without a decision. A resolution was passed: 'the Chamber, awaiting the communication which has been promised, adjourns till 6 p.m.' Déroulède spent the afternoon leading some 1500 of his Leaguers to shout '*Vive la Russie*' outside the Russian embassy, '*A bas Ferry*' outside the German, and then getting himself arrested in the rue de Rivoli. So too did the anarchist Louise Michel.

On December 2 at 3 p.m. Floquet read to the Chamber a long message in which the President laid down his office in order to avoid a possible conflict between the executive and Parliament: 'My duty and my right would be to resist, but in the circumstances. . . .' The message was received in icy silence.

Grévy was gone, but the succession was still far from settled. On the night 2/3 December there were crowds in the place de la Concorde, shouting against Ferry and calling for Boulanger. There were riots, and eventually the police and the Garde Républicaine cleared the square. Grévy in the meantime had evacuated the Elysée Palace and taken refuge in his mansion in the avenue d'Iéna. Most of the trouble came from the attempts of Rochefort's following to incite an indifferent crowd to make trouble. And in the meantime, Vaillant and his Blanquistes were conspiring in the Hôtel de Ville with a group of Paris deputies to organise a new Commune. A meeting of the Radical parliamentarians to select a candidate was boycotted by most of the Opportunists. Of 340 votes, 101 went to Floquet with Freycinet only seven behind him. It is said that Clemenceau had already put his finger on the possible dark horse, Sadi Carnot. Floquet was persuaded to withdraw; it was known that the Senate was fixed on Ferry and that he would get no further.

During the pourparlers with Boulanger, Mackau had agreed to forward the Royalist enterprise by throwing the votes of the Right to Freycinet. It seems that the latter had been approached, but believing that he would win anyhow, had refused Mackau's terms. In any case, owing to the misunderstanding, the claimant's agreement was not received in time. In consequence, without firm orders, the Right put up two candidates, General Saussier and General Appert.

At the full meeting of the Left in a small Versailles theatre there were four candidates, Floquet no longer standing. The first poll, concluded about 10 a.m., gave Ferry 200, Freycinet 193, Brisson (Gauche radicale) 81, and Carnot 61. More members had arrived by the end of the next poll which resulted in: Ferry 216, Freycinet 196, Brisson 79 and Carnot

61. The third poll was to be held at 1.30. It was vital to his enemies that Ferry should be beaten. An attempt was made to persuade Brisson to withdraw; he refused. Clemenceau perceived that by allowing himself to be put forward at the meeting of the Radicals on the previous evening, Freycinet had advertised his adherence to the Radicals, or rather theirs to him, and that he would receive no support from the Opportunists. This was the moment to lead out the dark horse. Which? Brisson or Carnot? 'Carnot is not very strong and what's more, he's a thorough reactionary: but, all the same, he bears a Republican name, and we have nothing better. We vote for him.' It was done. Freycinet found to his horror that he was deserted, and it was now too late to secure the Right votes he had neglected. At 1.30 Carnot stood at 162, while Ferry was down to 105, Freycinet to 171, and Brisson to 51. On this the plenary session of the whole National Assembly, Senate and Chamber, Left and Right, opened at 2 p.m. At 4 p.m. Carnot had 303, not yet the absolute majority, Ferry 212 (the whole Senate Republican vote with those of a few deputies), Saussier 148, Freycinet 76, and Appert 72.

(ii)

Outside the Palace, the crowd, hemmed in by troops, was bewildered. Who was Carnot? No one had ever heard of him. There were a few shouts of 'Down with Ferry', and that was all. Ferry — of all the leaders of the Third Republic the least self-seeking, and therefore the first to be deserted — threw in his hand, went to Carnot and told him that he had his, Ferry's, vote. The result of the second poll came at 6.20 p.m.: Carnot 616, Saussier 188. Ferry was crushed and Clemenceau had won an election. But he had won nothing more. Carnot had no more use for the Radical leader than Grévy had had. Moreover, Carnot could not be either bullied or flouted. He was of the authentic Republican élite, with his grandfather, Lazare, the 'Organiser of Victory', his father, Hippolyte, one of the figures of 1848. He himself was without ambition; he had fought as a volunteer in 1870. He had been an upright and courageous Minister of Finance to Freycinet in 1886. He had never sought either office or honours. Reactionary he might be, but he represented the best elements in the Republic, a republic which was being soiled by the representatives of the people. He asked no more than to do his duty.

His first move was to invite Goblet, then Fallières, to form a cabinet. Both failed.[5] He then tried Tirard. Tirard had never been a conspicuous politician. He had been maire of the Paris I arrondissement, and its deputy, Minister of Commerce and Agriculture in Freycinet's first cabinet and in Ferry's, and again in Freycinet's second. He had then been Minister of Finance until Ferry's defeat of March 1885. He was an excellent chairman, and given a strong team could control its members. Unfortunately the new cabinet was particularly colourless, 'modest and retiring'. Tirard kept Flourens at the Foreign Office. At the War Office, he accepted General Logerot, whom Boulanger believed to be friendly towards him. At the Interior, he placed Sarrien, the undistinguished lobby politician.

On December 10 Ferry was shot and severely wounded by a lunatic Alsatian in the vestibule of the Palais Bourbon. Though he recovered, his health was never again good.

Boulanger kept quiet, but not inactive. At the end of December he again met Mackau and Martimprey in Paris. The pact to overturn the cabinet, install one in which Boulanger should be Minister of War, carry out a *coup d'état*, and after a plebiscite (both Mackau and Martimprey were originally Imperialists) restore the monarchy, was confirmed. But Boulanger had not even tact in treachery. Within a week of this meeting, at the suggestion of a Bonapartist journalist, Thiébaud, he travelled in disguise to Prangins near Geneva to call on Prince Napoleon, to whom also he engaged himself for common action ending in a plebiscite. However, the prince had no money for adventures and in any case was sceptical of Boulanger's chances.

The silence that had fallen over the general's name since the period of his arrest was suddenly broken at the end of February when, in seven simultaneous bye-elections, it was found that without his being announced as a candidate, his name had been 'written in', and that in five departments he had received votes running from 4,000 up to 16,000. On being interrogated by Logerot, he replied that he was a complete stranger to the proceedings, and a few days later told the War Minister that he desired nothing more than to confine himself to his duties. Nevertheless, on March 12, there appeared a daily paper calling itself *La Cocarde, organe Boulangiste.* The Senate had already begun to press the Government. Hence, on March 17, on representations from Logerot, President Carnot had Boulanger put on half-pay and ordered to hand over his command. The grounds for this were that he had thrice visited Paris in the last six weeks in spite of having been refused permission, twice in disguise. Through the police, the Government was perfectly aware that Boulanger was carrying on a clandestine correspondence with Déroulède, Thiébaud and a certain Comte Dillon, whom he had known at Saint-Cyr, and who, after a period of financial vicissitude, had become the managing director of a transatlantic cable company founded by Pouyer-Quertier. The cabinet knew all about Boulanger's complicity in the matter of his candidatures.

Boulanger immediately asked Laguerre to collect a group of journalists and politicians, and hurried to Paris. Claiming that he could do nothing officially, he left them to produce a manifesto announcing the constitution of a Committee of National Protest against a government which was not inspired by patriotic sentiments, and recommending the candidature of Boulanger for the Chamber. They entered him for a bye-election in Bouches-du-Rhône, where he had not a chance, and another in Aisne for March 25. On this Tirard announced to the Chamber that a court of enquiry would look into the general's actions. On March 26, Boulanger was put on the retired list, culpable of having left the XIII Corps without troubling to hand over, as he had been ordered. The Boulanger committee had in the meantime withdrawn his two candidatures, but in the Aisne he headed the first poll with 45,000 votes.

On the day after Boulanger was relieved of his command, Daniel Wilson, who on March 2 had been condemned to two years imprisonment, a fine of 3,000 francs and deprivation of his civil rights for five years, was spared his punishment, since the court of appeal quashed the verdict. The superficial contrast between the freeing of a petty swindler who had abused a position of trust and the breaking of a gallant soldier for a trivial technical offence appeared iniquitous. From now there would be open war between the general and the régime.

(iii)

Boulanger had now become a symbol, but of what? There was plenty of discontent in France, but no one could say exactly to what it was due. There was unemployment and short time, there was a slump in agricultural and other prices, but the main cause seems to have been political, a movement of irritation with parliamentarism, of 'the party of the disgusted', 'the party of the discontented'. But there are other matters. First, there is the Boulangist committee, the men who had been familiar with him from his emergence from obscurity, the ambitious deputies, Laguerre, the rapidly-risen lawyer from the south, one of Clemenceau's young men, scarcely thirty, but extravagant and needy, Laisant, a retired army engineer officer and mathematician, Francis Laur, an engineer and something of an economist, Naquet, the chemist and mystic, a Jew who would find his way to anarchism, all Radical intellectuals, already beginning to look on Clemenceau as past his time. With them a number of well-known Paris journalists, Rochefort, Mayer of the *Lanterne*, Lalou, a coal-mine director and owner of *La France*, and later Arthur Meyer of the *Gaulois*. Behind these again a number of minor Radical deputies, two from Tulle, two from Nevers, and others. Also adventurers such as the Comte Dillon, and humbler rogues. Also Socialists from the Blanquiste group, Granger and Elie May. And most important of all, at least in Paris, Déroulède and the Ligue des Patriotes.

What is so mystifying is their faith in Boulanger. Boulanger was politically both inexperienced and unread, wholly ignorant. He was impulsive and silly: no soldier of his seniority, unless quite unreflecting, could have so light-heartedly broken every rule of discipline as he had done, or believed that if he were attacked, public opinion would rescue him. It was the total absence of positive qualities, the emptiness of the man, that seems to have misled his more intelligent supporters. They gave him what they had and saw in him their own reflection. They did not see, though many more aloof from him saw, that all the poor creature wanted was to be put back in his chair at the War Office in permanency. Instead they believed him to be a revolutionary, capable, for political ends, of subverting an army, which had amply demonstrated its loyalty to the State!

On March 30 the Tirard Government fell under a double attack from Right and Left. Carnot sent for Floquet, President of the Chamber, a little man with a handsome head which he believed resembled Mirabeau's and must thus contain Mirabeau's talents. He also tried to embody the qualities of other heroes of the Revolution, particularly Saint-Just. Having a ready tongue, he had been a successful President of the Chamber. But he was bombastic and silly and had earned himself the nickname of La Boursouflure. He had never held a portfolio, though he had been préfet of the Seine for a few months in 1882. It was entirely appropriate that the crisis should arise between two dummies. He had some trouble in mounting a cabinet, owing to the refusal of Rouvier, the only available financier, to suffer Goblet at the Foreign Office, on which Goblet danced on his hat and cursed the Opportunists.

In the end the Radical Peytral took the Finance Ministry, the Opportunists departed and a Radical-tinged ministry appeared. The novelty was the presence of Freycinet at the War Office, the first occasion a civilian had held the portfolio; he was to hold it for four years.

It is of the absurd nature of politics that Tirard had fallen as a result of a motion from Laguerre for the consideration of the revision of the constitution — Boulanger's project — which the Government had opposed, and that Floquet who ostensibly had come to power in order to implement the Chamber's desires should at once be driven to obtain an adjournment of the question. But the situation had completely changed with the imminent appearance of Boulanger in the Chamber. Not only had Clemenceau's group already expelled from their midst those who had signed the National Protest; in the face of the approaching catastrophe, as it appeared, they surrendered their prejudices, and refrained from attacking the Finance Minister on the Vatican embassy, the souspréfectures, and the secret service money.

Though the dismissal of Boulanger had stimulated the agitation, the difficulties of the protagonist, no longer a soldier, but a political adventurer, a role for which he had neither taste nor talent, increased. He was now the champion of Royalists, Bonapartists, dissident Radicals and the more violent Blanquistes. This confusion of support had the consequence that no serious programme could be proposed, and that all Boulanger stood for was contained in the slogan, 'Dissolution, Constituent [i.e. Constituent Assembly], Revision', a text which differed little from that of the Radicals. At first this did not appear to matter. In early April, he had been put up in both Dordogne and Aisne. In Dordogne, he was elected and at once resigned (in July, a Bonapartist substitute won the seat); in Aisne, having led at the first poll, he withdrew and the seat was eventually won by Paul Doumer, Republican. There followed a more important election. In Nord at a bye four months earlier, the Republican had won against a Conservative by 22,000 in 270,000. On April 15 Boulanger carried the seat with 173,000 against some 85,000 divided between a Republican and a Radical. This was staggering and could not be explained away. He had not even visited the constituency. A few members of the Boulanger Committee and a host of newspaper boys selling *Intransigeant, Lanterne* and *Cocarde* were enough. His false reputation as the man feared by Bismarck, coupled with his punishment, had made him.

The effects of this thundering victory were immediate. The Republicans, of course, were at sixes and sevens, but so were the Royalists.

u

In November Mackau had made an arrangement over the presidential election, which had gone astray. In December Boulanger had engaged himself to carry out a *coup d'état* of which, as soon as he was installed in the War Office in a cabinet led by one of the weak three, Goblet, Freycinet or Floquet, the Comte de Paris would be the beneficiary. The conditions had failed. After his dismissal in March, Boulanger had had a third interview with Mackau. Since his original plan had now crumbled, Boulanger told Mackau that he would stand for the deputation in several departments, thus organising a kind of plebiscite in his own name. He said his feelings as regards the monarchy had not changed. Mackau was not to know that Boulanger had already insisted on and was to repeat to Laguerre his devotion to the Republic.

Among the Royalists there was considerable hesitation. The claimant's older advisers were opposed, so too was his uncle Aumale: to work with Boulanger was dishonourable. On the other side, those who had come to royalism either from Bonapartism or from anti-republicanism, feared that if Boulanger was not brought in as an ally he might turn to the Bonapartist claimant. Worse, the present Royalist deputies, of which the Duc de la Rochefoucauld was the chief, were terrified of the consequences of opposing Boulangism in the constituencies: they might lose their seats! But the decisive contribution came from the Comte de Mun. De Mun had no illusions. In 1885, in desperation, perhaps, in any case sincerely, he had wanted to found a Catholic party akin to the Centre in the Reichstag. Leo XIII had deprecated it, and he had gone no further. But he knew that, without a transformation the royal cause was doomed. If it would perhaps adopt social Catholicism . . . 'but it is always the policies of 16 and 24 May'. Alone, royalism could offer nothing to an electorate based on universal suffrage. A popular idol, a Boulanger, was the vital ally. The claimant agreed. Nineteenth-century princes were slow in learning the demagogic arts.

In the meantime, things were not going too well for Boulangism. In Isère on May 14 the general had been defeated by a Republican, but then Isère had never elected any other kind. In June there was a vacancy in Charente. The general thought of standing, but the Committee (it had now renamed itself National Republican) was opposed. It feared this plebiscitary policy. It put up Déroulède. The local Imperialists wanted Boulanger. Since they could not have him, they put up their own candidate. At the first poll, the Imperialist led over the Republican with Déroulède at the bottom. For the second poll, the Committee insisted on the withdrawal of the President of the Ligue des Patriotes. The Imperialist won. The Charente Radicals had not rallied, as was hoped, to the Republican. It was seen that Boulanger the man was indispensable: no substitute could take his place and the future tactics must be built round him. It now became necessary for every seat to be discussed between the National Republican Committee and those of the Royalists and Imperialists.

In the Chamber Boulanger had not cut an impressive figure. On June 4 he had read to the deputies a long weak treatise on the revision of the constitution. It was heard with contempt. On July 12 he renewed the theme. He asked that the President should dissolve the Chamber, since the elections (due in September–October 1889) ought to take place before the opening of the Paris Exhibition in that year. Floquet could not be restrained from replying at length, and attacked the general's personality. Boulanger called him a liar. A meeting was arranged for the following morning. Neither could fence, and Boulanger ran onto the point of his myopic adversary's foil, while Clemenceau, who was Floquet's second, roared with laughter. Bleeding from the neck, he was taken from the field. In three days he was none the worse. The most astonishing result was that this soldier who had made himself ridiculous was not laughed out of public life.

On July 22 another bye-election took place, this time in Ardèche. Boulanger, having again resigned, appeared as a candidate. Ardèche is divided between Catholic and Protestant, the latter being the Republican element. The Orleanists there received their orders from the Comte de Paris very late, and in consequence there were many abstentions. Boulanger was handsomely defeated. Yet his star was on the point of blazing. Three further elections were pending, in Charente-inférieure, in Somme and again in Nord. On August 19 he was elected in all three.

It may be that, as many writers put it, the country was disgusted with the Government of the Centre and that they believed that Boulanger would sweep away all the alleged corruption. It is also true that the Boulanger episode occurred during the worst years of the depression. But the real factors in the elections, especially those of August 1888 and January 1889, are two. First, Boulanger to some extent 'stumped the country', a thing that had not been done for some years. In early May, he toured his newly-won Nord constituency, Lille, Dunkerque, Anzin, promising reforms. In early August before the elections, he had gone round Charente-inférieure and Somme. All these tours were carried out with great ostentation. That was due to the second factor, money. The general's war-chest had been lavishly filled by the Duchesse d'Uzès; she had put 3 million francs at the disposal of the Comte de Paris. The elections of August 19 cost her half a million. No one had ever spent thus on an election. In France candidates were on the whole frugal. Bodley[6] records that, in the two Sables d'Olonne constituencies of Vendée, successful election cost neither candidate as much as £60, or 1,500 francs. The money supplied by Madame d'Uzès (derived from the cellars of Madame Veuve Clicquot) and also by the Comte de Paris may, as has been suggested, have gone into the pockets of Boulanger's assistants. The fact remains that much money was spent and he was elected, while in the constituencies where no preparations were made, e.g. Ardèche and Isère, the general was beaten. It is not necessary to think that the countryside was seething with indignation and burning to get rid of the Opportunists. The byes before Boulanger came on to the electoral stage easily dispose of that myth.

The climax was reached in January 1889 with yet another bye-election, this time in Paris. Boulanger had of course the support of every anti-Opportunist group, Déroulède and his Ligue des Patriotes, Rochefort and the majority of the Blanquistes. The senior clergy would have liked a Catholic layman as their candidate. They were overborne by the lower ranks of the Church. Similarly the Royalists put forward no one. The Republicans found a candidate in the President of the Municipal Council, named Jacques, '*le pauvre Jacques*' and the minority Blanquistes joined with the followers of Jules Guesde of the Parti ouvrier, '*les maigres prolétaires*', in putting up one Boule. The campaign was conducted in a feverish atmosphere. Troops were brought into the capital. The duchess's money flowed out, another half-million. On the night of January 27, great crowds flooded into the rue Royale and the Place de la Madeleine, opposite Durand's where Boulanger awaited the results. The Government, or rather Floquet, sat anxiously in the Ministery of the Interior in the Place Beauvau. Anything might happen, the politicians believed: Clemenceau was heard asking a former Communard deportee what living conditions were like in Nouméa. Not so the Military Governor Saussier, who in spite of alarmists, trusted the soldiers. What was more, he trusted his knowledge of Boulanger. 'He'll be off to bed with his Madame de Bonnemain.' And so it was. The results were out at 11.15. Boulanger 245,000, Jacques 163,000, Boule 17,000. Ignoring the shouts of '*A l'Elysée!*' Boulanger went off to bed. Constans, waiting near the Elysée, said to his companion, '*Quel . . .*'

and he too went to bed. Boulanger had known all along that the army would not help him, and had said again and again that the Empire had died of its origins. It was not true, but it gave him an excuse for doing nothing. Indeed for the next ten days he did nothing at all. On February 11 a bill to return to *scrutin d'arrondissement* was brought before the Chamber by the Government: it was the last service Floquet could offer. The Radicals tried to bargain, but this was no time for nonsense. *Scrutin d'arrondissement* was voted by the Left, which in 1885 had voted for *scrutin de liste*. The bill was opposed by the Conservatives and also by the new Opportunist deputy Jean Jaurès and his Socialist-Radical friend, Millerand. The bill had a majority of forty, and on the same day was passed by the Senate. It became law on February 13.

Floquet's usefulness, such as it had been, was now over. On February 14 he introduced a bill for revision of the Constitution. By nearly a hundred votes the Chamber refused to discuss it and Floquet went off to hand his resignation to Carnot.

(iv)

Carnot invited Tirard again, and Tirard appeared on February 22 with a strong cabinet. The single survivor of the Floquet team was Freycinet at the War Office. The most striking entrants were Rouvier at Finance and Constans at the Interior. The Centre Republicans had obviously redeployed their forces with an eye to the October elections. Did it mean a break with the Radicals? Or an attack on the Boulangists? On March 7 the decree exiling the Duc d'Aumale was repealed. On an interpellation, Constans received the support of the Royalists and a majority of 200. At the same time, he countermanded the laicisation of two State hospices ordered by Floquet.

Constans had an ill reputation. It was said that he had made his fortune too quickly and by methods which should not be too closely scanned. In June 1886 he had been sent to Pekin on a diplomatic mission and in the following year had been appointed governor-general of Indo-China. Returning to Paris, in July 1888, he had criticised the Colonial under-secretary, but soon afterwards, his successor in Indo-China, Richaud, reported him to have filled his pockets by re-establishing and licensing Chinese gaming-houses. Richaud, recalled by the Tirard Government, died on the way home. The charges were never cleared up. The stigma remained.

The Boulangists had forgotten that Constans had been Minister of the Interior in Ferry's first ministry and that he had 'presided' over the magnificently successful election of 1881. They forgot his reputation as a hard but reliable master. His préfets had not. 'I don't ask you if it is possible. I tell you to do it. We understand each other, don't we, my dear préfet? That is all I have to say to you.' Laguerre, Rochefort, Déroulède thought they could challenge him and bring him down.

Shortly before this, a half-crazy Russian at the head of a body of volunteers attempted to cross the French colony of Obock with the intention of carrying the Orthodox faith into Ethiopia. He and his band were dispersed by shells from a French warship. On this, Déroulède accused the Government of the unpatriotic action of shedding friendly Russian blood. The Government, fully aware that the Tsar had no interest in the apostle, at once decided to prosecute the Ligue des Patriotes together with Laguerre, Laisant and Naquet.

Rochefort, as even his friendly admirers admitted, was politically imbecile, but it is amazing that neither Boulanger, nor Laisant nor Laguerre understood that they were in no position to defy the Minister of the Interior or that his action would be rapid, brutal and successful. Against the Government they could mobilise nothing better than a wavering, indeed disappointed public opinion in Paris already critical of Boulangist lethargy. True, the Government had little they could charge against their enemies, but their enemies were by no means clear in their consciences. Rumours began to spread that the intention was to arrest Boulanger. Between them, his committee came to the conclusion, first, that Boulanger must stay, then, that he must go. On the night of March 14 Boulanger suddenly went off to Brussels. Then, finding he was not pursued, came back to Paris. He encouraged Laguerre to attack Constans in the Chamber, Laguerre did so, not very effectively. In his reply, Constans said: 'According to you, I have made a great fortune in business. You, you have not yet made one, but while you wait for it, you live as if you had done so. Say and do whatever you like, I utterly despise your words and your accusations, and I cannot tell you to what lengths I shall go.'

The Government meantime prepared openly to bring the deputies before the High Court of Parliament, i.e. the Senate. The bill constituting it was voted on April 4. The procureur-général, Bouchez, refused to sign the request to the Chamber for the prosecution of Boulanger, but another, Quesnay de Beaurepaire, did so. In the meantime, every kind of rumour had assailed the general, that he would be arrested and that once in prison he would be poisoned. Finally Clemenceau's henchman, Granet, visited Constans, who during the interview was called away. Granet seized the opportunity of looking through Constans's papers and found a draft order to arrest Boulanger. No doubt this was a deliberately planted trap into which Granet tumbled. He at once warned the victim. On the evening of April 1 Boulanger took train to Brussels. This time he would not return. He joined Dillon and Rochefort, who had already fled, in London. 'He slipped out like an enema', said his disgusted agent, Thiébaud.

With Boulanger and Dillon in London and the majority of the Boulangist committee working for their own re-election, the preparations for the struggle limped. Moreover money was short. The Duchesse d'Uzès, enraged at the general's flight, would do no more than produce the last fractions of the famous three millions, a mere 350,000 francs. The financial resources were now in the hands of the Royalist committee, amounting, it is said, to four million francs. Of this two-and-a-half came from the Jewish financier, Baron Hirsch, who was persuaded by the claimant's secretary, the Marquis de Breteuil, himself partly Jewish, being the grandson of the former Finance Minister, Achille Fould, to replenish the war-chest. In return, he was to be elected to the Club of the rue Royale. He paid, but in the end he was not elected. Of this large sum, the Royalist committee gave 1.3 millions to Boulanger. It is possible he received other amounts, some large. The whole matter was wrapt in mystery. Boulanger and Dillon succeeded in keeping the more honest Republicans on the committee, such as Déroulède, in the dark as to the sources.

During August and September the ill-assorted allies quarrelled over the distribution of the constituencies, whether they should be allotted to Royalist or National candidates. For the public, the theme was the same: dissolution, revision. For the 'pure' Boulangists it was mortifying to find that, in the provinces, their candidates stood alongside Royalists and Clericals. By this time, neither the Comte de Paris nor Mackau believed in success, nor again did the more clear-sighted of Boulanger's adherents. In July, to remove yet another aid from the general, Parliament passed a law forbidding candidates to stand in more than one constituency. Jaurès once again protested and from Brisson received a severe rebuke. The last chance was the presence of Boulanger: whether he was left free or arrested, he must return to France. Angrily he repulsed all such suggestions, and to keep up his confidence, predicted a majority.

The first poll on September was disastrous for the cause. Eighteen Boulangists were elected in Paris, including the general and a couple of Blanquistes. There were victories in Bordeaux, Nancy (here a young Maurice Barrès) and Nevers, where the two old sitting Radicals called themselves by what they believed to be the popular label. The second poll on October 6 confirmed the first. The Boulangists had at best 53 seats. The Conservatives (Royalist and Bonapartist) held 141 as against 187 in 1885. They had lost 11 in Nord, 11 in Pas-de-Calais, 7 in Finistère, 5 in Oise, 4 each in Lot, Manche and Basses-Pyrenées. None of these were compensated by 19 Left-wing Boulangists, Radicals or Revolutionaries in Paris. Considering the fever of the election and the notorious expenditure of money, the Republican victors behaved with restraint. There were no more than 25 invalidations (there had been 24 in 1885). Included in this figure were the quite unconstitutional annul-ments of the elections of Boulanger and Dillon and the substitution of the losing Republican candidates. Of the rest, 11 were Boulangists, of whom 8 were re-elected. The Royalists were treated tenderly: only 6 were invalidated and of these 3 re-appeared. There is reason to believe that Constans came to an agreement with Mackau to smother charges of illegal pressure, though what was the *quid-pro-quo* is by no means certain; it is believed some tens of thousands of francs passed.

So far as Boulangism was concerned it was the end. The general moved from London to Jersey. He hoped to recover his position in the spring at the municipal elections in Paris. The Right put forward their own candidates. The Boulangists captured exactly two of eighty seats. The committee saw only one chance of revival, the return of the fugi-tive to France. Again he refused.

That autumn (1890) one of the Paris deputies, Terrail, published, under the pseudonym of Mermeix, in the *Figaro* a series of articles in which he revealed the whole double-crossing history of Boulanger, his negotiations with the Royalists, his visit to Prince Napoleon, the financial aid of the Duchesse d'Uzès, who in fact was one of Terrail's informers. It was all very awkward, especially for the Comte de Paris. Boulanger denied that there had ever been for him any question of a monarchical restoration. No one believed him; his complete disregard for the truth was now patent.

In the following year, Madame de Bonnemain became seriously ill. Boulanger took her to Brussels and here on July 19 she died. Two and a half months later, on the afternoon of September 30, Boulanger blew out his brains on her grave.

Thus ended a trivial and tedious episode which should never have happened and almost certainly never would have but for the absence of men of character and courage. It is surprising that after so much fret, so little resulted. The monarchist cause, as de Mun had observed, was finished. There was no sentiment for monarchy in the country and no restoration could possibly come about through universal suffrage. Mackau's attempt to revive Orleanism by tying it to the apparently young body of Boulangism was a last desperate throw, which could not but fail, for Boulangism was but a simulacrum of a young movement. The Monarchists had learned nothing and had no ideas. They wanted their old privileges as they had been before 1848 and they had failed to adapt themselves. Or had they? Was it possible that they were securing the real privileges of their names behind a mask of loyalty to a cause they had betrayed? As Drumont pointed out, while giving lip-service to the Pretender, they were well content with the Republic, and they were not going to risk their comfort. The Ralliement, coupled with the death of the Comte de Paris in September 1894, completed the liquidation of a cause which, since the failure of 1877, had been moribund.

The Imperialists had expected much from the plebiscitary technique of Boulanger. With Prince Napoleon distrusted and Prince Victor a nonentity, they had, so to speak, fled to Boulanger. When he had gone, there was nothing left. When Prince Napoleon died in March 1891, Bonapartism was dead and the survivors joined with the Boulangist remnants to form a dissident anti-republican movement in the name of patriotism.*

* Tirard quarrelled with Constans over a judicial appointment and Constans resigned on March 1, 1890. A fortnight later, the government was defeated in the Senate over a minor economic question and Tirard resigned. Freycinet stepped into his shoes, remaining at the War Office and bringing Constans back to the Interior. Ribot was appointed Foreign minister.

Chapter Eighteen

The Ralliement

Pius IX died in 1878 in the thick of the Kulturkampf, the fight with
the German government over the relationship of State and Church.
His successor was Cardinal Pecci, Archbishop of Perugia, whom he had
disliked. Leo XIII, as Pecci became, had a far wider knowledge of the
world than had Pius and was keenly aware of the problems of the State
in relation to both religion and insurgent demos. For him the most
important problem was that of the Eldest Daughter of the Church,
France, where the claims of the pretender to the throne were supported
by many of the French clergy, and where political reaction claimed that
only under a monarchy could the Catholic Church survive. The Pope
had seen far more clearly than his predecessor that the 'Scientific International', the corresponding societies of the physicists and chemists, the
interchanges of the statisticians and sociologists, of the biologists and
medical men, of the inventors and the technicians, the spread of the
learned journal, were rapidly transforming the world, and that the
spectacular growth of population was creating new problems for society
and for the Church, above all the Church. Should then the Church
continue to support claimants to the throne of France when they and
their partisans demonstrated constantly that their ideas were those of
the past? The cause of monarchy was dying; the reasons for its existence, unless greatly modified, were in question. 'The only corpse to
which the Church is perpetually attached is that of our Lord Jesus
Christ,' said the Pope.

In 1881 he made his first important declaration on the matter in the
Encyclical *Diuturnum*, in which he warned the heads of States that
attacks on the Church would in the end be transformed into attacks on
the Civil Power, and laid it down that provided it was based on justice,
the form of the State was a matter of indifference to Catholic doctrine.
This was followed in 1884 by a second encyclical addressed to the
Nobilissima Gallorum Gens.

Although for political and politico-religious purposes, the Right and
the French Catholic Church apparently worked hand in hand, behind
this superficial amity there was, among the more religious-minded, a

growing distrust of the alliance. It was true that should the Comte de Paris recover the throne, the Church would be heartened and strengthened, but the 1885 election had shown that even at its then best, the prospects of Monarchist success were remote.

Although he had tactfully discouraged de Mun's Catholic political party, the Pope had not withdrawn. On November 10, a month after the election, he issued *Immortale Dei*. 'Sovereignty is necessary to society, and the original sovereign is God, who is not concerned with any particular form of State. But, whatever the form of government, society owes a duty to God. The State owes respect to the religious society which is the depository of Christ's religion. In every country there are two independent powers equally necessary, since their purpose differs, the civil power and the ecclesiastical power. This they should recognise and each should respect the other.'

So far as the Republican Government was concerned, the Pope might as well have not spoken. The Minister of the Interior, Goblet, was doing his best to invalidate successful Right candidates on the grounds of clerical pressure, while in the 1886 budget, a credit for the salaries of the poorest parsons was struck out. In 1886 the bill to employ no members of religious congregations in primary schools, which had been on the stocks since it was promoted by Paul Bert in 1882, reached the statute book after tumultuous debates. The act excluded male and female religious teachers from primary schools in any department where an école normale had been established for four years, the men to be replaced at the end of five years from the promulgation of the law, the sisters as vacancies occurred. The rapporteur of the 1888 budget, Yves Guyot, cut the Public Worship budget by 15 millions — but the Senate replaced the money.

The tension between Church and State was largely obscured between 1887 and 1889 by the Boulanger episode, but the general's defeat and the non-success of the Radicals at the 1889 elections led the moderate Republicans to talk of conciliation.

At this point, the Pope believed he saw the occasion for which he had waited a dozen years, the occasion to come to a compromise with the French Republic. He sounded various high ecclesiastics as to a herald and was recommended Cardinal Lavigerie, Archbishop of Carthage and Algeria, who had negotiated with Freycinet on behalf of the congregations in 1880. Lavigerie had once been a champion of the uncompromising Royalists, but had learned much in the course of time. Yet it was doubtful whether he was the wisest choice. Lavigerie was a warrior; but he had spent most of his life in Africa: he knew little of conditions in France, and little of the problems of the metropolitan hierarchy.

On receipt of the Pope's message, he visited Paris and talked with Freycinet, Ribot and Constans, who seem to have welcomed the approach. He then went to Rome where, from September 10–14, 1890, he discussed with the Pope the policy to be followed. It was agreed that there should be a break with the political Right, that the Catholics should be invited to proclaim their adherence to the Republic and that a Catholic Union should be founded with, at its head, Emile Keller, a former Legitimist deputy for Haut Rhin and Belfort. The Pope was by no means certain that his views would prevail and feared that this counsel might anger some of the Church's most conscientious supporters. Lavigerie's dominant personality seems to have broken down Leo's doubts, yet he was willing only for a *ballon d'essai* to be sent up as from Lavigerie personally and without committing the Holy See.

On November 12, the French Mediterranean fleet under Vice-Admiral Duperré anchored off Algiers. Lavigerie offered lunch to the naval officers, the head of the garrison and the chief civil administrators. At the end, he made a speech in which he said that the Republic was clearly in accord with the will of the people, that it was vain to fight against the principles which alone vitalised the Christian and civilised countries and that it behoved all good Frenchmen to rally to it. On which he raised his glass to the French navy. The admiral, a Bonapartist by tradition and creed, very angrily limited his reply to: 'I drink to his Eminence the Cardinal and the clergy of Algeria', and sat down.

French political circles were startled by the reports of the speech. A few bishops at once made public their agreement with Lavigerie. Others feared that they were being invited to condone the anti-clerical policy of the Government. With rare exceptions the politicians and journalists of the Right abused Lavigerie without mercy or scruple, as, of course, did anti-clericals like Ranc and Pelletan. Keller refused Lavigerie's invitation on the ground that the French did not like the clergy intervening in politics! The Pope, seeing the effect, hesitated to commit himself and maintained a studious reserve.

It would be otiose to follow the confused and fruitless strivings of the next months. Whereas some of the Centre Republicans and some of the devout Catholics accepted the principle of the 'ralliement', the Extremists on both sides rejected it. The Radicals refused to put any trust in the promises implied in Lavigerie's speech.

In April 1890 Jacques Piou, a wealthy man, deputy for a Toulouse constituency, and a devout Catholic, had tried to form a 'constitutional Right' in the Chamber with half a dozen Conservative members. It had had little success, but incited by the Lavigerie speech, Piou in January 1891 went to Rome and saw the Pope. Leo gave him some vague encouragement, though he was far from specific. Early in February, a conference of the Right was held in Nîmes. At this, the Comte d'Haussonville, representing the Comte de Paris, declared that the Church could not exist without the monarchy, and that a 'conservative republic' was impossible, to which Piou rejoined that this came oddly from the leader of the Right chiefly responsible for bringing the Constitution of 1875 into being.

Few of the Right were whole-heartedly in favour of the Republic. Even men willing to rally did so with repugnance. How could they work with noisy bullies such as Ranc, who scoffed at their advances? 'If you are only a tiny minority in the Chamber, we shall despise you; if you are an imposing minority, we shall invalidate you; if you are a majority, we shall take our rifles and go down into the street.' With such as Ranc, accommodation was as impossible as it was with a Catholic like the journalist Jules Delahaye, a brute and a liar. As for the clergy, most bishops were at best lukewarm.

The rest of 1891 passed in discord and debate. Royalist Bishops such as Cabrières and Freppel, Cardinal Richard, vainly pressed Leo to disavow the toast of Algiers. In October, arising out of a gratuitous insult by a French Catholic pilgrim, there was a small fracas in Rome between Italian Anti-clericals and French Clericals. The Pope at once suspended the pilgrimage, and Fallières, Minister of Public Worship, circularised the French bishops inviting them to stop the pilgrimages for the time being. It was a clumsy letter which threw the blame on the bishops. It infuriated the Archbishop of Aix into inditing a letter to the press denouncing the Republican Governments. 'Peace is sometimes on your lips, hatred and persecution are always in your actions, since that daughter of Satan, Freemasonry, directs and commands.' Monsignor Gouthé-Soulard was forthwith prosecuted. The wiser bishops held their peace, but 59 belligerents, with the approval of their monarchist laity, encouraged the archbishop, who refused the recommendation of the Papal Nuncio that he should apologise. Monsignor Gouthé-Soulard made a triumphal journey through railway stations crowded with the faithful to Paris, where he was fined 3,000 francs by the Conseil d'Etat. The incident, intrinsically unimportant, led to interpellations in the

Senate and severe comments by the Prime Minister. The real effect was to lessen the chances of the 'ralliement'.

Then in January 1892 the five French cardinals (excluding Lavigerie) Richard, Archbishop of Paris, Langénieux, Archbishop of Reims, Foulon, Archbishop of Lyon, Desprez, Archbishop of Toulouse, and Place, Archbishop of Rennes, published a letter addressed to the faithful. In this, an opening sentence ran: 'In the first place, the duty of the Catholics is to cease from political disagreement and by putting themselves resolutely in the constitutional field, to intend above all the defence of their threatened faith.' Unhappily this admirable sentiment came in the second part of the document, the first being devoted to a series of considerations of the actions of the Republic towards the Church during the previous dozen years, in fact a denunciation of the anti-clerical legislation since 1880. It was published on January 21. The odd thing, however, was the fact that it could be read in a number of ways. Most of the bishops approved of it. So did the Monarchists who looked only at the list of grievances. So did the Moderate Republicans who read the acceptance of the constitution. The Radicals of course attacked it; that was common form. The publication being a joint work might infringe the article of the Concordat against collective circulars, but the Papal Nuncio persuaded Freycinet to defer action. The most disturbed individual was Leo XIII, who had been informed of the declaration too late to read it before publication.

But the Pope was to be more disturbed. Freycinet for reasons by no means clear and probably, like other Freycinet actions, ambivalent, in February laid before the Chamber a bill for the regulation of the associations, which might have led to the dissolution of a number of the congregations while nominally upholding the principle of liberty. On February 18, the Radicals moved for urgent passage to the discussion, which Freycinet accepted. Thereupon they voted against him since he refused to make any promises on the separation of Church and State. The Right, seeing the danger in the bill, also voted against the Government. Attacked by de Mun, who insisted that the bill was persecutive of the congregations, attacked by Clemenceau in a remarkable speech, ('the Church alone has the right to guide men without their consent being necessary, and since she is in possession of absolute truth ... she possesses *a fortiori* earthly truth. And it is you, a lay government, a government of *parvenus*, which wants to trick such a power, an eternal power, which holds the scales of justice in this world and the next! A fight is possible between the rights of Man and what are called the rights of God. An alliance is not. . . . You say a hand is held out to yours? Put yours in it: it will be so firmly grasped that you cannot withdraw. You can, you will be the captives of the Church. The Church will never be in your power.') Freycinet was defeated by a combination of Radicals and Right, and the ministry resigned.

On the previous evening, February 17, the *Petit Journal* had published an interview which the Pope had given to its correspondent, Ernest Judet; in this he gave as his opinion that all citizens should unite under the law and that while each might maintain his private preferences, in action it was the government given to France by Frenchmen that alone had the rights. A Republic was as legitimate a form as any other. Three days later, these summary views were published at length in the encyclical *Inter Innumeras Sollicitudines*. The central directive implied that while no objection could or should be raised to a form of government, in itself good, bad legislation, that is of course legislation aimed at the Church, should be contested by all legal means. But the *Petit Journal* article had done the work. It was this, according to Melchior de Vogüé, 'which put the cabinet to death. It terrified the Left and exasperated the Right'.

Ideally, the Pope's recommendations were perfect. Unfortunately the practical objections were overwhelming. The majority of lay Catholics while admitting the Pope's authority in matters of faith rejected it in matters of politics; they refused to believe that the monarchical cause was finished. Privately in the châteaux, the Pope was spoken of as 'the old Jacobin'. The bishops tactfully or bluntly answered that adhesion to the Republic was impossible: their work was too dependent on the charity of the châteaux. Many did their best to put on the encyclical an acceptable gloss. It is fair to say that more bishops than the twenty who publicly accepted would have done so — they had no objection to a Republic — but for the anti-clerical legislation. 'As Catholics, we have no opposition to the republican form,' said Monsignor d'Hulst, 'but our opposition to the body of doctrines you call republican is irreducible.'

On the other hand, the 'ralliés' found no welcome from the Moderate Republicans. 'We have done without you in the past and can very well do without you now.' The attitude of the Radicals was as might be expected, and was summed up by Léon-Bourgeois in a speech at Nantes: 'You say you rally to the Republic. So be it. But do you accept the Revolution?' Ferry, Positivist, though Conservative, could think only in terms of doing without God. Ricard, Minister of Public Worship in the new Government led by Emile Loubet, entered on a course of minor persecution, in which he was much assisted by the provocations of turbulent preachers. The failure of the Ralliement has been ably expressed by Dansette: 'The rallying of Albert de Mun, the withdrawal of Keller and Chesnelong illuminated the end of an epoch which the survivors prolong — the demise of a policy which sought its deathbed long before the disappearance of the claimant in whom it was incarnated. The attempt at the restoration of the monarchy and the great pilgrimages, the appeal of traditionalist France to the resurrection of a legendary past, the mystical union of throne and altar — Leo XIII had torn the faithful from these vast and melancholy memories for ever.'

Chapter Nineteen

Panama

(i)

La Compagnie universelle du Canal Interocéanique de Panama had been founded during the good days of 1880 before the crash of the Union Générale. Its founder was Ferdinand de Lesseps, with whose name was associated the construction of the highly successful Suez Canal, opened in 1869. In 1880 he was now seventy-five years of age; he had never been an engineer — his career had been that of a minor diplomat — but he was an accredited heroic figure. 'The Great Frenchman', as Gambetta had named him, felt inspired to organise a company to construct a canal through the isthmus of Panama from Colon to Balbao on the Pacific. Unfortunately, being in no sense a technician, he had vague views on the method of cutting through the isthmus, the cost and the time required. His intention was to build a canal without locks through a series of lakes, but, between the main Gatun lake and the exit to the Pacific, lay a massif of hill, La Culebra, some 350 feet high, which must be pierced by a trench of considerable depth. Into the Gatun lake also, there flowed a river, the Chagres, subject to violent flooding, while the tide at Panama was of some twenty feet, and that at Colon only two. The time for construction was variously estimated between eight and twelve years, and the cost between 1200 millions and 530 millions. De Lesseps had tried to found a company with a capital of 400 millions and had failed. He then realised that, for a flotation, there must be extensive preparation. This was carried out during 1880 and in December there were offered for public subscription 600,000 shares of 500 francs each, giving a capital of 300 millions. The further expenses, it was announced, would be covered by the issue of debentures.

From the beginning the company was in difficulties, both physical and financial. First, it was necessary to construct what was effectively a colony at Colon, to build a port, to provide from Europe the materials and tools, and to recruit and transport a labour force. That the area was unhealthy had not been seriously considered: swamp fever and yellow jack raged and took a high toll of the labourers, an even higher one

x

possibly of the white engineers. A force of 30,000 was needed; it was rarely above 15,000. Panama, wrote Edouard Drumont, 'thanks to these nameless corpses, has become an ossuary which one day will give birth to the idea of a battlefield on which every type of human being will be found.'

Within two years, the company found itself forced into purchasing the Panama Railroad, the one means of crossing from Colon to Panama, at the high price of 95 millions.

Nevertheless, the Panama board of directors continued to produce enthusiastic and optimistic bulletins. In 1881 the shareholders learned that a whole year had been gained and that they could count on an opening during 1888. This was repeated in October 1883. At the general meeting of 1884, de Lesseps advanced the date to January 1, 1888.

Meanwhile, more money was required, and, as will be recalled, the years 1882 and onwards were years in which capitalists and smaller investors were slowly recovering from the follies of the boom of 1881–1882. In September 1882 the Panama Company offered debentures; again in October 1883, and once more in September 1883, to a total of 409 millions. The last of these three was not taken up in full and the company was forced to dispose of the remainder at a discount.

By 1885 yet more money was needed. De Lesseps bethought himself of the attractiveness of a lottery loan to investors. A lottery loan required the sanction of Parliament. At the general meeting of shareholders in July 1885, de Lesseps persuaded them to allow him to request Parliament to authorise a lottery loan of 600 millions, which when received would make the indebtedness of the company 1300 millions, rather more than the highest estimate of 1879. He had already approached Allain-Targé, Minister of Finance, and as good as threatened that if the Government was recalcitrant, he, as the protagonist of a vast enterprise in which the interests of France were involved, would bring all the forces of public opinion into action and smash the ministry, in token of which he roused the shareholders to petition the Government. Brisson, Prime Minister, was impressed but prudent. He despatched Armand Rousseau, a conseiller-d'état and a Public Works expert, to Panama to report. Rousseau returned in April 1886.

Rousseau's report was a practical document. He allowed that construction should not be abandoned, not only for the sake of the shareholders, but because the work would be at once continued by a foreign company, which would seriously weaken French influence in America. The Government should therefore support the company with all the

'administrative and diplomatic means at its disposal', but should give
the board neither advice nor financial guarantee. But the completion of
the canal within the period and with the resources at the company's
disposal seemed worse than problematic, unless the board agreed to
limit and simplify the plans. Privately, Rousseau said that the position
was hopeless unless a locked canal was substituted. Simultaneously two
of the company's engineers put in reports that the canal without locks
could not be carried out with the limited resources of a private company. De Lesseps and his entourage rejected the advice and insisted
that with a new loan their project could be realised.

In June (1886) Baïhaut, Minister of Public Works in Freycinet's
cabinet, tabled a bill for authorisation of the lottery loan. The committee appointed to examine the details, having heard the views of the
engineers, demanded a full financial analysis. In consequence, the law
could not be voted before the end of the session.

The situation of the company was now perilous. De Lesseps once
more approached the public and, scornfully asserting that the great
work would not be delayed by the attitude of six deputies, called on his
hearers to find the 600 millions in debentures. To tempt them, the
debentures, nominally 500 francs, were to be repaid at 1000. The first
loan was issued in August for 225 millions. It produced 206. The second
followed in July 1887: of the 200 millions offered, only 114 were taken
up. Nevertheless the work continued, and de Lesseps at length gave
way enough to allow the canal through the Culebra defile to be fur-
nished with locks as at least a temporary and economical measure. A
contract for the construction of the locks was signed with Gustave
Eiffel of the Tower. There still remained the question of money.

De Lesseps once again approached the Government in November
1887. Tirard replied that the cabinet's view was that the matter was one
for Parliament, not the Government.

In March 1888, inspired by de Lesseps, a Radical deputy, Michel, put
forward a proposal for a lottery loan which the Chamber agreed to
discuss. The company, by now in desperate straits, could not wait. A
further loan of a mere 150 millions was issued; it brought in 35. Meanwhile the Chamber committee, having first negatived the bill, ended by
recommending it by seven votes to six. In April the Chamber, by 284
votes to 128, voted the issue of a lottery loan of 720 millions, in the face
of two extremely cogent attacks on the company's financial mismanagement. The Senate agreed early in June and on 23rd the subscription
opened. It was a catastrophic failure. For one thing, a false report of de

Lesseps' death was circulated, with the result that the company's shares quoted that morning at 370 fell heavily. For another, contrary to the wishes of de Lesseps and his advisers, the whole 720 millions were offered at once instead of in three portions. Only 254 millions were taken up, and of this sum 60 millions were already engaged.

De Lesseps continued to struggle, to proclaim that the canal could be completed in the following year. He himself was now, at the age of eighty-three, no longer able to address audiences. His place was taken by his son, Charles. A tour of the wealthiest cities of France was undertaken without success. In December a last despairing effort was made to raise money, 'the death-bed issue'. It did no better than 50%. On December 15, three days after the disaster, Peytral, Minister of Finance, tabled a bill for a three month moratorium on the company's debts. The Chamber rejected it. The company thereupon suspended payment (this was a few days after Boulanger's triumphant election in Paris). The Seine civil court appointed administrators with wide powers, including the contracting of loans. They failed to improve the company's position. In February 1889 de Lesseps tried to form a new company for the completion of the canal, without result. The Seine civil court stepped in and ordered the dissolution of the company and appointed a liquidator, Brunet, Minister of Commerce in Broglie's 1877 government.

For a year, the liquidator worked on the company's papers. In March 1890 a deputy asked the Government (Tirard's second) to appoint a commission to study a future renewal of the work. He was told that this was beyond the attributes of the Government. A little later a group of shareholders petitioned the Chamber to examine methods whereby their interests would be saved. The commission which examined the application showed no interest in continuing the work on the canal: it recommended that those responsible for the disaster be identified and the case laid before the Ministry of Justice. Fallières, the minister in question, replied that as soon as the liquidator's accounts were ready, it should be possible to determine the responsibilities, and if necessary to bring the culprits before the courts.

Although proceedings against the Panama board were begun, it was not until June 1891 that an examining magistrate was appointed. This officer, Prinet, was notoriously slow, and the ramifications of the case were enormous. In January 1892 Gauthier de Clagny, a Boulangist deputy, presented a batch of petitions from the shareholders. Once more the Chamber ignored the requests to study the rescue of the investments, but expressed its desire that the Government should take energetic action against all those whose responsibility was involved in the crash.

Unexpectedly, in June, Prinet presented the file of the case to the Procureur général, Quesnay de Beaurepaire, who on September 10 submitted his report to the Minister of Justice, Ricard, preferring the prosecution of the chief officers of the Panama Company, namely Ferdinand de Lesseps, his son, Charles, vice-president, Marius Fontane, the secretary, and a director, Baron Cottu. On the same day, the *Libre Parole*, Drumont's paper, published the first of a number of articles on the company over the signature 'Micros'. Micros was a provincial 'banker' named Martin who in 1885 had done much to push the idea of the lottery loan. He thought his services ill-rewarded, and now stated that the company had bribed a number of members of parliament. Of those who had been the company's go-betweens he named the Baron Jacques de Reinach and a kerb-broker named Arton.

It is fair to say that the Panama Company board of directors was in no way dishonest, nor in spite of later accusations were the expenses at Colon and Panama extravagant. On the other hand, de Lesseps was madly optimistic. Piercing the flat terrain of the Suez isthmus, where moreover the country was healthy and labour available, had presented no problems; even so, Suez had cost nearly three times the original estimate. Panama was wild hilly country and the lake area unhealthy. Labour was not easily available, was highly paid and ineffective. The original estimate of the cost was fantastically too low, as was the length of time required. The board was driven to borrowing within two years of the foundation of the company. Furthermore de Lesseps, although no engineer, persisted against advice in not employing the most economical means of construction.

The consequence of all this was that money was required at short intervals and, as has been said, at a time when money was short. He had therefore to pay at ever increasing rates. Furthermore, the French money market was far from being well organised. Not one of the company's loans seems to have been underwritten. Charles de Lesseps told the examining magistrate in 1892 that whereas they had been able to build Suez out of the company's own resources 'without syndicate, without bankers and with no other press expenditure than an announcement', for Panama they had been blackmailed and squeezed, by journalists, by bankers, by people in good society, and to carry on they had capitulated.

(ii)

'The terror of right-thinking men', such is the title Georges Bernanos gave to his biography of Edouard Drumont, a character Bernanos valued. In 1886 Drumont had suddenly sprung into notoriety with the publication of two fat volumes, *La France Juive*, a violent attack on the Jews, Jewish finance and the social evils he believed to derive from this source. Anyone, however, who has read through these tedious pages will be struck by the fact that the contemporary Jews assailed are the wealthy ones, the Rothschilds, the Ephrussi, the Cahen d'Anvers, the Bischoffsheims, and that the most vitriolic scorn is reserved for the aristocratic Christians who batten on Jewish finance.*

The Jews had in fact formed a tiny fraction of the French population. The Sephardic Jews were in the south: the Papal Jews in the former Comtat Venaissin, and the descendants of the exiled Portuguese in Bordeaux, Nantes and Toulouse. All these were completely assimilated. Most of the originally Eastern Jews, the Askenazim, had been in Alsace, and save for those who had come over into France after 1870, were now German citizens. That few had opted for France is witnessed by the reduction in the number of rabbinates between 1869 and 1872 from 120 to 50. In Alsace alone had there been anti-semitism and that had been there before the Revolution. In Paris there was the Jewish quarter, the Marais (Léon Blum was born there), but its Jewish character was fading. As Jacques-Emile Blanche in an autobiographic sketch of his childhood shows, no one in the seventies paid the faintest attention to this kind of thing. In any case, in this period there were no more than about eighty thousand Jews in the whole of France.

Change came in the eighties. The murder of Alexander II of Russia in 1881 was followed by persecution of the Jews and finally led to police-incited pogroms in Poland and the Ukraine. A large Jewish exodus began, and though most went elsewhere, some refugees settled in France. Their numbers were not large; by 1900 there were not two hundred thousand: but the immigrants, most of whom spoke nothing but Yiddish and wore the traditional garments, were conspicuous, and caused anxiety to the Jewish committees in Paris.

* Drumont had once been in the employment of the Pereire brothers, the Jewish railway financiers who had in the high days of the Second Empire waged war against Rothschilds. The one Jewish financier who is praised was the younger Pereire, Isaac, who had been Drumont's employer. It was the revenge of Saint-Simonianism on the Haute-Banque.

There was thus little substantial anti-semitism. Indeed apart from Paris, it was scarcely known, and it was only in legal and financial circles of the capital, of whose practitioners the Jews formed some ten per cent, a high proportion to that of their numbers in the total population, that the prejudice could be said to exist. In the *'gratin'* it had little existence. Such a sentiment could scarcely survive in a society in which the Duc de Gramont and the Duc de Wagram were married to Frankfort Rothschilds, and the Duc de Richelieu to a Heine; the Marquis de Breteuil's mother was a Fould, and Ferdinand de Faucigny-Lucinge et Coligny, Prince de Lucinge, had recently married Raphaela Cahen, and on her death would marry May Ephrussi.

This, of course, for a romantic such as Drumont was the very point. He never attacked the Hebrew religion, never insulted a rabbi. As fiercely as Marx, he hated the financier, the Rothschilds, the Ephrussi, the Erlangers, the Bambergers, who had destroyed the ancient French virtues and values: loyalty, religion, responsibility, modesty, work and thrift. He hated the ostentation of Agenor de Gramont, son of the Foreign Minister who had made and lost the war of 1870, an ostentation only possible through the wealth of Meyer-Karl Rothschild of Frankfort-on-Main. And he hated the whole humbug of republicanism and royalism. 'For twenty years we have lived with the idea that there were two parties: one, true Frenchmen, honourable, generous, alive to the greatness of their land; the other, the exploiters, cynical republicans, shameless tricksters, who persecute and oppress the true French. This conception is utterly wrong. In reality there are not two political parties — there is a system, the Jewish capitalist system, and the representatives of all the parties which struggle for power are members of it. From this system the Republicans, with more sagacity, because they are more needy, ask perhaps more immediate satisfactions: they show possibly more ruthlessness and impudence: but the Conservatives are no less attached to it than the Republicans; they have, it may be a greater, interest in its survival, and they have no intention of allowing hands to be laid on it.'

La France Juive had had an enormous success. Drumont followed it with other denunciatory volumes. In 1890 he had published *La Dernière Bataille*, a horrifying exposure of the physical and moral plight of the Panama Canal area. In April 1892 he founded *La Libre Parole*, an anti-semitic daily paper. Within a month, as the result of his attacks on Jewish officers in the army, there took place a number of duels, in one of which a Captain Mayer was killed by admittedly unfair means.

Now, in September, Drumont began his campaign against those who were believed to have profited from blackmail of the Panama Company.

(iii)

As Charles de Lesseps had said, the family had had no difficulty in getting money for Suez, but in the building of that canal there had been few hitches and no loans had been necessary until the work was within measurable distance of completion. In the case of Panama, money had been wanted within two years of beginning. The Panama board had employed as their first financial agent one Marcus Lévy-Cremieux, a director of the Franco-Egyptian bank. On this man's death, they turned to a prominent figure in the stock-market, Baron Jacques de Reinach, a son of a wealthy Jewish banker of Frankfort, Adolf Reinach, who had obtained a patent of nobility from the Italian government in 1866, a patent confirmed by the Prussian court in 1867, and who had also become a naturalised French citizen. The Baron Jacques had had his fingers in many pies, several of them none too savoury. There had been an odd affair in 1880, land-grants in Algeria, in which President Grévy's brother, Albert, the governor-general, was involved. There had been enterprises in Malaya, Siam, Venezuela, Greece. And there was the Chemin de fer du Sud, the peculiarities of whose administration would send a senator to jail; but that would occur after the baron's death. The baron was familiar with a number of senators and deputies, with the stage and with artists, and appears to have led a gay and extravagant existence.

It was after the comparative failure of the third Panama debenture issue in September 1884 that the intervention of the baron in the company's affairs became tortuous. The company's inability to underwrite its loan issues forced it to go direct to the public. To persuade the unsuspicious citizen to invest, all the forces of public persuasion must be enlisted. It was in this that Jacques de Reinach was useful. He obtained from the company money with which he bribed all whom he conceived to be useful, journalists, politicians, people in society, to speak encouragingly of Panama. Between 1885 and 1888 he seems to have received rather more than seven-and-a-half million francs, say £300,000, to employ in these services, the major part being used at the time of the campaign to secure the parliamentary authorisation of the lottery loan. Reinach himself seems to have dealt with the big fish; the smaller fry, obscure needy provincial deputies, he left to one Aaron, otherwise Arton, a flashy adventurer, who after a career of bank-ruptcies in Brazil and Paris, had become secretary of a dubious com-pany, the Société de Dynamite: he, too, was a Jew.

The third Jew in the business was the queerest. Cornelius Herz, born in 1845 in Besançon of Bavarian parents, had been taken as a child to the United States, of which he became a citizen. About 1866 he had re-turned to France. Here, after working in various humble capacities in pharmacy and medicine, he obtained during the later stages of the war the rank of aide-major in the Army of the Loire and was decorated with the Legion of Honour. ('Never' wrote one embittered soldier, 'were so many honours broadcast as rewards for this, our most humiliating defeat.') With this he had returned to America and obtained some kind of medical degree. (Even after the first World War, medical degrees in the United States could be purchased from penurious universities for quite modest fees.) In San Francisco, he ran into debt and found it wiser to return to his native land. In Paris his life became even more obscure, but eventually he emerged as an entrepreneur of inventions. His first effort, an attempt to amalgamate three electric-lamp companies, failed. His second, to secure the telephone monopoly, broke down. But as the owner of a quasi-scientific journal, he gradually made his way. In 1881 he obtained his first promotion in the Legion of Honour; in 1883 he was made Commander, and in 1886 Grand Officer. At some point he became a sleeping partner in Clemenceau's *Justice*: the Radical leader was always a bad judge of men. Fortunately he appears to have bought back Herz's shares before 1886.

Herz seems to have become linked with Reinach from about 1880. Whereas Reinach was an amateurish sort of rogue, Herz was a quite accomplished scoundrel. He seems to have been a greedy financier of government contracts, often in association with Reinach. If Ernest Judet is to be believed, though this is doubtful, Herz made a trade of buying the votes of deputies and then forcing the Minister of War, Freycinet, to give him a share in a contract unless he wanted to be defeated in the Chamber.[1] He soon turned his peculiar talents to the Panama company. When the lottery loan of 1885 was postponed, Herz assured Charles de Lesseps that he could obtain it. He asked for twelve millions for 'publicity'. De Lesseps refused. Reinach then came in with a request for twelve millions for Herz and himself. Charles offered two.

Herz however appears to have obtained a contract from Charles under which he would receive ten millions on the day the lottery loan was voted. Moreover, the document was in some way endorsed by Reinach. This seems to have been subject to the contingency that if no result was obtained within a stated time, the contract fell. According to de Lesseps, this took place in 1887 and the document was destroyed. Nevertheless in May 1888, two months after Michel's proposal, Reinach recognised that should the lottery loan be authorised, Herz would be entitled to ten million francs. From July, when the Chamber agreed to the loan, Herz's pressure began in earnest. It is clear that he had some very strong hold on the baron, since the wretched creature capitulated again and again. By November 1892 nearly 9,400,000 francs had been extorted and more was being demanded.

Long before this, however, Dr Herz had not only secured Reinach, but had also intimidated at least two ministers, Floquet and Freycinet.

(iv)

On September 10, 1892, Quesnay de Beaurepaire received from Prinet the file of the case against the board of the company, together with his conclusions. Nevertheless, after a thorough consideration of the points, he came to the decision that the directors of the company had been in no way fraudulent and that the collapse was not due to any criminal activity.

The Prime Minister was much relieved at the Procureur-général's report. Loubet, a stout Republican, had reason to be so. The last thing he desired was a thorough probing of the history of the company's finances. When, on the previous January 5, the Chamber, at the end of the debate on Gauthier's motion on behalf of the shareholders, had unanimously called on the Government to take energetic action against those responsible for the disaster, i.e. the board, Baron Cottu, after the two de Lesseps the most important of the directors, enraged at the behaviour of the deputies, had hurried to the Minister of the Interior, and handed to him a list of those parliamentarians whom he knew to have been softened by the attentions of Baron Reinach.

Constans — for it was that hard man — had no illusions as to the generosity of politicians. He knew himself to be efficient; he had killed Boulangism. But he also knew he was disliked and feared. He took precautions. He had Cottu's list photographed. When, on Freycinet's fall (February 18) he was not called on to form a government — Carnot hated him — nor was he continued at the Place Beauvau, he handed over to his successor, the Prime Minister, the damning list — damning because with one unimportant exception every name was that of a Republican. No wonder that Loubet was disturbed.

Nevertheless the question was primarily for the Minister of Justice. The Minister was Ricard, a Radical lawyer from Rouen, mean, plump, solemn, handsome, with magnificent white side-whiskers, known to the Chamber as 'la belle Fatma' for his resemblance to the performer of the 'danse du ventre' at the Colonial Exhibition. Now the Micros articles had appeared in the *Libre Parole* since Prinet had handed his report to Quesnay. Prinet, to whom all this was new, considered that a further examination should be made as to the circumstances of the votes in the Chamber and Senate on the lottery loan in 1888. He asked Ricard, and the latter consented.

Thus on November 4, Prinet summoned Reinach and examined him on the employment of some three million francs which he had received for publicity in connection with the lottery loan. Reinach's answers were unsatisfactory and since for the time being he refused to produce any accounts or instructions, Prinet charged him on the spot. On the following day he instructed the police to take steps to make the baron justify his actions. Since this was a Saturday, no action was taken, indeed no move was made until Tuesday 8. By that day, the Baron had taken himself off to the Riviera. Prinet decided to await his return.

The Procureur-général, however, on November 5, had informed Ricard of his conclusion against prosecution. As to what happened between this date and November 15, illuminating detail is missing. On November 10 the deputy for Chinon, Jules Delahaye, of the Extreme Right, had notified an interpellation on the slowness of the Ministry of Justice in throwing light on the company's activities. On November 11 Loubet asked Quesnay to let him have a few lines justifying the abandonment of a prosecution of the Panama directorate in favour of a civil suit. This Quesnay handed to Loubet on 14th. But on November 15, before (it seems) the cabinet meeting, Ricard instructed Quesnay to bring the case as soon as possible before the Paris Appeal Court.* This, he mentioned casually to his colleagues when they met. Now of these, four would be pilloried before the Chamber, Rouvier, Minister of Finance, Burdeau, Minister of Marine, Freycinet, Minister of War, and Jules Roche, Minister of Commerce. Loubet, having the Cottu list,

---

* Bearers of the Grand Cross of the Legion of Honour, such as Ferdinand de Lesseps, could only be tried by a Court of Appeal.

knew this, so possibly did Burdeau, who seems to have been Loubet's confidant. But what could they do? Whatever protest they made would betray their secret uselessly.

On November 19, when Floquet, President of the Chamber, was about to take his seat, he asked leave to make a personal statement before calling on the various interpellators. On the previous evening, the Boulangist paper, *La Cocarde*, edited by one Ducret, had accused him while Prime Minister of having taken from the Panama Company 300,000 francs for electoral purposes. Floquet indignantly denied that he had ever 'demanded, requested, received or distributed' anything at all. Unhappily, while he was delivering himself of this emphatic statement, there was being handed round the benches a copy of a Republican paper *Le Jour* in which a friend of Floquet had stated in an interview that Floquet did not reproach himself for having in a moment of danger to the Republic sought the financial aid of the great credit institutions, among which was the Panama Company.

Ricard then announced that the case of the Panama board had been handed over to the legal authorities and could not be discussed. On this, an ambitious young politician, the Béarnais lawyer Barthou, rejoined that in effect there was also a political side to the case, which should be answered in the Chamber. Ricard agreed and the discussion of the interpellations of Delahaye and others was set down for Monday, November 21.

On this day, the summonses for the four members of the Panama board and the Baron de Reinach should have been served. Loubet, whose fears had in no way been allayed, succeeded in delaying service until after the legal hour for this operation, and then talked with Quesnay. He asked him whether it was not possible to omit Reinach from the proceedings? Burdeau, who was also present, added his persuasions to those of the Prime Minister. He insisted that this was a Radical plot to attack the Baron's nephew, Joseph, through an assault on the uncle. Joseph Reinach, once a secretary to Gambetta, editor and part-owner of the Opportunist *République Française*, and one of the most active enemies of the late Boulanger, was hated equally by the Right and the Radicals and not much liked by anyone else. The Procureur replied that he had his instructions from his own minister, Ricard: if the Prime Minister insisted on this action, he would have no alternative but to resign. The honest Loubet could not allow this and reluctantly consented to the law taking its course. It would have been better if he had not spoken.

Before he left for the Riviera Baron Jacques de Reinach had told his lawyer Andrieux — this mischief-making ambitious rascal was a natural choice — that he would tell the *Libre Parole* all about his activities, provided the paper omitted him from their campaign. Andrieux, nominally a Radical — principles he had none, except that they be to his own advantage — saw Drumont, at that moment doing three months in Saint-Pélagie for insulting Burdeau, and squared him. Reinach's disclosures began to appear in the *Libre Parole* on November 8, by which time he had left Paris. At Nice, his alarms seem to have died down. At least, he returned to Paris, arriving on the afternoon of November 18. Here on arrival he found the article in the *Cocarde* with its accusations against Floquet. With the *Cocarde*'s editor, Ducret, it seems he had no link, and no doubt he guessed that the blood-sucking Herz was behind this new exposure: whether out of frivolity or by extortion, he appears to have divulged to the Doctor the names of the parliamentarians he had bribed, together with the sums he had paid them. He must somehow shut Herz's mouth.

So on the following morning, November 19,* the day of the opening of Parliament, he sought Rouvier, Minister of Finance, and asked him to put pressure on Herz to bring the press polemics to an end. Rouvier (since Herz claimed to be ill) agreed to accompany Reinach to Herz's house provided the conversation took place before a witness. They agreed on Clemenceau, whom they eventually found about four of the afternoon at the Palais Bourbon. Clemenceau said he would accompany them. They met at Herz's house. Reinach asked the Doctor to put an end to the campaigns of the *Libre Parole* whose articles derived from Reinach's own disclosures had reawakened curiosity, and the *Cocarde*, adding that Rouvier was as anxious as he was to stop them. Herz replied that if he had been warned earlier he might have done something, but by now it was too late. On this, Reinach turned to Clemenceau and said that since there was no solution here, would he take him to see Constans? Reluctantly Clemenceau agreed. The trio left Herz's house and Rouvier went home. Clemenceau and Reinach reached Constans's home about 7.30. Clemenceau explained that they had come because it was rumoured that Constans was at the bottom of the campaign. Constans flew into a temper and denied all knowledge of the matter. The two visitors left, and Reinach parted from Clemenceau groaning, 'I'm done for.' He drove to see his nephew who was also his

---

* The peregrinations of Reinach on November 19 are in part mysterious and without explanation; he behaved like a bat in a lighted room.

son-in-law, Joseph Reinach, who had already received from his friend Quesnay de Beaurepaire news of the issue of writs. It is said that uncle and nephew quarrelled; though it is of no importance. The baron left about eleven and called on two sisters, whom he was said to be keeping, in the rue Marbeuf. He reached his home at 1 a.m. At a quarter to seven in the morning, Sunday November 20, Reinach's man entered the bedroom to discover 'a member of the family' (was it Joseph?), who said: 'It's not worth while; the baron's dead.'

During the morning, Joseph passed a note to Adrien Hébrard, chairman and editor of *Le Temps*, who passed the information on to Cornelius Herz and Charles de Lesseps. That afternoon, the good Cornelius took the train for London. On his way to the station, he called on Andrieux to say that Joseph was at work on his uncle's papers and that he could be trusted to leave nothing likely to compromise his friends. By some strange influence three days passed before the judicial liquidator appointed at the request of the Reinach family sealed up the baron's papers.

(ν)

On Monday, November 21, the first interpellation came from Argeliès, a left-wing Boulangist, member for Corbeil, and soberminded. He insisted that Parliament with its bill of 1886 for the lottery loan, with its law of 1888, and with Peytral's suggested moratorium for the company, had engaged its moral responsibility in the future of the canal: the Government could not divest itself. His speech bored the audience.

He was followed by Jules Delahaye, perhaps the best hated man in the Chamber. Royalist, Boulangist, Clerical, he was without scruple. On several occasions he had been fined for libel. He had no hesitation in slandering anyone he conceived hostile to his violent political views: he had conspired with the lesser clergy to undermine the influence of bishops of Poitiers whom he believed to be Republican.

He opened by proposing the nomination of a commission of enquiry into the scandal of Panama. He alleged that the prosecutions which had begun had no other aim than to cover up the real facts.[2] The Daniel Wilson case was a trifle compared with the Panama evil. 'This is open squandering, the plunder in full light of day of the fortunes of citizens, of the poor, the needy, by men whose duty it is to protect and defend.

... I have discovered that the great deceivers have been the deceived, that the exploiters have been exploited with such cynicism, such greed, that if the misfortunes of the share and debenture holders permitted the uttering of the word pity ... it is for them that it should be reserved in the lamentable catastrophe in which they have foundered with the Panama enterprise.' From the beginning, the speaker had been assailed by shouts and abuse. Reiterated again and again was the cry 'the names! the names!' to which he monotonously answered 'Vote the enquiry'. He said enough to demonstrate that he knew more, but, well aware that more than he knew must follow if the commission was appointed, he stood his ground in the face of the uproar. Finally, challenged by Floquet to give the names, he rounded on the Boursouflure with 'I am astounded, Monsieur le président, that, after having been accused, you personally are not the first to join in my request for an enquiry'. He left the tribune in a storm of yells. After calm was restored, Loubet said that in the face of these accusations, the Government could not oppose a request for light. A commission of thirty-three was voted without a division.

On the following two days the Chamber elected the members of the Commission, seventeen Republicans, six Radicals, nine Right and one Boulangist. Brisson the austere was chosen president. According to Barrès,[3] the categories should be thirteen saviours of themselves and their party, all Republicans and Radicals except the old Bonapartist Jolibois, four who were weak, and the rest who were ignorant.

The commission had hardly got to work before rumours began to be spread that Reinach's death had not been natural. On November 28, a deputy of the Right asked the Minister of Justice to carry out an autopsy on the baron's body. Ricard read a report from a doctor that Reinach had died of a stroke, and fell back on details of procedure to refuse the invitation. Brisson returned that the Government had promised light on the case; they should carry out their promise. Loubet moved 'the order of the day pure and simple', which the Chamber rejected, after which they passed by a huge majority a motion associating the Chamber with the commission's request. Loubet resigned.

Carnot invited first Brisson to take Loubet's place, and on his failure to get support, Casimir-Périer. The latter also failed and Carnot's next choice, Léon Bourgeois, declined. Constans, whom Carnot detested, and perhaps feared, was not asked. Finally, Ribot, the Foreign Minister, succeeded in getting promises of support. He appeared on December 8 with a team almost identical with Loubet's. Loubet kept the Interior,

Rouvier Finance, Freycinet, Burdeau, Viette, Develle all remained. Ricard was very naturally dropped and Léon Bourgeois took Justice. What, it was asked, did Ribot intend, collaboration with the commission or hostility? Ribot in a speech filled with conventional phrases succeeded in getting a majority, and Léon Bourgeois, pressed to divulge the evidence on which Prinet and Quesnay had worked, was forced to a vague promise.

The autopsy was carried out on December 10: because of the decomposition of the body, it revealed nothing certain as to the cause of Reinach's death. It did not appear to have been a stroke, and most people concluded that poison had been administered, but by whom? Two days later *Figaro* revealed the visit of Reinach, Rouvier and Clemenceau to Herz on November 19. Clemenceau immediately published a plain statement in *Justice*. Rouvier resigned at once (the departure of the only serious financier in Parliament caused a panic on the Bourse)[4] and explained to the Chamber that, on November 19, he had no knowledge that Reinach was compromised, a not very probable statement.

There followed a few days later a strenuous attempt on the part of the Commission to secure for itself what was tantamount to judicial powers. Bourgeois and Ribot with great difficulty repulsed the proposal, but they only carried the day by a majority of six. Anxious to reestablish itself in the public esteem, the Government through Bourgeois ordered the arrest of Charles de Lesseps, Fontane and Cottu for corruption of State servants. In addition, they ordered that of Sans-Leroy, the deputy who in 1888 as a member of the committee on the lottery loan had changed his vote to one in favour of its authorisation. He was one of the few individuals Delahaye had denounced in giving the commission his evidence.

Now, on November 30, a banker named Thierrée who had taken over the finance house of Kohn, de Reinach et Cie., had told the commission that he had in his possession 26 cheques drawn by the baron in July 1888. These he had handed over on December 3. Two were in favour of the senators, Léon Renault, once Préfet of Police, and Albert Grévy, brother of the late President and former governor-general of Algeria: otherwise, except for that of Cornelius Herz, the names were those of nobodies. The commission asked Thierrée for the stubs of the cheques, which he said had been burned. But three days after the arrest of the Panama board, on December 19, he admitted to the examining magistrate in the de Lesseps case that he still had them. Whether this

admission was provided by Constans, enraged at being kept from office
or by the determination of the Panama directors to defend themselves
cannot be decided, but on the evidence before him the examining magistrate asked that the parliamentary immunity of five deputies should
be raised, Arène, Proust, Jules Roche, Rouvier (the last two recent
ministers) and Dugué de la Fauconnerie, the last a member of the Right.

That afternoon, December 20, Floquet asked the Chamber whether
it agreed to the removal of parliamentary immunity from these five. In
the debate that followed, the only intervention of interest was that of
Rouvier who said, in a sentence of which much was made, that he had
handled the great affairs of the country without his fortune having
swollen 'abnormally', and went on to tell the Chamber that when he
became Prime Minister in 1887 he found the secret fund so depleted
that he had to borrow from his acquaintances. 'As for those who inter-
rupt me, if they had been otherwise defended and served, it is possible
that they would not now be sitting on these benches.' Jules Roche, who
was not in the Chamber, had not even voted in the lottery loan division.

On the same day, the Government asked the Senate to raise the
immunity on Béral, Albert Grévy, Léon Renault, Thévenet, former
Minister of Justice, Dévès, a minister in three cabinets. It was done.

The dramatic surprises of the day were not yet at an end. After
Rouvier had spoken and the deputies involved had been placed at the
disposition of justice, Déroulède asked leave to interpellate the Government on the disciplinary measures to be taken by the Chancellor of the
Legion of Honour against Cornelius Herz. Leave being granted
Déroulède developed a long attack on Clemenceau. How, asked
Déroulède, had this little German Jew without patronage or patron
been advanced so rapidly; obviously he must have very powerful
friends. 'Now, this indefatigable and devoted intermediary, so active
and so dangerous, you all know him, his name is on all lips; but all the
same not one of you would name him, for there are three things that
you fear, his sword, his pistol, his tongue. Well, I brave all three and I
name him: it is M. Clemenceau.' He went on to speak of the Radical
leader's business relations with Herz, who, he said, had claimed to have
paid Clemenceau 400,000 francs. Finally he asserted that Herz was the
agent of a foreign power, and that Clemenceau, in his career of destruction ('It was to destruction that you consecrated your efforts. What
things, what people you have broken! Your career is built of ruins!'),
had been the helper of this spy.

Clemenceau called him a liar and then from the tribune gave his own

Y

version of his relations with Herz, that he had been a sleeping partner in *Justice* until 1885, when Clemenceau had bought back the shares at, admittedly, a low price, that he had never had any connection with Herz's business and never recommended him for decorations. As for the charge of attempting to harm his country, 'To this last charge, there is only one answer: M. Paul Déroulède, you have lied.' But though he was applauded by the Left, the applause found no echo on the Right or in the Centre: the Republicans were delighted that Clemenceau had met his match. A duel inevitably followed. Each fired three times and each missed. 'I've not killed Clemenceau,' said Déroulède, 'but I've done for his pistol.'

(*vi*)

Herz had taken refuge in England. The difficulties of Government, the fall of Loubet, the formation of the Ribot ministry, the coming and going between the legal authorities and the politicians, had meant that the rogue had been temporarily ignored, but not by those who saw that he might be useful. At some time in December, probably in the week beginning Monday 12, Louis Andrieux had gone to London and interviewed the Doctor. He had returned at the end of the week and on Sunday, December 18, called on Ernest Judet of the *Petit Journal*, to whom on behalf of Clemenceau and himself (so Judet says) he made the offer of an alliance. He, Andrieux, had in his possession a list of 123 members of Parliament among whom Reinach's agent, Arton, had distributed 1,340,000 francs. If Judet would co-operate, they would break the Opportunists; Rouvier would climb into the first tumbril. 'The list of Radicals who have had a share is in our hands and will stay there. We are sure of their fidelity, as they are of our silence.' Judet says he refused to concert with Clemenceau and Andrieux.[5]

Whether this story is true or not, on December 22 Andrieux read to the parliamentary commission a list of names which Reinach several years earlier had dictated to one of his employees and handed to Herz, from whom he, Andrieux, had obtained a photograph. This on the whole confirmed to a remarkable degree the indications on the cheques and the stubs provided by Thierrée. It also added several names, of which one was that of Sans-Leroy, the deputy who in the committee on the lottery loan changed his vote from No to Aye. He had taken 300,000 for his conversion.

One further exposure was made soon after the New Year. A representative of the Crédit Lyonnais, Blondin, was arrested on the charge
of having bribed Baïhaut, Minister of Public Works from 1883–85 and
again in 1886, when he had prepared and tabled a bill for a lottery loan
in June. The information came from Charles de Lesseps.

Meanwhile, a number of rumours had been spread regarding Freycinet. On January 10, Ribot resigned and at once re-formed his cabinet,
having dropped his embarrassing Minister of War and also Loubet,
whose attempt to hush the whole thing up had made him the target for
the opposition. With them went Burdeau, Minister of Marine, who
resigned; he was being surreptitiously accused of having written for
Henri Maret a favourable report on the canal.

(vii)

The trial of the board for fraud and abuse of trust began on January
7. The Advocate general in his opening, and later, was vicious in his
assault on the four men, whom he insisted on charging collectively. He
was unable to establish anything worse than over-optimism and error.
Up to 1888 the programme had been fulfilled. The accusation that de
Lesseps had used the money of the humble but not his own was shown
to be false: he had invested a million and three-quarters and had lost
300,000 francs, Charles was shown to be a relatively poor man. When
the Advocate-general said, 'You wasted the millions of the debenture-
holders intentionally,' Charles answered: 'With as much intention as
one hands over one's watch at the pistol point.' All the correspondence
demonstrated complete good faith: it was a case for the civil and not the
criminal courts. Nevertheless, poor men had lost their all; there were
suicides, and public opinion demanded punishment. On February 9
both de Lesseps were sentenced to five years imprisonment and fines of
3000 francs, Cottu and Fontane to two years and the same fine, while
Eiffel who, owing to the peculiarities of the contract for the locks, had
made a bigger profit than he would had he completed the work, was
given two years and fined 20,000 francs. All the defendants appealed.
On June 15 the Cour de Cassation reversed the sentence and ordered
the release of the prisoners. Long before the trial, Ferdinand de Lesseps,
now aged eighty-eight, had collapsed. He died a few months later.

During these weeks, the examining magistrate had gone into the
cases of many of the deputies and senators whose immunity had been

lifted. He found insufficient evidence to charge seven among them: Jules Roche, Rouvier, Emmanuel Arène, Thévenet, Devès, Albert Grévy, Léon Renault. It is pretty certain that Jules Roche and Devès were wholly innocent, their dealings with Reinach having been quite legitimate, while Rouvier's 'touch' had been on behalf of the Government. (All the same, his reputation suffered: he had been too astute; he did not re-appear on the Government benches until 1902.) Against Thévenet there was no evidence that he had ever heard of the cheque. In the cases of Léon Renault and Grévy, however, suspicion remained. It is to be noted that every one of the seven was politically important, and an Opportunist.

On the following day Godefroy Cavaignac, one of the newer members of the Chamber, deputy for a Sarthe constituency since 1885, and Minister of Marine in Loubet's cabinet, addressed the government on the white-washing of the seven in an energetic speech in which he quite properly insisted that the possibility that the Government should have borrowed from financial companies was disgraceful, and that the Chamber should give a guarantee that the procedure of 1887–89 should not re-occur. Ribot weakly agreed. It was the speech he had failed to make in December, and the Chamber knew it. Cavaignac, a stiff, solemn and ambitious prig, found his reputation enhanced.

The bribery trial began in March before the Assize Court. The chief defendants were Charles de Lesseps, Fontane, Baïhaut and his corrupter Blondin, Sans-Leroy and four others. De Lesseps who in the Court of Appeal had been discreet in the expectation that Ribot, in return for his silence, would influence the prosecution, now divulged as much as he could. He explained how Herz had deceived him, how he had black-mailed Reinach, the pressure exercised by Freycinet and Clemenceau and the crude extortion of Baïhaut, who had required a bribe of a million francs to carry through the lottery loan in 1886. Through Blondin, it was agreed that Baïhaut should receive 375,000 on tabling his bill, 250,000 on its passage through the Senate, and another 375,000 before the issue of the loan. Since it got no further than submission to the Chamber, he had got no more than 375,000, a reasonable compensation for the work involved. Baïhaut had fully admitted his crime to the examining magistrate and now made a full and fatuous confession in court.

Sans-Leroy on the other hand attempted to explain that his change of mind in the loan-lottery committee had been due to the pressure of his constituents and that 200,000 francs which had been paid into his bank account bore no relation to the case. His explanation was refuted by the Advocate-general. The other defendants put up very unconvincing exhibitions of virtue. Baïhaut was condemned to five years imprisonment, a fine of 750,000 francs and the repayment of 375,000 to the Panama Company. Blondin was given two years and Charles de Lesseps one, and both were made responsible should Baïhaut fail to repay the 375,000. Baïhaut, of course, failed; the Finance Ministry pursued Charles, who retreated to England. From this refuge he was able to arrive at a compromise, and return to watch over his interests in Suez. The rest, including the obviously guilty Sans-Leroy, were acquitted for lack of evidence!*

One curious incident was brought to light at the trial. Madame Cottu appeared and stated that in December she had been invited by an intermediary to visit the head of the Sûreté, Soinoury. The Government, he said, was anxious to close the case and would have a 'no case' verdict given by the examining magistrate if the members of the board held their tongues. Madame Cottu therefore went to the Sûreté on January 7. She alleged that after some fencing, Soinoury proposed that if she could compromise a member of the Right and give a name, Cottu would be released. Amid immense excitement, Soinoury was called and failed completely to make any serious explanation. The audience hooted him so loudly on his leaving the witness box that the court had to be

---

* Arton who had fled the country in June 1892 in consequence of a charge by the President of the Dynamite Society, disappeared completely. He still had allies in France. Through one of these, Arton suggested he might be of service to the Government. The Minister of the Interior agreed to allow the Sûreté to pursue the matter. But Arton soon discovered that he was to be arrested. Through January and part of February 1893 he flitted about east-central Europe. In mid-February, his traces were lost. In fact he got to England, and it was not until November 1895 that he was picked up in London. In the meantime he had been condemned to 20 years for forgery and fraud in the Dynamite Society case, and to five years for bribing Sans-Leroy (who had been acquitted). He was eventually acquitted in this case, but was given 8 years detention in that of the Dynamite Society. During the hearing of the former charge, he told the court that Andrieux's list of 104 was nonsense: there had been only 26 parliamentary 'chequards'. He claimed that when he had the money from Reinach, he had formed a committee of Le Guay, Barbe (both on the board of the Société de Dynamite) and Naquet to work on the members and he had later brought in Henry Maret, rapporteur of the lottery-loan proposition, and Burdeau, who in fact wrote the report. In the end, two deputies and two senators, together with five former deputies, were put on trial in December 1897, in the midst of the breaking of the scandals in the Dreyfus case. The evidence was thin, in some cases none was offered, and in the others the defendants, including Arton, were acquitted.

A second commission had been set up in March 1897 with Vallé, rapporteur of that of 1892, as president. Herz, now living at Bournemouth, invited the commission to take his evidence, but they eventually saw that the doctor was merely amusing himself, which he continued to do until death overtook him on July 6, 1898.

cleared. Léon Bourgeois two days later told the court that he was completely unaware of any of this, but in the Chamber, Ribot failed to
satisfy the members and was only saved by the intervention of a Radical
who managed to muddle the evidence. From what is known of the
history of the Paris police, it is probable that Madame Cottu's evidence
was true. But who gave Soinoury his orders?

In the Chamber de Mun properly upbraided Ribot for his dishonesty.
'You have not done your duty. You have spoken and behaved like the
leader of a party and not the leader of a government. . . . You could
have been an avenger. You preferred to be a rescuer, and you have
rescued nothing.'[6] The Chamber recognised the truth of de Mun's
criticism. On March 30 the Government was beaten on a financial
question and on April 4 Ribot resigned. His place was taken by Charles
Dupuy, another Republican, who himself took over the Ministry of the
Interior.*

One further episode caused a storm. It arose only indirectly out of
Panama. Déroulède and his foolish friend, the Boulangist Millevoye,
were still persuaded that Clemenceau was, through Herz, in the pay of
a foreign power. On June 21 Ducret printed in the *Cocarde* a statement
that important documents which demonstrated the treachery of some
politicians had been stolen from the embassy of a foreign power. On
the following day Millevoye read in the Chamber a number of letters
alleged to have been written from the British Foreign Office to the
Paris embassy, which included a list, dated June 10, of the sums paid to
prominent journalists and politicians, *Le Temps, Le Journal des Débats*,
Burdeau, Maret, Rochefort and Clemenceau, the last for £20,000. The
Chamber roared with laughter. Millevoye, nettled, called on the new
Foreign Minister, Develle, to whom he had shown the papers, to
support him. Develle, who seems to have allowed Millevoye to discredit himself, replied that the accuser had been deceived. Burdeau
and Clemenceau attacked Millevoye. Several members of the Right
disavowed their colleague and the Chamber passed a condemnatory
resolution by 384 to 2, on Millevoye and Déroulède, both of whom
resigned their seats. The documents in question had been manufactured
by Ducret in conjunction with a coloured man, a criminal, one Véron,
who called himself Norton. Both were tried, condemned, imprisoned
and fined.

*Ferry, who had been elected to the Senate in February 1891 and to its Presidency in
January of that year, died from the after-effects of his wound, on March 17.

(*viii*)

The Panama scandal has been swollen by the passions of some of those concerned in it as politicians and by most of those interested in it as writers. No one who reads Barrès's *Leurs Figures* can fail to be excited by his accounts of the Baron de Reinach's last day, of Rouvier's furious reply to the charge, of Delahaye's interpellation: they bear the mark of the first-class reporter (Boulangist deputy for Nancy 3, Barrès was sitting high up on the extreme left of the Chamber) and they stand out vividly in contrast to such puppets of his imagination as Sturel and Römerspacher. Barrès, however, was not writing history, while further-more parts of the book are based on Vallé's reports to the Commissions of Enquiry which themselves are slanted.

Other writers, Zévaès and Dansette, well versed in the documents, appear to start from a prejudiced standpoint. For Zévaès (*Le Scandale de Panama*, 1931), the whole matter is due to the capitalist system and all involved are equally villains. Dansette (*Les Affaires de Panama*, 1934) is more judicious, but he labours under the belief that the full amount of corruption has not been brought to light: his view is similar to that of Tweedledum on the Walrus.

The fact is that there is not sufficient valid evidence to come to any conclusion as to the amount of corruption. Andrieux said he had from Herz 104 names; Delahaye claimed to have 175; Arton said there were in fact less than 30 and that Reinach had given the others to Herz '*de chic*', while nobody has ever revealed the names of Cottu's list. The death of the baron and the rapid action in emergency of his nephew Joseph deprived the investigators of essential material. So far as the extent of the corruption, we are unlikely to have an answer. It is hinted that the examining magistrates or the judges were influenced by poli-tical considerations. It may be so, but we have no proof. It is clear that they themselves also suffered from the same lack. As Sans-Leroy, who was certainly guilty, said when challenged by the prosecutor: 'Prove it': the prosecutor could not. One has no doubt that the members of the committee on the lottery loan who voted in favour had received money: should then the 284 deputies and 158 senators who voted the law be tarred with the same brush? Wallon, Baudry d'Asson, Clemenceau, de Mun? Surely not.

Further, the amount of money involved is exaggerated by the ac-cusers. When the cost to the company of the flotation of the original shares and the subsequent loans is worked out, it is found to be a trifle under 8.2% for the amount received, almost exactly 6% for the amount expected to be brought in, which is just about the same as that needed to float the bonds of the Paris Exhibition of 1889.[7]

No definite conclusions can be drawn. All that can be said is that a company presided over by a vain and incompetent man made a series of bad miscalculations and huge blunders which, in spite of warnings, were persisted in, so that in the end a serious scheme was brought to naught and many people ruined.* De Lesseps rejected the advice of technical experts and was outraged when bankers after the failure of the 1884 loan would not underwrite new loans. Believing that his prestige was enough to give him political support, he pressed three Prime Ministers, Brisson, Rouvier, Tirard, to permit the legalising of the lottery loan. Failing to secure it, he put himself in the hands of one whose business was 'fixing'. From that rash move, the rest followed. Incompetence there may have been, but it does not appear that de Lesseps or any other member of the board was involved in peculation.

The details of what happened are of the least historical importance. Three corrupting rogues and perhaps thirty corrupted parasites, in a body of nearly nine hundred, are intrinsically without interest. The interest lies in the consequences. The core of the Republican party had been shaken by the Boulanger adventure, and although the Right had been defeated there were still enough of them to make trouble. Loubet, personally irreproachable, was deeply alarmed at the possible effects of the disclosure of the 'chequards' on the political situation, and within twelve months of a general election. In the Chamber, there were still too many enemies of the Republic. Should the Radicals from whim or pique join with them, the resulting confusion might produce an explosive situation. The economic position was no better. Unemployment and near starvation were still bad. Anarchism of the most violent kind would be active during the next two years. 1893 moreover would be a year of strikes and riots. Loubet's plans went astray. Had he consulted Rouvier instead of Burdeau, between November 11 and 15, it is possible that the prosecution of the Panama board would have been abandoned in accordance with Quesnay de Beaurepaire's second

---

* How many private investors were involved? Did the greater share of the capital come from them or from the bankers? Or did the bankers when they saw what was happening unload their holdings on to the small saver in the country? The activities of bond-salesmen had already been seen in connection with the Union Générale.

thoughts, and Ricard would have been stopped from his fatal action of
November 15.

(ix)

The election of August-September 1893 is important from its very
negativeness, from the absence of political excitement. In the spring
there had been disturbances. In April Dupuy had ordered the closing
of the Paris Bourse du Travail to prevent demonstrations on May 1. In
June there had been quarrels between the students of the Quartier
Latin and the police; one student was killed and there was talk about
agents-provocateurs. This was followed by more trouble over the
Bourse du Travail, and an attempted resistance of the syndicats to ful-
filling the requirements of the law of 1884 was answered by the occupation of the Bourse by the military.

Somewhat naturally there had been misgivings about the election. It
was thought that Charles Dupuy was not of big enough calibre to keep
a grip on the constituencies. The exclusion of Constans was regretted.
It was feared moreover that the Panama scandals might provoke the
electorate. The fears were misconceived. The sovereign people remained unprovoked. If truth be told, a number of people rather expected their deputy to feather his nest, when he could, and so long as he
continued to watch the interests of his constituents, they did not resent
it. The préfets had the country well in hand: too well some thought.
Apart from half a dozen constituencies where well-known politicians
were beaten, the election was without surprise, the quietest since 1881.
The poll was no better than 71%: in seven departments, 60% and even
less voted. Of the 581 successful candidates, 392 had sat in the previous
Chamber, and of the outgoing deputies who stood, only 39 failed to
secure re-election.*

In such an election, there could be little shift in the pattern of the
Chamber. Although in Paris the Boulangists were largely eliminated,

---

* It is erroneous to say as Caillaux does in his memoirs that the rising generation was
able to sweep out their predecessors and take their places at no cost to themselves. Of
those tainted by Panama, only Floquet (Paris XI, i) was defeated. Rouvier, Roche, Maret
and others came back. Both the accusers, Delahaye and Millevoye, lost their seats. At
Draguignan (Var) Clemenceau was beaten by a combination of revengeful Boulangists,
who fought him without scruple. He was opposed by five other so-called Radical candidates, also by the préfet, and, against the advice of Jaurès, by the local Socialists. He was
beaten at the second poll by a Marseille lawyer, who proved to be a thorough reactionary.
In Paris, his chief aide in the Chamber, Pichon, lost his seat to a left-wing Boulangist.

the Radicals did not regain the supremacy they had had in 1885: the seats, particularly those of the outer fringe and the suburbs, went to the Socialists of various persuasions. The Radicals, hitherto the chosen of the urban Extremist, now began the invasion of the rural constituencies, chiefly in the south-west where the transition from Bonapartism to Jacobinism was natural. This, as will appear, was merely a change of label. The Right destroyed itself by fighting the Ralliés. Though they severely damaged these 'deserters', whose leaders, Piou, de Mun and Lamy, were all beaten, the Right came back less than sixty strong. The victors were the mass of colourless Republicans who with mild Radicals and Ralliés brought the normal government vote to above 300.

There was no serious reason why the result should have been otherwise. There were no burning issues. There was now no alternative to the Republic. The deaths of Boulanger and Prince Napoleon since 1889 had deprived many Anti-republicans of figure-heads. The Comte de Paris would follow these rivals to the grave in 1894. The next generation of royal and imperial candidates, exiled since 1886, were known to few and in any case were negligible. Conservative in a conservative society, competent within their limitations, the Republicans reflected very faithfully the temper of the French arrondissements in the nineties. As yet they had no apprehension that this legislature would be their Indian summer and that the decade would go out in political storms with the Republican party riven.

(x)

In token of its conservative character, the Chamber elected Casimir-Périer, grandson of Louis-Philippe's minister, to the Presidency by a handsome majority over Brisson, but a few days later, on Dupuy's declaration of policy which amounted to little more than a confession of impotence, the three Radicals in the cabinet resigned, and Dupuy threw in his hand. A week later Casimir-Périer took office. Except for the Minister of Agriculture, Viger, the members of the cabinet were new, largely old-fashioned Republicans of the Gambetta *clientèle*, such as Raynal, Spuller and Dubost. There was not a touch of radicalism. No doubt a combination of the anarchist troubles, and the presence of fifty-odd so-called Socialists in the Chamber, led to a desire to strengthen the executive by a cabinet drawn from the 'governing classes': it would at least indicate a volte-face against a new Panama. But there were limits to the amount of reaction the Chamber would permit. Casimir-Périer, the biggest shareholder in Anzin, the biggest coal-mine in France, which had recently been oppressing its workers — at least the left-wing orators said so — was too much for some members to swallow, and Casimir-Périer's declaration of policy, which in fact was more liberal than Dupuy's, only escaped defeat with the aid of the votes of Conservatives and Ralliés. Forty government Republicans voted against him. This he could not afford.

Dupuy replaced him in the presidential chair. On December 9, a Saturday, in revenge for the execution of the Anarchist, Ravachol, a bomb was thrown into the well of the Chamber by the Anarchist Vaillant during the session, an example, jeered Clemenceau, 'of the democratic form of regicide.' It must have been a small bomb, since only one person, the Abbé Lemire, deputy for Hazebrouck, was injured. On Monday, the Minister of Justice submitted several bills for the repression of anarchism, the first against press propaganda. No text had been printed, nor was even a written one available, nor had it been discussed by a committee. All amendments were rejected without discussion by the government, which by the mouth of Casimir-Périer made this a matter of confidence. Bills against the manufacture of explosives and for the reinforcement of the police were passed by huge majorities in the Chamber and unanimously by the Senate (L. Dec. 12, 1893). A further bill passed on December 18 punished with hard labour the 'intention' to attack persons or property, even knowledge of the intention.

Vaillant's execution was followed by another bomb-throwing. The perpetrator was in turn guillotined. Then on June 24 in Lyon, President Carnot was fatally stabbed by yet another anarchist, an Italian, Caserio, whose presence in France had been known but for whose arrest no steps had been taken.*

Once more Parliament hurried to legislate. Anyone propagating anarchist theories was to be at once brought before a criminal tribunal, tried without a jury, and if necessary, at the magistrate's decision, despatched to the life-in-death penal settlement at Guyane. Press re-

---

* Casimir-Périer's cabinet had been defeated on May 22 and had been succeeded by one headed by Dupuy. The election of the successor to Carnot in accordance with the constitution was held at Versailles two days later. The candidates were Casimir-Périer, the candidate of the Conservative Republicans in Senate and Chamber, Brisson, Radical, and Charles Dupuy, an action of strange vanity. Dupuy claimed his friends would be disappointed if he did not stand. Casimir-Périer was elected with an absolute majority at the first poll.

ports of such trials were forbidden. The bill was far more strenuously resisted than those of December. The Socialists and the older Radicals, Brisson, Goblet and Pelletan, had every reason to suspect that by its very vagueness the law could be applied to socialism. The crux of the conflict was one of definition. What was 'anarchism'? Suspicion was increased when Deschanel proposed to identify 'anarchism' and 're-volutionary socialism'. The bill with amendments was eventually passed against strong minorities in the Chamber and by large majorities in the Senate. But it all amounted to little. A number of intellectuals professing anarchism, arrested and tried in a body during the summer recess, were acquitted. Politically, they were people of no importance. In any case, anarchism was fading out. Serious revolutionaries had no use for romantic terrorism and none for individual action. With the growth of the syndicats and the C.G.T., anarchism was seen to be without future. The laws dropped into desuetude.

Chapter Twenty

Labour and Socialism

(i)

The political history of the urban workers from 1871 up, indeed, to 1906 is one of confused debate. 'The true history of France', wrote Renan in 1849, 'begins in 1789 and nothing of importance happens in France that is not the direct consequence of that huge fact, which has profoundly affected the conditions of life in our country.' '*La Révolution est un bloc . . . dont on ne peut rien distraire*', said Clemenceau in the ridiculous debate on Sardou's *Thermidor* in 1889. There is the long list of dates which every Republican child learns: those of the Revolutionary calendar, Thermidor 9, Vendémiaire 13, Floréal 21, Fructidor 18, Brumaire 18. And the later revolutions, 1814, 1815 (twice), July 1830, February 1848, June 1848, December 1851, 1852, 1869, 1870: the abortive revolts, Lyon in 1831 and 1834, the rue Transnonain 1839, the barricades of June 1848, the failure of 1849, October 1870, January 1871 and the Commune of March to May: — a calendar of violence. 'The revolutionary philosophy' — again it is Renan — 'continued a belief in *violence*, an idea of justice based on a materialistic conception of property, a neglect of personal rights, all of which carries the germs of destruction, heralds the reign of mediocrity, the disappearance of initiative, just for the sake of superficial physical comfort, the conditions of which are really self-destructive.'

Up to 1870, and indeed in many cases later, to speak of a 'working-class' is a misnomer. In many trades the great proportion of workers were individuals, often domestic workers, often both artisan and agriculturist. For a long time concentrated trades were only those which were so by their nature, the extractive industries and those such as required large plant. At the beginning of the Franco-Prussian war, it is a travesty to speak of a working-*class*, or at least to pretend that it covers all manual workers. Perhaps no fact exemplifies this better than the continued existence of the *livret*, the pay-book in which the employer should enter the owner's wages and the changes in his employment and the reasons for them. It had fallen into desuetude before 1870, but was not legally abolished until 1890, until in fact it was wholly obsolete. Its importance lay in the fact that in it had been inscribed the amount of material given to a domestic worker by the *fabricant* to transform. As Georges Duveau showed, even in an industrial city such as Paris had become in the last years of the Second Empire, much of the old life, when the artisan was a *compagnon*, a journeyman with a guild, still survived. In conditions of this nature, before the transition to a working-class had been completed, social-industrial reform was scarcely possible. In the forties limitations on the hours of children's work had been laid down, but since no inspectorate had been appointed, the law had inevitably remained a dead letter. Who could inspect the homes of the *bonnetières* of Troyes?

Nevertheless change was in the air. The Chapelier law of 1791, the French equivalent of the English Combination Acts, had been reinforced by the Penal Code (Articles 414–16) and again by the law of April 10, 1834, which forbade associations of above twenty without government licence. Napoleon III, who had a *faiblesse* for the poor, partly from sentiment, partly from calculation, in 1864 insisted on the passage of a law (May 25) which struck the penalty for coalition from the Penal Code: trade unions would now be tolerated, provided there was no violence. In 1868 Article 1781 of the Code, which laid down that the evidence of the master was to be preferred to that of the employee, was expunged, also at the Emperor's instigation (Law of March 30). Beyond this, efforts were made to encourage the *mutualliste* (friendly society) movement. None of these reforms had any effect in reconciling employed and employer.

The gradual loosening of the imperial authority and the advent of the 'Liberal Empire' did not in any way placate either the political revolutionaries, the followers of Blanqui, or the French members of the International Workingmen's Association. There had been a moment in 1866 at Geneva when the International was Proudhonist to the marrow. Three years later at Basle, that liberal virus was eliminated. Marx had killed the anarchist influence.

The Commune, in spite of the influence of members of the International among the leaders in Paris towards the last weeks, was not a socialist movement. But the National Assembly, even the Republicans, preferred to think it was. Yet though Thiers had had the police disperse the *chambres syndicales*, tolerated under the Empire, the representatives in the National Assembly were not prepared to go to extremes. In June 1871 Peltereau-Villeneuve and Delsol introduced a motion for the repeal of the law of 1864, 'which has hampered industry and led to the destitution of considerable numbers of work-people.' It was rejected. This in no way implied a weakening in the direction of socialism, and in the following year (Law March 14) the International was outlawed. Affiliates were liable to two years in jail and fines up to 1000 francs, leaders to five years and 2000. A year later the Assembly refused to finance the visit of a workers' delegation to the Vienna Exhibition. The workers found the money themselves.

The politicians tried to ignore the existence of a social question. Its existence however had been brought harshly to the understanding of Comte Albert de Mun by the tragedy of the Commune. Together with a friend, the Marquis de La Tour du Pin, who had been brought up in the belief that *noblesse oblige* had a literal meaning in a material world, he founded a number of Christian social clubs for workers, with the further purpose of building up a new lay Christian order. He looked forward, as he told the Chamber, to the time when the Revolution 'which claims to build society upon the will of Man instead of the will of God' would be defeated by a Counter-Revolution, which based society upon the law of Christianity. Nobly inspired as he was, de Mun completely misunderstood the sentiment of the age. His move- ment stood for Church and Crown and drew its inspiration from the Syllabus of Common Errors. It aimed at a hierarchical, a corporative society of which the Christian faith as taught by the Roman Catholic Church should be the cement.

His initiative met with a mixed response. The bishops were reserved, while the parish priests, seeing a rival to themselves, were suspicious. The Legitimists of the Right considered that the movement smelt socialist. The more liberal Right thought it far too reactionary. Falloux put his finger on the spot when he said, 'Don't you know that the bulk of the public translates Counter-Revolution by Ancien Régime in the worst sense of the phrase?'

The clubs had an auspicious beginning. By 1875 some 15,000 workers were members. But they became bored and they were irked by the constant moral supervision of the directors. De Mun, as Drumont put it, in doffing his cuirassier's uniform had merely put on the gendarme's.

The movement lost its early energy. Though it continued to grow, its success was small compared with more violent and more material doctrines.

After the war, an attempt had been made to refound the mutuallist syndicates without much success, but some had revived, and in 1872 an attempt was made to found a workers' federation. This Cercle de l'Union ouvrière was suppressed by the Préfet of Police, Renault, in January 1873, and sixteen months later in Lyon, the Union des ouvriers sur metaux was dissolved by the magistrates, who held that toleration did not mean authorisation. In spite of this, a number of clandestine labour associations remained in existence: a compositors' syndicate from 1860, a union of Lyon silk-weavers, and a shadow union of coal-miners round Valenciennes, which was seriously weakened by a strike in 1878, but survived. The feebleness of these beginnings was in part due to the defeat of the several Communes of 1871. Of the militants some were dead, some in prison, some deported to New Caledonia and others refugees abroad.*

With the Republican triumph at the election of 1876, the beginning of greater indulgence was shown to workers' co-operative activity. The Government even showed some sympathy, by financing a co-operative delegation to the Philadelphia Exhibition, but the acceptance of the money was bitterly criticised by the refugees.

In these early years there was no agreed body of socialist doctrine and no clear vision of possibilities. In 1876 Lockroy proposed a law by which syndicates of masters and workmen could conclude conventions, and the simultaneous repeal of the Chapelier law. A workers' congress called in Paris in October attacked and voted the proposal down on the ground that since the names of members were to be registered, 'we are merely offered new chains, a new kind of police law.' They were better off under the legislation of 1868. A similar bill was presented by Cazot and Tirard in 1880 to permit the formation of syndicates and unions of syndicates. The Senate rejected the formation of unions, and during 1882 and 1883 the bill passed to and fro between the Luxembourg and the Palais Bourbon.

In 1877 Jules Guesde, a provincial journalist, who had favoured the Commune and gone into exile, returned. While abroad, he had come into contact with Karl Marx and although he disliked Marx's tyranny, was persuaded by his theories. In November, in conjunction with another communard, Gabriel Deville, he issued the first number of

---

* There still survived among the craftsmen watchmakers of the French and Swiss Jura, the Fédération jurassienne, which with the other anarchist groups had been expelled from the First International. This survived sufficiently long to be able to issue a poster during the crisis of 1877 warning the workers that the Republicans would either collapse or be hunted out unless the workers took up arms on their behalf. The Federation came to an end in 1880, though anarchist ideology survived in men such as Elisée Reclus and Prince Kropotkin, apart from the real haters like Louise Michel.

Egalité which included extracts from Marx's writings, and earned sharp criticism from the *Vorwarts* and the *Berliner Freie Presse*.

A second congress held in the following January at Lyon was dominated by the moderates and co-operators. The only violence was anti-clerical, and a resolution in favour of collectivism received only eight votes. It was asserted that the peasants had been freed so recently from the feudal yoke that they were unlikely to accept the collective. The single positive resolution was to invite the International to meet in Paris in September. This was forbidden by the police and when an attempt was made to hold it, the leaders, Guesde, Deville and others, were arrested. Guesde was given six months and fined 200 francs, the rest lighter sentences, and *Egalité*, which was fined 1,000 francs, ceased publication. In March of this year a writer in the *Economiste Français* ventured the belief that violent conflicts between capitalists and workers were to all intents things of the past. In April 1879, at a bye-election in Bordeaux, Blanqui, the '*Enfermé*', who had spent forty years of his life in prison and was now doing a spell in Clairvaux, was elected against Gambetta's nominee. Although he was invalidated, he was shortly released. Blanqui however was now no more than a name to excite the discontented; his career was over and in 1882 he died.

A great change was taking place. At the third congress at Marseille (October 1879), the revolutionaries, that is Guesde and his friends, supported by Blanqui's disciple, Dr Edouard Vaillant, appeared and denounced the elders, Louis Blanc and Tolain, now a senator. A large majority accepted the idea of collectivism.* A Parti ouvrier was founded and at the end Guesde presented the minimum programme he had worked out with Marx, Engels and Marx's son-in-law Jules Lafargue, which would be considered at the congress of 1880.

This programme was divided into two parts, political and economic, and headed a little optimistically: 'In expectation of the triumph of collectivism.' The political articles were (1) suppression of the Public Worship budget and confiscation of the property of the Orders; (2) abolition of the Public Debt; (3) suppression of standing armies; (4) the extension of communal powers. It was in fact a new version of the famous Belleville programme to which Gambetta had subscribed in 1869, already demanded by the Extreme Left. The only effective point was the appeal to the decentralising sentiment, which had the unforeseen consequence that in future provincial socialist groups would insist on

* Cf. note, p. 13.

z

their local autonomy. The economic points were (1) a weekly day of rest; (2) the eight-hour day; (3) annual fixing of a minimum wage; (4) equal wages for men and women; (5) participation by the workers in drafting of workshop regulations; (6) reversion of banks, railways and mines to the State; (7) direct taxes on income; (8) restriction of inheritance to 20,000 francs.

Guesde foresaw that the struggle for the accomplishment of a socialist society would be long, unrelenting and unscrupulous. Nothing therefore was to be gained by precipitate violence. It would lead to the shedding of the workers' blood to the profit of the capitalist, and would in fact be an error of tactics. The items on the programme, however desirable, could only be arrived at in a rational economy, and that lay a long way ahead. He was therefore uninterested in strikes over wages, hours and other immediate ends of the workers; in fact he was inclined to deprecate them as likely if successful to weaken the revolutionary spirit. On the other hand, he commended any action, whether pacific or violent, whether political or industrial, which would forward the grand design and the ultimate end. He had no objection to violence in itself: indeed he counted on violence for the final decision. Since that final decision was the capture of the State, in contrast to the anarchists who would destroy it, any action towards this objective, such as the foundation and organisation of a political party in the Chamber and Senate, should be fostered. The State must be seized before economic expropriation could be carried out. In his early years in exile, he had criticised Marx for his tyranny over the International in London, but with his conversion to the creed, Guesde too had become authoritarian and stiffly intellectual; Clovis Hugues' nickname, 'the Torquemada in spectacles' would be approved by any reader of his speeches. It also explains why Guesdism took root and flourished only in those areas where the industrial discipline of the machine had formed the workers, in the north, in some of the Paris suburbs, in the Centre from Le Creusot through Nevers, Bourges, Montluçon down to Limoges. In the casual workshops of the south, Guesdism obtained little but lip-service.

In May (1880) a demonstration organised by Guesde and his friends at the Mur des Fédérés in honour of the Communards was broken up by the police under the supervision of Andrieux. Clemenceau raised the matter in the Chamber, and put forward a motion criticising the Government for its lack of confidence in the wisdom of the people of Paris. It secured only twenty-eight supporters. Nevertheless a second demonstration on May 30 was not interfered with.

At this point, the anti-bourgeois movement was reinforced by the Communards who returned under the amnesty of July 12. In addition to Rochefort, there came back, among others, Jean Allemane, a compositor, and J. B. Dumay, a member of the International and a miner who had led a formidable strike at Le Creusot in 1870. Only the last joined the Guesde group. The sectarian quarrels flared up again. At the Le Havre congress in November, the co-operators not only rejected collectivism; they refused to validate the mandates of the Guesdists. These immediately opened a parallel congress in the city, at which a resolution to expropriate private property without compensation was noisily acclaimed. There were also abusive attacks on the 'vermin of society', the bourgeoisie and on Gambetta, 'the man who pays his cook 15,000 francs a year and says there is no social question' — he had said there was no one question, but a number which should be dealt with in order.

At the next Congress, at Reims in November 1881, the latent hostility to Guesde and his dogmatism came into the open. A group had already formed, of whom Benoit-Malon, Joffrin and Dr Paul Brousse were the most prominent. They criticised the drafters of the minimum programme for 'staying perched on the towers of Utopia and never seeing anything concrete or palpable coming along'. 'We prefer to abandon the *all-at-once* . . . which generally ends in *nothing-at-all*, to break up the ideal aim into several serious stages, and secure some of our *possible* claims.' Their proposals amounted to the nationalisation of public utilities. Guesde retorted that they were nothing better than 'opportunists', and sneeringly named them 'possibilists'.

From now onwards the split inside the party widened. The revolutionaries were incapable of agreeing on a common aim, a common doctrine, or a common policy. At the municipal elections of 1881, socialist candidates received in all no more than 12,000 votes in Paris and 20,000 elsewhere. At the general election, only 20,000 and 30,000 respectively. It was not much, but at a bye in May 1882, in a quarter of the XVIIIth Arrondissement, Joffrin was elected as a Socialist to the Paris municipal council.

At the Saint-Etienne congress in this year, the schism was completed. The Guesde-Marx programme was negatived and Guesde and his twenty-three followers withdrew amid the jeers of Brousse's supporters and went off to Roanne where they formally adopted the title of Parti ouvrier. They were joined soon afterwards by the rump of the Blanquists under Vaillant, which took the title of Parti socialiste révolutionnaire. The Possibilists or Broussists became formally the Fédération des Travailleurs socialistes de France, with a policy of winning parliamentary seats.

One clan of the anti-bourgeois revolt held itself apart from the quarrelling sects — the anarchists, followers of Bakunine, dead in 1876. These had, of course, left the International, or rather had been expelled by Marx and Engels. Their strength was in Italy and Spain. In France, the anarchists were of two kinds, one the almost puritanical Federation which ran through the Jura on both sides of the frontier, of the highly-skilled mechanical craftsmen which had dispersed in 1880. The other derived from the Communards, anti-authoritarians who detested the discipline of Marx and believed in violence, even murder, as a political weapon. They opposed Guesdists, Broussists and Blanquists, and advised the workers to give up trusting any parliamentarian. 'When there was fighting in 1871, what did Louis Blanc do? He said, "When the judges speak, all men should be silent." The beast! what he called judges were the machine-guns of the Lobau barracks.' Regarded as by far the most dangerous, the anarchist groups had been infiltrated by Andrieux's police, *agents-provocateurs*. In the autumn of 1882 there was a rash of strikes, at Saint-Etienne, Grenoble, Vienne, Le Creusot, Lyon, Villefranche. In September there were violent troubles at Montceau-les-Mines and Blanzy. In October a bomb was thrown in Lyon. The police swooped, picking up every known anarchist, including the famous Russian scholar, Prince Kropotkin, who was sentenced to five years and a fine of 2000 francs.

This did not prevent further violent disorder. In 1883 a demonstration of unemployed in Paris was encouraged by Louise Michel, the former Communard deportee to Nouméa, to plunder the local bakeries. There followed further outrages. Criminals discovered, too, that they might get some sympathy by proclaiming anarchist sympathies.

Trouble was increased by the adoption, by the revived International, of May 1 as a day for demonstrations in favour of the eight-hour day. On the first of these in 1890, there were anarchist-provoked riots at Vienne on the Rhône. On this same day, there were demonstrations at Fourmies, when the military, having failed to disperse a mob, opened fire, killing ten and wounding a number of others. In 1891, there was an affray between anarchists and police in Clichy-Levallois, followed by a trial and heavy penalties. It was in revenge for these that terrorism by bomb-throwing was begun in Paris by Ravachol with the purpose of intimidating the magistrature. Over the purity of Ravachol's motives there was considerable dissension among the anarchist intellectuals. Ravachol however went to the scaffold, though it was not a Parisian jury which sent him there, but a provincial, which had neither scruples nor fears. Other outrages followed, until Vaillant's bomb in December, 1893, convinced the majority of the Chamber that things had gone too far; this was too much. They voted a number of laws against anarchism and its propagation, and stopped trial by jury for the crime. The culminating infamy came in June 1894 when President Carnot was stabbed by an Italian, Caserio, in Lyon. It was anarchism's last demonstration. Pursued by the police, who had no longer reason for restraint, they went underground, disguising themselves as loyal syndicalists and propagating a policy of violent industrial action.

(iii)

Between 1872 and 1882, trade had flourished; there had been little unemployment. In the depression which followed the crash of 1882, the political immaturity of the professing revolutionaries is marked by the fact that, in a period of increasing short-time, they fostered strikes which had no chance of success. Revolutions are not made by classes in distress, only revolts. Revolutions are made by those classes whose ascent is impeded by reactionaries. Not one of the points on Guesde's minimum programme of 1880 would be secured before 1900.

By 1880 however it was clear that it was impossible to allow the outbreak of large-scale strikes without the existence of workers' representatives to negotiate. Strikes were often violent, and difficult to control because no one was responsible for their conduct. Local police were quite inadequate, and the calling out of troops to maintain order was costly. In 1880 Paul Cambon, then Préfet of Nord, had prevented rioting when the textile workers of the whole department came out, by using cavalry patrols to keep the strikers continuously on the move. In 1883 the bill which Cazot and Tirard had brought in in 1880 at last returned to the Chamber from the Senate. Throughout it had been dourly contested on points of detail. Many members believed that the syndicates would be tyrannical. There was a struggle over the abrogation of the article of the Penal Code on the penalties for concerted action to prevent 'free exercise of industry or labour', and opposition to the clause permitting the union of syndicates. The final text became law on March 21, 1884.

It legalised the formation of associations of masters and workmen either jointly or severally. It limited these associations to professional organisations only; religious and political associations were excluded from its terms. The law abolished the greater part of the anti-combination legislation as it affected syndicates, the laws of 1791, 1834 and 1849, and the relevant Penal Code articles. The earlier objections of the workers were met in that no more than the deposit of the statutes of the syndicate at the local mairie and the names of the syndicate officers were required. Except for its offices, the syndicate could not acquire house property or land. Further, syndicates could unite for the furtherance of their professional interests. These unions could register, but they could not possess offices. Neither syndicates nor unions would possess legal personality, and thus could not sue or be sued.

A number of questions were left unanswered, for example, the exact limits of a professional organisation were not defined. Waldeck-Rousseau told the préfets to let the syndicates work out their own methods: 'the role of a republican administration is to help, not to complicate.' A number of complications soon appeared. Men could not be coerced into joining, and Article 7 allowed any member to withdraw if his dues were paid up. Syndicates were unable to punish men for their refusal to join a strike. The Government invariably refused to press workers to syndicalise or to come to terms with employers, on the ground that this would be an infringement of the individual's liberty of action, while the courts would not sanction action by a syndicate against a man who refused to join. Consequently, collective bargaining was slow to be introduced and accepted, though this indeed was scarcely to be expected in a country where the small workshop predominated. Further, Syndicalists were loath to disclose the names of their officials as the law required, since this would expose them to their employers. Since every member of a syndicate must be an active member of the trade, an employer by dismissing him could deprive the syndicate of its secretary. The two mine leaders of Pas-de-Calais, Basly and Lamendin, had considerable difficulties until they were elected to the Chamber of Deputies.

There was no immediate haste to take advantage of the law. In a number of trades, the leaders looked on it as an instrument against the workers' interests. In 1885 there were four mixed (masters and workmen) syndicates, 285 of employers and 221 of industrial workers; the 39 agricultural syndicates were largely co-operatives. In 1890 the mixed syndicates were 97, the workers' 1,006, averaging about 140 members apiece, the masters' 1,004. It is significant that the local character of the syndicates is universally recognised, as indeed it still was in Great Britain, though to a lesser extent. In the Saint-Etienne coal-field for example there were at least three separate miners' syndicates of 800, 400 and 234 members. The law also failed to define economic interests, though political and religious were specifically excluded: legal judgements appear to permit syndicates to interest themselves in the election of prud'hommes, but not in those of deputies. Further, although a syndicate could not be an industrial or commercial organisation, it could create co-operatives: this particularly applied to non-profit-making agricultural organisations.

The growth of syndicates was slow. Although the law of 1884 allowed the formation of unions of syndicates, these restricted themselves to their own region. Unions did not offer help to others of their own profession when in trouble. In 1884 the Anzin coal-miners came out in protest against the dismissal, as an economy measure in a year of fallen dividends, of the maintenance men, old retired miners who looked after the timbering. The strike lasted for two months at the end of which the strikers capitulated. Neither the Pas-de-Calais nor the Loire unions offered any support although the Anzin company's action affected every pitman.

Although, from the crisis of 1882, the number of strikes was double that between 1874 and 1881, the great majority were short and involved few workers. By far the greater number were in the North, as might be expected, and the Paris area, and concerned chiefly the textile trades, and to a less extent mines, metals and building. In 1892 syndicate membership amounted to 31% of miners and 36% of engineers and foundrymen, but, of the million and a quarter textile workers, less than 3% belonged to a syndicate.

Much of this is due to the differences between the groups over aims and methods. In 1886 under Brousse's inspiration, the silk-weavers of Lyon organised a congress with a view to the constituting of a federation of syndicates. The Fédération nationale des syndicats de France was indeed instituted, but in the process the moderates were outvoted and the Federation fell under Guesdist influence and for a time was far from national. The syndicate leaders, however, by now were feeling that their interests were not those of the political revolutionaries. It was inescapable that the majority of the politicos were bourgeois — of the fifty-one self-styled Socialists elected to the Chamber of 1893, only eleven came from manual occupations. The antagonism between the political and industrial groups came to a head in 1888, only two years after the foundation of the Federation. At its congress at the Bordeaux suburb, Le Bouscat, two resolutions were passed. The first called on the workers to separate from the political parties 'which deceive them'; the second commended the general strike as the only weapon which could emancipate the toiler.

This nascent schism was complicated by the growth of the Bourses du Travail. The first of these had been instituted in Paris in 1887 by the Préfet of the Seine, Poubelle (after whom the ash-can is named) to act in some sort as a workers' club, a centre of professional instruction and a labour exchange. The example of Paris was followed by other municipalities; by 1892 there were fourteen. Since they were regional and had no professional basis, they could not avoid hindering the syndicates and unions, all the more because they were supported by municipal finance. In February of this year, at a meeting at Saint-Etienne, ten Bourses formed a federation. In September at a regional congress, Fernand Pelloutier, the founder of the Saint-Nazaire Bourse, obtained a vote in favour of the general strike as an anti-capitalist weapon, and of excluding the 'collaboration of the parliamentary Socialists'. There followed a break with the Guesdists. At the Nantes Congress in 1894, Pelloutier, who had now become assistant secretary to the Federation (aided by the as yet scarcely known Aristide Briand), succeeded in carrying the adoption of the general strike against Guesde and brought into the open the fundamental antagonism between the syndicalists and the politicians. In the following year, the older Fédération des syndicats, weakened by its connection with the Guesdists, called a congress at Limoges where the federation converted itself into the Confédération Générale du Travail (C.G.T.), to which some thirty organisations subscribed. In 1896 the C.G.T. completed the break with the politicians by voting in favour of the general strike. Pelloutier, who a year earlier had become the secretary of the Fédération des Bourses, held aloof from the C.G.T. for some years. Although both bodies were opposed to political action and were pledged to the general strike, their relationship was not easy, since the Bourses were based on regions and the members of the C.G.T. on trades: also the latter were industrial whereas Pelloutier, a dedicated revolutionary, was meditating the inclusion of the industrial workers attached to agriculture, smiths and wheelwrights, in his federation. Although the two organisations came together, their incompatibility was obvious and could not be remedied until after the death of Pelloutier in 1902. Meanwhile, two attempts in 1898 by members of the C.G.T. to organise general strikes had ignominiously failed.

It is manifest that in the nineties neither the parliamentary Socialists nor the Syndicalists had an idea outside revolution. The quarrel between them turned on whether the State was accepted or not. Certainly some of the syndicates were infected by the anti-authoritarianism of the anarchists who, after the repressive laws of 1892–94, had sought refuge in the syndicates. But although the liquidation of the capitalist system was the aim, one of the main hindrances to revolutionary action was the very weakness of the capitalist system in France. It is ironical to find Victor Griffuelhes, secretary general of the C.G.T., complaining in 1910 of the sterility of the French capitalists: 'their slow advance comes of their timidity; their uncertainty derives from their lack of initiative.' In the nineties there was not, indeed there could scarcely be, a labour movement. For that there must have been an active development of industry. 'In 1892 it could be said that in Paris there was no large-scale industry. There was a multitude of small businesses and a very intelligent and well-read body of artisans.' Large-scale industry was to be found scarcely anywhere in France. The 1896 census shows thirteen great enterprises. Of these six were coal-mines, five in the north, the sixth an adjunct of the single large iron and steel firm, Le Creusot. There was one shipyard near Marseille; the remaining five were the two government dockyards of Toulon and Brest, and Paris gas and transport companies. Of the 2,937,911 firms recorded, 96% employed fewer than ten workers, and of these nearly 600,000 had no employees at all. Everywhere there were the small workshops, usually family affairs. 'If you want to know what kind of a capitalist I am,' retorted a deputy to an insult from another, 'I employ four people, of whom one is my brother and another my father-in-law.' The total number of employees in industry in 1896 was about $5\frac{1}{2}$ million (men $3\frac{3}{4}$ million), while engaged in agriculture were $8\frac{1}{2}$ million (men $5\frac{3}{4}$). The number of syndicalists was perhaps 350,000.* In iron, steel and engineering in 1892 there were 36,000 syndicalists out of 99,000, 42,000 coal-miners out of 134,000, but of textile workers, reckoned at 1,166,000, only 31,500 were syndicalists, 2.6%. It could truly be said that, until industry grew, talk of revolution was purely romantic; and the growth of industry depended on other things than industry.

It may be this tradition of revolution and the idea of paradise round the corner that accounts for the absence of labour welfare legislation. It

* The British Trade Union Congress claimed 1,250,000 in 1892, but it was believed the figure should be nearer two million.

is reproached to Parliament that between 1871 and 1892 there were only two such laws, that of 1874, and that of November 2, 1892, both dealing with hours and child and women's labour. On December 28, 1892, a law which attempted to provide machinery for conciliation and arbitration between masters and workmen reached the statute book. It is difficult to resist the belief that later legislation came less from the appearance of increasing numbers of Socialists in the Chamber than from an increasing knowledge of labour conditions. At the instigation of Rouvier and Jules Roche, Minister of Commerce, there was instituted by the law of July 21, 1891, the Office du Travail as a branch of the Ministry of Commerce. Its purpose was the provision of accurate information, statistical, technical and international on labour questions. Its staff was drawn from men both within and without government service. To its head was appointed Arthur Fontaine, later to become the permanent head of the International Labour Office.

(iv)

For some years after March 1884 the syndicalist movement remained subordinate to the political. In May 1882 a Socialist, Joffrin, had been elected to the Paris municipal council, in 1884 Chabert and Vaillant. By this time, some of the Radicals on the council had begun to prefix to the word Radical the epithet *socialiste*. But the bulk of the Radicals held aloof. Socialism had made little impact on the electorate. Guesde had stood for the succession to Gambetta's seat at Belleville in 1883 and come out bottom of the poll. In 1884 Clemenceau refused publicly to subscribe to the Guesde doctrines; the Guesdists were on the wrong road, initiators of class-warfare. He professed not to believe in exclusive classes. Guesde retorted that neither did he; his class was wage-earning whether of labourers or Pasteurs. But Clemenceau repeated that he was for liberty, complete liberty. In July 1885 before the election, while speaking at Bordeaux, he held out a hand to the Socialists inviting them to a temporary alliance with the Radicals 'up to the point where the radical and collectivist doctrines divide. When the Radical and Socialist programme has been carried out through our common effort, each of us will then go the path we think we ought to follow.' Guesde refused. 'Since we do not believe in your peaceful methods, what would we be doing in your boat?'

The election of October, 1885, had been a bitter disappointment to Guesdists and Blanquists. The total socialist vote is recorded as 46,000 for fifteen lists. Compared with the Radical list, the candidature was weak, and some acknowledged or tentative Socialists were elected on Radical lists. In Paris, the last three on the second poll were Camelinat, a trade-union secretary, member of the International, Communard refugee; Emile-Joseph Basly, who in 1888 founded a coalminers syndicate at Lens, a strike-leader, a resolute, independent and worthy man; and the vaudevillist-journalist Rochefort, who resigned in the following February. In Bouches-du-Rhône, there were over 35,000 Socialist-Radical votes, but of eight candidates, only two, Clovis Hugues and Antide Boyer, ever showed a touch of socialism. In Loire there were 17,000 Socialist-Radical votes in a poll of 109,000. Otherwise the best count was 3,500 in Rhône. Nevertheless in March 1886 a manifesto was issued by a group of eighteen deputies, signed among others by Basly, Boyer, Camelinat, Hugues, Planteau, Prudhon, more or less socialists, and by Laguerre, Laisant and Michelin, Radicals who would turn Boulangist. The manifesto called for the repeal of the law banning the International; the regulation of children's labour; guarantees against unemployment, sickness, accidents and old age; reorganisation of the conseils des prud'hommes; guaranteed independence of miners' delegates; improvements in the conditions of seamen, the suppression of monopolies and the organisation of credit for labour. A new Republican deputy patronised by Ferry and his friends, Jean Jaurès, admitted some years later that for a moment he had considered joining this group, 'but I was deterred by the theoretical poverty of their published ideas and the thinness of their programme'. He was also distressed by the violence of their language, especially, in the middle of the Decazeville strike, by Basly's speech, which had in fact been edited by Guesde.

The last years of the eighties present a confused picture with the incursion of irrelevant and distracting movements, both political and social. The rise of Boulanger, the expulsion of Grévy and the anti-Ferry movement, the second Boulanger phase, are criss-crossed with either real or false anarchism, and with anti-semitism of both Left and Right, Guesde and Drumont appeared on the same platform; the internecine feuds of the socialist doctrinaires became more bitter as adherents deserted to rivals or to false prophets, or turned bourgeois in frustrated despair. During the Carnot election two revolutionary Socialists were given eighteen months for attacks on Ferry, and during 1888 four Blanquists seceded to Boulanger. In 1889 the Second International was founded. Brousse was ordered to organise an international congress in Paris under Guesdist direction. He naturally refused. Hence Paris was diverted by the spectacle of rival congresses, the Broussist with over 500 French delegates, but only 130 foreign, of whom 39 were British, and the Guesdist with only 220 Frenchmen, but 170 foreigners and much more distinguished ones, Vandervelde, Liebknecht, William Morris and Cunninghame-Grahame. From this date the influence of Brousse began to decline.

The decline was accentuated in the following year when, at Chatellerault, Jean Allemane threw over Brousse, who had condemned the general strike, and founded, with other dissidents, the Parti ouvrier socialiste révolutionnaire, more usually known as the Allemanists, with a programme relying on industrial action and in chief the general strike. Thus at the beginning of the nineties, the socialist movement consisted of a number of splinter groups, none of them as yet dominant. There is Guesde's Parti ouvrier of which the strength was chiefly in the industrial north, and in Isère round Grenoble. Closely connected with the Guesdists was Dr Edouard Vaillant's Parti social révolutionnaire, otherwise the Blanquists, of which the strongholds were in Paris and the Centre (Bourges with its arsenal and Montluçon), together with some influence in the south-west. The Broussists and Allemanists had little following outside Paris.

Except for Brousse, whose movement began to decline in the nineties, Guesde was at this time the dominant figure. None of the others were of his calibre. There were level-headed men like Allemane and Basly, good negotiators, but the majority were noisy in speech and empty of thought. In 1892, the Socialists found a recruit in Jean Jaurès. The egg 'hatched by Jules Ferry' had proved an ugly duckling, although it is not true that in 1885, or even in 1889, Jaurès was already a Socialist. Throughout his four years in the Chamber he had voted with the Centre on all the main questions. At the 1889 election he was defeated in Albi 2 by the president of the Carmaux coal-mines, the Vicomte de Solages. Solages resigned his seat at the end of 1892 and Jaurès was re-elected in January 1893 as a Socialist. Thereafter he became one of the principal socialist orators: apart from his speeches in the Chamber, he was used by Guesde all over the country. A brilliant speaker, he was encouraged to use all his eloquence in assemblies which appreciated oratory, whether the Chamber of Deputies or workers' meetings. His speech at the opening of the Chamber on November 14, 1893, remained famous: 'You have torn the people from the Chamber's guidance. . . . You have interrupted the old cradle-song which lulled human misery, and Poverty has awakened screaming. It stands before you and asks for its place, its large place in the sun.' (The theme of the lullaby had been used by Renan thirty years earlier, but no matter.) Guesde however found the new orator too romantic. He, Guesde, had consistently refused to forecast the society of the future. All that he would admit (somewhat aridly) was that it would be collectivised. Jaurès, on the other hand, held that revolutionary enthusiasm could not be roused without a vision. He was invited to join the Parti ouvrier, but declined. While adhering to the Marxist thesis, he, with a number of others unable to suffer Guesde's authoritarianism, Deville, Viviani, Millerand, Sembat, remained independent.

Yet Guesde was right. It was useless to encourage revolt when the rebels were not prepared, not disciplined to go through with it. Until the situation was ripe, only preaching and propaganda would be profitable. He failed to see that unless he paralleled his doctrine with action — not the general strike, but the eight-hour day — he would, as the Broussists said, merely be marking time in the same place.

Chapter Twenty-One

The Russian Alliance

(i)

In an article published in 1901, the historian Charles Seignobos drew attention to the Frenchman's marked lack of interest in foreign affairs.[1] Foreign affairs never figured in electoral campaigns. In the Chamber, apart from the debate on the Foreign Office budget (a debate usually devoted to demands for the suppression of the Vatican embassy), they were rarely mentioned. An interpellation was sometimes made by a friend in order to allow the Foreign Minister to make a pompous declaration, or by an enemy to embarrass him. Paul Cambon, writing to Delcassé in January 1899 told him that his recent speech was the first general survey of French foreign relations to have been given to the Chamber in twenty years.[2] One might think the subject dead. Seignobos was right. The mass of peasants and workers was interested in only one aspect, the maintenance of peace. The appeal was unvoiced but recognised, the appeal of a people which had learnt from generation to generation that prosperity and misfortune go hand in hand, and having gained a level at which they could exist without too much danger, would risk as little as possible. They belonged to a world in which 'honour' was the false face of honesty. This their deputies well understood, and from that came their mastery over governments. Inveigh as he might, Gambetta was impotent against the Chamber. For all his popularity, the Chamber of 1881 broke him. The same Chamber six months later rejected his advice and overthrew Freycinet on the question of Egypt. It broke Ferry because, among other things, it believed him to be running unjustifiable risks. Boulanger's popularity rested on the baseless belief that he had scared Bismarck, and he was eliminated by the politicians who knew the insubstantiality of the belief and the danger he presented.

The two obsessions at the Quai d'Orsay were fear of the German Empire and jealousy of Great Britain. With Germany terms could scarcely be cordial, but it does not seem that the political directorate discerned Bismarck's need to stabilise Europe in the pattern shaped by the wars of the fifties and sixties. This required the maintenance of peace, and to maintain peace, he must prevent a clash between Austria-Hungary and Russia in the Balkans. To this end, he had put Austria on the leash in 1879 with the Dual Alliance. This had been extended in 1882 by the inclusion of Italy in a Triple Alliance, which protected the Austrian rear in a conflict with Russia and bolstered up the monarchy in Italy. So far as France was concerned, Germany had promised to defend Italy against the French, and Italy had engaged herself to assist Germany in a case of French aggression. No French Foreign Minister, however pacific he might be, could entirely dismiss from his mind the rape of 1871 or fail to dream of the recovery of the lost departments by his instrumentality. What in the eighties he could not know was that Moltke, haunted by the possibility of a war on two fronts, had decided that, against the French new frontier defences a German attack would be too slow, and that therefore in future the German army would stand on the defensive in the west.

During 1883–85, Ferry had been judicious in his contacts with Berlin. After his defeat, Franco-German relations were disturbed by the activities of Déroulède and the Ligue des Patriotes in the Vosges. In spite of Freycinet's insistence to Hohenlohe in October 1885 on his way to take over the government of Alsace-Lorraine, that the French ministry disapproved of Déroulède, the Germans became more distant. Then in February 1887 the Protesters took all fifteen seats for Alsace-Lorraine in the Reichstag, and Boulangism began to grow into a movement. Hence, in 1888 the German authorities tightened up the passport regulations for French visitors to the lost provinces and let it be known semi-officially that 'Germany does not wish for war — only for more distant relations with France'. Nevertheless, as has been seen, the two brief periods of tension in January and April 1887 had been reduced by the good sense of Bismarck and Grévy.

With the British government, the French Foreign Office remained on *aigre-doux* terms, never friendly, rarely splenetic. In spite of Admiral Aube, the advocate of the destruction of English merchant shipping by French fast cruisers and torpedo boats, there was no probability of war between the two countries. Only unadmitted and unavowable hostilities were carried on by agents who in emergency could be disowned. French 'explorers' from the navy or marines, pushing on towards Lake Chad, met and sometimes fought with British 'agents' on the upper Niger. It was no more than minor irritation. As for the independent sultanate of Morocco, the French, alleging that as rulers of Algeria and protectors of Tunisia they were an important Moslem power, hoped to inherit its pieces when it disintegrated, if not as the only heir, at least as the major partner with Spain. They had no sympathy with the selfish British attempts to keep Morocco independent by reforming its government.

But so long as the British remained in Egypt, cordiality between the countries was not to be had. For the French, the removal of the British was a matter of prestige: the British must go, whether voluntarily or through pressure, it did not matter. Or if they remained then compensation must be given. Of what that compensation should consist they did not know and they could not produce a respectable formula. When, in 1887, the British offered the Turks a plan for the evacuation of Egypt, Flourens directed the French ambassador at Constantinople to join with the Russian ambassador in forcing the Sultan to reject the British terms. Although Flourens, immediately after the departure of the British plenipotentiary, repented, the situation had already changed and the British would not re-open negotiations.

With Italy, French relations were unvaryingly bad. The commercial treaty of 1881 between the two countries, though nominally to run for ten years, could be terminated at five. Although the Italians were doing well with exports of strong wine and raw silk into France, the Italian government needed more revenue. It was also ambitious. It had been enraged by the French occupation of Tunisia in 1881 and it was firm that no further extension should take place in North Africa without Italy getting a fair share of the spoils. But, as Bismarck had said, 'Italy grew her appetite before she grew her teeth.' Much more money than a country whose economy was based almost wholly on peasant production could afford, was being put into the army and the navy. Between 1875 and 1890, defence expenditure increased by some 25%. For these reasons, in December 1886 the Italians notified the French that they would terminate the commercial treaty in the following December and make an upward revision of the tariff scale by some 60% *ad valorem*. The negotiations which followed broke down in February 1888 and in spite of further conversations, a venomous tariff war of surtax against surtax began. The result was an abrupt halving of trade with the French who henceforward bought their cheap wines from Spain and Portugal, although Italian silk appears to have reached Lyon by a circuitous route through Switzerland. Italy was far more severely hit than France, and in December 1889 the contest was abandoned. Nevertheless the French maintained their reprisal surtaxes until January 1892.

This was, however, subsidiary to the diplomatic struggle. In 1887, in renewing the Triple Alliance, the German government promised that it would give support should the French try to extend their frontiers eastwards into Tripolitania or westwards into Morocco. At the same time, the English, irked by the French policy of pin-pricks in Egypt as well as French pressure on the Moroccan frontier, signed in February 1887 an agreement with Italy and in March one with Austria for the maintenance of the actual situation in the Mediterranean. The French, who had learned the terms of the Triple Alliance, now proceeded to put financial pressure on Italy in the hope of detaching it from its partners. In 1887 the French Finance Ministry refused authorisation for the placing of new Italian issues on the Paris Bourse and through 1888–89 the French banks disposed of some 700 millions of Italian securities. These proceedings so jeopardised Italian public finances that it was thought the army and navy would have to be reduced, but the German government came to the rescue not only in 1890, but again in 1892.

(ii)

In the fifteen years since the Treaty of Frankfort, the French army had been completely re-organised. The new frontier was covered with defences sufficient to withstand a surprise attack. The army was continuously being supplied with new weapons and new equipment. Yet no minister and no general could conceive of a war against Germany without the support of a strong ally. There were only two powers who were not tied to the enemy, Great Britain and Russia. Their interests clashed in the Near and Middle East, while British liberalism was odious to Russian autocracy. Further, for a continental war, the British had only a fleet, and that was obsolescent. On the other hand, although the late Tsar Alexander II was credited with having saved France from a new German invasion in 1875, there was little to indicate that Alexander III, a religious fanatic, would come to the rescue of an anti-clerical republic. Was there any common interest to link the two countries? Only a mutual hostility to Germany, and in the middle eighties Russia had no serious quarrel with Germany. Nevertheless, the wooing of Alexander III would be one of the major undertakings of foreign ministers from 1887 to 1894.

In the thirteen years between the fall of Ferry and the arrival in July

2A

1898 of Théophile Delcassé at the Quai d'Orsay, there were seventeen governments, of which the last survived for more than two years, and nine foreign ministers. Of these, five lasted but a few months. Of the others, Freycinet in 1885–86 was more interested in the army. In any case, he had offended the Tsar by releasing under an amnesty the anarchist Prince Kropotkin who was doing five years in Clairvaux, and by recalling the French Ambassador in Saint-Petersburg, General Appert, whom the Tsar liked and for whom he refused for some months to accept a replacement. Goblet, Freycinet's successor in December 1886, unwilling to go to the Quai d'Orsay himself, appointed the inexperienced but ambitious Gustave Flourens, a Conseiller d'Etat. In January 1887, during the short-lived war scare, Paul Lefebvre de Laboulaye, son of a member of the National Assembly and the new French Ambassador at Saint-Petersburg, sounded Giers, the Russian Foreign Minister, as to the support the French might expect in case of trouble. Flourens at once rebuked him for this indiscretion, saying that the initiative must come from the Russians: if approaches were made, Laboulaye was to say that he would ask for instructions. In the meantime, Flourens made much of the Russian ambassador, Mohrenheim. Nevertheless, there was no advance. The Russians let it be known that a French alliance was not to be thought of, and in June 1887 the so-called Reinsurance Treaty between Germany and Russia was signed by which Russia promised neutrality if Germany were to be attacked by France, and Germany likewise if Russia should be attacked by Austria. Furthermore, Goblet, the Prime Minister, clear-headed but prickly, who thought Flourens despicably servile to Bismarck during the Schnaebele trouble, firmly believed that so long as France did not wish to go to war, there was no interest in an alliance, 'which it would be difficult to conclude and which would come of itself if war were to break out.'[3]

In this year, 1887, the Russians who for revenue purposes had again and again raised their import duties, made yet another increase. Annoyed by this as well as by other actions which had hurt the East Prussian landlords, the German government struck Russian bonds off the list of securities acceptable by German banks as collateral for loans, while German holders threw large quantities of Russian shares on the market. Perpetually in financial straits, the Russian government sent its agents to the French. After some months, the Tirard Government (1887–88) authorised the listing of Russian government loans by the Paris Bourse. Six months later, in October 1888, the loan of a modest

500 million francs opened the formidable catalogue of Russian borrowings. In 1889 two further loans were launched, of 467 and 1200 millions, but there were no political approaches. The Boulanger episode had not yet come to its miserable end. Moreover, says Goblet, Freycinet at the War Office, who two years back asked for another year, was still not ready.

In March 1890 the smouldering quarrel between Bismarck and William II flared up and the Chancellor resigned. His successor, Caprivi, had no Bismarckian dexterity and would not renew the Reinsurance treaty with Russia. The refusal, which was not in any way unfriendly, caused the Tsar to reflect. In 1889, the Grand Duke Vladimir on a visit to Paris had sounded Freycinet, who had taken over the War Office in April 1888, on the possible purchase of the new French magazine rifle for the Russian army. Freycinet had been agreeable on the understanding that the rifles should never be used against French soldiers. It was a step towards a mutual interest, a gesture of confidence. The deal for 500,000 rifles was negotiated between December 1889 and December 1890.

In the same month that Bismarck resigned, Freycinet became Prime Minister, remaining at the War Office. To the Foreign Office he invited Ribot, the most conservative of Republicans, the most accomplished of hair-splitters. 'The misfortune is that he is imbued with the idea that truth is embodied in an assembly. . . . For minds of his type, parliamentary government does not consist in having and applying ideas with the check of the Chambers, but in seeking the ideas of the majority, which for most of the time don't exist, and giving to this nonentity an appearance.'[4] During the previous year, Laboulaye had been gradually gaining the confidence of Giers and the Tsar. More than once, Alexander had let fall some vague remark to the effect that France was necessary to Europe. In July 1890 the British signed a convention with the Germans by which in return for the handing over of Heligoland, the Germans gave up whatever rights they had in Zanzibar. This seemed to confirm what had been suspected, an adhesion of Great Britain to the Triple Alliance.

In August General Le Mouton de Boisdeffre, Sub-chief of the French Staff, attended Russian manoeuvres. He had been asked by Freycinet to make discreet enquiries as to what the Russians would do if war was declared on France. Boisdeffre wrote that someone, whose name he would give by word of mouth when he came home (presumably Alexander III), had said that Germany would be told that the existence of France was indispensable to the European equilibrium, a euphemism for Russian security. On the other hand, the Russian War Minister said Russians were alarmed by the constant changes of government in France. He also admitted that their interest was in Austria. And if the Germans put the bigger part of their eastern forces against the Russians, they would retreat.[5] This was far from what the French hoped. They would be committed to a defensive campaign, probably against the better part of the German army, while the Russians took the spoils from Austria. The talks were adjourned. But the French had no friends. They could not, or would not approach the British. They were on the worst of terms with the Italians. And they feared the volatile nature of William II.

The proponents of the Russian alliance were lucky. The Russian harvest of 1890 had been poor, that of 1891 threatened to be (and was) disastrous. The Government was desperate for money. In the spring the Paris Rothschilds refused to underwrite a new loan: it was said that their English cousins insisted that they should hold aloof until the Tsar promised to alleviate the miseries of the Russian Jews.*[6] The Russian government began to thaw, Giers started to talk suggestively to Laboulaye. In July, on a Russian invitation, a French squadron visited Kronstadt and was received by Alexander III. In the same month, Boisdeffre once more attended Russian manoeuvres, taking with him a plan. On this occasion, the Russian staff proposed simultaneous mobilisation if either partner were to be attacked by one member of the Triple Alliance. Giers, however, flinched from so positive an engagement as a military convention and substituted a political understanding. After considerable dilution of the original terms, an exchange of letters was made on August 27, agreeing to consult in case of danger, signed by Giers and Ribot, who throughout the summer had been urging Laboulaye to secure a decision. It was as little compromising an agreement as could be devised, but the French had a foot inside the door. In token of which, in October, the Russians got a loan of 600 millions, reluctantly sanctioned by Rouvier, the Finance Minister, and to which the Jewish financial houses raised no objection. The management of the loan was in the hands of the Crédit Foncier, but, though it was successful, much was left on the jobbers' hands, and a little later the bank was found to be buying up stock thrown on the market in order to support

---

* There had been increasing persecution of the Jews for some years. In March 1891 the Grand Duke Sergius, governor of Moscow, decreed the expulsion of all Jews from the city. It is also said that Freycinet and Ribot, to put pressure on the Tsar, asked the Paris Rothschilds to refuse.

the price. There was some talk of a military convention at this point, but though the French Chief of Staff sent a draft to Saint-Petersburg, the Tsar held back. Freycinet and Ribot became more pressing. Ribot, in the hope of frightening the Tsar, insinuated that the secrecy of the negotiations might be broken.

Undoubtedly, the Russians were being both cajoled and dragooned into an agreement which they did not really like. In the circumstances, it is surprising that the French were so insistent, most of all Boisdeffre. In 1882 he had been ADC to General Chanzy, then ambassador at Saint-Petersburg. He found that the great Russian empire needed five weeks to put no more than 500,000 men in the field and two months for 800,000. 'I believe we are forced to extreme prudence,' he had written. 'In the case of an alliance with France, it is no longer a question of the defensive, and for an effective offensive, it is absolutely necessary that Russia enters the battle two months before we do. Without that the battle will be fought out on our territory before this country [Russia] has been grazed.'[7] In 1887 the second military attaché, Commandant Moulin, warned General Ferron, the War Minister, that in a war against Germany the Russian high command would follow the strategy of 1812 and retire: there would be no counter-offensive until the second year of war. In any case, they could put no more than a third of their forces against Germany: at the moment there were only 204 battalions and 108 squadrons available.[8] A year later he reported his firm conviction that Russian military strength was not what, in the interests of France, it ought to be. It could not use its reserves because it could not equip them. It could not concentrate on the frontier fast enough. It would need six weeks to mobilise. Russia needed 500 million francs for railways and weapons.[9] In 1891 while Boisdeffre was struggling to persuade a reluctant War Minister and Chief of Staff, Moulin was reporting that the Tsar took absolutely no interest in the technical aspect of manoeuvres, so that nobody else cared, and that he hated riding. The Russian official reports bore no relation to the truth and the whole thing was totally unrealistic.[10] His last note said that the Russian general staff was still thinking entirely in terms of Austria, and that Obrutchev, the Chief of Staff, was not to be trusted. Freycinet, since he combined the duties of War Minister with that of Prime Minister, must have read these reports. Yet the only consequence, if consequence it be, was the insertion, in the final instrument, of the number of troops with which Russia would meet the German army in the event of a conflict with the Triple Alliance.

In August 1892 Boisdeffre went once more to Saint-Petersburg with a draft military convention. After weeks of argument, a compromise was reached that even should France alone be attacked by the Germans, the Russians would act against Germany, while should Russia be attacked by Austria, the French would mobilise, but not necessarily go to war. This latter term was only agreed by the French in order to prevent a complete failure of negotiations. The Russians would put 800,000 men in the field against Germany, the French 1,200,000 to 1,300,000. The agreement was to last as long as the Triple Alliance stood. It was, however, only between the two army staffs. It was signed neither by the Tsar, nor by Giers or Ribot. In October the Panama scandal burst and once more the Tsar was shaken in his faith in France. Moreover, the political trouble eliminated one by one Loubet, the Prime Minister, Freycinet and Ribot, the political sponsors of the pact. The negotiations hung fire, but there was no withdrawal: the alliance simply remained at its preliminary phase.

The delay was not prolonged. The Panama imbroglio was cleared up in the spring of 1893. The French produced another sweetener for the Russians, a mere 173 millions. During the summer, the new Prime Minister, Charles Dupuy, closed the Paris Bourse du Travail, which was said to be falling into the hands of violent revolutionaries. In the previous November a new German military bill, reducing service for infantry and artillery to two years, but adding 80,000 to the establishment, had been introduced and rejected by the Reichstag, which in consequence was dissolved. After the election, in July the bill was passed by the new Reichstag. This also appears to have disquieted the Tsar. In June he had agreed to send a Russian squadron to return the visit of the French warships in the previous year. The visit of the Russian sailors to Toulon and Paris in October produced the most extraordinary outburst of enthusiasm from the French populace, a genuine and spontaneous emotion, which was hailed by the French press as if this in itself made an alliance. There was much talk of the Slav genius. 'Events have thrust two peoples irresistibly towards each other; their hearts have spoken.' Dupuy's son, professor at the Polytechnic, who half a dozen years later would be suspended by Freycinet as a Dreyfusard, complimented the journalists on having disseminated 'the true image of great Russia', while Flourens claimed that it was 'an alliance concluded outside the stale formulae of protocols, outside the mysteries of chancelleries . . . the alliance of two great peoples, masters of their destinies, who have nothing to hide . . . it has made war henceforward impossible'. Even Clemenceau did not shrink from speaking of the unsubstantiated rumours as 'diplomacy in broad daylight . . . free from the vices and perils of the Triple Alliance'![11] In such phrases was the commitment to Russia commended to the French electorate, which in the previous month had sent to the Chamber a solid Conservative Republican majority. The Tsar was impressed, but he still did not accept the military convention. He still feared that the French might lead him into a conflict in which Russia had no interest. Then, on December 16, talking to Laboulaye's successor, Lannes de Montebello, he complimented the French nation on its patriotism and its dignity in adversity, but added that he deprecated the idea of a *revanchard* war. Having made this demonstration, on December 27 he agreed the convention. It was signed by Giers and, a week later, Montebello signed on behalf of France.

The signing of the convention was not divulged. The Tsar had insisted on secrecy, but secrecy was equally necessary for the French. Under Article 8 of the Constitutional Law of July 16, 1875, it need not come before the Chambers.

The alliance is one of the more spectacular blunders of French politicians. Between the two partners, there was scarcely a common interest. The interests of Russia lay in the Balkans, the Near and Middle East, those of France largely in the Mediterranean and Africa. They shared a common but not oppressive apprehension of Germany, and here from the beginning the French suspected with reason that they would be cast for the part of catspaw and that, in a war with the Triple Alliance, the Russians would throw their weight against the Austrians and leave the French to battle with the Germans and Italians.

Various individuals are advanced as the real authors of the alliance. William II and Alexander III are two. Paul Cambon, who distrusted the Russians ('Their national egoism is more ferocious than that of the English'), declared that the alliance was made by no one in France and 'those who boast of it were negligible. It was born of the resentment of the late Emperor [Alexander III] against Germany and it is he who made the decision'.[12] This shows that the part played by Freycinet and Ribot remained hidden. The Tsar was gradually edged into agreement half against his will, by the famine, the cholera, and the empty treasury. The men who imposed their country on Russia were Freycinet and Ribot, aided by Boisdeffre. Both Freycinet and Boisdeffre knew the state of the Russian army; so, not improbably, did Ribot. They knew in 1893 that with the best will in the world this ally could not be ready for war in less than two years. Yet they pressed the alliance relentlessly. Later Ribot was gradually to attenuate his share, even going so far as to tell the Chamber in 1903 that the Tsar had made 'offers'. Freycinet, 'megalomaniac, smitten with numbers and speculating exclusively on figures', Ribot, the corridor-conspirer, as Georges Gilbert, military correspondent of the *Nouvelle Revue* called him, and Boisdeffre, the eternal staff-officer, placed the French nation in a situation from which escape became more and more impossible. In a note to Freycinet in August 1891 Ribot had written: 'If we tighten up our understanding with Russia, it is not to let ourselves be committed to war about Afghanistan or even the Balkans.'[13] In August 1914 France was committed to a war undertaken by her ally on behalf of a Balkan state.

In 1895, when the existence of an alliance was publicly admitted, though not the terms, Ribot on June 10 in the Chamber said: 'We have joined the interests of France to the interests of a great nation: we have done it as a safeguard of peace and the maintenance of the equilibrium of Europe.' And this mendacious rhetoric was applauded. 'The voter', wrote Seignobos, 'knows nothing about Russia or its government; he does not trouble to find out if the two countries have common interests. But he fears war. . . . He believes that Russia is very powerful and will prevent Germany from attacking.' Had the elector had a glimpse of the reports of the military attaché, he might have been shaken in his beliefs, though seeing what Freycinet and Ribot believed, one is not sure.

(iii)

In July 1890 the German and British governments had signed an agreement by which, in exchange for the cession of Heligoland by the British, Germany waived her claims in Zanzibar and recognised the British protectorate of the island. Further, the Germans agreed to the definition of the northern boundary of the German East African colony and acknowledged the Sudan as a British sphere of influence as far north as the 'confines of Egypt' with defined boundaries to the east and west. A similar convention was agreed with Italy in 1891. This strengthened the British position in Egypt. The French, who also under a treaty of 1862 had claims in Zanzibar, tried to sell them to the British, asking *inter alia* that the British renounce their tariff treaty with the French Protectorate of Tunisia. The British refused unless they secured tariff autonomy in Egypt, which the French in turn rejected.

In the end the bargain was reduced to a British recognition of the

French protectorate over Madagascar and a large extension of the French frontiers in West Africa down to Lake Chad and a little north of Sokoto. There was no reference to the Egyptian Sudan in the agreement. None of this brought the countries closer together. When in 1891, Ribot accepted an invitation for the French squadron on its way back from Kronstadt to visit Portsmouth, he told Freycinet that 'we must not embroil ourselves with the English. We must go to Portsmouth in spite of the indignant outbursts in our press'.[13] The pinpricks in Egypt continued. In the winter of 1892–93, the French and Russian consuls-general encouraged the new young Khedive, Abbas II, to flout Sir Evelyn Baring in the appointment of a distrusted prime minister. Supported from London, Baring forced on Abbas the cancellation of the nomination and 'his fine-weather friends abandoned him', Baring grimly wrote. The Quai d'Orsay — the Minister was now Develle — tried through the Sultan of Turkey to intervene, but the Russians would not help. And though a French squadron visited Alexandria and Constantinople, Abdul Hamid was far too careful to invite trouble.

In 1890 the British had not cared to negotiate a treaty with the French similar to that with the Germans in the matter of the Upper Nile. The vast area to the west of Ethiopia, once partly garrisoned by Egyptian troops but abandoned after the killing of General Gordon in 1885, was dominated by the Mahdi and his following. The British had postponed reconquest until a more favourable time. In the spring of 1893 Commandant Monteil, who was now in Paris, had a long talk with President Carnot and Théophile Delcassé, Radical deputy for Foix and, since January, Under-secretary for Colonies. Impressed by Monteil's exposition of the situation, the President exclaimed: 'We must occupy Fashoda', a place on the Nile at least 300 miles beyond the nearest French outpost. Delcassé, energetic and ambitious, seized on the idea. Carnot's exclamation seems to have been at once adopted and a double expedition envisaged, one coming from the French Red Sea colony of Obock through Abyssinia, the other, commanded by Monteil, moving from the Upper Ubangui in French Equatoria. The intention was not to acquire a new province but to embarrass the English and force what was called 'the re-opening of the Egyptian question'. The project was purely in the diplomatic arena, a move in the game. How little serious hostilities with Britain were contemplated is shown by the scrupulous, cool and tactful behaviour of the French in a moment of British agitation in July over the status of Siam, caused by an erroneous telegram to the Foreign Office.[14]

Chapter Twenty-Two

The Pursuit of Self-sufficiency

(i)

Beneath the clamour and abuse, behind the posturing and cabotinage of the Boulangers, and the Déroulèdes, the Floquets and the Delahayes, the politicians and the journalists, there was coming into existence a France of a different character. The period between 1873 and, say, 1896 was for many years labelled the 'Great Depression', indeed until half a century later when another, deeper and more formidable, exposed the misinterpretation in the nineteenth-century title. The lamentations were exaggerated. The not so severe decline in prices, which afflicted the western industrial world, was due to a multiplicity of events, of which the most influential were the series of technical changes heralding the vigorous expansion of the first years of the twentieth century. The physical sciences were preparing to interfere decisively in the shaping of political society. The development of power, power to move men and materials in the exact amounts required; the power to convey information with immediacy and accuracy; the power to mould mechanically articles of iron and steel in series; the adoption of new elements, fuel oil and electricity; the discovery of new alloys, new syntheses and new substitutes. There was the new control of time, bringing the punctual arrival of ships and trains, with a consequent economy of freight charges and insurance; the power of accurate calculation of everything except Nature — weather, disease, parasites and insects, droughts, floods and men's tempers remained uncoercible. In all, the reduction of the uncertain element in manufacture, with a serious reduction in risk margins.

The developments were attended by consequences both pleasant and unpleasant, that is to say, for workers in an industry dying or being transformed there might be on the one hand unemployment, short time or reduced wage-rates, or, on the other, rising money earnings and a rising standard of real wages. Both were sporadic; unemployment, so far as can be judged from inadequate figures, varied from year to year, while prices, particularly of foodstuffs, fell steadily until beyond the end of the eighties.

In France this new phase of the industrial revolution was less visible than in Great Britain, Germany or the eastern United States. The fluctuations in external trade were less extreme than in the more industrialised countries, though bad harvests and the need to replace the wine lost as the phylloxera continued its inexorable march through the French vineyard, added heavily to the import bill in the early eighties and little less up to the middle of the nineties.* There were other

* Special Trade: Annual averages per quinquennium, in million francs

	Imports	Exports
1850–54	1,066	1,288
1855–59	1,732 + 63%	1,894 + 47%
1860–64	2,298 + 33%	2,402 + 32%
1865–69	2,984 + 30%	2,992 + 30%
[1870]	[2,868] —	[1,425] —
1871–75	3,547 + 19%	3,599 + 20%
1876–80	4,292 + 21%	3,239 – 6%
1881–85	4,584 + 7%	3,381 + 4%
1886–90	4,219 – 8%	3,440 + 2%
1891–95	4,076 – 4%	3,344 – 1%
1896–1900	4,288 + 5%	3,754 + 12%
1901–05	4,569 + 7%	4,367 + 21%
1906–10	6,182 + 33%	5,573 + 27%

Average cost of wine imports in million francs: 1875–79, 50; 1880–99, 356; 1900–09, 143.

In the six worst years 1886–91, imports averaged 11.5 million hectolitres (or 253 million gallons). Replanting had, of course, begun, but vines cannot produce in less than four years.

Average annual cost of wheat imports in million francs: 1870–77, 264; 1878–85, 785; 1886–93, 768; 1894–1901, 508; 1901–09, 286; 1910–14, 804.

The worst years were 1879 (22.34 million quintals); 1880 (20.4); 1891 (20.6); 1892 (19.45); 1898 (20.1); 1911 (21.7).

Of the ten chief imports at the end of the seventies, nine were still in place at the end of the century. These were cereals and wine, raw silk, wool and cotton, timber, coal and coke, skins and hides, and live animals apart from horses. In 1880, these ten items accounted for 60% of the value of retained imports. Nine of the ten remained more or less in position up to 1914. The single exception was animals, most of which had been for breeding. By the end of the century the new crossings of cattle and sheep had been established. The two consumption items, cereals and wines, were due to bad harvests and phylloxera. Cereals fell away as harvests improved and wine as phylloxera was dealt with. The only other consumption good was coffee. The rest of the commodities were raw materials for industry, silk, wool and cotton, hides, timber, coal and coke and ground nuts, a cheap substitute for various plant oils. Coal and coke went on increasing in volume up to 1914, a great deal coming in from Belgian fields through Jeumont on the Sambre. With the introduction of electricity there came at the end of the century an increasing demand for copper and rubber.

Of exports there was little change in the main money-makers before 1905. The ten leading commodities earned about half the total in 1880 and continued to do so until about 1905. In 1870–74, silk piece goods produced an annual average of 470 mn. francs, though thereafter Italian and Japanese competition brought prices down. Yet up to 1914 the revenue from this item rarely dropped below 250 mns. and was reinforced by a growing export of troubles. Although the immediate consequences of the Union Générale crash had been liquidated, and the railway agreements of 1883, the 'crooks' conventions', had relieved the State of responsibility for railway building and helped the Finance Ministry to convert the 5% rentes, the indemnity loan, to 4½%, the economic activity of the late seventies had slowed down. Saving was said to have dried up for five years. Prices, partly due to increased efficiency, partly to the great advance in quantitative production with the return of peace, particularly in America, had been falling from the middle seventies. Raw material prices were tumbling down: iron ore by 25%, cotton by 20%, silk by an eighth, wool by a third. On the other hand, money wages-rates, which had moved steadily up from 1871 to 1882, after a pause resumed their upward movement from 1886 to 1891, while after 1884 the cost of living fell sharply.*[1] These are the industrial wage-rates for men in work. What is not known is the incidence of unemployment. The only figures available are for coal-mining, which for the years 1882–89 show an average unemployment figure of 3.6% (in 1884 7%)** and for 1890–1899 4.6% (8% in 1893), figures better than those for Britain. But coal-mining in France employed not more than 4% of the male industrial population — in 1896 142,700 out of 3.71 millions.[2] Since a great number of industrial workers were artisans and some 40% of all active citizens called themselves 'patrons', no serious evidence is to be found. Certainly there were bad years. The expenses of the bureaux de bienfaisance rose sharply in 1886, and in the same year bankruptcies reached a peak not to be recorded again until 1932.[3] The probability is that unemployment, as in Great Britain, was patchy both as to trades and areas. There is evidence that Paris was perhaps the worst sufferer. In December 1883 Langlois,[4] Proudhon's executor, Extreme Left

---

raw silk. Woollen cloths were also high earners, though the export of merinos declined, but again in compensation the export of raw wool and yarns, less than 50 mn. francs in the seventies, quadrupled by 1900. Exports of cotton goods, very low in the seventies, gradually expanded until, after 1900, they were as profitable as silk; this was largely due to the development of the colonies. Wines and spirits produced a trifle under 300 mn. francs annually from 1873 to 1913. The other items had varying fortunes, largely due to the fluctuations of fashion. Clothing and lingerie, millinery and artificial flowers, toys, haberdashery and fancy goods were all money spinners, but leather goods fell away. Cheese and butter earned a steady 80/90 mns. It is not until after 1900 that new features began to encroach on the standard list, chemicals, rubber and automobiles.

* See the figures in Phelps Brown, 273. The standard of living index (1890 – 99 = 100) shows a steep rise from 1880 to 1882, (81–86), followed by a further rise to 1887 (to 98), then, after a regression to 1891 (95), a continuous upward movement to 1897 (105).

** The 1884 figure is probably due to the Anzin strike involving 11,000 men in February, just as the four months strike at Decazeville in 1886 raised the percentage to 6.

deputy for Pontoise, accused the Government of caring nothing for the sufferings of the working-classes. He found supporters on the Right who charged the Republic with breeding nothing but dissension and ruin. The united attacks led to a full-dress debate on the economic situation which occupied most of the second half of January 1884. In two vast speeches at the end of the month, Ferry defended the Government.[5] While admitting the existence of unemployment, he asserted that it was no worse than in the previous two years, offering as evidence the statistics of the municipal pawn-shops in Paris, presumably the only reliable record. He denied that unemployment was serious outside the capital. Paris lived on the building and luxury trades, and the luxury trades depended on fashion, which was a law to itself. He hazarded that perhaps too much money had gone into building, and that not unnaturally there was now a pause. He reproached the Paris municipal council for giving up building for the poorer classes. He believed, and here he was probably right, that there had been inflated profits in the past, and that the money had not been used to replace obsolescent and worn out machinery. The manufacturers preferred small turn-over and high profits. 'We suffer from the lack of industrial courage.' He rejected a plea for State-subsidised public works: it was this that had brought down the Government of 1848. 'We are less idealist nowadays.'

This was 1884 and the worst years, 1885 to 1889, were to come, when Ferry was discredited and influential only behind the scenes, the years when the industrial output appears at its lowest and both iron ore and coal were in the doldrums. It may well be that what had been the main public works, railway building, was employing fewer men. It is at least certain that against the 5660 kilometres of railway opened in 1881–84, only 3254 were added in 1885–88. The heavy import of railway iron in the earlier period — 30 million metric tons in 1882 — was succeeded by a large export in 1885, and iron and steel companies, which in expectation of a big expansion from the Freycinet plan had put in much modern machinery, were now engaged in cut-throat competition for survival.[6] The Longwy and Pont-à-Mousson iron-masters created a *comptoir* to dispose of surplus iron in 1876; and similar agencies were constituted in the early nineties.[7] Steel companies were paying lower dividends.[8] Chatillon-Commentry's fell from above 60 to 15 in 1888 and the market value of the share from 1000 to 330. Aciéries de Longwy, an 1880 amalgamation of five or six historic family firms, made a loss in 1887–88 and had to reorganise. Denain-Anzin was in trouble up to 1890.

The gloomy picture had its obverse. Much was preparing that would mature between 1897 and 1914. The Bessemer ores in France were being worked out, and the foundries of the Centre were too far from the sea to tap Spain and North Africa for as much as they needed. The steel companies adopting the Thomas method were moving from the Centre to Lorraine. While concessions had already been granted of 80% of the Longwy basin and 75% of the Nancy, the Briey area was only just being surveyed. With the exception of the Joeuf mine granted earlier to Wendel, the concessions began in the eighties: between May 1884 and February 1902 the whole basin, except for two reserved areas, was conceded in some forty lots,[9] but the basin's future remained problematical until the late nineties. In 1883 Aciéries de Longwy made its first run of Thomas steel at Mont Saint-Martin. In 1885 the same company began to use the gases from its blast furnaces for heating. 1882 is the year in which the Marquis de Dion took up with the engineer Georges-Thadée Bouton and built the first automobile factory at Puteaux. 1883 is the date of Laval's steam turbine. In 1884 Panhard and Levassor produced their first motorcar with a (German) Daimler engine. In 1885 Marcel Desprez transported electricity from Vizille to Grenoble, ten miles, and in the next year from Creil to Paris. In 1885 Héroult produced his electric oven and the electrolytic process which carried the annual output of aluminium from 7.2 tons in 1880–89 to 414 in 1890–99. In 1884 Farcy, a Radical deputy, put forward a proposition to end the government monopoly of arms manufacture. Adopted by the War Minister, General Lewal, it became the Law of August 26, 1885, and led to the great extension of Le Creusot as a rival to Krupp. Steel field-guns came from Schneider's works a year later. Further evidence is the continuing rise of coal consumption, from an average 17,470,000 tons raised in 1876–80 and 8,665,000 imported, to a production of 22,838,000 in 1886–90 coupled with an import of 10,616,000. In 1890 there was a rapid rise in consumption from 34 to 37 million tons. Last, in spite of the inaccuracy of figures, it is possible to discern from the censuses the growth of the younger industries, chemicals and rubber, oil refining, electric lighting, metallurgy and engineering, and the decline of the numbers engaged in the traditional occupations, such as textiles. There is change everywhere except in the fields.

(ii)

Louis-Napoleon's commercial treaties of the sixties, which had removed prohibitions on imports and lowered duties, had never been whole-heartedly accepted by French industrialists, even if they were loyal Bonapartists. Only those who profited by exports, the wine and silk interests, and possibly those who thrived on fashion, the jewellers and providers of lingerie and lace, of artificial flowers and feathers, of stays and stockings, made no grimaces. Thiers, whose interest was purely fiscal, had failed to persuade the National Assembly to return to the commercial system of his youth, and his success in bullying the representatives to vote duties on raw materials was repudiated as soon as he was out of office. Attempts to denounce the commercial treaties with England before the dates of their expiration had also failed, and the almost perpetual argument between the Ambassador, Lord Lyons, and the Ministries of Finance and Commerce remained inconclusive. But before the last treaty ran out in 1877, committees in both Senate and Chamber were preparing. The majority of both bodies was protectionist. At the back of every thinking Frenchman's mind lay the preoccupation with defence and the open eastern frontier. As they saw it, a France without allies, or with weak ones, must be self-sufficient, capable, as it were, of standing a siege. Hence both industry and agriculture must be fortified to resist foreign competition. At the end of the seventies, however, industrialists were far from united on the matter of protection. Enquiries from the Chambers of Commerce in April, 1875, showed that sixty-two were in favour of new commercial treaties against only fourteen that were not; these last included the textile towns of Rouen, Roubaix, Tourcoing and Amiens. Most of the rest merely wanted protection from specific articles, and the cloth industry was divided between the worsted and the woollen manufacturers. As yet, the agriculturists were not as hot as the industrialists, but in 1879 the indefatigable cotton-master Pouyer-Quertier, encouraged by the bad harvest, toured rural Normandy preaching the protectionist gospel and buying signatures to petitions from the peasants at 25 centimes a time — 'at that date', says Augé-Laribé,[10] 'twenty-five centimes represented the wages for an hour or more's work.' In the end the law of May 7, 1881, created a new general tariff, with, alongside, conventional tariffs for those countries with whom treaties were arranged. To the free-trading United Kingdom, which could not reciprocate in the reduction of duties, but which was by far the best customer for French goods, France granted 'most-favoured nation' treatment. The Chamber added from 10–30% duties on specific articles, including agricultural produce, but the Senate refused to follow the enthusiastic agrarians on the committees; duties were increased on beasts and meat, but not on cereals. Moreover, in the new treaties to be negotiated, neither livestock nor cereals were to be touched: the bad harvests of 1879 and 1880 had been a warning. During the next months treaties were negotiated with Belgium, Holland, Italy, Austria, Sweden and Switzerland, to last for ten years.

The partisans of protection were naturally not satisfied with this minor success. The Société des Agriculteurs — founded in 1867, it was less cultivating than landowning — did not withdraw from the campaign. Prices were falling, even in years of short harvests. In 1879, the smallest crop since 1871, the price had been lower than the average for the past ten years, and from 1881, the decline was more pronounced. The average of the seventies per quintal was 29.70 francs; in 1883 the price was under 25 and sinking.* After 1882 sugar prices dropped precipitously, with incidentally catastrophic consequences for the sugar islands, the value of whose exports to France, nine-tenths in sugar and rum, declined by a quarter. In France the lower price was partly but not adequately compensated by increasing production and consumption. Butter and cheese also cheapened. Nevertheless it is probable that many, if not most, of the small cultivators were little affected. To the small owner-occupier, money was rather a means of saving than an agent of commerce. When prices fell, wheat or rye was consumed.** The sufferers were the growers who supplied the millers, the cultivators of large arable farms, behind whom in many instances lay the landlord. They watched with fear the millions of quintals of wheat pouring into Marseille and Le Havre from Russia and America in 1879 and 1880. From the high levels of 1881 both rents and land-values began to fall. There were renewed appeals for the protection of the cereal farmer. There was talk of a 'flight from the land' and prophecies of approaching disasters. Lecouteux, Professor of Agriculture and prolific publicist, in 1881 claimed that of eight million landowners, three million were indigent.[12] The Marquis de Roys inveighed against the speculators in

---

* The prices of rye, maize, barley and oats did not touch bottom until 1890 (Res. Ret. 175).

** Zolla, the agricultural economist, stated that of 82 million quintals of wheat, 50.5 million came onto the market, and 31.5 million were consumed.[11]

grain. 'It is simply because of the speculation', retorted Rouvier, 'that there is no want.' In the debate of January 1884 Ferry declined to hold out hope, insisting that agriculture could expect little from manipulating customs duties. To propagate among the peasants the belief that 'a decree which raises the duties a few francs would be enough to produce agricultural prosperity would be a grievous blunder'.[13]

The Société des Agriculteurs, however, had an ally within the Government itself, the Minister of Agriculture, Jules Méline. Méline, a Vosges lawyer, deputy for Remiremont, would become notorious in republican French histories by his mishandling of the politics of the Dreyfus case in 1896–98. Practical knowledge of agriculture he had none. He had taken up agricultural protection in 1880 when one of the rapporteurs of the tariff committee, sitting there as the champion of the interests of the Vosges cotton-spinners. Like Pouyer-Quertier, he discovered allies among the farmers and in due time became the advocate of agricultural protection. 'He lives for nothing but cereals,' said an irreverent lobby-correspondent. 'He found his road to Damascus when he became Minister of Agriculture in Ferry's government of 1883–85.' In spite of Ferry's warning against raising the farmers' hopes by tariff legerdemain, Méline in 1884 ordered an enquiry into the farming situation in Aisne where, it was said, more than 800 farms were in hand and tenants could not be found even for the best.* In November of this year, in spite of Ferry, he succeeded in getting a vote from the Chamber in favour of the principle of duty on cereals. It was the first move to 'bogging agriculture down in the marshes of least effort'.[14] A law imposing duties of 3 francs a quintal on wheat, 6 francs on flour, and 1.50 francs on oats, rye and barley, was promulgated two days before Ferry's defeat. (L. March 28, 1885.) Alas! the market did not respond: prices showed no inclination to swell. The Protectionists, their faith unshaken in the panacea, demanded bigger doses. After a long debate in 1886, they secured the further increase of two francs on wheat (L. March 30, 1887). The fact that there was still no appreciable rise in prices did not induce them to think again. They looked forward to what might be achieved when the commercial treaties expired in 1892, and they acquired as allies a number of deputies from industrial constituencies, who hoped to be rewarded with increased protection for their own products. Léon Say took the preparations so seriously that he

---

* The report was much exaggerated, but the Soissons, Laon and Château-Thierry regions had been hit by the fall in the price of merino wool under competition from Plate and Australian wools. (Jenkins, 83.)

2B

abandoned his senatorial chair to stand for the Chamber in order to add authority to the Anti-protectionists.

(iii)

Immediately after the elections of 1889, Méline was elected to the presidency of both Republican and Right agricultural groups in the Chamber, which then fused, while in January 1890 a tariff committee of fifty-five, largely protectionist, was set up. After a year's work, Méline as chairman and rapporteur-general presented the committee's recommendations. Between April and July, these proposals were debated at enormous length.[15] The opposition was led by Lockroy, who had stigmatised the Société des Agriculteurs as the 'marquesses of the dear loaf', and attacked the whole principle of national self-sufficiency as a chimera. He was ably assisted by Aynard, the Lyonnais banker and spokesman of the silk trade, by Charles-Roux, the shipping magnate, on behalf of the interests of Marseille, and by Léon Say, who jeered at Méline's economics: '*Vous défendez le pain des ouvriers en le rendant plus cher, cela veut dire que vous défendez aux ouvriers d'avoir du pain.*' 'Protectionism', he said, 'is the socialism of the rich.' 'And free-trade', rejoined Méline, 'is the anarchism of millionaires.'[16] Méline's best supporter was the smooth Deschanel, who attacked all the other interests, shipping, which asked for subsidies for building, the Paris Chamber of Commerce which wanted protection of its own specialities, and so forth. Acloque, iron-master and chairman of the *Association de l'industrie française*, put the whole strength of the Chamber's industrialists at Méline's disposal. Méline at one point claimed that while he and his group did not forget the export trades, the one thing they could not do was to sacrifice, as in 1860, 'the domestic market, which constitutes by far the greatest share of French wealth.' As in most political debates where finance of trade is concerned, the speakers were at pains to disguise their true motives while animadverting on the egotism of their opponents. Throughout, the Government (now Freycinet's with Develle, a moderate Protectionist, at the Ministry of Agriculture) took an intermediate line: *it was not a party question.* 'I am a resigned Protectionist,' said Develle, 'convinced that in the present state of Europe and the world, we are condemned to the defence of the home market.' In the autumn, the bill was dealt with by the Senate, by temperament more friendly to agriculture than the Chamber. Some of the old 'liberal' senators, Jules Simon and Tirard, resisted, but they were overwhelmed. Ferry was among the bill's supporters. Few products escaped the net, these chiefly raw materials, silk, wool, wool, flax, hemp, hides and oil-seeds; but, if they were not protected, some of their producers were sweetened by subsidies. It is to be noted that the harvests of 1890 and 1891 were deficient, and to keep the nation from starving grain had to be imported in quantities nearly as large as in 1879 and 1880. A moderate Radical, Viger, who would himself later become Minister of Agriculture, brought in a bill for a temporary relaxation of the duties on wheat. It was carried (L. July 2, 1891) against an opposition vote of 129, of whom eighty were deputies from the main landlord-tenant area of Brittany, Normandy and Artois. The great tariff law which is known by Méline's name was carried at the end of the year by 386–105 and became the law of January 11, 1892. But this was by no means the end of the demands for protection, and the statute book shows a fine roll of amendments up to 1914, in spite of constant counter-attacks by the free-trade interests and the followers of Jaurès.

(iv)

Before the passage of the law, it was observed that unless the proposed system was extended to the colonies, a market for French goods would be lost. The colonies must therefore be 'assimilated' to the French system. The opinion of the Chambers of Commerce and other like associations in France was sought, but not a single organisation overseas was consulted. To French manufacturers and traders it was unthinkable that countries where the French were undisputed masters should compete. The Under-secretary for the Colonies, Eugène Etienne, born in Oran, deputy for Oran, and married into a great Marseillais shipping family, is regarded as one of the constructors of the French Empire. Yet in December 1891 he made no defence of colonial interests, telling the Chamber that since France had incurred considerable expenses in acquiring these overseas territories, they should be reserved for French products. 'Nowhere was there a colonial point of view, and nowhere, save perhaps vaguely in Etienne's mind, was there the concept that the colonies were a coherent organism of their own.'[17] Algeria and Indo-China had already had their tariffs assimilated in 1884 and 1887. Now the rest of the empire was to receive like benefits. But assimilation did not imply imperial free trade: tariffs would be manipulated in favour of the benefactor. In future all French goods would be admitted free into a colony. Those colonies, such as the sugar islands, which in the sixties had received tariff autonomy and were able to finance part of their administration out of a general *octroi de mer*, could no longer levy on French manufactures. On the other hand, goods described as 'colonial products', tea, coffee, cocoa, pepper, were subject to duties on entering France in the interests of French revenue, while cane-sugar and its derivatives were heavily burdened in the interests of the beet-sugar growers and refiners of northern France. These regulations were applied to all colonies with the exception of the as yet unconsolidated fragments of West Africa and Gaboon and the enclaves on the Indian sub-continent, this tenderness being due to the fact that control of smuggling was almost impossible.

(*v*)

Did the law of January 11, 1892, succeed in its objective? The protectionists claim that it did and point to the agricultural prosperity twenty years later. Critics reply that the recovery from the sharp fall in farm income after 1885, the year of the first high duty on grain, was impeded by the action of the new law. Prices did not begin to recover until after 1900, and did not return to the level of 1875, that is the lowest level of the seventies, until about 1910, when costs were considerably higher. The alleged 'drift from the land' was not arrested. Owners of property did not go, but the younger sons of the landless labourers, for whom agriculture promised no future, sought the town. Given the stubbornness of the peasant, even without the Méline Tariff he would not have moved. Neither prices of land nor rents ever returned to the 1881 high levels.

Certainly there were changes. There was reduction in the cost of food imports. From 1653 million francs in 1891, it dropped to 1063 millions in 1893, and thereafter to under 1000 millions, except for the years of bad harvests, up to 1910. The replanting after the passage of the phylloxera began to show results; the import of 12 million hectolitres of 1891 fell to 4½ million in 1894. The Marseillais complained that under this 'murderous régime' their shipping revenue had fallen by 15% by 1896 and that the new tariff had killed grain distilling, while the disappearance of grain offals was depressing the pig trade. That would not last, but it is true that the development of Marseille was slower than that of similar great ports in other countries.[18] The improvement in prices when they rose was due not to tariffs but to other stronger forces. For one, the growth of the urban market by 4½ million between 1881 and 1911, slow though it was, coupled with improvement in transport, played a part. For another, improvements in methods and increase in output. Between the years 1876–80 and 1906–10, the wheat area fell by a million acres, the rye by a million and a half, and the barley by 800,000, while on the other hand the area of oats had grown by 1,200,000, and that of lucerne, clover etc. had risen from 6½ million acres to above 10 million. The vine area continued to shrink; by 1914 it was little more than three-fifths of what it had been in 1874, but yields were as great. Some of the prosperity was due to the turning away from traditional agriculture and the discovery of new methods and new products, probably under duress. In the eighties, in the two Charente departments ruined by phylloxera, one Eugène Biraud persuaded a group of peasants to grub up their vine roots and turn to co-operative dairying. At that date, there was one co-operative of ninety members, who from 300 cows produced 31 tons of butter. By 1908 there were 112 societies in the two departments with 67,000 members producing 11,636 tons of butter. In 1905 nearly three-quarters of the butter consumed in Paris came from this region. In 1882 in the two departments there were over half a million acres under vine: in 1929 there were about 200,000.[19]

For the colonies, the effects of the new régime appear to have been either bad or negligible. The sugar islands were ruined,[20] while in New Caledonia the decline was so great that within twenty years the island had to be released from control. In Indo-China, the trade remained in the hands of the Chinese, who could easily outwit the French. Rice was the chief export, and to China. Cotton production remained in Chinese hands, and exports from France never made any serious progress. Although French trade with French colonies more than doubled between 1892 and 1911, the French share remained much the same. The growth was not what it might have been, as was demonstrated by the external commerce of Tunisia, which was governed by treaties from before the days of the protectorate and multiplied eight times between 1888 and 1913. The new system, however, made the colonies conscious of themselves as entities. It is from these years that a colonial movement begins and the formation of such bodies as the Comité Dupleix, the Congrès des Anciennes Colonies, Afrique Française and the organisation of the colonial groups in the Chamber and Senate.

Chapter Twenty-Three

The End of an Epoch

(i)

The middle nineties offer a brief period of political calm between the subsidence of the Right and the ascension of the Left. In this, the coherence of the Republic can be considered as a prelude to that period of rapid enrichment of the North Atlantic countries which culminated with the outbreak of war in 1914, a period in which French economy was, as it were, dragged onward by the vulgar appetites of the British, German and American peoples. Here pass a few years of scarcely vexed tranquillity between the period of defence against the past and that of resistance to the future.

The 'Revolution of the Fourth of September' 1870, memorialised by an ugly Paris street, which leads appropriately enough to the Bourse, was no revolution: at best it was the occupation of the vacant seat of government by a hitherto impotent opposition, itself united only in opposition. The lack of revolutionary dynamism was demonstrated by the inability of the several Communes to achieve even moderate success. The real revolution, such as it was, was unheard and unspectacular. Awakened by Gambetta's prophetic speech of 1872 at Grenoble, it reached its consummation, the occupation of the places of power by the lesser bourgeoisie, in the election of 1881. Once again there was occupation of an empty place, rather than a conquest. 'It is', wrote Francis Magnard of the *Figaro*, after the election of Barodet in 1873,[1] 'a seedy Third Estate . . . hemmed in between the worker and the bourgeois, having neither the hopes and the freedom of the first, nor the ease and indifference of the second. . . .'

After Gambetta, who died just in time to save his reputation, such political energy as had bubbled in the 'new social strata' evaporated. In his *Ancien Régime*, published in 1858, Alexis de Tocqueville described the French people as 'the most brilliant and most dangerous of the nations of Europe, and that best formed to become by turns the object of admiration, of hatred, of pity, of terror, but never of indifference'. By 1885 that characterisation was out of date. France had ceased to strive for the hegemony of Europe. It was generally felt that the average Frenchman was no longer concerned even about the liberation of Alsace-Lorraine. The age of crusading was past; that of mediocrity had set in. 'Take care,' Thiers had once said: 'The dictatorship of big men has destroyed you: that of little men will ruin you no less, and with them there is less glory.'[2]

(ii)

The reaction to anarchism had revealed one conversion, that of the Radical party. The elimination of Clemenceau at the election had removed the strongest personality among the Radical leaders, perhaps the single speaker in the Chamber who could call out the most generous (though also the most cowardly) sentiments from the deputies. But feller of ministries as he had been, he had only once been called on to form a government — by Grévy *in extremis*, and had naturally refused. To a party, however amorphous it might be, the inability of its doughtiest champion to secure the spoils was maddening. The Radicals had begun to perceive that not only did opposition on principle not pay, but that they must make themselves worthy of office by a sense of governmental responsibility. From the point of view of workaday Radicals, the loss of Clemenceau was something of a blessing. However regrettable his defeat, they were glad to see his back: some, indeed, were known to view the possibility of his return with horror.

He had now taken up journalism, with difficulty, writing in his own *Justice* and the *Dépêche de Toulouse* fierce articles on behalf of the indigent and destitute, holding up ministers, even the President of the Republic, to derision and contempt. He had been replaced as spokesman of the Radicals by a personage of a different complexion, Léon Bourgeois, deputy for Châlons-sur-Marne, whose career had included twenty years on the prefectorial ladder, culminating in the quasipolitical post of Préfet of Police in November 1887 from which he resigned three months later when elected to the Chamber at a bye. Only six weeks after his appearance at the Palais Bourbon, in April, he was appointed Under-secretary of the Interior, demonstrating to his fellow Radicals the truth of Madame de Genlis's remark: 'Nothing is so clever as impregnable conduct'. During another thirty years, his career would exhibit how a careful man could succeed by repeated refusals to occupy positions requiring courage and a sense of responsibility.*

This was the man who succeeded Clemenceau in the leadership of the former Extreme Left. It was thus not surprising that the Radical opponents of the *lois scélérates*, as the anti-anarchist legislation was nicknamed by the Socialists, were not Bourgeois, Cavaignac or Doumer, but older men such as Brisson and Goblet. Neo-Radical was but old Republican writ large. He had merely taken the scarcely perceptible shift to the side, so easy in an assembly, whose members sit cheek by jowl in a semi-circle, the shift that is not, as is the defiant crossing of the floor in the British Parliament, a test of character. For example, of the six Radicals elected for the department of Ain in 1893, three had been elected as Opportunists in 1889. Elsewhere in that Chamber were to be found thirty-five similar converts, while some former Boulangists had adopted the title of Rallié or Socialist-Radical. As a later statesman was to write: '*Un conflit de doctrine ne pèse rien contre une exigence professionnelle*'.³

(*iii*)

When, in May 1894, Casimir-Périer's Government fell because the Minister of Public Works, Jonnart, could not make up his mind as to the relationship between industrial employees of the State and trade unions, Paul Cambon, now Ambassador in Constantinople, wrote to his mother that this was only one more illustration of the impossibility of governing France as a parliamentary democracy. 'With its appetites, its paltriness, its parish-pump feuds, democracy can only be guided by a jackbooted master or a collection of ministerial mediocrities. We are on the point of retreating into that degrading concentration from which we have suffered since Jules Ferry's fall.'⁴

Cambon, of course, like all trained and competent *grands commis*, had a contempt for disorder. But in fact the cause of his complaint was older than the fall of Ferry and deeper seated. It lay in the structure of French society itself.

Although the technical growth of industry in France began as early

* During the Peace Conference of 1919, Bourgeois infuriated many allied delegates. Balfour once said to Clemenceau in a strong Anglo-Saxon accent, 'Oh, vous ne savez pas comme je déteste cet homme, c'est un imbécile.' To which the Tiger returned: 'Pas ça, mon ami, pas ça. C'est un homme de second plan comme il y a beaucoup ici.' (Stephen Bonsal, *Unfinished Business*, 195.)

as in other countries of continental Europe, it had developed more slowly. By the end of the nineteenth century, Germany, Belgium, Holland and Switzerland were relatively ahead of France. French scientists and inventors were in no way inferior to those of other nations, nor were they unpractical: in fuel economy and by-product recovery, for example, the French were in advance of the British. But French industrialists appeared unable or perhaps reluctant to adopt inventions or develop large-scale production. Even steel-making did not expand rapidly until the late nineties.

No doubt the absence of an increasing home-market (indeed, after 1870 it was a temporarily diminished one) was discouraging. In every other country of north-western Europe, population was rising at an unexampled pace after the middle of the century. Between 1881 and 1911, the population of Great Britain rose annually by 1.41%, of Germany by 1.45%, of Belgium by 1.15%. Including immigration, the French figure averaged no better than 0.24%. An increase of twelve millions between 1801 and 1911 compares ill with a growth of thirty-eight millions in England, Scotland and Wales, of which eight millions emigrated.

The slow increase of the population of France is paralleled by a similar slowness in the growth of cities. Alone of the European capitals, Paris did not double between 1875 and 1936. Berlin, Madrid, Rome, Copenhagen, Brussels, the Hague, even the already obese London grew enormously. Birmingham, Cologne, Milan trebled. There was no industrial concentration in France to compare with these. At the end of the century France was still predominantly rural. Internal migration was limited. Men might be abandoning sub-marginal land in the Alps and Pyrenees, but they were not seeking the towns. As elsewhere, the migrant was expelled rather than attracted: he moved slowly from hamlet to village, from village to *bourg*, and so on. Up to 1886 well over 80% of the population were living in the department in which they had been born. At the 1891 census the figure was still 82.6%.[5] It is only in Seine, Paris and its suburbs that immigration was active: in 1891 nearly two-thirds of the inhabitants had been born elsewhere. Professor T. H. Marshall once remarked that migration is conditioned 'not by rational calculation of economic advantages, but by the presence of a certain sensational quality in the appeal. There is romance in the call of London and the Colonies'. To the French man or woman, the colonies made no call. The only romantic summons came from the capital, '*Paname*'. Many found it a cruel city. True, wages in Paris were higher, but so were the costs, and the unemployment. There can hardly be a year between 1888 and 1896 without the publication of a score of sober articles on deaths by starvation or suicide: 1894 is the peak year for suicides before 1907. For the mass of countrymen, the town offered no attraction.*

Some have attributed this passivity to the inability of industry to expand owing to the lack of capital, and it is laid to the charge of the French bankers that they granted loans to foreigners with far greater ease than to their fellow countrymen. It is, of course, true that by 1894 the Russian government had extracted since 1890 some eight milliard francs from the French prudential saver, while other governments had also dipped into the French stocking. No doubt some of this was due to the activities of banks such as the Société Générale and the Crédit Lyonnais. The establishment of ever wider circles of branches made it almost inevitable that they should take the lead in the foreign loan business over such members of *Haute Banque* as Mallet, Vernes and Rothschild, for whose kind of business country branches were useless.[6] These new banks, of course, made their money out of the flotation and management of foreign government loans, and undoubtedly the prospect of good profits led them to take unjustifiable risks, as the future would show.

In the early nineties, however, this was largely irrelevant. The whole ethos of the industrialist was still opposed to borrowing as against financing out of profits. The years up to 1896, and even in some cases beyond, are those in which the prices of the main raw materials reached their nadir. The industrialists were not prepared to take risks and further they were not prepared to aggravate the prevailing unemployment by the institution of labour-saving machinery. Levasseur in an article in 1898[7] quoted the statement of a foreman at Le Creusot, who had visited Homestead and Chicago, that Schneiders could not put in the heavy hammers the Americans were using: if they did, they would have unemployment for nine months of the year. It is perhaps for such reasons that in 1895 the cotton-spinners in the Vosges were employing nearly nine hands per thousand spindles against less than six in Mulhouse and less than two-and-a-half in Lancashire. In such circumstances, the call for capital was not important and certainly not hampered by the loans to foreign governments and corporations.

It has been suggested[8] that possibly the drain of French savings into

---

* There were fairly rapid agglomerations in Alpes-maritimes, Bouches-du-Rhône and Nord largely due to foreign immigrants, who in 1896 were 20% of the population of the first and 14.5% of the other two.

foreign countries was in fact offset by many items of invisible export. It is doubtful if in the early nineties any of these, for example freight charges or tourist payments, were big enough to compensate. The amounts however remain invisible and unverifiable.

In point of fact, the lack of enterprise was largely due to the absence of pressures. France is still a country of which agriculture is the dominating interest. The agricultural population is largely that of owner-occupiers, and largely small-scale, certainly under-capitalised. Of these a number are subsistence farmers, getting a poor living, but independent. Agricultural technique is traditional rather than rational. More than two-fifths, nearly half the population, live from the land, and of these perhaps an eighth are vinegrowers and market-gardeners.[9] Industry was late in developing and both industry and commerce are more interested in preserving the home market than in running the risks of extending their trade. There are, of course, big firms in heavy industry, but they do not comprise more than 10% of the industrial personnel. The population was rising so slowly that there was no need for that rapid transformation which was forced on Britain and was being repeated in Germany and the United States. These countries developed because they were compelled by the needs of growing population.* France could accommodate her slowly rising population without trouble.

There were no urgent pressures, and therefore there were no vital interests, and in consequence no political parties, only incoherent groups.

(iv)

Thiers had said: 'the Republic will be conservative or it will not be.' All that had happened since 1879 seemed to prove it, though it was not the conservative Republic ('not Athenian; Florentine') Thiers had envisaged. Nevertheless, the outside world, and indeed many French observers, looking at the rapidly succeeding governments of the Republic, spoke of French governmental instability. To them it appeared that the ministries were defeated because the men composing them lacked character. This was a misunderstanding. There were not weak

---

* It may be objected that the United States developed much machinery especially agricultural from the very deficiency of labour. But the density of population in the eastern states was in many areas comparable to the densities in Europe.

or strong governments. Such are concepts of those who think only in terms of personalities, not of situations. All French governments must from their very constitution be weak, since all must be coalitions. These alliances could last only so long as the situation that brought the allies together continued. When their purpose was fulfilled, or the situation changed, the need for the coalition ceased. It could survive just so long as no new question came up on which the cabinet could not agree. It was thus not a matter of strong or weak governments, but of difficult or easy situations. In a difficult or dangerous situation, governments could survive for long; in fine political weather the groups could play politics.

From Dufaure's ministry of 1877 to Gambetta's of 1881 each cabinet emerged from the debris of its predecessor. Gambetta's was formed almost wholly of new men, not by his desire, but because of the desertion of Say and Freycinet. When Gambetta fell, Freycinet sought Gambetta's predecessors for his colleagues. The cabinets of new men are few. In fact the cleanest sweep is that carried out by Casimir-Périer in 1893, and that was an attempt to put the clock back ten years. Between the defeat of Ferry in April 1885 and that of Léon Bourgeois in April 1896, there were sixteen cabinets, surviving on the average eight months apiece. And there was no serious crisis, even at the zenith of Boulangism, even in the pit of Panama. When reproached for destroying them, Clemenceau rightly retorted: 'It was always the same one.' The new one never had fewer than two members of the previous cabinet. Freycinet had seven members of Tirard's in his cabinet of 1890, and Freycinet's provided six for Loubet's of 1892, while in the autumn Loubet handed on nine members (including himself) to Ribot, who in 1893 passed on eight old hands to Dupuy. All were concentrations of the Centre, the Opportunists, shifting a little from Left to Right and from Right to Left according to the political temperature.

Governments came in to administer rather than to inaugurate new policy, even when the Prime Minister was nominally a Radical. Programmes were nebulous. After Floquet had with difficulty got a team together in April 1888, Loubet remarked that a programme was needed, to which the aspiring Prime Minister returned that his cabinet were all Republicans and that the name of Floquet was enough.[10] Indeed, this might be true, for generally parliamentary activity was negative: anti-clericalism, anti-monarchism, anti-imperialism, anti-colonialism, and anti-socialism. Thibaudet recalled that Barrès once asserted in the Chamber that the Radicals had no policy, on which the respectable and simple Goblet huffily replied that they had — the separation of Church and State — and was taken aback when everyone laughed. The debates on Méline's tariff bill demonstrate that the project was defensive; it was to save, not to improve agriculture. The French statute book is largely barren of social legislation: there is no series of laws and orders dealing with industry, the factory, the mine, the workshop and the workers that is to be found in England and Germany. It is not until 1875 that the employment of children in mines and factories is seriously taken in hand, when for the first time factory inspectors were appointed. But effective legislation hardly begins before the nineties. This, although, as in other countries, there is callousness and indifference, is due rather to the slow growth of collectivised industry and urbanisation. Factories cannot be inspected when they do not exist, and domestic industry, as the English discovered, is uninspectable.

The lethargy of economic and social growth left a vacuum in French political life, which was almost inevitably filled by sterile controversies on forms of government, methods of representation and abstract principles in which the average citizen took no interest. These controversies gave rise to vast oratorical jousts in which many heroic or deplorable episodes of the past were fought over again. In his annual review for 1894, the eminent financial journalist Alfred Neymarck wrote: 'Parliament has spent all its time in discussions and otiose interpellations. . . . The Chamber has agitated itself in a vacuum. It is full of good intentions, but instead of occupying itself with realities, it chases chimeras and lets itself be distracted by some clever orator with the same ease it goes back on its votes'.[11] De Vogüé, a new member at the 1893 election (for Ardèche), showed in his dull but in some ways illuminating novel, Les Morts qui parlent, how the Chamber filled when an attractive orator went to the tribune and how it emptied when he had finished.

The negativeness was in part due to the absence of serious opposition and the domination of the ministry by the Chamber. The deputies had control, but did not know what to use it for. The Government looked to the deputies and the deputies looked to the elector. Except on local issues, the elector had no views. 'His first contact with the sovereign people enlightened him. The rhetoric of the journalists, their arbitrary classification of so-called parties, the advertised currents of opinion, all these townsman's fictions had no relation to the rural masses, except a few leaders. Conservative by instinct, with a passive deference to whichever government happened to exist, attached by tradition to religious customs, which must not be disturbed, but also not imposed, and yet on guard against the curé meddling in their private affairs, the masses were above all hungry for material rewards, and always on the look-out for a protector against their natural enemies, the tax-collector, the recruiting sergeant, the lawyer. . . . Jacques saw with brutal clarity the simplicity or the hypocrisy of those who feigned to ask political direction from the eternally directed.'[12]

In the great and passionate speech Clemenceau made to the electors of Salernes (Var) in August 1893, when he was fighting desperately for his political existence, he spoke contemptuously of the inert and un-leavened lump of the French bourgeoisie, but he admitted that in politics the leaders were pushed on more often than they drew forward. But who pushed them? One looks down the lists of ministers from 1888 to 1896 and sees many worthy and intelligent men, a Jules Roche, an Yves Guyot, a Develle, in their own offices excellent ministers; but unable and aware that they were unable to do more than mark time. 'The people care not what government they live under so as they may plough and go to market.'

Appendix I

ALSACE-LORRAINE (Chapter One)

By the Treaty of Frankfurt the inhabitants of the annexed provinces who desired to maintain their French nationality were permitted to elect before October 1, 1872, to remain French and to cross the frontier into France. Some 160,000 claimed French citizenship, but only about 60,000 were effective, those who could afford to emigrate. The better part of the 60,000 were from the professional and skilled-worker classes; for the small working landowner removal was impossible. The medical faculty of the University of Strasbourg moved to the University of Lyon. A number of owners of textile-factories, particularly Jews, came to Lille and Rouen — including the family of Léon Blum. Wool-manufacturers came from Bischweiler to Elbeuf, among them the family of André Maurois, the Fraenkels. The Sarreguemines pottery-works went to Digoin (Saône-et-Loire), and from Lorraine some 5000 peasants were moved to Algeria and provided with 250,000 acres of land. It is to be noted that of all the immigrants to Paris those from Alsace-Lorraine formed the biggest group. After 1875 emigration increased. It is reckoned that some quarter of a million came out between this date and 1910.

The consequence of the severance from France was the sundering of the economic unity of both provinces and of considerable population movements. The cotton-spinners of Alsace were divorced from the weavers of the Vosges. Longwy on the Luxembourg frontier was cut off from the iron area of Ottange, and Wendel's Moyeuvre stagnated for another twenty-five years. Sainte-Marie-aux-Mines, cut off from Saint-Dié, declined. Most of the communes on the eastern slopes of the Vosges from Ferrette on the Swiss frontier as far as Metz lost population. (See the map attached to the article by Vidal de la Blache in 25 *AG*.) The growth of Mulhouse slowed down. On the other hand, the valleys of the Meurthe from Saint-Dié to Nancy and the Moselle from Epinal to Pagny, and also the Belfort area, received an impulse hitherto wanting.

Appendix II

THE SIZE OF THE NATIONAL ASSEMBLY
(CHAPTER ONE)

THE full membership of the National Assembly on February 12, 1871, should have been 768. Owing to multiple elections and refusals to accept election, this number was reduced by eighty-seven. Then immediately after the ratification of peace preliminaries, the whole representation of Meurthe, Moselle, Bas-Rhin and Haut-Rhin, forty members, resigned, but nine, seven from Meurthe and two from Moselle, continued to sit as representatives of the newly-formed department of Meurthe-et-Moselle. During March and April there were further withdrawals, chiefly of Communards and such sympathisers as Clemenceau and Floquet. Further vacancies occurred through the death of members.

Hence by June 30 the Assembly was reduced to 618. The election on July 2 was for 120 seats, which included the new seat for the remnant of Haut-Rhin, the 'Territory of Belfort'. The Assembly, however, was not complete, owing to further multiple elections. In fact, the Assembly at no time from 1871 to 1875 can have sat as a whole; a number of members were always absent on duty, such as Le Flô, Ambassador at Saint-Petersburg. Further, from February 1875 no further bye-elections took place, except for an odd bye in Guadeloupe.

Appendix III

THE PREFECTORIAL SYSTEM

(CHAPTER ONE)

THE prefectorial system derived from the Ancien Régime. The endeavours of the monarchy to secure control go back many centuries, but up to 1789 had not succeeded. The system begun by Richelieu and improved by Colbert had no more than created a system of local governors. It is therefore not surprising that Louis XVI himself welcomed and showed a deep interest in the recasting of the provinces into departments in 1789. The Revolution, however, did little beyond laying the foundations of a new centralised government. '*Quand un peuple a détruit dans son sein l'aristocratie*', wrote Tocqueville, '*il court vers la centralisation comme de lui-même.*' It was left to Napoleon to clear the board, and by what Faguet called 'the terrible law of 28 pluviose, An VIII', February 17, 1800, erect the centralised machine which with little modification still stands.

The principle was simple. At the head of the State stood the chief executive, the Emperor. From him radiated hierarchically organised sub-governments; in each department a préfet, in each arrondissement a sous-préfet, in each commune a maire, each responsible to the next higher authority.[1] The préfets corresponded directly with each ministry in matters affecting it, but they were the servants of the Minister of the Interior, who appointed, transferred, relieved or dismissed them. Each préfecture had its own miniature replica of government, its secretary-general for administration, its *conseillers* to decide conflicts between public bodies or between the private citizen and the State, and its law officers, *procureur* and so on. Such verdicts as did not satisfy the litigants could be appealed to the Conseil d'Etat, in the lower ranks of which many préfets had begun their careers. Besides the préfet, in each department sat an elected *conseil-général*, with analogous councils in the arrondissements, cantons and communes: but their duties were purely advisory; they had no control over the préfet's actions. They met only twice a year, in the spring for a fortnight, in the autumn for a month, chiefly to allot taxes. The préfets were in fact, as Napoleon said, 'minor emperors; but since they had no connection with the territory they controlled, they had all the privileges of the erstwhile great absolute agents with none of their drawbacks.'

Endowed with a machine of this character, Louis XVIII, returning to an uneasy throne in 1814 and 1815, maintained the imperial system, Louis-Philippe scarcely modified it, and the Second Republic, for all its chatter

2C

about liberty, merely changed the title of its agents from préfet to commissioner. Napoleon III naturally not only accepted but strengthened the instrument, encouraged the préfets to be tough and increased their powers: they were a necessary part of the plebiscitary machine and were pressed to secure the necessary 'ayes' and the necessary representatives in the Corps législatif. Only official candidates were allowed to use white paper for their appeals to the electorate — the notorious *affiche blanche,* which was reserved for official notices and hence indicated government benevolence to the candidate. The maires were kept well in hand. 'When I was at Barcelonnette,' said the secretary-general of Vienne to Ludovic Halévy in 1869,[2] 'out of 4000 votes there were sixty opposition. In one commune there were seven. Next morning in came the maire to the sous-préfecture. "I can't go on as maire," he said; "I've come to resign. *Seven opposition votes!* I'm disgraced." '

As has been seen, after September 4, 1870, Gambetta replaced the imperial officials with his own nominees. Thiers in turn removed many of these in favour of his own men, and over the heads of his Ministers of the Interior corresponded directly with the departments. 'He liked', said Jules Simon,[3] 'to know his ministers' business a little before they did, which was not always to their liking.' When Broglie took office, he immediately ordered the transfer or revocation of those functionaries who had shown too great an enthusiasm for republicanism.

The office of préfet thus required men of tact and courage, and even more of foresight, since too much zeal on behalf of a defeated Government might be even more risky than luke-warmness, as the list of revocations and transfers with each change of Minister of the Interior testifies. Although the Third Republic, at least after 1877, deprecated publicly electoral pressure by governmental agencies, such action continued irregularly into the twentieth century. There are many peculiar incidents in electoral history, e.g. the officially stage-managed candidature of Ménard-Dorian at Lodève in 1889,[4] and the manoeuvres of the préfet of Var against Clemenceau in 1893. Adrien Hébrard,[5] editor of the *Temps* after the 1885 election, told of the maire of a Pyrenean village who made up the poll before the election, giving nine votes to the opposition candidate because he was a local man. 'You won't mind, will you?'

The political influence of the préfets has been exaggerated. Indeed, it would be truer to say that, after 1877, not many meddled in politics, save perhaps at the election of 1889, the *coup de grâce* of the Boulanger adventure, when Constans made it clear to government agents that should the general's candidates be returned in force, heads would roll. They were the Government's executives, appointed to see that governmental decrees were carried out, even of the most unpleasant nature, and order preserved. They were picked men, whose nomination derived from the unanimous agreement of the cabinet; the determined opposition of one minister might prevent the appointment. The great majority were like other civil servants in France, faithful representatives of the State, honourable and highly competent: the long list of governors-general and ambassadors who came from the prefectorial ranks far outweighs the occasional political adventurer of the Félix Granet type. To see the préfet at his best, one has only to read the correspondence of Paul Cambon, préfet of Aube, Doubs and Nord between 1872 and 1882, appointed by the Republic, but maintained, until his resignation, by the Broglie administration. There is Hendlé, one of the few Jewish préfets, who in the aristocratic-bourgeois department of Seine-inférieure, transformed himself from 'the' préfet to 'our' préfet.[6] If one asks why France remained a stable country between 1870 and 1940, during which time the average life of a Government was no more than eight months, one must look at the corps of préfets.

On the other hand, the system had its weaknesses. The better a préfet, the more successful, the quicker his transfer and promotion. As Faguet pointed out,[7] they grew no roots; they could only study their departments superficially. 'It would have been thought the height of folly to send M. Turgot, intendant of the Limousin, to Picardy about 1768 at the moment when he was set to transform the Limousin. But nowadays no inconvenience is felt; if the préfet is sent from Limoges to Lille in either the first or the tenth year of his term, in the last year he is doing exactly what he was doing in the first, and he will do in Lille exactly what he was doing in Limoges. Only, M. Turgot did something in the Limousin, and the modern préfets do nothing at all; they may labour, but they create absolutely nothing.' Faguet's diatribe is too severe, but it is true that they were no more than intermediaries between the departments and the all-powerful stifling State. They could administer, and, in two wars, many in the invaded regions did heroic work, but in creation they could have little share, while on the other hand, the State, which distrusted bodies within its own body, killed local initiative. Examine the career of Cazelles: in 1870 secretary-general at Nîmes, in 1878 préfet of Creuse, in 1879 of Hérault, transferred in the same year to Director of Penitentiary Administration. In 1880 he became Director of the Sûreté, in 1882 préfet of Meurthe-et-Moselle, in 1883 of Bouches-du-Rhône, in 1886 Director of Public Assistance, in 1887 a Conseiller-d'Etat, in 1889–92 Director of the Sûreté, in 1892–97 Conseiller-d'Etat.

For the times the préfets were well paid. The holders of the eleven first-class préfectures received 35,000 francs, while those of the second and third class received 24,000 and 18,000. In addition, there were expense-allowances of considerable value. The préfet of Seine, a quasi-political appointment, at least down to 1882, got 50,000 francs. As they rose, many achieved more highly considered appointments, embassies or colonial governorships. The less ambitious received towards the end of their careers such jobs as those of treasurer-general, 'superbly paid sinecures.'

Furthermore, in his department the préfet controlled much local patronage. Practically all the minor appointments in a department were in his gift; prison-warders and inspectors, doctors and officials of lunatic asylums, departmental architects and archivists, officials of charitable institutions, directors and teachers of art schools, museum officials, supernumerary inspectors of taxes, collectors of taxes up to 300,000 francs, small tobacco-bureaux and post-offices, forest-guards, veterinary surgeons and road-menders, and one-third of the lowest grades of school-teachers, all were appointed by the préfet. Though he might have to resist the pressures of senators and deputies, in the aggregate it was a power of great consequence.

Appendix IV

WAS THE NATIONAL ASSEMBLY 'CONSTITUENT'? (CHAPTER ONE)

ON September 8, 1870, the Government of National Defence issued a decree convoking the electoral colleges for October 16, for the purpose of electing a 'constituent National Assembly'. Two days later it issued a similar decree for the colonies. Three other decrees of September 15, 16 and 17, refer to '*the* Constituent Assembly'. Owing to the advance of the Germans, the elections for '*the* Constituent Assembly' were adjourned by decree of September 23, which added that a later date would be in due time announced.

On January 28, 1871, the terms of the armistice were signed. Article 2 laid down that '*a* National Assembly' should be convoked to consider the continuation of the war or the terms of peace.

On January 29 a decree stated in Article 1 that 'the electoral colleges are convoked for the purpose of electing *the* National Assembly etc.', while on February 5 a circular from the Ministry of the Interior (responsible for the elections) refers to 'an assembly which possibly may be called on to lay the foundations of our political institutions, for it is impossible to see where its duties will end'.

It is clear from all this that the Government intended a constituent Assembly in September and had in mind the same Assembly (mark the employment of 'the') in January. Hence Gambetta's claim that the Assembly had no mandate is flimsy: the reference to the terms of the armistice is irrelevant, since that instrument was between two Governments, while the French Government's decrees were given by itself to the electors. Gambetta's further claim that the trend of the elections was running in favour of the Republicans and that the Assembly must therefore be dissolved might be good propaganda, but could have no basis in any constitutional law. (Cf. Duguit et Monnier, *Les Constitutions etc.*, 111–13.)

Appendix V

THE CONSEIL D'ETAT (Chapter One)

THE nomination of the *conseillers en service ordinaire* was given back to the President under Article 4 of the constitutional law of February 25, 1875. On the debate on this article, Raudot, an intelligent member of the Right, an ardent decentraliser, and Raoul Duval, the best by far of the Appel au Peuple group, alone protested against the attempt to rush a matter of such profound importance. But the Assembly, exhausted by the polemics of the last month, ignored them and passed the article by a huge majority. Daniel Halévy (*République des Ducs*, 176–81) comments on this reaction from the previous attitude, and suggests that the Right, opposed in 1872 to nomination by Thiers, now saw that with MacMahon as President at a moment when a third of the councillors was due for re-election (May 1875), it was essential to put the power of appointment in the hands of the President, otherwise the now unreliable majority might elect Radical jurists, while, on the other hand, the Left, formerly distrustful of Thiers, now with their Pisgah-sight of power, were willing to uphold the centralised State. Robert Dreyfus, whose opinion is given by Halévy in his footnote to p. 181 cited above, claims that the Law of May 24, 1872, was directed against Thiers and not against the Conseil d'Etat as an institution. I incline to this reading of the situation. In my opinion, Halévy exaggerates the debates of 1872: 'The Assembly had deliberated three times, listened to immense speeches.' But three readings were normal, and the speeches from a body of men who loved the sound of their own voices were not, compared with many other debates, immense. Nevertheless, it is important to observe that '*les grands corps napoléoniens*', and the Conseil d'Etat in chief, were too valuable for any hopeful politician to discard. In France as elsewhere, the Susan Nippers know their place. '*Les pouvoirs réels*', wrote Halévy, '*sont discrets et savent triompher tout bas.*'

Appendix VI

THE ELECTION OF THE LIFE SENATORS
IN DECEMBER 1875 (CHAPTER TWO)

ALTHOUGH there are plenty of accounts of the negotiations for the election of Life Senators in December 1875, e.g. Bosq, *Souvenirs de l'Assemblée Nationale*; Daudet, *Souvenirs de la Présidence du Maréchal MacMahon*; de Meaux, *Souvenirs politiques*; while Hanotaux adds a few points, the details are somewhat contradictory. It is, however, almost certain that, contrary to many accounts, Jules Simon was not the principal in the negotiations, although the Republican committee met at his apartment. Testelin, representative for Nord, 'patriotic Jacobin' friend of Gambetta, is also mentioned, not convincingly. The most circumstantial account is that given in a letter from General de Galliffet to Ranc of November 14, 1886 (Ranc, *Correspondance*, 425–32), categorically affirming that the go-between was Duclerc, who at this date was probably the strongest individual of the Republican Left, very active in the corridors and with friends in all camps. The decisive evidence is that Galliffet says that Simon had to beg Gambetta, his mortal enemy, to procure his election, and Duclerc said to Gambetta: 'Nominate him, but I tell you we shall repent it.' During the voting between December 9 and 16, Simon's position on the list never came near election until December 15, when eighteen were elected and he was nineteenth. His alarm was obvious: according to Daudet, he was heard 'plaintively repeating that if he were not elected a Life Senator, he would be excluded from public life' (*op. cit.*, 85). He was elected fifth of ten on December 16, and sixty-fifth on the full list.

La Rochette, when his followers realised what he had done, was forced to resign from the leadership of the Extreme Right, and died shortly afterwards. Although supporting the coalition, the Bonapartists refused to bargain for seats for themselves. 'For a few seats in the Senate', said Rouher, 'we could not accept the suffrages of those who voted the forfeiture of the Empire and consolidated the Republic'. (Bosq, *op. cit.*, 323.)

It is said that as they left Versailles for Paris on the last evening, the Duc d'Aumale said in a bitter voice to Broglie: 'The only difference between those who serve us and those who served my father, is that they sent him off in a cab, while you make us go by train.'

Appendix VII

PARLIAMENTARY PROCEDURE (Chapter Two)

WHETHER French legislatures were unicameral (1871–76) or bicameral (1876–1940) procedure is important in that constitutional changes came rather from this source than through formal amendment in the National Assembly.

The rules of procedure (*le Règlement*) after 1870 were derived from the practice of 1789 as modified by subsequent régimes. The central point was, and remains, the Committee system, without an understanding of which much political history must be obscure. The National Assembly of 1871 was divided into fifteen bureaux by lot, the drawing taking place at the beginning of each session and thereafter monthly. After the passage of the Constitutional Laws and the division of Parliament into two houses, the bureaux numbered nine in the Senate and eleven in the Chamber of Deputies. From the bureaux were elected four monthly committees as follows: (1) the initiating committee (*commission d'initiative*), consisting of two members from each bureau; (2) the committee dealing with bills relating to local interests; (3) the committee dealing with petitions; (4) the committee dealing with requests for leave from parliamentary duties. The last three consisted of only one member from each bureau, and in the present connection have no interest. The initiating committee examined every bill emanating from a private member and reported on it to the full body with a recommendation as to whether it should be considered or not. Government bills, and from 1876 bills from the other Chamber, went direct to the full bureaux. These then elected their representatives to a committee whose duty it was to consider and report to the whole House on each bill. Thus each bill had its own committee, which elected a president and a *rapporteur*. When the examination was complete, the *rapport* was printed, giving the views of the committee and, in case of disagreement inside the committee, the opinions of both majority and minority. This was distributed and there followed a debate in the Chamber in which the bill as redrawn by the committee was defended by the *rapporteur*.

From this practice a number of peculiar consequences proceeded. Since the bureaux were drawn by lot, it might happen that the minority in the Chamber held the majority in the greater number of bureaux, and was thus able to pack the committee with a majority unfavourable to the bill, which would then produce an unfavourable report, bolstered up by the hostile *rapporteur*'s eloquence. Worse, a minister might, and not infrequently did, find that his bill had been so mishandled by the committee that a very different document was before the House. He would then be in the unenviable position of having to oppose the committee's bill, with, it might be, catastrophic results. He might indeed, as happened to Dufaure in 1876, find his bill amended in a sense contrary to his own, and then have to defend the amended version in the Senate.

Beyond this, it might well happen that the ministry had fallen long before the committee was ready with the bill, since there was in fact no method of forcing an unwilling committee to produce a report. The President of the Chamber (or Senate) alone could invite, no more, the committee to hurry, but the committee could ignore the invitation. (Pierre, *Traité de Droit politique*, Sec. 786.) Parliament seems never to have attempted to force the issue. As Pierre observes: 'Sometimes it is the larger prudence to leave sleeping in a committee a bill which has previously been greeted with enthusiasm.' Thus it is seen that the committees in effect had the real control of legislation.

From this certain corollaries followed. The procedure implied the unimportance of the Government. A ministry might go, but the bill survived. Caillaux's income-tax bill of 1907 had just come back to the Chamber from the Senate when he returned to the Ministry of Finance in December 1912. The bill to abolish the workman's *livret* was seven years getting on to the statute-book. The matter of the suppression of communal fallow-grazing seems to have taken some twenty years to reach finality. The bill for the erection of the Sacré Coeur at Montmartre was accepted by the Thiers Government in 1873, but was passed under that of MacMahon.

In the second place, the procedure brought about the gradual encroachment of the committees on the executive. In 1871, and formally until 1902, there was only one permanent committee, that of the Budget. Until 1877 this consisted of two members from each bureau, when the Chamber raised the number to three. Since its work required many months, it was elected annually, but since it demanded of its members some knowledge of public finance, it tended within limits to perpetuate itself. It did, however, like the others, suffer from election in the bureaux. It was open to the legislature to nominate a committee not in the bureaux, but by public vote of the whole body, as was done in the years 1871–75 for most of the Standing Committees (*Commissions de permanence*), which guarded the rights of the Assembly during recesses, for the committees for examining petitions for pardon after the Commune, and for the Committee of Thirty on the constitutional laws. At a later date, in November 1892, the Chamber committee on the Panama enquiry was also elected by this method. (Pierre, p. 777, fn. 1.) Yet although it was recognised that the luck of the draw might bring all the financial experts into one or two bureaux and thus deprive the Budget committee of the services of eminent members, the Chamber refused to modify its standing orders.

A further practice tended to the survival of the committees. Should a bill be presented which had some connection with another already before a committee, the new bill would be sent to it. Thus the committee might find itself receiving more work than it could finish in the time at its disposal. Nevertheless, once with a committee, a bill stayed with it, and though the committee might dissolve, as for example at the end of a legislature, it could still be reassembled in the new Chamber until its work was finished. It is probably due to this that the Army committee appears to have attained as great permanence as that of the Budget.

This procedure survived until 1910, when after some experiments the system of permanent committees was set up, a system which, with later modifications, had much to do with the sterility of parliamentary proceedings between 1919 and 1940. Thus, by their longevity compared with that of most ministries, the committees were effectively the masters of the executive.

Other points of procedure are important for the understanding of French political history. One is the method of voting. In 1871 there were three methods: (1) *par assis et levé*, when on the invitation of the President, the 'ayes' rose, while the 'noes' remained seated, followed by a rising of the 'noes', while the 'ayes' sat; (2) by public vote; (3) by secret vote. The last, which had some importance in the 1881 debates on elections, and which could be proposed in the Chamber by not less than fifty members, was discarded in 1885. The Senate abolished it in January 1887. For ordinary voting the members were provided with a number of slips with their names printed, white for 'aye', blue for 'no'. On the vote being taken, the ushers went round the House carrying urns into which the members put their slips. These were then counted by the secretaries to the House, and the result announced. In case of a tie, the motion was defeated, the President having no casting vote. It was the rule that only those members present could vote, a rule in fact rarely honoured, since a friend provided with the absent member's slips would put them in for him, leading sometimes to duplication of votes. Almost every issue of the Official Journal will be found to carry corrections from members stating that their names had appeared on the wrong list. These corrections, however, did not affect the original vote. After one division on July 3, 1899, the result was given as 274 to 262. On verification it was found that it should have been 244 to 248, on which Marcel Habert claimed that in a close vote war might be declared against the will of the Chamber. On the other hand, in cases (there were several at the time of the Panama scandal) in which the public wanted a certain vote that would be against the interest of the Chamber to carry, members negatived the motion and then in great numbers corrected their vote on the following day.

French legislative bodies took their duties seriously. A member drawing from the State a fee for loss of time and expenses (*indemnité*) which is not a salary, could not absent himself as he chose. He must obtain leave from the fourth committee. If absent without leave for six sittings, he could be brought before this body, and if his explanation was not accepted, he could be fined and the record printed in the Official Journal. Pairing was not permitted. 'Such a system', wrote Pierre (*op. cit.*, Sec. 1023), 'would hardly be understood in France: our logical and sensible country does not accept votes determined in advance. It more easily understands deputies of opposing parties struggling to convince each other than their mutual annulment in order to go running about after their private affairs.'

As regards abstention from voting (the Official Journal recorded both the abstainers and the absent) only one member, the President, must always be neutral: a Vice-President who happened to be in the chair might vote, but usually he did not. A President not occupying the chair, however, appears thereby to have become a private member. In the division of May 20, 1881, Gambetta voted.

On a vote of confidence ministers could but need not abstain. In January 1882 Gambetta and all his ministers abstained on the vote which brought his ministry down, but in 1904 Combes and his ministers voted and thus just escaped defeat. It was implied that members financially interested in a particular bill should not vote, but there was no obligation. On the other hand, organised abstention was strongly deprecated. 'The nation gives powers to its delegates to act, not to take refuge in silence.' (Pierre, *op. cit.*, Sec. 1024.) The *règlement* forbade collective abstentions, but no disciplinary action was possible. In 1878 Louis Blanc informed the Chamber that he and his friends would abstain on a motion, not as an action against the Government, but from conviction; and since the explanation was given before the vote, it was accepted. In 1892 the Boulangist rump tried to organise a mass abstention with the aid of the Right with the intention not only of defeating the Government, but of bringing about a dissolution. The Right refused, but apparently only because they thought the plan silly.

It is to be noted that ministers need not belong to either Chamber or Senate, although they usually did. 'The ministers may be chosen from the members of the two Chambers,' (Pierre, *op. cit.*, Sec. 98.) i.e. not 'must'. Flourens, Foreign Minister from December 1886 to April 1888, was elected to the Chamber only after leaving office. Hanotaux, too, from May 1894 to October 1895 and from April 1896 to July 1898 was extra-parliamentary. So too were many of the officers who sat as Ministers of War or the Marine.

In the French Parliament there was no equivalent of Questions in the House of Commons. Questions could be put verbally, but the minister need not reply. After 1876 questions were permitted by the President only after he had ascertained that the minister would reply. On the other hand, there existed the interpellation, which could be addressed to any minister as requiring an explanation of some matter within his purview. The request to interpellate had to be made in writing giving the object of the interpellation to the President of the Chamber, who would than read the gist to the members and ask that a date should be fixed for the discussion. In certain circumstances the President could refuse the request, as could also the ministers, but the latter must give their reason.

The interpellation is more than a question, in so far that from it may emerge a motion, in which the text, after embodying the motion in the name of the House, concludes with the phrase 'passes to the Order of the Day'. In critical political circumstances it might well happen that many more than one motion would be put forward. As a rule in such circumstances supporters of the Government might submit a text conveying confidence in the ministry, which would be accepted by the Government as that on which it would stand or fall. Occasionally the Government, knowing its position to be weak, would accept 'the Order of the Day, pure and simple', which took precedence of all other motions and allowed the original challenge to be ignored; the incident would then be quietly interred. On the other hand, in hot debates so many motions could be put forward that the confusion made any solution impossible. On November 1881, when Ferry was interpellated on the Tunisian expedition, eighteen different resolutions were submitted. Such was the chaos that the President of the Chamber, Gambetta, descended from the chair and himself put forward a motion, which would rally the majority in favour of the Government.

The important changes in the committee system which were made after 1900 and had a considerable influence on the existence of Governments between 1919 and 1940 will be considered later.

Appendix VIII

AGRICULTURAL WAGES (CHAPTER FOUR)

NOTHING of serious value can be said about the level of wages of the agricultural day-labourer in the seventies and eighties. The Enquête of 1882 gives the departmental wage-rates for winter and summer, both with and without food. Food appears to be reckoned at one franc a day everywhere. Winter rates appear quite capricious and do not seem to bear any relation to the wealth of the area. Summer-rates on the other hand reflect to some extent the economic needs of time and place. As would be expected, the rates round Paris are the highest, nearly five francs a day without food, while the adjacent departments are little worse. It is however noticeable that summer wages were nearly as high in some of the departments to the east of Paris, Marne, Aube, Yonne, Loiret and Haute Marne, the departments of small owners, where there was a shortage of labour. The wages in Brittany were very low; even at the height of '*la belle saison*'. Finistère, Côtes-du-Nord and Morbihan all paid less than two francs a day. The only other department to pay what appears above the normal rates was Calvados, where again there appears a shortage of labour.

The figures, however, mean little apart from employment, which was precarious. 300 days a year seems well above the average. In the Midi day-labourers were lucky to get 240. Women's wages were very low, usually less than half those paid to men.

The high earning period was of course the harvest and the *vendange*, during which men expected, as they often did, to earn double and treble ordinary rates.

The more permanent, or specialist staff, was hired by the year. Their pay varied enormously, but the level of specialists was rising all the time. There were many payments in kind, especially in the south: wine, oil, wheat or rye, salt. Shepherds, of whom there was a great deficiency, were allowed to run their own sheep with the flock. The champagne firm of Chandon at Epernay paid from March 1 to May 15, 6.75 francs a day with food and drink; from May 16 to July 31, 5.12 francs, also with food and drink. From August 1 to the vintage, pay fell to 3 francs a day and two bottles of wine, while for the winter, it sank to 2 francs also with two bottles.

The great part of the rural population, especially towards the south, lived largely on bread, soup and vegetables. Bread was that of the local cereal, where available wheat, but otherwise rye, and in the hills, maslin and even chestnut. Meat was usually salted, either pork or goose. The budget for a family of four at Gaillac (Tarn) was bread 280 francs, vegetables 50 francs, salt pork 75 francs and 40 francs to the butcher. The standard in the north was higher but everywhere there were deficiencies, particularly of meat and sugar.

Appendix IX

COMPARATIVE COSTS IN THE ENGLISH AND FRENCH WORSTED AND WOOL TRADES, 1876
(CHAPTER FIVE)

In their report to the Bradford Chamber of Commerce, Godwin and Illingworth presented the following table of wages in English currency. The formal rate of exchange at the date was 25.22 francs, but the Bradford delegates seem to have used a rate of their own, or at least varied it.

WAGES IN SHILLINGS AND PENCE

	French		*English*
	72 hours	56½ hours	56½ hours
Labourers	16.8	13.1	20.0
Ordinary mechanics	24.4	19.1	31.5–32.0
Superior ,,	31.0	24.4 Foremen	36.0
Sorters, men	23.9½	18.8	32.0
,, women	11.11	9.4	none
Washers, men	14.10	11.8	20.0
Backwashers, women	10.3	8.0	11.6–12.0
Cardfeeders	8.5	6.8	11.0
Drawers before combing	8.10	6.11	11.6
Combers	10.5	8.2	12.0
Combing, overlookers, men	36.0	28.3	30–40
Carding ,,	36.7	28.9	34.0
Drawers, men	26.4	20.8	30–33.0
,, women	9.9	7.8	11.6
Mule winders, men	26.4	20.8	30–33.0
Adult piecers, both sexes	12.4	9.8	13–18.6
Creelers, small piecers	6.10	5.4 (13–15 years)	8–9.0
Sorting per pack of 240 lbs.			
clean Port Philip	5.3		10.0
Sorting French, greasy	3.6		not used
Weaving			
Loom-minders	21.3	16.8	17.0
Beamers	17.10	14.0	
Sizers	39.0	34.9	
Twisting in	16.7	13.0	25.0
Warp putter, 100 looms	23.2	18.2	

	French		*English*
	72 hours	56½ hours	56½ hours
Overlooker, 50 looms	29.0	22.9 (45 looms)	36.0
Director, 360 looms	61.0	47.10⎫	60 at least
„ 500 „	68.8	53.10⎭	
Dyeing			
Black Dyer	152.6	114.4½	80–160.0
Colour „	76.3	57.2¼	100–200.0
First Process cleaning			
Foreman	61.0	45.9	40–50.0

Great care paid to dyeing and finishing in France and prices higher than in Bradford.

The delegates also noted that building land in and round Reims and Roubaix was considerably cheaper, up to 50%, than in and round Bradford. The cost of coal varied enormously according to quality and distance from the mine. Pit head coal was about 16.49 francs, or roughly 13 shillings, per metric ton. At Fourmies, the price in English currency was 13.9–17.7; at Saint-Quentin, 16.0–17.6; Reims 19.9–22.7; Amiens, 16.1. In all, they reckoned, French coal cost 17.0 on average compared to 9.4 in Bradford. Gas at Reims and Saint-Quentin was 6.9 per 1,000 cubic feet, with a discount of 25% after 10,000 feet. At Roubaix it was 6.3 and at Fourmies 3.4½ or the same as at Bradford. There was nowhere *octroi* on coal for industrial purposes, only for private consumption. The price of water was less than in England.

They concluded that in actual working French costs were only fractionally higher than in England, but that wages, except in weaving, gave the French a big advantage.

(*From the Foster Papers in the Library of the University of Leeds.*)

Appendix X

LIMITED LIABILITY (Chapter Five)

THE normal industrial or commercial undertaking was a partnership business, a *société en nom collectif,* in which each and every partner was personally responsible without limitation. Beyond this was the *société en commandite,* i.e. a firm with sleeping partners, who were only liable for the amount of their subscription, but were forbidden to take any part in the management. These two types were respectively 83% and 13% of all legally constituted *sociétés* in 1870.

The *société anonyme par actions,* the limited liability company, existed (under Sec. 29 of the Code de Commerce) from 1807, but had never shown a tendency to develop, largely owing to the need to obtain government authorisation. Under the law of May 23, 1863, this was waived for companies with a capital of less than 20 million francs, but required that one-third of the capital should be paid up. This was further amended by the law of July 24, 1867, which required authorisation in future only for insurance and tontine companies. Only the object of the association needed to be in the title, not the names of the direction. This law limited the liability to the amount of the share. The share unit for a company of less than 200,000 francs capital must be not less than 25 francs and fully paid up. Above this amount the share (until law of August 8, 1893, when it was reduced to 100 francs) had to be 500 francs, of which 25% must be paid up. These relaxations were slow to have effect. Up to the sixties, the *sociétés anonymes* were almost wholly confined to railway and insurance companies. Not more than ninety were registered between 1841 and 1865. In the next five years 126 companies appeared, and from that date this form of organisation became more general up to 976 in 1881, but with the Union générale crash of January 1882 there was an immediate decline.

A number of partnerships turned themselves into *sociétés en commandite par actions,* which while limiting the liability of the shareholder, gave him no control. A great number of the Pas-de-Calais mines were of this kind, and mostly partly paid up. The Courrières mine company, where there was a ghastly explosion with a thousand deaths in 1906, had its capital in shares of 1000 francs of which 300 only were paid up: these shares were divided into units of one-thirtieth in 1900; these were quoted on the Bourse at 2900 francs, i.e. the original 300 franc investment was now worth 87,000 francs. The Anzin values were of course infinitely more fantastic.

Appendix XI

THE SECRECY OF THE VOTE (Chapter Seven)

Although secrecy of the vote was laid down in the Organic Law of November 30, 1875, the vote was notoriously not so in the rural arrondissements, where in spite of the Decree of 1852 threatening bribers with up to two years imprisonment, bribery was normal. The agent wanted to know if the voter had gone back on his bargain. Further since it was laid down '*le bulletin est blanc et sans signe extérieur*', voting slips were frequently contested on the ground that the paper was ruled. Also by Law of April 5, 1884, '*sont nuls les bulletins dans lesquels les votants se font connaître*'. A polling clerk could make a dirty thumb mark on the paper and the vote could thus be challenged. There were no printed bulletins, owing to the large number of candidates.

Appendix XII

GAMBETTA AND LÉONIE LÉON
(Chapter Eight)

IN addition to his political difficulties, Gambetta had just emerged from an awkward contretemps. In 1869 he had been taken up by Jeanne-Marie Meersman, a woman of the half-world, eighteen years his senior. He had broken with her in 1872 when he met Léonie Léon. Meersman had a number of his papers and also a photograph on which he had written to the effect that for her he would sacrifice his country. In September 1877 she offered to sell these to Rouher. Gambetta's friends, hearing of this, tried to buy them, but failed. Finally, they were purchased by Madame Juliette Adam, and burned in her presence by Gambetta.

Léonie Léon, partly Creole, partly Jewish, was the same age as Gambetta. She had been the mistress of an imperial official by whom she had a son. She had known Gambetta from about 1868, but only became linked with him in 1872. She then wanted to marry him, but he refused. She remained his mistress. From 1879, Gambetta in turn wanted to marry her, but she now refused, at least until 1882 when she seems to have consented. The marriage had not taken place when he died. After his death, she lived in retirement until her death in 1906. Some hundred letters from Gambetta to her survive, but the major part of the correspondence was destroyed. It is impossible to estimate her influence on his political actions. From the surviving letters, it would appear to be very little, except that one gathers her part was to warn rather than encourage. It has been said that she pressed him towards an approach to Germany, but the evidence lends little support. It seems from Letter no. 403 that she was opposed to his becoming President of the Chamber, possibly the major error of his life.

NOTES AND REFERENCES

INTRODUCTION

1. Halévy, D., *Histoire d'une histoire*, 97.
2. Halévy, Ludovic, *Notes et Souvenirs*, 273.
3. Dauzat, *Le village et le paysan*, 137.
4. *J.O.*, *Assemblée Nationale*, Nov. 16–22, 1875, Annexe 3379.
5. Siegfried, *Tableau politique de la France de l'Ouest*, 101.
6. Taine, *Carnets de voyage*, 37 ff., 86, 164 ff.
7. Dumont, *Dépopulation et Civilisation*, 224–25.
8. Hamerton, *Round my House*, 228, 230–31.
9. Siegfried, *Géographie électorale de l'Ardèche*, 67; also Bodley, *France* (ed. of 1899), 567 fn.
10. Sarcy, in *Le Temps*, Aug. 28, 1882.
11. Siegfried, *op. cit.* (*Ouest*), Ch. XIII and XVI.
12. Thabault, *Mon Village*, 127.
13. Taine, *op. cit.*, 65.
14. de Woelmont, *Les marquis français*, 172.
15. Gramont, *Au temps des équipages*, 112.
16. *Id.*, 85–6.
17. de Tocqueville, *Souvenirs*, 211.
18. Quoted by Halévy, D., *La République des ducs*, 65–6.
19. Veuillot, *Les Odeurs de Paris*, in *Oeuvres diverses*, XI, 233.
20. Halévy, D., *Clemenceau*, 7.
21. Adam, *Mes souvenirs*, VI, 210.
22. Benoist, *Souvenirs*, II, 446.
23. September 16, 1870, printed in *RP*, July 15, 1939.
24. Benda, 'La jeunesse d'un clerc', in *NRF*, Aug. 1, 1936.
25. Duveau, *La vie ouvrière en France sous le Second Empire*, 414–15.

CHAPTER ONE

1. Haussonville, 'Souvenirs, II, 1869–71', in *RDM*, Nov. 1, 1923, 27.
2. Meaux, A. de, *Souvenirs politiques*, 4.
3. Gouault, *Comment la France est devenue républicaine*. 92.
4. Weiss, J. J., *Combat constitutionnel*, 75–6.
5. Duguit et Monnier, *Les Constitutions*, etc., 479.
6. *Id.*, 480.
7. *First DDF*, I, No. 1.
8. Thiers, *Discours parlementaires*, XIII, 91.

9. Bodley, *France*, 527.
10. Meaux, *op. cit.*, 10.
11. Audriffet-Pasquier, *La Maison de France*, 157–58.
12. Falloux, *Mémoires d'un royaliste*, II, 494.
13. Saint-Valry, *Souvenirs et réflexions politiques*, 248.
14. Thiers, quoted by Lajusan, *Revue d'histoire moderne*, VIII, 45, fn.
15. Veuillot, quoted by Halévy, *Fin des notables*, 52.
16. Falloux, *op. cit.*, II, 499.
17. Lacombe, *Journal politique*, January 19, 1872.
18. *Occupation et libération*, I, lxviii, Jany. 29, 1872.
19. *Id.*, 271, April 18, 1872.
20. *Id.*, I, cxli, June 1, 1872.
21. Monteilhet, *Les institutions militaires de la France*, 214.
22. Halévy et Pilliais, *Lettres de Gambetta*, No. 205, Sept. 5, 1874 and fn.
23. Freycinet, *Souvenirs*, I, 291.
24. Adam, Juliette, *Mes souvenirs*, V, 178.
25. Meaux, *op. cit.*, 243.
26. Gambetta, *Discours*, etc., III, 101 (Sept. 26, 1872).
27. Lajusan, *op. cit.*, 473, fn. 2.
28. Marion, M., *Histoire financière de la France*, etc., V, 574.
29. Halévy, L., *Trois dîners*, etc., 47. Also Lacombe, *op. cit.*, 155.
30. Gontaut-Biron, *Mon ambassade*, etc., 238–51.
31. Simon, J., *Le gouvernement de M. Thiers*, II, 385.
32. Quoted by Dreyfus, *La République de M. Thiers*, 185.
33. Charmes, *Questions historiques*, 329.
34. Audriffet-Pasquier, *op. cit.*, 97 ff.
35. *J.O.*, Annexe 1781, May 20, 1873.
36. Falloux, *op. cit.*, II, 540.
37. Halévy, D., *Le Courrier de M. Thiers*, 467.
38. Falloux, *op. cit.*, II, 542.

CHAPTER TWO

1. Daudet, E., *Souvenirs de la présidence du Maréchal de Macmahon*, 148.
2. Meaux, *Souvenirs politiques*, 150.
3. Broglie, *Mémoires*, II, 200–01.
4. *Id.*, 178–79.
5. Gontaut-Biron, *Mon ambassade*, etc., 356–57.
6. Lacombe, *Journal politique*, I, 187 (June 30, 1873).
7. Lajusan in *Rev. d'histoire moderne*, VIII, 425.
8. Broglie, *op. cit.*, 275–76.
9. Weiss, *Combat constitutionel*, 112.
10. Halévy et Pilliais, *Lettres de Gambetta*, No. 193, May 26, 1874, to Ranc.

11. *Revue bleue*, August 22, 1874.
12. Broglie, *op. cit.*, 328–31.
13. Cambon, P., *Correspondance*, I, 49, Dec. 5, 1874.
14. Broglie, *op. cit.*, 328–31.
15. Halévy et Pilliais, *op. cit.*, No. 232, Jany. 12, 1875, to Ranc.
16. Broglie, *op. cit.*, 343.
17. Saint-Valry, *Souvenirs et réflexions*, 88, March 30, 1875.
18. Broglie, *op. cit.*, 361–62.
19. This oversimplifies. The complexities can be seen in Paul Cambon's letter of Feby. 25 (which should be 26), *op. cit.*, 58–61.
20. Saint-Valry, *op. cit.*, 116 (April 26) and 121 (May 5).
21. Halévy, L., *Trois diners*, etc., 21; Goblet, 'Souvenirs de ma vie politique' in 136 *RPP* (1928), 373.

CHAPTER THREE

1. Glass, D. V., 'Reproduction Rates in France' in *Eugenics Review*, July 1945, 61.
2. Corbon, A., *Le secret du peuple de Paris*, 62–3.
3. Horace de Viel Castel.
4. *J.O., Chambre, Débuts*, May 12, 1891, col. 872.
5. Fraix de Figon, P. de, *Le métayage en Bourbonnais*, 67.
6. Siegfried, A., *Tableau des partis en France*, 31.
7. Chevalier, L., *La formation de la population parisienne au XIXe siècle*, 54 n.
8. Chevalier, *Id.*, Charts, 82–4.
9. *J.O., Assemblée Nationale*, Rapport Ducarre, November 18, 1875.
10. Baudrillart, M. H., *Les populations agricoles de la France*, III, 286 ff. and 318.
11. Baudrillart, *op. cit.*, I, 110–11 and 340.
12. Bourgin in *R.P.P.*, September 1898.

CHAPTER FOUR

Unless otherwise stated, figures employed are from the *Statistique agricole de la France (Algérie et Colonies)* . . . *Résultats généraux de l'Enquête décennale de 1882*, supplemented by similar Inquests of 1862, 1892 and 1929. It is referred to as either the Enquête or Inquest. The French agricultural statistics are similar to those of other countries in the nineteenth century in point of accuracy, except that the French complicate the deficiencies by an inability to add. The defects of the French reports have been sharply criticised by all commentators, notably by M. Augé-Laribé from his *Evolution de la France agricole* of 1912 to his *Politique agricole de la France, 1880–1940* of 1950. It is also fair to the editor of this and the *Enquête* of 1892, Eugène Tisserand, the Conseiller d'Etat for the Ministry of Agriculture, that he was much alive to the shortcomings of the report and that his commentary on it is full of warnings. It is however the only document of its kind, and if one does not take the figures *au pied de la chiffre*, one obtains a credible if impressionistic picture of the situation, which is not in its main lines contradicted by independent witnesses.

1. Sagnac, P., *La formation de la société moderne*, II, 13.
2. Bloch, Marc, *Les caractères originaux de l'histoire rurale française*, 223 ff. and 227. See also Bloch, M., 'La lutte pour l'individualisme agraire dans la France du XVIIIe siècle' in *Annales*, 1930, 329 ff. and 511 ff.
3. Lizerand, G., *Le régime rural de l'ancienne France*, 128–33.
4. Marion, M., *La vente des biens nationaux pendant la Révolution*, 228.
5. Royal Commission on Agriculture, 1882, C-3375, I, 64 (Druce's report); also Bateman, J., *The Great Landowners of Great Britain and Ireland* (which corrects the official 'Return of Landowners'), *passim*.
6. Lavergne, L. de, *Economie rurale de la France depuis 1789*, 360–61; *Encyclopédie des Bouches-du-Rhône*, VII, 15–39; Richardson, G. G., *The Corn and Cattle Producing Districts of France*, 285; Gramont, E. de, *Au temps des équipages*, 85.
7. 38 *AG* (1929), 387.
8. Richardson, *op. cit.*, 282.
9. Siegfried, André, *Tableau politique de la France de l'Ouest sous la Troisième République*, Ch. III, Sec. 1.
10. Augé-Laribé, M., *La politique agricole de la France de 1880 à 1940*, 87 and 89.
11. Quoted by A. de Foville, *Le morcellement*, 259.
12. Anon. (Léon Faucher), 'De la propriété en France' in *RDM*, 1836, 309–321.
13. Lefebvre, G., *Questions agraires au temps de la Terreur*, Ch. III, 103 ff.
14. Fraix de Figon, P. de, *Le métayage en Bourbonnais*, 67–75.
15. Baudrillart, M. H., *Les populations agricoles de la France*, III, 616.
16. See Garidel, B., in Larminat, L. de, *Le métayage dans le département de l'Allier*, Domaine A.
17. Marion, M., *op. cit.*, 418, fn. 1.
18. Demangeon, A., *La Picardie*, 351–52; Jenkin's report in *R.C. on Agriculture*, C-3375, IV, 99–100.
19. Augé-Laribé, *op. cit.*, 49.
20. Reinhard, M., 'Le Pays d'Auge' in 32 *AG* (1923), 33–40.
21. Siegfried, *op. cit.*, 12; Baudrillart, *op. cit.*, II, 187.
22. Marshall, *Rural Economy of Yorkshire*, I, 57.
23. Jenkins in *R.C. on Agriculture*, IV, 114.

24. Tricart, J., 'Asnières-sous-Bois, Yonne' in *Population*, 1949, 495 ff. and *J.O. Chambre, Débats*, Feby. 27, 1890 (Bourgeois and Faye).

25. Sentou, J., 'La révolution agricole dans le Narbonnais' in Faucher, D., *France méridionale et pays ibériques*, II, 651 ff.

26. Baudrillart, *op. cit.*, III, 610–14; *Statistique agricole*, 1892, 200.

27. Thabault, R., *Mon village*, 147.

28. Augé-Laribé, *op. cit.*, 56–7.

29. Large, E. C., *The Advance of the Fungi*, Ch. XI.

30. Bateman, A. E., 'A Note on the Statistics of Wine Production in France', in *JRSS*, 1883, 113 ff.

31. Isnard, H., 'Vignes et colonisation en Algérie, 1880–1947' in *Annales*, 1947, 288 ff.

32. Baudrillart, *op. cit.*, III, 286 and 318.

33. Baudrillart, *op. cit.*, III, 549–50.

34. Thabault, *op. cit.*, 151.

35. Foville, A. de, *op. cit.*, App. XIII, 261.

36. Cambiaire, A. de, *L'autoconsommation en France*, 163 ff.

37. Manry, A. G., 'En Limagne entre 1865 et 1905' in *Annales*, 1950, 114 ff.

38. Foville, *op. cit.*, 137.

39. Siegfried, André, *Tableau des partis en France*, 34.

40. Bourgin in *RPP*, September 1898.

41. Siegfried, André, *Géographie électorale de l'Ardèche sous la Troisième République*, 29–30.

CHAPTER FIVE

1. Dunham, A. L., *La révolution industrielle en France (1815–48)*, Ch. VIII, and p. 98.

2. Dunham, *op. cit.*, Chs. II and III.

3. Blanchard, Marcel, 'La politique ferroviare du Second Empire' in *Annales*, 1934, 529 ff., and 'Aux origines de nos chemins de fer', *Annales*, 1938, 97 ff.

4. Girard, Louis, *La politique des Travaux Publics du Second Empire*, 51.

5. Girard, *op. cit.*, Part II, Ch. I.

6. Girard, *op. cit.*, Part II, Ch. III.

7. Corbon, A., *Le secret du peuple de Paris*, 209–10.

8. Girard, *op. cit.*, 100–16.

9. Girard, *op. cit.*, 163, fn. 4 and 5.

10. Labasse, Jean, *Les capitaux et la région*, 25.

11. Labasse, *op. cit.*, 32.

12. Labasse, *op. cit.*, 28.

13. Labasse, *op. cit.*, 30.

14. Bouvier, Jean, 'Les réflexes sociaux des milieux d'affaires' in *Revue historique*, 1953, 297, fn. 4.

15. Girard, *op. cit.*, 241 ff. and Ashley, Percy, *Modern Tariff History*, 298–312.

16. Dunham, A. L., *The Anglo-French Treaty of Commerce of 1860*, 150.

17. Rouff, Marcel, *Les mines de charbon en France au XVIIIe siècle*, 368–69, and Monniot, S., 'Le rôle de la forêt' in *Etudes sur ... l'Ancien Régime*, 173–82.

18. Block, Maurice, *Dictionnaire de l'administration française* under 'Mines'.

19. Reybaud, Louis, *Le Fer et la Houille*, 30–2; Chevalier, Jean, *Le Creusot*, Ch. I; Perrin, M., 'Le Creusot' in 43 *AG*, 1934.

20. Le Play, F., *Les ouvriers européens*, V, 313–19.

21. Dunham, A. L., *Révolution industrielle*, 352–55.

22. Perrin, *loc. cit.*; Duveau, Georges, *La vie ouvrière sous le Second Empire*, 157–58 and 158, fn. 2.

23. Institut national de la statistique, *Résumé rétrospectif* (1946), 174.

24. Girard, *op. cit.*, 145.

25. *Résumé rétrospectif*, 106.

26. Comité des Forges, *La sidérurgie française*, I, 171.

27. Vacher, A., 'Montluçon' in 13 *AG*, 1904, 121–37.

28. Levasseur, E., *Questions ouvrières*, etc., 41 and n.; *Sidérurgie*, I, 171; Perrin, M., 'Le Bassin houiller de la Loire' in 31 *AG*, 1930, 359–75; *Journal of the Iron and Steel Institute*, 1888, II, 43; Burn, D. L., *Economic History of Steelmaking*, 52–4.

29. Levasseur, *op. cit.*, 40 and fn.; *Sidérurgie*, 199.

30. Levasseur, *op. cit.*, 41–2.

31. Emerit, Marcel, *Les Saint-Simoniens en Algérie*, 184, and 'La Compagnie des Minerais de Fer magnétique de Mokta-el-Hadid' in *RPP*, vol. 167, (1936), 584 ff.

32. *Sidérurgie*, 145–49; Sömme, Axel, *La Lorraine métallurgique*, 6–7.

33. Picard, Alfred, *Le bilan d'un siècle, 1801–1900*, IV, 87.

34. Bulard, Marcel, 'L'industrie du fer dans la Haute-Marne' in 13 *AG*, 1904.

35. *Sidérurgie*, 171; Sömme, Axel, *loc. cit.*

36. Bulard, *loc. cit.*

37. Launay, Louis, *De Wendel*,

38. Du Fou, Raoul, *Le mouvement de concentration de la sidérurgie*, 22–3, 26.

39. *Sidérurgie*, 176.

40. *Encyclopédie des Bouches-du-Rhône*, VIII, 394 ff.

41. Haber, L. F., *The Chemical Industry during the Nineteenth Century*, 41 ff.

42. Haber, *op. cit.*, 42.

43. Haber, *op. cit.*, 89 and 109.

44. Haber, *op. cit.*, 112.

45. Haber, *op. cit.*, 114.

46. Morazé, P., 'The Treaty of 1860 and the Industry of the Department of the North' in 10 *Eco. Hist. Rev.*, (1940), 18–28.

47. *Enquête parlementaire sur le régime économique*, I, *Industries textiles*, May 23, 1870, quoted by Dunham, *Anglo-French Treaty*, 208 fn.

48. Delaisi, F., *Le Pétrole*, 139–40.

49. Picard, A., *op. cit.*, IV, 207.

50. Baudrillart, *op. cit.*, III, 538–43 and 549–50; *Statistique de la France*, Nouvelle Série, Tome VIII, 1878.

51. Henry Illingworth's notebook is in the collection of papers from John Foster & Son of Queensbury, Halifax, now in the library of the University of Leeds. (Cf. Appendix IX.) See also *R.C. on the Depression of Trade and Industry*, 1886, evidence of Sir Jacob Behrens, Bousfield and H. Mitchell. Also Sigsworth, E. M., *Black Dyke Mills*, passim.

52. Bergner in annual report of the Commerce Commission, 1909, 326.

53. Dunham, *Anglo-French Treaty*, 186 ff.

54. *Enquête parlementaire sur le régime économique*, 1870, I, 358.

55. Sion, J., *Les paysans de la Normandie orientale*, 334.

56. Levasseur, *op. cit.*, 121, fn. 3.

57. Demangeon, A., *La Picardie*, etc.

58. Combe, J., 'Thiers et la vallée industrielle de la Durolle' in 31 *AG* (1922), 360–65.

59. Baudrillart, *op. cit.*, III.

60. Meynier, A., 'Trois centres de ganterie' in 43 *AG* (1934).

61. Péguy, C., from *L'argent* in Oeuvres, III, 389.

62. Dunham, *Anglo-French Treaty*, Chs. XV and XVI.

63. Dunham, *op. cit.*, 207.

64. Direction des Douanes, *Tableau générale du Commerce de la France* (annual).

CHAPTER SIX

1. Maurain, J., *La politique ecclésiastique du Second Empire*, etc., 453.

2. *Id.*, 455.

3. Bettenson, *Documents of the Christian Church*, 381.

4. Maurain, *op. cit.*, 875, fn. 1.

5. *Id.*, 710.

6. Block, M., *Statistique de la France*, ed. 1875, I, 246: Lizerand, G., *Vergigny*, 72.

7. *Enquête parlementaire sur les conditions du travail*, 1872 (*J.O.*, 1875) sub Eure and Ille-et-Vilaine.

8. Illingworth notebook (cf. p. 392).

9. Simon, J., *Le gouvernement de M. Thiers*, II, 80 ff.

10. Lecanuet, *L'Eglise de France sous la Troisième République*, I, 288 ff.

11. Baudrillart, *Les populations agricoles*, III, 316.

12. See Le Bras, *Etudes de sociologie religieuse*; Boulard, abbé F. in *Rencontres*, No. 16; Fauvet and Mendras, *Les paysans et la politique dans la France contemporaine.*

13. Maurain, *op. cit.*, 310, prefectorial report.

CHAPTER SEVEN

1. Thibaudet, *Les idées politiques de France*, 80.

2. Halévy et Pilliais, *op. cit.*, No. 267, Feby. 8, 1876.

3. Daudet, E., *Souvenirs*, etc., 157.

4. *Id.*, 158 fn.

5. Gambetta, *Discours*, etc., V, 205-07.

6. Cambon, P., *Correspondance*, I, 71, Feby. 25, 1876.

7. Adam, J., *Mes Souvenirs*, VI, 367.

8. Ferry, *Discours*, II, 206-332.

8a. Hanotaux, *Histoire de la Troisième République*, III, 646; Cambon, *op. cit.*, I, 73; Freycinet, *Souvenirs*, I, 336-52.

9. Simon, J., *Au soir de ma journée*, 238.

10. Ferry, *op. cit.*, 239.

11. Cambon, *op. cit.*, I, 80, April 22, 1877.

12. Daudet, *op. cit.*, 156 fn.

13. Simon, *op. cit.*, 242.

14. Meaux, *Souvenirs politiques*, 311.

15. Seché, *Jules Simon*, 239-40.

16. Simon, *op. cit.*, 249.

17. Daudet, *op. cit.*, 166 fn.

18. *Id.*, 165 fn.

19. Meaux, *op. cit.*, 315.

20. Saint-Valry, *Souvenirs*, etc., 275.

21. *Id.*, 198.

22. Caillaux, J., *Mes mémoires*, I, 62.

23. Carter, H., 'The Metz Interview of May 9, 1877' in *American Hist. Review*, and Hohenlohe, *Memoirs*, Sept. 9, 1877.

24. Meaux, *op. cit.*, 393-94.

25. Valon, Comtesse de, *Souvenirs de sa vie*, 345.

27. Marcère, *De la fin de l'Assemblée Nationale au 16 mai 1877*, 227-30; Halévy, D., *La république des ducs*, 325.

26. Hohenlohe, *op. cit.*, Feby. 10, 1880.

28. Daudet, *op. cit.*, 163 f.n.; Pierre, E., *Traité de droit politique et parlementaire*, Supplement, 86.

29. Bonnard, R., 'De l'homogénéité et de la solidarité ministérielles à propos du ministère Barthou' in *Rev. du Droit Public*, July–Sept. 1913.

CHAPTER EIGHT

1. January 8, 1878 (*Discours*, VIII, 4).
2. Adam, *Souvenirs*, VII, 141–45, Feby. 8, 1878.
3. *Id.*, 138, Feby. 1, 1878.
4. *Id.*, 229, Sept. 4, 1878.
5. Gambetta, *Discours*, VIII, 243.
6. Cambon, *Correspondance*, I, 89, Oct. 22, 1878.
7. Adam, *op. cit.*, VII, 179; and Freycinet, *Souvenirs*, II, 32.
8. *First DDF.* II, No. 332, July 21, 1878.
9. *Id.*, No. 334, July 24, 1878.
10. Newton, *Lord Lyons*, Letter of July 20, 1878.
11. *First DDF.* II, No. 342, Sept. 7, 1878.
12. *Id.*, No. 352, Oct. 13, 1878.
13. Halévy et Pilliais, *Lettres de Gambetta*, No. 401, to Léonie Léon, Jany. 19, 1879.
14. Daudet, *Souvenirs*, 209.
15. Halévy et Pilliais, *op. cit.*, No. 402, Jany. 20, 1879.
16. Adam, *op. cit.*, VII, 294–96.
17. Cambon, *op. cit.*, I, 96, Feby. 1, 1879.
18. Halévy, et Pilliais, *op. cit.* No. 403, to Léonie Léon, Jany. 31, 1879.
19. Halévy, L., *Trois dîners, etc.*, 36.
20. Freycinet, *op. cit.*, II, 86–96.

CHAPTER NINE

1. Blum, Léon, 'L'Article 7', in *Revue Blanche*, April 1, 1900, reprinted in his *Oeuvre*, I. 375.
2. Freycinet, *Souvenirs*, II. 124–25.
3. Tournier, J., *Le Cardinal Lavigerie et son action politique*, 55.
4. Tournier, *op. cit.*, 73.
5. Freycinet, *op. cit.*, 133–40.
6. Tournier, *op. cit.*, 91.
7. Freycinet, *op. cit.*, 150–53.
8. Tournier, *op. cit.*, 105.
9. Tournier, *op. cit.*, 109.
10. Cambon, P., *Correspondance*, I, 124–32.
11. *J. O. Chambre*, November 11, 1880.
12. Ferry, J., *Lettres*, November 10, 1880, 306–07.
13. Cambon, *op. cit.*, I, 376, June 25, 1894.

CHAPTER TEN

1. Raymond, A., 'Les tentatives anglaises de pénétration économique en Tunisie, 1856–77' in 214 *R. Hist.*, 1955, 48–67 and Roberts, S. H., *History of French Colonial Policy*, Ch. VII.
2. Ferry, J., *Discours*, IV, 532 ff.
3. Halévy, L., *Trois dîners, etc.*, 26.
4. Dietz, J., 'Jules Ferry et la tradition républicaine' in 135 *RPP*, Oct. 1935, 100–01.
5. Weiss, J. J., in *RB*, Oct. 22, 1881, reprinted in *Combat constitutionnel*, 163 ff.
6. Vogüé, E. M. de, *Journal*, 254.
7. *J. O.*, *Chambre*, July 27, 1881, 1786 ff.
8. Gambetta, *Discours etc.*, IX, 430 ff.
9. Dietz, *loc. cit.*,
10. Ferry, J., *Lettres*, 310–15 (Sept. 1881).
11. Reinach, J., *Le ministère Gambetta*, Ch. III; Michel, G., *Léon Say, sa vie, ses oeuvres*, 364; Freycinet, C. de, *Souvenirs*, II, 190–98.
12. Marcellin-Pellet, E. A., 'Souvenirs sur Gambetta' in *R. de France*, Nov. 15, 1927.
13. Reinach, J., *Le ministère Gambetta*, 141–42 and 149 ff.
14. Cambon, P., *Correspondance*, I, 150, Jany. 4, 1880.
15. Marion, M., *Histoire financière de la France depuis 1715*, VI, 14.
16. *Economiste français*, July 30, 1882, 129.
17. *Id.*, July 1881–April 1882; also Say, Léon, *Les Finances de la France*, III.
18. *Id.*, Sept. 20, 1884.
19. *Id.*, July 30, 1882.
20. Claveau, A., *Souvenirs politiques*, etc., II, 402.
21. Michel, G., *op. cit.*, 365, fn. 2.

CHAPTER ELEVEN

1. Soulier, A., *L'instabilité ministérielle sous la Troisième République 1871–1938*, 280.
2. Cambon, P., *Correspondance*, I, 335, June 8, 1892 on Ribot.
3. Leveau, R., '*Enseignement et Vulgarisation agricoles*', in Fauvet, J. and Mendras, H., *Les paysans et la politique*, etc., 269.
4. Gouault, J., *Comment la France est devenue républicaine*, 134–35.
5. Duverger, M., *L'influence des systèmes electorales sur la vie politique*, 318–320.
6. Richardson, G. G., *The Corn and Cattle producing Districts of France*, 29.
7. Meaux, Vicomte A. de, *Souvenirs politiques*, 296; Saint-Aulaire, Comte de, *Confession d'un vieux diplomate*, 768.

CHAPTER TWELVE

1. Michel, G., *Léon Say, sa vie, ses oeuvres*, 367.
2. Freycinet, *Souvenirs*, II, Ch. VII.
3. *J. O.*, *Chambre*, July 20, 1882.
4. Ferry, J., *Lettres*, Aug. 1, 1882, 320–21.
5. Newton, Lord, *Lord Lyons*, 473.
6. Marion, *Histoire financière*, etc., VI, 44–8.
7. Ferry, *op. cit.*, Jany. 8, 1883, 330–31; Charmes, Francis, quoted by Jules Clarétie in his *Journal*, Nov. 1, 1906.
8. Halévy, L., *Carnets*, Jany. 6, 1883, in *RDM*, 1938, XLIII, 603–04.

CHAPTER THIRTEEN

1. Martet, J., *Clemenceau peint par lui-même*, 147–48.
2. Cf. Direction générale des Douanes. *Tableau général du commerce de la France.*
3. Marion, M., *Histoire financière*, VI, 61.
4. Marion, *op. cit.*, 47–8.
5. Drumont, E., *La fin d'un monde*, 268.
6. Ferry, *Discours*, etc.
7. Freycinet, *Souvenirs*, II, 67.
8. Colson, C., 'Les chemins de fer et le budget' in *RDM*, Dec. 15, 1895, 859 ff.; Marion, *op. cit.*, 52 ff.
9. Marion, *op. cit.*, 57.
10. Dietz, Jean, 'Jules Ferry: la révision de la constitution et le scrutin de liste' in 166–167 *RPP*, 1936, March and April.

CHAPTER FOURTEEN

1. Deschamps, Léon, *Histoire de la question coloniale*, 350.
2. Roberts, Stephen H., *History of French Colonial Policy, 1870–1925*, Chs. I–IV.
3. Roberts, *op. cit.*, Ch. VI; and Wahl, M., *L'Algérie*, 254 ff.
4. Halévy, Daniel, *Visites aux paysans du Centre*, 120.
5. Isnard, H., 'Vigne et colonisation en Algérie', in *Annales*, 1947, 290.
6. Roberts, *op. cit.*, 183 ff.
7. Roberts, *op. cit.*, 302 ff.
8. Brunel, J. M., *Le général Faidherbe*, 140.
9. Delavignette, R. and Julien, C. A., *Les constructeurs de la France d'Outremer*, 237; Monteil, Col. P. L., 'Contribution d'un vétéran à l'histoire coloniale' in *RP*, Sept. 1, 1923.

10. Ferry, *Discours*, V, 555.
11. Ferry, *op. cit.*, V, 172–225 (July 28, 1885).
12. Roberts, *op. cit.*, 19.
13. Bac, F., *Intimités de la Troisième République*, I, 455.
14. Taylor, A. J. P., *Bismarck*, 240.
15. *First DDF*, V, No.
16. Rambaud, A., *Jules Ferry*, Chaps. XXII–XXIV. Also Thompson, Virginia, *French Indo-China*.
17. Monteil, *loc. cit.*

CHAPTER FIFTEEN

1. Goblet, René, 'Souvenirs de ma vie politique', VI, in 138 *RPP*, Jany. 1939, 367.
2. Dansette, A., *Histoire religieuse de la France contemporaine*, II, 111–12.
3. *Encyclopédie des Bouches-du-Rhône*, X, 473–75.
4. Blum, Léon, *Nouvelles conversations avec Eckermann* in *L'oeuvre de Léon Blum*, I, 232.

CHAPTER SIXTEEN

The most competent book on these years is Adrien Dansette's *Le Boulangisme*, which should be read with his *L'Affaire Wilson et la chute du Président Grévy*. In addition may be read with advantage Paul Cambon's *Correspondance*, 1, 214–89, and Goblet's 'Souvenirs de ma vie politique', in the *Revue politique et parlementaire*, vols. 137, 138, 139, 141.

CHAPTER SEVENTEEN

As for Chapter Sixteen, the reader is referred to Dansette's *Le Boulangisme* and *L'Affaire Wilson et la chute du President Grévy*.

1. Halévy, L., *Carnets*, I, 187–88.
2. Marion, M., *Histoire financière*, etc., VI, 97–9. Owing to the political crisis, the conversion was a partial failure.
3. Goblet, René, 'Souvenirs de ma vie politique' in 141 *RPP* (Nov. 1929).
4. Siegfried, A., *Tableau politique de la France de l'Ouest*, 102.
5. Siegfried, A., 'Une crise ministérielle en 1887, d'après le journal de mon père' [Jules Siegfried] in 11 *Hommes et Mondes* (1950), 484–96.
6. Bodley, *France*, 374 and fn.

CHAPTER EIGHTEEN

In the context of the French people, the ralliement, like so many doctrinal quarrels, is of small importance in the long run. Its importance in the short is scarcely more; the defeat of the Freycinet government — which amounted to little more than a change in the name of the Prime Minister, since Freycinet remained at the War Office. The only thing that emerges is that in political quarrels, religion counts for little: it is only powerful in terms of centuries — '*in saecula saeculorum.*'

As earlier, the main general history is Dansette's; in more or perhaps richer detail, Lecanuet's volumes. Tournier's life of Cardinal Lavigerie probably gives the best detail of the attempted transaction. Freycinet's *Souvenirs* are even more obscure than usual.

CHAPTER NINETEEN

In addition to the books discussed on p. 321, the history of the canal itself is given in Edger-Bonnet, G., *Le Canal de Panama*, while a vivid attack on the company before the breaking of the scandal is to be read in Drumont's *La dernière bataille* (1890). A judicious examination of the finances of the company is Marlio, L., *La véritable histoire de Panama.*

1. Judet, E., *Le véritable Clemenceau*, 196–200.
2. Dansette, *op. cit.*, prints most of Delahaye's speech *in extenso*.
3. Barrès, *Leurs Figures*, Appendix.
4. Marion, M., *Histoire financière*, etc., VI, 152 and fn. 2.
5. Judet, *op. cit.*, 159.
6. *J. O.*, *Chambre, Débats*, Feby. 9.,
7. Marlio, L., *La véritable histoire de Panama.*

CHAPTER TWENTY

The books consulted include:
Dolléans, E., *Histoire du mouvement ouvrier*, I (1830–71), and II (1871–1936).
Duveau, G., *La vie ouvrière en France sous le Second Empire.*
Louis, P., *Histoire du Socialisme en France.*
Laroque, P., *Les rapports entre patrons et ouvriers.*
Lecanuet, P., *La Fin du Pontificat de Pie IX*, Chapter 10.
Bouglé, C., *Socialismes français.*
Pirou, G., *Les doctrines économiques en France.*
Humbert, S., *Les 'Possibilistes'.*
Zévaès, A., *De la semaine sanglante au Congrès de Marseille.*
Zévaès, A., *Les 'Guesdistes'.*
Zévaès, A., 'Jules Guesde et Jean Jaurès' in *RP* (1936), July 1.

CHAPTER TWENTY-ONE

1. 'La politique internationale des partis en France' in *L'Européen*, Dec. 7, 1901, reprinted in *Etudes de politique et d'histoire*,

2. Cambon, *Correspondance*, II, 17, Jany. 13, 1899.
3. Goblet, R., 'Souvenirs, etc.' in 137 *RPP* (1928), 345.
4. Cambon, *op. cit.*, I, 355, June 8, 1892.
5. *First DDF*, VIII, No. 165, Aug. 15/27, 1890.
6. Daudet, E., *Histoire diplomatique de l'alliance franco-russe, 1873–93*, 261.
7. Quoted by Contamine, *La Revanche*, 50.
8. *First DDF*, VI bis, No. 46, June 23, 1887.
9. *Id.*, VII, App. III, June 6, 1888.
10. *Id.*, VIII, No. 504, August 19, 1891.
11. All quoted by Michon, *L'alliance franco-russe*, Ch. IV.
12. Cambon, *op. cit.*, I, 423, Dec. 16, 1896.
13. *First DDF*, VIII, No. 485, Aug. 11, 1891.
14. On the preliminaries to Fashoda, P. Renouvin, 'Les origines de l'expédition de Fachoda' in 200 *Rev. historique* (1948), 180 ff., and Taylor, A. J. P., 'Prelude to Fashoda' in *EHR*, 1948, reprinted in *Rumours of War*, 81 ff.

Beyond the works quoted above, see Taylor, A. J. P., *Struggle for Mastery*, etc.; Langer, W. L., *The Franco-Russian Alliance, 1890–94*; Cromer, Lord, *Egypt*; Robinson, R. and Gallagher, J., *Africa and the Victorians*.

CHAPTER TWENTY-TWO

1. Phelps Brown and Hopkins, 'The Course of Wage-Rates in Five Countries, 1860–1939' in *Oxford Economic Papers*, II, (1950), 273.
2. *Evolution de la population active en France*, etc. in *Etudes et Conjunctures*, May–June 1953.
3. *Résumé rétrospectif*, (1946), 58 and 68.
4. Ferry, *Discours*, VI, 196.
5. *Id.*, VI, 196 ff.
6. Comité des Forges, *Sidérurgie, Tableaux statistiques*, 104 and 199.
7. Du Fou, *Le mouvement de concentration dans la sidérurgie lorraine*, 115.
8. Vignes, M., 'Le bassin de Briey et la politique de ses entreprises sidérurgiques' (Second article) in 27 *Rev. d'économie pol.*, (1913), 314. Also *Aciéries de Longwy, 1880–1930*.
9. *Annales des Mines*, Ser. X, Vol. I, 313–16.
10. Augé-Laribé, *Politique agricole*, 233.
11. Zolla, D., *Crise agricole*, 205; Cambiaire, A. de, *L'autoconsommation*, 170–71.
12. Jenkins, in *R.C. on Agriculture*, C-3375, IV, 71.
13. Ferry, *op. cit.*, VI, 253 (Oct. 18, 1884).
14. Augé-Laribé, *op. cit.*, 237.
15. *Id.*, Part I, Ch. V, 4; Golob, E. O., *The Méline Tariff*, Ch. VI.
16. *Id.*, 218.

17. Roberts, S. H., *History of French Colonial Policy*, 48.
18. *Encyclopédie des Bouches-du-Rhône*, VIII, 217.
19. Arqué, P., *Géographie du Midi Aquitain*, 113–14; Lamartine Yates, *Food Production*, 266–67.
20. Roberts, *op. cit.*, 502–09 and 516–30.

CHAPTER TWENTY-THREE

1. *Figaro*, April 15/16, 1873, quoted by Halévy, D., *Fin des notables*, 237 fn.
2. Simon, J., *Le Gouvernement de M. Thiers*, II, 402.
3. Tardieu, A., *La révolution à refaire*, II, 52.
4. Cambon, *Correspondance*, I, 372, May 24, 1894.
5. Chevalier, L., *La formation de la population parisienne*, etc., 55, fn. 1.
6. White, H. D., *The French International Accounts*, 279.
7. Levasseur, E., article in 8 *RPP* (1896).
8. White, *op. cit.*, 301.
9. Leroy-Beaulieu, P., 'De la population rurale, etc.' in *Economiste français*, Dec. 6, 1884.
10. Legrand-Girarde, Gen., *Un quart de siècle au service de la France*, 200.
11. Neymarck, A., *Finances contemporains*, I, 336.
12. Vogüé, E. M. de, *Les morts qui parlent*, 89.

APPENDIX III TO CHAPTER ONE

1. The arrondissement was created by the law of December 22, 1789: it was suppressed in 1795 but revived in 1800. The sous-préfet was the successor to the delegate of the intendant. He was assisted by an elected council, renewed by half every three years. The council composed of one member from each canton, distributes the taxes between the communes. The canton, also created by the law of 1789, is a division of an arrondissement and consists of several communes. It is the district of a justice of the peace and a financial district with a tax-collector.
2. L. Halévy, *Carnets*, II, 79.
3. *Gouvernement de M. Thiers*, II, 241.
4. Bodley, *France*, 371–72.
5. Goncourt, *Journal*, Nov. 3, 1885.
6. Siegfried, *Ouest*, 287–88 (and see also 404–06 on the political limitations of the préfet's power). In 1882 Ernest Charles Hendlé (1844–1900), then préfet of Saône-et-Loire, intervened in a strike at Montceau-les-Mines, largely stimulated by anarchists, which turned to anti-religious riots. After they were over, Hendlé told Schneider that if he did not re-employ

the strikers, he would stop all litigation in which Le Creusot had an
interest, at the Conseil de Préfecture (Anon. 'La République en 1883',
RDM, February 1, 1883, p. 565, fn. 1). He also played an active part on
behalf of the moderate Republicans of Seine-inférieure. Cf. also Halévy,
D., *La fin des notables*, 97 fn.
7. 'Décentralisateurs et Fédéralistes' in *Questions politiques*,

BIBLIOGRAPHY

ABBREVIATIONS

AG:	Annales de Géographie
Annales:	Annales d'Histoire économique et sociale, 1928–38; Annales d'Histoire sociale, 1939–41; Mélanges d'Histoire sociale, 1942–45; Annales, Economies-Sociétés-Civilisations, 1946–
First DDF:	Documents diplomatiques français; First Series, 1871–1900
JRSS:	Journal of the Royal Statistical Society
JO:	Journal Officiel (Sénat, Chambre, Debats, Documents)
NRF:	Nouvelle Revue Française
RB:	Revue politique et littéraire (Revue bleue)
RDM:	Revue des Deux Mondes
RF:	Revue de France
R.hist.:	Revue historique
RP:	Revue de Paris
RPP:	Revue politique et parlementaire

OFFICIAL PUBLICATIONS, BOOKS OF REFERENCE, ETC.

Unless otherwise stated, the place of all French publications is Paris, of English London.

Direction générale des Douanes. *Tableau général du commerce de la France* (annual).

Enquête parlementaire sur le régime économique; Industries textiles (1870), 1876.

Enquête parlementaire sur les conditions du travail en France, JO, 16–22 Nov., 1875, Annexe 3379.

Ministère des Affaires etrangères. *Documents diplomatiques francais, 1e serie.*

Ministère de l'Intérieur, *Dénombrement de la population*, 1881.

Ministère de l'Agriculture, *Statistique agricole de la France...Résultats généraux de l'Enquête décennale de 1882*, 1887. (Similar *enquêtes* held in 1862, 1892 and 1929. The 1862 was republished with that of 1882. 1892 was published in 1897, and 1929 in 1934).

Statistique de la France, Nouvelle série (annually from 1871).

Direction de la Statistique générale. *Annuaire statistique, Résumé rétrospectif* (annual).

Royal Commission on Agriculture, Final Report, 1882, C-3309, and reports of Assistant Commissioners, on Southern District of England (Druce), C-3375, I, and on Denmark and Northern France (Jenkins), C-3375, IV.

Royal Commission on the Depression in Trade and Industry, 1886, C-4621, 4715, 4797, 4893.

Balteau, J. etc. *Dictionnaire de biographie française* (in progress).

Robert, A., and Cougny, G. *Dictionnaire des parlementaires français depuis le premier mai, 1789 jusqu'au premier mai, 1889*, 1889–93.

Vapereau, G. *Dictionnaire universel des contemporains*, 4, 5 and 6 eds.

Duguit, L., Monnier, H., and Bonnard, R., *Les constitutions et les principales lois politiques de la France depuis 1789.*

Duvergier, J. B. *Collection des lois, décrets, ordonnances, réglements et avis du Conseil d'Etat* (annual since 1788).

Block, Maurice, *Dictionnaire de l'administration française*, 2v. 5ème ed. 1905.

——, *Statistique de la France*, 2v., 1870; 2ème ed., 1875.

Daniel, André (*ps.* André Lebon), *L'année politique* (1874–1905 annual).

GENERAL PUBLICATIONS

(Anon.) *Aciéries de Longwy, 1880–1930*, Mulhouse-Dornach, 1930.

Adam, Juliette, *Mes souvenirs*, Vols. 5, 6 and 7, 1904–08.

Ariès, P., *Histoire des populations françaises et leurs attitudes devant la vie depuis le XVIIIe siècle*, 1948.

Arqué, P., *Géographie du Midi Aquitain*, 1939.

Ashley, P., *Modern Tariff History*, 1904.

Audriffet-Pasquier, le duc d', *La maison de France et l'Assemblée nationale, Souvenirs*, 1938.

Auge-Laribé, M., *L'évolution de la France agricole*, 1912.

——, *La politique agricole de la France de 1880 à 1940*, 1950.

Bac, Ferdinand, *Intimités de la 3ème République*, 3v., 1935.

Barnard, A., *The Australian Wool Market, 1840–1900*, Melbourne, 1958.

Barrès, M., *Les déracinés*, 1897.

——, *L'appel au soldat*, 1899.

——, *Leurs figures*, 1902.

Bateman, J., *The Great Landowners of Great Britain and Ireland*, 1883.

Baudrillart, M. H., *Les populations agricoles de la France*, 3v. I, *La Normandie*, 1880; II, *Maine, Anjou, Touraine, Poitou, Flandre, Artois, Picardie, Ile-de-France*, 1888; III, *Les populations du Midi*, 1893.

Bell, I. Lowthian, *The Principles of the Manufacture of Iron and Steel*, 1884.

Benoist, Charles, *Souvenirs*, 3v. 1932–33.

Benoit, Fernand, *Histoire de l'outillage rural et artisanal*, 1947.

Bernanos, G., *La grande peur des bien-pensants* (Drumont), 1931.

Bernard, P., *Economie et sociologie de la Seine-et-Marne, 1850–1950*, 1953.

Bettenson, Henry, *Documents of the Christian Church*, Oxford, 1943.

Bloch, Marc, *Les caractères originaux de l'histoire rurale française*, 1931.

Blum, Léon, *L'oeuvre de*, 2v., 1954.

Bodley, J. E. C., *France*, 2nd ed., 1899.

Bonnard, R. *Les réglements des Assemblées législatives de la France depuis 1789, Notes historiques et textes*, 1926.

Bosq, P., *Nos chers souverains*, 1898.

——, *Souvenirs de l'Assemblée nationale*, 1908.

Bouglé, C., *Socialismes français*, 1932.

Boulard, Abbé F., *Problèmes missionaires de la France rurale*, Rencontres 16, 1945.

Brogan, D. W., *The Development of Modern France, 1870–1940*, 1940.

Broglie, J. V. A., duc de, *Mémoires*, 2v., 1938–41.

Brunel, J. M., *Le général Faidherbe*, 1890.

Burn, D. L., *The Economic History of Steelmaking, 1867–1939*, Cambridge, 1940.

Byrnes, R. F., *Anti-semitism in Modern France*, New Brunswick, 1950.

Caillaux, Joseph, *Mes mémoires*, 3v., 1942–47.

Cambiaire, A. de, *L'autoconsommation agricole en France*, 1953.

Cambon, Paul, *Correspondance, 1870–1924*, 3v., 1940–46.

Cassin, René, and others, *Le Conseil d'Etat, livre jubiliaire, 4 Nivôse An VIII–24 decembre, 1949*, 1952.

Chapman, Brian, *The Prefects and Provincial France*, London, 1955.

Chantriot, E., *La Champagne*, 1906.

Charmes, Francis, *Questions historiques*,

Chevalier, Jean, *Le Creusot*, 1946.

Chevalier, Louis, *La formation de la population parisienne au XIXe siècle*, 1950.

Clapham, J. H., *The Economic Development of France and Germany, 1815–1914*, Cambridge, ed. of 1936.

Claveau, A., *Souvenirs politiques et parlementaires d'un témoin, II, Le principat de M. Thiers, 1871–73*, 1914.

Clermont-Tonnerre, E. duchesse de, (E. Gramont) *Mémoires, I, Au temps des équipages*, 1928; II, *Les marronniers en fleur*, 1929.

Comité des Forges de France, I, *La sidérurgie française*; II, *Tableaux statistiques sur la production minière et sidérurgique des principaux pays, 1864–1913*, n.d. [1920].

Contamine, Henry, *La revanche, 1871–1914*, 1957.

Corbon, A., *Le secret du peuple de Paris*, 1863.

Cunéo d'Ornano, G., *La République de Napoléon*, 1894.

Dansette, Adrien, *L'affaire Wilson et la chute du président Grévy*, 1936.

——, *Les affaires de Panama*, 1934.

——, *Le Boulangisme*, 1946.

Dansette, Adrien, *Histoire religieuse de la France contemporaine sous la Troisième République*, 1951.

Daudet, Ernest, *Histoire diplomatique de l'alliance franco-russe, 1873–93*, 1894.

——, *Souvenirs de la présidence du Maréchal de Mac-Mahon*, 1880.

Dauzat, A., *Le Village et le paysan*, 1941.

Delaisi, F., *Le pétrole*, 1931.

Delavignette, R. and Julien, C. A. J., *Les constructeurs de la France d'outremer*, 1946.

Demangeon, A., *La Picardie et les régions voisines*, 1905.

Deschamps, L., *Histoire de la question coloniale*, 1891.

Deslandres, M., *Histoire constitutionelle de la France: l'avènement de la Troisième République; la Constitution de 1875*, 1937.

Dolléans, E., *Histoire du mouvement ouvrier*, 3v., I, *1830–71*; II, *1871–1936*, 1938.

Dreyfus, Robert, *La république de Monsieur Thiers*, 1930.

Drumont, E., *La France juive*, 2v., 1886.

——, *La fin d'un monde*, 1889.

——, *La dernière bataille*, 1890.

Dubreuil, L., *Paul Bert*, 1935.

Du Fou, R., *Le mouvement de concentration dans la sidérurgie de Lorraine*, 1934.

Dumont, Arsène, *Dépopulation et civilisation*, 1890.

Dunham, A. L., *The Anglo-French Treaty of Commerce of 1860 and the Progress of the Industrial Revolution in France*, Ann Arbor (Mich.), 1930.

——, *La révolution industrielle en France, 1815–48*, 1933.

Duveau, Georges, *Les instituteurs*, 1957.

——, *La vie ouvrière en France sous le Second Empire*, 1946.

Duverger, M., *L'influence des systèmes électoraux sur la vie politique*, 1950.

Emerit, Marcel, *Les Saint-Simoniens en Algérie*, 1941.

Faguet, Emile, *Questions politiques*, 1899.

Falloux, comte de, *Mémoires d'un royaliste*, II, 1888.

Faucher, D., *France méridionale et pays ibériques*, 2v., Toulouse, 1949.

Fauvet, J. et Mendras, H., *Les paysans et la politique dans la France contemporaine*, 1958.

Ferry, J., *Discours et opinions de*, ed. by P. Robiquet, 6v., 1895–96.

Foville, A. de, *Le morcellement*, 1885.

Fraix de Figon, P. de, *Le métayage en Bourbonnais au point de vue économique et social*, 1911.

Freycinet, C. de, *Souvenirs*, 2v., 1911–13.

Gambetta, Leon, *Discours et plaidoyers*, ed. by J. Reinach, 11v., 1883 etc.

Gendarme, René, *Le région du Nord: essai d'analyse économique*, 1954.

Girard, L., *La politique des Travaux publics du Second Empire*, 1952.

Goguel, F., *Géographie des élections francaises 1870–1951*, 1951.

Golob, E. O., *The Méline Tariff: French Agriculture and Nationalist Economic Policy*, New York, 1944.

Gontaut-Biron, le vicomte de, *Mon ambassade en Allemagne, 1872–73*, 1906.

Gouault, J., *Comment le France est devenue républicaine. Les élections générales et partielles à l'assemblée nationale, 1870–75*, 1954.

Gramont, see under Clermont-Tonnerre.

Haber, L. F., *The Chemical Industry during the Nineteenth Century*, Oxford, 1958.

Halévy, Daniel, *Clemenceau*, Abbeville, 1934.

——, *La fin des notables*, 1930.

——, *La république des ducs*, 1937.

——, *Histoire d'une histoire, esquissée pour le troisième cinquantenaire de la Révolution française*, 1939.

——, *Visites aux paysan du Centre, 1907–,34*, 1935.

——, et Pilliais, E., *Lettres de Gambetta, 1868–82*, 1938.

Halévy, Ludovic, *Carnets, 1867–70*, ed. by D. Halévy, 2v., 1935.

——, *Notes et souvenirs, 1871–72*, 1889.

——, *Trois diners avec Gambetta*, ed. by D. Halévy, 1929.

Hamerton, P. G., *Round my House*, 1876.

Hanotaux, G., *Histoire de la France contemporaine*, 4v., 1903–08.

Henry, P., *Histoire des préfets*, 1950.

Huber, M., *La population de la France*, n.d. [1938].

Humbert, S., *Les 'Possibilistes'*, 1911.

Jaurès, J., *Discours parlementaires*, with preface 'Le socialisme et le radicalisme en 1885', 1904.

Judet, Ernest, *Le véritable Clemenceau*, 1920.

Labasse, J., *Les capitaux et la région; essai sur le commerce et la circulation des capitaux dans la région lyonnaise*, 1955.

Lacour-Gayet, J. (ed.), *Histoire du commerce*, V, 1952.

Lacombe, Charles de, *Journal politique*, 2v. ed. by A. Helot, 1908.

Large, E. C., *The Advance of the Fungi*, 1940.

Larminat, L. de, *Le métayage dans le département de l'Allier*, Moulins, 1881.

Laroque, P., *Les rapports entre patrons et ouvriers*, 1938.

Launay, Louis, *De Wendel*, Vaucresson, 1938.

Lavergne, Léonce de, *Economie rurale de la France depuis 1789*, 1865.

Le Bras, Gabriel, *Etudes de sociologie religieuse*, 2v., 1955.

Lecanuet, R. P., *Les dernières années du pontificat de Pie IX, 1870–78,* 1930.
——, *Les premières années du pontificat de Léon XIII, 1878–94,* 1930.
——, *La vie de l'Eglise sous Léon XIII,* 1930.
Lefebvre, G., *Questions agraires au temps de la Terreur,* Strasbourg, 1932.
——, *La revolution française et les paysans,* Cahiers de la Révolution française, No. 1, 1934.
Legrand-Girarde, Gen., *Un quart de siècle au service de la France,* 1954.
Le Play, F., *Les ouvriers européens,* V, Tours, 1878.
Levasseur, E., *Questions ouvrières et industrielles en France sous la Troisième République,* 1907.
Lizerand, G., *Le régime rural de l'ancienne France,* 1942.
——, *Un siècle de l'histoire d'une commune rurale; Vergigny,* n.d. [1949].
Louis, Paul, *Histoire du socialisme en France,* 5th ed., 1950.

Marcère, E. de, *L'Assemblée nationale de 1871,* 2v., 1904.
——, *Histoire de la République, 1876–79,* 2v., 1909–10.
Marion, M., *Histoire finançiere de la France depuis 1715,* 6v., 1931.
——, *La vente des biens nationaux pendant la Révolution,* 1908.
Marlio, L., *La véritable histoire de Panama,* 1932.
Marshall, W., *The Rural Economy of Yorkshire,* 2v., 1788.
Martet, Jean, *Clemenceau peint par lui-même,* 1929.
Masson, Paul, *Les Bouches-du-Rhône; Encyclopédie départementale,* 12v, Marseille, 1925–32.
Maurain, J., *La politique ecclésiastique du Second Empire de 1852 à 1869,* 1930.
Meaux, M. C. A., vicomte de, *Souvenirs politiques, 1871–77,* 1905.
Michel, G., *Léon Say, sa vie, ses oeuvres,* 1899.
Michon, G., *L'alliance franco-russe, 1891–1917,* 1927.
Millaud, Edouard, *Le journal d'un parlementaire, 1864–1906,* 4v., 1914–20.
Monteilhet, J., *Les institutions militaires de la France, 1814–1924,* ed. of 1932.
Municipalité bordelaise, La, *Bordeaux,* 3v., Bordeaux, 1892.
Musset, René, *Le Bas-Maine,* 1917.

Newton, Lord, *Lord Lyons: a record of British diplomacy,* 2v., 1913.
Neymarck, A., *Finances contemporains,* 2v., 1903.

Péguy, Charles, *Notre jeunesse,* ed. 1926.
L'argent, Oeuvres, III.
Picard, Alfred, *Le bilan d'un siècle, 1801–1900,* 6v., 1906.
Pierre, Eugène, *Traité de droit politique, électoral et parlementaire,* 1893.
Pirou, G., *Les doctrines économiques en France depuis 1870,* 1934.
Pounds, N. J. G., and Parker, W. N., *Coal and Steel in Western Europe,* 1957.

Rambaud, A., *Jules Ferry,* 1903.
Ranc, Arthur, *Souvenirs et correspondance, 1831–1908,* 1913.

Reinach, Joseph, *Le ministère Gambetta: histoire et doctrine*, 1884.

Reybaud, L., *Le fer et la houille*, 1874.

Richardson, G. G., *The Corn and Cattle Producing Districts of France*, n.d. [1877].

Roberts, S. H., *History of French Colonial Policy, 1870–1925*, 2v., 1929.

Robinson, R. and Gallagher, J., *Africa and the Victorians: the Official Mind of Imperialism*, 1961.

Rouff, M., *Les mines de charbon en France au XVIIIe siècle, 1744–91*, 1922.

Sagnac, P., *La formation de la société moderne*, 2v.

Saint-Aulaire, le comte de Beaupoil de, *Confession d'un vieux diplomate*, 1953.

Saint-Valry, Gaston de, *Souvenirs et réflexions politiques*, 2v., 1886.

Say, Léon, *Les finances de la France sous la Troisième République*, 3v., 1900.

Séché, Léon, *Jules Simon*, 1898.

Seignobos, C., *Le déclin de l'Empire et l'établissement de la Troisième République*, Vol. 7 in Lavisse, *Histoire de la France contemporaine L'évolution de la Troisième République*, Vol. 8 in same.

——, *Etudes de politique et d'histoire*, 1934.

Sentou, J., 'La révolution agricole dans le Narbonnais' see above under Faucher, D.

Siegfried, André, *Tableau politique de la France de l'Ouest sous la Troisième République*, 1913.

——, *Tableau des partis en France*, 1930.

——, *Géographie électorale de l'Ardèche sous la Troisième République*, 1949.

Simon, Jules, *Le soir de ma journée*, n.d. [1901].

——, *Le gouvernement de M. Thiers*, 2v.

Sion, J., *Les paysans de la Normandie orientale*, 1909.

Sömme, Axel, *La Lorraine métallurgique*, 1930.

Soulier, A., *L'instabilité ministérielle sous la Troisième République*, 1939.

Taine, H., *Carnets de voyage; notes sur la province, 1863–65*, 1913.

Tardieu, André, *La révolution à refaire*, 2v., 1936.

Taylor, A. J. P., *Bismarck: the Man and the Statesman*,

——, *Rumours of Wars*, 1952.

——, *The Struggle for the Mastery of Europe*, 1954.

Thabault, Roger, *Mon village, 1848–1914* (Mazières-en-Gâtine), 1945.

Thibaudet, A., *Les idées politiques de la France*, 1932.

——, *La république des professeurs*, 1927.

Thiers, A., *Discours de*, ed. by Calmon, 15v., 1880–83.

Thompson, Virginia, *French Indo-China*, 1937.

Tocqueville, A. de, *Souvenirs*, ed. by Luc Monnier, 1942.

Tournier, J., *Le Cardinal Lavigerie et son action politique, 1863–92*, 1913.

Valon, la comtesse de, *Souvenirs de sa vie*, ed. by G. Clement-Simon, 1909.
Varennes, H., *De Ravachol à Caserio* (*Notes d'audience*) n.d. [1895].
Veuillot, Louis, *Oeuvres diverses*, XI, 1926.
Vogüé, vicomte E. M. de, *Journal Paris-Saint Petersbourg*, *1877–83*, 1925.
———, *Les morts qui parlent*, 1899.

Wahl, Maurice, *L'Algérie*, 1897.
Weiss, J. J., *Combat constitutionel*, 1893.
White, Harry Dexter, *The French International Accounts*, *1880–1913*, Harvard, 1933.
Woelmont, Baron Henry de, *Les marquis français*, 1919.

Yates, F. Lamartine, *Food Production in Western Europe*, 1940.

Zévaès, Alexandre, *Les 'Guesdistes'*, 1909.
———, *De la semaine sanglante au Congrès de Marseille*, 1908.
———, *Clemenceau*, 1949.

ARTICLES

Allain-Targé, H., 'Le ministère Waddington', in *RP*, 1 March, 1904.
Baraud, F., 'L'industrie à Montluçon', 43 *AG*, 1934, 364 ff.
Bateman, A. E., 'A note on the statistics of wine production in France', in 46 *JRSS*, March, 1883, 113 ff.
Benda, J., 'La jeunesse d'un clerc', in *NRF*, 1 Aug., 1936.
Bertillon, Jacques, 'Le problème de la dépopulation', in 12 *RPP*, 1897, 531.
Blanchard, M., 'La politique ferroviaire du Second Empire', in *Annales*, 1934, 529 ff.
———, 'Aux origines de nos chemins de fer: Saint-Simoniens et banquiers', in *Annales*, 1938, 97 ff.
Blanche, J. E., 'Tableau d'une existence', in *RP*, 15 Sept., 1931.
Bloch, Marc, 'La lutte pour l'individualisme agraire dans la France du XVIIIe siècle' in *Annales*, 1930, 329 ff. and 511 ff.
Bonnard, Roger, 'De l'homogenéité et de la solidarité ministérielles à propos du ministère Barthou' in *Revue du Droit public et de la science politique*, July, 1913.
Bouvier, J., 'Les réflexes sociaux des milieux d'affaires' in 210 *R.hist.*, 1953, 271–301.
Brown, E. H. Phelps and Hopkins, Sheila v., 'The Course of Wage-rates in Five countries, 1860–1939' in 2 *Oxford Economic Papers*, 1950, 226 ff.
Bulard, M., 'L'industrie de fer dans la Haute-Marne' in *AG*, 1904.
Combe, J., 'Thiers et la vallée de la Durolle', in 31 *AG*, 1922, 360–65.

Coutin, P., 'La notion d'exploitation agricole familiale: l'exemple de la Limagne', in *Annales*, 1946, 342 ff.

Dietz, J., 'Jules Ferry: sa première [seconde] présidence du conseil', in 165 *RPP*, Oct.–Dec., 1935.

——, 'Jules Ferry: la révision de la constitution et le scrutin de liste', in 166–167 *RPP*, March–April, 1936.

Faucher, Léon [Anon.], 'De la propriété en France', in *ROM*, 1836, 309–21.

Glass, D. V., 'Reproduction Rates in France', in *Eugenics Review*, July, 1945, 61.

Goblet, R., 'Souvenirs de ma vie politique' in 136–139, 141, 145, 149 *RPP*, Sept., Nov.–Dec., 1928–April, 1929; Oct.–Nov., 1929; Dec., 1930; Nov., 1931.

Haussonville, comte O. d', 'Souvenirs, *II*, 1869–71' in *RDM*, 1 Nov., 1923, 27.

Hérault, A., 'Souvenirs' in *RP*, 1–15 June, 1930.

Isnard, H., 'Vignes et colonisation en Algérie, 1880–1947, in *Annales*, 1947, 288 ff.

Jacques, F., 'De la propriété et des servitudes rurales d'après la loi de 1890', in *Rev. critique de la Législation et de Jurisprudence*, 1890, 192, 549, 626 ff. and 1891, 88, 456, 640 ff.

Javal, A., 'La grande misère de la petite culture' in *RP*, 15 March, 1933.

Lajusan, A., 'Les origines de la Troisième République: quelques éclaircissements' in 5 *Rev. d'histoire moderne*, 1930, 419 ff.

Manry, A. G., 'En Limagne, entre 1865 et 1905', in *Annales*, 1950, 114 ff.

Martignon, J., 'L'élevage du mouton dans la champagne berrichonne' in 31 *AG*, 1922, 364–66.

Meynier, A., 'Trois centres de ganterie, Millau, Niort, Saint-Junien', in 43 *AG*, 1934.

Monteil, Col. P. L., 'Contribution d'un vétéran à l'histoire coloniale', in *RP*, Sept. 1, 1923.

Morazé, P., 'The Treaty of 1860 and the Industry of the Department of the North', in 10 *Ec. Hist. Rev.*, 1940, 18 ff.

Pellet, E. A., Marcellin-, 'Souvenirs sur Gambetta', in *RF*, Nov. 15, 1927.

Perrin, M., 'Le bassin houiller de la Loire' in 39 *AG*, 1930, 359–75.

——, 'Le Creusot', in 43 *AG*, 1934, 255–74.

Raymond, A., 'Les tentatives anglaises de pénétration économique en Tunisie, 1856–77', in 214 *R. hist.*, 1955, 48–67.

Renouvin, P., 'Les origines de l'expédition de Fachoda', in 200 *R.hist.* 1948, 180–97.

Siegfried, A., 'Une crise ministérielle en 1887, d'après le journal de mon père [Jules Siegfried]', in 11 *Hommes et Mondes*, 1950, 477 ff.

Taylor, A. J. P., 'Les premières années de l'alliance russe, 1892–95' in 204 *R.hist.*, 1950, 67–76.

Tricart, J., 'Exemple d'évolution d'une société rurale en 'milieu répulsif': Asnières-sous-Bois (Yonne)', in 4 *Population*, 1949, 495 ff.

Vaucher, P., 'La politique agricole française' in *La France Libre*, Nov., 1942.

Vignes, M., 'Le bassin de Briey et la politique de ses entreprises sidérurgiques', in *Rev. d'économie politique*, 1912, 669 ff., and 1913, 304 ff., 578 ff., 681 ff.

Vidal de la Blache, 'Evolution de la population en Alsace-Lorraine et dans les départements limitrophes' in 25 *AG*, 1916.

Zévaès, A., 'Jules Guesde et Jean Jaurès' in *RP*, July 1, 1936, 79 ff.

INDEX OF PERSONS

INDEX OF SUBJECTS AND PLACES

PRINTED IN GREAT BRITAIN
BY ROBERT MACLEHOSE AND CO. LTD
THE UNIVERSITY PRESS, GLASGOW